Financial Aid
for Asian Americans
2006-2008

RSP FINANCIAL AID DIRECTORIES
OF INTEREST TO MINORITIES

College Student's Guide to Merit and Other No-Need Funding, 2005-2007
Selected as one of the "Outstanding Titles of the Year" by *Choice,* this directory describes 1,300 no-need funding opportunities for college students. 464 pages. ISBN 1-58841-102-8. $32.50, plus $6 shipping.

Directory of Financial Aids for Women, 2005-2007
Nearly 1,500 funding programs set aside for women are described in this biennial directory, which *School Library Journal* calls "the cream of the crop." 528 pages. ISBN 1-58841-131-1. $45, plus $6 shipping.

Financial Aid for African Americans, 2006-2008
Nearly 1,400 scholarships, fellowships, grants, and internships open to African Americans are described in this award-winning directory. 542 pages. ISBN 1-58841-133-8. $40, plus $6 shipping.

Financial Aid for Asian Americans, 2006-2008
This is the source to use if you are looking for financial aid for Asian Americans; more than 1,000 funding opportunities are described. 402 pages. ISBN 1-58841-134-6. $37.50, plus $6 shipping.

Financial Aid for Hispanic Americans, 2006-2008
More than 1,200 funding programs open to Americans of Mexican, Puerto Rican, Central American, or other Latin American heritage are described here. 484 pages. ISBN 1-58841-135-4. $40, plus $6 shipping.

Financial Aid for Native Americans, 2006-2008
Detailed information is provided on 1,400 funding opportunities open to American Indians, Native Alaskans, and Native Pacific Islanders. 562 pages. ISBN 1-58841-136-2. $42.50, plus $6 shipping.

Financial Aid for Research and Creative Activities Abroad, 2005-2007
Described here are 1,000 scholarships, fellowships, grants, etc. available to support research, professional, or creative activities abroad. 278 pages. ISBN 1-58841-107-9. $45, plus $6 shipping.

Financial Aid for Study and Training Abroad, 2005-2007
This directory, which *Children's Bookwatch* calls "invaluable," describes nearly 1,000 financial aid opportunities available to support study abroad. 358 pages. ISBN 1-58841-094-3. $39.50, plus $5 shipping.

Financial Aid for the Disabled and Their Families, 2006-2008
Named one of the "Best Reference Books of the Year" by *Library Journal,* this directory describes in detail more than 1,200 funding opportunities. 502 pages. ISBN 1-58841-148-6. $40, plus $6 shipping.

Financial Aid for Veterans, Military Personnel, and Their Dependents, 2006-2008
According to *Reference Book Review,* this directory (with its 1,100 entries) is "the most comprehensive guide available on the subject." 443 pages. ISBN 1-58841-143-5. $40, plus $6 shipping.

High School Senior's Guide to Merit and Other No-Need Funding, 2005-2007
Here's your guide to 1,100 funding programs that *never* look at income level when making awards to college-bound high school seniors. 416 pages. ISBN 1-58841-100-1. $29.95, plus $5 shipping.

How to Pay for Your Degree in Education & Related Fields, 2006-2008
Here's hundreds of funding opportunities to support undergraduate and graduate students preparing for a career in teaching, guidance, etc. 222 pages. ISBN 1-58841-146-X. $30, plus $6 shipping.

Money for Christian College Students, 2005-2007
This is the only directory to describe nearly 800 funding opportunities available to support Christian students working on an undergraduate or graduate degree (secular or religious). 238 pages. ISBN 1-58841-118-4. $30, plus $6 shipping.

Money for Graduate Students in the Social & Behavioral Sciences, 2005-2007
Described here are the 1,100 biggest and best funding opportunities available to students working on a graduate degree in the social or behavioral sciences. 332 pages. ISBN 1-58841-141-9. $42.50, plus $6 shipping.

RSP Funding for Nursing Students, 2006-2008
You'll find 500+ scholarships, fellowships, loans, grants, and awards here that can be used for study, research, professional, or other nursing activities. 198 pages. ISBN 1-58841-157-5. $30, plus $6 shipping.

Financial Aid for Asian Americans 2006-2008

Gail Ann Schlachter
R. David Weber

A List of Scholarships, Fellowships, Loans, Grants, Awards, and Internships Open Primarily or Exclusively to Asian Americans and a Set of Six Indexes (Program Title, Sponsoring Organizations, Residency, Tenability, Subject, and Deadline Date)

Reference Service Press
El Dorado Hills, California
2006

ISBN: 1-58841-134-6

10 9 8 7 6 5 4 3 2 1

Reference Service Press (RSP) began in 1977 with a single financial aid publication *(The Directory of Financial Aids for Women)* and now specializes in the development of financial aid resources in multiple formats, including books, large print books, disks, CD-ROMs, print-on-demand reports, eBooks, and online sources. Long recognized as a leader in the field, RSP has been called, by the *Simba Report on Directory Publishing,* "a true success in the world of independent directory publishers." Both Kaplan Educational Centers and Military.com have hailed RSP as "the leading authority on scholarships."

Reference Service Press
El Dorado Hills Business Park
5000 Windplay Drive, Suite 4
El Dorado Hills, CA 95762
   (916) 939-9620
   Fax: (916) 939-9626
   E-mail: info@rspfunding.com
Visit our web site: www.rspfunding.com

Manufactured in the United States of America
Price: $37.50, plus $6 shipping.

ACADEMIC INSTITUTIONS, LIBRARIES, ORGANIZATIONS AND OTHER QUANTITY BUYERS:
Discounts on this book are available for bulk purchases. Write or call for information on our discount programs.

Contents

Introduction

PURPOSE OF THE DIRECTORY

Despite the recent steps taken to curtail affirmative action and equal opportunity programs, the financial aid picture for minorities has never looked brighter. Currently, billions of dollars are set aside specifically for Asian Americans and other minorities. This funding is open to applicants at any level (high school through postdoctoral and professional) for study, research, travel, training, career development, or innovative effort.

While numerous directories have been prepared to identify and describe general financial aid programs (those open to all segments of society), they have never covered more than a small portion of the programs designed primarily or exclusively for minorities. Before *Financial Aid for Asian Americans* and its predecessor (*Directory of Financial Aids for Minorities*) were published, many advisors, librarians, scholars, researchers, and students were unaware of the extensive funding opportunities available to Asian Americans and other minorities. Now, with the ongoing publication of *Financial Aid for Asian Americans,* up-to-date and detailed information is available in a single volume about the special resources set aside for members of this group.

Financial Aid for Asian Americans is prepared biennially as part of Reference Service Press' four-volume *Minority Funding Set* (the other volumes cover funding for African Americans, Hispanic Americans, and Native Americans). Each of the volumes in this set is sold separately, or the complete set can be purchased at a discounted price (for more information contact Reference Service Press's marketing department).

No other source, in print or online, offers the coverage provided by these titles. That's why the Grantsmanship Center labeled the set "a must for every organization serving minorities" and *Reference Books Bulletin* selected each of the volumes in the *Minority Funding Set* as the "Editor's Choice." *Financial Aid for Asian Americans,* itself, has also received rave reviews. *Al Jahdid* called the directory "an excellent resource," the Miami-Dade Public Library System included it in its list of "Essential Titles for the College Bound," and *Small Press* found it both "inclusive" and "valuable." Perhaps *Choice* sums up the critical reaction best: "a unique and valuable resource; highly recommended."

EXTENT OF UPDATING IN THE 2006-2008 EDITION

The preparation of each new edition of *Financial Aid for Asian Americans* involves extensive updating and revision. To insure that the information included in the 2006-2008 edition of the directory is both reliable and current, the editors at Reference Service Press 1) reviewed and updated all relevant programs covered in the previous edition of the directory, 2) collected information on all programs open to Asian Americans that were added to Reference Service Press' funding database since the last edition of the directory, and then 3) searched extensively for new program leads in a variety of sources, including printed directories, news reports, journals, newsletters, house organs, annual reports, and sites on the Internet. Since all program descriptions included in the directory are written directly from information supplied by the sponsoring organizations (no information is ever taken from secondary sources), we contacted all sponsoring organizations identified in this process up to four times in writing and, if necessary, up to 3 times by telephone. Unfortunately, despite our best efforts, some sponsoring organizations failed to respond to our data requests; consequently, their programs are not included in this edition of the directory.

The 2006-2008 edition of *Financial Aid for Asian Americans* completely revises and updates the previous edition. Programs that have ceased operations have been dropped from the listing. Profiles of continuing programs have been rewritten to reflect operations in 2006-2008; more than 80 percent of the continuing programs reported substantive changes in their locations, requirements (particularly application deadline), benefits, or eligibility requirements since 2003. In addition, more than 350 new entries have been added to the program section of the directory. The resulting listing describes more than 1,000 scholarships, fellowships, loans, grants, awards, and internships.

WHAT MAKES THIS DIRECTORY UNIQUE?

The 2006-2008 edition of *Financial Aid for Asian Americans* will help Americans with origins from Asia or subcontinent Asia and Pacific island nations (e.g., Japan, China, the Philippines, Vietnam, Korea, Laos, Cambodia, Taiwan, Burma, Thailand, Malaysia, Indonesia, Singapore, Brunei, Macao, Hong Kong, Indian, Pakistan, Bangladesh, Tonga) tap into the billions of dollars available to them, as minorities, to support study, research, creative activities, past accomplishments, future projects, professional development, work experience, and many other activities. The listings cover every major subject area, are sponsored by more than 800 different private and public agencies and organizations, and are open to Asian Americans at any level, from college-bound high school students through professionals and postdoctorates.

In addition to its extensive and focused coverage, *Financial Aid for Asian Americans* offers several other unique features. Covered here are hundreds of funding opportunities not listed in any other source (so even if you have checked other directories, you will want to look through the listings here). Unlike other funding directories, which generally follow a straight alphabetical arrangement, this one groups entries by type (scholarships, grants, awards, etc.), making it easy to search for appropriate programs. The same convenience is offered in the indexes, where title, organization, geographic, subject, and deadline date entries are each subdivided by type of funding. Finally, we have tried to anticipate all the ways you might wish to search for funding. The volume is organized so you can identify programs not only by type, but by specific subject, sponsoring organization, program title, residency requirements, where the money can be spent, and even deadline date. Plus, we've included all the information you'll need to decide if a program is right for you: purpose, eligibility requirements, financial data, duration, special features, limitations, number awarded, and application date. You even get fax numbers, toll-free numbers, e-mail addresses, and web sites (when available), along with complete contact information.

ARRANGEMENT OF THE DIRECTORY

Financial Aid for Asian Americans is divided into two sections: 1) a descriptive list of funding opportunities open to Asian Americans and 2) a set of six indexes.

Financial Aid Programs Open to Asian Americans. The first section of the directory describes 1,023 funding opportunities open to Asian Americans. The focus is on financial aid available to American citizens or permanent residents and tenable in the United States. The programs described here are sponsored by more than 800 different government agencies, professional organizations, corporations, sororities and fraternities, foundations, religious groups, educational associations, and military/veterans organizations. All areas of the sciences, social sciences, and humanities are covered.

Entries in this section are grouped into the following six categories, to help you in your search for a specific kind of financial assistance (e.g., a scholarship for undergraduate study, a grant for independent research, an award for outstanding literary achievement):

> ***Scholarships:*** Programs that support studies at the undergraduate level in the United States. Usually no return of service or repayment is required. For information on funding for research on the undergraduate level, see the Grants category below.

Fellowships: Programs that support studies at the graduate level in the United States, including work on a master's degree, doctorate, professional degree (e.g., law, medicine), or specialist's certificate. Usually no return of service or repayment is required. For information on funding for research on the graduate level, see the Grants category below.

Loans: Programs that provide money that eventually must be repaid—in cash or in service and with or without interest. Forgivable loans (along with scholarship/loans and loans-for-service) are also described in this part of the directory.

Grants: Programs that provide funds to support Asian Americans' innovative efforts, travel, projects, creative activities, or research on any level (from undergraduate to postdoctorate, professional, or other). In some cases, proposals must be submitted by institutions or organizations only; in others, individual minority group members may submit proposals directly.

Awards: Competitions, prizes, and honoraria granted in recognition of Asian Americans' personal accomplishments, professional contributions, or public service. Prizes received solely as the result of entering contests are excluded.

Internships: Work experience programs for Asian American undergraduates, graduate students, and recent graduates. Only salaried positions are described.

Programs that supply more than one type of assistance are listed in all relevant subsections. For example, both undergraduate and graduate students may apply for the Abe and Esther Hagiwara Student Aid Award, so the program is described in both the scholarship and the fellowship subsections.

Entries in each subsection are arranged alphabetically by program title. Each program entry (see the sample entry on page 7) has been designed to provide a concise profile that includes information (when available) on program title, organization address and telephone numbers (including toll-free and fax numbers), e-mail addresses, web site, purpose, eligibility, money awarded, duration, special features, limitations, number of awards, and application deadline. The information reported for each of the programs in this section was supplied in response to research inquiries distributed through the first quarter of 2006. While this listing is intended to be as comprehensive as possible, some sponsoring organizations did not respond to our research requests and, consequently, are not included in this edition of the directory.

The focus of the directory is on "portable" (noninstitution-specific) programs open primarily or exclusively to Asian Americans or to minority pools that specifically include Asian Americans. Excluded from this listing are:

Awards for which American citizens would be ineligible: Programs open only to nationals from other countries (e.g., Asian nations) are not covered.

Awards tenable only outside the United States: Since there are comprehensive and up-to-date directories that describe available funding for study and research abroad (see the list of Reference Service Press titles opposite the directory's title page), only programs that fund activities in the United States are covered here.

Minority programs that specifically exclude Asian Americans: Programs that are open to specific minority groups, but not to Asian Americans (e.g., programs only for African Americans), are excluded.

Programs that are open equally to all segments of the population: Only funding opportunities set aside primarily of exclusively for Asian Americans are included here.

Programs open to residents in a very restricted geographic location: In general, programs are excluded if they are open only to the residents of mid-sized or smaller counties or cities.

Programs administered by individual academic institutions solely for their own students: The directory identifies "portable" programs—ones that can be used at any number of schools. Financial aid administered by individual schools specifically for their currently-enrolled students is not covered. Write directly to the schools you are considering to get information on their offerings.

Indexes. The six indexes included in *Financial Aid for Asian Americans* will help you target appropriate financial aid opportunities. Program Title, Sponsoring Organization, Residency, Tenability, Subject, and Calendar Indexes each follow a word-by-word alphabetical arrangement and pinpoint the entry numbers (not page numbers) that you should check.

> *Program Title Index.* If you know the name of a particular funding program and want to find out where it is covered in the directory, use the Program Title Index. To assist you in your search, every program is listed by all its known names, former names, and abbreviations. Since one program can be included in several subsections (e.g., a program providing assistance to both undergraduate and graduate students is described in both the scholarships and the fellowships subsections), each entry number in the index has been coded to indicate program type (e.g., "F" = Fellowships; "A" = Awards). By using this coding system, you can avoid duplicate entries and turn directly to the programs that match your financial interests.

> *Sponsoring Organization Index.* This index makes it easy to identify agencies that offer funding primarily or exclusively to Asian Americans. More than 800 organizations are indexed here. As in the Program Title Index, we've used a code to help you determine which organizations offer scholarships, fellowships, loans, grants, awards, and/or internships.

> *Residency Index.* Some programs listed in this book are restricted to Asian Americans in a particular city, county, state, or region. Others are open to Asian Americans wherever they live. This index helps you identify programs available only to residents in your area as well as programs that have no residency requirements. Further, to assist you in your search, we've also indicated the type of funding offered to residents in each of the areas listed in the index.

> *Tenability Index.* This index identifies the geographic locations where the funding described in *Financial Aid for Asian Americans* may be used. Index entries (city, county, state, province, region, country, continent) are arranged alphabetically (word by word) and subdivided by program type. Use this index when you are looking for money to support your activities in a particular geographic area.

> *Subject Index.* This index allows you to identify the subject focus of each of the financial aid opportunities described in *Financial Aid for Asian Americans.* More than 200 different subject terms are listed. Extensive "see" and "see also" references, as well as type-of-program subdivisions, will help you locate appropriate funding opportunities.

> *Calendar Index.* Since most financial aid programs have specific deadline dates, some may have closed by the time you begin to look for funding. You can use the Calendar Index to determine which programs are still open. This index is arranged by program type (e.g., scholarship, loan, internship) and subdivided by month during which the deadline falls. Filing dates can and quite often do vary from year to year; consequently, this index should be used only as a guide for deadlines beyond 2008.

TIPS ON HOW TO USE THE DIRECTORY

To Locate Programs Offering a Particular Type of Assistance. If you are looking for programs offering a particular type of financial aid (e.g., a scholarship for undergraduate courses, a grant for independent research, an award for outstanding literary achievement), turn first to the definitions of the various program types on pages 4-5 in the Introduction and then browse through the entries in each of the appropriate categories in the first section of the directory (scholarships, fellowships, loans, grants, awards, or internships). Keep in mind that more than one of these subsections may contain funding leads for you. For example, if you are a graduate student looking for money to help you pay for the educational and research costs associated with your master's degree, you will not want to overlook the opportunities described in the fellowships, loans, grants, and even awards subsections. Note: since programs with multiple purposes are listed in every appropriate location, each of these subsections functions as a self-contained entity. As a result, you can browse through any of the subsections in the directory without first consulting an index.

SAMPLE ENTRY

(1) **[37]**

(2) **ASIAN & PACIFIC ISLANDER AMERICAN SCHOLARSHIPS**

(3) Asian & Pacific Islander American Scholarship Fund
P.O. Box 57
San Francisco, CA 94104
(415) 808-0805   Toll-free: (877) 808-7032
E-mail: scholarshipquestions@apiasf.org
Web: www.apiasf.org

(4) **Purpose** To provide financial assistance to Asian and Pacific Islander Americans who are entering college for the first time.

(5) **Eligibility** This program is open to U.S. citizens, nationals, permanent residents, and citizens of the Freely Associated States who are first-time incoming college students. Applicants must be enrolling full time in an accredited 2-year or 4-year college or university in the United States, Guam, American Samoa, U.S. Virgin Islands, or the Commonwealth of the Northern Mariana Islands. They must have a GPA of 2.7 or higher or the GED equivalent. Along with their application, they must submit an essay of 275 words or less that describes an experience in their life that either demonstrates their character or helped to shape it. Selection is based on the essay, academic record, academic plans and career goals, community service, a letter of recommendation, and financial need.

(6) **Financial data** The stipend is $2,000.

(7) **Duration** 1 year.

(8) **Additional information** These scholarships were first offered in 2005. Support for this program is provided by such sponsors as the AT&T Foundation, Wells Fargo and Company, the Coca-Cola Company, Wal-Mart Stores, Hilton Hotels Foundation, General Mills Foundation, and the Asian McDonald's Owners/Operators Association.

(9) **Number awarded** 1 or more each year.

(10) **Deadline** February of each year.

DEFINITION

(1) **Entry number:** Consecutive number assigned to the funding profiles and used to index the entry.

(2) **Program title:** Title of scholarship, fellowship, loan, grant, award, or internship.

(3) **Sponsoring organization:** Name, address, and telephone number, toll-free number, fax number, e-mail address, and/or web site (when information was available) for organization sponsoring the program.

(4) **Purpose:** Identifies the major program requirements; read the rest of the entry for additional detail.

(5) **Eligibility:** Qualifications required of applicants, plus information on application procedure and selection process.

(6) **Financial data:** Financial details of the program, including fixed sum, average amount, or range of funds offered, expenses for which funds may and may not be applied, and cash-related benefits supplied (e.g., room and board).

(7) **Duration:** Period for which support is provided; renewal prospects.

(8) **Additional information:** Any unusual (generally nonmonetary) benefits, features, restrictions, or limitations associated with the program.

(9) **Number awarded:** Total number of recipients each year or other specified period.

(10) **Deadline:** The month by which applications must be submitted.

To Locate a Particular Financial Aid Program. If you know the name of a particular financial aid program, and the type of assistance offered by the program (scholarship, fellowship, grant, etc.), then go directly to the appropriate category in the first section of the directory, where you will find the program profiles arranged alphabetically by title. But be careful: program titles can be misleading. For example, the Darshan S. Bhatia Memorial Award is actually a scholarship, not an award, and the Elichi Matsushita Memorial Scholarship is really a fellowship rather than a scholarship. So, if you are looking for a specific program and do not find it in the subsection you have checked, be sure to refer to the Program Title Index to see if it is covered elsewhere in the directory. To save time, always check the Program Title Index first if you know the name of a specific award but are not sure under which subsection it has been listed. Since we index each program by all its known names and abbreviations, you'll also be able to track down a program there when you only know the popular rather than official name.

To Locate Programs Sponsored by a Particular Organization. The Sponsoring Organization Index makes it easy to identify agencies that provide financial assistance to Asian Americans or to identify specific financial aid programs offered by a particular organization. Each entry number in the index is coded to identify program type, so that you can easily target appropriate entries.

To Browse Quickly Through the Listings. Turn to the type of funding that interests you (scholarships, fellowships, awards, etc.) and read the "Purpose" paragraph in each entry. In seconds, you'll know if this is an opportunity that you might want to pursue. If it is, be sure to read the rest of the information in the entry, to make sure you meet all of the program requirements before writing or going on the Internet for an application form. Please, save your time and energy. Don't apply if you don't qualify!

To Locate Funding Available to Asian Americans from or Tenable in a Particular City, County, or State. The Residency Index identifies financial aid programs open to Asian Americans in a particular city, county, state, region, etc. The Tenability Index shows where the money can be spent. In both indexes, "see" and "see also" references are used liberally, and index entries for a particular geographic area are subdivided by type of program (scholarships, fellowships, loans, grants, awards, internships) to help you identify the funding that's right for you. When using these indexes, always check the listings under the term "United States," since the programs indexed there have no geographic restrictions and can be used in any area.

To Locate Financial Aid Programs Open to Asian Americans in a Particular Subject Area. Turn to the Subject Index first if you are interested in identifying financial aid programs for Asian Americans in a particular subject area (more than 200 different subject fields are listed there). To facilitate your search, the type of funding available (scholarships, fellowships, loans, grants, awards, internships) is clearly labeled. Extensive cross-references are provided. As part of your search, be sure to check the listings in the index under the heading "General Programs;" those programs provide funding in any subject area (although they may be restricted in other ways).

To Locate Financial Aid Programs for Asian Americans by Deadline Date. If you are working with specific time constraints and want to weed out the financial aid programs whose filing dates you won't be able to meet, turn first to the Calendar Index and check the program references listed under the appropriate program type and month. Keep in mind: not all sponsoring organizations supplied deadline information, so not all programs are indexed in this section. To identify every relevant financial aid program, regardless of filing date, read through all the entries in each of the program categories (scholarships, fellowships, etc.) that apply.

To Locate Financial Aid Programs Open to All Segments of the Population. Only programs available to Asian Americans are listed in this publication. However, there are thousands of other programs that are open equally to all segments of the population. To identify these programs, talk to your local librarian, check with your financial aid office on campus, or use a computerized scholarship or grant search service.

PLANS TO UPDATE THE DIRECTORY

This volume, covering 2006-2008, is the fifth edition of *Financial Aid for Asian Americans.* The next biennial edition will cover the years 2008-2010 and will be issued in mid-2008.

OTHER RELATED PUBLICATIONS

In addition to *Financial Aid for Asian Americans,* Reference Service Press publishes several other titles dealing with fundseeking, including the award-winning *Directory of Financial Aids for Women; Financial Aid for the Disabled and Their Families;* and *Financial Aid for Veterans, Military Personnel, and Their Dependents.* Since each of these titles focuses on a separate population group, there is very little duplication in the listings. For more information on Reference Service Press' award-winning publications, write to the company at 5000 Windplay Drive, Suite 4, El Dorado Hills, CA 95762, give us a call at (916) 939-9620, fax us at (916) 939-9626, send us an e-mail at info@rspfunding.com, or visit our expanded web site: www.rspfunding.com.

ACKNOWLEDGEMENTS

A debt of gratitude is owed all the organizations that contributed information to the 2006-2008 edition of *Financial Aid for Asian Americans.* Their generous cooperation has helped to make this publication a current and comprehensive survey of awards.

ABOUT THE AUTHORS

Dr. Gail Ann Schlachter has worked for more than three decades as a library administrator, a library educator, and an administrator of library-related publishing companies. Among the reference books to her credit are the biennially-issued *Directory of Financial Aids for Women* and two award-winning bibliographic guides: *Minorities and Women: A Guide to Reference Literature in the Social Sciences* (which was chosen as an "outstanding reference book of the year" by *Choice*) and *Reference Sources in Library and Information Services* (which won the first Knowledge Industry Publications "Award for Library Literature"). She was the reference book review editor for *RQ* (now *Reference and User Services Quarterly*) for 10 years, is a past president of the American Library Association's Reference and User Services Association, is the former editor-in-chief of the *Reference and User Services Association Quarterly,* and is currently serving her third term on the American Library Association's governing council. In recognition of her outstanding contributions to reference service, Dr. Schlachter has been awarded both the Isadore Gilbert Mudge Citation and the Louis Shores/Oryx Press Award.

Dr. R. David Weber teaches economics and history at East Los Angeles College (Wilmington, California), where he directed the Honors Program for many years. He has written a number of critically-acclaimed reference works, including *Dissertations in Urban History* and the three-volume *Energy Information Guide.* With Gail Schlachter, he is the author of Reference Service Press' *Financial Aid for the Disabled and Their Families,* which was selected by *Library Journal* as one of the "best reference books of the year," and a number of other financial aid titles, including the *College Student's Guide to Merit and Other No-Need Funding,* which was chosen as one of the "outstanding reference books of the year" by *Choice.*

Financial Aid Programs
Open to Asian Americans

Scholarships ●
Fellowships ●
Loans ●
Grants ●
Awards ●
Internships ●

Scholarships

Described here are 395 funding programs open to Asian Americans that are available to fund studies on the undergraduate level in the United States. Usually no return of service or repayment is required. Note: other funding opportunities for Asian American undergraduates are also described in the Loans, Grants, Awards, and Internships sections. So, if you are looking for a particular program and don't find it in this section, be sure to check the Program Title Index to see if it is covered elsewhere in the directory.

[1]
AAJAZ SCHOLARSHIPS

Asian American Journalists Association-Arizona
  Chapter
c/o Kristin Go
Arizona Republic
200 East Van Buren Street
Phoenix, AZ 85004
(602) 444-7967
E-mail: kristin.go@arizonarepublic.com
Web: www.aajaz.org/scholarships

Purpose To provide financial assistance to Asian American students majoring in fields related to journalism at colleges and universities in Arizona.

Eligibility This program is open to students of Asian descent who are studying journalism, broadcasting, or communications at a college or university in Arizona.

Financial data The stipend is $500.

Duration 1 year.

Number awarded 3 each year.

Deadline December of each year.

[2]
ABE AND ESTHER HAGIWARA STUDENT AID AWARD

Japanese American Citizens League
Attn: National Scholarship Awards
1765 Sutter Street
San Francisco, CA 94115
(415) 921-5225   Fax: (415) 931-4671
E-mail: jacl@jacl.org
Web: www.jacl.org/scholarships.html

Purpose To provide financial assistance for college or graduate school to student members of the Japanese American Citizens League (JACL) who can demonstrate severe financial need.

Eligibility This program is open to JACL members who are enrolled or planning to enroll in a college, university, trade school, or business college. Applicants must be undergraduate or graduate students who are able to demonstrate that, without this aid, they will have to delay or terminate their education. They must submit a statement describing their current level of involvement in the Japanese American community or Asian Pacific community and how they will continue their involvement in future years. Selection is based on financial need, academic record, extracurricular activities, and community involvement.

Financial data The stipend depends on the availability of funds but usually ranges from $1,000 to $5,000.

Duration 1 year; nonrenewable.

Additional information Applications must be submitted to the JACL National Scholarship Program, c/o San Diego JACL Chapter, 1031 25th Street, San Diego, CA 92102.

Number awarded At least 1 each year.

Deadline March of each year.

[3]
ACAP LEADERSHIP/COMMUNITY SERVICE SCHOLARSHIP

Association of Chinese American Professionals
Attn: Leadership Scholarship Committee
10202 Westoffice Drive
Houston, TX 77042-5306
(713) 789-4995
Web: www.acap-usa.org

Purpose To provide financial assistance for college to Chinese Americans who can demonstrate leadership in community service activities.

Eligibility This program is open to Chinese American students who are juniors or seniors in high school or freshmen, sophomores, or juniors in college. Applicants must have demonstrated leadership in community service to promote the social and/or political status of Chinese Americans or Asian Americans in the United States. Along with their application, they must submit an essay of 500 to 1,000 words on their leadership and community service experiences. Financial need is also considered in the selection process.

Financial data Stipends are at least $500.

Duration 1 year; nonrenewable.

Additional information The Association of Chinese American Professionals (ACAP) was founded in 1978. It recruits most of its members from Arkansas, Louisiana, Mississippi, Oklahoma, and Texas. Information on this scholarship is also available from Simon Tung, (713) 842-4003, E-mail: simonytung@yahoo.com

Number awarded 2 each year: 1 to a current high school student and 1 to a college student.

Deadline April of each year.

[4]
ACCOUNTANCY BOARD OF OHIO EDUCATION ASSISTANCE PROGRAM

Accountancy Board of Ohio
77 South High Street, 18th Floor
Columbus, OH 43215-6128
(614) 466-4135   Fax: (614) 466-2628
Web: acc.ohio.gov/edrule.html

Purpose To provide financial assistance to minority and financially disadvantaged students enrolled in an accounting education program at Ohio academic institutions approved by the Accountancy Board of Ohio.

Eligibility This program is open to minority and financially disadvantaged Ohio residents enrolled full time as sophomores, juniors, or seniors in an accounting program at an accredited college or university in the state. Students who remain in good standing at their institutions and who enter a qualified fifth-year program are also eligible, if funds are available. Minority is defined as people with significant ancestry from Africa (excluding the Middle East), Asia (excluding the Middle East), Central America and the Caribbean islands, South America, and the islands of the Pacific Ocean. Financial disadvantage is defined according to information provided on the Free Application for Federal Student Aid (FAFSA). U.S. citizenship or permanent resident status is required.

Financial data The amount of the stipend is determined annually but does not exceed the in-state tuition at Ohio public universities.

Duration 1 year; nonrenewable.
Number awarded Several each year.
Deadline May or November of each year.

[5]
AETNA/NCEMNA SCHOLARS PROGRAM

National Coalition of Ethnic Minority Nurse
Associations
c/o Dr. Betty Smith Williams, President
6101 West Centinela Avenue, Suite 378
Culver City, CA 90230
(310) 258-9515   Fax: (310) 258-9513
E-mail: bwilliams@ncemna.org
Web: www.ncemna.org/scholarships.html

Purpose To provide financial assistance to nursing students who are members of constituent organizations of the National Coalition of Ethnic Minority Nurse Associations (NCEMNA) working on a 4-year or master's degree.
Eligibility This program is open to members of the 5 associations that comprise NCEMNA: the Asian American/Pacific Islander Nurses Association, Inc. (AAPINA), the National Alaska Native American Indian Nurses Association, Inc. (NANAINA), the National Association of Hispanic Nurses, Inc. (NAHN), the National Black Nurses Association, Inc. (NBNA), and the Philippine Nurses Association of America, Inc. (PNAA). Applicants must be currently attending or applying to a 4-year or master's degree program in nursing. Along with their application, they must submit a letter of reference, demonstration of leadership and involvement in the ethnic community, and statement of career goals.
Financial data The stipend is $2,000.
Duration 1 year.
Additional information This program was established in 2004 with a grant from the Aetna Foundation.
Number awarded 5 each year: 1 nominee from each of the constituent associations.

[6]
AFSCME/UNCF UNION SCHOLARS PROGRAM

United Negro College Fund
Attn: Corporate Scholars Program
P.O. Box 1435
Alexandria, VA 22313-9998
Toll-free: (866) 671-7237   E-mail: internship@uncf.org
Web: www.uncf.org/internships/index.asp

Purpose To provide financial assistance to students of color who are interested in working during the summer on an organizing campaign for the American Federation of State, County and Municipal Employees (AFSCME).
Eligibility This program is open to students of color, including African Americans, Hispanic Americans, Asian/Pacific Islander Americans, and American Indians/Alaskan Natives. Applicants must be second semester sophomores or juniors and majoring in ethnic studies, women's studies, labor studies, American studies, sociology, anthropology, history, political science, psychology, social work, or economics. They must have a GPA of 2.5 or higher and be interested in working on a union organizing campaign at 1 of several locations in the United States.
Financial data The program provides a stipend of $4,000, on-site housing at their location, a week-long orientation

and training, and (based on successful performance during the organizing campaign) a $5,000 scholarship.
Duration 10 weeks for the organizing assignment; 1 year for the scholarship.
Number awarded Varies each year.
Deadline February of each year.

[7]
AIA-NJ SCHOLARSHIPS

Association of Indians in America-New Jersey Chapter
c/o Deepa Mehrotra
192 Midland Avenue
Glen Ridge, NJ 07028
(973) 748-5310   E-mail: ravim2@verizon.net
Web: www.aianj.org

Purpose To provide financial assistance for college to high school seniors in New Jersey who are of Asian Indian ancestry.
Eligibility This program is open to seniors graduating from high schools in New Jersey who are of Asian Indian ancestry or origin. Applicants must have 1) a GPA of 3.5 or higher or class standing in the top 10% of their class; 2) an excellent SAT or ACT score; and 3) a record of active participation in at least 2 non-academic extracurricular activities, such as varsity sports, social service, volunteer work, or cultural activities.
Financial data The stipend is $1,000.
Duration 1 year.
Number awarded 3 each year.
Deadline February of each year.

[8]
AIA/AAF MINORITY/DISADVANTAGED
SCHOLARSHIP PROGRAM

American Institute of Architects
Attn: American Architectural Foundation
1735 New York Avenue, N.W.
Washington, DC 20006-5292
(202) 626-7511   Fax: (202) 626-7420
E-mail: info@archfoundation.org
Web: www.archfoundation.org

Purpose To provide financial assistance to high school and college students from minority and/or disadvantaged backgrounds who are interested in studying architecture in college.
Eligibility This program is open to students from minority and/or disadvantaged backgrounds who are high school seniors, students in a community college or technical school transferring to an accredited architectural program, or college freshmen entering a professional degree program at an accredited program of architecture. Students who have completed 1 or more years of a 4-year college curriculum are not eligible. Initially, candidates must be nominated by 1 of the following organizations or persons: an individual architect or firm, a chapter of the American Institute of Architects (AIA), a community design center, a guidance counselor or teacher, the dean or professor at an accredited school of architecture, or the director of a community or civic organization. Nominees are reviewed and eligible candidates are invited to complete an application form in which they write an essay describing the reasons they are inter-

ested in becoming an architect and provide documentation of academic excellence and financial need. Selection is based primarily on financial need.

Financial data Awards range from $500 to $2,500 per year, depending upon individual need. Students must apply for supplementary funds from other sources.

Duration 9 months; may be renewed for up to 2 additional years.

Additional information This program is offered jointly by the American Architectural Foundation (AAF) and the AIA.

Number awarded Up to 20 each year.

Deadline Nominations are due by December of each year; final applications must be submitted in January.

[9]
AIKO SUSANNA TASHIRO HIRATSUKA MEMORIAL SCHOLARSHIP

Japanese American Citizens League
Attn: National Scholarship Awards
1765 Sutter Street
San Francisco, CA 94115
(415) 921-5225   Fax: (415) 931-4671
E-mail: jacl@jacl.org
Web: www.jacl.org/scholarships.html

Purpose To provide financial assistance for undergraduate education in the performing arts to student members of the Japanese American Citizens League (JACL).

Eligibility This program is open to JACL members who are working on undergraduate study in the performing arts. Applicants should provide published performance reviews and/or evaluations by their instructor. They must also submit a statement describing their current level of involvement in the Japanese American community or Asian Pacific community and how they will continue their involvement in future years. Selection is based on academic record, extracurricular activities, and community involvement. Professional artists are not eligible.

Financial data The stipend depends on the availability of funds but usually ranges from $1,000 to $5,000.

Duration 1 year; nonrenewable.

Additional information Applications must be submitted to the JACL National Scholarship Program, c/o San Diego JACL Chapter, 1031 25th Street, San Diego, CA 92102.

Number awarded 1 each year.

Deadline March of each year.

[10]
AIMMS EXCELLENCE SCHOLARSHIPS

Maryland State Department of Education
Attn: Achievement Initiative for Maryland's Minority
   Students Council
200 West Baltimore Street
Baltimore, MD 21201
(410) 887-2446
Web: www.msde.state.md.us

Purpose To provide financial assistance for college to Maryland high school seniors who have demonstrated leadership in addressing diversity.

Eligibility This program is open to seniors in high schools in Maryland who plan to attend a community college, university, college, or technical/vocational school. Applicants

must have a GPA of 3.0 or higher. They must submit an essay about their leadership in 1 or more of the following areas: 1) academic, school, or community support for diverse students; 2) promotion of positive intergroup relations and understanding; or 3) performance of services to increase success among diverse groups of students. Diverse groups include race/ethnicity, gender, age, disability, or poverty. Selection is based on academic success and contributions to better understanding and appreciation among diverse groups.

Financial data Stipends are $1,000 or $500.

Duration 1 year.

Additional information This program began in 1999. The scholarship for $1,000 is designated the Barbara Dezmon Scholarship

Number awarded 11 each year: 1 at $1,000 and 10 at $500.

Deadline July of each year.

[11]
AIR PRODUCTS AND CHEMICALS SCHOLARSHIP FOR DIVERSITY IN ENGINEERING

Association of Independent Colleges and Universities
   of Pennsylvania
101 North Front Street
Harrisburg, PA 17101-1405
(717) 232-8649   Fax: (717) 233-8574
E-mail: info@aicup.org
Web: www.aicup.org

Purpose To provide financial assistance to women and minority students at member institutions of the Association of Independent Colleges and Universities of Pennsylvania (AICUP) who are majoring in designated fields of engineering.

Eligibility This program is open to full-time undergraduate students at designated AICUP colleges and universities who are women and/or members of the following minority groups: American Indians, Alaska Natives, Asians, Blacks/African Americans, Hispanics/Latinos, Native Hawaiians, or Pacific Islanders. Applicants must be juniors majoring in chemical or mechanical engineering with a GPA of 2.7 or higher. Along with their application, they must submit an essay on their characteristics, accomplishments, primary interests, plans, and goals, and what sets them apart.

Financial data The stipend is $7,500 per year.

Duration 1 year; may be renewed 1 additional year if the recipient maintains appropriate academic standards.

Additional information This program, sponsored by Air Products and Chemicals, Inc., is available at the following AICUP colleges and universities: Bucknell University, Carnegie Mellon University, Drexel University, Gannon University, Geneva College, Grove City College, Lafayette College, Lehigh University, Messiah College, Swarthmore College, Villanova University, Widener University, and Wilkes University.

Number awarded 2 each year.

Deadline April of each year.

[12]
AKRON BEACON JOURNAL MINORITY SCHOLARSHIP PROGRAM

Akron Beacon Journal
Attn: Educational Services Manager
44 East Exchange Street
P.O. Box 640
Akron, OH 44309-0640
(330) 996-3860   E-mail: rkelly@thebeaconjournal.com
Web: www.ohio.com/mld/beaconjournal

Purpose To provide financial assistance to minority high school seniors in the Akron, Ohio area interested in preparing for a career in the newspaper industry.

Eligibility This program is open to minority high school seniors in the Ohio counties of Medina, Portage, Stark, Summit, and Wayne. Applicants must be interested in attending college and majoring in business, finance, communications, graphics, photography, journalism, marketing, or other areas related to the newspaper industry. They must submit up to 5 samples of work with bylines; 2 letters of recommendation; transcripts; SAT/ACT scores; and an essay covering their reasons for wanting to prepare for a career in the news or business side of the newspaper industry, their knowledge of Knight Ridder, and how they see themselves working in Knight Ridder.

Financial data The stipend is $1,000.

Duration 1 year; nonrenewable.

Additional information The recipients of these scholarships are automatically entered into competition for the Knight Ridder Minority Scholarship Program of $40,000 over 4 years.

Number awarded 2 each year.

Deadline January of each year.

[13]
ALICE YURIKO ENDO MEMORIAL SCHOLARSHIP

Japanese American Citizens League
Attn: National Scholarship Awards
1765 Sutter Street
San Francisco, CA 94115
(415) 921-5225   Fax: (415) 931-4671
E-mail: jacl@jacl.org
Web: www.jacl.org/scholarships.html

Purpose To provide financial assistance to student members of the Japanese American Citizens League (JACL) who are working on an undergraduate degree, particularly in public or social service.

Eligibility This program is open to JACL members who are currently enrolled or planning to reenter a college, university, trade school, business college, or other institution of higher learning. Applicants must submit a statement describing their current level of involvement in the Japanese American community or Asian Pacific community and how they will continue their involvement in future years. Selection is based on academic record, extracurricular activities, financial need, and community involvement. Preference is given to students planning a future in public or social service and/or residing in the Eastern District Council area.

Financial data The stipend depends on the availability of funds but usually ranges from $1,000 to $5,000.

Duration 1 year; nonrenewable.

Additional information Applications must be submitted to the JACL National Scholarship Program, c/o San Diego JACL Chapter, 1031 25th Street, San Diego, CA 92102.

Number awarded 1 each year.

Deadline March of each year.

[14]
ALLISON TRANSMISSION AND INDIANAPOLIS METAL CENTER SCHOLARSHIPS

National FFA Organization
Attn: Scholarship Office
6060 FFA Drive
P.O. Box 68960
Indianapolis, IN 46268-0960
(317) 802-4321   Fax: (317) 802-5321
E-mail: scholarships@ffa.org
Web: www.ffa.org

Purpose To provide financial assistance for college to FFA members who are from an ethnic minority group and interested in majoring in selected fields.

Eligibility This program is open to members who are graduating high school seniors planning to enroll full time in college. Applicants must be members of ethnic minority groups and interested in working on a 4-year degree in the following areas of agriculture: management, finance, science, engineering, and related specialties, although non-agricultural majors are also eligible. They must have a GPA of 3.0 or higher and be able to demonstrate financial need. Selection is based on academic achievement (10 points for GPA, 10 points for SAT or ACT score, 10 points for class rank), leadership in FFA activities (30 points), leadership in community activities (10 points), and participation in the Supervised Agricultural Experience (SAE) program (30 points). U.S. citizenship is required.

Financial data The stipend is $5,000 per year. Funds are paid directly to the recipient.

Duration 1 year; nonrenewable.

Additional information Funding for these scholarships is provided by the Allison Transmission and Indianapolis Metal Center of General Motors Corporation.

Number awarded 2 each year.

Deadline February of each year.

[15]
ALMA EXLEY SCHOLARSHIP

New Britain Foundation for Public Giving
Attn: Donor Relations Manager
29 Russell Street
New Britain, CT 06052-1312
(860) 229-6018   Fax: (860) 229-2641
E-mail: cfarmer@nbfoundation.org
Web: www.nbfoundation.org

Purpose To provide financial assistance to minority college students in Connecticut who are interested in preparing for a teaching career.

Eligibility This program is open to students of color in Connecticut who have passed the Praxis examination and have been admitted to a certified teacher preparation program at an accredited 4-year college or university in the state.

Financial data A stipend is awarded (amount not specified).

Duration 1 year.

Number awarded 1 each year.

[16]
AMBASSADOR MINERVA JEAN FALCON HAWAI'I SCHOLARSHIP

Hawai'i Community Foundation
Attn: Scholarship Department
1164 Bishop Street, Suite 800
Honolulu, HI 96813
(808) 537-6333   Toll-free: (888) 731-3863
Fax: (808) 521-6286
E-mail: scholarships@hcf-hawaii.org
Web: www.hawaiicommunityfoundation.org

Purpose To provide financial assistance to Hawaii residents of Filipino ancestry who are interested in attending college.

Eligibility This program is open to Hawaii residents of Filipino ancestry who are enrolled in or planning to enroll in an accredited college or university in Hawaii. Applicants must be full-time students at the undergraduate level and able to demonstrate academic achievement (GPA of 2.7 or higher), good moral character, and financial need. In addition to filling out the standard application form, applicants must write a 2-page essay on how they plan to be involved in the community as a Filipino-American student.

Financial data The amounts of the awards depend on the availability of funds and the need of the recipient; recently, the stipend was $1,000.

Duration 1 year.

Additional information This scholarship was first offered in 2001.

Number awarded Varies each year; recently, 1 of these scholarships was awarded.

Deadline February of each year.

[17]
AMELIA KEMP MEMORIAL SCHOLARSHIP

Women of the Evangelical Lutheran Church in America
Attn: Scholarships
8765 West Higgins Road
Chicago, IL 60631-4189
(773) 380-2730   Toll-free: (800) 638-3522, ext. 2730
Fax: (773) 380-2419   E-mail: womenelca@elca.org
Web: www.womenoftheelca.org

Purpose To provide financial assistance to lay women of color who are members of Evangelical Lutheran Church of America (ELCA) congregations and who wish to study on the undergraduate, graduate, professional, or vocational school level.

Eligibility These scholarships are available to ELCA lay women of color who are at least 21 years of age and have experienced an interruption of at least 2 years in their education since high school. Applicants must have been admitted to an educational institution to prepare for a career in other than a church-certified profession. U.S. citizenship is required.

Financial data The amount of the award varies, depending on the availability of funds.

Duration Up to 2 years.

Number awarded Varies each year, depending upon the funds available.

Deadline February of each year.

[18]
AMERICAN ASSOCIATION OF JAPANESE UNIVERSITY WOMEN SCHOLARSHIP PROGRAM

American Association of Japanese University Women
c/o Ms. Reiko Yamashita, Scholarship Committee Co-Chair
15325 South Menlo Avenue
Gardena, CA 90247-4240

Purpose To provide financial assistance to female students currently enrolled in upper-division or graduate classes in California.

Eligibility This program is open to female students enrolled in accredited colleges or universities in California. They must have junior, senior, or graduate standing. Applicants must be a contributor to U.S.-Japan relations, cultural exchanges, and leadership development in the areas of their designated field of study. To apply, they must submit a current resume, an official transcript of the past 2 years of college work, 2 letters of recommendation, and an essay (up to 2 pages in English or 1,200 characters in Japanese) on 1 of the following topics: 1) what I hope to accomplish in my field of study to develop leadership and role model qualities; or 2) thoughts on how my field of study can contribute to U.S.-Japan relations and benefit international relations.

Financial data The stipend is $1,000.

Duration 1 year.

Additional information The association was founded in 1970 to promote the education of women as well as to contribute to U.S.-Japan relations, cultural exchanges, and leadership development. Requests for applications must include a stamped self-addressed envelope.

Number awarded 1 or more each year.

Deadline September of each year.

[19]
AMERICAN DENTAL HYGIENISTS' ASSOCIATION INSTITUTE MINORITY SCHOLARSHIPS

American Dental Hygienists' Association
Attn: Institute for Oral Health
444 North Michigan Avenue, Suite 3400
Chicago, IL 60611
(312) 440-8918   Toll-free: (800) 735-4916
Fax: (312) 440-8929   E-mail: institute@adha.net
Web: www.adha.org/institute/Scholarship/index.htm

Purpose To provide financial assistance to minority students and males of any race enrolled in undergraduate programs in dental hygiene.

Eligibility This program is open to members of groups currently underrepresented in the dental hygiene profession (Native Americans, African Americans, Hispanics, Asians, and males) who are active members of the Student American Dental Hygienists' Association (SADHA) or the American Dental Hygienists' Association (ADHA). Applicants must have a GPA of 3.0 or higher, be able to document financial need of at least $1,500, and have completed at least 1 year of full-time enrollment in an accredited dental hygiene program in the United States. Along with their application, they must submit a statement that covers their long-term career goals, their intended contribution to the dental hygiene profession, their professional interests, and the manner in which their degree will enhance their professional capacity.

Financial data Stipends range from $1,000 to $2,000.
Duration 1 year; nonrenewable.
Number awarded 2 each year.
Deadline April of each year.

[20]
AMERICAN PHILOLOGICAL ASSOCIATION MINORITY SCHOLARSHIP

American Philological Association
Attn: Executive Director
University of Pennsylvania
291 Logan Hall
249 South 36th Street
Philadelphia, PA 19104-6304
(215) 898-4975   Fax: (215) 573-7874
E-mail: apaclassics@sas.upenn.edu
Web: www.apaclassics.org

Purpose To prepare minority undergraduates during the summer for advanced work in the classics.

Eligibility Eligible to apply are minority (African American, Hispanic American, Asian American, and Native American) undergraduate students who wish to engage in summer study as preparation for graduate work in the classics. Applicants may propose participation in summer programs in Italy, Greece, Egypt, or other classical centers; language training at institutions in the United States or Canada; or other relevant courses of study. Selection is based on academic qualifications, especially in classics; demonstrated ability in at least 1 classical language; quality of the proposal for study with respect to preparation for a career in classics; and financial need. Applications must be endorsed by a member of the American Philological Association (APA).

Financial data The maximum award is $3,000.
Duration 1 summer.
Number awarded 1 each year.
Deadline February of each year.

[21]
ANA MULTICULTURAL EXCELLENCE SCHOLARSHIP FUND

American Association of Advertising Agencies
Attn: Manager of Diversity Programs
405 Lexington Avenue, 18th Floor
New York, NY 10174-1801
(212) 682-2500   Toll-free: (800) 676-9333
Fax: (212) 682-8391   E-mail: tiffany@aaaa.org
Web: www.aaaa.org/diversity/foundation/funds.htm

Purpose To provide financial assistance to multicultural students who are working on an undergraduate degree in advertising.

Eligibility This program is open to undergraduate students who are U.S. citizens of proven multicultural heritage and have at least 1 grandparent of multicultural heritage. Final selection of recipients is made by advertising agencies that are chosen as winners of Multicultural Excellence Awards by the Association of National Advertisers (ANA). For that competition, advertising firms submit samples of their campaigns that ran for at least 3 months and were directed at multicultural markets. Entries are submitted in 5 categories: African American, Asian, Hispanic, General (e.g., Native American, Russian, Polish), or Campaign with Significant Results. Winners of those awards select recipients of these scholarships on the basis of demonstrated academic ability.

Financial data A stipend is awarded (amount not specified).
Duration 1 year.
Additional information This program was established by ANA in 2001. The American Association of Advertising Agencies (AAAA) assumed administration in 2003.
Number awarded 5 each year.

[22]
ANGELFIRE SCHOLARSHIP

Datatel Scholars Foundation
4375 Fair Lakes Court
Fairfax, VA 22033
(703) 968-9000, ext. 4549   Toll-free: (800) 486-4332
Fax: (703) 968-4573   E-mail: scholars@datatel.com
Web: www.datatel.com

Purpose To provide financial assistance to graduating high school seniors, continuing college students, and graduate students who will be studying at a Datatel client school and are veterans, veterans' dependents, or refugees from southeast Asia.

Eligibility This program is open to 1) veterans who served in the Asian theater (Vietnam, Cambodia, or Laos) between 1964 and 1975; 2) their spouses and children; 3) refugees from Vietnam, Cambodia, or Laos; and 4) veterans who served in Operation Desert Storm, Operation Enduring Freedom, and/or Operation Iraqi Freedom. Applicants must attend a Datatel client college or university during the upcoming school year. They must first apply to their institution, which selects 2 semifinalists and forwards their applications to the sponsor. Along with they application, they must include a 1,000-word personal statement that discusses how the conflict has affected them personally, summarizes how the conflict has impacted their educational goals, and describes how being awarded this scholarship will help them achieve their goals. Selection is based on the quality of the personal statement (40%), academic merit (30%), achievements and civic involvement (20%), and 2 letters of recommendation (10%).

Financial data Stipends are $2,400, $1,600, or $1,000, depending upon the cost of undergraduate tuition at the participating institution. Funds are paid directly to the institution.
Duration 1 year.
Additional information Datatel, Inc. produces advanced information technology solutions for higher education. It has more than 470 client sites in the United States and Canada. This scholarship was created to commemorate those who lost their lives in Vietnam or Iraq and is named after a memorial administered by the Disabled American Veterans Association in Angelfire, New Mexico.

Number awarded Varies each year. Recently, 10 of these scholarships were awarded: 7 at $2,400, 2 at $1,600, and 1 at $1,000.

Deadline Students must submit online applications to their institution or organization by January of each year.

[23]
ANHEUSER-BUSCH FOUNDATION SCHOLARSHIPS

Chicago Urban League
Attn: Education Department
4510 South Michigan Avenue
Chicago, IL 60653-3898
(773) 451-3565   Fax: (773) 285-7772
E-mail: info@cul-chicago.org
Web: www.cul-chicago.org

Purpose To provide financial assistance to Illinois residents of color interested in full-time study at a 4-year college or university.

Eligibility This program is open to minority residents of Illinois who will be full-time freshmen at a 4-year college or university. Applicants must have a GPA of 2.5 or higher and be able to demonstrate financial need. An interview is required.

Financial data The stipend is $2,500 per year.

Duration 4 years.

Additional information This program is supported by the Anheuser-Busch Foundation, which makes the final decision on selection of recipients.

Number awarded Varies each year.

Deadline May of each year.

[24]
ANNA GRACE SAWYER MINORITY SCHOLARSHIP

Presbytery of Chicago
Attn: Scholarship Coordinator
100 South Morgan Street
Chicago, IL 60607-2619
(312) 243-8300   Fax: (312) 243-8409
E-mail: roseblaney@chicagopresbytery.org
Web: www.chicagopresbytery.org

Purpose To provide financial assistance for college to minority students from the Chicago area who are affiliated with the Presbyterian Church (USA).

Eligibility This program is open to confirmed members of a Presbyterian Church in the Chicago Presbytery and, for nonmembers, participants in the youth program of those churches. Applicants must be African Americans, Hispanic Americans, Asian Americans, or Native Americans who have been accepted or are currently enrolled as a full-time undergraduate at an accredited college, university, or vocational school. They must demonstrate a volunteer spirit through service to others. Selection is based on the applicant's personal and financial situation and current and potential service to others.

Financial data Stipends range from $100 to $1,000. The exact amount awarded depends on the availability of funds.

Duration 1 year; recipients may reapply.

Additional information The Presbytery of Chicago covers Cook, DuPage, and Lake counties.

Number awarded 1 or more each year.

Deadline April of each year.

[25]
ANNE FORD SCHOLARSHIP

National Center for Learning Disabilities
Attn: Scholarship
381 Park Avenue South, Suite 1401
New York, NY 10016-8806
(212) 545-7510   Fax: (212) 545-9665
E-mail: AFScholarship@ncld.org
Web: www.ld.org

Purpose To provide financial assistance for college to high school seniors (particularly minorities and women) with learning disabilities.

Eligibility This program is open to high school seniors with learning disabilities who plan to work on a university degree. Applicants must submit an essay (750 to 1,000 words in length) describing their learning disability and how it has affected their life, including scholastic development, relationships with family and friends, community involvement, and future aspirations. They should specify their positive and negative experiences with a learning disability, and elaborate on how they have coped with the negative aspects. Their essay should demonstrate how they meet the program's goal of supporting "a person who has faced the challenges of having a learning disability and who, through hard work and perseverance, has created a life of purpose and achievement." If they prefer, they may submit a video or audio tape (up to 15 minutes in length) with accompanying script or outline that describes their experiences with a learning disability. Other required submissions include high school transcripts, portfolios (if applicable), 3 letters of recommendation, a financial statement (financial need is strongly considered in the selection process), and SAT and/or ACT scores. U.S. citizenship is required. Minorities and women are specifically encouraged to apply.

Financial data The stipend is $2,500 per year.

Duration 4 years, provided the recipient submits annual reports (written or in video format) detailing their progress in school and describing their insights about their personal growth.

Additional information This program was established in 2002.

Number awarded 1 each year.

Deadline December of each year.

[26]
APIO SCHOLARSHIP PROGRAM

Asian Pacific Islander Organization
3003 North Central Avenue, Suite 103
PMB 111
Phoenix, AZ 85012-2901
Web: www.apio.org/scholarships.htm

Purpose To provide financial assistance to Asian Pacific Americans who are interested in studying designated fields in college.

Eligibility This program is open to Asian Pacific American students who are working on or planning to work on a bachelor's degree in agriculture, computer science, engineering, or any field related to natural resource conservation. Preference is given to students working on a computer science or engineering degree with an emphasis on geographic information systems (GIS), natural resources, or conservation in their academic program. Selection is based on academic achievement, personal strengths, leadership abilities, and career goals.

Financial data　The stipend is $500.

Duration　1 year.

Additional information　The Asian Pacific Islander Organization (APIO) was established in 1998 as a professional society of employees of the Natural Resources Conservation Service of the U.S. Department of Agriculture. Information on this program is also available from San Ly, Scholarship Committee Chair, USDA-Natural Resources Conservation Service, 44 West Street, Suite 1, Walton, NY 13856, (607) 865-7090, ext. 236, Fax: (607) 865-5535, E-mail: sam.ly@ny.usda.gov.

Number awarded　3 each year.

Deadline　July of each year.

[27]
APPRAISAL INSTITUTE MINORITIES AND WOMEN EDUCATIONAL SCHOLARSHIP PROGRAM

Appraisal Institute
Attn: Minorities and Women Scholarship Fund
550 West Van Buren Street, Suite 1000
Chicago, IL 60607
(312) 335-4121　　　　　　Fax: (312) 335-4118
E-mail: sbarnes@appraisalinstitute.org
Web: www.appraisalinstitute.org

Purpose　To provide financial assistance to women and minority undergraduate students majoring in real estate or allied fields.

Eligibility　This program is open to members of groups underrepresented in the real estate appraisal profession. Those groups include women, American Indians, Alaska Natives, Asians, Black or African Americans, Hispanics or Latinos, and Native Hawaiians or other Pacific Islanders. Applicants must be full- or part-time students enrolled in real estate courses within a degree-granting college, university, or junior college. They must submit evidence of demonstrated financial need and a GPA of 2.5 or higher. U.S. citizenship is required.

Financial data　The stipend is $1,000 per year. Funds are paid directly to the recipient's institution to be used for tuition and fees.

Duration　1 year.

Number awarded　At least 1 each year.

Deadline　April of each year.

[28]
ARKANSAS CONFERENCE ETHNIC LOCAL CHURCH CONCERNS SCHOLARSHIPS

United Methodist Church-Arkansas Conference
Attn: Ethnic Local Church Concerns
Two Trudie Kibbe Reed Drive
Little Rock, AR 72202-3770
(501) 324-8000　　　　　Toll-free: (877) 646-1816
Fax: (501) 324-8018　　　　E-mail: mallen@arumc.org
Web: www.arumc.org

Purpose　To provide financial assistance for college to ethnic minority Methodist students from Arkansas.

Eligibility　This program is open to ethnic minority undergraduate students who are active members of local congregations affiliated with the Arkansas Conference of the United Methodist Church. Applicants must be currently enrolled in an institution of higher education. Along with their application, they must submit a transcript and documentation of participation in local church activities.

Financial data　The stipend is $1,000.

Duration　1 year; may be renewed.

Number awarded　1 or more each year.

Deadline　September of each year.

[29]
ARKANSAS GAME AND FISH SCHOLARSHIP

Arkansas Game and Fish Commission
Two Natural Resources Drive
Little Rock, AR 72205
(501) 223-6300　　　　　Toll-free: (800) 364-4263
Web: www.agfc.com

Purpose　To provide financial assistance to high school seniors and undergraduates (particularly minorities) from Arkansas interested in preparing for a career in fish and wildlife management.

Eligibility　Applicants must be high school seniors or college undergraduates interested in preparing for a career in the field of natural resource conservation and/or wildlife law enforcement, including fishery management, environmental education and interpretation, and related fields. They must be Arkansas residents, have at least a 2.5 GPA, and intend to attend school on a full-time basis. Selection is based on merit. Minorities are particularly encouraged to apply. Full-time employees of the Arkansas Game and Fish Commission, their spouses, and their children are not eligible for these scholarships.

Financial data　The stipend is $1,000 per year. Funds are to be used for tuition, books, fees, and lodging.

Duration　1 year; may be awarded for up to 4 additional years.

Additional information　Applicants must not have received a full scholarship from another source. They must attend or be accepted for admission at an accredited 4-year college or university in the state.

Number awarded　25 each year.

Deadline　October of each year.

[30]
ARTHUR H. GOODMAN MEMORIAL SCHOLARSHIPS

CDC Small Business Finance
Attn: Memorial Scholarship Program
925 Fort Stockton Drive
San Diego, CA 92103
(619) 291-3594　　　　　Toll-free: (800) 611-5170
Fax: (619) 291-6954
Web: www.cdcloans.com/scholar.htm

Purpose　To provide financial assistance to women and minority college students from southern California who are interested in preparing for a career related to community development.

Eligibility　This program is open to women and minorities who are residents of or attending school in Imperial, Orange, Riverside, San Bernardino, or San Diego counties. Applicants must have completed 2 years of community college study with a GPA of 3.0 or higher and be ready to transfer to a 4-year college or university. They must be interested in preparing for a career in business, government, nonprofit, public service, or other profession that will improve their community. Along with their application, they must submit 2 letters of recommendation (including 1 from a supervisor or mentor of a community service or economic development project with which they have volunteered or worked); official transcripts of community college courses; a personal statement that covers their career goal, why they have chosen that as their path, an individual or event that has influenced their decision to attend college and/or select their desired career, their personal perspective on the role of community involvement and volunteerism, and why they feel they are a strong candidate for this scholarship.

Financial data Stipends range from $1,500 to $3,000.

Duration 1 year.

Additional information This program was established in 1998 with a fund administered through the San Diego Foundation.

Number awarded Approximately 4 each year.

Deadline May of each year.

[31]
ASCE MAINE SECTION SCHOLARSHIP

American Society of Civil Engineers-Maine Section
c/o Holly Anderson, P.E.
Maine Department of Transportation
Urban and Arterial Highway Program
16 State House Section
Augusta, ME 04333-0016
(207) 624-3349   E-mail: holly.anderson@state.me.us

Purpose To provide financial assistance to high school seniors (particularly minorities and women) in Maine who are interested in studying civil engineering in college.

Eligibility This program is open to graduating high school seniors who are Maine residents and who intend to study civil engineering in college. Women and minorities are especially encouraged to apply. Applicants must submit a 200-word statement describing why they have chosen civil engineering as a career and what they hope to accomplish by being a civil engineer. Selection is based on the statement, academic performance, extracurricular activities, and letters of recommendation.

Financial data The stipend is $2,000.

Duration 1 year; nonrenewable.

Number awarded 1 each year.

Deadline January of each year.

[32]
ASEI UNDERGRADUATE SCHOLARSHIPS

American Society of Engineers of Indian Origin
c/o Ramu Ramamurthy, Scholarship Committee Chair
47790 Pavillon Road
Canton, MI 48188
(248) 226-6895   Fax: (248) 226-7166
E-mail: awards@aseimichigan.org.
Web: www.aseio.org

Purpose To provide financial assistance to undergraduate students of Indian origin (from India) who are majoring in architecture, engineering, or related areas.

Eligibility This program is open to undergraduate students of Indian origin (by birth, ancestry, or relation). They must be enrolled full time at an accredited college or university in the United States and majoring in engineering, architecture, computer science, or allied science with a GPA of 3.2 or higher. Selection is based on demonstrated ability, academic achievement (including GPA, honors, and awards), career objectives, faculty recommendations, involvement in science fair and campus activities, and industrial exposure (including part-time work and internships).

Financial data The stipend is $1,000.

Duration 1 year.

Number awarded Several each year.

Deadline June of each year.

[33]
ASIA PACIFIC EXCHANGE SCHOLARSHIPS

Eastman Kodak Company
Attn: Asia Pacific Exchange
343 State Street
Rochester, NY 14650-1193
(585) 724-9388   Fax: (585) 724-9416
E-mail: mimi.lee@kodak.com
Web: www.kodak.com

Purpose To provide financial assistance and work experience to Asian American high school seniors from the Rochester, New York area who are interested in studying selected business, engineering, or science fields in college.

Eligibility This program is open to Asian American residents of the Rochester, New York area who are graduating high school seniors. Applicants must be planning to enroll full time in an approved degree program in accounting, chemical engineering, chemistry, computer engineering, computer science, electrical engineering, finance, information systems, logistics, manufacturing engineering, mechanical engineering, optical engineering, optics science, or software engineering. They must have an ACT score of 25 or higher (or the equivalent on the SAT). Selection is based on academic achievement and leadership within the community.

Financial data The stipend is $10,000 per year.

Duration 4 years, provided the recipient maintains a GPA of 3.0 or higher, full-time enrollment in an approved degree program, and timely progress toward completion of the degree.

Additional information Recipients are required to complete at least 1 cooperative internship with Kodak.

Number awarded 1 each year.

Deadline February of each year.

[34]

ASIAN AMERICAN SCHOLARSHIP

US Pan Asian American Chamber of Commerce
Attn: Scholarship Coordinator
1329 18th Street, N.W.
Washington, DC 20036
(202) 296-5221   Fax: (202) 296-5225
E-mail: administrator@uspaacc.com
Web: www.uspaacc.com

Purpose To provide financial assistance for college to Asian American high school seniors who demonstrate financial need.

Eligibility This program is open to high school seniors of Asian heritage who are U.S. citizens or permanent residents. Applicants must be planning to begin full-time study at an accredited postsecondary educational institution in the United States. Along with their application, they must submit a 500-word essay on "Why I need this scholarship." Selection is based on academic excellence (GPA of 3.3 or higher), leadership in extracurricular activities, community service involvement, and financial need.

Financial data The maximum stipend is $5,000. Funds are paid directly to the recipient's college or university.

Duration 1 year.

Additional information This program was established in 1989. Funding is not provided for correspondence courses, Internet courses, or study in a country other than the United States.

Number awarded 1 each year.

Deadline February of each year.

[35]

ASIAN CHURCH MULTIPLICATION TEAM SCHOLARSHIPS

Southern Baptist Convention
North American Mission Board
Attn: Church Multiplication Team
4200 North Point Parkway
Alpharetta, GA 30022-4176
(770) 410-6235   Fax: (770) 410-6012
E-mail: jdoyle@namb.net
Web: www.namb.net

Purpose To provide financial assistance to Asian American Baptists interested in religious vocations.

Eligibility This program is open to Asian Americans who are U.S. citizens involved in some type of approved Baptist ministry. Applicants must be able to demonstrate financial need. Only students in accredited institutions working toward a basic college (bachelor's) or seminary (M.Div.) degree are eligible. As part of the selection process, applicants must submit an essay describing their interest in and commitment to a Christian vocation.

Financial data The maximum grants are $500 per year for students attending accredited colleges, $600 per year for students in non-Southern Baptist Convention seminaries, and $850 per year for students at 1 of the 6 Southern Baptist Convention seminaries.

Duration 1 year; renewable.

Additional information The 6 Southern Baptist seminaries are Golden Gate Baptist Theological Seminary (Mill Valley, California), Midwestern Baptist Theological Seminary (Kansas City, Missouri), New Orleans Baptist Theological Seminary (New Orleans, Louisiana), Southeastern Baptist Theological Seminary (Wake Forest, North Carolina), Southern Baptist Theological Seminary (Louisville, Kentucky), and Southwestern Baptist Theological Seminary (Fort Worth, Texas).

Number awarded Varies each year.

Deadline Applications may be submitted at any time, but they must be received at least 1 month (preferably sooner) before the student enrolls in a school.

[36]

ASIAN COMMUNITY DEVELOPMENT SCHOLARSHIPS

Asian Business Association of Orange County
Attn: Asian Community Development
2960 South Daimler Street
Santa Ana, CA 92705
(949) 222-2291   Fax: (949) 222-2293
Web: www.abaoc.org/scholarship.html

Purpose To provide financial assistance for college to residents of Orange County, California who are of Asian descent.

Eligibility To program is open to residents of Orange County, California who have at least 1 Asian parent and are either graduating from high school or enrolled in their first or second year of college. Applicants must a transcript, a resume, and 2 letters of recommendation. They must also submit an essay on a topic that is presented to them at the time of an interview. Selection is based on academic performance, community involvement, and proficiency and quality of the essay.

Financial data The stipend is $1,000.

Duration 1 year.

Additional information Information is also available from Maria Erlinda C. Sarno, Scholarship Committee Chair, P.O. Box 1023, Artesia, CA 90702.

Number awarded 2 each year.

Deadline July of each year.

[37]

ASIAN & PACIFIC ISLANDER AMERICAN SCHOLARSHIPS

Asian & Pacific Islander American Scholarship Fund
P.O. Box 57
San Francisco, CA 94104
(415) 808-0805   Toll-free: (877) 808-7032
E-mail: scholarshipquestions@apiasf.org
Web: www.apiasf.org

Purpose To provide financial assistance to Asian and Pacific Islander Americans who are entering college for the first time.

Eligibility This program is open to U.S. citizens, nationals, permanent residents, and citizens of the Freely Associated States who are first-time incoming college students. Applicants must be enrolling full time in an accredited 2-year or 4-year college or university in the United States, Guam, American Samoa, U.S. Virgin Islands, or the Commonwealth of the Northern Mariana Islands. They must have a GPA of 2.7 or higher or the GED equivalent. Along with their application, they must submit an essay of 275 words or less that describes an experience in their life that either demonstrates their character or helped to shape it. Selection is based on the essay, academic record, academic plans and career goals, community service, a letter of recommendation, and financial need.

Financial data The stipend is $2,000.

Duration 1 year.

Additional information These scholarships were first offered in 2005. Support for this program is provided by such sponsors as the AT&T Foundation, Wells Fargo and Company, the Coca-Cola Company, Wal-Mart Stores, Hilton Hotels Foundation, General Mills Foundation, and the Asian McDonald's Owners/Operators Association.

Number awarded 1 or more each year.

Deadline February of each year.

[38]
ASIAN PACIFIC ISLANDER UNIVERSITY SCHOLARSHIP OF THE CALIFORNIA STATE FAIR

California State Fair
Attn: Friends of the Fair Scholarship Program
1600 Exposition Boulevard
P.O. Box 15649
Sacramento, CA 95852
(916) 274-5969   E-mail: wross@calexpo.com
Web: www.bigfun.org

Purpose To provide financial assistance to California residents of Asian Pacific Islander heritage who plan to attend a 4-year college or university in the state.

Eligibility This program is open to Asian Pacific Islanders who are currently enrolled in a high school or community college in California. Applicants must be planning to attend a 4-year college or university in the state in the following fall. They must have a GPA of 3.0 or higher. Along with their application, they must submit a 2-page statement on their Asian Pacific Islander background, community involvement, career goals, and desire to give back to their community. Selection is based on personal commitment, goals established for their chosen field, leadership potential, and civic accomplishments.

Financial data The stipend is $1,000.

Duration 1 year.

Additional information The Friends of the Fair Scholarship Program was established in 1993.

Number awarded 1 each year.

Deadline March of each year.

[39]
ASIAN PACIFIC STATE EMPLOYEES ASSOCIATION SCHOLARSHIPS

Asian Pacific State Employees Association
Attn: APSEA Foundation Scholarship Committee
P.O. Box 22188
Sacramento, CA 95822
(916) 554-0791
E-mail: apseascholarship@eudoramail.com
Web: www.apsea.org/foundation-scholarship.htm

Purpose To provide financial assistance for college to members of the Asian/Pacific Islander community in the greater Sacramento region of California.

Eligibility This program is open to high school seniors and continuing community college students who live in the greater Sacramento region of California. Applicants must be planning to attend a college, university, vocational school, or community college in the following academic year. They must have ties to the Asian/Pacific Islander community. Along with their application, they must submit a 200-word essay on how their cultural heritage has influenced their educational goals.

Financial data The stipend is $1,000.

Duration 1 year.

Additional information Scholarship winners must attend the awards dinner in Sacramento in April.

Number awarded 1 or more each year.

Deadline February of each year.

[40]
ASIAN REPORTER FOUNDATION SCHOLARSHIPS

Asian Reporter
Attn: AR Foundation
922 North Killingsworth Street, Suite 1-A
Portland, OR 97217
(503) 283-4440   Fax: (503) 283-4445
E-mail: arfoundation@asianreporter.com
Web: www.asianreporter.com

Purpose To provide financial assistance for college to residents of Oregon and Clark County, Washington who are of Asian descent.

Eligibility This program is open to 2 categories of students: 1) Oregon residents attending Oregon schools of higher education; and 2) residents of Oregon or Clark County, Washington attending schools of higher education in Oregon or Washington. Applicants must be of Asian descent, have a GPA of 3.0 or higher, be a graduating high school senior or current college student working on or planning to work on an undergraduate degree as a full-time student, have a record of involvement in community- or school-related activities, and be able to demonstrate financial need.

Financial data Stipends are $1,000 or $500.

Duration 1 year; nonrenewable.

Number awarded Varies each year; recently, 15 of these scholarships were awarded.

Deadline March of each year.

[41]
ASSOCIATED COLLEGES OF ILLINOIS SCHOLARSHIP PROGRAM

Associated Colleges of Illinois
Attn: Executive Director
20 North Wacker Drive, Suite 1456
Chicago, IL 60606
(312) 263-2391, ext. 23   Fax: (312) 263-3424
E-mail: aci@acifund.org
Web: www.acifund.org

Purpose To provide financial assistance to minority and other students attending or planning to attend an academic institution affiliated with the Associated Colleges of Illinois (ACI).

Eligibility Eligible to apply are students entering or currently enrolled at the 24 private colleges and universities that are members of ACI. The program includes 5 categories of awards: 1) first-generation and minority scholarships, to support students who are the first in their family to attend college and encourage minority achievement and graduation; 2) college-to-work scholarships, to attract more students to specific fields of study and career paths; 3) basic needs scholarships, to address students' unmet financial needs; 4) emergency assistance scholarships, to direct critical financial support to students experiencing personal or family emergencies; and 5) academic merit scholarships, to reward the best and the brightest students.

Financial data Awards depend on the availability of funds and the need of the recipient.

Duration 1 year; may be renewed.

Additional information Members of ACI are Augustana College, Aurora University, Concordia University, Dominican University, Elmhurst College, Eureka College, Greenville College, Illinois College, Illinois Wesleyan University, Knox College, Lake Forest College, Lewis University, McKendree College, Millikin University, Monmouth College, North Central College, North Park University, Olivet Nazarene University, Principia College, Quincy University, Rockford College, Saint Xavier University, Trinity Christian College, and University of St. Francis. This program includes the following named scholarships: the A. Montgomery Ward Scholarship, the Betty A. DeVries Memorial Fund, the Carole B. Whitcomb Endowed Scholarship, the Fifth Third Bank Scholarship Award, the Grover Hermann Foundation Scholarship, HSBC Scholars, the James S. Copley Foundation Scholarship, MB Financial Bank Scholarship, the McGraw Foundation Emergency Award, the Michelle and Peter Willmott Fund for Minority Leadership, the Motorola Scholarship, the Motorola Minority Scholarship, the Nick Amatangelo Scholarship, the Paul Hucko Memorial Scholarship, the Pepper Family Scholarship, the Polk Brothers Minority Scholarship, the UPS Scholarship, the Vulcan Materials Scholarship, and the Ward Scholarship.

Number awarded Varies each year; since 1990, this program has awarded more than $2 million in financial aid to 1,600 students.

[42]
ASSOCIATED FOOD DEALERS OF MICHIGAN MINORITY SCHOLARSHIPS

Associated Food Dealers of Michigan
Attn: AFD Foundation
18470 West Ten Mile Road
Southfield, MI 48075
(248) 557-9600   Toll-free: (800) 666-6233
Fax: (248) 557-9610   E-mail: info@afdom.org
Web: www.afdom.org

Purpose To provide financial assistance to minority high school seniors and currently-enrolled college students in Michigan.

Eligibility This program is open to high school seniors as well as college freshmen, sophomores, and juniors. Applicants must be members of at least 1 of the following minority groups: African American, Hispanic Americans, Asian American, Native American, or Arab/Chaldean American. Preferential consideration is given to applicants who are either employed by a company (for at least 6 months) or whose parent is employed by a company (for at least 1 year) that is an AFD member; however, membership is not required. Selection is based on academic performance,

leadership, and participation in school and community activities.

Financial data The stipend is $1,000.

Duration 1 year; recipients may reapply.

Additional information This program is administered by Scholarship Program Administrators, Inc., 1201 Eighth Avenue South, P.O. Box 23737, Nashville, TN 27202-3737, (615) 320-3149, Fax: (615) 320-3151, E-mail: info@spaprog.com. Recipients must attend college on a full-time basis.

Number awarded At least 10 each year.

Deadline March of each year.

[43]
ATLANTA CHAPTER OF AAJA SCHOLARSHIPS

Asian American Journalists Association-Atlanta Chapter
c/o Patti Tom, President
Primedia Business Magazines
6151 Powers Ferry Road, Suite 200
Atlanta, GA 30339
(770) 618-0310   (770) 618-0204
E-mail: ptom@primediabusiness.com
Web: chapters.aaja.org/Atlanta

Purpose To provide financial assistance to Asian American undergraduate and graduate students in the Southeast who are interested in preparing for a career in journalism.

Eligibility This program is open to Asian American graduate or undergraduate students enrolled in an accredited college or university in the Southeast. Applicants must be interested in preparing for a career in print, photo, or broadcast journalism.

Financial data Stipends are $1,000 or $250.

Duration 1 year.

Number awarded Varies each year. Recently, 4 of these scholarships were awarded: 3 at $1,000 and 1 at $250.

Deadline October of each year.

[44]
AVON GRANT SCHOLARSHIPS

Chicago Urban League
Attn: Education Department
4510 South Michigan Avenue
Chicago, IL 60653-3898
(773) 451-3565   Fax: (773) 285-7772
E-mail: info@cul-chicago.org
Web: www.cul-chicago.org

Purpose To provide financial assistance to Illinois residents who are women of color interested in full-time study at a 4-year college or university.

Eligibility This program is open to minority women residents of Illinois who will be full-time freshmen at a 4-year college or university. Applicants must have a GPA of 2.5 or higher, be a head of household, and be able to demonstrate financial need. An interview is required.

Financial data The stipend is $1,000 per year.

Duration 1 year.

Number awarded 2 each year.

Deadline May of each year.

[45]
BAKER FAMILY FOUNDATION SCHOLARSHIP

Baker Family Foundation
17 Gelnnon Farm Lane
Lebanon, NJ 08833
E-mail: info@bakerfamilyfoundation.org
Web: www.baakerfamilyfoundation.org

Purpose To provide financial assistance to high school students (especially minorities) facing obstacles when trying to attend college.

Eligibility Open to high school seniors interested in attending college. While the foundation does not target any specific ethnic group, the majority of the recipients come from urban minority groups. The first step in the application process is to find a sponsor, who will then submit part 1 of the preliminary application. If selected for the next stage, students submit part 2 of the application, as well as financial, academic, and any other necessary documentation. References are contacted and the candidates are interviewed. From this group, finalists are selected. Selection is based on financial need, desire to achieve, and academic performance (generally a GPA of 3.0 or higher).

Financial data The amount awarded varies, depending upon several factors: personal and family resources, the applicant's financial aid package, other outside scholarships, and any unusual circumstances that might have financial impact. The foundation attempts to "fill the gap" between the true costs of attending school and all other sources of financial aid. Funds may be used for tuition, room and board, transportation, day care expenses, family assistance, computer training, and college prep classes.

Duration 1 year; may be renewed if the recipient maintains at least a "B" average, continues to demonstrate financial need, and remains a student in good standing.

Number awarded Varies each year.

Deadline While applications may be submitted at any time, students are encouraged to submit their applications as soon after the first of the new year as possible.

[46]
BANATAO FILIPINO AMERICAN EDUCATION FUND COLLEGE SCHOLARSHIPS

Asian Pacific Fund
Attn: Scholarship Coordinator
225 Bush Street, Suite 590
San Francisco, CA 94104
(415) 433-6859   Toll-free: (800) 286-1688
Fax: (415) 433-2425
E-mail: scholarship@asianpacificfund.org
Web: www.asianpacificfund.org

Purpose To provide financial assistance to high school seniors of Filipino heritage in designated northern California counties who are interested in studying computer science, engineering, or physical science in college.

Eligibility This program is open to seniors at high schools in the following northern California counties: Alameda, Contra Costa, Marin, Merced, Monterey, Napa, Sacramento, San Francisco, San Joaquin, San Mateo, Santa Clara, Santa Cruz, Solano, Sonoma, and Stanislaus. Applicants must be of at least 50% Filipino heritage, have a GPA of 3.0 or higher, and plan to enroll in a 4-year college or university to major in computer science, mathematics, or physical sci-

ence. Selection is based on academic achievement, personal strengths (such as maturity and motivation), potential to succeed, interest in engineering or science as a career, participation in family and community activities, honors, work experience, a statement of educational and career goals, an outside appraisal, and financial need.

Financial data The stipend is $5,000 per year.

Duration 1 year; may be renewed for up to 3 additional years if the recipient continues to meet the eligibility criteria.

Number awarded 5 each year.

Deadline February of each year.

[47]
BASF AGRICULTURAL PRODUCTS SCHOLARSHIPS

National FFA Organization
Attn: Scholarship Office
6060 FFA Drive
P.O. Box 68960
Indianapolis, IN 46268-0960
(317) 802-4321   Fax: (317) 802-5321
E-mail: scholarships@ffa.org
Web: www.ffa.org

Purpose To provide financial assistance to women and minority FFA members who are interested in studying specified agribusiness fields in college.

Eligibility This program is open to members who are either graduating high school seniors planning to enroll in college or students already enrolled in college. Applicants must 1) be interested in working full time on a 4-year degree in agricultural marketing, merchandising, or sales; 2) be women or members of a minority group; 3) have a GPA of 3.0 or higher; 4) have participated in community service; and 5) be able to demonstrate strong leadership skills and financial need. Selection is based on academic achievement (10 points for GPA, 10 points for SAT or ACT score, 10 points for class rank), leadership in FFA activities (30 points), leadership in community activities (10 points), and participation in the Supervised Agricultural Experience (SAE) program (30 points). U.S. citizenship is required.

Financial data The stipend is $1,000. Funds are paid directly to the recipient.

Duration 1 year; nonrenewable.

Additional information Funding for these scholarships is provided by BASF Agricultural Products.

Number awarded 7 each year.

Deadline February of each year.

[48]
BELVA DAVIS DIVERSITY SCHOLARSHIP

American Women in Radio and Television-Golden Gate
    Chapter
c/o Jackie Wright
UPN Bay Area, KBHK-TV
855 Battery Street
San Francisco, CA 94111-1597
(415) 765-8725   E-mail: jwright@kbhktv.com
Web: www.awrtgold.org/pages/scholarship.htm

Purpose To provide financial assistance to minority students in the San Francisco Bay area who are interested in a career as a broadcast journalist.

Eligibility This program is open to students who have been enrolled for at least 2 years in a San Francisco Bay area high school, 4-year college or university, or graduate school. Applicants must be members of minority groups who are preparing for a career as a broadcast journalist. Selection is based on educational achievements, journalistic achievements and plans, leadership experience, extracurricular activities, community involvement, academic goals, overall future plans and goals, and financial need.
Financial data A stipend is awarded.
Duration 1 year.
Additional information This program was established in 1999.
Number awarded 1 each year.
Deadline May of each year.

[49]
BEVERLY YIP SCHOLARSHIPS

Union of Pan Asian Communities
Attn: Development Coordinator
1031 25th Street
San Diego, CA 92102
(619) 232-6454   Fax: (619) 235-9002
E-mail: info@upacsd.com
Web: www.upacsd.com/programs.html

Purpose To provide financial assistance to Asian and Pacific Islander residents of San Diego County, California who are interested in studying designated fields in college.
Eligibility This program is open residents of San Diego County, California who are Asian, Pacific Islander, or of refugee status. Applicants may be high school seniors, undergraduates, or graduate student, but they must be studying health and human services, international relations, psychology, social work, criminal justice, health promotion and disease prevention, engineering, business, or science. Along with their application, they must submit an autobiographical statement, documentation of financial need, and 2 letters of recommendation.
Financial data The stipend is $1,000.
Duration 1 year.
Number awarded 3 each year.
Deadline February of each year.

[50]
BILOXI SUN HERALD MINORITY SCHOLARSHIP PROGRAM

Biloxi Sun Herald
Attn: Scholarship Committee
P.O. Box 4567
Biloxi, MS 39535-4567
(228) 896-2365   Fax: (228) 896-2151
Web: www.sunherald.com

Purpose To provide financial assistance to minority high school students in Mississippi who are interested in attending college to prepare for a career in the newspaper industry.
Eligibility This program is open to minority high school seniors graduating from high schools in Mississippi. They must be interested in attending college to prepare for a career in the news or business aspects of the newspaper industry. Along with their application, they must submit a

500-word essay on why they want to prepare for a career in the newspaper industry. Selection is based on the essay, 2 letters of recommendation, a transcript of grades (including SAT/ACT scores), journalism or business experience, and extracurricular activities.
Financial data The stipend is $1,000.
Duration 1 year.
Additional information The recipients of these scholarships are automatically entered into competition for the Knight Ridder Minority Scholarship Program of $40,000 over 4 years.
Number awarded 1 each year.
Deadline January of each year.

[51]
BLUE CROSS BLUE SHIELD OF WISCONSIN NURSING SCHOLARSHIPS

Wisconsin League for Nursing
2121 East Newport Avenue
Milwaukee, WI 53211-2952
(414) 332-6271
Web: www.cuw.edu/wln/scholarship.htm

Purpose To provide financial assistance to residents (especially minorities) of Wisconsin attending a school of nursing in the state.
Eligibility This program is open to residents of Wisconsin who working on an undergraduate degree at an accredited school of nursing in the state. Applicants must have completed at least half the credits needed for graduation. They may obtain applications only from their school of nursing; no applications are sent from the sponsor's office. Ethnic minority students are especially encouraged to apply. Selection is based on scholastic ability, professional abilities and/or community service, understanding of the nursing profession, goals upon graduation, and financial need.
Financial data Stipends range from $500 to $1,000.
Duration 1 year.
Additional information Information is also available from Mary Ann Tanner, P.O. Box 107, Long Lake, WI 53542-0107. This program is sponsored by Blue Cross Blue Shield of Wisconsin.
Number awarded Varies each year. Recently, 5 of these scholarships were awarded.
Deadline July of each year.

[52]
BOB STANLEY AND AL COMPTON MINORITY AND INTERNATIONAL SCHOLARSHIP

Baptist Communicators Association
Attn: Scholarship Committee
1715-K South Rutherford Boulevard, Suite 295
Murfreesboro, TN 37130
(615) 904-0152   E-mail: bca.office@comcast.net
Web: www.baptistcommunicators.org/scholar.htm

Purpose To provide financial assistance to minority and international students who are working on an undergraduate degree to prepare for a career in Baptist communications.
Eligibility This program is open to undergraduate students of minority ethnic or international origin. Applicants must be majoring in communications, English, journalism,

or public relations with a GPA of 2.5 or higher. Their vocational objective must be in Baptist communications. Along with their application, they must submit a statement explaining why they desire to receive this scholarship.

Financial data The stipend is $1,000.

Duration 1 year; recipients may reapply.

Additional information This program was established in 1996.

Number awarded 1 each year.

Deadline January of each year.

[53]
BOOKER T. WASHINGTON SCHOLARSHIPS

National FFA Organization
Attn: Scholarship Office
6060 FFA Drive
P.O. Box 68960
Indianapolis, IN 46268-0960
(317) 802-4321   Fax: (317) 802-5321
E-mail: scholarships@ffa.org
Web: www.ffa.org

Purpose To provide financial assistance to minority FFA members who are interested in studying agriculture in college.

Eligibility This program is open to members who are graduating high school seniors planning to enroll full time in college. Applicants must be members of a minority ethnic group (African American, Asian American, Pacific Islander, Hispanic, Alaska Native, or American Indian) planning to work on a 4-year degree in agriculture. Selection is based on academic achievement (10 points for GPA, 10 points for SAT or ACT score, 10 points for class rank), leadership in FFA activities (30 points), leadership in community activities (10 points), and participation in the Supervised Agricultural Experience (SAE) program (30 points). U.S. citizenship is required.

Financial data Scholarships are either $10,000 or $5,000. Funds are paid directly to the recipient.

Duration 1 year; nonrenewable.

Number awarded 4 each year: 1 at $10,000 and 3 at $5,000.

Deadline February of each year.

[54]
BOSTON CHAPTER SIGNIFICANT ACHIEVEMENT AND FUTURE LEADERSHIP AWARDS

National Association of Asian American Professionals-
   Boston Chapter
Attn: Scholarship Committee
P.O. Box 381435
Cambridge, MA 02238-1435
(781) 937-7072   E-mail: naaap@naaapboston.org
Web: www.naaapboston.org

Purpose To provide financial assistance for college to Asian American high school seniors from Massachusetts.

Eligibility This program is open to seniors of Asian heritage who attend high school in Massachusetts. Applicants must submit official high school transcripts that include standardized test scores and 2 letters of recommendation. They must also submit essays of 500 words each on themselves and on how they think being an Asian American has

shaped their perspective and will shape their contributions to society in the future. Selection is based on the essays, academic achievement, community service, and extracurricular activities. Personal interviews are required. U.S. citizenship or permanent resident status is required.

Financial data The stipend is at least $1,000.

Duration 1 year.

Additional information Information is also available from May Yu, Scholarship co-chair, E-mail: myu@mba2006.hbs.edu.

Number awarded 1 or more each year.

Deadline February of each year.

[55]
BRADENTON HERALD SCHOLARSHIP FOR MINORITIES

Bradenton Herald
Attn: Angela Regnier
102 Manatee Avenue West
Bradenton, FL 34205-8894
(941) 748-0411   Fax: (941) 745-7062
E-mail: aregnier@bradentonherald.com
Web: www.bradentonherald.com

Purpose To provide financial assistance to minority high school seniors in selected areas of Florida who are interested in attending college to prepare for a career in the newspaper industry.

Eligibility This program is open to minority seniors graduating from high schools in Manatee County and portions of Hillsborough or Sarasota counties in Florida. Applicants must be interested in attending college to prepare for a career in the news or business aspects of the newspaper industry. Along with their application, they must submit a 500-word essay on why they want to prepare for a career in the newspaper industry. Selection is based on the essay, 2 letters of recommendation, a transcript of grades (including SAT/ACT scores), journalism or business experience, and extracurricular activities.

Financial data The stipend is $500.

Duration 1 year.

Additional information The recipients of these scholarships are automatically entered into competition for the Knight Ridder Minority Scholarship Program of $40,000 over 4 years.

Number awarded 1 each year.

Deadline January of each year.

[56]
BREAKTHROUGH TO NURSING SCHOLARSHIPS FOR RACIAL/ETHNIC MINORITIES

National Student Nurses' Association
Attn: NSNA Foundation
45 Main Street, Suite 606
Brooklyn, NY 11201
(718) 210-0705   Fax: (718) 210-0710
E-mail: nsna@nsna.org
Web: www.nsna.org

Purpose To provide financial assistance to disadvantaged minority undergraduate and graduate students who wish to prepare for careers in nursing.

Eligibility This program is open to students currently enrolled in state-approved schools of nursing or pre-nursing associate degree, baccalaureate, diploma, generic doctorate, or generic master's programs. Graduating high school seniors are not eligible. Support for graduate education is provided only for a first degree in nursing. Applicants must be able to demonstrate that they are from a disadvantaged background, including membership in a racial or ethnic minority underrepresented among registered nurses (American Indian or Alaska Native, Hispanic or Latino, Native Hawaiian or other Pacific Islander, Black or African American, or Asian). Selection is based on academic achievement, financial need, and involvement in student nursing organizations and community health activities.

Financial data Stipends range from $1,000 to $2,500. A total of $120,000 is awarded each year by the foundation for all its scholarship programs.

Duration 1 year.

Additional information Applications must be accompanied by a $10 processing fee.

Number awarded Varies each year. Approximately 14 of these scholarships were awarded recently.

Deadline January of each year.

[57]
BROWN AND CALDWELL MINORITY SCHOLARSHIP

Brown and Caldwell
Attn: Scholarship Program
201 North Civic Drive, Suite 115
P.O. Box 8045
Walnut Creek, CA 94596
(925) 937-9010   Fax: (925) 937-9026
E-mail: scholarships@brwncald.com
Web: www.brownandcaldwell.com

Purpose To provide financial assistance to minority students working on an undergraduate degree in an environmental or engineering field.

Eligibility This program is open to members of minority groups (African Americans, Hispanics, Asians, Pacific Islanders, Native Americans, and Alaska Natives) who are full-time students in their junior year at an accredited 4-year college or university. Applicants must have a GPA of 3.0 or higher with a declared major in civil, chemical, or environmental engineering or an environmental science (e.g., biology, ecology, geology, hydrogeology, industrial hygiene, toxicology). Along with their application, they must submit an essay (up to 250 words) on why they chose to major in an environmental discipline. They must be U.S. citizens or permanent resident and available to participate in a summer internship at a Brown and Caldwell office. Financial need is not considered in the selection process.

Financial data The stipend is $3,000.

Duration 1 year.

Additional information As part of the paid summer internship at a Brown and Caldwell office at 1 of more than 40 cities in the country, the program provides a mentor to guide the intern through the company's information and communications resources.

Number awarded 1 each year.

Deadline February of each year.

[58]
BROWN FOUNDATION COLLEGE SCHOLARSHIPS

Brown Foundation for Educational Equity, Excellence
and Research
1515 S.E. Monroe
Topeka, KS 66612
(785) 235-3939   Fax: (785) 235-1001
E-mail: brownfound@juno.com
Web: brownvboard.org/foundatn/sclrbroc.htm

Purpose To provide financial assistance to currently-enrolled college juniors of color who are interested in preparing for a teaching career.

Eligibility To be eligible for this scholarship, applicants must meet the following requirements: be a minority; be a college junior; be admitted to a teacher education program; be enrolled in an institution of higher education with an accredited program in education; have at least a 3.0 GPA; be enrolled at least half time; and submit 2 recommendations (from a teacher, counselor, or other school official and from a person familiar with the applicant). Selection is based on GPA, extracurricular activities, career plans, essays, and recommendations.

Financial data The stipend is $500 per year.

Duration 2 years (junior and senior years).

Additional information The first Brown Foundation Scholarships were awarded in 1989.

Number awarded 1 each year.

Deadline March of each year.

[59]
BROWN FOUNDATION HIGH SCHOOL SCHOLARSHIPS

Brown Foundation for Educational Equity, Excellence
and Research
1515 S.E. Monroe
Topeka, KS 66612
(785) 235-3939   Fax: (785) 235-1001
E-mail: brownfound@juno.com
Web: brownvboard.org/foundatn/sclrbroc.htm

Purpose To provide financial assistance to high school seniors of color who are interested in preparing for a teaching career.

Eligibility To be eligible for this scholarship, applicants must meet the following requirements: be a minority; have demonstrated a commitment to entering a teaching program (e.g., volunteer experience, work experience, statements by references); be graduating from a public or private high school; be accepted at an institution of higher education with an accredited program in education; have at least a 3.0 GPA; and submit 2 recommendations (from a teacher, counselor, or other school official and from a person familiar with the applicant). Selection is based on GPA, extracurricular activities, career plans, essays, and recommendations.

Financial data The stipend is $300 or $500.

Duration 1 year; nonrenewable.

Additional information The first Brown Foundation Scholarships were awarded in 1989.

Number awarded 1 each year.

Deadline March of each year.

[60]
BUFFETT FOUNDATION SCHOLARSHIP PROGRAM

Buffett Foundation
Attn: Scholarship Office
P.O. Box 4508
Decatur, IL 62525
(402) 451-6011   E-mail: buffettfound@aol.com
Web: www.BuffettScholarships.org

Purpose To provide financial assistance to entering or currently-enrolled college students (preference given to minorities) in Nebraska.

Eligibility This program is open to U.S. citizens who are Nebraska residents. Applicants must be entering or currently enrolled in a state school, community college, or trade school in Nebraska. They must be in financial need, be the only family member presently receiving a grant from the foundation, have at least a 2.5 GPA, and have applied for federal financial aid. Selection is based on academic performance and financial need. Preference is given to minority students, students with disabilities, and married or unmarried students with dependents.

Financial data The maximum stipend is $2,500 per semester. Funds are sent directly to the recipient's school and must be used to pay tuition and fees; they may not be used to pay for books or other expenses.

Duration Up to 5 years for a 4-year college, or up to 3 years for a 2-year school. Students on scholarship may not drop out for a period of time and be reinstated as a scholarship recipient; they must reapply along with first-time students.

Additional information Students on a 12-month program or the quarter system may use the scholarship for summer tuition; students on the semester system may not use funds for summer school. Students who are not working must enroll in at least 12 credit hours; students who are working must enroll in at least 9 credit hours.

Deadline April of each year.

[61]
BUNCHIRO TAMESA SCHOLARSHIP

Japanese American Citizens League-Seattle Chapter
P.O. Box 18558
Seattle, WA 98118-0558
(206) 622-4098   E-mail: email@jaclseattle.org
Web: www.jaclseattle.org

Purpose To provide financial assistance for college or graduate school to residents of the Seattle, Washington area who are of Japanese ancestry or from a family that is a member of the Japanese American Citizens League (JACL).

Eligibility This program is open to Seattle (Washington) area residents who are of Japanese ancestry or members of JACL families. Applicants must be entering their freshman year of college or graduate school. As part of their application, they must submit a list of extracurricular and community activities, 2 letters of recommendation, a list of awards or recognitions they have earned, and a 500-word essay on the legacy of the Japanese American community in American society.

Financial data The stipend is $1,000.

Duration 1 year.

Additional information Information is also available from May Namba, 2324 N.W. 94th Street, Seattle, WA 98117.

Number awarded 1 each year.

Deadline March of each year.

[62]
BUSINESS REPORTING INTERN PROGRAM FOR MINORITY COLLEGE SOPHOMORES AND JUNIORS

Dow Jones Newspaper Fund
P.O. Box 300
Princeton, NJ 08543-0300
(609) 452-2820   Fax: (609) 520-5804
E-mail: newsfund@wsj.dowjones.com
Web: DJNewspaperFund.dowjones.com

Purpose To provide work experience and financial assistance to minority college students who are interested in careers in journalism.

Eligibility This program is open to college sophomores and juniors who are U.S. citizens interested in careers in journalism and participating in a summer internship at a daily newspaper as a business reporter. Applicants must be members of a minority group (African American, Hispanic, Asian American, Pacific Islander, American Indian, or Alaskan Native) enrolled as full-time students. They must submit a resume, 3 to 5 recently-published clips, an list of courses with grades, and a 500-word essay.

Financial data Interns receive a salary of $350 per week during the summer and a $1,000 scholarship at the successful completion of the program.

Duration 10 weeks for the summer internship; 1 year for the scholarship.

Number awarded Up to 12 each year.

Deadline October of each year.

[63]
CAAM SCHOLARSHIPS

Chinese American Association of Minnesota
Attn: Scholarship Program
P.O. Box 582584
Minneapolis, MN 55458-2584
Web: www.caam.org/pages/scholarships.htm

Purpose To provide financial assistance for college or graduate school to Minnesota residents of Chinese descent.

Eligibility This program is open to Minnesota residents of Chinese descent who are enrolled or planning to enroll full time at a postsecondary school, college, or graduate school. Applicants must submit an essay on the role their Chinese heritage has played in their work, study, and accomplishments. Selection is based on academic record, leadership qualities, and community service; financial need is also considered for some awards. Membership in the Chinese American Association of Minnesota (CAAM) is not required. Priority is given to applicants who have not previously received a CAAM scholarship.

Financial data The stipend is $1,000.

Duration 1 year.

Additional information Recipients who are not CAAM members are expected to become members for at least 2 years.

Number awarded At least 5 each year.

Deadline September of each year.

[64]
CALIFORNIA REAL ESTATE ENDOWMENT FUND SCHOLARSHIP PROGRAM

California Community Colleges
Attn: Student Financial Assistance Programs
1102 Q Street
Sacramento, CA 95814-6511
(916) 324-0925   E-mail: rquintan@cccco.edu
Web: www.cccco.edu

Purpose To provide financial assistance to disadvantaged California community college students who are studying real estate.

Eligibility This program is open to students at community colleges in California who are majoring in real estate or (if their college does not offer a real estate major) business administration with a concentration in real estate. Applicants must have completed at least a 3-unit college course in real estate with a grade of "C" or better and must be enrolled in at least 6 semester units of real estate for the semester of the scholarship. Students must meet 1 of the following financial need criteria: 1) have completed the Free Application for Federal Student Aid (FAFSA) and been determined by their college to have financial need; 2) come from a family with an income less than $12,885 for 1 person, $17,415 for 2 persons, $21,945 for 3 persons, $26,475 for 4 persons, or an additional $4,530 for each additional family member; or 3) come from a family with an income less than $50,000 and be from a disadvantaged group (have low economic status and/or have been denied opportunities in society for reasons of gender, race, ethnicity, economics, language, education, physical disabilities, or other mitigating factors). Scholarships are awarded on a first-come, first-served basis.

Financial data Awards up to $400 per semester are available.

Duration 1 semester; may be renewed if the student remains enrolled in at least 6 units of real estate with a GPA of 2.0 or higher.

Additional information Students apply to their community college, not to the sponsoring organization.

Number awarded From 75 to 90 each year; approximately $60,000 per year is available for this program.

Deadline April of each year.

[65]
CANFIT PROGRAM SCHOLARSHIPS

California Adolescent Nutrition, Physical Education, and
    Culinary Arts Scholarships
2140 Shattuck Avenue, Suite 610
Berkeley, CA 94704
(510) 644-1533   Toll-free: (800) 200-3131
Fax: (510) 644-1535   E-mail: info@canfit.org
Web: www.canfit.org/scholarships.html

Purpose To provide financial assistance to minority undergraduate and graduate students who are studying nutrition, physical education, or culinary arts in California.

Eligibility Eligible to apply are American Indians/Alaska Natives, African Americans, Asians/Pacific Islanders, and Latinos/Hispanics who are enrolled in either: 1) an approved master's or doctoral graduate program in nutrition, public health nutrition, or physical education or in a preprofessional practice program approved by the American Dietetic Association at an accredited university in California; or, 2) an approved bachelor's or professional certificate program in culinary arts, nutrition, or physical education at an accredited university or college in California. Graduate student applicants must have completed at least 12 units of graduate course work and have a cumulative GPA of 3.0 or higher; undergraduate applicants must have completed 50 semester units or the equivalent of college credits and have a cumulative GPA of 2.5 or higher. Selection is based on financial need, academic goals, and community nutrition or physical education activities.

Financial data Graduate stipends are $1,000 each and undergraduate stipends are $500 per year.

Additional information A goal of the California Adolescent Nutrition and Fitness (CANFit) program is to improve the nutritional status and physical fitness of California's low-income multi-ethnic youth aged 10 to 14. By offering these scholarships, the program hopes to encourage more students to consider careers in adolescent nutrition and fitness.

Number awarded 5 graduate scholarships and 10 undergraduate scholarships are available each year.

Deadline March of each year.

[66]
CARL A. SCOTT BOOK SCHOLARSHIPS

Council on Social Work Education
Attn: Chair, Carl A. Scott Memorial Fund
1725 Duke Street, Suite 500
Alexandria, VA 22314-3457
(703) 683-8080   Fax: (703) 683-8099
E-mail: eafrancis@cswe.org
Web: www.cswe.org

Purpose To provide financial assistance to ethnic minority social work students in their last year of study for a baccalaureate or master's degree.

Eligibility This program is open to students from ethnic groups of color (African American, Asian American, Mexican American, Puerto Rican, and American Indian) who are in the last year of study for a social work degree in an accredited baccalaureate or master's degree program. Applicants must have a cumulative GPA of 3.0 or higher and be enrolled full time. They must demonstrate a commitment to work for equity and social justice in social work.

Financial data The award is $500.

Duration This is a 1-time award.

Number awarded 2 each year.

Deadline May of each year.

[67]
CAROLE SIMPSON SCHOLARSHIP

Radio and Television News Directors Foundation
1600 K Street, N.W., Suite 700
Washington, DC 20006-2838
(202) 467-5218   Fax: (202) 223-4007
E-mail: karenb@rtndf.org
Web: www.rtndf.org

Purpose To provide financial assistance to outstanding undergraduate students, especially minorities, who are interested in preparing for a career in electronic journalism.

Eligibility Eligible are sophomore or more advanced undergraduate students enrolled in an electronic journalism sequence at an accredited or nationally-recognized college or university. Applicants must submit 1 to 3 examples of reporting or producing skills on audio or video cassette tapes (no more than 15 minutes total), a description of their role on each story and a list of who worked on each story and what they did, a statement explaining why they are seeking a career in broadcast or cable journalism, and a letter of endorsement from a faculty sponsor that verifies the applicant has at least 1 year of school remaining. Preference is given to undergraduate students of color.

Financial data The stipend is $2,000, paid in semiannual installments of $1,000 each.

Duration 1 year.

Additional information The Radio and Television News Directors Foundation (RTNDF) also provides an all-expense paid trip to the Radio-Television News Directors Association (RTNDA) annual international conference. It defines electronic journalism to include radio, television, cable, and online news. Previous winners of any RTNDF scholarship or internship are not eligible.

Number awarded 1 each year.

Deadline April of each year.

[68]
CARSON PURIEFOY MEMORIAL FUND

Philadelphia Foundation
1234 Market Street, Suite 1800
Philadelphia, PA 19107-3794
(215) 563-6417   Fax: (215) 563-6882
Web: www.philafound.org

Purpose To provide financial assistance for college to high school seniors from the Philadelphia area who are minority group members involved in golf.

Eligibility This program is open to minority seniors graduating from high schools in the Philadelphia area. Applicants must be involved in golf.

Financial data A stipend is awarded (amount not specified).

Duration 1 year.

Additional information This fund was established in 1998.

Number awarded 1 or more each year.

[69]
CATERPILLAR SCHOLARS AWARD

Society of Manufacturing Engineers
Attn: SME Education Foundation
One SME Drive
P.O. Box 930
Dearborn, MI 48121-0930
(313) 425-3304   Toll-free: (800) 733-4763, ext. 3304
Fax: (313) 425-3411   E-mail: foundation@sme.org
Web: www.sme.org

Purpose To provide financial assistance to undergraduates (special attention given to minorities) enrolled in a degree program in manufacturing engineering or manufacturing engineering technology.

Eligibility Applicants must be full-time students attending a degree-granting institution in North America and preparing for a career in manufacturing engineering. They must have completed at least 30 units in a manufacturing engineering or manufacturing engineering technology curriculum with a minimum GPA of 3.0. Minority applicants may apply as incoming freshmen. Need is not considered in awarding scholarships (unless 2 or more applicants have equal qualifications).

Financial data The stipend is $2,000.

Duration 1 year; may be renewed.

Additional information This program is sponsored by Caterpillar, Inc.

Number awarded 5 each year.

Deadline January of each year.

[70]
C.C. MIAO AND ROSALIND MIAO SCHOLARSHIP

Communities Foundation of Texas
Attn: Scholarship Department
5500 Caruth Haven Lane
Dallas, TX 75225-8146
(214) 750-4222   Fax: (214) 750-4210
E-mail: grants@cftexas.org
Web: www.cftexas.org/recc.html

Purpose To provide financial assistance for college to Chinese Americans in the Dallas, Texas area.

Eligibility This program is open to Dallas, Texas area high school seniors and currently-enrolled college students who have a GPA of 3.0 or higher. Applicants must either have been born in China, Hong Kong, or Taiwan or have been born in the United States and have parents or grandparents who were born in China, Hong Kong, or Taiwan. Along with their application, they must submit an essay of 200 to 500 words on the topic, "As a Chinese descendant, how can I make America a better place in which to live?" Selection is based on academic ability and financial need. Preference may be given to students born in China, Hong Kong, or Taiwan.

Financial data The amount of the stipend varies.

Duration 1 year; may be renewed for up to 3 additional years provided the recipient maintains full-time enrollment and a GPA of 3.0 or higher.

Additional information Recipients must attend a college or university in Texas.

Number awarded Up to 12 each year.

Deadline March of each year.

[71]
CELEBRATING DIVERSITY SCHOLARS PROGRAM

McDonald's Family Restaurants of Greater Washington, D.C.
c/o GolinHarris
2200 Clarendon Boulevard, Suite 1100
Arlington, VA 22201
(703) 741-7500   E-mail: molear@golinharris.com
Web: www.mcdonaldsexpo.com

Purpose To provide financial assistance for college to high school seniors in the greater Washington, D.C. area who have helped to develop an appreciation for cultural diversity.

Eligibility This program is open to college-bound seniors graduating from high schools in Washington, D.C. and designated counties or cities in Maryland, Virginia, and West Virginia. Applicants must be able to demonstrate academic achievement (GPA of 3.0 or higher), leadership, character, and community service. Along with their application, they must submit 200-word essays on 1) how education is important in developing an appreciation for cultural diversity, and 2) the best lessons they have learned from their community service experiences.

Financial data The stipend is $1,500. Funds are paid directly to the recipient's college or university.

Duration 1 year.

Additional information A goal of this program is to honor diversity and award scholarships across ethnic groups. It is available to residents of the District of Columbia; the Maryland counties of Alleghany, Calvert, Carroll, Charles, Cumberland, Frederick, Garrett, Montgomery, Prince George's, St. Mary's, and Washington; the Virginia counties of Arlington, Clarke, Culpeper, Fairfax, Fauquier, Frederick, King George, Loudoun, Page, Prince William, Rappahannock, Shenandoah, Spotsylvania, Stafford, Warren, and Westmoreland; the independent Virginia cities of Alexandria, Fairfax, Falls Church, Fredericksburg, Manassas, Manassas Park, and Winchester; and the West Virginia counties of Berkeley, Grant, Hampshire, Hardy, Jefferson, Mineral, and Morgan.

Number awarded At least 50 each year.

Deadline February of each year.

[72]
CHARLOTTE OBSERVER MINORITY SCHOLARSHIPS

Charlotte Observer
Attn: Zaira Goodman
600 South Tryon Street
P.O. Box 30308
Charlotte, NC 28230-3038
(704) 358-5715   Fax: (704) 358-5707
E-mail: zgoodman@charlotteobserver.com
Web: www.charlotteobserver.com

Purpose To provide financial assistance to minority high school seniors in North and South Carolina who are interested in preparing for a career in the newspaper field.

Eligibility This program is open to minority seniors at high schools in the service area of the *Charlotte Observer* (North and South Carolina). Applicants must be planning to attend college to study advertising, finance, human resources, information/Internet technology, marketing, or other field related to journalism and business communications. They must submit an original essay explaining why they want to prepare for a career in journalism or business communications, what they know about Knight Ridder and how they see themselves contributing to the company in the future, 2 letters of recommendation, a transcript, SAT/ACT scores, and up to 3 samples of work with bylines. Selection is based primarily on GPA and involvement in school publications.

Financial data The stipend is $1,000 per year.

Duration 1 year.

Additional information The recipients of these scholarships are automatically entered into competition for the Knight Ridder Minority Scholarship Program of $40,000 over 4 years.

Number awarded 2 each year.

Deadline November of each year.

[73]
CHERRY BLOSSOM SCHOLARSHIPS

Northern California Cherry Blossom Scholarship
    Committee
c/o Steven Hirabayashi
2441 Farrol Avenue
Union City, CA 94587-5258
(510) 471-7324   E-mail: yshiraba@yahoo.com

Purpose To provide financial assistance for college to high school seniors of Japanese descent in northern California.

Eligibility Applicants must be high school seniors in northern California and of Japanese American descent. They must have a GPA of 2.5 or higher and should be actively involved in their local community. Selection is based on community involvement, personal character, academic achievement, and 2 separate 500-word essays: 1) why it is important to be involved in the community and 2) the most important issue or concern facing the Japanese American community today.

Financial data The stipend is $2,000.

Duration 1 year.

Number awarded 2 each year.

Deadline March of each year.

[74]
CHINESE AMERICAN CITIZENS ALLIANCE FOUNDATION SCHOLARSHIPS

Chinese American Citizens Alliance
Attn: Scholarship Foundation
763 Yale Street
Los Angeles, CA 90012
(323) 876-4083
Web: www.cacanational.org/foundation-scholar.html

Purpose To provide financial assistance to Chinese American undergraduate students at colleges and universities in California.

Eligibility This program is open to students of Chinese descent who have completed the sophomore year at a college or university in California. Applicants must provide information on their volunteer work, accomplishments and honors received in college, organizational membership and offices held, previous scholarship awards, career plans, and how they will benefit from the scholarship. Financial need is not considered. Applicants must be available for an in-person interview in Los Angeles.

Financial data The stipend is $1,000.

Duration 1 year.

Additional information This program consists of the following named scholarships: the Yoke Quong Jung Memorial Scholarship, the Huan Lin Cheng Memorial Scholarship, the Y.C. Hong Memorial Scholarship, the Collin and Susan Lai Scholarship, the Julian and Eleanor Sue Scholarship, and the Robert and Edith Jung Scholarship.

Number awarded 6 each year.

Deadline July of each year.

[75]
CHINESE PROFESSIONAL CLUB SCHOLARSHIPS

Chinese Professional Club of Houston
Attn: John Loh, Scholarship Committee Chair
P.O. Box 941682
Houston, TX 77094-8682
(832) 428-8832
Web: www.cpchouston.com/scholarship.htm

Purpose To provide financial assistance to high school seniors of Chinese descent in the Houston, Texas area who are interested in attending college.

Eligibility To qualify, applicants must be students of Chinese descent (minimum 1/4), residents of the greater Houston metropolitan area, and currently enrolled in an accredited high school. They must be planning to attend college (anywhere in the United States) on a full-time basis. Semifinalists are interviewed. Selection is based on scholastic achievement, leadership qualities, writing proficiency, and a personal interview. Of the scholarships awarded, 4 are designated specifically for applicants with demonstrated financial need and 1 for an applicant interested in a career in education.

Financial data Stipends range from $1,000 to $2,000. Funds are sent directly to the recipient's school.

Duration 1 year.

Additional information The association will reimburse all financial need award applicants for copying expenses.

Number awarded At least 10 each year.

Deadline November of each year.

[76]
CHUNGHI HONG PARK SCHOLARSHIP

Korean-American Scientists and Engineers Association
1952 Gallows Drive, Suite 300
Vienna, VA 22182
(703) 748-1221   Fax: (703) 748-1331
E-mail: sejong@ksea.org
Web: www.ksea.org

Purpose To provide financial assistance to women who are undergraduate or graduate student members of the Korean-American Scientists and Engineers Association (KSEA).

Eligibility This program is open to women who are Korean American undergraduate or graduate students, graduated from a high school in the United States, are KSEA members, and are majoring in science, engineering, or a related field. Along with their application, they must submit a 500-word essay on either of the following topics: 1) their career goals and intended contributions to society, or 2) the meaning of Korean heritage in their life. Selection is based on the essay (20%), work experience and extracurricular activities (20%), recommendation letters (30%), and academic performance (30%).

Financial data The stipend is $1,000.

Duration 1 year.

Number awarded 2 each year.

Deadline February of each year.

[77]
CJAAA SCHOLARSHIP PROGRAM

California Japanese American Alumni Association
Attn: Ron Yamada
P.O. Box 15235
San Francisco, CA 94115-0235
(650) 802-0939   E-mail: scholarships@cjaaa.org
Web: www.cjaaa.org/scholarship.html

Purpose To provide financial assistance to undergraduate or graduate students of Japanese American descent who are currently enrolled at 1 of the University of California campuses.

Eligibility This program is open to continuing or returning undergraduate or graduate students of Japanese American descent who are attending 1 of the University of California campuses. They must be American citizens and may be studying in any field or discipline. A GPA of 3.0 or higher is strongly recommended but not required. Applicants interested in participating in the University of California Education Abroad Program in Japan must have a GPA of 3.5 or higher. Selection is based on academic excellence, commitment to community and social concerns, personal attributes, and financial need (in that order).

Financial data Stipends range from $1,000 to $3,000. The Moriaki "Mo" Noguchi Memorial Scholarship of $3,000 is given to the top overall candidate. The George Kondo Award is at least $1,000 and is awarded to the applicant with the best community service record. The Yori Wada Award is $2,000 and is awarded to the applicant with the most outstanding record of public service. The stipend for a student accepted to the University of California Education Abroad Program ranges from $2,500 to $5,000.

Duration 1 year; nonrenewable.

Number awarded 5 to 15 each year.

Deadline April of each year.

[78]
CLEVELAND ADVERTISING ASSOCIATION EDUCATION FOUNDATION SCHOLARSHIPS

Cleveland Advertising Association
Attn: Education Foundation
20325 Center Ridge Road, Suite 670
Cleveland, OH 44116
(440) 673-0020   Fax: (440) 673-0025
E-mail: adassoc@clevead.com
Web: www.clevead.com/education/scholarships.php

Purpose To provide financial assistance to undergraduate students (especially minorities) who are residents of Ohio majoring in a field related to advertising at a college or university in the state.

Eligibility This program is open to residents of Ohio who are full-time seniors, juniors, or second-semester sophomores at colleges and universities in the state. Applicants must be majoring in advertising or a related communications/marketing field and have a GPA of 3.0 or higher. They must submit transcripts, 2 letters of recommendation, and an essay describing their career goals. Financial need is not considered in the selection process. Some of the scholarships are set aside for U.S. citizens of African, Asian, Hispanic, Native American, or Pacific Island descent.

Financial data Stipends range from $1,000 to $2,500.

Duration 1 year.

Additional information This program includes the following named scholarships: the Arras Group Minority Scholarship, the Wyse Advertising Scholarship, the Thomas Brennan Memorial Scholarship, the Hitchcock Fleming and Associates Scholarship, the Innis Maggiore Scholarship, the Marcus Thomas Scholarship, the Laurie Mitchell and Company Scholarship, and the Plain Dealer Bob Hagley Scholarship.

Number awarded Varies each year. Recently, this program awarded 11 scholarships: 2 at $2,500, 1 at $2,000, 3 at $1,500, and 5 at $1,000.

Deadline October of each year.

[79]
CLEVELAND JAPANESE AMERICAN SCHOLARSHIPS

Japanese American Citizens League-Cleveland Chapter
c/o Bill Sadataki
4066 Brush Road
Richfield, OH 44286
(330) 659-3880
Web: www.lkwdpl.org/jacl/scholarship.htm

Purpose To provide financial assistance for college to high school seniors in the Cleveland (Ohio) area who are members of the Japanese American Citizens League (JACL), dependents of members, or of Japanese descent.

Eligibility This program is open to seniors graduating from high schools in the following Ohio counties: Cuyahoga, Geauga, Lake, Lorain, Medine, Portage, and Summit. Applicants must be a JACL member, a dependent of a member, or a U.S. citizen of Japanese descent. They must be planning to attend a college, university, business/trade school, or any other institution of higher learning. Financial need is considered in the selection process.

Financial data A stipend is awarded (amount not specified).

Duration 1 year.

Additional information This program is jointly sponsored by the Cleveland Chapter of the JACL and the Cleveland Japanese American Foundation.

Number awarded 1 or more each year.

Deadline June of each year.

[80]
COLGATE "BRIGHT SMILES, BRIGHT FUTURES" MINORITY SCHOLARSHIPS

American Dental Hygienists' Association
Attn: Institute for Oral Health
444 North Michigan Avenue, Suite 3400
Chicago, IL 60611
(312) 440-8918   Toll-free: (800) 735-4916
Fax: (312) 440-8929   E-mail: institute@adha.net
Web: www.adha.org/institute/Scholarship/index.htm

Purpose To provide financial assistance to minority students and males of any race enrolled in undergraduate programs in dental hygiene.

Eligibility This program is open to members of groups currently underrepresented in the dental hygiene profession (Native Americans, African Americans, Hispanics, Asians, and males) who are active members of the Student American Dental Hygienists' Association (SADHA) or the American Dental Hygienists' Association (ADHA). Applicants must have a GPA of 3.0 or higher, be able to document financial need of at least $1,500, and have completed at least 1 year of full-time enrollment in an accredited dental hygiene program in the United States. Along with their application, they must submit a statement that covers their long-term career goals, their intended contribution to the dental hygiene profession, their professional interests, and the manner in which their degree will enhance their professional capacity.

Financial data Stipends range from $1,000 to $2,000.

Duration 1 year; nonrenewable.

Additional information These scholarships are sponsored by the Colgate-Palmolive Company.

Number awarded 2 each year.

Deadline April of each year.

[81]
COLORADO SOCIETY OF CPAS ETHNIC DIVERSITY SCHOLARSHIPS FOR HIGH SCHOOL STUDENTS

Colorado Society of Certified Public Accountants
Attn: CSCPA Educational Foundation
7979 East Tufts Avenue, Suite 500
Denver, CO 80237-2845
(303) 741-8613   Toll-free: (800) 523-9082 (within CO)
Fax: (303) 773-6344   E-mail: gmantz@cocpa.org
Web: www.cocpa.org

Purpose To provide financial assistance to minority high school seniors in Colorado who plan to study accounting in college.

Eligibility This program is open to African American, Hispanic, Asian American, American Indian, and Pacific Islander high school seniors in Colorado planning to major in accounting at a college or university in the state. Applicants must have a GPA of 3.0 or higher. Selection is based primarily on scholastic achievement.

Financial data The stipend is $1,000.

Duration 1 year; nonrenewable.

Number awarded 3 each year.

Deadline February of each year.

[82]
COMMUNITY COLLEGE SCHOLARSHIP OF THE CALIFORNIA STATE FAIR

California State Fair
Attn: Friends of the Fair Scholarship Program
1600 Exposition Boulevard
P.O. Box 15649
Sacramento, CA 95852
(916) 274-5969   E-mail: wross@calexpo.com
Web: www.bigfun.org

Purpose To provide financial assistance to California residents of Asian Pacific Islander heritage who plan to attend a community college in the state.

Eligibility This program is open to Asian Pacific Islanders who are currently enrolled in a high school or community college in California. Applicants must be planning to attend a community college in the state in the following fall. They must have a GPA of 3.0 or higher. Along with their application, they must submit a 2-page statement on their Asian Pacific Islander background, community involvement, career goals, and desire to give back to their community. Selection is based on personal commitment, goals established for their chosen field, leadership potential, and civic accomplishments.

Financial data The stipend is $500.

Duration 1 year.

Additional information The Friends of the Fair Scholarship Program was established in 1993.

Number awarded 2 each year.

Deadline March of each year.

[83]
COMMUNITY SERVICE AWARD

Indian American Heritage Foundation
3818 Gleneagles Drive
Tarzana, CA 91356
(818) 708-3885   E-mail: ashok4u@aol.com
Web: www.la-indiacenter.com

Purpose To recognize and reward high school seniors in southern California who are of Asian Indian descent and have participated in community service activities.

Eligibility This award is available to seniors graduating from high schools in southern California (south of Fresno) who have at least 1 parent of Asian Indian descent. Applicants must have participated in community service activities and have a GPA of 2.0 or higher. They must attend a function of the sponsoring organization at which they take a quiz on India, based on material supplied by the organization. Along with their application, they must submit a 2-page essay on how their volunteer services affected, impacted, or changed their own life. and lifestyle. Selection is based on their quiz score (15%), the essay (15%), the total number of hours of volunteer services performed (10%), the type of services rendered at each institution (10%), motivation for providing volunteer services (15%), results achieved at each institution (15 points), how the individuals or institutions were impacted by their services (10%), and honors and awards (10%).

Financial data The award is $250 or $500.

Duration 1 year.

Additional information Material about India for the quiz is sent to the applicant after receipt of a check for $10 and the completed application.

Number awarded 1 each year.

Deadline April of each year.

[84]
CONNECTICUT EDUCATION FOUNDATION SCHOLARSHIPS FOR MINORITY COLLEGE STUDENTS

Connecticut Education Foundation, Inc.
c/o Connecticut Education Association
21 Oak Street, Suite 500
Hartford, CT 06106-8001
(860) 525-5641   Toll-free: (800) 842-4316
Fax: (860) 725-6388   E-mail: phila@cea.org
Web: www.cea.org/cef/minguidelines.html

Purpose To provide financial assistance to minority college students in Connecticut who are interested in preparing for a teaching career.

Eligibility This program is open to minority students (Blacks, Native Americans or Alaskan Natives, Asian or Pacific Islanders, and Hispanics or Latinos) who have been accepted into a teacher preparation program at an accredited college or university in Connecticut. Applicants must have earned a GPA of 2.75 or higher. Finalists may be interviewed. Financial need is considered in the selection process.

Financial data The stipend is $750.

Duration 1 year; may be renewed.

Number awarded At least 1 each year.

Deadline April of each year.

[85]
CONNECTICUT EDUCATION FOUNDATION SCHOLARSHIPS FOR MINORITY HIGH SCHOOL STUDENTS

Connecticut Education Foundation, Inc.
c/o Connecticut Education Association
21 Oak Street, Suite 500
Hartford, CT 06106-8001
(860) 525-5641   Toll-free: (800) 842-4316
Fax: (860) 725-6388   E-mail: phila@cea.org
Web: www.cea.org/cef/minguidelines.html

Purpose To provide financial assistance to minority high school students in Connecticut who are interested in preparing for a teaching career.

Eligibility This program is open to minority students (Blacks, Native Americans or Alaskan Natives, Asian or Pacific Islanders, and Hispanics or Latinos) who have been accepted at an accredited 2- or 4-year college or university in Connecticut. Applicants must intend to enter the teaching profession. They must have earned a GPA of 2.75 or higher. Finalists may be interviewed. Financial need is considered in the selection process.

Financial data The stipend is $500.

Duration 1 year; may be renewed.

Number awarded At least 1 each year.

Deadline April of each year.

[86]
CONNECTICUT MINORITY TEACHER INCENTIVE PROGRAM

Connecticut Department of Higher Education
Attn: Office of Student Financial Aid
61 Woodland Street
Hartford, CT 06105-2326
(860) 947-1855   Fax: (860) 947-1838
E-mail: mtip@ctdhe.org
Web: www.ctdhe.org/SFA/sfa.htm

Purpose To provide financial assistance and loan repayment to minority upper-division college students in Connecticut who are interested in teaching at public schools in the state.

Eligibility This program is open to minority juniors and seniors enrolled full time in Connecticut college and university teacher preparation programs. Students must be nominated by the education dean at their institution.

Financial data The maximum stipend is $5,000 per year. In addition, if recipients complete a credential and teach at a public school in Connecticut, they may receive up to

$2,500 per year, for up to 4 years, to help pay off college loans.

Duration Up to 2 years.

Number awarded Varies each year.

Deadline September of each year.

[87]
CONNECTICUT SPECIAL EDUCATION TEACHER INCENTIVE GRANT

Connecticut Department of Higher Education
Attn: Education and Employment Information Center
61 Woodland Street
Hartford, CT 06105-2326
(860) 947-1846   Toll-free: (800) 842-0229 (within CT)
Fax: (860) 947-1311   E-mail: setig@ctdhe.org
Web: www.ctdhe.org/SFA/sfa.htm

Purpose To provide financial assistance to undergraduate and graduate students (particularly underrepresented minorities) in Connecticut who are preparing for a career as a special education teacher.

Eligibility This program is open to full-time juniors and seniors and full- or part-time graduate students who are residents of Connecticut. Applicants must be enrolled in 1) special education teacher preparation programs at selected universities in Connecticut; or 2) out-of-state teacher preparation programs seeking cross-endorsement for teaching "low-incidence student" areas. They must be nominated by the dean of education at their school and have a stated intent to teach in a Connecticut public school, an approved private special education facility, or a Regional Educational Service Center. Priority is given to minority (African American, Hispanic/Latino, Asian American, and Native American) and bilingual students and to Connecticut residents enrolled in an approved out-of-state program.

Financial data The stipend is $5,000 per year for full-time study or $2,000 per year for part-time graduate study.

Duration 1 year.

Additional information The approved in-state programs are at Central Connecticut State University, Fairfield University, Saint Joseph College, Southern Connecticut State University, University of Connecticut, and University of Hartford. The programs for students seeking cross-endorsement certification for teaching students who are blind and partially-sighted or visually impaired are at Hunter College of CUNY (New York, New York), Dominican College (Orangeburg, New York), Teachers College of Columbia University (New York, New York), and University of Northern Colorado (Greeley, Colorado). The programs for students seeking cross-endorsement certification for teaching students who are deaf or hearing-impaired are at Hunter College, Teachers College, Clarke School for the Deaf at Smith College (Northampton, Massachusetts), and Boston University (Boston, Massachusetts).

Number awarded Varies each year.

Deadline August of each year.

[88]
CONNTESOL SCHOLARSHIPS

Connecticut Teachers of English to Speakers of Other Languages
c/o Sue Goldstein
42 Crosswinds Drive
Noank, CT 06340
E-mail: goldstei@galaxyinternet.net

Purpose To provide financial assistance for college to Connecticut high school seniors whose native language is not English.

Eligibility This program is open to seniors graduating from high schools in Connecticut whose first language is not English. Selection is based on academic achievement, community service, an essay, and financial need.

Financial data The stipend is at least $250 for students at 2-year colleges or $500 for students at 4-year colleges and universities.

Duration 1 year.

Number awarded 2 each year.

Deadline May of each year.

[89]
CONTRA COSTA TIMES MINORITY SCHOLARSHIP

Contra Costa Times
Attn: Cathy Singh
2640 Shadelands Drive
Walnut Creek, CA 94598
(925) 943-8100   Fax: (925) 977-8444
E-mail: csingh@cctimes.com
Web: www.cctimes.com

Purpose To provide financial assistance to minority high school seniors in selected northern California counties who are interested in attending college to prepare for a newspaper career.

Eligibility This program is open to college-bound minority seniors graduating from high schools in Alameda, Contra Costa, and Solano counties in California. Applicants must be able to demonstrate interest in a communications career with an emphasis on journalism, advertising, circulation, finance, or production. Along with their application, they must submit letters of recommendation, transcripts, 5 samples of work with bylines, and an essay on why they are interested in a career in the newspaper industry.

Financial data The stipend is $500.

Duration 1 year.

Additional information The recipients of these scholarships are entered into competition for the Knight Ridder Minority Scholarship Program of $40,000 over 4 years.

Number awarded 1 each year.

Deadline January of each year.

[90]
CORA AGUDA MANAYAN FUND

Hawai'i Community Foundation
Attn: Scholarship Department
1164 Bishop Street, Suite 800
Honolulu, HI 96813
(808) 537-6333   Toll-free: (888) 731-3863
Fax: (808) 521-6286
E-mail: scholarships@hcf-hawaii.org
Web: www.hawaiicommunityfoundation.org

Purpose To provide financial assistance to Hawaii residents of Filipino ancestry who are interested in preparing for a career in the health field.

Eligibility This program is open to Hawaii residents of Filipino ancestry who are interested in studying in Hawaii as full-time students and majoring in a health-related field (on the undergraduate or graduate school level). They must be able to demonstrate academic achievement (GPA of 2.7 or higher), good moral character, and financial need. In addition to filling out the standard application form, they must write a short statement indicating their reasons for attending college, their planned course of study, and their career goals.

Financial data The amounts of the awards depend on the availability of funds and the need of the recipient; recently, stipends averaged $1,000.

Duration 1 year.

Number awarded Varies each year; recently, 15 of these scholarships were awarded.

Deadline February of each year.

[91]
COX FOUNDATION SCHOLARSHIPS

Asian American Journalists Association
Attn: Student Programs Coordinator
1182 Market Street, Suite 320
San Francisco, CA 94102
(415) 346-2051, ext. 102   Fax: (415) 346-6343
E-mail: brandons@aaja.org
Web: www.aaja.org

Purpose To provide financial assistance to student members of the Asian American Journalists Association (AAJA) interested in careers in broadcast, photo, or print journalism.

Eligibility This program is open to AAJA members who are high school seniors or college students (graduate or undergraduate) enrolled full time in accredited institutions. Applicants must submit a 500-word essay on their involvement or interest in the Asian American community and how, if they are awarded this scholarship, they would contribute to the field of journalism and/or media issues involving the Asian American and Pacific Islander community. Selection is based on scholastic ability, commitment to journalism, sensitivity to Asian American and Pacific Islander issues as demonstrated by community involvement, journalistic ability, and financial need.

Financial data The stipend is $2,500.

Duration 1 year; may be renewed.

Additional information This program is supported by the Cox Foundation.

Number awarded Varies each year.

Deadline April of each year.

[92]
COX NEWSPAPER DIVISION MINORITY JOURNALISM SCHOLARSHIP

Cox Newspapers, Inc.
Attn: Scholarship Administrator
6205 Peachtree Dunwoody Road
P.O. Box 105720
Atlanta, GA 30348
(678) 645-0000
Web: www.coxnews.com

Purpose To provide work experience and financial assistance to minority undergraduate and graduate students from areas served by selected Cox Enterprises newspapers who are preparing for a career in the newspaper industry.

Eligibility This program is open to minority (African American, Hispanic, Asian American, Native American) undergraduate and graduate students interested in newspaper careers. Applicants must be interested in continuing their program of study as well as working as an intern at a participating Cox newspaper. Cox employees and their families are eligible. Each newspaper establishes its own criteria regarding GPA requirements, supporting documentation, and essay requirements. In general, applicants must have demonstrated an interest in the department (newsroom, online, advertising, accounting, marketing, or information technology) in which they would like to intern and be able to demonstrate experience with campus publications and/or daily deadlines.

Financial data All educational expenses are paid for 4 years of college, including room, board, books, and tuition. The approximate total value of the award is $40,000.

Duration The scholarship is awarded for 4 years. The recipient is expected to intern at the newspaper during the summer and holiday breaks throughout the 4 years of college.

Additional information The scholarship is administered by major newspapers owned by the sponsor: the *Atlanta Journal and Constitution, Austin American-Statesman,* and *Palm Beach Post.* Applications are available from the Cox Newspapers headquarters in Atlanta, the offices of the various Cox-owned newspapers, and from guidance offices of high schools in the city selected for the scholarship for that year.

Number awarded 1 each year.

Deadline April of each year.

[93]
CSCPA ETHNIC DIVERSITY SCHOLARSHIPS FOR COLLEGE STUDENTS

Colorado Society of Certified Public Accountants
Attn: CSCPA Educational Foundation
7979 East Tufts Avenue, Suite 500
Denver, CO 80237-2845
(303) 741-8613   Toll-free: (800) 523-9082 (within CO)
Fax: (303) 773-6344   E-mail: gmantz@cocpa.org
Web: www.cocpa.org

Purpose To provide financial assistance to minority undergraduate or graduate students in Colorado who are studying accounting.

Eligibility This program is open to African Americans, Hispanics, Asian Americans, American Indians, and Pacific Islanders studying at a college or university in Colorado at the associate, baccalaureate, or graduate level. Applicants must have completed at least 1 intermediate accounting class, be declared accounting majors, have completed at least 8 semester hours of accounting classes, and have a GPA of at least 3.0. Selection is based first on scholastic achievement and second on financial need.

Financial data The stipend is $1,000. Funds are paid directly to the recipient's school to be used for books, tuition, room, board, fees, and expenses.

Duration 1 year; recipients may reapply.

Number awarded 2 each year.

Deadline June of each year.

[94]
C.T. LANG JOURNALISM MINORITY SCHOLARSHIP AND INTERNSHIP

Albuquerque Journal
Attn: Scholarship Committee
7777 Jefferson Street, N.E.
P.O. Drawer J
Albuquerque, NM 87103
(505) 823-7777

Purpose To provide financial assistance and work experience to minority upper-division students in journalism programs at universities in New Mexico.

Eligibility This program is open to minority students majoring or minoring in journalism at a New Mexico university in their junior year with a GPA of 2.5 or higher. Applicants must be enrolled full time. They must be planning a career in newswriting, photography, design, copy editing, or online. Selection is based on clips of published stories, a short autobiography that explains the applicant's interest in the field, a grade transcript, and a letter of recommendation.

Financial data The scholarship is $1,000 per semester; the recipient also receives a paid internship and moving expenses.

Duration The scholarship is for 2 semesters (fall and spring). The internship is for 1 semester.

Additional information This program is funded by the *Albuquerque Journal,* where the internship takes place.

Number awarded 1 each year.

Deadline December of each year.

[95]
DAMON P. MOORE SCHOLARSHIP

Indiana State Teachers Association
Attn: Scholarships
150 West Market Street, Suite 900
Indianapolis, IN 46204
(317) 263-3400   Toll-free: (800) 382-4037
Fax: (317) 655-3700   E-mail: kmcallen@ista-in.org
Web: www.ista-in.org

Purpose To provide financial assistance to ethnic minority high school seniors in Indiana who are interested in studying education in college.

Eligibility This program is open to ethnic minority public high school seniors in Indiana who are interested in studying education in college. Selection is based on academic achievement, leadership ability as expressed through co-curricular activities and community involvement, recom-

mendations, and a 300-word essay on their educational goals and how they plan to use this scholarship.

Financial data The stipend is $1,000.

Duration 1 year; may be renewed for 2 additional years if the recipient maintains at least a "C+" GPA.

Additional information This program was established in 1987.

Number awarded 1 each year.

Deadline February of each year.

[96]
DARSHAN S. BHATIA MEMORIAL AWARD

India American Cultural Association
1281 Cooper Lake Road, S.E.
Smyrna, GA 30082
(770) 436-3719   (770) 436-4272
Web: www.myiaca.org/scholarships.html

Purpose To provide financial assistance for college to high school seniors in Georgia whose parents or grandparents came from what is now India.

Eligibility This program is open to high school seniors who 1) are living in Georgia and 2) whose parents or grandparents came from present day India. For the purposes of this program, citizens of Pakistan and Bangladesh are not included. Applicants must be planning to attend a 4-year college or university as a full-time student. Along with their application, they must submit official school transcript, resume, SAT score report, the best essay they submitted to a college to which they applied, and documentation of financial need. Selection is based primarily on financial need.

Financial data The stipend is $1,250 per year.

Duration 4 years.

Additional information This program was established in 1993. Information is also available from the Indian American Scholarship Fund, 719 Vinings Estates Drive, Mableton, GA 30126, E-mail: manochaa@bellsouth.net. Membership in the India American Cultural Association (IACA) is not required to apply, but recipients must become members of the association.

Number awarded 1 each year.

Deadline May of each year.

[97]
DCNNOA/GENERAL DYNAMICS SCHOLARSHIP

National Naval Officers Association-Washington, D.C.
    Chapter
Attn: Scholarship Program
9805 Fox Run Drive
Clinton, MD 20735-3087
(202) 874-4994   E-mail: willie.evans@occ.treas.gov
Web: www.dcnnoa.org

Purpose To provide financial assistance to minority high school seniors from the Washington, D.C. area who are interested in majoring in engineering in college.

Eligibility This program is open to minority seniors at high schools in the Washington, D.C. metropolitan area who plan to enroll full time in an engineering program at an accredited 2-year or 4-year college or university. Applicants must have a GPA of 3.0 or higher and be U.S. citizens or permanent residents. Selection is based on academic achievement, community involvement, and financial need.

Financial data The stipend is $5,000 per year.

Duration 1 year; nonrenewable.

Additional information Recipients are not required to join or affiliate with the military in any way. This program is sponsored by General Dynamics.

Number awarded 1 each year.

Deadline March of each year.

[98]
DELL/UNCF CORPORATE SCHOLARS PROGRAM

United Negro College Fund
Attn: Corporate Scholars Program
P.O. Box 1435
Alexandria, VA 22313-9998
Toll-free: (866) 671-7237 E-mail: internship@uncf.org
Web: www.uncf.org/internships/index.asp

Purpose To provide financial assistance and work experience to undergraduate and graduate students, especially minorities, majoring in designated fields and interested in an internship at Dell Computer Corporation's corporate headquarters near Austin, Texas.

Eligibility This program is open to rising juniors and graduate students who are enrolled full time at institutions that are members of the United Negro College Fund (UNCF) or at any other 4-year college or university. Applicants must be majoring in business administration, computer science, engineering (computer, electrical, or mechanical), finance, human resources, management information systems, marketing, or supply chain management with a GPA of 3.0 or higher. Along with their application, they must submit a 1-page essay about themselves and their career goals, including information about their personal background and any particular challenges they have faced. Finalists are interviewed by a team of representatives from Dell, the program's sponsor.

Financial data The program provides a paid summer internship, housing accommodations in Austin, round-trip transportation to and from Austin, and (based on financial need and successful internship performance) a $10,000 scholarship.

Duration 10 to 12 weeks for the internship; 1 year for the scholarship.

Number awarded Varies each year.

Deadline January of each year.

[99]
DETROIT FREE PRESS MINORITY SCHOLARSHIPS

Detroit Free Press
Attn: High School Journalism Directors
600 West Fort Street
Detroit, MI 48226
(313) 222-6428 Toll-free: (800) 678-6400, ext. 6428
Fax: (313) 222-8874
E-mail: highschools@freepress.com
Web: www.freep.com

Purpose To provide financial assistance for college to minority high school seniors the circulation area of the *Detroit Free Press* who are interested in a career in journalism or newspaper business operations.

Eligibility This program is open to minority high school seniors in Michigan, the greater Toledo metropolitan area, and the greater Windsor metropolitan area. Applicants must be planning to attend a 4-year college or university to major in journalism, communications, or a related field. They must be interested in preparing for a career in journalism or newspaper business operations. Along with their application, they must submit 2 letters of recommendation, a transcript of grades, SAT/ACT scores, up to 5 samples of work with bylines (for journalism applicants), and an essay on "Why Journalism or the Newspaper Business is the Life for Me."

Financial data The stipend is $1,000.

Duration 1 year.

Additional information The recipients of these scholarships may be entered into competition for the Knight Ridder Minority Scholarship Program of $40,000 over 4 years.

Number awarded 3 each year, of whom at least 2 are nominated for the national scholarships.

Deadline January of each year.

[100]
DIABLO VALLEY CHAPTER SCHOLARSHIPS

Japanese American Citizens League-Diablo Valley
    Chapter
Attn: Scholarship Chair
P.O. Box 5386
Walnut Creek, CA 94596
Web: www.dvjacl.org/info/scholarship.html

Purpose To provide financial assistance for college to high school seniors in Contra Costa County, California who are members or children of members of the Japanese American Citizens League (JACL).

Eligibility This program is open to seniors at high schools in Contra Costa County, California. Applicants and/or their parents must be paid members of the Diablo Valley Chapter of JACL. They must be planning to enroll full time in a 4-year college or university.

Financial data A stipend is awarded (amount not specified).

Duration 1 year.

Number awarded 1 or more each year.

Deadline March of each year.

[101]
DON SAHLI–KATHY WOODALL MINORITY STUDENT SCHOLARSHIPS

Tennessee Education Association
801 Second Avenue North
Nashville, TN 37201-1099
(615) 242-8392 Toll-free: (800) 342-8267
Fax: (615) 259-4581
Web: www.teateachers.org

Purpose To provide financial assistance to minority high school seniors in Tennessee who are interested in majoring in education.

Eligibility This program is open to minority high school seniors in Tennessee who are planning to major in education. Application must be made by either a Future Teachers of America chapter affiliated with the Tennessee Education Association (TEA) or by the student with the recommendation of an active TEA member. Selection is based on academic record, leadership ability, economic need, and demonstrated interest in becoming a teacher.

Financial data The stipend is $1,000.

Duration 1 year.

Number awarded 1 each year.

Deadline February of each year.

[102]
DOUVAS MEMORIAL SCHOLARSHIP

Wyoming Department of Education
Attn: Director, Programs Unit
2300 Capitol Avenue
Cheyenne, WY 82002-0050
(307) 777-7168   Fax: (307) 777-6234

Purpose To provide financial assistance to high school seniors or students in Wyoming who are first-generation Americans.

Eligibility This program is open to first-generation youth in Wyoming who demonstrate need and are motivated to attend college. First-generation Americans are those born in the United States but whose parents were not born here. Applicants must be high school seniors or between the ages of 18 and 22. They must be Wyoming residents and be willing to use the scholarship at Wyoming's community colleges or the University of Wyoming.

Financial data The stipend is $500, payable in 2 equal installments. Funds are paid directly to the recipient's school.

Duration 1 year.

Additional information This scholarship was first awarded in 1995.

Number awarded 1 each year.

Deadline April of each year.

[103]
DR. AND MRS. YANG HO RHEE SCHOLARSHIP

Community Foundation of the Great River Bend
Attn: Scholarship Programs
111 East Third Street, Suite 710
Davenport, IA 52801-1524
(563) 326-2840   Fax: (563) 326-2870
E-mail: info@cfgrb.org
Web: www.cfgrb.org

Purpose To provide financial assistance for college to Korean high school seniors in Rock Island County, Illinois and Scott County, Iowa.

Eligibility This program is open to seniors of Korean descent who are graduating from high schools in Rock Island County, Illinois and Scott County, Iowa. Children of 1 or 2 Korean biological parents are preferred, but as little as 25% Korean ancestry is acceptable. Applicants must have a GPA of 3.0 or higher or be in the upper third of their graduating class. They must be planning to enroll as a full-time student working on a bachelor's degree. Financial need is considered in the selection process.

Financial data The stipend is $1,000.

Duration 1 year.

Number awarded 1 each year.

Deadline Applications must be submitted to high school counselors or principals by January of each year.

[104]
DR. HILDEGARD E. PEPLAU SCHOLARSHIP

American Psychiatric Nurses Association
Attn: APN Foundation
1555 Wilson Boulevard, Suite 515
Arlington, VA 22209
(703) 243-2443   Fax: (703) 243-3390
E-mail: inform@apna.org
Web: www.apna.org/foundation/scholarships.html

Purpose To provide financial assistance to students and registered nurses (especially minorities) working on a degree in nursing.

Eligibility This program is open to students and registered nurses enrolled in an NLN-accredited program in nursing. Applicants must submit 3 essays (each up to 500 words) on the following topics: 1) their career goals, how education will enhance those goals, and their contribution to the profession; 2) their professional activities, involvement, continuing education, and scholarly contributions; and 3) their voluntary community activities. Financial need is not considered in the selection process. Minorities are especially encouraged to apply.

Financial data The stipend is $1,000.

Duration 1 year.

Number awarded 1 or more each year.

Deadline January of each year.

[105]
DR. HO DA-FU SCHOLARSHIP

Professor Chen Wen-Chen Memorial Foundation
Attn: Scholarship Committee
P.O. Box 6223
Lawrenceville, NJ 08648
(609) 936-1352   E-mail: mkao@comcast.net
Web: www.cwcmf.org

Purpose To provide financial assistance to students at North American colleges and universities who have been involved in the Taiwanese community and are physically challenged or have physically challenged or single parents.

Eligibility This program is open to students who have participated in Taiwanese social-political movements or have made significant contributions to the Taiwanese community in North America. Applicants must be currently enrolled at a college or university in North America. They must 1) be physically challenged, 2) have physically-challenged parents, or 3) have single parents. Selection is based on academic achievement.

Financial data The stipend is $1,500.

Duration 1 year.

Additional information Information is also available from Dr. Long R. Mark Kao, 3 Worchester Lane, Princeton Junction, NJ 08550.

Number awarded 2 each year.

Deadline May of each year.

[106]
DR. SCHOLL FOUNDATION SCHOLARSHIPS

Chicago Urban League
Attn: Education Department
4510 South Michigan Avenue
Chicago, IL 60653-3898
(773) 451-3565   Fax: (773) 285-7772
E-mail: info@cul-chicago.org
Web: www.cul-chicago.org

Purpose To provide financial assistance to Illinois residents of color enrolled at a 4-year college or university.

Eligibility This program is open to Illinois residents of color who are full-time undergraduate students at a 4-year college or university with at least a 2.5 GPA. Applicants may be majoring in any field. They must be able to demonstrate financial need.

Financial data The stipend is $2,000 per year.

Duration 1 year.

Additional information This program is offered as part of the Chicago Urban League's Whitney M. Young, Jr. Memorial Scholarship Fund, established in 1970. It is sponsored by the Dr. Scholl Foundation.

Number awarded Varies each year.

Deadline May of each year.

[107]
DR. SYNGMAN RHEE SCHOLARSHIP

Dong Ji Hoi Society
c/o Dianne Lim, Scholarship Chair
91-201 Kaana Place
Kapolei, HI 96707-1931

Purpose To provide financial assistance to Korean Americans in Hawaii who are interested in pursuing postsecondary education.

Eligibility This program is open to graduating high school seniors in Hawaii who are at least 50% Korean ancestry. Applicants must be planning to attend a 4-year college or university. Selection is based on academic achievement, community service, extracurricular activities, and SAT scores.

Financial data The stipend is $1,500 per year.

Duration Up to 4 years.

Additional information Recipients may study in Hawaii or on the mainland. Requests for applications must be accompanied by a self-addressed stamped envelope.

Number awarded 10 to 16 each year.

Deadline June of each year.

[108]
DR. THOMAS T. YATABE MEMORIAL SCHOLARSHIP

Japanese American Citizens League
Attn: National Scholarship Awards
1765 Sutter Street
San Francisco, CA 94115
(415) 921-5225   Fax: (415) 931-4671
E-mail: jacl@jacl.org
Web: www.jacl.org/scholarships.html

Purpose To provide financial assistance for college to student members of the Japanese American Citizens League (JACL).

Eligibility This program is open to JACL members who are currently enrolled or planning to reenter a college, university, trade school, business college, or other institution of higher learning. Applicants must submit a statement describing their current level of involvement in the Japanese American community or Asian Pacific community and how they will continue their involvement in future years. Selection is based on academic record, extracurricular activities, financial need, and community involvement.

Financial data The stipend depends on the availability of funds but usually ranges from $1,000 to $5,000.

Duration 1 year; nonrenewable.

Additional information Applications must be submitted to the JACL National Scholarship Program, c/o San Diego JACL Chapter, 1031 25th Street, San Diego, CA 92102.

Number awarded At least 1 each year.

Deadline March of each year.

[109]
DRS. POH SHIEN AND JUDY YOUNG SCHOLARSHIP

US Pan Asian American Chamber of Commerce
Attn: Scholarship Coordinator
1329 18th Street, N.W.
Washington, DC 20036
(202) 296-5221   Fax: (202) 296-5225
E-mail: administrator@uspaacc.com
Web: www.uspaacc.net

Purpose To provide financial assistance for college to Asian American high school seniors who demonstrate financial need.

Eligibility This program is open to high school seniors of Asian heritage who are U.S. citizens or permanent residents. Applicants must be planning to begin full-time study at an accredited postsecondary educational institution in the United States. Along with their application, they must submit a 500-word essay on "Why I need this scholarship." Selection is based on academic excellence (GPA of 3.5 or higher), leadership in extracurricular activities, community service involvement, and financial need.

Financial data The maximum stipend is $4,000. Funds are paid directly to the recipient's college or university.

Duration 1 year.

Additional information Funding is not provided for correspondence courses, Internet courses, or study in a country other than the United States.

Number awarded 1 each year.

Deadline February of each year.

[110]
EARL P. ANDREWS, JR. MEMORIAL SCHOLARSHIP

Central Alabama Community Foundation
Attn: Executive Director
434 North McDonough Street
P.O. Box 11587
Montgomery, AL 36111
(334) 264-6223   Fax: (334) 263-6225
Web: www.cacinfo@cacfscholarships.shtml

Purpose To provide financial assistance for college to minority high school seniors in central Alabama.

Eligibility This program is open to minority high school seniors in central Alabama who have at least a 3.5 GPA and a minimum ACT score of 23 or the SAT equivalent. Applicants must submit a completed application form, a high school transcript, and an essay outlining career goals. Finalists are interviewed. Selection is based on academic achievement and financial need.

Financial data The stipend ranges from $500 to $1,000 per year.

Duration 1 year.

Additional information This program was funded in 1989.

Number awarded 1 each year.

Deadline March of each year.

[111]
EARL PHILLIPS SCHOLARSHIPS

YMCA of Greater Seattle
Attn: College Scholarship Committee
909 Fourth Avenue
Seattle, WA 98104-1194
(206) 382-5003, ext. 4700   Fax: (206) 382-7283
Web: www.seattleymca.org

Purpose To provide financial assistance for college to Christian minority students from King and south Snohomish counties in Washington who are preparing for a career with the YMCA.

Eligibility This program is open to minority residents of King and south Snohomish counties in Washington who are Christians and preparing for employment with the YMCA. Appropriate courses of study in college include: human services, child development, physical education, health/fitness, psychology, education, recreation, sociology, business administration, and related fields. Applicants may be high school seniors, high school/GED program graduates, or currently-enrolled college undergraduates. Along with their application, they must submit a current (or most recent) high school or college transcript, a 1-page essay on their future educational and career goals, a list of leadership and volunteer experiences (including YMCA experiences and involvement), a short statement about why they are seeking financial support for their college education, documentation of financial need, and 2 references.

Financial data The stipend is $2,500 per year.

Duration Up to 4 years.

Number awarded 4 each year.

Deadline March of each year.

[112]
EAST OHIO CONFERENCE BOARD OF ORDAINED MINISTRY ETHNIC MINORITY GRANTS

United Methodist Church-East Ohio Conference
Attn: Board of Ordained Ministry
8800 Cleveland Avenue, N.W.
P.O. Box 2800
North Canton, OH 44720
(330) 499-3972   Toll-free: (800) 831-3972
Fax: (330) 499-3279
Web: www.eocumc.com

Purpose To provide financial assistance to ethnic minority undergraduate and graduate students who are preparing for ordained ministry in the East Ohio Conference.

Eligibility This program is open to ethnic minority college and graduate students who are preparing for ordained ministry in the East Ohio Conference. Students must be recommended to receive this aid either by their District Superintendent or by the District Committee on Ordained Ministry where they hold their relationship. Applicants must attend a college or seminary that is fully accredited by the University Senate. They do not need to be certified candidates. Ethnic minority undergraduate pre-theological students are also eligible.

Financial data The stipend is $500 per year.

Duration 1 year.

Additional information Information is also available from Preston Forbes, Seminary Scholarships and Grants Secretary, 9071 Inverrary Drive, Warren, OH 44484, (330) 856-2631, E-mail: forbes@onecom.com.

Number awarded 1 or more each year.

Deadline September of each year.

[113]
EAST OHIO CONFERENCE COMMISSION ON RELIGION AND RACE SCHOLARSHIPS

United Methodist Church-East Ohio Conference
Attn: Commission on Religion and Race
8800 Cleveland Avenue, N.W.
P.O. Box 2800
North Canton, OH 44720
(330) 499-3972, ext. 116
Toll-free: (800) 831-3972, ext. 116
Fax: (330) 499-3279   E-mail: tony@eocumc.com
Web: www.eocumc.com

Purpose To provide financial assistance for college to racial minorities in east Ohio who are members of the United Methodist Church.

Eligibility This program is open to high school seniors and current college undergraduates who are members of minority groups (Asian, Hispanic, Native American, African American). Applicants must be active members of a United Methodist Church in east Ohio and admitted to an accredited university, college, or licensed technical or vocational institute. They must submit a 100-word statement on how their faith in Christ has had an impact on their life and how it might affect their future development. Selection is based on academic standing and ability, indication of commitment to Christian vocation, relationship and involvement with their local church, involvement in school and campus activities, general character, and financial need.

Financial data A stipend is awarded (amount not specified).
Duration 1 year.
Number awarded 1 or more each year.
Deadline April of each year.

[114]
EAST OHIO RACIAL ETHNIC MERIT SCHOLARSHIP

United Methodist Church-East Ohio Conference
Attn: Board of Higher Education and Campus Ministry
8800 Cleveland Avenue, N.W.
P.O. Box 2800
North Canton, OH 44720
(330) 499-3972, ext. 120
Toll-free: (800) 831-3972, ext. 120
Fax: (330) 499-3279   E-mail: gary@eocumc.com
Web: www.eocumc.com/highered/scholarships.htm

Purpose To provide financial assistance for college to outstanding racial minorities in east Ohio who are members of the United Methodist Church.

Eligibility This program is open to minorities who are active members of a United Methodist Church in east Ohio and admitted to or attending a United Methodist college or university. Students may also attend non-Methodist schools, provided they are pursuing a course of study not available at a Methodist institution. Applicants must be recommended by a local United Methodist Church. Along with their application, they must submit an administrative board recommendation form, a 500-word statement on how their faith journey has helped them set priorities in their life, and a personal letter of recommendation from a pastor or church lay leader. Selection is based on school activities and achievements, church involvement, community volunteer service, college honors and achievements, and financial need.

Financial data A stipend is awarded (amount not specified).
Duration 1 year; recipients may reapply.
Number awarded Several each year.
Deadline March of each year.

[115]
EASTERN REGION KOREAN AMERICAN SCHOLARSHIPS

Korean American Scholarship Foundation
Eastern Region
c/o William S. Lee, Scholarship Committee Chair
10301 Georgia Avenue, Suite 303
Silver Spring, MD 20902
(703) 748-5935   Fax: (703) 748-1874
E-mail: kasfdc@hotmail.com
Web: www.kasf.org

Purpose To provide financial assistance to Korean American undergraduate and graduate students who attend school in the eastern states.

Eligibility This program is open to Korean American students who are currently enrolled in a college or university in an eastern state as a full-time undergraduate or graduate student. Applicants may reside anywhere in the United States as long as they attend school in the eastern region: Delaware, District of Columbia, Kentucky, Maryland, North

Carolina, Pennsylvania, Virginia, and West Virginia. Selection is based on academic achievement, school activities, community service, and financial need.

Financial data Stipends range from $350 to $5,000.
Duration 1 year; renewable.
Number awarded Varies each year. Recently, 65 of these scholarships were awarded: 1 at $5,000, 20 at $2,000, 3 at $1,500, 33 at $1,000, 2 at $500, and 6 at $350.
Deadline May of each year.

[116]
EATON MULTICULTURAL SCHOLARS PROGRAM

Eaton Corporation
Attn: EMSP
1111 Superior Avenue
Cleveland, OH 44114-2584
(216) 523-4354   E-mail: mildredneumann@eaton.com
Web: www.eatonjobs.com/career/career_choices.asp

Purpose To provide financial assistance and work experience to minority college students interested in a career as an engineer.

Eligibility This program is open to full-time minority students who are U.S. citizens or permanent residents. Applicants must have completed 1 year in an accredited program and have 3 remaining years of course work before completing a bachelor's degree. They must be majoring in computer science/data processing, electrical engineering, or mechanical engineering. Selection is based on academic performance, the student's school recommendation, and an expressed interest in pursuing challenging and rewarding internship assignments.

Financial data Stipends range from $500 to $3,000 per year. Funds are paid directly to the recipient's university to cover the cost of tuition, books, supplies, equipment, and fees.

Duration 3 years.

Additional information In addition to the scholarships, recipients are offered paid summer internships at company headquarters in Cleveland. The target schools participating in this program recently were Cornell, Detroit-Mercy, Florida A&M, Georgia Tech, Illinois at Chicago, Illinois at Urbana-Champaign, Lawrence Technological, Marquette, Massachusetts Institute of Technology, Michigan at Ann Arbor, Michigan at Dearborn, Michigan State, Milwaukee School of Engineering, Minnesota, Morehouse College, North Carolina A&T State, North Carolina State, Northwestern, Notre Dame, Ohio State, Purdue, Southern, Tennessee, Western Michigan, and Wisconsin at Madison. This program was established in 1994. Until 2002, it was known as the Eaton Minority Engineering Scholars Program.

Number awarded Varies each year.
Deadline December of each year.

[117]
ED BRADLEY SCHOLARSHIP

Radio and Television News Directors Foundation
1600 K Street, N.W., Suite 700
Washington, DC 20006-2838
(202) 467-5218   Fax: (202) 223-4007
E-mail: karenb@rtndf.org
Web: www.rtndf.org

Purpose To provide financial assistance to outstanding undergraduate students, especially minorities, who are preparing for a career in electronic journalism.

Eligibility Eligible are sophomore or more advanced undergraduate students enrolled in an electronic journalism sequence at an accredited or nationally-recognized college or university. Applicants must submit 1 to 3 examples of reporting or producing skills on audio or video cassette tapes (no more than 15 minutes total), a statement explaining why they are interested in a career in broadcast or cable journalism, and a letter of endorsement from a faculty sponsor that verifies the applicant has at least 1 year of school remaining. Preference is given to undergraduate students of color.

Financial data The stipend is $10,000, paid in semiannual installments of $5,000 each.

Duration 1 year.

Additional information The Radio and Television News Directors Foundation (RTNDF) also provides an all-expense paid trip to the Radio-Television News Directors Association (RTNDA) annual international conference. It defines electronic journalism to include radio, television, cable, and online news. Previous winners of any RTNDF scholarship or internship are not eligible.

Number awarded 1 each year.

Deadline April of each year.

[118]
EDUCATIONAL ADVANCEMENT BSN SCHOLARSHIPS

American Association of Critical-Care Nurses
Attn: Educational Advancement Scholarships
101 Columbia
Aliso Viejo, CA 92656-4109
(949) 362-2000, ext. 338
Toll-free: (800) 899-AACN, ext. 338
Fax: (949) 362-2020   E-mail: info@aacn.org
Web: www.aacn.org

Purpose To provide financial assistance to members of the American Association of Critical-Care Nurses (AACN) who are working on a B.S.N. degree in nursing.

Eligibility This program is open to registered nurses who are current members of the association and enrolled in an accredited B.S.N. degree program. Applicants must be nurses who hold an active R.N. license and are currently working in critical care or have 1 year's experience in the last 3 years. They must have a cumulative GPA of 3.0 or higher and plan to hold junior or upper-division status in the fall semester. Along with their application, they must submit narratives on 1) how they see their nursing practice changing as a result of their baccalaureate degree; and 2) their contributions to critical care nursing, including work, community, and profession-related activities. Financial need is

not considered in the selection process. Qualified ethnic minority candidates receive at least 20% of these awards.

Financial data The stipend is $1,500 per year. The funds are sent directly to the recipient's college or university and may be used only for tuition, fees, books, and supplies.

Duration 1 year; recipients may reapply.

Number awarded Varies each year; recently, 5 of these scholarships were awarded.

Deadline March of each year.

[119]
EDWARD D. STONE, JR. AND ASSOCIATES MINORITY SCHOLARSHIP

Landscape Architecture Foundation
Attn: Scholarship Program
818 18th Street, N.W., Suite 810
Washington, DC 20006-3520
(202) 331-7070   Fax: (202) 331-7079
E-mail: rfigura@lafoundation.org
Web: www.laprofession.org

Purpose To provide financial assistance to minority college students who wish to study landscape architecture.

Eligibility This program is open to African American, Hispanic, Native American, and minority college students of other cultural and ethnic backgrounds, if they are entering their final 2 years of undergraduate study in landscape architecture. Applicants must submit a 500-word essay on a design or research effort they wish to pursue (explaining how it will contribute to the advancement of the profession and to their ethnic heritage), 4 to 8 35mm color slides or black-and-white photographs of their best work, and 2 letters of recommendation. Selection is based on professional experience, community involvement, extracurricular activities, and financial need.

Financial data The stipend is $1,000.

Duration 1 year.

Number awarded 2 each year.

Deadline April of each year.

[120]
EDWARD DAVIS SCHOLARSHIP FUND

Edward Davis Education Foundation
585 East Larned Street, Suite 100
Detroit, MI 48226
(313) 963-2209   Toll-free: (877) 847-9060
Web: www.automag.com/EDEFoundation/default.asp

Purpose To provide financial assistance to minority students interested in preparing for a career in an automotive-related profession.

Eligibility Applicants must be minority high school seniors or currently-enrolled college students who are interested in preparing for a career in the automotive industry. High school students must have a GPA of 3.0 or higher; college students must have at least a 2.5. To apply, students must complete an application; provide proof of acceptance or enrollment in an accredited college, university, vocational institute, or technical school; and submit an essay (up to 200 words) on "The Importance of Diversity in the Automobile Industry."

Financial data A stipend is awarded (amount not specified). Since its inception, the program has awarded more than $200,000 in stipends.

Duration 1 year.

Additional information This scholarship, established in 1998, honors the first African American to own a new car dealership.

Deadline November of each year.

[121]
EDWARD S. ROTH MANUFACTURING ENGINEERING SCHOLARSHIP

Society of Manufacturing Engineers
Attn: SME Education Foundation
One SME Drive
P.O. Box 930
Dearborn, MI 48121-0930
(313) 425-3304   Toll-free: (800) 733-4763, ext. 3304
Fax: (313) 425-3411   E-mail: foundation@sme.org
Web: www.sme.org

Purpose To provide financial assistance to students (especially minorities) enrolled or planning to enroll in a degree program in manufacturing engineering at selected universities.

Eligibility This program is open to U.S. citizens who are graduating high school seniors or currently-enrolled undergraduate or graduate students. Applicants must be enrolled or planning to enroll as a full-time student at 1 of 13 selected 4-year universities to work on a bachelor's or master's degree in manufacturing engineering. They must have a GPA of 3.0 or higher. Preference is given to 1) students demonstrating financial need, 2) minority students, and 3) students participating in a co-op program. Some preference may also be given to graduating high school seniors and graduate students.

Financial data The stipend is $2,500.

Duration 1 year; may be renewed.

Additional information The eligible institutions are California Polytechnic State University at San Luis Obispo, California State Polytechnic State University at Pomona, University of Miami (Florida), Bradley University, Central State University (Ohio), Miami University (Ohio), Boston University, Worcester Polytechnic Institute, University of Massachusetts, St. Cloud State University, University of Texas-Pan American, Brigham Young University, and Utah State University.

Number awarded 1 each year.

Deadline January of each year.

[122]
EIRO YAMADA MEMORIAL SCHOLARSHIP

Hawai'i Community Foundation
Attn: Scholarship Department
1164 Bishop Street, Suite 800
Honolulu, HI 96813
(808) 537-6333   Toll-free: (888) 731-3863
Fax: (808) 521-6286
E-mail: scholarships@hcf-hawaii.org
Web: www.hawaiicommunityfoundation.org

Purpose To provide financial assistance for college or graduate school to Hawaii residents who are descendants of World War II Japanese American veterans.

Eligibility This program is open to Hawaii residents who are interested in attending college on the undergraduate or graduate school level. Applicants must be a direct descendant of a World War II veteran of the 100th, 442nd, MIS, or 1399th units. They must be able to demonstrate academic achievement (GPA of 2.7 or higher), good moral character, and financial need. In addition to filling out the standard application form, applicants must write a short essay on "The Values I Have Learned from My Japanese American Forefathers" and their personal reflections on the Japanese American experience during World War II.

Financial data The amounts of the awards depend on the availability of funds and the need of the recipient; recently, stipends averaged $500.

Duration 1 year.

Additional information Recipients may attend college in Hawaii or on the mainland. Recipients must be full-time students.

Number awarded Varies each year; recently, 30 of these scholarships were awarded.

Deadline February of each year.

[123]
EIZO AND TOYO SAKUMOTO TRUST SCHOLARSHIPS

Hawai'i Community Foundation
Attn: Scholarship Department
1164 Bishop Street, Suite 800
Honolulu, HI 96813
(808) 537-6333   Toll-free: (888) 731-3863
Fax: (808) 521-6286
E-mail: scholarships@hcf-hawaii.org
Web: www.hawaiicommunityfoundation.org

Purpose To provide financial assistance to Hawaii residents of Japanese ancestry who are interested in attending college or graduate school.

Eligibility This program is open to Hawaii residents of Japanese ancestry who are enrolled in or planning to enroll in an accredited college or university in Hawaii. Applicants must be full-time undergraduate or graduate students and able to demonstrate academic achievement (GPA of 2.7 or higher), good moral character, and financial need. They must have been born in Hawaii.

Financial data The amounts of the awards depend on the availability of funds and the need of the recipient; recently, the stipend was $1,000.

Duration 1 year.

Number awarded Varies each year; recently, 57 of these scholarships were awarded.

Deadline February of each year.

[124]
ELLEN MASIN PERSINA SCHOLARSHIP
National Press Club
Attn: General Manager's Office
529 14th Street, N.W.
Washington, DC 20045
(202) 662-7532   E-mail: jbooze@press.org
Web: www.press.org/programs/aboutscholarship.cfm

Purpose To provide funding to minority high school seniors interested in preparing for a journalism career in college.

Eligibility This program is open to minority high school seniors who have been accepted to college and plan to prepare for a career in journalism. Applicants must 1) demonstrate an ongoing interest in journalism through work in high school and/or other media; 2) submit a 1-page essay on why they want to prepare for a career in journalism; and 3) have a GPA of 2.75 or higher in high school. Financial need is considered in the selection process.

Financial data The stipend is $5,000 per year.

Duration 4 years.

Additional information The program began in 1991. In the past, the Press Club has drawn on the Washington Association of Black Journalists and Youth Connections (a nationwide organization that produces free papers written by high school students).

Number awarded 1 or more each year.

Deadline February of each year.

[125]
ENCOURAGE MINORITY PARTICIPATION IN OCCUPATIONS WITH EMPHASIS ON REHABILITATION
Courage Center
Attn: EMPOWER Scholarship Program
3915 Golden Valley Road
Minneapolis, MN 55422
(763) 520-0214   Toll-free: (888) 8-INTAKE
Fax: (763) 520-0392   TTY: (763) 520-0245
E-mail: suep@courage.org
Web: www.courage.org

Purpose To provide financial assistance to students of color interested in preparing for a career in the medical rehabilitation field.

Eligibility This program is open to ethnically diverse students accepted at or enrolled in an institution of higher learning. Applicants must demonstrate a career interest in the medical rehabilitation field by completing at least 200 hours of career-related volunteer service. They must have a GPA of 2.0 or higher. Selection is based on career intentions and achievements, not academic rank.

Financial data The stipend is $1,500.

Duration 1 year.

Additional information This program is also identified by its acronym as the EMPOWER Scholarship Award.

Number awarded 2 each year.

Deadline April of each year.

[126]
ENVIRONMENTAL EDUCATIONAL SCHOLARSHIP PROGRAM
Missouri Department of Natural Resources
Attn: Environmental Educational Scholarship Program
P.O. Box 176
Jefferson City, MO 65102
(573) 526-8411   Toll-free: (800) 334-6946
TDD: (800) 379-2419
E-mail: daspec@dnr.state.mo.us
Web: www.dnr.state.mo.us/eesp

Purpose To provide financial assistance to underrepresented and minority students from Missouri who are or will be working on a bachelor's or master's degree in an environmental field.

Eligibility This program is open to minority and underrepresented residents of Missouri who have graduated from an accredited high school with a GPA of 3.0 or higher. Students who are already enrolled in college must have a GPA of 2.5 or higher and must be full-time undergraduate or graduate students. Applicants may be 1) engineering students in civil, chemical, environmental, mechanical, or agricultural engineering; 2) environmental students in geology, biology, wildlife management, planning, natural resources, or a closely-related course of study; 3) chemistry students in the field of environmental chemistry; or 4) law enforcement students in environmental law enforcement. They must submit a 1-page essay on their environmental education career goals. Selection is based on the essay, GPA and test scores, school and community activities, leadership, and character.

Financial data A stipend is $2,000 per year.

Duration 1 year; may be renewed if the recipient maintains a GPA of 2.5 or higher and full-time enrollment.

Number awarded Varies each year.

Deadline June of each year.

[127]
ERNST & YOUNG LLP MINORITY LEADERSHIP AWARDS
New Jersey Society of Certified Public Accountants
Attn: Student Programs Coordinator
425 Eagle Rock Avenue, Suite 100
Roseland, NJ 07068-1723
(973) 226-4494, ext. 209   Fax: (973) 226-7425
E-mail: njscpa@njscpa.org
Web: www.njscpa.org

Purpose To provide financial assistance to minority undergraduates in New Jersey who are preparing for a career as a certified public accountant.

Eligibility This program is open to African American, Asian, Hispanic, and Native American residents of New Jersey who are attending a college or university in the state. Applicants must be sophomores who are majoring or concentrating in accounting and have completed at least 3 credits in accounting courses. Along with their application, they must submit a letter of recommendation from an accounting professor, an official transcript indicating a GPA of 3.2 or higher, a resume, and an essay of 250 to 500 words on what motivated them to choose accounting as a career choice.

Financial data The stipend is $5,000.

Duration 1 year.

Additional information This program is sponsored by Ernst & Young.

Number awarded 2 each year.

Deadline January of each year.

[128]
ESTER BOONE MEMORIAL SCHOLARSHIPS

National Naval Officers Association-Washington, D.C.
    Chapter
Attn: Scholarship Program
9805 Fox Run Drive
Clinton, MD 20735-3087
(202) 874-4994   E-mail: willie.evans@occ.treas.gov
Web: www.dcnnoa.org

Purpose To provide financial assistance to minority high school seniors from the Washington, D.C. area.

Eligibility This program is open to minority seniors at high schools in the Washington, D.C. metropolitan area who plan to enroll full time at an accredited 2-year or 4-year college or university. Applicants must have a GPA of 2.5 or higher. Selection is based on academic achievement, community involvement, and financial need.

Financial data The stipend is $1,000 per year.

Duration 1 year. This program includes the Ester Boone Memorial Sustaining Scholarship, which is renewable.

Additional information Recipients are not required to join or affiliate with the military in any way.

Number awarded 11 each year: 10 nonrenewable scholarships and 1 that is renewable.

Deadline March of each year.

[129]
ETHNIC AWARENESS COMMITTEE SCHOLARSHIP

Washington Financial Aid Association
c/o James D. Flowers, Scholarship Committee
University of Washington
105 Schmitz, Box 355880
Seattle, WA 98195-5880
(206) 616-2309   E-mail: jflowers@washington.edu
Web: www.wfaa.org/ethnicawareness.html

Purpose To provide financial assistance for college to high school seniors or currently-enrolled college students of color in Washington.

Eligibility Open to graduating high school seniors or currently-enrolled college students of color who are or will be attending a college or university belonging to the Washington Financial Aid Association. Applicants must be able to demonstrate leadership abilities, have at least a 3.0 GPA, have financial need, and enroll or plan to enroll at least half time at an eligible private or public community college, technical school, college, or university. To apply, they must submit a typed personal statement, 2 letters of recommendation, and an official college and/or high school transcript.

Financial data Stipends range up to $1,000.

Duration 1 year.

Number awarded 1 or more each year.

Deadline June of each year.

[130]
ETHNIC MINORITY BACHELOR'S SCHOLARSHIPS IN ONCOLOGY NURSING

Oncology Nursing Society
Attn: ONS Foundation
125 Enterprise Drive
Pittsburgh, PA 15275-1214
(412) 859-6100, ext. 8503   Toll-free: (866) 257-4ONS
Fax: (412) 859-6160   E-mail: foundation@ons.org
Web: www.ons.org

Purpose To provide financial assistance to ethnic minorities interested in working on undergraduate studies in oncology nursing.

Eligibility The candidate must 1) demonstrate an interest in and commitment to cancer nursing; 2) be enrolled in an undergraduate nursing degree program at an NLN- or CCNE-accredited school of nursing (the program must have application to oncology nursing); 3) have a current license to practice as a registered nurse or a practical (vocational) nurse; 4) not have previously received a bachelor's scholarship from this sponsor; and 5) be a member of an ethnic minority group (Native American, African American, Asian American, Pacific Islander, Hispanic/Latino, or other ethnic minority background). Applicants must submit an essay of 250 words or less on their role in caring for persons with cancer and a statement of their professional goals and their relationship to the advancement of oncology nursing. Financial need is not considered in the selection process.

Financial data The stipend is $2,000.

Duration 1 year.

Additional information This program includes a mentoring component with an individual in the applicant's area of clinical interest. When appropriate, efforts are made to match the applicant and mentor by ethnicity. At the end of each year of scholarship participation, recipients must submit a summary describing their educational activities. Applications must be accompanied by a $5 fee.

Number awarded 3 each year.

Deadline January of each year.

[131]
ETHNIC MISSIONS SCHOLARSHIP PROGRAM

Baptist General Convention of Texas
Attn: Ethnic Missions
333 North Washington
Dallas, TX 75246-1798
(214) 828-5342   Toll-free: (800) 352-5342
Fax: (214) 828-5284   E-mail: porraz@bgct.org
Web: www.bgct.org/ethnic_missions

Purpose To provide financial assistance for college or seminary education to ethnic and deaf students in Texas who are members of Texas Baptist ethnic congregations.

Eligibility This program is open to members of Texas Baptist congregations who are Asian, Hispanic, or deaf and have a "sense of call" as a lay person or minister. Applicants must be U.S. citizens or permanent residents, have resided in Texas for at least 1 year, demonstrate financial need, and plan to attend or be attending a Texas Baptist university or the Southwestern Baptist Theological Seminary. Students still in high school must have a GPA of at least 3.0; students previously enrolled in a college or seminary must have at least a 2.0 GPA. Applicants must submit brief essays on what they, as a Baptist, believe about God, Jesus, sin, salvation, church membership, and baptism. They must also explain how they became a Christian, why they are seeking a Christian university education, and what they plan to do following graduation.

Financial data The grant for full-time students is $800 per year or $400 per semester. Part-time students receive $27 per credit hour.

Duration 1 year; may be renewed.

Additional information The scholarships are funded through the Week of Prayer and the Mary Hill Davis Offering for state missions sponsored annually by Women's Missionary Union of Texas.

[132]
EXTENDED OPPORTUNITY PROGRAMS AND SERVICES GRANTS

California Community Colleges
Attn: Student Services and Special Programs Division
1102 Q Street
Sacramento, CA 95814-6511
(916) 323-0453   Fax: (916) 327-8232
Web: www.ccccco.edu/ss/ss.htm

Purpose To provide financial assistance to disadvantaged students attending community colleges in California.

Eligibility To receive support under this program, students must be residents of California, be enrolled full time in a California community college, not have completed more than 70 units of course work in any combination of postsecondary institutions, be educationally disadvantaged, and be able to demonstrate financial need. Up to 10% of the EOPS students at each college may enroll for only 9 units; students with disabilities may enroll for fewer units, based on their disability. Educationally disadvantaged students include those who are not qualified to enroll in the minimum level English or mathematics course at their college, did not graduate from high school or obtain the GED, graduated from high school with a GPA below 2.5, previously enrolled in remedial education, or met other factors described in their college's plan, such as first-generation college student, member of underrepresented group at the college, or English not the primary language.

Financial data Individual grants are determined by participating community colleges, but they are generally small (rarely in excess of $500 per year) and are usually limited to such purposes as purchase of books.

Duration 1 year; may be renewed.

Additional information EOPS students are also eligible for other support in the form of counseling, tutoring, registration assistance, orientation, child care, transportation, and cultural activities. Students apply to their community college, not to the sponsoring organization.

Number awarded Varies each year; recently, 26,137 students received support through this program.

Deadline Varies by participating institution.

[133]
FAPAC SCHOLARSHIPS

Federal Asian Pacific American Council
Attn: Scholarship and Internship Chair
P.O. Box 23184
Washington, DC 20026-3184
E-mail: fapac@fapac.org
Web: www.fapac.org

Purpose To provide financial assistance for college to Asian American and other students.

Eligibility This program is open to high school seniors and students currently enrolled in college. Applicants must submit an essay of 500 to 750 words on the FAPAC topic "Salute to Liberty," including the importance of promoting equal opportunity and cultural diversity for American Pacific Islanders in government. Selection is based on academic achievement, personal merit, leadership in school and leadership in civic and other extracurricular volunteer activities.

Financial data The stipend is $1,000.

Duration 1 year.

Additional information Only 1 award is made to a family. FAPAC is an inter-agency organization founded in 1985 to promote equal opportunity and cultural diversity for Asian Pacific Americans within the federal and District of Columbia governments. Scholarships are awarded at the annual FAPAC Congressional Seminar and Leadership Training Conference. Information is also available from Mai Nguyen, (202) 267-7666, E-mail: Mai.Nguyen@faa.gov.

Number awarded 3 each year.

Deadline March of each year.

[134]
FATHER JOHN HINES AND DEACON FRANCIS CHAO MEMORIAL SCHOLARSHIP

Boston Chinese Catholic Community
c/o Rev. Denis Como, Chinese Catholic Pastoral
    Center
78 Tyler Street
Boston, MA 02111-1831
(617) 482-2949   Fax: (617) 482-2949
E-mail: pastoralcenter@aol.com
Web: www.rc.net/boston/bccc-stjames

Purpose To provide financial assistance for college to members of the Boston Chinese Catholic Community.

Eligibility This program is open to college-bound high school seniors who are members of the Boston Chinese Catholic Community. Selection is based on academic achievement, service to the Boston Chinese Catholic Community, service to the community, character and leadership demonstrated in an essay, transcripts, and recommendations.

Financial data The stipend is $500.

Duration 1 year.

Number awarded 1 to 3 each year.

Deadline April of each year.

[135]
FIFTH THIRD BANK INDIANA SCHOLARSHIPS

National FFA Organization
Attn: Scholarship Office
6060 FFA Drive
P.O. Box 68960
Indianapolis, IN 46268-0960
(317) 802-4321   Fax: (317) 802-5321
E-mail: scholarships@ffa.org
Web: www.ffa.org

Purpose To provide financial assistance for college to FFA members from designated counties of Indiana who are members of ethnic minority groups.

Eligibility This program is open to ethnic minorities who are FFA members and either graduating high school seniors planning to enroll full time or college students already enrolled on a full-time basis. Applicants must be residents of the following counties in Indiana: Adams, Allen, Bartholomew, Benton, Boone, Brown, Clay, Dearborn, Decatur, Fayette, Franklin, Greene, Hamilton, Hancock, Hendricks, Jackson, Jennings, Johnson, Lawrence, Madison, Marion, Monroe, Morgan, Orange, Owen, Parke, Putnam, Ripley, Rush, Shelby, Steuben, Sullivan, Tippecanoe, Vermillion, or Vigo. They must be planning to work on a 4-year degree in any field at a university in the state. Selection is based on academic achievement (10 points for GPA, 10 points for SAT or ACT score, 10 points for class rank), leadership in FFA activities (30 points), leadership in community activities (10 points), and participation in the Supervised Agricultural Experience (SAE) program (30 points). U.S. citizenship is required.

Financial data The stipend is $1,000. Funds are paid directly to the recipient.

Duration 1 year; nonrenewable.

Additional information Funding for these scholarships is provided by Fifth Third Bank.

Number awarded 5 each year.

Deadline February of each year.

[136]
FILIPINO AMERICAN LEAGUE OF ENGINEERS AND ARCHITECTS SCHOLARSHIP PROGRAM

Filipino American League of Engineers and Architects
94-518 Kupuohi Street, No. 102
Waipahu, HI 96797
(808) 688-0290   Fax: (808) 688-0290
Web: www.falea.org

Purpose To provide financial assistance to Hawaii residents who are of Filipino descent and are interested in preparing for a career in engineering, architecture, or a related field.

Eligibility Eligible to apply for this program are high school seniors or currently-enrolled college students who are Hawaii residents and of Filipino descent. They must be attending or planning to attend a college or university on a full-time basis, to work on a degree in engineering, architecture, surveying, or a related field. Selection is based on academic record, personality, letters of recommendation, leadership, and community involvement.

Financial data The stipend is $1,000.

Duration 1 year.

Additional information This program was started in 1994.

Number awarded 1 or more each year.

Deadline September of each year.

[137]
FILIPINO CHAMBER OF COMMERCE OF HAWAII SCHOLARSHIPS

Filipino Chamber of Commerce of Hawaii
1136 Union Mall, Suite 804
Honolulu, HI 96819
(808) 792-8876   Fax: (808) 599-7785
E-mail: camberfilipino@yahoo.com

Purpose To provide financial assistance for college to high school seniors in Hawaii who have been involved with Filipino culture.

Eligibility This program is open to seniors at high schools in Hawaii who have a GPA of 3.5 or higher and have been accepted at a postsecondary institution. Applicants must be involved with and seek to perpetuate the Filipino culture. Selection is based on academic achievement, high school activities, awards and honors, and an essay on their community service.

Financial data Stipends range from $1,000 to $1,500.

Duration 1 year.

Number awarded 1 or more each year.

Deadline February of each year.

[138]
FILIPINO EMPLOYEES ASSOCIATION SCHOLARSHIPS

Pacific Gas and Electric Company
Filipino Employees Association
Attn: Zenaida Arcayena
Mailcode B16A
P.O. Box 770000
San Francisco, CA 94177-0001
(415) 973-0557   E-mail: zpa1@pge.com
Web: www.pge.com/scholarships

Purpose To provide financial assistance to graduating high school seniors in Pacific Gas and Electric Company's (PG&E) service area who can demonstrate Filipino community involvement.

Eligibility This program is open to college-bound high school seniors who reside in PG&E's service area. Applicants must have a GPA of 3.25 or higher and a record of active participation as a leader in school and the Filipino community. They must submit an essay of 300 to 400 words on a topic that changes annually; recently, the topic was "How Can California Improve Its National Test Results by Enhancing Its Educational System?"

Financial data The stipend is $1,000.

Duration 1 year.

Number awarded 8 each year.

Deadline May of each year.

[139]
FILIPINO NURSES' ORGANIZATION OF HAWAII SCHOLARSHIP

Hawai'i Community Foundation
Attn: Scholarship Department
1164 Bishop Street, Suite 800
Honolulu, HI 96813
(808) 537-6333   Toll-free: (888) 731-3863
Fax: (808) 521-6286
E-mail: scholarships@hcf-hawaii.org
Web: www.hawaiicommunityfoundation.org

Purpose To provide financial assistance to Hawaii residents of Filipino ancestry who are interested in preparing for a career as a nurse.

Eligibility This program is open to Hawaii residents of Filipino ancestry who are interested in studying in Hawaii or the mainland as full-time students and majoring in nursing. They must be able to demonstrate academic achievement (GPA of 2.7 or higher), good moral character, and financial need.

Financial data The amounts of the awards depend on the availability of funds and the need of the recipient.

Duration 1 year.

Number awarded Varies each year.

Deadline February of each year.

[140]
FIRST DATA WESTERN UNION FOUNDATION SCHOLARSHIP

First Data Western Union Foundation
Attn: Scholarship Program
6200 South Québec Street, Suite 370 AU
Greenwood Village, CO 80111
(303) 967-6606
Web: www.firstdatawesternunion.org

Purpose To provide financial assistance to immigrant students so they can realize their educational dreams.

Eligibility This program is open to immigrant students, from high school seniors to currently-enrolled college students. Applicants must have a high school diploma or GED and live within the United States or Puerto Rico. Selection is based on personal challenges overcome, initiative, commitment to learning and working hard, and financial need. Special consideration is given to applicants who "show academic promise and a strong desire for advancing their educational and career goals."

Financial data Stipends range from $500 to $3,000. Funds must be used for tuition, fees, or books and must be used within 1 year of the award date.

Duration Both 1-time and renewable scholarships (up to 4 years) are offered.

Additional information Recipients must attend school on a full-time basis.

Deadline February, May, or November of each year.

[141]
FISHER BROADCASTING SCHOLARSHIPS FOR MINORITIES

Fisher Communications
Attn: Minority Scholarship
100 Fourth Avenue North, Suite 510
Seattle, WA 98109
(206) 404-7000   Fax: (206) 404-6037
E-mail: Info@fsci.com
Web: www.fsci.com/x100.xml

Purpose To provide financial assistance to minority college students in selected states who are interested in preparing for a career in broadcasting, marketing, or journalism.

Eligibility This program is open to students of non-white origin who are U.S. citizens, have a GPA of 2.5 or higher, and are at least sophomores enrolled in 1) a broadcasting, marketing, or journalism curriculum leading to a bachelor's degree at an accredited 4-year college or university; 2) a broadcast curriculum at an accredited community college, transferable to a 4-year baccalaureate degree program; or 3) a broadcast curriculum at an accredited vocational/technical school. Applicants must be either 1) residents of Washington, Oregon, Idaho, or Montana; or 2) attending a school in those states. They must submit an essay that explains their financial need, education and career goals, and school activities; a copy of their college transcript; and 2 letters of recommendation. Selection is based on need, academic achievement, and personal qualities.

Financial data A stipend is awarded (amount not specified).

Duration 1 year; recipients may reapply.

Additional information This program began in 1987.

Number awarded Varies; a total of $10,000 is available for this program each year.

Deadline April of each year.

[142]
FLORIDA SOCIETY OF NEWSPAPER EDITORS MINORITY SCHOLARSHIP PROGRAM

Florida Society of Newspaper Editors
c/o Florida Press Association
2636 Mitcham Drive
Tallahassee, FL 32308
(850) 222-5790   Fax: (850) 224-6012
E-mail: info@fsne.org
Web: www.fsne.org/minorityscholar.html

Purpose To provide financial assistance and summer work experience to minority upper-division students majoring in journalism at a college or university in Florida.

Eligibility This program is open to minority students in accredited journalism or mass communication programs at Florida 4-year colleges and universities. Applicants must be full-time students in their junior year, have at least a 3.0 GPA, and be willing to participate in a paid summer internship at a Florida newspaper. Along with their application, they must submit a 300-word autobiographical essay explaining why they want to prepare for a career in print journalism and provide a standard resume, references, and clips or examples of relevant classroom work.

Financial data Winners are given a paid summer internship at a participating newspaper between their junior and senior year. Upon successfully completing the internship, the students are awarded a $3,000 scholarship (paid in 2 equal installments) to be used during their senior year.

Duration 1 summer for the internship; 1 academic year for the scholarship.

Additional information Information is also available from Rosemary Armao, FSNE Scholarship Committee, c/o The Sarasota Herald Tribune, 801 South Tamiami Trail, Sarasota, FL 34230.

Number awarded 1 each year.

Deadline March of each year.

[143]
FLORIDA YES TEACH! SCHOLARSHIP PROGRAM

Florida Independent College Fund
929 North Spring Garden Avenue, Suite 165
DeLand, FL 32720-0981
(386) 734-2745   Fax: (386) 734-0839
E-mail: yesteach@ficf.org
Web: www.ficf.org/yesteach

Purpose To provide financial assistance to college graduates (particularly minorities) who have degrees in fields other than education and wish to become teachers by returning to school at designated private colleges and universities in Florida to obtain professional certification.

Eligibility This program is open to people in Florida who have a college degree in a field other than education and wish to become a teacher. Applicants must be interested in enrolling in 1 of 27 designated independent colleges or universities in Florida that offer alternative teacher certification training, continuing education courses, advanced degrees, online course offerings, and online support services. They must register with the Yes Teach! web site. Priority is given to the first 200 people who complete the "1st Class Tutorial" and get teaching jobs in Florida. Selection is based on 5 factors: 1) did the participant get a job as a Florida teacher; 2) is the participant working on a professional certificate; 3) is the new teacher employed in a targeted high-need school; 4) is this new teacher teaching a high-need subject; and 5) is this teacher from an underrepresented population.

Financial data The stipend depends on the 5 selection factors. The largest awards go to teachers who qualify on all 5 factors.

Duration 1 year.

Additional information This program is cosponsored by the Florida Department of Education and the Florida Independent College Fund (FICF). For a list of the 27 eligible institutions, contact the FICF.

Number awarded Varies each year.

[144]
FORE DIVERSITY SCHOLARSHIPS

American Health Information Management Association
Attn: Foundation of Research and Education
233 North Michigan Avenue, Suite 2150
Chicago, IL 60601-5806
(312) 233-1168   Fax: (312) 233-1090
E-mail: fore@ahima.org
Web: www.ahima.org/fore/programs.cfm

Purpose To provide financial assistance to minority members of the American Health Information Management Association (AHIMA) who are interested in working on an undergraduate or graduate degree in health information administration or technology.

Eligibility This program is open to AHIMA members who are enrolled in a health information administration or health information technology program accredited by the Commission on Accreditation of Allied Health Education Programs. Applicants must be minorities, be working on an undergraduate or graduate degree on at least a half-time basis, and have a GPA of 3.0 or higher. U.S. citizenship is required. Selection is based (in order of importance) on GPA and academic achievement, volunteer and work experience, commitment to the health information management profession, suitability to the health information management profession, quality and suitability of references provided, and clarity of application.

Financial data Stipends range from $1,000 to $5,000.

Duration 1 year; nonrenewable.

Number awarded Varies each year. Recently, 5 of these scholarships were awarded: 4 to undergraduates and 1 to a graduate student.

Deadline May of each year.

[145]
FORTUNE BRANDS SCHOLARS PROGRAM

United Negro College Fund
Attn: Corporate Scholars Program
P.O. Box 1435
Alexandria, VA 22313-9998
Toll-free: (866) 671-7237   E-mail: internship@uncf.org
Web: www.uncf.org/internships/index.asp

Purpose To provide financial assistance and work experience to minorities who are either juniors majoring in fields related to business or law students interested in an internship at corporate headquarters of Fortune Brands.

Eligibility This program is open to juniors and first- and second-year law students who are members of minority groups. Applicants must have a GPA of 3.0 or higher and an undergraduate major in accounting, finance, human resources, information systems, information technology, or marketing. They must be attending a designated college, university, or law school and be interested in an internship at Fortune Brands corporate headquarters in Lincolnshire, Illinois. Along with their application, they must submit a resume, 2 letters of recommendation, and official transcripts.

Financial data The program provides a paid internship and (based on successful internship performance) a $7,500 scholarship.

Duration 8 to 10 weeks for the internship; 1 year for the scholarship.

Additional information Eligible undergraduate institutions are Florida A&M University, Florida State University, Hampton University, Howard University, Morehouse College, North Carolina A&T State University, Northwestern University, Spelman College, University of Chicago, and University of Wisconsin. Participating law schools are those at Howard University, Northwestern University, University of Chicago, and University of Wisconsin.

Number awarded Varies each year.

Deadline February of each year.

[146]
FORUM FOR CONCERNS OF MINORITIES SCHOLARSHIPS

American Society for Clinical Laboratory Science
Attn: Forum for Concerns of Minorities
6701 Democracy Boulevard, Suite 300
Bethesda, MD 20817
(301) 657-2768   Fax: (301) 657-2909
E-mail: ascls@ascls.org
Web: www.ascls.org/leadership/awards/fcm.asp

Purpose To provide financial assistance to minority students in clinical laboratory scientist and clinical laboratory technician programs.

Eligibility This program is open to minority students who are enrolled in a program in clinical laboratory science, including clinical laboratory science/medical technology (CLS/MT) and clinical laboratory technician/medical laboratory technician (CLT/MLT). Applicants must be able to demonstrate financial need. Membership in the American Society for Clinical Laboratory Science is encouraged but not required.

Financial data Stipends depend on the need of the recipients and the availability of funds.

Duration 1 year.

Number awarded 2 each year: 1 to a CLS/MT student and 1 to a CLT/MLT student.

Deadline March of each year.

[147]
FRANK ODA MEMORIAL SCHOLARSHIP

Japanese American Citizens League-Sonoma County
    Chapter
Attn: Scholarship Committee
P.O. Box 1915
Santa Rosa, CA 95402
E-mail: info@sonomacojacl.org
Web: www.sonomacojacl.org/Pages/scholars.htm

Purpose To provide financial assistance for college to members of the Sonoma County (California) Chapter of the Japanese American Citizens League (JACL) and their children.

Eligibility This program is open to graduating high school seniors in Sonoma County, California who are planning to attend a college, university, or vocational/technical school. Applicants must be members of the Sonoma County JACL or have parents who are members. Along with their application, they must submit a 250-word personal statement on their personality, why they have selected their major, why they desire to attend the college(s) they have applied to, and their view of themselves and the world in which they live.

Their statement should emphasize their Japanese ancestry and/or their connection with the Asian/Japanese American community and how it has affected or impacted who they are as well as their personal goals. Financial need is considered in case of a tie.

Financial data A stipend is awarded (amount not specified).

Duration 1 year.

Additional information Information is also available from Margaret E. Wallman, 1720 Mariposa Drive, Santa Rosa, CA 95405, (707) 544-9368.

Number awarded 1 each year.

Deadline February of each year.

[148]
FRED G. LEE MEMORIAL SCHOLARSHIP

Chinese American Citizens Alliance-Portland Lodge
11453 S.E. Hazel Hill Road
Clackamas, OR 97015
(503) 698-2315   Fax: (503) 698-3488
E-mail: info@cacaportland.org
Web: www.cacaportland.org

Purpose To provide financial assistance for college to high school seniors of Chinese descent in Oregon and Clark County, Washington.

Eligibility This program is open to seniors graduating from high schools in Oregon and Clark County, Washington. Applicants must be a U.S. citizen or permanent resident, have at least 1 parent who is full-blooded Chinese, be active in school and community affairs, and have a GPA of 3.5 or higher. Along with their application, they must submit 2 essays of approximately 250 words: the relationship of their educational plans or goals to their Chinese heritage, and their personal philosophy and how their Chinese heritage has affected their perspective. Selection is based on scholarship, leadership in school, community activities, and financial need.

Financial data The stipend is $1,000 per year.

Duration Either 4 years or 1 year.

Number awarded 3 each year: 1 for 4 years and 2 for 1 year.

Deadline March of each year.

[149]
FUTURE BUILDING INITIATIVE SCHOLARSHIPS

Asian American Journalists Association-Philadelphia
    Chapter
c/o Murali Balaji
950 West Basin Road
New Castle, DE 19720
(302) 324-2553   E-mail: aajaphilly@yahoo.com
Web: chapters.aaja.org/Philadelphia

Purpose To provide financial assistance to members of the Asian American Journalists Association (AAJA) in the Delaware Valley area who are studying or planning to study journalism in college.

Eligibility This program is open to AAJA members enrolled in high schools or colleges in the tri-state area of Pennsylvania, New Jersey, and Delaware. Applicants must have a GPA of 3.0 or higher and a stated interest in journalism. They must have demonstrated leadership and initiative by starting an AAJA student chapter at their high school or college. Along with their application, they must submit a letter of intent stating their interest in journalism and the benefits they see in being involved in AAJA, a letter of recommendation, and an unofficial copy of their transcript.

Financial data A stipend is awarded (amount not specified).

Duration 1 year.

Number awarded 4 each year.

Deadline January of each year.

[150]
GARTH REEVES JR. MEMORIAL SCHOLARSHIP

Society of Professional Journalists-South Florida
Chapter
c/o Oline Cogdill
The Sun-Sentinel
200 East Las Olas Boulevard
Fort Lauderdale, FL 33301
(954) 356-4886   E-mail: ocogdill@sun-sentinel.com
Web: home.earthlink.net/~news30/spj/scholapp.htm

Purpose To provide financial assistance to south Florida minority college students interested in journalism as a career.

Eligibility This program is open to minority residents of south Florida who are high school seniors or current college students. Applicants must be interested in a career in journalism. Along with their application, they must submit a list of their journalism experience, documentation of financial need, a statement of their career goals in journalism, 2 letters of recommendation, samples of their work, and school transcripts.

Financial data The stipend ranges from $500 to $1,000 per year, depending upon the recipient's educational requirements and financial need.

Duration 1 year; recipients may reapply.

Number awarded 1 or more each year.

Deadline March of each year.

[151]
GATES MILLENNIUM UNDERGRADUATE SCHOLARS PROGRAM

Bill and Melinda Gates Foundation
P.O. Box 10500
Fairfax, VA 22031-8044
Toll-free: (877) 690-GMSP
Web: www.gmsp.org

Purpose To provide financial assistance to outstanding low-income minority students, particularly those interested in majoring in specific fields in college.

Eligibility This program is open to African Americans, Alaska Natives, American Indians, Hispanic Americans, and Asian Pacific Islander Americans who are graduating high school seniors with a GPA of 3.3 or higher. Principals, teachers, guidance counselors, tribal higher education representatives, and other professional educators are invited to nominate students with outstanding academic qualifications, especially those likely to succeed in the fields of mathematics, science, engineering, education, or library science. Nominees should have significant financial need and demonstrated leadership abilities through participation in community service, extracurricular, or other activities. U.S. citizenship or permanent resident status is required. Nominees must be planning to enter an accredited college or university as a full-time, degree-seeking freshman in the following fall.

Financial data The program covers the cost of tuition, fees, books, and living expenses not paid for by grants and scholarships already committed as part of the recipient's financial aid package.

Duration 4 years or the completion of the undergraduate degree, if the recipient maintains at least a 3.0 GPA.

Additional information This program, established in 1999, is funded by the Bill and Melinda Gates Foundation and administered by the United Negro College Fund with support from the American Indian Graduate Center, the Hispanic Scholarship Fund, and the Organization of Chinese Americans.

Number awarded Under the Gates Millennium Scholars Program, a total of 4,000 students receive support each year.

Deadline January of each year.

[152]
GEORGE CHOY MEMORIAL/GAY ASIAN PACIFIC ALLIANCE SCHOLARSHIP

Horizons Foundation
870 Market Street, Suite 728
San Francisco, CA 94102
(415) 398-2333   Fax: (415) 398-4733
E-mail: info@horizonsfoundation.org
Web: www.horizonsfoundation.org

Purpose To provide financial assistance to gay, lesbian, bisexual, and transgender Asian and Pacific Islanders who are living in the San Francisco Bay area and entering their first year of postsecondary education.

Eligibility Applicants must be self-identified as Asian/Pacific Islander (at least 25% ancestry), be entering the first or second year of postsecondary education (at a college, university, or vocational school), have a GPA of 2.75 or higher, and be living in 1 of the following 9 counties in California: Alameda, Contra Costa, Marin, San Francisco, San Mateo, Santa Clara, Napa, Sonoma, or Solano. Priority is given to applicants who self-identify as lesbian, gay, bisexual, or transgender or are involved in those communities. To apply, students must fill out the foundation's scholarship application form, supply their most recent transcripts, attach a letter of recommendation, and write a 500-word essay describing how someone can contribute to the understanding of the lesbian, gay, bisexual, and/or transgender communities in a diverse society. Financial need is also considered in the selection process.

Financial data The stipend is currently $1,000.

Duration 1 year.

Additional information This program, established in 1997, is funded by the Gay Asian Pacific Alliance and administered by the Horizons Foundation.

Number awarded 1 each year.

Deadline June of each year.

[153]
GEORGE M. BROOKER COLLEGIATE SCHOLARSHIP FOR MINORITIES

Institute of Real Estate Management Foundation
Attn: Foundation Coordinator
430 North Michigan Avenue
Chicago, IL 60611-4090
(312) 329-6008   Toll-free: (800) 837-0706, ext. 6008
Fax: (312) 410-7908   E-mail: kholmes@irem.org
Web: www.irem.org

Purpose To provide financial assistance to minorities interested in preparing (on the undergraduate or graduate school level) for a career in the real estate management industry.

Eligibility This program is open to junior, senior, and graduate minority (non-Caucasian) students majoring in real estate, preferably with an emphasis on management, asset management, or related fields. Applicants must be interested in beginning a career in real estate management upon graduation. They must have earned a GPA of 3.0 or higher in their major, have completed at least 2 college courses in real estate, and write an essay (up to 500 words) on why they want to follow a career in real estate management. U.S. citizenship is required. Selection is based on academic success and a demonstrated commitment to a career in real estate management.

Financial data Stipends are $1,000 for undergraduates or $2,500 for graduate students. Funds are disbursed to the institution the student attends to be used only for tuition expenses.

Duration 1 year; nonrenewable.

Number awarded 3 each year: 2 undergraduate awards and 1 graduate award.

Deadline March of each year.

[154]
GEORGE RUCK SCHOLARSHIP

United Methodist Church-Eastern Pennsylvania
   Conference
Attn: Foundation Executive Director
P.O. Box 820
Valley Forge, PA 19482-0820
(610) 666-9090, ext. 247   Toll-free: (800) 828-9093
Fax: (610) 666-9093   E-mail: kathleen@epaumc.org
Web: www.epaumc.org

Purpose To provide financial assistance for college to ethnic minority members of the United Methodist Church in eastern Pennsylvania.

Eligibility This program is open to undergraduate students who are members of ethnic minority groups (Asian, Black, Hispanic, or Native American). Applicants must have been a member of a United Methodist church in eastern Pennsylvania for at least 2 years. They must submit documentation of financial need, 2 letters of recommendation, transcripts, and a 200-word essay on their involvement in the church and how achievement of their educational goals will provide leadership to the church and society.

Financial data The stipend is $1,000 per year.

Duration 1 year; may be renewed.

Number awarded 1 or more each year.

Deadline February of each year.

[155]
GEORGIA SPACE GRANT CONSORTIUM FELLOWSHIPS

Georgia Space Grant Consortium
c/o Georgia Institute of Technology
Aerospace Engineering
Paul Weber Space Science and Technology Building,
   Room 210
Atlanta, GA 30332-0150
(404) 894-0521   Fax: (404) 894-9313
E-mail: wanda.pierson@aerospace.gatech.edu
Web: www.ae.gatech.edu/research/gsgc

Purpose To provide financial assistance for undergraduate and graduate study of space-related fields to students (particularly minorities, women, and students with disabilities) at member institutions of the Georgia Space Grant Consortium (GSGC).

Eligibility This program is open to U.S. citizens who are undergraduate and graduate students at member institutions of the GSGC. Applicants must be working on a degree in mathematics, science, engineering, computer science, or a technical discipline related to space. Selection is based on transcripts, 3 letters of reference, and an essay of 100 to 500 words on the applicant's professional interests and objectives and their relationship to the field of aerospace. Awards are provided as part of the Space Grant program of the U.S. National Aeronautics and Space Administration, which encourages participation by women, minorities, and people with disabilities.

Financial data A stipend is awarded (amount not specified).

Additional information Institutions that are members of the GSGC include Albany State University, Clark Atlanta University, Columbus State University, Fort Valley State University, Georgia Institute of Technology, Kennesaw State University, Mercer University, Morehouse College, Spelman College, State University of West Georgia, and the University of Georgia. This program is funded by NASA.

Number awarded 1 each year.

[156]
GILBERT MARTINEZ DIVERSITY SCHOLARSHIPS

Colorado Educational Services and Development
   Association
P.O. Box 40214
Denver, CO 80204
Web: www.cesda.org

Purpose To provide financial assistance for college to high school seniors in Colorado who are first-generation college students and/or members of underrepresented ethnic or racial minorities.

Eligibility This program is open to seniors graduating from high schools in Colorado who are 1) the first member of their family to attend college; 2) members of an underrepresented ethnic or racial minority (African American, Asian-Pacific Islander, American Indian, Hispanic/Chicano/Latino); and/or 1) able to demonstrate financial need. Applicants must have a GPA of 2.8 or higher and be planning to enroll at a 2- or 4-year college or university in Colorado. U.S. citizenship or permanent resident status is required. Selection is based on leadership and community service (particularly within minority communities), past academic performance, personal and professional accomplishments, personal attributes, special abilities, academic goals, and financial need.

Financial data The stipend is $1,000.

Duration 1 year; nonrenewable.

Additional information Information is also available from Marianna Bagge, Scholarship Committee, P.O. Box 621146, Littleton, CO 80162, (303) 225-8576, (800) 888-2787, ext. 8576.

Number awarded 6 each year.

Deadline February of each year.

[157]
GILLETTE/NATIONAL URBAN LEAGUE SCHOLARSHIP FOR MINORITY STUDENTS

National Urban League
Attn: Scholarship Coordinator
120 Wall Street
New York, NY 10005
(212) 558-5300   Toll-free: (888) 839-0467
Fax: (212) 344-5332   E-mail: info@nul.org
Web: www.nul.org

Purpose To provide financial assistance to minority students who are interested in completing their college education in designated areas of business and engineering.

Eligibility Eligible to apply are minority students who are pursuing full-time studies leading to a bachelor's degree at an accredited institution of higher learning. They must be juniors or third-year students at the time the scholarship award begins, have a GPA of 3.0 or higher, be U.S. citizens or permanent residents or have a student visa, be able to demonstrate financial need, and be majoring in business-related fields (e.g., accounting, business administration, economics, engineering, finance, human resource management, ITS, manufacturing operations, marketing, MIS, public relations). Applications must be endorsed by an Urban League affiliate.

Financial data The stipend is $2,500 per year. Funds must be used for tuition, room, board, and the purchase of required educational materials and books.

Duration 2 years.

Number awarded Approximately 5 each year.

Deadline January of each year.

[158]
GONGORO NAKAMURA MEMORIAL SCHOLARSHIP

Japanese American Citizens League
Attn: National Scholarship Awards
1765 Sutter Street
San Francisco, CA 94115
(415) 921-5225   Fax: (415) 931-4671
E-mail: jacl@jacl.org
Web: www.jacl.org/scholarships.html

Purpose To provide financial assistance for college to student members of the Japanese American Citizens League (JACL) who are high school seniors.

Eligibility This program is open to JACL members who are high school seniors interested in attending a college, university, trade school, business college, or other institution of higher learning. Applicants must submit a statement describing their current level of involvement in the JACL or Asian Pacific community and how they will continue their involvement in future years. Selection is based on academic record, extracurricular activities, and community involvement. Preference is given to students with an interest in public speaking or debate. Applicants must submit a statement describing their current level of involvement in the Japanese American community or Asian Pacific community and how they will continue their involvement in future years. Selection is based on academic record, extracurricular activities, financial need, and community involvement.

Financial data The stipend depends on the availability of funds but usually ranges from $1,000 to $5,000.

Duration 1 year; nonrenewable.

Additional information Applications must be submitted to the local JACL chapter.

Number awarded At least 1 each year.

Deadline February of each year.

[159]
GORDON STAFFORD SCHOLARSHIP IN ARCHITECTURE

Stafford King Wiese Architects
Attn: Scholarship Selection Committee
622 20th Street
Sacramento, CA 95814
(916) 443-4829   Fax: (916) 443-0719
E-mail: connie_van_berkel@skwaia.com
Web: www.skwaia.com

Purpose To provide financial assistance to members of minority groups interested in studying architecture in college.

Eligibility This program is open to students accepted by an accredited school of architecture as first-year or transfer students. Applicants must be U.S. citizens or permanent residents who are ethnic persons of color (defined as Black, Hispanic, Native American, Pacific-Asian, or Asian-Indian). They must submit a 500-word statement expressing their desire to study architecture. Finalists are interviewed and must travel to Sacramento, California at their own expense.

Financial data The stipend is $2,000 per year. That includes $1,000 deposited in the recipient's school account and $1,000 paid to the recipient's directly.

Duration 1 year; may be renewed up to 4 additional years.

Additional information This program was established in 1995 to celebrate the 50th anniversary of the architectural firm that sponsors it.

Number awarded Up to 5 of these scholarships may be active at a time.

Deadline June of each year.

[160]
GRACE BYRNE UNDERGRADUATE SCHOLARSHIP

Women's Transportation Seminar-Puget Sound Chapter
c/o Lorelei Mesic, Scholarship Co-Chair
W&H Pacific
3350 Monte Villa Parkway
Bothell, WA 98021-8972
(425) 951-4872   Fax: (425) 951-4808
E-mail: lmesic@whpacific.com
Web: www.wtspugetsound.org/nscholarships.html

Purpose To provide financial assistance to women (particularly women of color) undergraduate students from Washington working on a degree related to transportation.

Eligibility This program is open to women who are residents of Washington, studying at a college in the state, or working as an intern in the state. Applicants must be currently enrolled in an undergraduate degree program in a transportation-related field, such as engineering, planning, finance, or logistics. They must have a GPA of 3.0 or higher and plans to prepare for a career in a transportation-related field. Minority candidates are encouraged to apply. Along with their application, they must submit a 500-word statement about their career goals after graduation and why they think they should receive this scholarship award. Selection is based on that statement, academic record, and transportation-related activities or job skills. Financial need is not considered.

Financial data The stipend is $1,500.

Duration 1 year.

Additional information The winner is also nominated for scholarships offered by the national organization of the Women's Transportation Seminar.

Number awarded 1 each year.

Deadline October of each year.

[161]
HAE WON PARK MEMORIAL SCHOLARSHIP

W.O.R.K.: Women's Organization Reaching Koreans
c/o KIWA
3465 West Eighth Street
Los Angeles, CA 90005
Toll-free: (866) 251-5152, ext. 8739
E-mail: workla@onebox.com
Web: www.work-la.org/scholarship.html

Purpose To provide financial assistance to undergraduate and graduate women of Korean heritage.

Eligibility This program is open to women of Korean heritage who are enrolled at an undergraduate or graduate institution and have demonstrated a desire and commitment to serve their community. Applicants must submit 1 letter of recommendation, their transcript, a description of their community involvement, a 250-word statement about themselves, and a 500-word essay on the challenges facing Korean American women and how they would address those.

Financial data The stipend is $1,000.

Duration 1 year.

Additional information This scholarship was established in 1992.

Number awarded 1 each year.

Deadline May of each year.

[162]
HANA SCHOLARSHIPS

United Methodist Church
Attn: General Board of Higher Education and Ministry
Office of Loans and Scholarships
1001 19th Avenue South
P.O. Box 340007
Nashville, TN 37203-0007
(615) 340-7344   Fax: (615) 340-7367
E-mail: umscholar@gbhem.org
Web: www.gbhem.org

Purpose To provide financial assistance to upper-division and graduate Methodist students who are of Hispanic, Asian, Native American, Alaska Native, or Pacific Islander ancestry.

Eligibility This program is open to full-time juniors, seniors, and graduate students at accredited colleges and universities in the United States who have been active, full members of a United Methodist Church for at least 1 year prior to applying. Applicants must have at least 1 parent who is Hispanic, Asian, Native American, Alaska Native, or Pacific Islander. They must be able to demonstrate involvement in their Hispanic, Asian, or Native American (HANA) community. Selection is based on that involvement, academic ability, and financial need. U.S. citizenship or permanent resident status is required.

Financial data The stipend is $1,000 for undergraduates or $3,000 for graduate students.

Duration 1 year; recipients may reapply.

Number awarded 50 each year.

Deadline March of each year.

[163]
HARRISON LEE MEMORIAL SCHOLARSHIP AWARD

Chinese American Citizens Alliance-Washington, DC
   Lodge
9302 Christopher Street
Fairfax, VA 22301
(703) 273-7510

Purpose To recognize and reward outstanding essays on "Being an American" written by Chinese American high school seniors in the Washington, D.C. area.

Eligibility Chinese American high school seniors in the metropolitan Washington, D.C. area (including parts of Virginia and Baltimore, Maryland) are invited to write an essay, in English, on "What Does Being an American Mean to Me." Essays must be no more than 500 words. Selection is based on originality, clarity of thought, and expression.

Financial data First prize is $500, second $300, and third $200.

Duration The competition is held annually.

Number awarded 3 each year.

Deadline December of each year.

[164]
HAWAII CHAPTER OF AAJA SCHOLARSHIPS

Asian American Journalists Association-Hawaii Chapter
Attn: President
P.O. Box 22592
Honolulu, HI 96823-2592
(808) 536-9979   E-mail: aajahawaii@yahoo.com
Web: www.slider.net/~aaja/scholarships.html

Purpose To provide financial assistance to Asian/Pacific Islander students in Hawaii who are interested in careers in broadcast or print journalism.

Eligibility These scholarships are open to Asian/Pacific Islander students in Hawaii who are planning a career in broadcast or print journalism. Applicants may be high school seniors, college undergraduates, or graduate students. They must submit 2 essays of 250 to 500 words each on the following topics: 1) why they want to be a journalist, challenges they foresee, how they can contribute to the profession, and personal characteristics that will prepare them for a journalism career; and 2) involvement or interest in the Asian Pacific American community, how they can contribute to that community in the future, how they can improve coverage of the community as a journalist, and how their ethnic heritage may influence their journalistic perspective. Selection is based on academic achievement, financial need, work samples, recommendations, and the essays.

Financial data Stipends are up to $750.

Duration 1 year; may be renewed.

Number awarded 2 each year.

Deadline April of each year.

[165]
HENRY AND CHIYO KUWAHARA CREATIVE ARTS AWARD

Japanese American Citizens League
Attn: National Scholarship Awards
1765 Sutter Street
San Francisco, CA 94115
(415) 921-5225   Fax: (415) 931-4671
E-mail: jacl@jacl.org
Web: www.jacl.org/scholarships.html

Purpose To provide financial assistance to student members of the Japanese American Citizens League (JACL) interested in working on an undergraduate or graduate degree in the creative arts.

Eligibility This program is open to JACL members who are interested in working on an undergraduate or graduate degree in the creative arts. Professional artists are not eligible. Applicants must submit a detailed proposal on the nature of their project, including a time-plan, anticipated date of completion, and itemized budget. They must also submit a statement describing their current level of involvement in the Japanese American community or Asian Pacific community and how they will continue their involvement in future years. Selection is based on academic record, extracurricular activities, and community involvement. Preference is given to students who are interested in creative projects that reflect the Japanese American experience and culture.

Financial data The stipend depends on the availability of funds but usually ranges from $1,000 to $5,000.

Duration 1 year; nonrenewable.

Additional information Applications must be submitted to the JACL National Scholarship Program, c/o San Diego JACL Chapter, 1031 25th Street, San Diego, CA 92102.

Number awarded At least 1 each year.

Deadline March of each year.

[166]
HENRY AND CHIYO KUWAHARA MEMORIAL SCHOLARSHIPS

Japanese American Citizens League
Attn: National Scholarship Awards
1765 Sutter Street
San Francisco, CA 94115
(415) 921-5225   Fax: (415) 931-4671
E-mail: jacl@jacl.org
Web: www.jacl.org/scholarships.html

Purpose To provide financial assistance for undergraduate or graduate study to members of the Japanese American Citizens League (JACL).

Eligibility This program is open to JACL members who are high school seniors, undergraduates, or graduate students. Applicants must be attending or planning to attend a college, university, trade school, or business college. They must submit a statement describing their current level of involvement in the Japanese American community or Asian Pacific community and how they will continue their involvement in future years. Selection is based on academic record, extracurricular activities, financial need, and community involvement.

Financial data The stipend depends on the availability of funds but usually ranges from $1,000 to $5,000.

Duration 1 year; nonrenewable.

Additional information Applications from high school seniors must be submitted to the local JACL chapter. All other applications must be submitted to the JACL National Scholarship Program, c/o San Diego JACL Chapter, 1031 25th Street, San Diego, CA 92102.

Number awarded 6 each year: 2 each to entering freshmen, continuing undergraduates, and entering or currently-enrolled graduate students.

Deadline February of each year for graduating high school seniors; March of each year for current undergraduate or graduate students.

[167]
HERBERT JENSEN SCHOLARSHIP

Japanese American Citizens League-Arizona Chapter
c/o Michele Namba, Scholarship Committee Secretary
5414 West Glenn Drive
Glendale, AZ 85301
E-mail: webmaster@azjacl.org
Web: www.azjacl.org

Purpose To provide financial assistance to graduating high school seniors in Arizona who are of Japanese American or other ethnic background and whose parents are affiliated with the Japanese American Citizens League.

Eligibility This program is open to graduating high school seniors in Arizona who are U.S. citizens, have at least a 3.0 GPA, and have a parent who has been a member of the Arizona Chapter of the Japanese American Citizens League for at least 3 consecutive years prior to the application deadline. Applicants may be of Japanese American or other ethnic background. Financial need is not considered in the selection process.

Financial data   A stipend is awarded (amount not specified).

Duration   1 year.

Additional information   Recipients must attend the association's scholarship awards banquet and accept the award in person; failure to do so results in forfeiture of the award.

Number awarded   1 each year.

Deadline   February of each year.

[168]
HMONG NATIONAL DEVELOPMENT EDUCATIONAL SCHOLARSHIPS

Hmong National Development, Inc.
Attn: Educational Scholarships
1112 16th Street, N.W., Suite 110
Washington, DC 20036
(202) 463-2118   Fax: (202) 463-2119
E-mail: info@hndlink.org
Web: www.hndlink.org/scholarships.htm

Purpose   To provide financial assistance for college or graduate school to Hmong students in the United States.

Eligibility   This program is open to Hmong students who are entering or enrolled in an accredited college or university as a full-time undergraduate or graduate student. Applicants must submit 1) an official transcript; 2) a letter of recommendation; 3) a 1-page resume on their employment history, involvement with community and extracurricular activities, and honors received; and 4) a 3-page essay on a potential goal they plan to achieve within the next 5 years and their plans for overcoming potential obstacles and ultimately achieving their goals.

Financial data   The stipend is $500.

Duration   1 year.

Number awarded   10 each year.

Deadline   January of each year.

[169]
HORACE AND SUSIE REVELS CAYTON SCHOLARSHIP

Public Relations Society of America-Puget Sound
     Chapter
c/o Diane Beins
1006 Industry Drive
Seattle, WA 98188-4801
(206) 623-8632
E-mail: prsascholarship@asi-seattle.net
Web: www.prsapugetsound.org/cayton

Purpose   To provide financial assistance to minority upper-classmen from Washington who are interested in preparing for a career in public relations.

Eligibility   This program is open to U.S. citizens who are members of minority groups, defined as African Americans, Asian Americans, Hispanic/Latino Americans, Native Americans, and Pacific Islanders. Applicants must be juniors or seniors attending a college in Washington or Washington students (who graduated from a Washington high school or whose parents live in the state year-round) attending col-

lege elsewhere. They must be able to demonstrate aptitude in public relations and related courses, activities, and/or internships. Along with their application, they must submit a description of their career goals and the skills that are most important in general to a public relations career (15 points in the selection process); a description of their activities in communications in class, on campus, in the community, or during internships, including 3 samples of their work (15 points); a statement on the value of public relations to an organization (10 points); a description of any barriers, financial or otherwise, they have encountered in pursuing their academic or personal goals and how they have addressed them (15 points); a discussion of their heritage, and how their cultural background and/or the discrimination they may have experienced has impacted them (15 points); a certified transcript (15 points); and 2 or more letters of recommendation (15 points).

Financial data   The stipend is $2,500.

Duration   1 year.

Additional information   This program was established in 1992.

Number awarded   1 each year.

Deadline   March of each year.

[170]
HOUSTON CHAPTER COLLEGE SCHOLARSHIP PROGRAM

National Association of Asian American Professionals-
     Houston Chapter
Attn: Scholarship Committee
P.O. Box 540601
Houston, TX 77254-0601
E-mail: naaap@naaaphouston.org
Web: www.naaaphouston.org

Purpose   To provide financial assistance for college to high school seniors of Asian Pacific descent in the Houston metropolitan area.

Eligibility   This program is open to seniors of Asian Pacific descent graduating from high schools in the Texas counties of Chambers, Fort Bend, Harris, Liberty, Montgomery, and Waller. Applicants must submit 2 essays of 500 words each on an experience that shaped who they are today and a problem or challenge faced by the Asian American community and how they would address or solve the issue. Selection is based on academic achievement, community service, honors, work experience, and extracurricular activities.

Financial data   The stipend is $1,000.

Duration   1 year.

Number awarded   1 or more each year.

Deadline   April of each year.

[171]
HUN KWAN GOH MEMORIAL SCHOLARSHIPS

Humboldt Area Foundation
Attn: Scholarship Coordinator
373 Indianola Road
Bayside, CA 95524
(707) 442-2993   Fax: (707) 442-3811
Web: www.hafoundation.org

Purpose To provide financial assistance for college to Asian American high school seniors in Humboldt County, California.

Eligibility This program is open to seniors graduating from high schools in Humboldt County, California who are of Asian or part-Asian descent. Applicants must have a GPA of 3.3 or higher and be planning to enroll in an accredited 4-year college or university. Financial need is considered in the selection process.

Financial data The maximum stipend is $1,000.

Duration 1 year.

Number awarded 2 or 3 each year.

Deadline March of each year.

[172]
HYATT HOTEL FUND FOR MINORITY LODGING MANAGEMENT STUDENTS

American Hotel & Lodging Educational Foundation
Attn: Manager of Foundation Programs
1201 New York Avenue, N.W., Suite 600
Washington, DC 20005-3931
(202) 289-3188   Fax: (202) 289-3199
E-mail: ahlef@ahlef.org
Web: www.ahlf.org/scholarships

Purpose To provide financial assistance to minority college students working on a degree in hotel management.

Eligibility Applicants must be attending a 4-year college or university that is a member of the Council on Hotel, Restaurant and Institutional Education. They must be minorities and majoring in hotel management. Each member university may nominate 1 student. The most outstanding students receive this scholarship.

Financial data The stipend is $2,000.

Duration 1 year.

Additional information Funding for this program is provided by Hyatt Hotels & Resorts.

Number awarded Varies each year; recently, 18 of these scholarships were awarded.

Deadline March of each year.

[173]
IASF FINANCIAL AID SCHOLARSHIPS

India American Cultural Association
1281 Cooper Lake Road, S.E.
Smyrna, GA 30082
(770) 436-3719   (770) 436-4272
Web: www.myiaca.org/scholarships.html

Purpose To provide financial assistance for college to high school seniors in Georgia whose parents or grandparents came from what is now India.

Eligibility This program is open to high school seniors who 1) are living in Georgia and 2) whose parents or grand-parents came from present day India. For the purposes of this program, citizens of Pakistan and Bangladesh are not included. Applicants must be planning to attend a 4-year college or university as a full-time student. Along with their application, they must submit official school transcript, resume, SAT score report, the best essay they submitted to a college to which they applied, and documentation of financial need. Selection is based primarily on financial need.

Financial data Stipends range from $500 to $1,250.

Duration 1 year; nonrenewable.

Additional information This program was established in 1993. Information is also available from the Indian American Scholarship Fund (IASF), 719 Vinings Estates Drive, Mableton, GA 30126, E-mail: manochaa@bellsouth.net. Membership in the India American Cultural Association (IACA) is not required to apply, but recipients must become members of the association.

Number awarded Several each year.

Deadline May of each year.

[174]
IDAHO STATE BROADCASTERS ASSOCIATION SCHOLARSHIPS

Idaho State Broadcasters Association
270 North 27th Street, Suite B
Boise, ID 83702-4741
(208) 345-3072   Fax: (208) 343-8946
E-mail: isba@rmci.net
Web: www.idahobroadcasters.org/scholarships.aspx

Purpose To provide financial assistance to students at Idaho colleges and universities who are preparing for a career in the broadcasting field.

Eligibility This program is open to full-time students at Idaho schools who are preparing for a career in broadcasting, including business administration, sales, journalism, and engineering. Applicants must have a GPA of at least 2.0 for the first 2 years of school or 2.5 for the last 2 years. Along with their application, they must submit a letter of recommendation from the general manager of a broadcasting state that is a member of the Idaho State Broadcasters Association and a 1-page essay describing their career plans and why they want the scholarship. Applications are encouraged from a wide and diverse student population. The Wayne C. Cornils Scholarship is reserved for a less advantaged applicant.

Financial data The stipend for the general scholarships is $1,000. The amount of the Wayne C. Cornils Scholarship depends on the need of the recipient.

Duration 1 year.

Number awarded 3 each year: 2 general scholarships and the Cornils Scholarship.

Deadline March of each year.

[175]
ILLINOIS MINORITY REAL ESTATE SCHOLARSHIP

Illinois Association of Realtors
Attn: Illinois Real Estate Educational Foundation
3180 Adloff Lane, Suite 400
P.O. Box 19451
Springfield, IL 62794-9451
(217) 529-2600　　　　　E-mail: IARaccess@iar.org
Web: www.illinoisrealtor.org/iar/about/minority.htm

Purpose To provide financial assistance to Illinois residents who are members of minority groups and preparing for a career in real estate.

Eligibility This program is open to residents of Illinois who are African American, Hispanic or Latino, Native American, or Asian. Applicants must be interested in preparing for a career in real estate by pursuing: 1) courses to meet Illinois salesperson license requirement; 2) course work to meet Illinois broker license requirement; 3) course work required for Illinois appraisal licensing/certification; 4) professional development unrelated to obtaining license/certification; or 5) an undergraduate or graduate program of study. Along with their application, they must submit information on their employment history, transcripts, evidence of financial need, and an essay that describes their career goals and explains why they believe they should receive scholarship assistance through this program.

Financial data The maximum stipend is $500.

Duration Funds must be used within 24 months of the award date.

Deadline Applications may be submitted at any time, but they must be received at least 12 weeks prior to the beginning of the school term for which financial assistance is requested.

[176]
INDIA HERITAGE AWARD FOR HIGH SCHOOL GRADUATES

Indian American Heritage Foundation
3818 Gleneagles Drive
Tarzana, CA 91356
(818) 708-3885　　　　　E-mail: ashok4u@aol.com
Web: www.la-indiacenter.com

Purpose To provide financial assistance for college to high school seniors in southern California who are of Asian Indian descent.

Eligibility This program is open to seniors graduating from high schools in southern California (south of Fresno) who have at least 1 parent of Asian Indian descent. Applicants must have a GPA of 3.0 or higher. They must attend a function of the sponsoring organization at which they take a quiz on India, based on material supplied by the organization. Selection is based on their quiz score (15%), SAT1 score (17.5%), SAT2 score (17.5%), extracurricular activities (15%), and GPA (35%).

Financial data Stipends are $2,000, $1,000, $750, or $500.

Duration 1 year.

Additional information Material about India for the quiz is sent to the applicant after receipt of a check for $10 and the completed application.

Number awarded 8 each year: 1 at $2,000, 1 at $1,000, 1 at $750, and 5 at $500.

Deadline April of each year.

[177]
INDIAN AMERICAN SCHOLARSHIP FUND MERIT SCHOLARSHIPS

India American Cultural Association
1281 Cooper Lake Road, S.E.
Smyrna, GA 30082
(770) 436-3719　　　　　　　　　(770) 436-4272
Web: www.myiaca.org/scholarships.html

Purpose To provide financial assistance for college to high school seniors in Georgia whose parents or grandparents came from what is now India.

Eligibility This program is open to high school seniors who 1) are living in Georgia and 2) whose parents or grandparents came from present day India. For the purposes of this program, citizens of Pakistan and Bangladesh are not included. Applicants must be planning to attend a 4-year college or university as a full-time student. Along with their application, they must submit official school transcript, resume, SAT score report, and the best essay they submitted to a college to which they applied. Financial need is not considered in the selection process.

Financial data Stipends range from $500 to $1,250.

Duration 1 year; nonrenewable.

Additional information This program was established in 1993. Information is also available from the Indian American Scholarship Fund (IASF), 719 Vinings Estates Drive, Mableton, GA 30126, E-mail: manochaa@bellsouth.net. Membership in the India American Cultural Association (IACA) is not required to apply, but recipients must become members of the association.

Number awarded Several each year.

Deadline April of each year.

[178]
INTERNATIONAL COMMUNICATIONS INDUSTRIES ASSOCIATION COLLEGE SCHOLARSHIPS

International Communications Industries Association, Inc.
Attn: Director of Strategic Initiatives
11242 Waples Mill Road, Suite 200
Fairfax, VA 22030
(703) 273-7200　　　　　Toll-free: (800) 659-7469
Fax: (703) 278-8082　　E-mail: dwilbert@infocomm.org
Web: www.infocomm.org

Purpose To provide financial assistance to college students and entering graduate students (especially minorities and women) who are interested in preparing for a career in the audiovisual industry.

Eligibility This program is open to 1) college juniors completing their bachelor's degree in the following year; 2) college seniors who plan to enter graduate school; and 3) students in their final year of study for an associate degree. Applicants must have a GPA of 2.75 or higher in a program of audio, visual, audiovisual, electronics, telecommunications, technical theater, data networking, software development, or information technology. Students in other programs, such as journalism, may be eligible if they can demonstrate a relationship to career goals in the audiovisual industry. Along with their application, they must submit essays on why they are applying for this scholarship, why they are interested in the audiovisual industry, and their professional plans following graduation. Minority and women candidates are especially encouraged to apply. Selection is based on the essays, presentation of the application, GPA, work experience, and letters of recommendation.

Financial data The stipend is $2,500.

Duration 1 year.

Additional information Recipients are required to work during the summer as paid interns with a manufacturer, dealer, designer, or other firm that is a member of the International Communications Industries Association.

Number awarded Varies each year; recently, 7 of these scholarships were awarded.

Deadline April of each year.

[179]
INTERNATIONAL COMMUNICATIONS INDUSTRIES ASSOCIATION HIGH SCHOOL SCHOLARSHIPS

International Communications Industries Association, Inc.
Attn: Director of Strategic Initiatives
11242 Waples Mill Road, Suite 200
Fairfax, VA 22030
(703) 273-7200   Toll-free: (800) 659-7469
Fax: (703) 278-8082   E-mail: dwilbert@infocomm.org
Web: www.infocomm.org

Purpose To provide financial assistance for college to high school seniors (especially minorities and women) interested in preparing for a career in the audiovisual industry.

Eligibility This program is open to graduating high school seniors who have a GPA of 2.75 or higher. Applicants must have been accepted by an accredited postsecondary institution to work on a certificate or degree in audio, visual, audiovisual, electronics, telecommunications, technical theater, data networking, software development, or information technology. Students in other programs, such as journalism, may be eligible if they can demonstrate a relationship to career goals in the audiovisual industry. Along with their application, they must submit 1) an essay of 150 to 200 words on the career path they see themselves pursuing in the next 5 years and why, and 2) an essay of 250 to 300 words on the experience or person that most influenced them in selecting the audiovisual industry as their career of choice. Minority and women candidates are especially encouraged to apply. Selection is based on the essays, presentation of the application, GPA, work experience, and letters of recommendation.

Financial data The stipend is $500.

Duration 1 year.

Additional information Recipients are also offered a paid internship with a manufacturer, dealer, designer, or other firm that is a member of the International Communications Industries Association.

Number awarded Varies each year; recently, 9 of these scholarships were awarded.

Deadline April of each year.

[180]
JACKIE CHAN SCHOLARSHIPS

US Pan Asian American Chamber of Commerce
Attn: Scholarship Coordinator
1329 18th Street, N.W.
Washington, DC 20036
(202) 296-5221   Fax: (202) 296-5225
E-mail: administrator@uspaacc.com
Web: www.uspaacc.com

Purpose To provide financial assistance for college to Asian American high school seniors who demonstrate special talents.

Eligibility This program is open to high school seniors of Asian heritage who are U.S. citizens or permanent residents. Applicants must be planning to begin full-time study at an accredited postsecondary educational institution in the United States. Along with their application, they must submit a 500-word essay on "How do you plan to use your special talents to achieve your professional goals?" Selection is based on academic excellence (GPA of 3.3 or higher), leadership in extracurricular activities, community service involvement, and financial need.

Financial data The maximum stipend is $8,000. Funds are paid directly to the recipient's college or university.

Duration 1 year.

Additional information Funding is not provided for correspondence courses, Internet courses, or study in a country other than the United States.

Number awarded 2 each year.

Deadline February of each year.

[181]
JACKIE ROBINSON SCHOLARSHIPS

Jackie Robinson Foundation
Attn: Education and Leadership Development Program
3 West 35th Street, 11th Floor
New York, NY 10001-2204
(212) 290-8600   Fax: (212) 290-8081
E-mail: general@jackierobinson.org
Web: www.jackierobinson.org

Purpose To provide financial assistance for college to minority high school seniors.

Eligibility This program is open to members of an ethnic minority group who are high school seniors accepted at a 4-year college or university. Applicants must be able to demonstrate high academic achievement (ACT score of 21 or higher or the equivalent on the SAT), financial need, and leadership potential. U.S. citizenship is required.

Financial data The stipend is $6,000 per year.

Duration 4 years.

Additional information The program also offers personal and career counseling on a year-round basis, a week of interaction with other scholarship students from around the country, and assistance in obtaining summer jobs and permanent employment after graduation. It was established in 1973 by a grant from Chesebrough-Pond.

Number awarded 100 or more each year.

Deadline March of each year.

[182]
JAMES CARLSON MEMORIAL SCHOLARSHIP

Oregon Student Assistance Commission
Attn: Grants and Scholarships Division
1500 Valley River Drive, Suite 100
Eugene, OR 97401-2146
(541) 687-7395   Toll-free: (800) 452-8807, ext. 7395
Fax: (541) 687-7419
E-mail: awardinfo@mercury.osac.state.or.us
Web: www.osac.state.or.us

Purpose To provide financial assistance to Oregon residents (particularly minorities) majoring in education on the undergraduate or graduate school level.

Eligibility This program is open to residents of Oregon who are U.S. citizens or permanent residents. Applicants must be either 1) college seniors or fifth-year students majoring in elementary or secondary education or 2) graduate students working on an elementary or secondary certificate. Full-time enrollment and financial need are required. Priority is given to 1) members of African American, Asian American, Hispanic, or Native American ethnic groups; 2) dependents of members of the Oregon Education Association; and 3) applicants committed to teaching autistic children.

Financial data Stipend amounts vary; recently, they were at least $1,300.

Duration 1 year.

Additional information This program is administered by the Oregon Student Assistance Commission (OSAC) with funds provided by the Oregon Community Foundation, 1221 S.W. Yamhill, Suite 100, Portland, OR 97205, (503) 227-6846, Fax: (503) 274-7771.

Number awarded Varies each year; recently, 3 of these scholarships were awarded.

Deadline February of each year.

[183]
JAMES ECHOLS SCHOLARSHIP

California Association for Health, Physical Education,
   Recreation and Dance
Attn: Chair, Scholarship Committee
1501 El Camino Avenue, Suite 3
Sacramento, CA 95815-2748
(916) 922-3596   Toll-free: (800) 499-3596 (within CA)
Fax: (916) 922-0133   E-mail: cahperd@cahperd.org
Web: www.cahperd.org

Purpose To provide financial assistance to minority student members of the California Association for Health, Physical Education, Recreation and Dance.

Eligibility This program is open to California residents who have been members of the association for at least 60 days and are attending a 2-year or 4-year college or university in California. Applicants must be undergraduate or graduate students majoring in health, physical education, recreation, or dance and have completed at least 60 semester hours of college work. Selection is based on scholastic proficiency (a GPA of 3.0 or higher); leadership ability in school, community, and professional activities; and personal qualities of enthusiasm, cooperativeness, responsibility, initiative, and ability to work with others. This scholarship is awarded to the highest-ranked minority (Asian, African American, Latino, or Native American) applicant.

Financial data The stipend is $750.

Duration 1 year.

Additional information Information is also available from Nicolas Fraire, CAHPERD Scholarship Chair, 3792 Willowpark Drive, San Jose, CA 95118.

Number awarded 1 each year.

Deadline December of each year.

[184]
JAMES G.K. MCCLURE EDUCATIONAL AND DEVELOPMENT FUND SCHOLARSHIPS

James G.K. McClure Educational and Development
   Fund, Inc.
Attn: Executive Director
Sugar Hollow Farm
11 Sugar Hollow Lane
Fairview, NC 28730
(828) 628-2114   E-mail: jager@ioa.com

Purpose To provide financial assistance to Christian students (particularly students of color) in western North Carolina who are interested in attending college.

Eligibility This program is open to students from the following counties in North Carolina: Alleghany, Ashe, Avery, Buncombe, Burke, Caldwell, Cherokee, Clay, Graham, Haywood, Henderson, Jackson, Macon, Madison, McDowell, Mitchell, Polk, Rutherford, Swain, Transylvania, Watauga, or Yancey. Applicants must be entering the freshman class at 1 of the following schools: Asheville-Buncombe Community Technical College, Appalachian State University, Berea College, Blue Ridge Community College, Brevard College, Caldwell Community College, East Tennessee State, Gardner-Webb College, Haywood Community College, Isothermal Community College, Lees-McRae College, Mars Hill College, Mayland Community College, McDowell Community College, Montreat-Anderson College, North Carolina School of the Arts, North Carolina State University, Southwestern Community College, Tri-County Community College, University of North Carolina-Asheville, University of North Carolina-Greensboro, Warren Wilson College, Western Carolina University, Western Piedmont Community College, Wilkes Community College, or Young Harris College. Selection is based on scholarship, leadership, Christian character, financial need, intellectual promise, the desire to be of service to humanity, and demonstrated ambition. A special effort is made to offer scholarships to minority students from the region and to students entering nursing or other health care careers. Students facing a sudden and catastrophic financial problem may apply for a hardship grant to finish their course of study.

Financial data Awards for students at 4-year colleges and universities are either $750 or $1,500 per year; stipends at technical or community colleges are $300 per year; health careers scholarships are either $300 or $750 per year; hardship scholarships and minority scholarships are $1,000 per year. Funds are paid directly to the recipient's college.

Duration 1 year; may be renewed.

Additional information Interested students should first contact the financial aid office at their college, not the fund.

Number awarded Varies each year; recently, the fund awarded 39 scholarships to students at 4-year institutions for a total of $44,700, 22 scholarships to students at community colleges for $6,600, 25 health careers scholarships (at both 4-year and 2-year institutions) for $9,300, 1 designated minority scholarship (although some of the other scholarships went to minorities), and 1 hardship scholarship.

Deadline April of each year.

[185]
JAMES J. WYCHOR SCHOLARSHIPS

Minnesota Broadcasters Association
Attn: Scholarship Program
3033 Excelsior Boulevard, Suite 301
Minneapolis, MN 55416
(612) 926-8123   Toll-free: (800) 245-5838
Fax: (612) 926-9761
E-mail: meischen@minnesotabroadcasters.com
Web: www.minnesotabroadcasters.com

Purpose To provide financial assistance to Minnesota residents interested in studying broadcasting in college.

Eligibility This program is open to residents of Minnesota who are accepted or enrolled at an accredited postsecondary institution offering a broadcast-related curriculum. Applicants must have a high school or college GPA of 2.5 or higher and must submit a 200-word essay on why they wish to prepare for a career in broadcasting or electronic media. Employment in the broadcasting industry is not required, but students who are employed must include a letter from their general manager describing the duties they have performed as a radio or television station employee and evaluating their potential for success in the industry. Financial need is not considered in the selection process. Some of the scholarships are awarded only to minority and women candidates.

Financial data The stipend is $1,500.

Duration 1 year; recipients who are college seniors may reapply for an additional 1-year renewal.

Number awarded 10 each year, distributed as follows: 3 within the 7-county metro area, 5 allocated geographically throughout the state (northeast, northwest, central, southeast, southwest), and 2 reserved specifically for women and minority applicants.

Deadline May of each year.

[186]
JAPANESE MEDICAL SOCIETY OF AMERICA NURSING STUDENT SCHOLARSHIP

Japanese Medical Society of America, Inc.
c/o Yuzuru Anzai, M.D., Scholarship Committee Chair
285 Central Park West, Apartment 3W
New York, NY 10024
(212) 263-8682   Fax: (212) 883-5852
E-mail: yuzuru.anzai@med.nyu.edu
Web: www.jmsa.org

Purpose To provide financial assistance to Japanese American nursing school students.

Eligibility This program is open to Japanese Americans who are accepted at or currently enrolled in a nursing school in the United States. Applicants must submit a 1-page essay about themselves and how they will be involved in the sponsoring organization's activities. Selection is based on academic excellence, community activities, financial need, and interest in the organization.

Financial data A stipend is awarded (amount not specified).

Duration 1 year.

Deadline February of each year.

[187]
JASUMATI B. PATEL MEMORIAL AWARD

India American Cultural Association
1281 Cooper Lake Road, S.E.
Smyrna, GA 30082
(770) 436-3719   (770) 436-4272
Web: www.myiaca.org/scholarships.html

Purpose To provide financial assistance for college to high school seniors in Georgia whose parents or grandparents came from what is now India.

Eligibility This program is open to high school seniors who 1) are living in Georgia and 2) whose parents or grandparents came from present day India. For the purposes of this program, citizens of Pakistan and Bangladesh are not included. Applicants must be planning to attend a 4-year college or university as a full-time student. Along with their application, they must submit official school transcript, resume, SAT score report, the best essay they submitted to a college to which they applied, and documentation of financial need. Selection is based on financial need and academic excellence.

Financial data The stipend is $1,000 per year.

Duration 4 years.

Additional information This program was established in 1993. Information is also available from the Indian American Scholarship Fund, 719 Vinings Estates Drive, Mableton, GA 30126, E-mail: manochaa@bellsouth.net. Membership in the India American Cultural Association (IACA) is not required to apply, but recipients must become members of the association.

Number awarded 1 each year.

Deadline May of each year.

[188]
JEAN MARSHALL MINORITY SCHOLARSHIPS

New Jersey State Nurses Association
Attn: Institute for Nursing
1479 Pennington Road
Trenton, NJ 08618-2661
(609) 883-5335, ext. 15
Toll-free: (888) UR-NJSNA, ext. 15
Fax: (609) 883-5343   E-mail: vickie@njsna.org
Web: www.njsna.org/institute/institute.htm

Purpose To provide financial assistance to minority undergraduates in New Jersey who are preparing for a career as a nurse.

Eligibility All applicants must be New Jersey residents currently enrolled in an associate degree, baccalaureate, or diploma nursing program located in New Jersey. They must be members of 1 of the following groups: African American, Hispanic, American Indian or Alaskan Native, Asian, or Pacific Islander. Applicants who are R.N.s must be members of the New Jersey State Nurses Association (a copy of their membership card must be submitted with their application). Selection is based on financial need, academic achievement, and leadership potential.

Financial data A stipend is awarded (amount not specified).
Duration 1 year.
Number awarded Varies each year; recently, 1 of these scholarships was awarded.
Deadline November of each year.

[189]
JERE W. THOMPSON, JR. SCHOLARSHIP
Dallas Foundation
Attn: Scholarship Administrator
900 Jackson Street, Suite 150
Dallas, TX 75202
(214) 741-9898   Fax: (214) 741-9848
E-mail: cmcnally@dallasfoundation.org
Web: www.dallasfoundation.org
Purpose To provide financial assistance and work experience to disadvantaged students who are majoring in civil engineering at public universities in Texas.
Eligibility This program is open to disadvantaged students in civil engineering or construction engineering at public colleges and universities in Texas; special consideration is given to residents of counties in the service area of the North Texas Tollway Authority: Collin, Dallas, Denton, or Tarrant. At the time of application, students must be full-time sophomores. Finalists may be interviewed. Financial need is considered in the selection process.
Financial data Stipends range up to $2,000 per semester, beginning in the recipient's junior year; the maximum award is $8,000 over 4 semesters.
Duration 1 semester; may be renewed for up to 3 additional semesters, provided the recipient remains a full-time student, maintains at least a 2.5 GPA, and submits a grade report within 45 days after the end of each semester.
Additional information Recipients of the Thompson Scholarship are given an opportunity for a paid internship in the Dallas area during the summer between their junior and senior year. Assignments are available at the scholarship's sponsors: North Texas Tollway Authority, Brown and Root Services, Carter & Burgess, Inc., and HNTB Companies.
Number awarded 1 each year.
Deadline March of each year.

[190]
JIMMY A. YOUNG MEMORIAL EDUCATION RECOGNITION AWARD
American Association for Respiratory Care
Attn: American Respiratory Care Foundation
9425 North MacArthur Boulevard, Suite 100
Irving, TX 75063-4706
(972) 243-2272   Fax: (972) 484-2720
E-mail: info@aarc.org
Web: www.aarc.org/awards/young.html
Purpose To provide financial assistance to college students, especially minorities, interested in becoming respiratory therapists.
Eligibility Candidates must be enrolled in an accredited respiratory therapy program, have completed at least 1 semester/quarter of the program, and have a GPA of 3.0 or higher. Preference is given to nominees of minority origin.

Applications must include 6 copies of an original referenced paper on some aspect of respiratory care and letters of recommendation. The foundation prefers that the candidates be nominated by a school or program, but any student may initiate a request for sponsorship by a school (in order that a deserving candidate is not denied the opportunity to compete simply because the school does not initiate the application).
Financial data The stipend is $1,000. The award also provides airfare, 1 night's lodging, and registration for the association's international congress.
Duration 1 year.
Number awarded 1 each year.
Deadline June of each year.

[191]
JOE ALLMAN SCHOLARSHIP
Japanese American Citizens League-Arizona Chapter
c/o Michele Namba, Scholarship Committee Secretary
5414 West Glenn Drive
Glendale, AZ 85301
E-mail: webmaster@azjacl.org
Web: www.azjacl.org
Purpose To provide financial assistance to graduating high school seniors in Arizona who are of Japanese heritage.
Eligibility This program is open to graduating high school seniors in Arizona. Applicants or their parents must have been members of 1 of the following organizations for at least the preceding 3 years: Arizona Chapter of the Japanese American Citizens League (JACLA), the Phoenix Japanese Free Methodist Church, the Arizona Buddhist Church, a youth group of JACLA, a youth group of the Phoenix Free Methodist Church, or a youth group of the Arizona Buddhist Church. Financial need is not considered in the selection process. Special consideration is given to students currently involved in Scouting.
Financial data A stipend is awarded (amount not specified).
Duration 1 year.
Additional information Recipients must attend the association's scholarship awards banquet and accept the award in person; failure to do so results in forfeiture of the award.
Number awarded 1 each year.
Deadline February of each year.

[192]
KAHULUI FILIPINO COMMUNITY ASSOCIATION SCHOLARSHIP PROGRAM
Kahului Filipino Community Association
Attn: President
P.O. Box 1610
Kahului, HI 96732
Purpose To provide financial assistance to high school seniors in Hawaii who are of Filipino descent and interested in attending college.
Eligibility This program is open to graduating high school seniors on the island of Maui who are of Filipino descent, have earned at least a 3.0 GPA, and have applied to an accredited college or university. Selection is based on aca-

demic record, school and community activities, awards and honors, financial need, and letters of recommendation.

Financial data The stipend is $300 or $500.

Duration 1 year.

Additional information Information is also available from the scholarship committee, 457 West One Street, Karukui, HI 96732.

Number awarded 10 each year.

Deadline April of each year.

[193]
KAISER PERMANENTE ASIAN ASSOCIATION SCHOLARSHIP PROGRAM

Kaiser Permanente Asian Association
Attn: Suzanne Furuya, Scholarship Chair
KP Care Management Institute
One Kaiser Plaza, 16th Floor
Oakland, CA 94612
E-mail: scholarship@kpaaonline.org
Web: www.KPAAonline.org

Purpose To provide financial assistance for college to high school seniors of Asian descent from northern California.

Eligibility This program is open to seniors graduating from high schools in the service area of Northern California Kaiser Permanente (zip codes from 93230 to 95961). Applicants must be of Asian descent, although there is no requirement as to extent of Asian ancestry. They must have a GPA of 2.5 or higher and be planning to attend an accredited college, university, or trade or technical school. Along with their application, they must submit a personal statement that reflects their view and experiences about how their Asian heritage has shaped who they are today and how they feel it will help them meet their future career goal of holding a leadership position.

Financial data The stipend is $2,000.

Duration 1 year.

Additional information This program was established in 2000.

Number awarded 5 each year, including 1 reserved for a child or dependent of a Kaiser Permanente physician or employee in the Northern California region.

Deadline February of each year.

[194]
KANSAS ESOL/BILINGUAL EDUCATION SCHOLARSHIP

Kansas Association of Migrant Directors
c/o Cynthia Adcock
USD 305
P.O. Box 797
Salina, KS 67402
(785) 309-4718   E-mail: Cynthia.Adcock@ksde.org

Purpose To provide financial assistance for college to seniors graduating from high schools in Kansas who have been enrolled in a bilingual or English for Speakers of Other Languages (ESOL) program.

Eligibility This program is open to seniors graduating from high schools in Kansas who are currently in a bilingual or ESOL program. Applicants must be planning to attend a college or university in Kansas as a full-time student. Along

with their application, they must submit a paragraph about their educational goals, explaining why they want to go to college and describing their plans after graduation. Selection is based on the essay, GPA, school performance, and financial need.

Financial data The stipend is $250 per semester ($500 per year).

Duration 4 semesters (2 years).

Number awarded Varies each year; recently, 3 of these scholarships were awarded.

Deadline March of each year.

[195]
KANSAS ETHNIC MINORITY SCHOLARSHIP PROGRAM

Kansas Board of Regents
Attn: Student Financial Aid
1000 S.W. Jackson Street, Suite 520
Topeka, KS 66612-1368
(785) 296-3518   Fax: (785) 296-0983
E-mail: dlindeman@ksbor.org
Web: www.kansasregents.com

Purpose To provide financial assistance to minority students in Kansas who are interested in attending college in the state.

Eligibility Eligible to apply are Kansas residents who fall into 1 of these minority groups: American Indian, Alaskan Native, African American, Asian, Pacific Islander, or Hispanic. Applicants may be current college students (enrolled in community colleges, colleges, or universities in Kansas), but high school seniors graduating in the current year receive priority consideration. Minimum academic requirements include 1 of the following: 1) ACT score of 21 or higher or SAT equivalent; 2) cumulative GPA of 3.0 or higher; 3) high school rank in upper 33%; 4) completion of the Kansas Scholars Curriculum (4 years of English, 3 years of mathematics, 3 years of science, 3 years of social studies, and 2 years of foreign language); 5) selection by the National Merit Corporation in any category; or 6) selection by the College Board as a Hispanic Scholar.

Financial data A stipend of up to $1,850 is provided, depending on financial need and availability of state funds.

Duration 1 year; may be renewed for up to 3 additional years (4 additional years for designated 5-year programs) if the recipient maintains a 2.0 cumulative GPA and has financial need.

Additional information There is a $10 application fee.

Number awarded Approximately 200 each year.

Deadline April of each year.

[196]
KATU THOMAS R. DARGAN MINORITY SCHOLARSHIP

KATU-TV
Attn: Human Resources
2153 N.E. Sandy Boulevard
P.O. Box 2
Portland, OR 97207-0002
(503) 231-4222
Web: www.katu.com/insidekatu/scholarship.asp

Purpose To provide financial assistance and work experience to minority students from Oregon and Washington who are studying broadcasting or communications in college.

Eligibility This program is open to Native Americans, African Americans, Hispanic Americans, or Asian Americans who are U.S. citizens, currently enrolled in the first, second, or third year at a 4-year college or university or an accredited community college in Oregon or Washington, or, if a resident of Oregon or Washington, at a school in any state. Applicants must be majoring in broadcasting or communications and have a GPA of 3.0 or higher. Community college students must be enrolled in a broadcast curriculum that is transferable to a 4-year accredited university. Finalists will be interviewed. Selection is based on financial need, academic achievement, and an essay on personal and professional goals.

Financial data The stipend is $4,000. Funds are sent directly to the recipient's school.

Duration 1 year; recipients may reapply if they have maintained a GPA of 3.0 or higher.

Additional information Winners are also eligible for a paid internship in selected departments at Fisher Broadcasting/KATU in Portland, Oregon.

Number awarded 1 each year.

Deadline April of each year.

[197]
KEN INOUYE SCHOLARSHIP

Society of Professional Journalists-Greater Los Angeles
  Professional Chapter
c/o Christopher Burnett, Scholarship Chair
California State University at Long Beach
Department of Journalism
1250 Bellflower Boulevard
Long Beach, CA 90840-4601
(562) 985-5779   E-mail: cburnett@csulb.edu
Web: www.spj.org/losangeles

Purpose To provide financial assistance to minority undergraduate and graduate students in southern California who are interested in preparing for careers in journalism.

Eligibility Minority college juniors, seniors, or graduate students who are interested in careers in journalism (but not public relations, advertising, publicity, law, or a related field) are eligible to apply if they are residents of or attending school in Los Angeles, Ventura, or Orange counties, California. Applicants should be enrolled as journalism majors, but if their university does not offer such a major they may present other evidence of intent to prepare for a career in the field. Selection is based on evidence of unusual accomplishment and potential to advance in a news career; finan-

cial need is considered only if 2 or more applicants are equally qualified.

Financial data Stipends range from $500 to $1,000.

Duration 1 year; may be renewed.

Additional information The sponsor reserves the right to split the scholarship equally if 2 or more applicants appear equally qualified or to make no award if there are no promising applicants.

Number awarded 1 each year.

Deadline April of each year.

[198]
KEN KASHIWAHARA SCHOLARSHIP

Radio and Television News Directors Foundation
1600 K Street, N.W., Suite 700
Washington, DC 20006-2838
(202) 467-5218   Fax: (202) 223-4007
E-mail: karenb@rtndf.org
Web: www.rtndf.org

Purpose To provide financial assistance to outstanding undergraduate students, especially minorities, who are interested in preparing for a career in electronic journalism.

Eligibility Eligible are sophomore or more advanced undergraduate students enrolled in an electronic journalism sequence at an accredited or nationally-recognized college or university. Applicants must submit 1 to 3 examples of reporting or producing skills on audio or video cassette tapes (no more than 15 minutes total), a description of their role on each story and a list of who worked on each story and what they did, a statement explaining why they are seeking a career in broadcast or cable journalism, and a letter of endorsement from a faculty sponsor that verifies the applicant has at least 1 year of school remaining. Preference is given to undergraduate students of color.

Financial data The stipend is $2,500, paid in semiannual installments of $1,250 each.

Duration 1 year.

Additional information The Radio and Television News Directors Foundation (RTNDF) also provides an all-expense paid trip to the Radio-Television News Directors Association (RTNDA) annual international conference. It defines electronic journalism to include radio, television, cable, and online news. Previous winners of any RTNDF scholarship or internship are not eligible.

Number awarded 1 each year.

Deadline April of each year.

[199]
KENJI KAJIWARA MEMORIAL SCHOLARSHIP

Japanese American Citizens League
Attn: National Scholarship Awards
1765 Sutter Street
San Francisco, CA 94115
(415) 921-5225   Fax: (415) 931-4671
E-mail: jacl@jacl.org
Web: www.jacl.org/scholarships.html

Purpose To provide financial assistance for college to student members of the Japanese American Citizens League (JACL).

Eligibility This program is open to JACL members who are currently enrolled or planning to reenter a college, university, trade school, business college, or other institution of higher learning. Applicants must submit a statement describing their current level of involvement in the Japanese American community or Asian Pacific community and how they will continue their involvement in future years. Selection is based on academic record, extracurricular activities, financial need, and community involvement.

Financial data The stipend depends on the availability of funds but usually ranges from $1,000 to $5,000.

Duration 1 year; nonrenewable.

Additional information Applications must be submitted to the JACL National Scholarship Program, c/o San Diego JACL Chapter, 1031 25th Street, San Diego, CA 92102.

Number awarded At least 1 each year.

Deadline March of each year.

[200]
KENJI KASAI MEMORIAL SCHOLARSHIP

Japanese American Citizens League
Attn: National Scholarship Awards
1765 Sutter Street
San Francisco, CA 94115
(415) 921-5225   Fax: (415) 931-4671
E-mail: jacl@jacl.org
Web: www.jacl.org/scholarships.html

Purpose To provide financial assistance for college to student members of the Japanese American Citizens League (JACL) who are high school seniors.

Eligibility This program is open to JACL members who are high school seniors interested in attending a college, university, trade school, business college, or other institution of higher learning. Applicants must submit a statement describing their current level of involvement in the Japanese American community or Asian Pacific community and how they will continue their involvement in future years. Selection is based on academic record, extracurricular activities, and community involvement.

Financial data The stipend depends on the availability of funds but usually ranges from $1,000 to $5,000.

Duration 1 year; nonrenewable.

Additional information Applications must be submitted to the local JACL chapter.

Number awarded At least 1 each year.

Deadline February of each year.

[201]
KENTUCKY ANNUAL CONFERENCE ETHNIC SCHOLARSHIPS

United Methodist Church-Kentucky Annual Conference
Attn: Commission on Higher Education and Campus
    Ministry
7400 Floydsburg Road
Crestwood, KY 40014-8202
(502) 425-3884   Toll-free: (800) 530-7236
Fax: (502) 426-5181
Web: www.kyumc.org

Purpose To provide financial assistance for college to ethnic minority residents of Kentucky who are members of the United Methodist Church.

Eligibility This program is open to ethnic minority residents of Kentucky who are members of the United Method-

ist Church and attending or planning to attend a college or university. Candidates must be nominated by their pastor, Wesley Foundation director, and/or chair of their local church higher education and campus ministry work area. Each church may nominate only 1 person. The letter of nomination must include information on the candidate's academic achievements, local church involvement, community involvement, goals and plans, and financial need.

Financial data The stipend is $500.

Duration 1 year.

Additional information Recipients must attend the Annual Conference session to receive the award.

Number awarded 2 each year.

Deadline April of each year.

[202]
KNIGHT RIDDER MINORITY SCHOLARS PROGRAM

Knight Ridder, Inc.
Attn: Office of Diversity
50 West San Fernando Street, Suite 1200
San Jose, CA 95113
(408) 938-7734   Fax: (408) 938-7755
Web: www.knightridderscholars.com

Purpose To provide financial assistance and work experience to minority high school seniors who are interested in going to college to prepare for a career in journalism.

Eligibility This program is open to minority seniors graduating from high schools in areas served by Knight Ridder. Applicants must be interested in attending college to prepare for a career in the newspaper industry. They first apply to their local Knight Ridder newspaper and compete for local scholarships; selected winners are then nominated for this award. Both "news" and "business" students are eligible.

Financial data The stipend is $5,000 per year for the freshman and sophomore year and $15,000 per year for the junior and senior year.

Duration 1 year; may be renewed for up to 3 additional years, if the recipient maintains a GPA of 3.0 or higher and satisfactory performance on internships.

Additional information Recipients are offered an internship opportunity at a Knight Ridder newspaper during the summer. News scholars work in the newsroom, writing and editing stories, taking photographs, crafting illustrations, and designing news pages. Business scholars complete internships in advertising, marketing, information technology, circulation, and other areas essential to the industry. At the end of the sophomore year, recipients must agree to work at a Knight Ridder newspaper for 1 year after graduation.

Number awarded Up to 5 each year: 2 for news, 2 for business, and 1 for either.

[203]
KP-APAN SCHOLARSHIP PROGRAM

Kaiser Permanent Asian Pacific American Network
Attn: Scholarship Committee
P.O. Box 950
Pasadena, CA 91102-0950
E-mail: christina.c.lin@kp.org
Web: xnet.kp.org

Purpose To provide financial assistance for college to high school seniors of Asian descent from southern California.

Eligibility This program is open to seniors graduating from high schools in the service area of Southern California Kaiser Permanente (those portions of Kern, Los Angeles, Orange, Riverside, San Bernardino, San Diego, Tulare, and Ventura counties in zip codes from 90001 to 93599). Applicants must be of Asian descent, although there is no requirement as to extent of Asian ancestry. They must have a GPA of 3.0 or higher and be planning to attend an accredited college, university, or trade or technical school. Along with their application, they must submit a personal statement that reflects their view and experiences about how their Asian heritage has shaped who they are today and how they feel it will help them meet their future career goal of holding a leadership position.

Financial data The stipend is $2,000.

Duration 1 year.

Number awarded 2 each year, including 1 reserved for a dependent or sibling of a Kaiser Permanente physician or employee in the Southern California region.

Deadline April of each year.

[204]
KSEA SCHOLARSHIPS

Korean-American Scientists and Engineers Association
1952 Gallows Drive, Suite 300
Vienna, VA 22182
(703) 748-1221   Fax: (703) 748-1331
E-mail: sejong@ksea.org
Web: www.ksea.org

Purpose To provide financial assistance to undergraduate and graduate student members of the Korean-American Scientists and Engineers Association (KSEA).

Eligibility This program is open to Korean American undergraduate and graduate students who graduated from a high school in the United States, are KSEA members, and are majoring in science, engineering, or a related field. Along with their application, they must submit a 500-word essay on either of the following topics: 1) their career goals and intended contributions to society, or 2) the meaning of Korean heritage in their life. Selection is based on the essay (20%), work experience and extracurricular activities (20%), recommendation letters (30%), and academic performance (30%).

Financial data The stipend is $1,000.

Duration 1 year.

Additional information This program includes the following named scholarships: the Inyong Ham Scholarship, the Yohan and Rumie Cho Scholarship, the Shoon Kyung Kim Scholarship, the Nam Sook and Je Hyun Kim Scholarship, and the Hyundai Scholarships.

Number awarded Varies each year.

Deadline February of each year.

[205]
KYUTARO AND YASUO ABIKO MEMORIAL SCHOLARSHIP

Japanese American Citizens League
Attn: National Scholarship Awards
1765 Sutter Street
San Francisco, CA 94115
(415) 921-5225   Fax: (415) 931-4671
E-mail: jacl@jacl.org
Web: www.jacl.org/scholarships.html

Purpose To provide financial assistance for college to student members of the Japanese American Citizens League (JACL), especially those majoring in journalism or agriculture.

Eligibility This program is open to JACL members who are currently enrolled or planning to reenter a college, university, trade school, business college, or other institution of higher learning. Applicants must submit a statement describing their current level of involvement in the Japanese American community or Asian Pacific community and how they will continue their involvement in future years. Selection is based on academic record, extracurricular activities, financial need, and community involvement. Preference is given to students majoring in journalism or agriculture.

Financial data The stipend depends on the availability of funds but usually ranges from $1,000 to $5,000.

Duration 1 year; nonrenewable.

Additional information Applications must be submitted to the JACL National Scholarship Program, c/o San Diego JACL Chapter, 1031 25th Street, San Diego, CA 92102.

Number awarded At least 1 each year.

Deadline March of each year.

[206]
LAGRANT FOUNDATION SCHOLARSHIPS

LAGRANT FOUNDATION
555 South Flower Street, Suite 700
Los Angeles, CA 90071-2423
(323) 469-8680   Fax: (323) 469-8683
Web: www.lagrantfoundation.org

Purpose To provide financial assistance to minority high school seniors or college students who are interested in majoring in advertising, public relations, or marketing.

Eligibility This program is open to African Americans, Asian Pacific Americans, Hispanics, or Native Americans who are full-time students at a 4-year accredited institution or high school seniors planning to attend a 4-year accredited institution on a full-time basis. Applicants must have a GPA of 2.5 or higher and be majoring or planning to major in advertising, marketing, or public relations. They must submit 1) a 1- to 2-page essay outlining their career goals; what steps they will take to increase ethnic representation in the fields of advertising, marketing, and public relations; and the role of an advertising, marketing, or public relations practitioner; 2) a paragraph explaining how they are financing or planning to finance their education and why they need financial assistance; 3) a paragraph explaining the high school, college, and/or community activities in which they are involved; 4) a brief paragraph describing any honors and awards they have received; 5) if they are currently employed, a paragraph indicating the hours worked each week, responsibilities, and if the job will be kept while attending school; 6) a resume; and 7) an official transcript. Applicants majoring in public relations must write an essay on the importance and relevance of the Arthur W. Page Society Principles.

Financial data The stipend is $5,000 per year.

Duration 1 year.

Number awarded 10 each year.

Deadline March of each year.

[207]
LANDMARK SCHOLARS PROGRAM

Landmark Publishing Group
c/o Rich Martin, Managing Editor
The Roanoke Times
201 West Campbell Avenue
Roanoke, VA 24011
(540) 981-3211   Toll-free: (800) 346-1234
E-mail: rich.martin@roanoke.com
Web: www.landmarkcommunications.com

Purpose To provide work experience and financial aid to minority undergraduates who are interested in preparing for a career in journalism.

Eligibility This program is open to minority college sophomores, preferably those with ties to the mid-Atlantic states (Delaware, Maryland, North Carolina, South Carolina, Virginia, and Washington, D.C.). Applicants must be full-time students with a GPA of 2.5 or higher. They must be interested in preparing for a career in print journalism and in an internship as a reporter, photographer, graphic artist, sports writer, copy editor, or page designer.

Financial data The stipend is $5,000 per year. During the summers following their sophomore and junior years, recipients are provided with paid internships. Following graduation, they are offered a 1-year internship with full benefits and the possibility of continued employment.

Duration 2 years (the junior and senior years of college).

Additional information The internships are offered at the *News & Record* in Greensboro, North Carolina, the *Virginian-Pilot* in Norfolk, Virginia, or the *Roanoke Times* in Roanoke, Virginia.

Number awarded 1 or more each year.

Deadline November of each year.

[208]
LAWRENCE R. FOSTER MEMORIAL SCHOLARSHIP

Oregon Student Assistance Commission
Attn: Grants and Scholarships Division
1500 Valley River Drive, Suite 100
Eugene, OR 97401-2146
(541) 687-7395   Toll-free: (800) 452-8807, ext. 7395
Fax: (541) 687-7419
E-mail: awardinfo@mercury.osac.state.or.us
Web: www.osac.state.or.us

Purpose To provide financial assistance for college or graduate school to residents of Oregon (particularly minorities) who are interested in preparing for a public health career.

Eligibility This program is open to residents of Oregon who are attending a 4-year college or university in any state to prepare for a career in public health (not private practice). First preference is given to applicants who are either working in public health or enrolled as graduate students in that field. Second preference is given to undergraduates entering the junior or senior year of a health program, including nursing, medical technology, and physician assistant. A general preference is given to applicants from diverse cultures. Along with their application, they must submit a 1- to 2-page essay on their interest, experience, and future plans for a public health career

Financial data Stipend amounts vary; recently, they were at least $4,167.

Duration 1 year.

Additional information This program is administered by the Oregon Student Assistance Commission (OSAC) with funds provided by the Oregon Community Foundation, 1221 S.W. Yamhill, Suite 100, Portland, OR 97205, (503) 227-6846, Fax: (503) 274-7771.

Number awarded Varies each year; recently, 6 of these scholarships were awarded.

Deadline February of each year.

[209]
LEON C. HART MEMORIAL SCHOLARSHIP

Gravure Association of America
Attn: Gravure Education Foundation
1200-A Scottsville Road
Rochester, NY 14624
(585) 436-2150   Fax: (585) 436-7689
E-mail: lwshatch@gaa.org
Web: www.gaa.org/GEF/scholarships.htm

Purpose To provide financial assistance to college students, especially those from diverse ethnic backgrounds, who are interested in a career in printing.

Eligibility This program is open to students who are enrolled full time in a field related to printing at a designated learning resource center supported by the Gravure Education Foundation (GEF) of the Gravure Association of America. Applicants must have a GPA of 3.0 or higher. Along with their application, they must submit a 250-word essay on "How Involvement in my Community/School Has Made a Difference." Selection is based on the essay, financial need, transcripts, and either extracurricular involvement in school activities or community involvement. Preference is given to students of diverse ethnic backgrounds and to students who show an interest in printing education as a career path.

Financial data The stipend is $1,000.

Duration 1 year.

Additional information GEF learning resource centers are located at the following universities: Rochester Institute of Technology, Western Michigan University, California Polytechnic State University at San Luis Obispo, Arizona State University, Clemson University, Murray State University, and the University of Wisconsin at Stout. This program is named in honor of a former executive director of the GEF who began his career as a printer for the Afro-American Newspaper in Baltimore, Maryland.

Number awarded 1 each year.

Deadline May of each year.

[210]
LEONARD M. PERRYMAN COMMUNICATIONS SCHOLARSHIP FOR ETHNIC MINORITY STUDENTS

United Methodist Communications
Attn: Communications Resourcing Team
810 12th Avenue South
P.O. Box 320
Nashville, TN 37202-0320
(615) 742-5481   Toll-free: (888) CRT-4UMC
Fax: (615) 742-5485
E-mail: scholarships@umcom.org
Web: www.umcom.org

Purpose To provide financial assistance to minority United Methodist college students who are interested in careers in religious communications.

Eligibility This program is open to United Methodist ethnic minority students enrolled in accredited institutions of higher education as juniors or seniors. Applicants must be interested in preparing for a career in religious communications. For the purposes of this program, "communications" is meant to cover audiovisual, electronic, and print journalism. Selection is based on Christian commitment and involvement in the life of the United Methodist church, academic achievement, journalistic experience, clarity of purpose, and professional potential as a religious journalist.

Financial data The stipend is $2,500 per year.

Duration 1 year.

Additional information The scholarship may be used at any accredited institution of higher education.

Number awarded 1 each year.

Deadline March of each year.

[211]
LEWIS DAVIS SCHOLARSHIPS

Florida Institute of CPAs Educational Foundation, Inc.
Attn: Senior Director of Administration
325 West College Avenue
P.O. Box 5437
Tallahassee, FL 32314
(850) 224-2727, ext. 200
Toll-free: (800) 342-3197, ext. 200
Fax: (850) 222-8190
Web: www.ficpa.org

Purpose To provide financial assistance to minority students from south Florida who are majoring in accounting.

Eligibility Eligible to apply for this support are minority residents of south Florida who are fourth- or fifth-year accounting students enrolled full time in an accounting program at a college or university in the state. A faculty member in the accounting department of their college must nominate them. Applicants should be planning to sit for the C.P.A. exam and indicate a desire to work in Florida. Selection is based on financial need, educational achievement, and demonstrated professional, social, and charitable activities.

Financial data The maximum stipend is $1,250.

Duration 1 year; recipients may reapply for 1 additional year of support.

Number awarded Varies each year.

[212]
LEXINGTON HERALD-LEADER MINORITY SCHOLARSHIP

Lexington Herald-Leader
Attn: Paula Anderson
100 Midland Avenue
Lexington, KY 40508
(859) 231-1323   Fax: (859) 231-3584
E-mail: panderson@herald-leader.com
Web: www.kentucky.com/mld/heraldleader

Purpose To provide financial assistance for college to minority high school seniors in eastern and central Kentucky, especially those interested in studying journalism.

Eligibility This program is open to minority high school seniors from eastern and central Kentucky who are planning to attend a 4-year college or university. Applicants must submit 2 letters of recommendation, transcripts, SAT/ACT scores, and an essay explaining why they want to go to college and the kind of career they hope to pursue upon graduation. Students who intend to major in journalism or business to prepare for a newspaper career are considered for additional scholarships; they should also submit 5 samples of their writing. Financial need is not considered in the selection process.

Financial data The stipend is $1,000 per year.

Duration 1 year; nonrenewable.

Additional information If the recipients of these scholarships indicate an interest in a journalism career, they are automatically entered into competition for the 4-year $40,000 Knight Ridder Minority Scholarship Program.

Number awarded 2 each year.

Deadline January of each year.

[213]
LOS ANGELES CHAPTER OF AAJA GENERAL SCHOLARSHIPS

Asian American Journalists Association-Los Angeles
   Chapter
231 East Third Street
Los Angeles, CA 90013-1494
Web: www.aaja-la.org/scholarshipandfellowship

Purpose To provide financial assistance to Asian/Pacific Islander students in southern California who are interested in careers in journalism.

Eligibility These scholarships are open to Asian/Pacific Islander students who are planning a career in broadcast, photo, or print journalism. Applicants may be high school seniors, college undergraduates, or graduate students who are either permanently residing in or attending a school in the southern California region. They do not need to be a journalism, photojournalism, or communications major, but applicants must intend to pursue a journalism career. Selection is based on commitment to the field of journalism, scholastic achievement, journalistic ability and potential, a sensitivity to Asian American issues, community involvement, and financial need.

Financial data Stipends range from $500 to $1,000.

Duration 1 year; may be renewed.

Additional information Information is also available from Henry Fuhrmann, Los Angeles Times, 202 West First Street, Los Angeles, CA 90012, E-mail: henry.fuhrmann@latimes.com.

Number awarded Varies each year. Recently, 9 of these scholarships were awarded: 1 at $1,000, 4 at $750, and 4 at $500.

Deadline May of each year.

[214]
LOUIS B. RUSSELL, JR. MEMORIAL SCHOLARSHIP

Indiana State Teachers Association
Attn: Scholarships
150 West Market Street, Suite 900
Indianapolis, IN 46204
(317) 263-3400   Toll-free: (800) 382-4037
Fax: (317) 655-3700   E-mail: kmcallen@ista-in.org
Web: www.ista-in.org

Purpose To provide financial assistance to ethnic minority high school seniors in Indiana who are interested in pursuing vocational education.

Eligibility This program is open to ethnic minority high school seniors in Indiana who are interested in continuing their education in the area of industrial arts, vocational education, or technical preparation at an accredited postsecondary institution. Selection is based on academic achievement, leadership ability as expressed through co-curricular activities and community involvement, recommendations, and a 300-word essay on their educational goals and how they plan to use this scholarship.

Financial data The stipend is $1,000.

Duration 1 year; may be renewed for 1 additional year.

Number awarded 1 each year.

Deadline February of each year.

[215]
LOUISE MORITZ MOLITORIS LEADERSHIP AWARD

Women's Transportation Seminar
Attn: National Headquarters
1666 K Street, N.W., Suite 1100
Washington, DC 20006
(202) 496-4340   Fax: (202) 496-4349
E-mail: wts@wtsnational.org
Web: www.wtsnational.org

Purpose To provide financial assistance to undergraduate women (particularly women of color) interested in a career in transportation.

Eligibility This program is open to women who are working on an undergraduate degree in transportation or a transportation-related field (e.g., transportation engineering, planning, finance, or logistics). Applicants must have a GPA of 3.0 or higher. They must submit a 500-word statement about their career goals after graduation and why they think they should receive the scholarship award; their statement should specifically address the issue of leadership. Applications must be submitted first to a local chapter; the chapters forward selected applications for consideration on the national level. Minority candidates are encouraged to apply. Selection is based on transportation involvement and goals, job skills, academic record, and leadership potential; financial need is not considered.

Financial data The stipend is $3,000.

Duration 1 year.

Additional information Local chapters may also award additional funding to winners for their area.

Number awarded 1 each year.

Deadline Applications must be submitted by November to a local WTS chapter.

[216]
MANAA MEDIA SCHOLARSHIPS

Media Action Network for Asian Americans
P.O. Box 11105
Burbank, CA 91510
(213) 486-4433   E-mail: manaaletters@yahoo.com
Web: www.manaa.org

Purpose To provide financial assistance to Asian Pacific Islander students interested in advancing a positive image of Asian Americans in the mainstream media.

Eligibility This program is open to Asian Pacific Islander college students interested in preparing for careers in filmmaking and in television production (but not in broadcast journalism). Applicants must be interested in advancing a positive and enlightened understanding of the Asian American experience in the mainstream media. Along with their application, they must submit a 1,000-word essay that addresses the following questions: Where do you see yourself 10 years from now? What accomplishments and strides will you hope to have made in your career in the film and television industry? How will you have worked to advance more positive images of Asian Americans in the mainstream media? Selection is based on academic and personal merit, a desire to uplift the image of Asian Americans in film and television as demonstrated in the essay, potential as demonstrated in a work sample, and financial need.

Financial data The stipend is $1,000.

Duration 1 year.

Additional information This program began in 2001.

Number awarded 2 each year.

Deadline May of each year.

[217]
MARI AND JAMES MICHENER SCHOLARSHIP

Japanese American Citizens League
Attn: National Scholarship Awards
1765 Sutter Street
San Francisco, CA 94115
(415) 921-5225   Fax: (415) 931-4671
E-mail: jacl@jacl.org
Web: www.jacl.org/scholarships.html

Purpose To provide financial assistance for college to student members of the Japanese American Citizens League (JACL).

Eligibility This program is open to JACL members who are currently enrolled or planning to reenter a college, university, trade school, business college, or other institution of higher learning. Applicants must submit a statement describing their current level of involvement in the Japanese American community or Asian Pacific community and how they will continue their involvement in future years. Selection is based on academic record, extracurricular activities, financial need, and community involvement.

Financial data The stipend depends on the availability of funds but usually ranges from $1,000 to $5,000.

Duration 1 year; nonrenewable.

Additional information Applications must be submitted to the JACL National Scholarship Program, c/o San Diego JACL Chapter, 1031 25th Street, San Diego, CA 92102.

Number awarded 1 each year.

Deadline March of each year.

[218]
MARTIN LUTHER KING, JR. MEMORIAL SCHOLARSHIP FUND

California Teachers Association
Attn: Human Rights Department
P.O. Box 921
Burlingame, CA 94011-0921
(650) 552-5370   E-mail: scholarships@cta.org
Web: www.cta.org

Purpose To provide financial assistance for college or graduate school to racial and ethnic minorities in California who are members of the California Teachers Association (CTA), children of members, or members of the Student CTA.

Eligibility This program is open to members of a racial or ethnic minority group who are 1) active CTA members; 2) dependent children of active, retired-life, or deceased CTA members; or 3) members of Student CTA. Applicants must be interested in preparing for a teaching career in public education or already engaged in such a career.

Financial data Stipends vary each year, depending upon the amount of contributions received and the financial need of individual recipients.

Duration 1 year.

Number awarded Varies each year. Recently, 23 of these scholarships were awarded: 10 to CTA members, 8 to children of CTA members, and 5 to Student CTA members.

Deadline March of each year.

[219]
MARTIN LUTHER KING, JR. SCHOLARSHIP

North Carolina Association of Educators, Inc.
Attn: Minority Affairs Commission
700 South Salisbury Street
P.O. Box 27347
Raleigh, NC 27611-7347
(919) 832-3000, ext. 211
Toll-free: (800) 662-7924, ext. 211
Fax: (919) 839-8229
Web: www.ncae.org

Purpose To provide financial assistance for college to minority and other high school seniors in North Carolina.

Eligibility Applicants must be North Carolina residents enrolled as seniors in high school. They must be planning to continue their education upon graduation. Applications are considered and judged by members of the association's Minority Affairs Commission. Selection is based on character, personality, and scholastic achievement.

Financial data The amount of the stipend depends on the availability of funding.

Duration 1 year.

Number awarded 1 each year.

Deadline January of each year.

[220]
MARY MOY QUAN ING MEMORIAL SCHOLARSHIP

Asian American Journalists Association
Attn: Student Programs Coordinator
1182 Market Street, Suite 320
San Francisco, CA 94102
(415) 346-2051, ext. 102   Fax: (415) 346-6343
E-mail: brandons@aaja.org
Web: www.aaja.org

Purpose To provide financial assistance to graduating high school seniors who are members of the Asian American Journalists Association (AAJA) and interested in majoring in journalism in college.

Eligibility This program is open to graduating high school seniors who are AAJA members enrolling in college to study journalism. Applicants must submit a 500-word essay on their involvement or interest in the Asian American community and how, if they are awarded this scholarship, they would contribute to the field of journalism and/or media issues involving the Asian Pacific American and Pacific Islander community. Selection is based on scholastic ability, commitment to journalism, sensitivity to Asian American and Pacific Islander issues as demonstrated by community involvement, journalistic ability, and financial need.

Financial data The stipend is $2,000.

Duration 1 year.

Number awarded 1 each year.

Deadline April of each year.

[221]
MAS AND MAJIU UYESUGI MEMORIAL SCHOLARSHIP

Japanese American Citizens League
Attn: National Scholarship Awards
1765 Sutter Street
San Francisco, CA 94115
(415) 921-5225   Fax: (415) 931-4671
E-mail: jacl@jacl.org
Web: www.jacl.org/scholarships.html

Purpose To provide financial assistance for college to student members of the Japanese American Citizens League (JACL) who are high school seniors.

Eligibility This program is open to JACL members who are high school seniors interested in attending a college, university, trade school, business college, or other institution of higher learning. Applicants must submit a statement describing their current level of involvement in the Japanese American community or Asian Pacific community and how they will continue their involvement in future years. Selection is based on academic record, extracurricular activities, and community involvement.

Financial data The stipend depends on the availability of funds but usually ranges from $1,000 to $5,000.

Duration 1 year; nonrenewable.

Additional information Applications must be submitted to the local JACL chapter.

Number awarded At least 1 each year.

Deadline February of each year.

[222]
MASAO AND SUMAKO ITANO MEMORIAL SCHOLARSHIP

Japanese American Citizens League
Attn: National Scholarship Awards
1765 Sutter Street
San Francisco, CA 94115
(415) 921-5225   Fax: (415) 931-4671
E-mail: jacl@jacl.org
Web: www.jacl.org/scholarships.html

Purpose To provide financial assistance for college to student members of the Japanese American Citizens League (JACL) who are high school seniors.

Eligibility This program is open to JACL members who are high school seniors interested in attending a college, university, trade school, business college, or other institution of higher learning. Applicants must submit a statement describing their current level of involvement in the Japanese American community or Asian Pacific community and how they will continue their involvement in future years. Selection is based on academic record, extracurricular activities, and community involvement.

Financial data The stipend depends on the availability of funds but usually ranges from $1,000 to $5,000.

Duration 1 year; nonrenewable.

Additional information Applications must be submitted to the local JACL chapter.

Number awarded At least 1 each year.

Deadline February of each year.

[223]
MASTERFOODS USA UNDERGRADUATE MENTORED SCHOLARSHIPS FOR COLLEGE STUDENTS

Institute of Food Technologists
Attn: Scholarship Department
525 West Van Buren, Suite 1000
Chicago, IL 60607
(312) 782-8424   Fax: (312) 782-8348
E-mail: info@ift.org
Web: www.ift.org

Purpose To provide financial assistance to minority undergraduates interested in studying food science or food technology.

Eligibility This program is open to members of minority groups (African Americans, Native Indians, Hispanic Americans, and Asian Americans) who are entering the junior year of a food science or food technology program at an educational institution in the United States. Applicants may be transferring from another program in a 4-year college or from a 2-year junior college. Along with their application, they must submit an essay on their career aspirations; a list of awards, honors, and scholarships they have received; a list of extracurricular activities and/or hobbies; and a summary of their work experience. Financial need is not considered in the selection process.

Financial data The stipend is $4,000 per year. Recipients are also invited to attend the annual meeting of the Institute of Food Technologists (IFT); travel expenses up to $550 are reimbursed.

Duration 1 year; may be renewed if the recipient maintains a GPA of 3.0 or higher and participates in a mentoring program.

Additional information Completed applications must be submitted to the department head of the educational institution the applicant is attending. The department forwards the application to IFT along with a plan for mentoring the student if a scholarship is awarded.

Number awarded 5 each year.

Deadline January of each year.

[224]
MASTERFOODS USA UNDERGRADUATE MENTORED SCHOLARSHIPS FOR HIGH SCHOOL SENIORS

Institute of Food Technologists
Attn: Scholarship Department
525 West Van Buren, Suite 1000
Chicago, IL 60607
(312) 782-8424   Fax: (312) 782-8348
E-mail: info@ift.org
Web: www.ift.org

Purpose To provide financial assistance to minority high school seniors interested in studying food science or food technology in college.

Eligibility This program is open to high school seniors planning to enroll in a food science or food technology program at an educational institution in the United States. Applicants must be members of minority groups (African American, Native Indian, Hispanic American, or Asian American) with a GPA of 3.0 or higher and scores of at least 25 on the ACT or the equivalent on the SAT. Along with their application, they must submit a brief biographical sketch and a statement on why they would like to become a food technologist. Financial need is not considered in the selection process.

Financial data The stipend is $4,000 per year. Recipients are also invited to attend the annual meeting of the Institute of Food Technologists (IFT); travel expenses up to $550 are reimbursed.

Duration 1 year; may be renewed if the recipient maintains a GPA of 3.0 or higher and participates in a mentoring program.

Additional information Completed applications must be submitted to the department head of the educational institution the applicant is attending. The department forwards the application to IFT along with a plan for mentoring the student if a scholarship is awarded.

Number awarded 2 each year.

Deadline May of each year.

[225]
MEFUSA SCHOLARSHIPS FOR ASIAN AMERICANS

Minority Educational Foundation of the United States
    of America
Attn: Scholarship Program
3160 Wedgewood Court
Reno, NV 89509-7103

Purpose To provide financial assistance to Asian American high school seniors who are interested in attending a community college.

Eligibility This program is open to Asian Americans graduating from high schools anywhere in the United States. Applicants must be planning to attend a community college on a full-time basis. As part of the selection process, they must submit a 1,000-word essay on their educational and career goals, how a community college education will help them to achieve those goals, and how they plan to serve the Asian American community after completing their education. Selection is based on the essay, high school GPA (2.5 or higher), SAT or ACT scores, involvement in the African American community, and financial need.

Financial data The stipend is $5,000 per year.

Duration 1 year; may be renewed 1 additional year if the recipient maintains full-time enrollment and a GPA of 2.5 or higher.

Additional information The Minority Educational Foundation of the United States of America (MEFUSA) was established in 2001 to meet the needs of minority students who "show a determination to get a college degree," but who, for financial or other personal reasons, are not able to attend a 4-year college or university. Requests for applications should be accompanied by a self-addressed stamped envelope, the student's e-mail address, and the source where they found the scholarship information.

Number awarded Up to 100 each year.

Deadline April of each year.

[226]
MERCEDES-BENZ SCHOLARSHIPS

Chicago Urban League
Attn: Education Department
4510 South Michigan Avenue
Chicago, IL 60653-3898
(773) 451-3565   Fax: (773) 285-7772
E-mail: info@cul-chicago.org
Web: www.cul-chicago.org

Purpose To provide financial assistance to Illinois residents of color interested in studying a field related to automotive technology in college.

Eligibility This program is open to Illinois residents of color who are graduating high school seniors with a GPA of 2.5 or higher and planning to enroll as full-time undergraduate students at a 4-year college or university, Triton College, or 1 of the City Colleges of Chicago. Applicants must be planning to major in automotive technology or a field related to the automotive industry (e.g., engineering, computer science, business, or accounting). They must be able to demonstrate financial need.

Financial data The stipend is $1,000 per year.

Duration 4 years.

Additional information This program is offered as part of the Chicago Urban League's Whitney M. Young, Jr. Memorial Scholarship Fund, established in 1970.

Number awarded 4 each year.

Deadline May of each year.

[227]
MERCURY NEWS MINORITY BUSINESS/FINANCE SCHOLARSHIP

Mercury News
Human Resource Department
Attn: Scholarship Coordinator
750 Ridder Park Drive
San Jose, CA 95190
(408) 920-5555   Fax: (408) 271-3689
E-mail: info@mercscholars.com
Web: www.mercscholars.com

Purpose To provide financial assistance to minority students in northern California who are interested in preparing for newspaper careers in business or finance.

Eligibility This program is open to minority high school seniors in the California counties of Alameda, Contra Costa, Monterey, Sacramento, San Benito, San Francisco, San Joaquin, San Mateo, Santa Clara, and Santa Cruz. Applicants must be interested in majoring in business or finance in college and preparing for a career in newspaper production, finance, circulation management, human resources, marketing, electronic media or advertising. They must submit a 500-word essay on why they want to prepare for a career in business. Financial need is not considered in the selection process.

Financial data The stipend is $1,000.

Duration 1 year.

Additional information The *Mercury News* selects its winners by February of each year and submits their applications to the Knight Ridder Minority Scholarship Program. These winners are given the chance to compete for a 4-year Knight Ridder scholarship/internship of $40,000 and the promise of a job in journalism upon graduation. The internship takes place at a Knight Ridder paper in the recipient's community; interns work each year during the summer.

Number awarded 1 each year.

Deadline January of each year.

[228]
MERCURY NEWS MINORITY JOURNALISM SCHOLARSHIP

Mercury News
Human Resource Department
Attn: Scholarship Coordinator
750 Ridder Park Drive
San Jose, CA 95190
(408) 920-5555   Fax: (408) 271-3689
E-mail: info@mercscholars.com
Web: www.mercscholars.com

Purpose To provide financial assistance to minority students in northern California who are interested in preparing for careers in journalism.

Eligibility This program is open to minority high school seniors in the California counties of Alameda, Contra Costa, Monterey, Sacramento, San Benito, San Francisco, San Joaquin, San Mateo, Santa Clara, and Santa Cruz. Applicants must be interested in majoring in journalism in college and preparing for a career as a reporter, editor, copy editor, photographer, or graphic artist. They must submit 5 samples of their work and a 500-word essay on why they want to prepare for a career in journalism. Financial need is not considered in the selection process.

Financial data The stipend is $1,000.

Duration 1 year.

Additional information The *Mercury News* selects its winners by February of each year and submits their applications to the Knight Ridder Minority Scholarship Program. These winners are given the chance to compete for a 4-year Knight Ridder scholarship/internship of $40,000 and the promise of a job in journalism upon graduation. The internship takes place at a Knight Ridder paper in the recipient's community; interns work each year during the summer.

Number awarded 1 each year.

Deadline January of each year.

[229]
MICHAEL BAKER CORPORATION SCHOLARSHIP PROGRAM FOR DIVERSITY IN ENGINEERING

Association of Independent Colleges and Universities
  of Pennsylvania
101 North Front Street
Harrisburg, PA 17101-1405
(717) 232-8649   Fax: (717) 233-8574
E-mail: info@aicup.org
Web: www.aicup.org

Purpose To provide financial assistance to women and minority students at member institutions of the Association of Independent Colleges and Universities of Pennsylvania (AICUP) who are majoring in designated fields of engineering.

Eligibility This program is open to full-time undergraduate students at designated AICUP colleges and universities who are women and/or members of the following minority groups: American Indians, Alaska Natives, Asians, Blacks/African Americans, Hispanics/Latinos, Native Hawaiians, or Pacific Islanders. Applicants must be juniors majoring in architectural, civil, or environmental engineering with a GPA of 3.0 or higher. Along with their application, they must submit an essay on what they believe will be the greatest challenge facing the engineering profession over the next decade, and why.

Financial data The stipend is $1,000 per year.

Duration 1 year; may be renewed 1 additional year if the recipient maintains appropriate academic standards.

Additional information This program, sponsored by the Michael Baker Corporation, is available at the following AICUP colleges and universities: Bucknell University, Carnegie Mellon University, Drexel University, Gannon University, Geneva College, Grove City College, Lafayette College, Lehigh University, Messiah College, Swarthmore College, Villanova University, Widener University, and Wilkes University.

Number awarded 1 each year.

Deadline April of each year.

[230]
MID-ATLANTIC CHAPTER AWARDS

Chinese American Medical Society-Mid-Atlantic
  Chapter
c/o Richard Change, Scholarship Committee Chair
12522 Stratford Garden Drive
Silver Spring, MD 20904
(301) 424-0136   E-mail: orthochang62@hotmail.com

Purpose To provide financial assistance for college to high school students of Chinese descent in the greater Washington, D.C. metropolitan area.

Eligibility This program is open to juniors and seniors at high schools in Washington, D.C., northern Virginia, and southern Maryland who are of Chinese descent. Applicants must submit an updated transcript, scores on national tests (e.g., PSAT, SAT), and a list of honors, extracurricular activities, and awards. They must also submit a 2-page essay on either of these topics: 1) how cultural stereotypes of Asian youth have affected them or influenced their development to the present, or 2) the relevance of their Asian heritage.

Financial data A stipend is awarded (amount not specified).

Duration 1 year.

Number awarded Varies each year.

Deadline December of each year.

[231]
MIDEASTERN REGION KOREAN AMERICAN SCHOLARSHIPS

Korean American Scholarship Foundation
Mideastern Region
c/o Chang S. Choi, Scholarship Committee Chair
6410 Lahser Road
Bloomfield Hills, MI 48301
(248) 752-3180   Fax: (248) 644-0507
E-mail: cschoi@comcast.net
Web: www.kasf.org

Purpose To provide financial assistance to Korean American undergraduate and graduate students who attend school in Indiana, Michigan, or Ohio.

Eligibility This program is open to Korean American students who are currently enrolled in a college or university as full-time undergraduate or graduate students. Applicants may reside anywhere in the United States as long as they attend school in Indiana, Michigan, or Ohio. Selection is based on academic achievement, school activities, community service, and financial need.

Financial data Stipends range from $1,000 to $2,000.

Duration 1 year; renewable.

Number awarded Varies each year. Recently, the midwestern regional chapter (which then included the current mideastern regional chapter) awarded 69 of these scholarships.

Deadline March of each year.

[232]
MIDWESTERN REGION KOREAN AMERICAN SCHOLARSHIPS

Korean American Scholarship Foundation
Midwestern Region
c/o Tony S. Hahm, Scholarship Committee Chair
P.O. Box 0416
Northbrook, IL 60065-0416
(847) 797-1291   Fax: (847) 797-1304
E-mail: tonyhahm@yahoo.com
Web: www.kasf.org

Purpose To provide financial assistance to Korean American undergraduate and graduate students who attend school in the Midwest.

Eligibility This program is open to Korean American students who are currently enrolled in a college or university in the midwestern states as full-time undergraduate or graduate students. Applicants may reside anywhere in the United States as long as they attend school in the midwest region: Illinois, Iowa, Kansas, Minnesota, Missouri, Nebraska, North Dakota, South Dakota, and Wisconsin. Selection is based on academic achievement, school activities, community service, and financial need.

Financial data Stipends range from $1,000 to $2,000.

Duration 1 year; renewable.

Number awarded Varies each year. Recently, the midwestern regional chapter (which then included the current mideastern regional chapter) awarded 69 of these scholarships.

Deadline June of each year.

[233]
MINORITIES IN GOVERNMENT FINANCE SCHOLARSHIP

Government Finance Officers Association
Attn: Scholarship Committee
203 North LaSalle Street, Suite 2700
Chicago, IL 60601-1210
(312) 977-9700   Fax: (312) 977-4806
Web: www.gfoa.org/services/scholarships.shtml

Purpose To provide financial assistance to minority upper-division and graduate students who are preparing for a career in state and local government finance.

Eligibility This program is open to upper-division and graduate students who are preparing for a career in public finance with a major in public administration, accounting, finance, political science, economics, or business administration (with a specific focus on government or nonprofit management). Applicants must be members of a minority group, citizens or permanent residents of the United States or Canada, and able to provide a letter of recommendation from a representative of their school. Selection is based on career plans, academic record, plan of study, letters of recommendation, and GPA. Financial need is not considered.

Financial data The stipend is $5,000.

Duration 1 year.

Additional information Funding for this program is provided by Fidelity Investments Tax-Exempt Services Company.

Number awarded 1 or more each year.

Deadline February of each year.

[234]
MINORITY ARCHITECTS RESOURCE COMMITTEE SCHOLARSHIP

Dallas Architectural Foundation
1444 Oaklawn Avenue, Suite 600
Dallas, TX 75207
(214) 742-DAIA   Fax: (214) 742-3253
E-mail: info@dallasaia.org
Web: www.dallasaia.org

Purpose To provide financial assistance to minority architecture students who are residents of the Dallas-Irving area of Texas.

Eligibility This program is open to graduates of high schools in the Dallas and Irving Independent School Districts who are current enrolled or accepted in an accredited architecture program. Applicants must be members of a minority group that is underrepresented in relation to the general population. They must be able to demonstrate significance financial need. Along with their application, they must submit a 250-word essay on their architectural aspirations and their latest transcript.

Financial data The stipend is $1,000 per semester ($2,000 per year).

Duration 1 semester; may be renewed up to 3 additional semesters if the recipient remains enrolled full time with a GPA of 2.0 or higher.

Number awarded 1 each year.

Deadline March of each year.

[235]
MINORITY COMMUNITY COLLEGE TRANSFER SCHOLARSHIPS

State University System of Florida
Attn: Office of Academic and Student Affairs
325 West Gaines Street, Suite 1501
Tallahassee, FL 32399-1950
(850) 245-0467   Fax: (850) 245-9667
E-mail: we're.listening@fldoe.org
Web: www.fldoe.org

Purpose To provide financial assistance to minority community college students in Florida who are interested in transferring to a school within the State University System of Florida (SUS).

Eligibility This program is open to minority community college students who complete A.A. or A.S. degrees from an accredited Florida community college between December and August of the current year. Applicants must have been admitted as degree-seeking junior-level students at an SUS institution. All recipients must have participated in, received a waiver for, or passed the College-Level Academic Skills Test program. In addition, male applicants must have complied with the Selective Service System registration requirements. Students may apply for need awards, merit/need awards, or merit awards. The minimum cumulative GPA on postsecondary credits is 2.0 for need-based applicants or 3.0 for merit/need and merit applicants.

Financial data A stipend is awarded (amount not specified); funds are paid in 2 equal installments.

Duration Up to 6 semesters, provided the need recipient maintains at least a 2.0 GPA and the need/merit or merit recipient maintains at least a 3.0 average.

Additional information This program is administered by the equal opportunity program at each of the 11 SUS 4-year institutions. Contact that office for further information.

Number awarded Several each year.

Deadline May of each year.

[236]
MINORITY NURSE MAGAZINE SCHOLARSHIP PROGRAM

Minority Nurse Magazine
Attn: Career Recruitment Media
211 West Wacker Drive, Suite 900
Chicago, IL 60606
(312) 525-3095   Fax: (312) 429-3336
E-mail: pam.chwedyk@careermedia.com
Web: www.minoritynurse.com

Purpose To provide financial assistance to members of minority groups who are working on a bachelor's degree in nursing.

Eligibility This program is open to minority nursing students currently enrolled in 1) the third or fourth year of an accredited B.S.N. program; 2) an accelerated program leading to a B.S.N. degree (e.g., R.N. to B.S.N., B.A. to B.S.N.); or 3) an accelerated master's entry nursing program (e.g., R.N. to M.S.N., B.S. to M.S.N.) Selection is based on academic excellence (GPA of 3.0 or higher), demonstrated commitment of service to the student's minority community, and financial need. U.S. citizenship of permanent resident status is required.

Financial data The stipends are $1,000 or $500.

Duration 1 year.

Additional information These scholarships were first offered in 2000. Winners are announced in the fall issue of *Minority Nurse* magazine

Number awarded 4 each year: 2 at $1,000 and 2 at $500.

Deadline June of each year.

[237]
MINORITY SCHOLARSHIP AWARD IN PHYSICAL THERAPY

American Physical Therapy Association
Attn: Department of Minority/International Affairs
1111 North Fairfax Street
Alexandria, VA 22314-1488
(703) 706-3144   Toll-free: (800) 999-APTA, ext. 3144
Fax: (703) 706-8519   TDD: (703) 683-6748
E-mail: min-intl@apta.org
Web: www.apta.org

Purpose To provide financial assistance to minority students who are interested in becoming a physical therapist or physical therapy assistant.

Eligibility This program is open to minority students who are in the final year of a professional physical therapy or physical therapy assistant education program. Applicants must submit an essay outlining their professional goals and minority service. U.S. citizenship or permanent resident status is required. Selection is based on 1) demonstrated evidence of contributions in the area of minority affairs and services with an emphasis on contributions made while enrolled in a physical therapy program; 2) potential to con-

tribute to the profession of physical therapy; and 3) scholastic achievement.

Financial data The stipend varies; recently, minimum awards were $1,500 for physical therapy students or $750 for physical therapy assistant students.

Duration 1 year.

Number awarded Varies each year; recently, 6 of these awards were granted to physical therapy students and 4 to physical therapy assistant students.

Deadline November of each year.

[238]
MINORU TAZUMA SCHOLARSHIP

Japanese American Citizens League-Seattle Chapter
P.O. Box 18558
Seattle, WA 98118-0558
(206) 622-4098   E-mail: email@jaclseattle.org
Web: www.jaclseattle.org

Purpose To provide financial assistance for college or graduate school to residents of the Seattle, Washington area who are of Japanese ancestry or from a family that is a member of the Japanese American Citizens League (JACL).

Eligibility This program is open to Seattle (Washington) area residents who are of Japanese ancestry or members of JACL families. Applicants must be entering their freshman year of college or graduate school. As part of their application, they must submit a list of extracurricular and community activities, 2 letters of recommendation, a list of awards or recognitions they have earned, and a 500-word essay on the legacy of the Japanese American community in American society.

Financial data The stipend is $1,000.

Duration 1 year.

Additional information Information is also available from May Namba, 2324 N.W. 94th Street, Seattle, WA 98117.

Number awarded 1 each year.

Deadline March of each year.

[239]
MINORU YASUI MEMORIAL SCHOLARSHIP AWARD

Asian American Journalists Association
Attn: Student Programs Coordinator
1182 Market Street, Suite 320
San Francisco, CA 94102
(415) 346-2051, ext. 102   Fax: (415) 346-6343
E-mail: brandons@aaja.org
Web: www.aaja.org

Purpose To provide financial assistance to male Asian American students who are members of the Asian American Journalists Association (AAJA) and interested in a career in broadcast journalism.

Eligibility This program is open to Asian American male high school seniors, undergraduates, or graduate students enrolled full time at an accredited college or university in a broadcast journalism program. Applicants must be AAJA members. Along with their application, they must submit a 500-word essay on their involvement or interest in the Asian American community and how, if they are awarded this scholarship, they would contribute to the field of journalism and/or media issues involving the Asian American and

Pacific Islander community. Selection is based on scholastic ability, commitment to journalism, sensitivity to Asian American and Pacific Islander issues as demonstrated by community involvement, journalistic ability, and financial need.

Financial data The stipend is $2,000.

Duration 1 year.

Additional information This scholarship honors Minoru Yasui, a civil rights advocate and attorney who was 1 of 3 Nisei to challenge the internment of Japanese Americans during World War II.

Number awarded 1 each year.

Deadline April of each year.

[240]
MITSUYUKI YONEMURA MEMORIAL SCHOLARSHIP

Japanese American Citizens League
Attn: National Scholarship Awards
1765 Sutter Street
San Francisco, CA 94115
(415) 921-5225   Fax: (415) 931-4671
E-mail: jacl@jacl.org
Web: www.jacl.org/scholarships.html

Purpose To provide financial assistance for college to student members of the Japanese American Citizens League (JACL) who are high school seniors.

Eligibility This program is open to JACL members who are high school seniors interested in attending a college, university, trade school, business college, or other institution of higher learning. Applicants must submit a statement describing their current level of involvement in the Japanese American community or Asian Pacific community and how they will continue their involvement in future years. Selection is based on academic record, extracurricular activities, and community involvement.

Financial data The stipend depends on the availability of funds but usually ranges from $1,000 to $5,000.

Duration 1 year; nonrenewable.

Additional information Applications must be submitted to the local JACL chapter.

Number awarded At least 1 each year.

Deadline February of each year.

[241]
MNACC STUDENT OF COLOR SCHOLARSHIP

Minnesota Association of Counselors of Color
Attn: Rudy Hernandez, Scholarship Co-Chair
University of Minnesota
128 Pleasant Street, S.E.
Minneapolis, MN 55455
(612) 626-1513   Toll-free: (800) 752-1000
E-mail: r-hern@umn.edu
Web: www.mnacc.org

Purpose To provide financial assistance to high school seniors of color in Minnesota who plan to attend college in the area.

Eligibility This program is open to seniors graduating from public and private high schools in Minnesota who are U.S. citizens or permanent residents of ethnic minority (African American/Black, American Indian or Alaskan Native,

Asian or Pacific Islander, Hispanic/Chicano-Latino) descent. Applicants must be planning to attend a 4-year college or university, a 2-year college, or a trade or technical college that is a member of the Minnesota Association of Counselors of Color (MnACC). Along with their application, they must submit an essay, up to 500 words in length, on 1 of the following topics: 1 of their most meaningful achievements, their future goals, or their involvement within their community.

Financial data The stipend is $500.

Duration 1 year; nonrenewable.

Additional information These scholarships may be used at approximately 45 MnACC colleges, universities, and technical schools in Minnesota, Michigan Technological University (Houghton), North Dakota State College of Science (Wahpeton), North Dakota State University (Fargo), the University of North Dakota (Grand Forks), the University of Wisconsin at River Falls, or the University of Wisconsin at Superior.

Number awarded Varies each year.

Deadline March of each year.

[242]
MONICA AND ADRIAN ARIMA SCHOLARSHIPS

Organization of Chinese Americans of San Mateo County
P.O. Box 218
San Mateo, CA 94401
(650) 342-8336
E-mail: scholarships@ocasanmateo.org
Web: www.ocasanmateo.org

Purpose To provide financial assistance for college to high school students of Chinese descent in San Mateo County, California.

Eligibility Seniors of Chinese descent graduating from high schools in San Mateo County, California are eligible to apply for these scholarships. They must be planning to attend an accredited postsecondary institution. Selection is based on outstanding leadership and extensive community involvement through high school activities, community organizations, or religious affiliations.

Financial data The stipend is at least $250 (and may be $500 or more).

Duration 1 year.

Additional information Applications for this program are available only through high school counselors.

Number awarded 4 each year.

Deadline April of each year.

[243]
MONSIGNOR PHILIP KENNEY SCHOLARSHIP FUND

New Hampshire Charitable Foundation
37 Pleasant Street
Concord, NH 03301-4005
(603) 225-6641   Toll-free: (800) 464-6641
Fax: (603) 225-1700   E-mail: info@nhcf.org
Web: www.nhcf.org

Purpose To provide financial assistance for college to minority and other students from New Hampshire.

Eligibility This program is open to New Hampshire students who are economically disadvantaged, with a preference for Hispanics and other minorities who are enrolled in undergraduate study. Nontraditional students, both full and part time, are encouraged to apply. At least 1 scholarship is designated for a minority student from Merrimack County.

Financial data The scholarship designated for a minority student from Merrimack has a stipend of $1,000. Other stipends vary.

Duration 1 year; recipients may reapply.

Number awarded Varies; in addition to the 1 scholarship for a minority student from Merrimack County, a total of $10,000 is available each year.

Deadline April of each year.

[244]
MONTEREY COUNTY HERALD/KNIGHT RIDDER MINORITY SCHOLARSHIP PROGRAM

Monterey County Herald
Attn: Human Resources Department
8 Upper Ragsdale Drive
P.O. Box 271
Monterey, CA 93942
(831) 646-4480   Fax: (831) 648-1153
E-mail: gvalenzuela@montereyherald.com
Web: www.montereyherald.com

Purpose To provide financial assistance to minority high school seniors in Monterey County, California who are interested in attending college to prepare for a career in the newspaper industry.

Eligibility This program is open to minority seniors graduating from high schools in Monterey County, California. Applicants must be planning to attend college to prepare for a career in the newspaper industry, including both journalism and business (e.g., advertising, circulation, computer science, marketing, production). Along with their application, they must submit a transcript of grades, SAT and/or ACT scores, 2 letters of recommendation, up to 5 writing samples (for journalism applicants), and an essay on why they want a career in the business of journalism.

Financial data A stipend is awarded (amount not specified).

Duration 1 year.

Additional information The recipients of these scholarships are entered into competition for the Knight Ridder Minority Scholarship Program of $40,000 over 4 years.

Number awarded 1 each year.

Deadline January of each year.

[245]
MORRIS SCHOLARSHIP

Morris Scholarship Fund
Attn: Scholarship Selection Committee
525 S.W. Fifth Street, Suite A
Des Moines, IA 50309-4501
(515) 282-8192   Fax: (515) 282-9117
E-mail: morris@assoc-mgmt.com
Web: www.morrisscholarship.org

Purpose To provide financial assistance to minority undergraduate, graduate, and law students in Iowa.

Eligibility This program is open to minority students (African Americans, Asian/Pacific Islanders, Hispanics, or Native Americans) who are interested in studying at a college, graduate school, or law school. Applicants must be either Iowa residents and high school graduates who are attending a college or university anywhere in the United States or non-Iowa residents who are attending a college or university in Iowa; preference is given to native Iowans who are attending an Iowa college or university. Along with their application, they must submit an essay of 250 to 500 words on why they are applying for this scholarship, activities or organizations in which they are involved, and their future plans. Selection is based on the essay, academic achievement (GPA of 2.5 or higher), community service, and financial need.

Financial data The stipend is $1,500 per year.

Duration 1 year; may be renewed.

Additional information This fund was established in 1978 in honor of the J.B. Morris family, who founded the Iowa branch of the National Association for the Advancement of Colored People and published the *Iowa Bystander* newspaper.

Number awarded Varies each year; recently, 11 of these scholarships were awarded.

Deadline January of each year.

[246]
MR. AND MRS. TAKASHI MORIUCHI SCHOLARSHIP

Japanese American Citizens League
Attn: National Scholarship Awards
1765 Sutter Street
San Francisco, CA 94115
(415) 921-5225   Fax: (415) 931-4671
E-mail: jacl@jacl.org
Web: www.jacl.org/scholarships.html

Purpose To provide financial assistance for college to student members of the Japanese American Citizens League (JACL) who are high school seniors.

Eligibility This program is open to JACL members who are high school seniors interested in attending a college, university, trade school, business college, or other institution of higher learning. Applicants must submit a statement describing their current level of involvement in the Japanese American community or Asian Pacific community and how they will continue their involvement in future years. Selection is based on academic record, extracurricular activities, and community involvement.

Financial data The stipend depends on the availability of funds but usually ranges from $1,000 to $5,000.

Duration 1 year; nonrenewable.

Additional information Applications must be submitted to the local JACL chapter.

Number awarded At least 1 each year.

Deadline February of each year.

[247]
MVSNA STUDENT SCHOLARSHIP

Missouri Vocational Special Need Association
c/o Shawn Brice
Missouri Department of Elementary and Secondary
  Education
Division of Career Education–Special Needs
205 Jefferson Street
P.O. Box 480
Jefferson City, MO 65102-0480
(573) 522-1775   Fax: (573) 526-4261
E-mail: Shawn.Brice@dese.mo.us
Web: dese.mo.gov

Purpose To provide financial assistance to vocational/technical students in Missouri who are members of designated special populations.

Eligibility This program is open to Missouri vocational/technical students who are members of special populations, defined as individuals who are academically or economically disadvantaged, have limited English proficiency, or are nontraditional, disabled, pregnant teenagers, single/teen parents, or foster children. Applicants must submit brief essays on their professional or career goals; the challenges they have had to overcome to reach their educational goals; how they have received help from their school, teachers, or community; and how the award will help them in pursuing continued education. Selection is based on realism of career goal, financial need, unusual circumstances, and personal references.

Financial data A stipend is awarded (amount not specified).

Duration 1 year.

Additional information Information is also available from Cindy Grizzell, MVSNA Awards Chair, Waynesville Technical Academy, 810 Roosevelt, Waynesville, MO 65583, (573) 774-6106, E-mail: cgrizzell@waynesville.k12.mo.us.

Number awarded 1 each year.

Deadline April of each year.

[248]
NAAAP-NY SCHOLARSHIP PROGRAM

National Association of Asian American Professionals-
  New York Chapter
Attn: Scholarship Committee
P.O. Box 772, Knickerbocker Station
New York, NY 10002
Toll-free: (866) 841-9139, ext. 3037
E-mail: naaapny@naaapny.org
Web: www.naaapny.org/jfk/scholarship.asp

Purpose To provide financial assistance for college to Asian American high school seniors in the greater New York metropolitan area.

Eligibility This program is open to Asian Americans in their senior year at a public, private, or parochial high school in the New York metropolitan area who have demonstrated outstanding academic achievement and a commitment to community service. Applicants must be U.S. citizens or permanent residents who plan to attend an accredited 4-year college or university. Selection is based on academic achievement, essays, community service, and financial need. Finalists are interviewed.

Financial data The stipend is $2,500. Funds may be used to pay for tuition, room and board, books, and other costs of education.

Duration 1 year; nonrenewable.

Additional information This program was established in 2001. The New York metropolitan area is defined to include New York City and Nassau, Putnam, Rockland, Suffolk, and Westchester counties in New York; Bergen, Essex, Hudson, Middlesex, Passaic, and Union counties in New Jersey; and Fairfield County in Connecticut.

Number awarded Varies each year; recently, 2 of these scholarships were awarded.

Deadline January of each year.

[249]
NAAAP-SEATTLE CHAPTER SCHOLARSHIPS

National Association of Asian American Professionals-
  Seattle Chapter
Attn: Scholarship Committee
P.O. Box 14344, International Station
Seattle, WA 98104
(425) 450-4882   E-mail: pr@naaapseattle.org
Web: seattle.naaap.org

Purpose To provide financial assistance for college to Asian American high school seniors from King County, Washington.

Eligibility This program is open to Asian American seniors at high schools in King County, Washington. Applicants must provide information on their academics, community involvement, activities, work experience, educational goals, and financial need. They must also submit the names of 2 references and a 2-page essay on how they could promote or encourage the development of more Asian American leaders.

Financial data Stipends are $2,000 or $1,000 per year.

Duration 1 year.

Number awarded 2 each year: 1 at $2,000 and 1 at $1,000.

Deadline October of each year.

[250]
NAAPAE SCHOLARSHIPS

National Association for Asian and Pacific American
  Education
P.O. Box 3366
Daley City, CA 94015-3366
E-mail: jlu69@jps.net

Purpose To provide financial assistance for college to high school seniors and college students of Asian or Pacific Islander descent.

Eligibility This program is open to high school seniors and college juniors and seniors who 1) are of Asian or Pacific Islander descent; 2) are actively involved in extracurricular activities; 3) have outstanding academic records; and 4) are young leaders who show concern and commitment to Asian and Pacific communities. Applicants must submit high school and/or college transcripts, 2 letters of recommendation, a 50-word statement of career goals, a 300-word essay on how to end hate crime or how they can best serve the Asian Pacific community, and a list of their most important school and/or community activities and services over the past 2 years. Financial need is not considered in the selection process.

Financial data For high school seniors, the stipend is $500; for college juniors and seniors, the stipend is $1,000.

Duration 1 year.

Additional information Information is also available from Clara Park, NAAPAE Scholarship Committee, California State University at Northridge, College of Education, 18111 Nordhoff Street, Northridge, CA 91330-8265, (818) 677-2500, E-mail: clara.park@csun.edu.

Number awarded 4 of these scholarships are awarded each year: 2 to high school seniors and 2 to college juniors and seniors.

Deadline January of each year.

[251]
NARA BANK SCHOLARSHIPS

Nara Bank Scholarship Foundation
c/o Nara Bancorp, Inc.
3701 Wilshire Boulevard, Suite 220
Los Angeles, CA 90010
(213) 389-2000   Fax: (213) 639-1717
Web: www.narabank.com

Purpose To provide financial assistance for college to high school seniors (especially those of Korean heritage) from California, New York City, and New Jersey.

Eligibility This program is open to seniors, particularly those of Korean heritage, graduating from high schools in communities served by a Nara Bank (Los Angeles, Orange, Alameda, and Santa Clara counties in California; Queens and New York counties in New York; and New Jersey). Applicants must be U.S. citizens or permanent residents, have a family income that is less than 80% of their area's median income, plan to attend an accredited 4-year college or university, and have a GPA of 3.3 or higher. Selection is based on financial need, academic excellence, and leadership in the community.

Financial data The stipend is $1,000 per year.

Duration 1 year; nonrenewable.

Additional information The sponsor works closely with the Korean Youth Community Center (KYCC) to promote this program. Officials of KYCC serve as judges on the selection committee. This program began in 2001.

Number awarded Up to 100 each year.

Deadline December of each year.

[252]
NATIONAL TONGAN AMERICAN SOCIETY SCHOLARSHIPS

National Tongan American Society
Attn: Director
2480 South Main Street, Suite 108
Salt Lake City, UT 84115
(801) 467-8712
Web: www.planet-tonga.com/NTAS/education.htm

Purpose To provide financial assistance to undergraduate and graduate students of Tongan background.

Eligibility Applicants must be of Tongan background and enrolled full time as an undergraduate or graduate student. They must submit a completed application, a college and/or high school transcript, a Student Aid Report (SAR), and 2

letters of recommendation. Selection is based on GPA (10 points), extracurricular activities (25 points), statement of goals (10 points), letters of recommendation (5 points), financial need (25 points), and special considerations (e.g., single parent home, disability, etc., 25 points).

Financial data Stipends are awarded (amounts not specified).

Duration 1 year.

Number awarded Several each year.

Deadline May of each year.

[253]
NAVESNP/PINEY MOUNTAIN PRESS STUDENT AWARD

National Association of Vocational Education Special
    Needs Personnel
c/o Marjorie Eckman, Awards Chair
719 Gulf Lab Road
Cheswick, PA 15024
(412) 323-3970   E-mail: ME50@aol.com
Web: www.specialpopulations.org/award.htm

Purpose To provide financial assistance to vocational/technical students who are members of a special population.

Eligibility This program is open to vocational/technical students who are members of a special population, defined to include those who are academically or economically disadvantaged, limited English proficient, nontraditional, disabled, pregnant teenagers, single/teen parents, or foster children. Applicants must demonstrate how they have overcome barriers to achieve their highest potential for success. Selection is based on their choice of a realistic career goal, financial need, unusual circumstances, and letters of reference.

Financial data The stipend is $1,000.

Duration 1 year.

Additional information Piney Mountain Press supports half the stipend.

Number awarded 1 each year.

Deadline October of each year.

[254]
NELLIE STONE JOHNSON SCHOLARSHIP

Minnesota State University Student Association
Attn: Scholarship
108 Como Avenue
St. Paul, MN 55103-1820
(651) 224-1518   Fax: (651) 224-9753
E-mail: nsj@msusa.net
Web: www.msusa.net/nellie_stjo.html

Purpose To provide financial assistance to racial minority union members and their families who are interested in working on an undergraduate or graduate degree at a Minnesota state college or university.

Eligibility This program is open to students in 2-year, undergraduate, and graduate programs at a Minnesota state university, community college, or consolidated campus. Applicants must be a minority (Asian, American Indian, Alaska Native, Black/African American, Hispanic/Latino, Native Hawaiian, or Pacific Islander) union member or the child, grandchild, or spouse of a minority union member.

They must submit a 2-page statement about their background, educational goals, career goals, and other activities that may impact the cause of human or civil rights. Awards may be reserved for women. Preference is given to Minnesota residents. A personal or telephone interview may be required.

Financial data   Stipends range from $500 to $2,000.

Duration   1 year; may be renewed up to 3 additional years for student working on a bachelor's degree, 1 additional year for students working on a master's degree, or 1 additional year for students in a community or technical college program.

Number awarded   1 or more each year. If multiple awards are made, at least 1 recipient must be female.

Deadline   March of each year.

[255]
NETIP-NY SCHOLARSHIP

Network of Indian Professionals-New York
P.O. Box 3165
New York, NY 10163
(212) 969-6221   E-mail: cr@netip-ny.org
Web: www.kintera.org/htmlcontent.asp?cid=32140

Purpose   To provide financial assistance for college to South Asian high school students in New York.

Eligibility   South Asian high school students in New York who are planning to attend an accredited college are eligible to apply for this support.

Financial data   Stipends are at least $1,000.

Duration   1 year.

Additional information   This scholarship was first awarded in 1998.

Number awarded   1 or more each year.

[256]
NEW YORK CHAPTER HIGH SCHOOL
SCHOLARSHIP PROGRAM

Asian American Journalists Association-New York
   Chapter
c/o Charles Choi, Scholarship Coordinator
21-20 36th Street, First Floor
Astoria, NY 11105
(917) 328-7810   E-mail: aajanyc@hotmail.com
Web: chapters.aaja.org/NewYork/applications.shtml

Purpose   To provide financial assistance to Asian American high school seniors from New York interested in a career in journalism.

Eligibility   This program is open to Asian American high school seniors from the New York City area who will be enrolled in an accredited college or university in the next academic year. Applicants need not be journalism majors, but they must show a serious interest in a career in journalism. Along with their application, they must submit 4 essays of 200 words or less: how the scholarship will help them to pursue their journalism studies, their career goals, their participation in the Asian American Journalists Association (AAJA) or other Asian American activities in school or in their community, and their financial need. Selection is based on interest in journalism, writing or other journalism skills, participation in AAJA, other participation in Asian American issues, letters of recommendation, and financial need.

Financial data   Stipends are $3,000 or $1,000.

Duration   1 year; nonrenewable.

Additional information   Scholarship recipients are expected to give back to the organization through future volunteer activity.

Number awarded   3 each year: 1 at $3,000 and 2 at $1,000.

Deadline   April of each year.

[257]
NEW YORK UNIVERSITY URBAN JOURNALISM
WORKSHOP SCHOLARSHIP

New York University
Department of Journalism and Mass Communication
Attn: Urban Journalism Workshop
10 Washington Place
New York, NY 10003-6636
(212) 998-7980   Fax: (212) 995-4148
E-mail: pn1@nyu.edu
Web: journalism.nyu.edu/ujw

Purpose   To provide financial assistance for college to minority high school students from the New York City metropolitan area who participate in a summer journalism workshop.

Eligibility   This program is open to minority high school juniors and seniors from New York City, Westchester County, New Jersey, and Connecticut. Applicants must be interested in participating in a journalism workshop that includes exercises and lectures in news and feature writing taught by faculty of New York University (NYU) and visiting professionals; interviews and work sessions with reporters and editors from major New York newspapers and magazines; field trips to newsrooms and news sources; assignments for interviewing New York City newsmakers; writing, editing, and producing an 8-page newspaper; and full room and board at an NYU. They must submit an essay of 500 to 750 words on their interest in attending the workshop and preparing for a career in journalism. At the end of the workshop, the participant judged most outstanding receives this scholarship.

Financial data   The stipend is $1,000.

Duration   The workshop lasts 10 days, in July. The scholarship is for 1 year.

Additional information   Funding for the scholarship is provided by the Dow Jones Newspaper Fund.

Number awarded   20 students participate in the workshop; 1 of them receives the scholarship.

Deadline   April of each year.

[258]
NEWSROOM DIVERSITY SCHOLARSHIP

Society of Professional Journalists-Kansas Professional Chapter
c/o Lori O'Toole Buselt, Scholarship Chair
The Wichita Eagle
P.O. Box 820
Wichita, KS 67201-0820
(316) 268-6327   Fax: (316) 268-6627
E-mail: kansas@spj.org
Web: www.spj.org/kansas/scholarship.htm

Purpose To provide financial assistance to minority students at colleges and universities in Kansas who are interested in a career in journalism.

Eligibility This program is open to members of racial minority groups who are juniors and seniors at colleges and universities in Kansas. Sophomores may apply, designating the award for their junior year. Applicants do not have to be journalism or communication majors, but they must demonstrate a strong and sincere interest in print journalism, broadcast journalism, or photojournalism. They must have a GPA of 2.5 or higher and participate in outside journalism-related activities demonstrated by involvement in student or trade organizations and/or student or other news organizations or publications. Along with their application, they must submit 4 to 6 examples of their best work (clips or stories, copies of photographs, tapes or transcripts of broadcasts). Selection is based on the quality of work submitted, academic standing, references, and financial need.

Financial data The stipend is $1,000.

Duration 1 year.

Number awarded 1 each year.

Deadline March of each year.

[259]
NISEI VETERANS' COMMITTEE SCHOLARSHIP PROGRAM

Nisei Veterans' Committee, Inc.
Attn: Debbie McQuilken
6336 N.E. 138th Place
Seattle, WA 98144
(206) 721-5359   E-mail: debbiemcqu@aol.com

Purpose To provide financial assistance for college or graduate school to Japanese Americans and others in Seattle who are related to members of the Nisei Veterans' Committee (NVC).

Eligibility This program is open to Japanese Americans and others who are direct descendants or relatives of a member of the Nisei Veterans' Committee or its Women's Auxiliary. The Nisei Veterans' Committee Scholarship and the Women's Auxiliary Scholarship are limited to high school seniors. The Shiro Kashino Memorial Scholarships are also open to college and graduate students. Applicants must be residents of the Seattle area. Selection is based on leadership ability, activity in the Japanese American community, volunteer service to the NVC, pride in their Japanese American heritage, personality, athletic excellence, academic standards, and humanitarian qualities.

Financial data The stipend is normally $1,500 per year.

Duration 1 year.

Number awarded 6 each year, including 4 designated as Shiro Kashino Memorial Scholarships.

Deadline January of each year.

[260]
NMJGSA SCHOLARSHIPS

National Minority Junior Golf Scholarship Association
Attn: Scholarship Committee
4950 East Thomas Road
Phoenix, AZ 85018
(602) 258-7851   Fax: (602) 258-3412
E-mail: sdean@nmjgsa.org
Web: www.nmjgsa.org/scholarships.html

Purpose To provide financial assistance to minority high school seniors and undergraduate students who excel at golf.

Eligibility This program is open to minority high school seniors and undergraduate students already enrolled in college. Applicants are asked to write a 500-word essay on this question: "One of the principal goals of education and golf is fostering ways for people to respect and get along with individuals who think, dress, look, and act differently. How might you make this goal a reality?" Selection is based on academic achievement; personal recommendations; participation in golf, school, and community activities; and financial need.

Financial data Stipends range from 1-time awards of $1,000 to 4-year awards of $6,000 per year. Funds are paid directly to the recipient's college.

Duration 1 year or longer.

Additional information This program was established in 1984. Support is provided by the Jackie Robinson Foundation, PGA of America, Anheuser-Busch, the Tiger Woods Foundation, and other cooperating organizations.

Number awarded Varies; generally 80 or more each year.

Deadline April of each year.

[261]
NNOA/BOOZ-ALLEN & HAMILTON SCHOLARSHIP

National Naval Officers Association-Washington, D.C. Chapter
Attn: Scholarship Program
9805 Fox Run Drive
Clinton, MD 20735-3087
(202) 874-4994   E-mail: willie.evans@occ.treas.gov
Web: www.dcnnoa.org

Purpose To provide financial assistance to minority high school seniors from the Washington, D.C. area who are interested in majoring in computer sciences in college.

Eligibility This program is open to minority seniors at high schools in the Washington, D.C. metropolitan area who plan to enroll full time in a computer science program at an accredited 2-year or 4-year college or university. Applicants must have a GPA of 3.0 or higher and be U.S. citizens or permanent residents. Selection is based on academic achievement, community involvement, interpersonal and leadership skills, creativity, drive, and maturity.

Financial data The stipend is $5,000 per year.

Duration 1 year; nonrenewable.

Additional information Recipients are not required to join or affiliate with the military in any way. This program is sponsored by Booz-Allen & Hamilton, and recipients have an option to work with the firm as a summer intern.

Number awarded 1 each year.
Deadline March of each year.

[262]
NOBUKO R. KODAMA FONG MEMORIAL SCHOLARSHIP

Japanese American Citizens League
Attn: National Scholarship Awards
1765 Sutter Street
San Francisco, CA 94115
(415) 921-5225   Fax: (415) 931-4671
E-mail: jacl@jacl.org
Web: www.jacl.org/scholarships.html

Purpose To provide financial assistance for college to student members of the Japanese American Citizens League (JACL), particularly those in the Pacific Northwest.
Eligibility This program is open to JACL members who are currently enrolled or planning to reenter a college, university, trade school, business college, or other institution of higher learning. Applicants must submit a statement describing their current level of involvement in the Japanese American community or Asian Pacific community and how they will continue their involvement in future years. Selection is based on academic record, extracurricular activities, financial need, and community involvement. Preference is given to residents of the Pacific Northwest District.
Financial data The stipend depends on the availability of funds but usually ranges from $1,000 to $5,000.
Duration 1 year; nonrenewable.
Additional information Applications must be submitted to the JACL National Scholarship Program, c/o San Diego JACL Chapter, 1031 25th Street, San Diego, CA 92102.
Number awarded 1 each year.
Deadline March of each year.

[263]
NORTHEASTERN REGION KOREAN AMERICAN SCHOLARSHIPS

Korean American Scholarship Foundation
NorthEastern Region
c/o William Kim, Scholarship Committee Chair
51 West Overlook
Port Washington, NY 11050
(516) 883-1142   Fax: (516) 883-1964
E-mail: wkim@alson.com
Web: www.kasf.org

Purpose To provide financial assistance to Korean American undergraduate and graduate students who attend school in the northeastern states.
Eligibility This program is open to Korean American students who are currently enrolled in a college or university in a northeastern state as a full-time undergraduate or graduate student. Applicants may reside anywhere in the United States as long as they attend school in the northeastern region: Connecticut, Maine, Massachusetts, New Hampshire, New Jersey, New York, Rhode Island, and Vermont. Selection is based on academic achievement, school activities, community service, and financial need.
Financial data Stipends range from $1,000 to $2,000.
Duration 1 year; renewable.

Number awarded Varies each year; recently, 60 of these scholarships were awarded
Deadline June of each year.

[264]
NORTHWEST JOURNALISTS OF COLOR SCHOLARSHIP AWARDS

Northwest Journalists of Color
c/o Michael Ko
The Seattle Times
1120 John Street
Seattle, WA 98109
(206) 515-5653   E-mail: mko@aajaseattle.org
Web: www.aajaseattle.org

Purpose To provide financial assistance to minority students from Washington state who are interested in careers in journalism.
Eligibility These scholarships are open to minority (Asian American, African American, Native American, and Latino) students from Washington state who are planning a career in broadcast, photo, or print journalism. Applicants may be high school seniors or college undergraduates who are residents of Washington state, although they may attend college anywhere in the country. Along with their application, they must submit 1) a brief essay about themselves, including why they want to be a journalist, challenges they foresee, how they think they can contribute to the profession, and the influence their ethnic heritage might have on their perspective as a working journalist; 2) the kinds of experience they are seeking from this fellowship and why they are a good candidate for it; 3) up to 3 work samples; 4) reference letters; and 5) documentation of financial need.
Financial data Stipends range up to $1,000.
Duration 1 year; may be renewed.
Additional information This program, established in 1986, is sponsored by the Seattle chapters of the Asian American Journalists Association, the Native American Journalists Association, the National Association of Black Journalists, and the Latino Media Association. It includes the Walt and Milly Woodward Memorial Scholarship donated by the Western Washington Chapter of the Society of Professional Journalists. Other funding is provided by KING/5 Television, the *Seattle Post-Intelligencer*, and the *Seattle Times*.
Number awarded Varies each year; recently, 11 of these scholarships were awarded.
Deadline April of each year.

[265]
NSRCF SCHOLARSHIPS

Nisei Student Relocation Commemorative Fund, Inc.
19 Scenic Drive
Portland, CT 06480
E-mail: info@nsrcfund.org
Web: www.nsrcfund.org

Purpose To provide financial assistance for college to high school seniors in specific geographic areas who are southeast Asian refugees.
Eligibility Each year, this program operates in a different city or state. Within the selected area, graduating high school seniors are eligible to apply if they are southeast

Asian refugees of Cambodian, Hmong, Laotian, or Vietnamese ancestry. Applicants must have a high school GPA of 2.5 or higher and be planning to attend an accredited 2-year or 4-year college or university. Selection is based on academic record, references, extracurricular activities, work experience, financial need, and an essay on educational and career goals. Finalists may be interviewed.

Financial data Recently, stipends ranged from $500 to $1,000.

Duration 1 year.

Additional information The 2006 program is scheduled for the Phoenix/Tempe area of Arizona.

Number awarded Varies each year; recently, this program awarded 12 scholarships to students in the Oregon/Clark County, Washington area and 24 scholarships to students in Michigan.

Deadline March of each year.

[266]
NYMRAD MINORITY SCHOLARSHIPS

New York Market Radio
261 Madison Avenue, 23rd Floor
New York, NY 10016
(646) 254-4493　　　　　　Fax: (646) 254-4498
E-mail: db@nymrad.org
Web: www.nymrad.org/scholarship.html

Purpose To provide financial assistance and work experience to upper-division minority students in the New York City area who are majoring in communications.

Eligibility Applicants must be members of a minority group; be a declared communications major, with an expressed interest in pursuing a radio career; have a GPA of 3.0 or higher; permanently reside in the New York City metropolitan area; and be juniors or seniors at colleges in the New York City area.

Financial data The stipend is $3,000. Funds are sent to the recipient's school.

Duration 1 year.

Additional information New York Market Radio (NYMRAD) is the voice of the radio industry in the New York market. Its members include major radio stations, station representatives, and radio networks. Recipients must accept a paid internship with the sponsor.

Number awarded 1 each year.

Deadline May of each year.

[267]
OAHU COUNCIL OF FILIPINO CATHOLIC CLUBS SCHOLARSHIP PROGRAM

Oahu Council of Filipino Catholic Clubs
Attn: Josie Rayray, Information and Education
　　Committee
47-464 Poomau Street
Kaneohe, HI 96744
(808) 266-9893

Purpose To provide financial assistance for high school, college, or seminary to descendants of members of the Oahu Council of Filipino Catholic Clubs.

Eligibility This program is open to high school, college, and seminary students from Hawaii whose parents or grandparents have been members of the organization for at

least 1 year. Applicants must be 1) Filipino Catholics attending Catholic colleges or high schools or non-Catholic colleges, or 2) Filipino students attending a seminary or convent. They must have a GPA of 3.0 or higher and be able to demonstrate financial need. Along with their application, they must submit an essay about their significant experiences, accomplishments, future goals, and service to school, church, and community. An interview is required.

Financial data A stipend is awarded (amount not specified).

Duration 1 year.

Number awarded Several each year.

Deadline July of each year.

[268]
OCA-DFW ESSAY CONTEST

Organization of Chinese Americans, Inc.-Dallas/Fort
　　Worth Chapter
Attn: Executive Vice-president
P.O. Box 1281
Rockwall, TX 75087
(972) 577-6538　　　　　　E-mail: info@ocadfw.org
Web: www.ocadfw.org

Purpose To recognize and reward (with college scholarships) high school students in the Dallas-Fort Worth Metroplex area who submit outstanding essays on a topic of interest to the Dallas/Fort Worth Chapter of the Organization of Chinese Americans (OCA-DFW).

Eligibility This competition is open to juniors and seniors at public and private high schools in the Metroplex area of Dallas and Fort Worth, Texas. Applicants must submit an essay, up to 500 words in length, on a topic that changes annually but reflects the concerns of OCA-DFW; a recent topic was "What it means to be an American."

Financial data Prizes are $1,500, $750, and $500 scholarships.

Duration The competition is held annually.

Additional information This competition was first held in 2004. The Dallas-Fort Worth Metroplex area is officially defined to include Collin, Dallas, Denton, Ellis, Henderson, Hood, Hunt, Johnson, Kaufman, Parker, Rockwall, and Tarrant counties in Texas.

Number awarded 6 each year: 1 at $1,500, 1 at $750, and 4 at $500.

Deadline March of each year.

[269]
OCA/AVON SCHOLARSHIPS

Organization of Chinese Americans, Inc.
1001 Connecticut Avenue, N.W., Suite 601
Washington, DC 20036
(202) 223-5500　　　　　　Fax: (202) 296-0540
E-mail: oca@ocanatl.org
Web: www.ocanatl.org

Purpose To provide financial assistance to Asian Pacific American women entering their first year at a 2-year or 4-year college.

Eligibility This program is open to Asian Pacific American women (including east Asian Americans, Filipino Americans, Pacific Islander Americans, south Asian Americans, and southeast Asian Americans) who are entering their first year of college. Applicants must be U.S. citizens or permanent residents who have earned a GPA of 3.0 or higher in high school. Selection is based on academic achievement, community service, and financial need.

Financial data The stipend is $2,000.

Duration 1 year.

Additional information This program, established in 1995, is administered by the Organization of Chinese Americans (OCA), Inc. and funded by the Avon Foundation. Recipients must write a paper by the end of their freshman year describing their college experience as an Asian Pacific American woman.

Number awarded 15 each year.

Deadline April of each year.

[270]
OCA/AXA ACHIEVEMENT SCHOLARSHIPS

Organization of Chinese Americans, Inc.
1001 Connecticut Avenue, N.W., Suite 601
Washington, DC 20036
(202) 223-5500   Fax: (202) 296-0540
E-mail: oca@ocanatl.org
Web: www.ocanatl.org

Purpose To provide financial assistance for college to Asian Pacific Americans who are entering their first year of college and can demonstrate academic merit.

Eligibility This program is open to Asian Pacific American students entering their first year of college, university, or community college in the following fall. Applicants must be able to demonstrate academic achievement, leadership ability, and community service. They must have a cumulative GPA of 3.0 or higher and be a U.S. citizen or permanent resident.

Financial data The stipend is $2,000.

Duration 1 year.

Additional information This program, established in 2004, is funded by the AXA Foundation and administered by the Organization of Chinese Americans (OCA). Asian Pacific Americans are defined to include east Asian Americans, Filipino Americans, Pacific Islander Americans, south Asian Americans, and southeast Asian Americans.

Number awarded 6 each year.

Deadline April of each year.

[271]
OCA/SYSCO SCHOLARSHIPS

Organization of Chinese Americans, Inc.
1001 Connecticut Avenue, N.W., Suite 601
Washington, DC 20036
(202) 223-5500   Fax: (202) 296-0540
E-mail: oca@ocanatl.org
Web: www.ocanatl.org

Purpose To provide financial assistance for college to Asian Pacific Americans who are entering their first year of college and can demonstrate financial need.

Eligibility This program is open to Asian Pacific American students entering their first year of college, university, or community college in the following fall. Applicants must be able to demonstrate financial need, have a cumulative GPA of 3.0 or higher, and be a U.S. citizen or permanent resident.

Financial data The stipend is $2,000.

Duration 1 year.

Additional information This program, established in 2004, is funded by SYSCO Corporation and administered by the Organization of Chinese Americans (OCA). Asian Pacific Americans are defined to include east Asian Americans, Filipino Americans, Pacific Islander Americans, south Asian Americans, and southeast Asian Americans.

Number awarded 6 each year.

Deadline April of each year.

[272]
OCA/VERIZON SCHOLARSHIPS

Organization of Chinese Americans, Inc.
1001 Connecticut Avenue, N.W., Suite 601
Washington, DC 20036
(202) 223-5500   Fax: (202) 296-0540
E-mail: oca@ocanatl.org
Web: www.ocanatl.org

Purpose To provide financial assistance for college to Asian Pacific Americans who are entering their first year of college and have significant financial need.

Eligibility This program is open to Asian Pacific American students entering their first year of college, university, or community college in the following fall. Applicants must be able to demonstrate significant financial need, have a cumulative GPA of 3.0 or higher, and be a U.S. citizen or permanent resident.

Financial data The stipend is $2,000.

Duration 1 year.

Additional information This program, established in 2002, is funded by the Verizon Foundation and administered by the Organization of Chinese Americans (OCA). Asian Pacific Americans are defined to include east Asian Americans, Filipino Americans, Pacific Islander Americans, south Asian Americans, and southeast Asian Americans.

Number awarded 25 each year.

Deadline April of each year.

[273]
OHIO NEWSPAPERS FOUNDATION MINORITY SCHOLARSHIPS

Ohio Newspapers Foundation
1335 Dublin Road, Suite 216-B
Columbus, OH 43215-7038
(614) 486-6677   Fax: (614) 486-4940
E-mail: kpouliot@ohionews.org
Web: www.ohionews.org/scholarships.html

Purpose To provide financial assistance for college to minority high school seniors in Ohio planning to prepare for a career in journalism.

Eligibility This program is open to high school seniors in Ohio who are members of minority groups (African American, Hispanic, Asian American, or American Indian) and planning to prepare for a career in newspaper journalism. Applicants must have a high school GPA of 2.5 or higher and demonstrate writing ability in an autobiography of 750 to 1,000 words that describes their academic and career interests, awards, extracurricular activities, and journalism-related activities.

Financial data The stipend is $1,500.

Duration 1 year; nonrenewable.

Additional information This program was established in 1990.

Number awarded 3 each year.

Deadline March of each year.

[274]
ORGANIZATION OF CHINESE AMERICANS OF SAN MATEO COUNTY SCHOLARSHIP

Organization of Chinese Americans of San Mateo
  County
P.O. Box 218
San Mateo, CA 94401
(650) 342-8336
E-mail: scholarships@ocasanmateo.org
Web: www.ocasanmateo.org

Purpose To provide financial assistance for college to high school students of Chinese descent in San Mateo County, California.

Eligibility Seniors of Chinese descent graduating from high schools in San Mateo County, California with a minimum GPA of 3.0 are eligible to apply for these scholarships. They must be planning to attend an accredited postsecondary institution. Selection is based on good citizenship, extracurricular activities, community service, and active membership in Young OCA.

Financial data The stipend is $1,000.

Duration 1 year.

Additional information Applications for this program are available only through high school counselors.

Number awarded 1 each year.

Deadline April of each year.

[275]
PAGE EDUCATION FOUNDATION GRANTS

Page Education Foundation
P.O. Box 581254
Minneapolis, MN 55458-1254
(612) 332-0406   E-mail: info@page-ed.org
Web: www.page-ed.org

Purpose To provide funding for college to students of color in Minnesota.

Eligibility This program is open to students of color who are graduating from high school in Minnesota and planning to attend a postsecondary school in the state. Applicants must submit an essay of 400 to 500 words that deals with why they believe education is important, their plans for the future, and the service-to-children project they would like to complete in the coming school year. Selection is based on the essay, 3 letters of recommendation, and financial need.

Financial data Stipends range from $900 to $2,500 per year.

Duration 1 year; may be renewed up to 3 additional years.

Additional information This program was founded in 1988 by Alan Page, a former football player for the Minnesota Vikings. While attending college, the Page Scholars fulfill a service-to-children contract that brings them into contact with K-8 grade school students of color.

Number awarded Varies each year; recently, 570 Page Scholars were enrolled, of whom 61% were African Ameri-

can, 27% Asian American, 11% Chicano/Latino, and 1% American Indian.

Deadline April of each year.

[276]
PATRICIA AND GAIL ISHIMOTO MEMORIAL SCHOLARSHIP

Japanese American Citizens League
Attn: National Scholarship Awards
1765 Sutter Street
San Francisco, CA 94115
(415) 921-5225   Fax: (415) 931-4671
E-mail: jacl@jacl.org
Web: www.jacl.org/scholarships.html

Purpose To provide financial assistance for college to student members of the Japanese American Citizens League (JACL) who are high school seniors.

Eligibility This program is open to JACL members who are high school seniors interested in attending a college, university, trade school, business college, or other institution of higher learning. Applicants must submit a statement describing their current level of involvement in the Japanese American community or Asian Pacific community and how they will continue their involvement in future years. Selection is based on academic record, extracurricular activities, and community involvement.

Financial data The stipend depends on the availability of funds but usually ranges from $1,000 to $5,000.

Duration 1 year; nonrenewable.

Additional information Applications must be submitted to the local JACL chapter.

Number awarded At least 1 each year.

Deadline February of each year.

[277]
PDEF MICKEY WILLIAMS MINORITY STUDENT SCHOLARSHIP

Society of Nuclear Medicine
Attn: Committee on Awards
1850 Samuel Morse Drive
Reston, VA 20190-5316
(703) 708-9000, ext. 1255   Fax: (703) 708-9020
E-mail: grantinfo@snm.org
Web: www.snm.org

Purpose To provide financial support to minority students working on an associate or bachelor's degree in nuclear medicine technology.

Eligibility This program is open to students accepted or enrolled in a baccalaureate or associate degree program in nuclear medicine technology. Applicants must be members of a minority group: African American, Native American (including American Indian, Eskimo, Hawaiian, and Samoan), Hispanic American, Asian American, or Pacific Islander. They must have a cumulative GPA of 2.5 or higher and be able to demonstrate financial need. U.S. citizenship or permanent resident status is required.

Financial data The stipend is $5,000.

Duration 1 year; may be renewed for 1 additional year.

Additional information This program is supported by corporate sponsors of the Professional Development and

Education Fund (PDEF) of the Society of Nuclear Medicine Technologist Section

Number awarded 1 each year.

Deadline October of each year.

[278]
PETALUMA JAPANESE SUNDAY SCHOOL SCHOLARSHIPS

Japanese American Citizens League-Sonoma County Chapter
Attn: Scholarship Committee
P.O. Box 1915
Santa Rosa, CA 95402
E-mail: info@sonomacojacl.org
Web: www.sonomacojacl.org/Pages/scholars.htm

Purpose To provide financial assistance for college to high school seniors in Sonoma County, California who are of Japanese ancestry.

Eligibility This program is open to graduating high school seniors in Sonoma County, California who are planning to attend a college, university, or vocational/technical school. Applicants must be of Japanese ancestry. Along with their application, they must submit a 250-word personal statement on their personality, why they have selected their major, why they desire to attend the college(s) they have applied to, and their view of themselves and the world in which they live. Their statement should emphasize their Japanese ancestry and/or their connection with the Asian/Japanese American community and how it has affected or impacted who they are as well as their personal goals. For 1 of the scholarships, applicants must reside in and attend school in the Rohnert Park/Cotati or Petaluma High School District. Financial need is considered in case of a tie.

Financial data A stipend is awarded (amount not specified).

Duration 1 year.

Additional information Information is also available from Margaret E. Wallman, 1720 Mariposa Drive, Santa Rosa, CA 95405, (707) 544-9368.

Number awarded 3 each year: 1 reserved for a student in the Rohnert Park/Cotati or Petaluma High School District and 2 for any qualifying resident of Sonoma County.

Deadline February of each year.

[279]
PFIZER/UNCF CORPORATE SCHOLARS PROGRAM

United Negro College Fund
Attn: Corporate Scholars Program
P.O. Box 1435
Alexandria, VA 22313-9998
Toll-free: (866) 671-7237 E-mail: internship@uncf.org
Web: www.uncf.org/internships/index.asp

Purpose To provide financial assistance and work experience to minority undergraduate and graduate students majoring in designated fields and interested in an internship at a Pfizer facility.

Eligibility This program is open to sophomores, juniors, graduate students, and first-year law students who are African American, Hispanic American, Asian/Pacific Islander American, or American Indian/Alaskan Native. Applicants

must have a GPA of 3.0 or higher and be enrolled at an institution that is a member of the United Negro College Fund (UNCF) or at another targeted college or university. They must be working on 1) a bachelor's degree in animal science, business, chemistry (organic or analytical), human resources, logistics, microbiology, organizational development, operations management, pre-veterinary medicine, or supply chain management; 2) a master's degree in chemistry (organic or analytical), finance, human resources, or organizational development; or 3) a law degree. Eligibility is limited to U.S. citizens, permanent residents, asylees, refugees, and lawful temporary residents. Along with their application, they must submit a 1-page essay about themselves and their career goals, including information about their interest in Pfizer (the program's sponsor), their personal background, and any particular challenges they have faced.

Financial data The program provides an internship stipend of up to $5,000, housing accommodations near Pfizer Corporate facilities, and (based on successful internship performance) a $15,000 scholarship.

Duration 8 to 10 weeks for the internship; 1 year for the scholarship.

Additional information Opportunities for first-year law students include the summer internship only.

Number awarded Varies each year.

Deadline January of each year.

[280]
PHI TAU PHI EAST AMERICAN CHAPTER UNDERGRADUATE SCHOLARSHIP AWARDS

Phi Tau Phi Scholastic Honor Society-Eastern America Chapter
c/o Thomas T. Shen, Scholarship Selection Committee
146 Fernbank Avenue
Delmar, NY 12054
(518) 439-2362   Fax: (518) 439-2362
E-mail: cs.tt.shen@worldnet.att.net
Web: www.phitauphi.org

Purpose To provide financial assistance to college juniors and seniors of Chinese heritage at colleges and universities in eastern states.

Eligibility This program is open to juniors and seniors enrolled at an accredited institution of higher education east of a line along Ohio, Kentucky, and Alabama. Applicants must be of Chinese heritage or interested in and committed to Chinese heritage and culture, have a GPA of 3.4 or higher, and be sponsored by a member of Phi Tau Phi. Along with their application, they must submit a 1-page essay on their professional goals, achievements, financial need, and Chinese cultural interests.

Financial data Stipends are $1,000 or $500.

Duration 1 year.

Additional information Phi Tau Phi, first organized in 1921 in China and reestablished in 1964 in the United States, is a relatively small honor society of scholars, mainly of Chinese heritage, in various disciplines of science, technology, art, and humanity. Students who have difficulty in locating a sponsor should contact the Scholarship Selection Committee

Number awarded Varies each year; recently, 3 of these scholarships were awarded: 2 at $1,000 and 1 at $500.

Deadline September of each year.

[281]
PHILIP AND LOUISE WANG SCHOLARSHIPS

Organization of Chinese Americans of San Mateo
    County
P.O. Box 218
San Mateo, CA 94401
(650) 342-8336
E-mail: scholarships@ocasanmateo.org
Web: www.ocasanmateo.org

Purpose To provide financial assistance for college to
high school students of Chinese descent in San Mateo
County, California.

Eligibility Seniors of Chinese descent graduating from
high schools in San Mateo County, California with a minimum GPA of 3.3 are eligible to apply for these scholarships.
They must be planning to attend an accredited postsecondary institution. Selection is based on good citizenship,
extracurricular activities, community service, and financial
need.

Financial data The stipend is $1,000.

Duration 1 year.

Additional information Applications for this program are
available only through high school counselors.

Number awarded 5 each year.

Deadline April of each year.

[282]
PHILIPPINE-AMERICAN ASSOCIATION OF LORAIN COUNTY SCHOLARSHIP

Community Foundation of Greater Lorain County
Attn: Scholarship Program Associate
1865 North Ridge Road East, Suite A
Lorain, OH 44055
(440) 277-0142   Toll-free: (888) 695-7645
Fax: (440) 277-6955
E-mail: foundation@peoplewhocare.org
Web: www.peoplewhocare.org

Purpose To provide financial assistance for college to
members of the Philippine-American Association of Lorain
County (Ohio).

Eligibility This program is open to members of the association who are enrolled or planning to enroll in a college,
vocational school, or technical school. Applicants must
have a GPA of 2.5 or higher. Along with their application,
they must submit an official transcript from their present or
most recently attended school, documentation of financial
need, a list of extracurricular activities, ACT or SAT scores
(high school students only), letters of recommendation, and
an essay of 250 words or less describing their pride in their
Philippine American heritage. Selection is based on academic achievement, financial need, and community involvement.

Financial data A stipend is awarded (amount not specified). Funds are paid directly to the recipient's school.

Duration 1 year.

Number awarded 1 or more each year.

Deadline February of each year.

[283]
PILOT SCHOLARSHIP PROGRAM

Department of Agriculture
Natural Resources Conservation Service
Attn: Outreach Division
5601 Sunnyside Avenue, STOP 5474
Beltsville, MD 20705
(301) 504-2229

Purpose To provide tuition support to students (especially Asian Pacific Islanders) interested in studying agriculture or natural resources at designated universities to prepare for a career with the Natural Resources Conservation
Service (NRCS) of the U.S. Department of Agriculture.

Eligibility This program is open to students currently
enrolled at the College of Tropical Agriculture and Human
Resources of the University of Hawaii at Manoa and the University of Hawaii at Hilo, California State Polytechnic University at Pomona, the University of Minnesota-Twin Cities, and
the University of Wisconsin at River Falls. Applicants must
be majoring in agriculture, agricultural business and management, agricultural economics, agricultural engineering or
mechanics, agricultural production and technology, agron-
omy or crop science, botany, farm and range management,
horticulture, natural resources management, and soil conservation and science. They must be U.S. citizens, have a
high school diploma or GED, be in good academic standing
with a GPA of 3.0 or higher, and have a strong career interest in agriculture and natural resources within NRCS. Along
with their application, they must submit an essay of 500 to
800 words on their motivation for applying for the scholarship, why the Asian Pacific Islander Pilot program is important to them, their academic and career goals, and the skills
they bring to NRCS.

Financial data Full tuition scholarships are provided.

Duration 2 to 4 years; recipients are obligated to 1 year
of service to the NCRS for each year of financial support.

Additional information The program, established in
2004, also provides an internship with NCRS, employee
benefits, mentoring, career development, leadership training, and use of a personal computer.

Number awarded Varies each year.

Deadline July of each year.

[284]
PNI KNIGHT RIDDER MINORITY SCHOLARS PROGRAM

Philadelphia Newspapers, Inc.
Attn: Ivan Sample
400 North Broad Street
P.O. Box 8263
Philadelphia, PA 19101
(215) 854-2429   Fax: (215) 854-2578
E-mail: isample@phillynews.com
Web: www.philly.com/mld/philly/living/education

Purpose To provide financial assistance to minority high
school seniors from the circulation area of Philadelphia
Newspapers Inc. (PNI) who are interested in a career in journalism or communications.

Eligibility This program is open to minority seniors graduating from high schools in the service area of the PNI newspapers (the *Philadelphia Inquirer* and the *Philadelphia Daily
News*) in Delaware, New Jersey, and Pennsylvania. Appli-

cants must be interested in majoring in journalism in college. Along with their application, they must submit 2 letters of recommendation, transcripts of grades, SAT or ACT scores, up to 5 samples of work with bylines, and an essay on why they want to prepare for a career in the journalism or communication business.

Financial data The stipend is $1,000.

Duration 1 year; nonrenewable.

Additional information The recipients of these scholarships are automatically entered into competition for the Knight Ridder Minority Scholarship Program of $40,000 over 4 years.

Number awarded 3 each year.

Deadline January of each year.

[285]
PORTLAND CHAPTER AAJA SCHOLARSHIPS

Asian American Journalists Association-Portland
   Chapter
c/o Tracy Jan
The Oregonian
Metro East News Bureau
295 N.E. Second Street
Gresham, OR 97030
(503) 294-5970
E-mail: tracyjan@news.oregonian.com
Web: chapters.aaja.org/Portland/scholar.html

Purpose To provide financial assistance to undergraduate and graduate journalism students in Oregon and southwestern Washington area who have been involved in the Asian American community.

Eligibility This program is open to high school seniors, undergraduates, and graduate students who live or attend school in Oregon or the Vancouver, Washington area. Applicants must be enrolled or planning to enroll full time in a journalism program and be able to demonstrate involvement in the Asian American community. Along with their application, they must submit an essay (up to 750 words) on how they became interested in journalism or how they see themselves contributing to the Asian American community. They must also submit work samples (print: up to 3 articles; radio: up to 3 different stories on standard audio tapes; television: up to 3 different stories on a VHS tape; photojournalism: a portfolio of up to 15 entries). Selection is based on scholastic ability, commitment to journalism, sensitivity to Asian American issues as demonstrated by community involvement, journalistic ability, and financial need.

Financial data Stipends up to $2,000 are available.

Duration 1 year.

Number awarded 1 each year.

Deadline March of each year.

[286]
PORTLAND PRESS HERALD/MAINE SUNDAY TELEGRAM SCHOLARSHIP FUND

Maine Community Foundation
Attn: Program Director
245 Main Street
Ellsworth, ME 04605
(207) 667-9735   Toll-free: (877) 700-6800
Fax: (207) 667-0447   E-mail: info@mainecf.org
Web: www.mainecf.org/scholar.html

Purpose To provide financial assistance to students of color who are interested in studying journalism at a college or university in Maine.

Eligibility This program is open to students of color from anywhere in the United States who are interested in majoring in journalism, media studies, or related majors. First priority is given to students at the University of Southern Maine, but if no qualifying candidates apply from that school, students attending other 4-year postsecondary educational institutions in Maine are considered. Preference is given to applicants entering or currently enrolled as full-time students preparing for a career in print journalism. Selection is based on academic potential, financial need, and a demonstrated interest in and aptitude for print journalism.

Financial data A stipend is paid (amount not specified).

Duration 1 year; may be renewed.

Additional information This program was established in 2000.

Number awarded 1 or more each year.

Deadline May of each year.

[287]
PRIVATE COLLEGES & UNIVERSITIES MAGAZINE MULTICULTURAL SCHOLARSHIP

Private Colleges & Universities, Inc.
Attn: *PC&U* Multicultural Edition Scholarship Program
2 LAN Drive, Suite 100
P.O. Box 349
Westford, MA 01886
(978) 692-5092
E-mail: mc.scholar@privatecolleges.com
Web: www.privatecolleges.com

Purpose To provide financial assistance to high school seniors and graduates of color who are planning to enroll as a freshman in a private college or university.

Eligibility All students of color who are currently residents of the United States or its territories and who plan to enroll in a baccalaureate degree program at a participating private college or university (for a list, write to the sponsor) are eligible. Applicants must submit a 1,000-word statement about their community service activities, a high school transcript, and a recommendation by someone in their community (not a family member). Selection is based on academic merit (transcripts, class rank, and GPA) and on service to the community.

Financial data The stipend is $2,000.

Duration 1 year; nonrenewable.

Number awarded 5 each year.

Deadline December of each year.

[288]
PROFESSOR CHEN WEN-CHEN SCHOLARSHIPS

Professor Chen Wen-Chen Memorial Foundation
Attn: Scholarship Committee
P.O. Box 6223
Lawrenceville, NJ 08648
(609) 936-1352   E-mail: mkao@comcast.net
Web: www.cwcmf.org

Purpose To provide financial assistance to students at North American colleges and universities who have been involved in the Taiwanese community.

Eligibility This program is open to students who have participated in Taiwanese social-political movements or have made significant contributions to the Taiwanese community in North America. Applicants must be currently enrolled at a college or university in North America. Selection is based on academic achievement.

Financial data The stipend is $1,500.

Duration 1 year.

Additional information Information is also available from Dr. Long R. Mark Kao, 3 Worchester Lane, Princeton Junction, NJ 08550.

Number awarded 4 each year.

Deadline May of each year.

[289]
PUBLIC RELATIONS STUDENT SOCIETY OF AMERICA MULTICULTURAL AFFAIRS SCHOLARSHIPS

Public Relations Student Society of America
Attn: Director of Education
33 Irving Place, Third Floor
New York, NY 10003-2376
(212) 460-1474   Fax: (212) 995-0757
E-mail: prssa@prsa.org
Web: www.prssa.org

Purpose To provide financial assistance to minority college students who are interested in preparing for a career in public relations.

Eligibility This program is open to minority (African American/Black, Hispanic/Latino, Asian, Native American, Alaskan Native, or Pacific Islander) students who are at least juniors at an accredited 4-year college or university. Applicants must be attending full time, be able to demonstrate financial need, and have earned a GPA of 3.0 or higher. Membership in the Public Relations Student Society of America is preferred but not required. A major or minor in public relations is preferred; students who attend a school that does not offer a public relations degree or program must be enrolled in a communications degree program (e.g., journalism, mass communications).

Financial data The stipend is $1,500.

Duration 1 year.

Additional information This program was established in 1989.

Number awarded 2 each year.

Deadline April of each year.

[290]
P.V. JAGANNATHA RAO MEMORIAL AWARD

India American Cultural Association
1281 Cooper Lake Road, S.E.
Smyrna, GA 30082
(770) 436-3719   (770) 436-4272
Web: www.myiaca.org/scholarships.html

Purpose To provide financial assistance for college to high school seniors in Georgia whose parents or grandparents came from what is now India.

Eligibility This program is open to high school seniors who 1) are living in Georgia and 2) whose parents or grandparents came from present day India. For the purposes of this program, citizens of Pakistan and Bangladesh are not included. Applicants must be planning to attend a 4-year college or university as a full-time student. Along with their application, they must submit official school transcript, resume, SAT score report, the best essay they submitted to a college to which they applied, and documentation of financial need. Selection is based on financial need and demonstrated excellence and dedication in a particular endeavor.

Financial data The stipend is $1,250 per year.

Duration 4 years.

Additional information This program was established in 1993. Information is also available from the Indian American Scholarship Fund, 719 Vinings Estates Drive, Mableton, GA 30126, E-mail: manochaa@bellsouth.net. Membership in the India American Cultural Association (IACA) is not required to apply, but recipients must become members of the association.

Number awarded 1 each year.

Deadline May of each year.

[291]
RACIAL ETHNIC EDUCATIONAL SCHOLARSHIPS

Synod of the Trinity
Attn: Scholarships
3040 Market Street
Camp Hill, PA 17011-4599
(717) 737-0421, ext. 232
Toll-free: (800) 242-0534, ext. 232
Fax: (717) 737-8211   E-mail: Pnash@syntrinity.org
Web: www.syntrinity.org

Purpose To provide financial assistance for college to ethnic minority students in Pennsylvania, West Virginia, and designated counties in Ohio.

Eligibility This program is open to members of a racial minority group (African American, Asian, Hispanic, Latino, Middle Eastern, or Native American) who are attending or planning to attend an accredited college or vocational school as a full-time student. Applicants may be of any religious denomination, but they must be residents of the Presbyterian Church (USA) Synod of the Trinity, which covers all of Pennsylvania; West Virginia except for the counties of Berkeley, Grant, Hampshire, Hardy, Jefferson, Mineral, Morgan, and Pendleton; and the Ohio counties of Belmont, Harrison, Jefferson, Monroe, and the southern sector of Columbiana. They must be able to demonstrate financial need and U.S. citizenship or permanent resident status.

Financial data Awards range from $100 to $1,000 per year, depending on the need of the recipient.

Duration 1 year; may be renewed up to 3 additional years, provided that the recipient maintains a GPA of 1.75 or higher for the second year and 2.0 or higher for the third and fourth years.

Number awarded Varies each year.

Deadline April of each year.

[292]
RAMA SCHOLARSHIP FOR THE AMERICAN DREAM

American Hotel & Lodging Educational Foundation
Attn: Manager of Foundation Programs
1201 New York Avenue, N.W., Suite 600
Washington, DC 20005-3931
(202) 289-3188   Fax: (202) 289-3199
E-mail: ahlef@ahlef.org
Web: www.ahlf.org/scholarships

Purpose To provide financial assistance to minority college students working on a degree in hotel management at designated schools.

Eligibility Applicants must be attending 1 of 15 designated hospitality management schools, which select the recipients. Preference is given to students of Asian-Indian descent and other minority groups and to JHM Hotel employees.

Financial data The stipend varies at each of the participating schools.

Duration 1 year.

Additional information The participating institutions are Bethune-Cookman College, California State Polytechnic University at Pomona, Cornell University, Florida International University, Georgia State University, Greenville Technical College, Howard University, Johnson & Wales University (Charleston, South Carolina), Johnson & Wales University (Providence, Rhode Island), Michigan State University, New York University, University of Central Florida, University of Houston, University of South Carolina, and Virginia Polytechnic Institute and State University. This program is funded by JHM Hotels, Inc.

Number awarded Varies each year; recently, 28 of these scholarships were awarded.

[293]
RAYMOND H. TROTT SCHOLARSHIP FOR BANKING

Rhode Island Foundation
Attn: Scholarship Coordinator
One Union Station
Providence, RI 02903
(401) 274-4564   Fax: (401) 751-7983
E-mail: libbym@rifoundation.org
Web: www.rifoundation.org

Purpose To provide financial assistance to Rhode Island undergraduates of color interested in preparing for a career in banking.

Eligibility This program is open to minority residents of Rhode Island who are entering their senior year in college. Applicants must plan to prepare for a career in banking and be able to demonstrate financial need. Along with their application, they must submit an essay (up to 300 words)

on the impact they would like to have on the banking industry.

Financial data The stipend is $1,000.

Duration 1 year; nonrenewable.

Additional information This program was established in 1980.

Number awarded 1 each year.

Deadline June of each year.

[294]
RCA ETHNIC SCHOLARSHIP FUND

Reformed Church in America
Attn: Policy, Planning, and Administration Services
475 Riverside Drive, Room 1814
New York, NY 10115
(212) 870-3243   Toll-free: (800) 722-9977, ext. 3243
Fax: (212) 870-2499   E-mail: kbradsell@rca.org
Web: www.rca.org/aboutus/councils/scholarships.php

Purpose To provide assistance to minority student members of the Reformed Church in America (RCA) who are interested in working on an undergraduate degree.

Eligibility Applicants must be a member of a minority group (American Indian, African American, Hispanic, or Pacific or Asian American), be admitted to a college or other institution of higher learning, and be a member of an RCA congregation or be admitted to an RCA college. Priority is given to applicants who will enter colleges or universities and students enrolled in occupational training programs. Selection is based primarily on financial need.

Financial data The stipend depends on the need of the recipient, but is at least $500.

Duration 1 academic year; may be renewed until completion of an academic program.

Number awarded Several each year.

Deadline April of each year.

[295]
RDW GROUP, INC. MINORITY SCHOLARSHIP FOR COMMUNICATIONS

Rhode Island Foundation
Attn: Scholarship Coordinator
One Union Station
Providence, RI 02903
(401) 274-4564   Fax: (401) 751-7983
E-mail: libbym@rifoundation.org
Web: www.rifoundation.org

Purpose To provide financial assistance to Rhode Island students of color interested in preparing for a career in communications.

Eligibility This program is open to minority undergraduate and graduate students who are Rhode Island residents. Applicants must intend to major in communications (including computer graphics, art, cinematography, or other fields that would prepare them for a career in advertising). They must be able to demonstrate financial need and a commitment to a career in communications. Along with their application, they must submit an essay (up to 300 words) on the impact they would like to have on the communications field.

Financial data The stipend is $2,000.

Duration 1 year; nonrenewable.

Additional information This program is sponsored by the RDW Group, Inc.

Number awarded 1 each year.

Deadline April of each year.

[296]
RICHARD B. FISHER SCHOLARSHIP

Morgan Stanley
c/o Joyce Arencibia, IT College Recruiting
750 Seventh Avenue, 30th Floor
New York, NY 10019
(212) 762-4000
E-mail: diversityrecruiting@morganstanley.com
Web: www.morganstanley.com

Purpose To provide financial assistance and work experience to members of minority groups who are preparing for a career in technology within the financial services industry.

Eligibility This program is open to members of minority groups who are enrolled in their sophomore or junior year of college (or the third or fourth year of a 5-year program). Applicants must be enrolled full time and have a GPA of 3.0 or higher. They must be willing to commit to a paid summer internship in the Morgan Stanley Information Technology Division. All majors and disciplines are eligible, but preference is given to students preparing for a career in technology within the financial services industry. Along with their application, they must submit 1-page essays on 1) why they are applying for this scholarship and why they should be selected as a recipient; 2) a technical project on which they worked, either through a university course or previous work experience, their role in the project, and how they contributed to the end result; and 3) a software, hardware, or new innovative application of existing technology that they would create if they could and the impact it would have. Financial need is not considered in the selection process.

Financial data The stipend is $5,000.

Duration 1 year.

Additional information The program includes a paid summer internship in the Morgan Stanley Information Technology Division in the summer following the time of application.

Number awarded 1 or more each year.

Deadline February of each year.

[297]
RICHARD S. SMITH SCHOLARSHIP

United Methodist Church
Attn: Division on Ministries with Young People
P.O. Box 340003
Nashville, TN 37203-0003
(615) 340-7184   Toll-free: (877) 899-2780, ext. 7184
Fax: (615) 340-1764   E-mail: umyouthorg@gbod.org
Web: www.umyouth.org/scholarships.html

Purpose To provide financial assistance to minority high school seniors who wish to prepare for a Methodist church-related career.

Eligibility This program is open to graduating high school seniors who are members of racial/ethnic minority groups and have been active members of a United Methodist church for at least 1 year. Applicants must have been admitted to an accredited college or university to prepare for a church-related career. They must have maintained at least a "C" average throughout high school and be able to demonstrate financial need. Along with their application, they must submit brief essays on their participation in church projects and activities, a leadership experience, the role their faith plays in their life, the church-related vocation to which God is calling them, and their extracurricular interests and activities. U.S. citizenship or permanent resident status is required.

Financial data The stipend is $1,000.

Duration 1 year; nonrenewable.

Additional information This scholarship was first awarded in 1997. Recipients must enroll full time in their first year of undergraduate study.

Number awarded 2 each year.

Deadline May of each year.

[298]
RICHARD W. MITCHELL MEMORIAL SCHOLARSHIP

Poughkeepsie Area Chamber of Commerce
Attn: Chair, Scholarship Committee
110 Main street
Poughkeepsie, NY 12601
(914) 454-1700   Fax: (914) 454-1702

Purpose To provide financial assistance for college to residents of Dutchess County, New York who have overcome physical, emotional, or economic obstacles.

Eligibility Residents of Dutchess County, New York are eligible to apply if they have overcome a significant economic, physical developmental, or emotional barrier and is interested in pursuing further education. Applicants may be of any age. Financial need is considered in the selection process.

Financial data Stipends range up to $1,000. Funds may be used tuition, books, learning aids, child care, or transportation.

Duration 1 year.

Number awarded Varies each year; recently, 7 of these scholarships were awarded.

Deadline April of each year.

[299]
RISING BUSINESS STAR SCHOLARSHIP

Howard County Committee for Business and Economic Diversity
c/o Center for Business and Technology Development
9250 Bendix Road, North
Columbia, MD 21045
(410) 313-6550   Fax: (410) 313-7515
E-mail: ccardwell@hceda.org
Web: www.hceda.org/thecenter/cbed.html

Purpose To provide financial assistance to women, minority, and disabled high school seniors in Howard County, Maryland who have demonstrated an entrepreneurial spirit.

Eligibility This program is open to seniors graduating from high schools in Howard County, Maryland who are planning to begin full- or part-time college study in the following fall. Applicants must be a woman, minority, and/or person with a disability. They must have demonstrated business achievement by starting a small business, assisting an existing business in a significant way, or developing a creation or invention targeted at business. Along with their application they must submit a 300-word essay in which they describe an activity (work, school, community) in which they have demonstrated their entrepreneurial spirit and their 10-year professional goal.

Financial data The stipend is $1,000.

Duration 1 year.

Number awarded 1 each year.

Deadline March of each year.

[300]
ROBERT R. CHURCH SCHOLARSHIP FUND

Community Foundation of Greater Memphis
Attn: Director of Programs
1900 Union Avenue
Memphis, TN 38104
(901) 722-0054　　　　　Fax: (901) 722-0010
E-mail: mwolowicz@cfgm.org
Web: www.cfgm.org

Purpose To provide financial assistance to minority and other high school seniors in Memphis and Shelby County, Tennessee who are interested in majoring in business in college.

Eligibility This program is open to residents of Memphis and Shelby County, Tennessee who are juniors or seniors in high school. Applicants must have completed applied economics with a "C" average by the end of the first semester of their senior year. They must be planning to work on a degree in business at a college, university, or junior college in Tennessee. Along with their application, they must submit a letter or recommendation from their applied economics instructor, a letter describing why they are applying for the scholarship and their career goals; their most recent high school transcript; a copy of their most recent income tax return; and 2 signed letters of recommendation from teachers, clergy, or persons other than family members who are familiar with their skills and abilities. An interview may be required. Selection is based on academic record and financial need.

Financial data Stipends range from $1,000 to $2,500.

Duration 1 year; recipients may reapply.

Additional information This program honors the first African American millionaire in Memphis, who died in 1912. It is funded by the Mid-South Minority Business Council, 158 Madison Avenue, Suite 300, Memphis, TN 38103, (901) 525-6512, E-mail: dgordon@mmbc-memphis.org. Applications for this scholarship must be submitted to the Business Council; the foundation does not accept applications.

Number awarded Varies each year; recently, a total of $9,000 in these scholarships was awarded.

Deadline March of each year.

[301]
RONALD H. BROWN MEMORIAL SCHOLARSHIP

Travel Industry Association of America
Attn: TIA Foundation
1100 New York Avenue, N.W., Suite 450
Washington, DC 20005-3934
(202) 408-8422　　　　　Fax: (202) 408-1255
Web: www.tia.org

Purpose To provide financial assistance to minority undergraduate students interested in studying travel and tourism.

Eligibility This program is open to minorities who are interested in working on an undergraduate degree in the travel and tourism field. Candidates must first be nominated by a department head at a 4-year college or university that has a travel and tourism program. Nominees are then contacted by the foundation and invited to complete an application, including an essay on what segment of the tourism industry interests them and why.

Financial data The stipend is $3,000 per year.

Duration 1 year.

Number awarded 1 each year.

[302]
ROSEWOOD FAMILY SCHOLARSHIP FUND

Florida Department of Education
Attn: Office of Student Financial Assistance
1940 North Monroe Street, Suite 70
Tallahassee, FL 32303-4759
(850) 410-5200　　　　　Toll-free: (888) 827-2004
Fax: (850) 487-1809　　　　　E-mail: osfa@fldoe.org
Web: www.FloridaStudentFinancialAid.org

Purpose To provide financial assistance for undergraduate education to needy minority students who wish to study in Florida.

Eligibility This program is open to residents of any state who wish to attend state universities, public community colleges, or public postsecondary vocational/technical schools in Florida. Applicants must be a minority, defined as Black but not of Hispanic origin, Asian, Pacific Islander, Hispanic, American Indian, or Alaskan Native. Preference is given to descendants of African American Rosewood families (whose members were killed by a mob in January 1923). Other minority undergraduate students are considered if funds remain available after awarding Rosewood descendants. Financial need must be demonstrated.

Financial data Awards cover the actual costs of tuition and fees, up to $4,000 per year.

Duration 1 year; may be renewed up to 3 additional years provided the student maintains full-time enrollment and a GPA of 2.0 or higher.

Number awarded 25 each year.

Deadline March of each year.

[303]
ROYCE OSBORN MINORITY STUDENT SCHOLARSHIPS

American Society of Radiologic Technologists
Attn: ASRT Education and Research Foundation
15000 Central Avenue, S.E.
Albuquerque, NM 87123-3917
(505) 298-4500   Toll-free: (800) 444-2778, ext. 2541
Fax: (505) 298-5063   E-mail: foundation@asrt.org
Web: www.asrt.org

Purpose To provide financial assistance to minority students enrolled in entry-level radiologic sciences programs.

Eligibility This program is open to African Americans, Native Americans (including American Indians, Eskimos, Hawaiians, and Samoans), Hispanic Americans, Asian Americans, and Pacific Islanders who are enrolled in an entry-level radiologic sciences program. Applicants must have a GPA in radiologic sciences core courses of 3.0 or higher and be able to demonstrate financial need. They may not have a previous degree or certificate in the radiologic sciences. Along with their application, they must submit an essay of 450 to 500 words on their reason for entering the radiologic sciences, career goals, and financial need. Only U.S. citizens, nationals, and permanent residents are eligible.

Financial data The stipend is $4,000.

Duration 1 year; may be renewed for 1 additional year.

Number awarded 5 each year.

Deadline January of each year.

[304]
RUTH MU-LAN CHU AND JAMES S.C. CHAO SCHOLARSHIP

US Pan Asian American Chamber of Commerce
Attn: Scholarship Coordinator
1329 18th Street, N.W.
Washington, DC 20036
(202) 296-5221   Fax: (202) 296-5225
E-mail: administrator@uspaacc.com
Web: www.uspaacc.com

Purpose To provide financial assistance for college to female Asian American high school seniors who demonstrate financial need.

Eligibility This program is open to female high school seniors of Asian heritage who are U.S. citizens or permanent residents. Applicants must be planning to begin full-time study at an accredited postsecondary educational institution in the United States. Along with their application, they must submit a 500-word essay on "Why I need this scholarship." Selection is based on academic excellence (GPA of 3.5 or higher), community service involvement, and financial need.

Financial data The maximum stipend is $5,000. Funds are paid directly to the recipient's college or university.

Duration 1 year.

Additional information Funding is not provided for correspondence courses, Internet courses, or study in a country other than the United States.

Number awarded 1 each year.

Deadline February of each year.

[305]
RYU FAMILY FOUNDATION SCHOLARSHIP GRANTS

Ryu Family Foundation, Inc.
901 Murray Road
East Hanover, NJ 07936
(973) 560-9696   Fax: (973) 560-0661

Purpose To provide financial assistance to Korean and Korean American undergraduate and graduate students in the Northeast.

Eligibility To qualify for this assistance, applicants must be Korean American (U.S. citizen) or Korean (permanent resident status); be enrolled full time and working on an undergraduate or graduate degree; have a GPA of 3.5 or higher; be able to document financial need; and be either residing or attending college in 1 of the following 10 northeastern states: Connecticut, Delaware, Maine, Massachusetts, New Hampshire, New Jersey, New York, Pennsylvania, Rhode Island, or Vermont. All applicants must submit a 500-word essay on a subject that changes annually.

Financial data A stipend is awarded (amount not specified). Checks are made out jointly to the recipient and the recipient's school.

Duration 1 year; may be renewed for 1 additional year.

Additional information Recipients who reside in the designated northeastern states may attend school in any state.

Deadline November of each year.

[306]
SABURO KIDO MEMORIAL SCHOLARSHIP

Japanese American Citizens League
Attn: National Scholarship Awards
1765 Sutter Street
San Francisco, CA 94115
(415) 921-5225   Fax: (415) 931-4671
E-mail: jacl@jacl.org
Web: www.jacl.org/scholarships.html

Purpose To provide financial assistance for college to student members of the Japanese American Citizens League (JACL).

Eligibility This program is open to JACL members who are currently enrolled or planning to reenter a college, university, trade school, business college, or other institution of higher learning. Applicants must submit a statement describing their current level of involvement in the Japanese American community or Asian Pacific community and how they will continue their involvement in future years. Selection is based on academic record, extracurricular activities, financial need, and community involvement.

Financial data The stipend depends on the availability of funds but usually ranges from $1,000 to $5,000.

Duration 1 year; nonrenewable.

Additional information Applications must be submitted to the JACL National Scholarship Program, c/o San Diego JACL Chapter, 1031 25th Street, San Diego, CA 92102.

Number awarded At least 1 each year.

Deadline March of each year.

[307]
SAJA SCHOLARSHIPS

South Asian Journalists Association
c/o Sreenath Sreenivasan
Columbia Graduate School of Journalism
2950 Broadway
New York, NY 10027
(212) 854-5979   Fax: (212) 854-7837
E-mail: ss221@Columbia.edu
Web: www.saja.org/scholarships.html

Purpose   To provide financial assistance for undergraduate and graduate study to journalism students of south Asian descent.

Eligibility   This program is open to students of south Asian descent (including Bangladesh, Bhutan, India, Maldives, Nepal, Pakistan, and Sri Lanka; Indo-Caribbeans are also eligible). Applicants must be serious about preparing for a journalism career and must provide evidence they plan to do so through courses, internships, or freelancing. They may be 1) high school seniors about to enroll in an accredited college or university; 2) current students in an accredited college or university in the United States or Canada; or 3) students enrolled or about to enter a graduate program in the United States or Canada. Applicants with financial hardship are given special consideration. Selection is based on interest in journalism, writing skills, participation and enthusiasm in the sponsoring organization, reasons for entering journalism, and financial need.

Financial data   The stipends are $1,000 for high school seniors and current college students or $1,500 for graduate students.

Duration   1 year.

Additional information   Recipients are expected to give back to the South Asian Journalists Association (SAJA) by volunteering at the annual convention or at other events during the year.

Number awarded   3 each year: 1 to a high school senior entering college, 1 to a current college student, and 2 to graduate students.

Deadline   February of each year.

[308]
SALINAS CHAPTER SCHOLARSHIPS

Chinese American Citizens Alliance-Salinas Chapter
Attn: Scholarship Committee
P.O. Box 754
Salinas, CA 93902
Web: www.cacasalinas.org/scholar.html

Purpose   To provide financial assistance for college to high school seniors of Chinese descent in Monterey County, California.

Eligibility   This program is open to seniors graduating from high schools in Monterey County, California who plan to attend a postsecondary accredited trade school, junior or community college, or 4-year college or university. Applicants must be of Chinese descent. Selection is based on scholarship (30%), financial need (20%), extracurricular school activities (10%), community service/work (10%), a personal essay (15%), letters of recommendation (5%), and special or unusual circumstances (10%).

Financial data   The maximum stipend is $800.

Duration   1 year.

Additional information   Information is also available from Elena Fujii, 7 Alameda Place, Salinas, CA 93901.

Number awarded   Up to 6 each year.

Deadline   May of each year.

[309]
SAM S. KUWAHARA MEMORIAL SCHOLARSHIP

Japanese American Citizens League
Attn: National Scholarship Awards
1765 Sutter Street
San Francisco, CA 94115
(415) 921-5225   Fax: (415) 931-4671
E-mail: jacl@jacl.org
Web: www.jacl.org/scholarships.html

Purpose   To provide financial assistance to student members of the Japanese American Citizens League (JACL) who are working on or planning to work on an undergraduate degree, particularly in agriculture.

Eligibility   This program is open to JACL members who are either high school seniors or current undergraduates. Applicants must be enrolled or planning to enter or reenter a college, university, trade school, business college, or other institution of higher learning. They must submit a statement describing their current level of involvement in the Japanese American community or Asian Pacific community and how they will continue their involvement in future years. Selection is based on academic record, extracurricular activities, financial need, and community involvement. Preference is given to students who wish to study agriculture or a related field.

Financial data   The stipend depends on the availability of funds but usually ranges from $1,000 to $5,000.

Duration   1 year; nonrenewable.

Additional information   Applications from high school seniors must be submitted to the local JACL chapter. Other applications must be submitted to the JACL National Scholarship Program, c/o San Diego JACL Chapter, 1031 25th Street, San Diego, CA 92102.

Number awarded   2 each year: 1 for a graduating high school senior and 1 for a continuing undergraduate.

Deadline   February of each year for graduating high school seniors; March of each year for current college students.

[310]
SAN DIEGO CHINESE WOMEN'S ASSOCIATION SCHOLARSHIP

San Diego Chinese Women's Association
Attn: Director
P.O. Box 881882
San Diego, CA 92168-1882
(619) 421-7539   E-mail: jungwon@cox.net
Web: members.cox.net/jungwon/Scholarship.pdf

Purpose   To provide financial assistance for college to Chinese American students in the San Diego County, California area.

Eligibility   This program is open to seniors graduating from high schools in San Diego County, California, Applicants must be at least one quarter Chinese, be planning to attend a community college or 4-year school, and have a GPA of 3.0 or higher. Along with their application, they must submit a 2-page essay describing their Chinese heritage, involvement in activities, future goals and plans, and something about themselves. Financial need is not considered in the selection process.

Financial data The scholarships for a 4-year college or university are $1,000; the scholarships for a community college or vocational/technical school are $500.

Duration 1 year.

Number awarded Up to 12 each year: up to 8 to attend a 4-year college or university and up to 4 to attend a community college or vocational/technical school.

Deadline March of each year.

[311]
SAN FRANCISCO BAY AREA CHAPTER OF AAJA SCHOLARSHIPS

Asian American Journalists Association-San Francisco Bay Area Chapter
c/o Nerissa Pacio, Scholarship Co-Chair
San Jose Mercury News
750 Ridder Park Drive
San Jose, CA 95190
(408) 920-5827   Fax: (408) 271-3786
E-mail: aaja@aajasf.org
Web: www.aajasf.org

Purpose To provide financial assistance to Asian American students in the San Francisco Bay area who are interested in careers in broadcast or print journalism.

Eligibility These scholarships are open to Asian American students who either attend school in the San Francisco Bay area or reside in northern California and attend school elsewhere. Applicants may be high school seniors entering college in the following fall, undergraduates, or graduate students. Students do not need to be majoring in journalism, radio/television, photojournalism, or mass communications, but they must demonstrate serious intent to prepare for a career in journalism. Selection is based on scholastic achievement, commitment to journalism, sensitivity to Asian American issues as demonstrated by community involvement, journalistic ability, and financial need.

Financial data Stipends range from $500 to $2,500.

Duration 1 year; may be renewed.

Number awarded Varies each year. Recently, 9 of these scholarships were awarded: 1 at $2,500 (the Ken Wong Memorial Award), 3 at $2,000 (AAJA ChevronTexaco Awards), 2 at $1,500 (AAJA Shamrock Awards), and 3 at $500.

Deadline April of each year.

[312]
SAN FRANCISCO LODGE HIGH SCHOOL SCHOLARSHIPS

Chinese American Citizens Alliance-San Francisco Lodge
1044 Stockton Street
San Francisco, CA 94108
(415) 434-2232   Fax: (415) 434-2232
E-mail: info@cacasf.org
Web: www.cacasf.org

Purpose To provide financial assistance for college to Chinese American high school seniors from the San Francisco area.

Eligibility This program is open to high school seniors in the San Francisco area who are of Chinese descent and planning to attend college. Selection is based on academic record, school and community involvement, career outlook, and financial need.

Financial data Stipends vary but are generally between $500 and $1,000 per year.

Duration 1 year; nonrenewable.

Number awarded Varies each year; recently, 10 of these scholarships were awarded.

Deadline April of each year.

[313]
SARA HUTCHINGS CLARDY SCHOLARSHIP AWARDS

Japanese American Citizens League-Arizona Chapter
c/o Michele Namba, Scholarship Committee Secretary
5414 West Glenn Drive
Glendale, AZ 85301
E-mail: webmaster@azjacl.org
Web: www.azjacl.org

Purpose To provide financial assistance to graduating high school seniors in Arizona who are of Japanese heritage.

Eligibility This program is open to graduating high school seniors in Arizona who have a GPA of 3.0 or higher. Applicants or their parents must have been members of 1 of the following organizations for at least the preceding 3 years: Arizona Chapter of the Japanese American Citizens League (JACLA), the Phoenix Japanese Free Methodist Church, the Arizona Buddhist Church, a youth group of JACLA, a youth group of the Phoenix Free Methodist Church, or a youth group of the Arizona Buddhist Church. Financial need is not considered in the selection process.

Financial data A stipend is awarded (amount not specified).

Duration 1 year.

Additional information Recipients must attend the association's scholarship awards banquet and accept the award in person; failure to do so results in forfeiture of the award.

Number awarded 4 each year.

Deadline February of each year.

[314]
SCHOLARSHIPS FOR DEPENDENTS OF ICIA MEMBERS

International Communications Industries Association, Inc.
Attn: Director of Strategic Initiatives
11242 Waples Mill Road, Suite 200
Fairfax, VA 22030
(703) 273-7200   Toll-free: (800) 659-7469
Fax: (703) 278-8082   E-mail: dwilbert@infocomm.org
Web: www.infocomm.org/Foundation/Scholarships

Purpose To provide financial assistance for college to dependents of minority and other members of the International Communications Industries Association (ICIA) interested in preparing for a career in the audiovisual industry.

Eligibility This program is open to graduating high school seniors and current college students who are the children, stepchildren, and spouses of employees at ICIA member companies. Applicants must have a GPA of 2.75 or higher and be majoring or planning to major in audio, visual, audiovisual, electronics, telecommunications, technical theater, data networking, software development, or information technology. Students in other programs, such as journalism, may be eligible if they can demonstrate a relationship to career goals in the audiovisual industry. Along with their application, they must submit 1) an essay of 150 to 200 words on the career path they see themselves pursuing in the next 5 years and why, and 2) an essay of 250 to 300 words on the experience or person that most influenced them in selecting the audiovisual industry as their career of choice. Minority and women candidates are especially encouraged to apply. Selection is based on the essays, presentation of the application, GPA, work experience, and letters of recommendation.

Financial data The stipend is $1,500.

Duration 1 year.

Number awarded Varies each year; recently, 3 of these scholarships were awarded.

Deadline April of each year.

[315]
SCIENCE AWARD

Indian American Heritage Foundation
3818 Gleneagles Drive
Tarzana, CA 91356
(818) 708-3885   E-mail: ashok4u@aol.com
Web: www.la-indiacenter.com

Purpose To recognize and reward high school seniors in southern California who are of Asian Indian descent and are interested in science.

Eligibility This award is available to seniors graduating from high schools in southern California (south of Fresno) who have at least 1 parent of Asian Indian descent. Applicants must have participated in science activities and have a GPA of 2.0 or higher. They must attend a function of the sponsoring organization at which they take a quiz on India, based on material supplied by the organization. Along with their application, they must submit a 2-page essay on how learning and training in science has affected and influenced their life. Selection is based on their quiz score (15%); the essay (15%); training in science in school, research laboratory, or science workshop (20%); evidence of science projects undertaken (15%); evidence of participation in science fairs (10%); evidence of exhibits of science projects (10%), and honors and awards in science (15%).

Financial data The award is $500 or $250.

Duration 1 year.

Additional information Material about India for the quiz is sent to the applicant after receipt of a check for $10 and the completed application.

Number awarded 1 each year.

Deadline April of each year.

[316]
SCOTTS COMPANY SCHOLARS PROGRAM

Golf Course Superintendents Association of America
Attn: Scholarship and Student Programs Manager
1421 Research Park Drive
Lawrence, KS 66049-3859
(785) 832-3678   Toll-free: (800) 472-7878, ext. 3678
E-mail: psmith@gcsaa.org
Web: www.gcsaa.org

Purpose To provide financial assistance and summer work experience to high school seniors and college students, particularly those from diverse backgrounds, who are preparing for a career in golf management.

Eligibility This program is open to high school seniors and college students (freshmen, sophomores, and juniors) who are interested in preparing for a career in golf management (the "green industry"). Applicants should come from diverse ethnic, cultural, and socioeconomic backgrounds, defined to include women, minorities, and people with disabilities. Selection is based on cultural diversity, academic achievement, extracurricular activities, leadership, employment potential, essay responses, and letters of recommendation. Financial need is not considered. Finalists are selected for summer internships and then compete for scholarships.

Financial data Each intern receives a $500 award. Scholarship stipends are $2,500.

Duration 1 year.

Additional information The program is funded by a permanent endowment established by Scotts Company. Finalists are responsible for securing their own internships.

Number awarded 5 interns and 2 scholarship winners are selected each year.

Deadline February of each year.

[317]
SEATTLE HIROSHIMA CLUB SCHOLARSHIPS

Seattle Hiroshima Club
P.O. Box 14167
Seattle, WA 98114

Purpose To provide financial assistance for college to high school seniors from King County, Washington who have ties to the Hiroshima prefecture in Japan.

Eligibility Eligible to apply are high school seniors in King County, Washington, provided at least 1 of their parents, grandparents, or ancestors lived in the Hiroshima prefecture. In addition, the applicant's parent or guardian must be a member of the Seattle Hiroshima Club by the time the scholarship is submitted (membership is $5). All applicants must have a GPA of 3.6 or higher. To apply, students must submit a completed application, their latest high school transcript, 2 letters of recommendation, and an essay (at least 200 words) on "What Hiroshima Means to Me." Selection is based on academic achievement, school recognition and awards, extracurricular activities, community involvement, recommendations, and the essay.

Financial data The stipend is $1,000.

Duration 1 year.

Additional information Information is also available from Beth Kawahara, Seattle Hiroshima Club Scholarship Administrator, P.O. Box 1566, Mercer Island, WA 98040.

Number awarded 3 each year.

Deadline January of each year.

[318]
SEO SCHOLARS PROGRAM

Sponsors for Educational Opportunity
Attn: Director, Scholars Program
126 East 31st Street
New York, NY 10016
(212) 532-2454   E-mail: bcullen@seo-usa.org
Web: www.seo-usa.org

Purpose To provide financial assistance for college to students of color in New York City who participate throughout high school in an academic enrichment program.

Eligibility This program is open to students of color at public high schools in New York City who participate in weekly after-school and Saturday activities for 4 years as well as intervening summers. Those activities provide core academic success skills, college guidance, and leadership development. Students who meet the program's requirements while in high school are eligible to apply for college scholarships.

Financial data Stipends are awarded (amount not specified).

Duration 1 year; may be renewed.

Additional information This program was launched in 2002 as a replacement for the College Preparation Program, originally established in 1963. It includes the Franklin H. Williams Scholarship, the Andrew Golkin Memorial Scholarship, and the Martha M. Innes Scholarship.

Number awarded Varies more than 500 high school and college students are active in the program each year.

[319]
SERVICE LEAGUE MINORITY NURSING SCHOLARSHIP

Akron General Medical Center
Attn: Human Resources Department, Nurse
    Recruitment
400 Wabash Avenue
Akron, OH 44307
(330) 344-6867   E-mail: rkovalchik@agmc.org
Web: www.agmc.org/scholar.asp

Purpose To provide financial assistance to minority nursing students from Ohio who are working on a baccalaureate degree.

Eligibility This program is open to graduates of high schools in Ohio who have been accepted by an accredited baccalaureate nursing program in the state. Employees of Akron General Medical Center and their children and spouses are also eligible. Applicants must have a GPA of 2.8 or higher and be a member of a racial or ethnic minority group (African American, Hispanic, Asian/Pacific Islander, American Indian/Alaskan Native). They must submit a short essay on the reason they chose nursing as a career and why they believe they have the qualities and skills necessary to be a successful nurse. Selection is based on academic achievement and financial need.

Financial data A stipend is awarded (amount not specified).

Duration 1 year.

Number awarded 1 or more each year.

Deadline February of each year.

[320]
SHARE AND CARE SCHOLARSHIPS

Share and Care Foundation
Attn: Scholarship Committee
211 East 35th Street, Apt. 3F
New York, NY 10016
(908) 598-0390
Web: www.shareandcare.org

Purpose To provide financial assistance for college to high school seniors of Asian-Indian origin.

Eligibility This program is open to graduating high school seniors who are of Asian-Indian origin, have been accepted at an accredited 4-year college, achieved an ACT score of 23 or higher (or the SAT equivalent), and come from a family whose annual gross income is less than $60,000. Selection is based on financial need, academic potential, personal integrity, enthusiasm for learning, and a desire to better humanity.

Financial data The stipend is $1,500 per year.

Duration 4 years, provided the recipient successfully completes the previous year's courses.

Number awarded Varies each year.

Deadline May of each year.

[321]
SHARON D. BANKS MEMORIAL UNDERGRADUATE SCHOLARSHIP

Women's Transportation Seminar
Attn: National Headquarters
1666 K Street, N.W., Suite 1100
Washington, DC 20006
(202) 496-4340   Fax: (202) 496-4349
E-mail: wts@wtsnational.org
Web: www.wtsnational.org

Purpose To provide financial assistance to minority and other undergraduate women interested in a career in transportation.

Eligibility This program is open to women who are working on an undergraduate degree in transportation or a transportation-related field (e.g., transportation engineering, planning, finance, or logistics). Applicants must have at least a 3.0 GPA and be interested in a career in transportation. They must submit a 500-word statement about their career goals after graduation and why they think they should receive the scholarship award. Applications must be submitted first to a local chapter; the chapters forward selected applications for consideration on the national level. Minority candidates are encouraged to apply. Selection is based on transportation involvement and goals, job skills, and academic record; financial need is not considered.

Financial data The stipend is $3,000.

Duration 1 year.

Additional information This program was established in 1992. Local chapters may also award additional funding to winners for their area.

Number awarded 1 each year.

Deadline Applications must be submitted by November to a local WTS chapter.

[322]
S.I. NEWHOUSE FOUNDATION SCHOLARSHIPS

Asian American Journalists Association
Attn: Student Programs Coordinator
1182 Market Street, Suite 320
San Francisco, CA 94102
(415) 346-2051, ext. 102   Fax: (415) 346-6343
E-mail: brandons@aaja.org
Web: www.aaja.org

Purpose To provide financial assistance and summer work experience in print journalism to members of the Asian American Journalists Association (AAJA) who are undergraduate or graduate students.

Eligibility This program is open to all students but especially welcomes applications from historically underrepresented Asian Pacific American groups, including southeast Asians (Vietnamese, Cambodians, and Hmong), south Asians, and Pacific Islanders. Applicants may be graduating high school seniors who declare journalism as a major or undergraduate or graduate students working on a degree in journalism and a career in print journalism. AAJA membership is required. Along with their application, they must submit a 500-word essay on their involvement or interest in the Asian American community and how, if they are awarded this scholarship, they would contribute to the field of journalism and/or media issues involving the Asian American and Pacific Islander community. Selection is based on scholastic ability, commitment to journalism, sensitivity to Asian American and Pacific Islander issues as demonstrated by community involvement, journalistic ability, and financial need.

Financial data Stipends range from $1,000 to $5,000.

Duration 4 years for a graduating high school senior; 1 year for current undergraduate or graduate students.

Additional information This program began in 1994; it is funded by Newhouse News Service and administered by AAJA. Recipients are also eligible for summer internships with a Newhouse publication.

Number awarded Varies each year; recently, 7 of these scholarships (2 at $5,000, 3 at $4,000, 1 at $2,000, and 1 at $1,000) were awarded.

Deadline April of each year.

[323]
SODEXHO PAN ASIAN NETWORK GROUP SCHOLARSHIP

US Pan Asian American Chamber of Commerce
Attn: Scholarship Coordinator
1329 18th Street, N.W.
Washington, DC 20036
(202) 296-5221   Fax: (202) 296-5225
E-mail: administrator@uspaacc.com
Web: www.uspaacc.com/sodexho

Purpose To provide financial assistance and work experience to Asian American college students

Eligibility This program is open to college sophomores and juniors of Asian heritage who are U.S. citizens or permanent residents. Applicants must be enrolled in full-time study at an accredited 4-year college or university in the United States and working on a degree in business management, preferably food service management, hotel restaurant institution management, facilities management, or similar program leading to a bachelor's degree. They must be willing to commit to a paid internship with Sodexho during the summer. Along with their application, they must submit a 500-word essay on how they plan to use their special talents to achieve their professional goals. Selection is based on academic excellence (GPA of 3.0 or higher), leadership in extracurricular activities, and community service involvement.

Financial data The stipend is $5,000. Funds are paid directly to the recipient's college or university. An additional stipend is paid for the internship.

Duration 1 academic year for the scholarship; 8 weeks for the internship.

Additional information This program, established in 2005, is sponsored by Sodexho and its Pan Asian Network Group (PANG). Funding is not provided for correspondence courses, Internet courses, or study in a country other than the United States.

Number awarded 1 each year.

Deadline February of each year.

[324]
SOLEDAD FERNANDEZ SCHOLARSHIP FUND

Asian Pacific Fund
Attn: Scholarship Coordinator
225 Bush Street, Suite 590
San Francisco, CA 94104
(415) 433-6859   Toll-free: (800) 286-1688
Fax: (415) 433-2425
E-mail: scholarship@asianpacificfund.org
Web: www.asianpacificfund.org

Purpose To provide financial assistance to high school seniors of Filipino heritage in designated northern California counties who are interested in attending a 4-year college or university.

Eligibility This program is open to seniors at public high schools in the following northern California counties: Alameda, Contra Costa, Marin, Merced, Monterey, Napa, Sacramento, San Francisco, San Joaquin, San Mateo, Santa Clara, Santa Cruz, Solano, Sonoma, and Stanislaus. Applicants must be of at least 50% Filipino heritage, have a GPA of 3.0 or higher, and plan to enroll in a 4-year college or university. They should be able to demonstrate the qualities associated with Soledad Fernandez: resourcefulness, responsibility, thoughtfulness about Filipino heritage, overcoming hardships or appreciating advantages, independence, commitment to lifelong learning, motivation, and maturity. Selection is based on merit and financial need. Finalists must be available for an interview.

Financial data The stipend is $5,000 per year.

Duration 1 year.

Number awarded 1 to 3 each year.

Deadline January of each year.

[325]
SONOMA COUNTY JACL MEMORIAL SCHOLARSHIP

Japanese American Citizens League-Sonoma County
   Chapter
Attn: Scholarship Committee
P.O. Box 1915
Santa Rosa, CA 95402
E-mail: info@sonomacojacl.org
Web: www.sonomacojacl.org/Pages/scholars.htm

Purpose To provide financial assistance for college to members of the Sonoma County (California) Chapter of the Japanese American Citizens League (JACL) and their children.

Eligibility This program is open to graduating high school seniors in Sonoma County, California who are planning to attend a college, university, or vocational/technical school. Applicants must be members of the Sonoma County JACL or have parents who are members. Along with their application, they must submit a 250-word personal statement on their personality, why they have selected their major, why they desire to attend the college(s) they have applied to, and their view of themselves and the world in which they live. Their statement should emphasize their Japanese ancestry and/or their connection with the Asian/Japanese American community and how it has affected or impacted who they are as well as their personal goals. Financial need is considered in case of a tie.

Financial data A stipend is awarded (amount not specified).

Duration 1 year.

Additional information Information is also available from Margaret E. Wallman, 1720 Mariposa Drive, Santa Rosa, CA 95405, (707) 544-9368.

Number awarded 1 each year.

Deadline February of each year.

[326]
SONOMA COUNTY JACL STUDENT GRANT

Japanese American Citizens League-Sonoma County
   Chapter
Attn: Scholarship Committee
P.O. Box 1915
Santa Rosa, CA 95402
E-mail: info@sonomacojacl.org
Web: www.sonomacojacl.org/Pages/scholars.htm

Purpose To provide financial assistance for college to high school seniors in Sonoma County, California who are of Japanese ancestry.

Eligibility This program is open to graduating high school seniors in Sonoma County, California who are planning to attend a college, university, or vocational/technical school. Applicants must be of Japanese ancestry. Along with their application, they must submit a 250-word personal statement on their personality, why they have selected their major, why they desire to attend the college(s) they have applied to, and their view of themselves and the world in which they live. Their statement should emphasize their Japanese ancestry and/or their connection with the Asian/Japanese American community and how it has affected or impacted who they are as well as their personal goals. Financial need must be demonstrated.

Financial data A stipend is awarded (amount not specified).

Duration 1 year.

Additional information Information is also available from Margaret E. Wallman, 1720 Mariposa Drive, Santa Rosa, CA 95405, (707) 544-9368.

Number awarded 1 each year.

Deadline February of each year.

[327]
SOUTH FLORIDA CHAPTER AIA SCHOLARSHIP PROGRAM

Association of Indians in America-South Florida
   Chapter
Attn: Scholarship Program
11851 N.W. Tenth Place
Coral Springs, FL 33071
E-mail: aiaflorida@myacc.net
Web: www.aiaflorida.org/scholarship.htm

Purpose To provide financial assistance for college to high school seniors in south Florida who are affiliated with the Association of Indians in America (AIA).

Eligibility This program is open to permanent residents or naturalized U.S. citizens whose parents migrated to the United States after the independence of India on August 15, 1947. Applicants must be seniors graduating from high schools in Broward, Dade, or Palm Beach counties in Florida. They must have been individual or family members of the AIA for at least 1 year; have a GPA of 3.0 or higher; have an excellent SAT score; and have been involved in a humanitarian community service project that reflects the mission of AIA: "Indian Heritage and American Commitment." Along with their application, they must submit a 500-word essay on their impressions of adjusting to the American culture while still preserving their Indian heritage. The AIA membership, GPA, and SAT requirements are waived if the applicant can demonstrate financial hardship.

Financial data The stipend is $1,000.

Duration 1 year; nonrenewable.

Additional information Information is also available from Joyce Campos, 10224 Vestal Court, Coral Springs, FL 33071, (954) 752-7573.

Number awarded Varies each year; recently, 14 of these scholarships were awarded.

Deadline April of the year.

[328]
SOUTH PARK JAPANESE COMMUNITY SCHOLARSHIP

Japanese American Citizens League
Attn: National Scholarship Awards
1765 Sutter Street
San Francisco, CA 94115
(415) 921-5225   Fax: (415) 931-4671
E-mail: jacl@jacl.org
Web: www.jacl.org/scholarships.html

Purpose To provide financial assistance for college to student members of the Japanese American Citizens League (JACL) who are high school seniors.

Eligibility This program is open to JACL members who are high school seniors interested in attending a college, university, trade school, business college, or other institution of higher learning. Applicants must submit a statement describing their current level of involvement in the Japanese American community or Asian Pacific community and how they will continue their involvement in future years. Selection is based on academic record, extracurricular activities, and community involvement.

Financial data The stipend depends on the availability of funds but usually ranges from $1,000 to $5,000.

Duration 1 year; nonrenewable.

Additional information This scholarship was established by the Japanese American Citizens League group in Seattle, Washington. Applications must be submitted to the local JACL chapter.

Number awarded At least 1 each year.

Deadline February of each year.

[329]
SOUTHERN REGION KOREAN AMERICAN SCHOLARSHIPS

Korean American Scholarship Foundation
Southern Region
c/o Dr. Sam Sook Chung, Scholarship Committee Chair
2989 Preston Drive
Rex, GA 30273
(770) 968-6768   E-mail: southern@kasf.org
Web: www.kasf.org

Purpose To provide financial assistance to Korean American undergraduate and graduate students who attend school in the southern states.

Eligibility This program is open to Korean American students who are currently enrolled in a college or university in the southern states as full-time undergraduate or graduate students. Applicants may reside anywhere in the United States as long as they attend school in the southern region: Alabama, Arkansas, Florida, Georgia, Louisiana, Mississippi, Oklahoma, South Carolina, Tennessee, and Texas. Selection is based on academic achievement, school activities, community service, and financial need.

Financial data Stipends range from $1,000 to $2,000.

Duration 1 year; renewable.

Number awarded Varies each year. Recently, 39 of these scholarships, worth $42,700, were awarded.

Deadline June of each year.

[330]
SPORTS JOURNALISM INSTITUTE

Associated Press Sports Editors
c/o Sandy Bailey
Sports Illustrated
135 West 50th Street
New York, NY 10020
(212) 522-6407   E-mail: Sandy_Bailey@simail.com
Web: apse.dallasnews.com/news/sjiapplication.html

Purpose To provide student journalists (especially those of color) with an opportunity to learn more about sports journalism during the summer.

Eligibility This program is open to college juniors and sophomores, especially members of ethnic and racial minority groups. Applicants must be interested in participating in a summer program that includes a crash course in

sports journalism followed by an internship in the sports department of a daily newspaper. They must submit a current college transcript, 2 letters of recommendation, up to 7 writing samples or clips, and an essay of up to 500 words stating why they should be chosen to participate in the program. Selection is based on academic achievement, demonstrated interest in sports journalism as a career, and the essay. Eligibility is not limited to journalism majors.

Financial data All expenses are paid during the crash course segment. A salary is paid during the internship portion. At the conclusion of the program, participants receive a $500 scholarship for the following year of college.

Duration 10 days for the crash course (at the end of June); 7 weeks for the internship (July through mid-August); 1 year for the college scholarship.

Additional information The crash course takes place during the annual convention of the Associated Press Sports Editors (ASPE), which provides funding for this program, along with the Times Mirror Foundation and the New York Daily News. The institute works with the National Association of Black Journalists (NABJ), the Asian American Journalists Association (AAJA), and the National Association of Hispanic Journalists (NAHJ).

Number awarded 10 each year.

Deadline December of each year.

[331]
SPRINT SCHOLARSHIP PROGRAM

North Carolina Community College System
Attn: Student Development Services
200 West Jones Street
5016 Mail Service Center
Raleigh, NC 27699-5016
(919) 807-7106   Fax: (919) 807-7164
E-mail: littlep@ncccs.cc.nc.us
Web: www.ncccs.cc.nc.us

Purpose To provide financial assistance to North Carolina residents (particularly minorities) studying at publicly-supported technical or vocational schools in the state.

Eligibility This program is open to North Carolina residents enrolled full time in the 34 community colleges in Sprint's local service areas in the state. Applicants must be enrolled or planning to enroll in a course of study leading to an associate of applied science degree or vocational diploma. Priority is given to women, "displaced workers," and minorities (defined by Sprint as African Americans, Hispanics, American Indians/Native Alaskans, Pacific Islanders, and Asians). Selection is based on scholastic achievements, individual financial need, participation in outside activities, and demonstrated interest in a technical or vocational career.

Financial data The stipend is $700 per year.

Duration 1 year; may be renewed 1 additional year if the recipient maintains a GPA at or above the level required for graduation

Additional information Recipients are encouraged to seek employment with Sprint (the program's sponsor) after graduation. There are no special application forms for the scholarship. Students apply to their local community college, not to the system office. Each eligible school selects its own recipients from applicants meeting the above criteria.

Number awarded 34 each year: 1 at each participating community college.

[332]
ST. PAUL PIONEER PRESS SCHOLARSHIP FOR MINORITIES

St. Paul Pioneer Press
Attn: Dan Baltzer
345 Cedar Street
St. Paul, MN 55101-1057
(651) 228-5006   Fax: (651) 228-5197
E-mail: dbaltzer@pioneerpress.com
Web: www.pioneerpress.com

Purpose To provide financial assistance to minority students in selected areas of Minnesota who are interested in going to college to prepare for a career in journalism or business.

Eligibility This program is open to minority high school seniors interested in preparing for a career in journalism or business. Applicants must reside in the circulation area of the *St. Paul Pioneer Press* (Anoka, Chisago, Dakota, Ramsey, and Washington counties in Minnesota; Pierce, Polk, and St. Croix counties in Wisconsin). Applicants must submit an essay on why they want to prepare for a career in newspapering, what they know about Knight Ridder, and how they see themselves working in Knight Ridder. Selection is based on the essay, transcripts, standardized test scores, extracurricular activities, 2 letters of recommendation, and (for journalism applicants) up to 5 samples of work with bylines.

Financial data The stipend is $500.

Duration 1 year; nonrenewable.

Additional information Recipients work as paid interns during the summer at the *Pioneer Press.* They also are nominated as candidates for Knight Ridder scholarships of $40,000 over 4 years.

Number awarded 2 each year: 1 in journalism and 1 in business.

Deadline January of each year.

[333]
STAN BECK FELLOWSHIP

Entomological Society of America
Attn: Entomological Foundation
9332 Annapolis Road, Suite 210
Lanham, MD 20706-3150
(301) 459-9082   Fax: (301) 459-9084
E-mail: melodie@entfdn.org
Web: www.entfdn.org/beck.html

Purpose To assist "needy" students working on an undergraduate or graduate degree in science who are nominated by members of the Entomological Society of America (ESA).

Eligibility This program is open to students working on an undergraduate or graduate degree in entomology at a college or university in Canada, Mexico, or the United States. Candidates must be nominated by members of the society. They must be "needy" students; for the purposes of this program, need may be based on physical limitations, or economic, minority, or environmental conditions.

Financial data The stipend is $2,000 per year.

Duration 1 year; may be renewed up to 3 additional years.

Additional information Recipients are expected to be present at the society's annual meeting, where the award will be presented.

Number awarded 1 or more each year.

Deadline June of each year.

[334]
STANLEY E. JACKSON SCHOLARSHIP AWARD FOR ETHNIC MINORITY GIFTED/TALENTED STUDENTS WITH DISABILITIES

Council for Exceptional Children
Attn: Yes I Can! Foundation for Exceptional Children
1110 North Glebe Road, Suite 300
Arlington, VA 22201-5704
(703) 620-3660   Toll-free: (800) 224-6830, ext. 462
Fax: (703) 264-9494   TTY: (866) 915-5000
E-mail: yesican@cec.sped.org
Web: yesican.sped.org/scholarship/index.html

Purpose To provide financial assistance for college to gifted minority students with disabilities.

Eligibility Applicants must be gifted or talented in 1 or more of the following categories: general intellectual ability, specific academic aptitude, creativity, leadership, or visual or performing arts. They must be disabled, financially needy, ready to begin college, and a member of an ethnic minority group (e.g., Asian, African American, Hispanic, or Native American). Candidates must submit a 200-word statement of philosophical, educational, and occupational goals as part of the application process. Selection is based on academic achievement, ability, promise, and financial need. U.S. citizenship is required.

Financial data The stipend is $500.

Duration 1 year; nonrenewable.

Additional information Scholarships may be used for 2- or 4-year college programs or for vocational, technical, or fine arts training programs. Recipients must enroll full time.

Number awarded 1 or more each year.

Deadline January of each year.

[335]
STANLEY E. JACKSON SCHOLARSHIP AWARD FOR ETHNIC MINORITY STUDENTS WITH DISABILITIES

Council for Exceptional Children
Attn: Yes I Can! Foundation for Exceptional Children
1110 North Glebe Road, Suite 300
Arlington, VA 22201-5704
(703) 620-3660   Toll-free: (800) 224-6830, ext. 462
Fax: (703) 264-9494   TTY: (866) 915-5000
E-mail: yesican@cec.sped.org
Web: yesican.sped.org/scholarship/index.html

Purpose To provide financial assistance for college to minority students with disabilities.

Eligibility Applicants must be students with disabilities who intend to enroll for the first time on a full-time basis in a college, university, vocational/technical school, or fine arts institute and are able to document financial need. Only minority (African American, Asian, Native American, or Hispanic) students are eligible for the award. Candidates must submit a 200-word statement of philosophical, educational, and occupational goals as part of the application process. Selection is based on academic achievement, ability, promise, and financial need. U.S. citizenship is required.

Financial data The stipend is $500.

Duration 1 year; nonrenewable.

Additional information Scholarships may be used for 2- or 4-year college programs or for vocational, technical, or fine arts training programs. Recipients must enroll full time.

Number awarded 1 or more each year.

Deadline January of each year.

[336]
STAR-TELEGRAM/DIARIO LA ESTRELLA/NIE/KNIGHT RIDDER MINORITY SCHOLARSHIPS

Fort Worth Star-Telegram
Attn: Minority Scholarships
400 West Seventh Street
Fort Worth, TX 76102-4793
(817) 390-7878   Fax: (817) 336-3739
Web: www.star-telegram.com

Purpose To provide financial assistance to minority high school seniors in the circulation area of the *Fort Worth Star-Telegram* who are interested in attending college to prepare for a career in the newspaper industry.

Eligibility This program is open to minority seniors graduating from high schools in the Fort Worth-Arlington Metropolitan area (Hood, Johnson, Parker, and Tarrant counties) as well as 14 adjoining counties in north Texas. Applicants must be planning to attend college to prepare for a career in the newspaper industry, including both journalism and business (e.g., advertising, circulation, computer science, marketing, production). Along with their application, they must submit a transcript of grades, SAT and/or ACT scores, 2 letters of recommendation, up to 5 writing samples (for journalism applicants), and a 750-word essay on why they want to prepare for a career in journalism or the newspaper business.

Financial data The stipend is $1,000.

Duration 1 year.

Additional information This program is sponsored by the *Star-Telegram,* its Spanish-language affiliate *Diario La Estrella,* and its Newspapers in Education (NIE) program. The recipients of these scholarships are entered into competition for the Knight Ridder Minority Scholarship Program of $40,000 over 4 years.

Number awarded Up to 5 each year.

Deadline January of each year.

[337]
THE STATE NEWSPAPER AND KNIGHT RIDDER MINORITY SCHOLARSHIP PROGRAM

The State Newspaper
Attn: Tanya Fogg Young
1401 Shop Road
P.O. Box 1333
Columbia, SC 29202-1333
(803) 771-8659   Fax: (803) 540-3041
E-mail: tfyoung@thestate.com
Web: www.thestate.com

Purpose To provide financial assistance to minority high school seniors in South Carolina interested in attending college to prepare for a newspaper career.

Eligibility This program is open to minority seniors graduating from high schools in South Carolina. Applicants must be interested in attending college to prepare for a career in journalism or business communications. Along with their application, they must submit a transcript with grades and SAT/ACT scores, 2 letters of recommendation, up to 5 samples of work (for journalism students), a list of any journalism or business experience, a description of extracurricular activities, and an essay on why they want to prepare for a career in journalism or business communications.

Financial data The stipend is $500.

Duration 1 year.

Additional information The recipients of these scholarships are entered into competition for the Knight Ridder Minority Scholarship Program of $40,000 over 4 years.

Number awarded 1 each year.

Deadline January of each year.

[338]
STUDENT OPPORTUNITY SCHOLARSHIPS FOR ETHNIC MINORITY GROUPS

Presbyterian Church (USA)
Attn: Office of Financial Aid for Studies
100 Witherspoon Street, Room M-052
Louisville, KY 40202-1396
(502) 569-5745   Toll-free: (888) 728-7228, ext. 5745
Fax: (502) 569-8766   E-mail: KSmith@ctr.pcusa.org
Web: www.pcusa.org

Purpose To provide financial assistance for college to high school seniors of racial/ethnic minority heritage who are Presbyterians.

Eligibility This program is open to members of the Presbyterian Church (USA) who are from racial/ethnic minority groups (Asian American, African American, Hispanic American, Native American, Alaska Native). Applicants must be able to demonstrate financial need, be high school seniors entering college as full-time students, and be U.S. citizens or permanent residents. They must submit a recommendation from their high school guidance counselor, a high school transcript, and an essay (up to 500 words in length) on their career goals and how they plan to achieve them.

Financial data Stipends range from $100 to $1,000 per year, depending upon the financial need of the recipient.

Duration 1 year; may be renewed for up to 3 additional years if the recipient continues to need financial assistance and demonstrates satisfactory academic progress.

Number awarded Varies each year.

Deadline April of each year.

[339]
SUMMER WORKSHOPS WRITING COMPETITION FOR MINORITY HIGH SCHOOL STUDENTS

Dow Jones Newspaper Fund
P.O. Box 300
Princeton, NJ 08543-0300
(609) 452-2820   Fax: (609) 520-5804
E-mail: newsfund@wsf.dowjones.com
Web: DJNewspaperFund.dowjones.com

Purpose To recognize and reward (with college scholarships) outstanding participants in journalism workshops for minority high school students.

Eligibility Each summer, workshops on college campuses around the country allow minority high school students to experience work on a professional-quality publication. Students are taught to write, report, design, and layout a newspaper on topics relevant to youth. The director of each workshop nominates 1 student who submits an article from the workshop newspaper and an essay on why he/she wants to pursue journalism as a career. The students whose articles and essay are judged most outstanding receive these college scholarships.

Financial data The award is a college scholarship of $1,000.

Duration Workshops normally last 2 weeks during the summer. Scholarships are for 1 year and may be renewed for 1 additional year if the recipient maintains a GPA of 2.5 or higher and an interest in journalism.

Additional information Recently, workshops were held on college campuses in Alabama, Arizona, Arkansas, California, Florida, Illinois, Kentucky, Massachusetts, Minnesota, Mississippi, Missouri, New Jersey, New York, Ohio, Oklahoma, Pennsylvania, South Dakota, Texas, Virginia, Washington, and Wisconsin. For the name and address of the director of each workshop, contact the Newspaper Fund.

Number awarded 8 each year.

[340]
SYNOD OF THE COVENANT ETHNIC STUDENT SCHOLARSHIPS

Synod of the Covenant
Attn: CECA Ethnic Scholarship Committee
1911 Indianwood Circle, Suite B
Maumee, OH 43537-4063
(419) 754-4050
Toll-free: (800) 848-1030 (within MI and OH)
Web: www.synodofthecovenant.org

Purpose To provide financial assistance to ethnic students working on an undergraduate degree (with priority given to Presbyterian applicants from Ohio and Michigan).

Eligibility This program is open to ethnic minority students working full or part time on a baccalaureate degree or certification at a college, university, or vocational school. Applicants must have a GPA of 3.0 or higher and be able to demonstrate participation in a Presbyterian church. Priority is given to Presbyterian applicants from the states of Michigan and Ohio. Financial need is considered in the selection process.

Financial data The maximum amount allowed within a calendar year is $600 (for full-time students in their first year), $800 (for renewals to full-time students), or $400 (for part-time students). Funds are made payable to the session for distribution.

Duration Students are eligible to receive scholarships 1 time per year, up to a maximum of 5 years. Renewals are granted provided 1) the completed application is received before the deadline date, 2) the recipient earned at least a 2.0 GPA last year, and 3) the application contains evidence of Presbyterian church participation and continued spiritual development.

Number awarded Varies each year.

Deadline September of each year for fall semester; February of each year for spring semester.

[341]
TEACHERS FOR TOMORROW SCHOLARSHIP PROGRAM

Edison International
Attn: Educational Relations
P.O. Box 800
Rosemead, CA 91770
(626) 302-3382   Fax: (626) 302-3007
Web: www.edison.com

Purpose To provide financial assistance to minority and other students at designated campuses of the California State University (CSU) system who are working on their teaching credential.

Eligibility This program is open to students enrolled as a full-time CSU student in a teacher preparation program (single subject, multiple subject, or special education credential) at designated campuses in southern California. Applicants must have a cumulative GPA of 3.0 or higher and be able to demonstrate financial need. Preference is given to applicants who are economically and educationally disadvantaged. Selection is based on 2 letters of reference, a 2-page essay describing reasons for entering the teaching profession, and a 1-page statement that reflects a commitment to education and service to the community.

Financial data The stipend is $5,000 per year.

Duration 1 year.

Additional information The eligible CSU campuses are those at Dominguez Hills, Fullerton, Long Beach, Los Angeles, Northridge, Pomona, and San Bernardino. This program was established in 1999.

Number awarded 25 each year.

Deadline Students must apply to the financial aid office of their university by January of each year; each financial aid officer must submit the nominations from that institution by February of each year.

[342]
TELAMON SCHOLARSHIP

US Pan Asian American Chamber of Commerce
Attn: Scholarship Coordinator
1329 18th Street, N.W.
Washington, DC 20036
(202) 296-5221   Fax: (202) 296-5225
E-mail: administrator@uspaacc.com
Web: www.uspaacc.com/web/programs/telamon.htm

Purpose   To provide financial assistance for college to Asian American high school seniors.

Eligibility   This program is open to high school seniors of Asian heritage who are U.S. citizens or permanent residents. Applicants must be planning to begin full-time study at an accredited postsecondary educational institution in the United States. Along with their application, they must submit a 500-word essay on "What are the characteristics or qualities needed in order to achieve success?" Selection is based on academic excellence (GPA of 3.5 or higher), leadership in extracurricular activities, community service involvement, and financial need.

Financial data   The maximum stipend is $3,500. Funds are paid directly to the recipient's college or university.

Duration   1 year.

Additional information   This program was established in 2001. Funding is not provided for correspondence courses, Internet courses, or study in a country other than the United States.

Number awarded   1 each year.

Deadline   February of each year.

[343]
TEXAS CHAPTER SCHOLARSHIPS

Asian American Journalists Association-Texas Chapter
c/o Julie Tam, Scholarship Chair
KLTV-TV ABC 7
105 West Ferguson
P.O. Box 957
Tyler, TX 75710
(903) 597-5588   Fax: (903) 510-7847
E-mail: julie@julietam.com
Web: chapters.aaja.org/Texas/schol.html

Purpose   To provide financial assistance to members of the Asian American Journalists Association (AAJA) in Texas who are working on an undergraduate or graduate degree in journalism.

Eligibility   This program is open to graduating high school seniors, undergraduates, and graduate students who are either Texas residents or planning to attend an accredited college or university in Texas. Applicants must be AAJA members. Along with their application, they must submit a 250-word autobiography that explains why they are interested in a career in journalism, a 500-word essay on the role of ethnic diversity in news coverage (both for the subjects of the news events and also the journalists involved), their most recent official transcript, a statement of financial need, 2 letters of recommendation, and a resume. Work samples to be submitted are 2 legible clips from print journalism students; 3 to 5 prints or slides with captions or descriptions from print photojournalism students; 2 VHS taped excerpts with corresponding scripts from television broadcast students; 2 edited VHS excepts from television photojournal-

ism students; 3 taped cassette excerpts with corresponding scripts from radio broadcast students; or 3 legible online articles from web journalism students. Selection is based on commitment to the field of journalism, awareness of Asian American issues, journalistic ability, scholastic ability, and financial need.

Financial data   The stipend is $1,000 per year.

Duration   1 year.

Number awarded   2 each year.

Deadline   April of each year.

[344]
THIRD WAVE FOUNDATION WOODLAKE SCHOLARSHIPS

Third Wave Foundation
511 West 25th Street, Suite 301
New York, NY 10002
(212) 675-0700   Fax: (212) 255-6653
E-mail: info@thirdwavefoundation.org
Web: www.thirdwavefoundation.org

Purpose   To provide educational assistance to undergraduate and graduate women of color who have been involved as social change activists.

Eligibility   This program is open to full-time and part-time students under 30 years of age who are enrolled in, or have been accepted to, an accredited university, college, vocational/technical school, community college, or graduate school. Applicants must be women of color who place greater emphasis on social justice and the struggle for justice and equality over academic performance and who integrate social justice into all areas of their lives. They must submit 500-word essays on 1) their current social change involvement and how it relates to their educational and life goals; and 2) if they would describe themselves as a feminist and why. Graduate students and students planning to study abroad through a U.S. university program are also eligible. Selection is based on financial need and commitment to social justice work.

Financial data   Stipends are $3,000 or $1,000 per year.

Duration   1 year.

Number awarded   Varies each year. Recently, 8 of these scholarships were awarded: 6 at $3,000 and 2 at $1,000.

Deadline   March or September of each year.

[345]
THZ FO FARM FUND

Hawai'i Community Foundation
Attn: Scholarship Department
1164 Bishop Street, Suite 800
Honolulu, HI 96813
(808) 537-6333   Toll-free: (888) 731-3863
Fax: (808) 521-6286
E-mail: scholarships@hcf-hawaii.org
Web: www.hawaiicommunityfoundation.org

Purpose   To provide financial assistance to Hawaii residents of Chinese descent who are interested in studying gerontology on the undergraduate or graduate school level.

Eligibility   This program is open to high school seniors, high school graduates, and college students in Hawaii who are of Chinese ancestry and are interested in studying gerontology as full-time undergraduate or graduate students.

They must be able to demonstrate academic achievement (GPA of 2.7 or higher), good moral character, and financial need. In addition to filling out the standard application form, applicants must write a short statement indicating their reasons for attending college, their planned course of study, and their career goals.

Financial data The amounts of the awards depend on the availability of funds and the need of the recipient; recently, stipends averaged $1,500.

Duration 1 year.

Additional information Recipients may attend college in Hawaii or on the mainland.

Number awarded Varies each year; recently, 2 of these scholarships were awarded.

Deadline February of each year.

[346]
TILLIE GOLUB-SCHWARTZ MEMORIAL SCHOLARSHIP FOR MINORITIES

Golub Foundation
c/o Price Chopper Scholarship Office, Mailbox 60
501 Duanesburg Road
P.O. Box 1074
Schenectady, NY 12301
(518) 356-9450   Toll-free: (877) 877-0870
Web: www.pricechopper.com

Purpose To provide financial assistance for college to minority high school seniors in selected areas of several states: Connecticut, Massachusetts, New Hampshire, New York, Pennsylvania, and Vermont.

Eligibility This program is open to high school seniors in areas of Connecticut, Massachusetts, New Hampshire, New York, Pennsylvania, and Vermont served by Price Chopper Supermarkets who plan to attend an accredited 2-year or 4-year college or university in those states. Applicants must be Alaskan Native, American Indian, Asian, Pacific Islander, Black (not of Hispanic origin), Puerto Rican, Mexican American, or other Hispanic. Along with their application, they must submit information on their educational history, including grades, Regents marks (if applicable), rank in class, and SAT and/or ACT scores; honors and awards; participation in school, extracurricular, civic, and/or leadership activities; 3 reference letters; and a 1,000-word essay on how they have demonstrated a commitment to humanity through their involvement in community, church, and/or school activities.

Financial data The stipend is $2,000 per year.

Duration 4 years.

Additional information The Golub Corporation is the parent company of Price Chopper Supermarkets, which operates in the following counties: in Connecticut, Litchfield, New Haven, and Windham; in Massachusetts, Berkshire, Hampden, Hampshire, Middlesex, and Worcester; in New Hampshire, Cheshire, Grafton, and Sullivan; in New York, Albany, Broome, Cayuga, Chenango, Clinton, Columbia, Cortland, Delaware, Dutchess, Essex, Franklin, Fulton, Greene, Hamilton, Herkimer, Jefferson, Lewis, Madison, Montgomery, Oneida, Onondaga, Orange, Oswego, Otsego, Rensselaer, St. Lawrence, Saratoga, Schenectady, Sullivan, Schoharie, Tioga, Tompkins, Ulster, Warren, and Washington; in Pennsylvania, Lackawanna, Luzerne, Susquehanna, Wayne, and Wyoming; in Vermont, Addison, Bennington, Caledonia, Chittenden, Essex, Franklin, Grand Isle, Lamoille, Orange, Orleans, Rutland, Washington, Windham, and Windsor.

Number awarded 1 each year.

Deadline March of each year.

[347]
T.P. WANG SCHOLARSHIP

Chinese Professional Club of Houston
Attn: John Loh, Scholarship Committee Chair
P.O. Box 941682
Houston, TX 77094-8682
(832) 428-8832
Web: www.cpchouston.com/scholarship.htm

Purpose To provide financial assistance for college, graduate school, or other study activities to members of the Chinese Professional Club (CPC) of Houston and their families.

Eligibility This program is open to CPC members and their offspring who are interested in undergraduate, graduate, leadership, or community service development studies. Applicants for undergraduate or graduate study must submit 2 essays (1 on themselves and their aspirations, 1 on either being a Chinese American living in the United States or a person or event that has had the greatest influence on their lives); transcripts; a list of academic honors, awards, and scholarships; a list of extracurricular activities and personal initiatives; and 2 letters of recommendation. Applicants for non-academic study must submit a personal resume, 2 letters of recommendation, and an essay, of 300 to 500 words, on their aspirations and how the scholarship can help to achieve their goals.

Financial data A stipend is awarded (amount not specified). Funds must be used for payment of tuition.

Duration 1 year.

Additional information This scholarship was established in 2002.

Number awarded 1 each year.

Deadline November of each year.

[348]
TRIBUNE/KNIGHT RIDDER MINORITY SCHOLARSHIP PROGRAM

San Luis Obispo Tribune
Attn: Devon Goetz
3825 South Higuera Street
San Luis Obispo, CA 93406
(805) 781-7805   Fax: (805) 781-7966
E-mail: dgoetz@thetribunenews.com
Web: www.thetribunenews.com

Purpose To provide financial assistance to minority high school seniors in San Luis Obispo County, California who are interested in attending college to prepare for a career in the newspaper industry.

Eligibility This program is open to minority seniors graduating from high schools in San Luis Obispo County, California. Applicants must be planning to attend college to prepare for a career in journalism, photography, graphic design, marketing, advertising, production, or other newspaper-related field. They should be able to demonstrate grades that reflect a collegiate standard and participation in the school and community. Along with their application, they must submit an essay on why they want to prepare for a career in journalism or the newspaper business, including what they know about Knight Ridder and how they see themselves making a difference at Knight Ridder.

Financial data The stipend is $1,000.

Duration 1 year.

Additional information The recipients of these scholarships are entered into competition for the Knight Ridder Minority Scholarship Program of $40,000 over 4 years.

Number awarded 1 each year.

Deadline January of each year.

[349]
TU'IPELEHAKE LEADERSHIP SCHOLARSHIP

National Tongan American Society
Attn: Director
2480 South Main Street, Suite 108
Salt Lake City, UT 84115
(801) 467-8712
Web: www.planet-tonga.com/NTAS/education.htm

Purpose To provide financial assistance for college to high school seniors of Tongan background who reside in Utah or Tonga.

Eligibility This program is open to financially disadvantaged Tongan students with leadership skills residing in Utah who are qualified and determined to graduate with a degree from an accredited college/university. Also eligible to apply are qualified and financially disadvantaged students residing in Tonga who are potential leaders, graduating from high school, and seeking to attend a college or university. All applicants must have a cumulative GPA of 3.0 or better, be able to demonstrate leadership ability, and have a record of community service and extracurricular activities.

Financial data The stipend is $1,000 for recipients from Utah and full-tuition scholarships at Tonga colleges for recipients from Tonga.

Duration 1 year.

Additional information This scholarship was first awarded in 2006.

Number awarded Several each year.

Deadline January of each year for Utah residents; November of each year for residents of Tonga.

[350]
TYLER WARD MINORITY JOURNALISM SCHOLARSHIP

Society of Professional Journalists-Mid-Florida Chapter
c/o Randy Miller, Scholarship Committee Chair
University of South Florida
School of Mass Communications
4202 East Fowler Avenue, CIS 1040
Tampa, FL 33620-7800
(813) 974-6791   Fax: (813) 974-2592
E-mail: rmiller@chuma.cas.usf.edu
Web: www.spj.org/midflorida/tylerinfo.htm

Purpose To provide financial assistance to minority students in mid-Florida who are interested in preparing for a career in journalism.

Eligibility This program is open to minority college students who are from the mid-Florida (between Gainesville

and Sarasota) region or who attend colleges or universities there. Applicants must submit an essay on their goals for a journalism career and a reference letter from a journalism professor or a campus media adviser.

Financial data The stipend is $1,000.

Duration 1 year.

Number awarded 1 each year.

Deadline May of each year.

[351]
UNCF/HOUSEHOLD CORPORATE SCHOLARS PROGRAM

United Negro College Fund
Attn: Corporate Scholars Program
P.O. Box 1435
Alexandria, VA 22313-9998
Toll-free: (866) 671-7237   E-mail: internship@uncf.org
Web: www.uncf.org/internships/index.asp

Purpose To provide financial assistance and work experience to minority and other students majoring in fields related to business.

Eligibility This program is open to rising juniors majoring in accounting, business, computer science, finance, human resources, or marketing with a GPA of 3.0 or higher. Applicants must be interested in an internship with Household International, the program's sponsor, at 1 of the following sites: Bridgewater, New Jersey; Charlotte, North Carolina; Chesapeake, Virginia; Chicago, Illinois; Dallas, Texas; Indianapolis, Indiana; Jacksonville, Florida; Monterey, California; New Castle, Delaware; San Diego, California; or Tampa, Florida. Preference is given to applicants who reside in those areas, but students who live in other areas are also considered. African Americans, Hispanic Americans, American Indians, and Asian Americans are encouraged to apply. Along with their application, students must submit an essay on their personal and career goals and objectives, a letter of recommendation, and an official transcript.

Financial data This program provides a stipend of up to $10,000 per year and a paid internship.

Duration 8 to 10 weeks for the internships; 1 year for the scholarships, which may be renewed.

Number awarded Varies each year.

Deadline February of each year.

[352]
UNCF/SPRINT SCHOLARS PROGRAM

United Negro College Fund
Attn: Corporate Scholars Program
P.O. Box 1435
Alexandria, VA 22313-9998
Toll-free: (866) 671-7237   E-mail: internship@uncf.org
Web: www.uncf.org/internships/index.asp

Purpose To provide financial assistance and work experience to minority students who are majoring in selected business and science fields.

Eligibility This program is open to members of minority groups who are enrolled full time as juniors or seniors at a 4-year college or university in the United States. Applicants must have a GPA of 3.0 or higher and be majoring in accounting, business, computer engineering, computer information systems, computer science, economics, electrical engineering, finance, industrial engineering, journalism, marketing, management information systems, public relations, or statistics. They must be interested in a summer internship at Sprint. Along with their application, they must submit a 1-page personal statement describing their career interests and goals, a current resume, a letter of recommendation, official transcripts, and a financial need statement.

Financial data This program provides a paid internship and (upon successful completion of the internship) a need-based stipend of up to $7,500.

Duration 10 to 12 weeks for the internships; 1 year for the scholarships.

Additional information This program is sponsored by Sprint. Recipients may attend any of the 39 member institutions of the United Negro College Fund (UNCF), other Historically Black Colleges and Universities (HBCUs), or an accredited majority 4-year college or university.

Number awarded Varies each year.

Deadline October of each year.

[353]
UNITED METHODIST ETHNIC MINORITY SCHOLARSHIPS

United Methodist Church
Attn: General Board of Higher Education and Ministry
Office of Loans and Scholarships
1001 19th Avenue South
P.O. Box 340007
Nashville, TN 37203-0007
(615) 340-7344   Fax: (615) 340-7367
E-mail: umscholar@gbhem.org
Web: www.gbhem.org

Purpose To provide financial assistance to undergraduate Methodist students who are of ethnic minority ancestry.

Eligibility This program is open to full-time undergraduate students at accredited colleges and universities in the United States who have been active, full members of a United Methodist Church for at least 1 year prior to applying. Applicants must have at least 1 parent who is African American, Hispanic, Asian, Native American, Alaska Native, or Pacific Islander. They must have a GPA of 2.5 or higher and be able to demonstrate financial need. U.S. citizenship, permanent resident status, or membership in a central conference of the United Methodist Church is required.

Financial data A stipend is awarded (amount not specified).

Duration 1 year; recipients may reapply.

Number awarded Varies each year.

Deadline April of each year.

[354]
UNITED METHODIST SCHOLARSHIP PROGRAM

United Methodist Church
Attn: General Board of Higher Education and Ministry
Office of Loans and Scholarships
1001 19th Avenue South
P.O. Box 340007
Nashville, TN 37203-0007
(615) 340-7344   Fax: (615) 340-7367
E-mail: umscholar@gbhem.org
Web: www.gbhem.org

Purpose To provide financial assistance to undergraduate and graduate students attending schools affiliated with the United Methodist Church.

Eligibility This program is open to U.S. citizens and permanent residents who have been active, full members of a United Methodist Church for at least 1 year prior to applying; members of the A.M.E., A.M.E. Zion, and other "Methodist" denominations are not eligible. Undergraduates must have been admitted to a full-time degree program at a United Methodist-related college or university and have a GPA of 2.5 or above. Most graduate scholarships are designated for persons working on a degree in theological studies (M.Div., D.Min., Ph.D.) or higher education administration, or for older adults changing their careers. Some scholarships are designated for racial ethnic undergraduate or graduate students. Applications are available from the financial aid office of the United Methodist school the applicant attends or from the chair of their annual conference Board of Higher Education and Campus Ministry.

Financial data The funding is intended to supplement the students' own resources.

Duration 1 year; renewal policies are set by participating universities.

Number awarded Varies each year.

[355]
UNITED PARCEL SERVICE SCHOLARSHIP FOR MINORITY STUDENTS

Institute of Industrial Engineers
Attn: Chapter Operations Department
3577 Parkway Lane, Suite 200
Norcross, GA 30092
(770) 449-0461, ext. 118   Toll-free: (800) 494-0460
Fax: (770) 263-8532   E-mail: srichards@iienet.org
Web: www.iienet.org

Purpose To provide financial assistance to minority undergraduates who are studying industrial engineering at a school in the United States, Canada, or Mexico.

Eligibility Eligible to be nominated are minority undergraduate students enrolled in any school in the United States and its territories, Canada, or Mexico, provided the school's engineering program is accredited by an agency recognized by the Institute of Industrial Engineers (IIE) and the student is pursuing a full-time course of study in industrial engineering with a GPA of at least 3.4. They must have at least 5 full quarters or 3 full semesters remaining until graduation. Students may not apply directly for these awards; they must be nominated by the head of their industrial engineering department. Nominees must be IIE members. Selection is based on scholastic ability, character, leadership, potential service to the industrial engineering profession, and need for financial assistance.

Financial data The stipend is $4,000.

Duration 1 year.

Additional information Funding for this program is provided by the UPS Foundation.

Number awarded 1 each year.

Deadline November of each year.

[356]
UPS DIVERSITY SCHOLARSHIPS

American Society of Safety Engineers
Attn: ASSE Foundation
1800 East Oakton Street
Des Plaines, IL 60018
(847) 768-3441   Fax: (847) 296-9220
E-mail: mrosario@asse.org
Web: www.asse.org

Purpose To provide financial assistance to minority undergraduate student members of the American Society of Safety Engineers (ASSE).

Eligibility This program is open to ASSE student members who are enrolled in a 4-year degree program in occupational safety and health or a closely-related field (e.g., safety engineering, safety management, systems safety, environmental science, industrial hygiene, ergonomics, fire science). Applicants must be U.S. citizens and members of a minority ethnic or racial group. They must be full-time students who have completed at least 60 semester hours with a GPA of 3.0 or higher. As part of the selection process, they must submit 2 essays of 300 words or less: 1) why they are seeking a degree in safety, a brief description of their current activities, and how those relate to their career goals and objectives; and 2) why they should be awarded this scholarship (including career goals and financial need).

Financial data Stipends range from $4,000 to $6,000 per year.

Duration 1 year; nonrenewable.

Additional information Funding for this program is provided by the UPS Foundation.

Number awarded Varies each year; recently, 2 of these scholarships at $5,250 each were awarded.

Deadline November of each year.

[357]
UPS GOLD MOUNTAIN SCHOLARSHIP

Organization of Chinese Americans, Inc.
1001 Connecticut Avenue, N.W., Suite 601
Washington, DC 20036
(202) 223-5500   Fax: (202) 296-0540
E-mail: oca@ocanatl.org
Web: www.ocanatl.org

Purpose To provide financial assistance for college to Asian Pacific Americans who are the first person in their family to attend an institution of higher education.

Eligibility This program is open to Asian Pacific American students entering their first year of college in the following fall. Applicants must be the first person in their immediate family to attend college, have a cumulative GPA of 3.0 or higher, be in financial need, and be a U.S. citizen or permanent resident.

Financial data The stipend is $2,000.

Duration 1 year.

Additional information This program is funded by the UPS Foundation and administered by the Organization of Chinese Americans (OCA). Asian Pacific Americans are defined to include east Asian Americans, Filipino Americans, Pacific Islander Americans, south Asian Americans, and southeast Asian Americans.

Number awarded 12 each year.

Deadline April of each year.

[358]
USA FUNDS ACCESS TO EDUCATION SCHOLARSHIPS

Scholarship America
Attn: Scholarship Management Services
One Scholarship Way
P.O. Box 297
St. Peter, MN 56082
(507) 931-1682   Toll-free: (800) 537-4180
Fax: (507) 931-9168
E-mail: scholarship@usafunds.org
Web: www.usafunds.org

Purpose To provide financial assistance to undergraduate and graduate students, especially those who are members of ethnic minority groups or have physical disabilities.

Eligibility This program is open to high school seniors and graduates who plan to enroll or are already enrolled in full-time undergraduate or graduate course work at an accredited 2- or 4-year college, university, or vocational/technical school. Half-time undergraduate students are also eligible. Up to 50% of the awards are targeted at students who have a documented physical disability or are a member of an ethnic minority group, including but not limited to Native Hawaiian, Alaskan Native, Black/African American, Asian, Pacific Islander, American Indian, or Hispanic/Latino. Residents of 49 states (residents of Hawaii are eligible for a separate program), the District of Columbia, Puerto Rico, Guam, the U.S. Virgin Islands, and all U.S. territories and commonwealths are eligible. Preference is given to applicants from the following states: Arizona, Indiana, Kansas, Maryland, Mississippi, Nevada, and Wyoming. Applicants must also be U.S. citizens or eligible noncitizens and come from a family with an annual adjusted gross income of $35,000 or less. In addition to financial need, selection is based on past academic performance and future potential, leadership and participation in school and community activities, work experience, career and educational aspirations, and goals.

Financial data The stipend is $1,500 per year for full-time undergraduate or graduate students or $750 per year for half-time undergraduate students. Funds are paid jointly to the student and the school.

Duration 1 year; may be renewed until the student receives a final degree or certificate or until the total award to a student reaches $6,000, whichever comes first. Renewal requires the recipient to maintain a GPA of 2.5 or higher.

Additional information This program, established in 2000, is sponsored by USA Funds, which serves as the education loan guarantor and administrator in the 7 states where the program gives preference.

Number awarded Varies each year; recently, a total of $2.85 million was available for this program.

Deadline March of each year.

[359]
USA FUNDS HAWAII SILVER ANNIVERSARY SCHOLARSHIPS

Scholarship America
Attn: Scholarship Management Services
One Scholarship Way
P.O. Box 297
St. Peter, MN 56082
(507) 931-1682   Toll-free: (800) 537-4180
Fax: (507) 931-9168
E-mail: scholarship@usafunds.org
Web: www.usafunds.org

Purpose To provide financial assistance to undergraduate and graduate students from Hawaii, especially those who are members of ethnic minority groups or have physical disabilities.

Eligibility This program is open to high school seniors and graduates who are residents of Hawaii planning to enroll or already enrolled in full-time undergraduate or graduate course work at an accredited 2- or 4-year college, university, or vocational/technical school. Half-time undergraduate students are also eligible. Up to 50% of the awards are targeted at students who have a documented physical disability or are a member of an ethnic minority group, including but not limited to Native Hawaiian, Alaskan Native, Black/African American, Asian, Pacific Islander, American Indian, or Hispanic/Latino. Applicants must also be U.S. citizens or eligible noncitizens and come from a family with an annual adjusted gross income of $50,000 or less. In addition to financial need, selection is based on past academic performance and future potential, leadership and participation in school and community activities, work experience, career and educational aspirations, and goals.

Financial data The stipend is $1,500 per year for full-time undergraduate or graduate students or $750 per year for half-time undergraduate students. Funds are paid jointly to the student and the school.

Duration 1 year; may be renewed until the student receives a final degree or certificate or until the total award to a student reaches $6,000, whichever comes first. Renewal requires the recipient to maintain a GPA of 2.5 or higher.

Additional information This program, first offered in 2004, is sponsored by SMS Hawaii, the USA Funds affiliate that serves as the education loan guarantor and administrator in Hawaii and 7 other states. Information is also available from SMS Hawaii, 1314 South King Street, Suite 861, Honolulu, HI 96814, (808) 593-2262, (866) 497-USAF, ext. 7573, Fax: (808) 593-8268, E-mail: lteniya@usafunds.org.

Number awarded Varies each year; recently, a total of $300,000 was available for this program.

Deadline March of each year.

[360]
VATE MINORITY SCHOLARSHIP AWARD

Virginia Association of Teachers of English
Attn: Chuck Miller, Executive Secretary
1417 Birchwood Drive
Crozet, VA 22932
(434) 823-1483   E-mail: CMillerCrz@adelphia.net
Web: www.seva.net/~vate/Recognition.html

Purpose To provide financial assistance to minority students at colleges and universities in Virginia who are preparing for a career as a teacher of English language arts.

Eligibility This program is open to minority students enrolled in a teacher preparation program at a Virginia college or university. Applicants must be preparing to teach English language arts on the elementary or secondary level. Membership in the Virginia Association of Teachers of English (VATE) is required. Along with their application, they must submit a resume, 2 professional recommendations, and a statement (from 100 to 500 words) on what they will contribute in the classroom.

Financial data A stipend is awarded (amount not specified).

Duration 1 year.

Additional information Information is also available from Robert Williams, Radford University, Department of English, P.O. Box 6935, Radford, VA 24142, (540) 831-6700, E-mail: rohwilli@radford.edu.

Number awarded 1 each year.

Deadline August of each year.

[361]
VENTURA COUNTY JACL SCHOLARSHIPS

Japanese American Citizens League-Ventura County Chapter
Attn: Scholarship Committee
P.O. Box 1092
Camarillo, CA 93011
E-mail: vcjacl@hotmail.com
Web: www.vcjacl.org

Purpose To provide financial assistance for college to high school seniors in Ventura County, California who are members of the Japanese American Citizens League (JACL) or of Japanese ancestry.

Eligibility This program is open to seniors graduating from public or private high schools in Ventura County, California who are planning to attend a 2- or 4-year college, university, or trade school. Applicants must be members of JACL or of Japanese ancestry. Along with their application, they must submit a description of their involvement in JACL, a letter of recommendation, a transcript, a personal statement, and a list of activities, honors, and awards. Applicants who have special financial concerns (e.g., single parent, unemployment) may also describe those.

Financial data A stipend is awarded (amount not specified).

Duration 1 year.

Additional information Information is also available from Jennifer Kuo, (805) 373-4536, E-mail: benjenkuo@earthlink.net.

Number awarded 1 or more each year.

Deadline March of each year.

[362]

VERIZON WORKFORCE RESPONSE SCHOLARSHIPS

Independent Colleges of Washington
600 Stewart Street, Suite 600
Seattle, WA 98101
(206) 623-4494   Fax: (206) 625-9621
E-mail: info@icwashington.org
Web: www.icwashington.org

Purpose To provide financial assistance to minority students preparing for a career in teaching or nursing at colleges and universities that are members of Independent Colleges of Washington (ICW).

Eligibility This program is open to students completing their junior year at ICW-member colleges and universities. Applicants must be members of underserved or minority populations. They must be majoring in education or nursing. Along with their application, they must submit a 1-page essay on why they chose to prepare for a career in teaching and/or nursing. Preference is given to community college graduates. Financial need is considered in the selection process.

Financial data The stipend is $2,500.

Duration 1 year; nonrenewable.

Additional information The ICW-member institutions are Gonzaga University, Heritage College, Pacific Lutheran University, Saint Martin's College, Seattle Pacific University, Seattle University, University of Puget Sound, Walla Walla College, Whitman College, and Whitworth College.

Number awarded 4 each year.

Deadline October of each year.

[363]

VIETNAMESE PHYSICIAN ASSOCIATION OF NORTHERN CALIFORNIA SCHOLARSHIP

Vietnamese Physician Association of Northern
   California
c/o Thao Duong, Scholarship Program
Department of Physical Medicine and Rehabilitation
751 South Bascom Avenue
San Jose, CA 95128
E-mail: thao.duong@hhs.co.santa-clara.ca.us

Purpose To provide financial assistance for college to high school seniors in northern California who are of Vietnamese descent.

Eligibility This program is open to seniors graduating from high schools in northern California who are of Vietnamese descent. Applicants must have a GPA of 3.5 or higher and be planning to attend a college or university. Along with their application, they must submit an essay, high school transcript, 2 letters of recommendation, and documentation of financial need.

Financial data The stipend is $1,000.

Duration 1 year.

Number awarded 1 or more each year.

Deadline April of each year.

[364]

VIRGINIA HIGHER EDUCATION TEACHER ASSISTANCE PROGRAM

State Council of Higher Education for Virginia
Attn: Financial Aid Office
James Monroe Building
101 North 14th Street, Ninth Floor
Richmond, VA 23219-3659
(804) 225-2600   Toll-free: (877) 515-0138
Fax: (804) 225-2604   TDD: (804) 371-8017
E-mail: fainfo@schev.edu
Web: www.schev.edu

Purpose To provide financial assistance to minority and other residents of Virginia who are enrolled or interested in enrolling in a K-12 teacher preparation program in college.

Eligibility This program is open to residents of Virginia who are enrolled, or intend to enroll, full time in an eligible K-12 teacher preparation program at a public or private Virginia college or university. Applicants must 1) be U.S. citizens or eligible noncitizens; 2) demonstrate financial need; 3) have a cumulative college GPA of 2.5 or higher; and 4) be nominated by a faculty member. Preference is given to applicants enrolled in a teacher shortage content area (recently including special education, mathematics, chemistry, physics, earth and space sciences, foreign languages, and technology education), minority students enrolled in any content area for teacher preparation, and males enrolled in any approved elementary or middle school teacher preparation program.

Financial data Stipends are $2,000 per year for students at 4-year institutions or $1,000 per year for students at 2-year institutions.

Duration 1 year; may be renewed if funds are available and the recipient maintains satisfactory academic progress.

Additional information Applications and further information are available at the financial aid office of colleges and universities in Virginia. This program, established in 2000, is funded in part with federal funds from the Special Leveraging Educational Assistance Partnership (SLEAP) program.

Number awarded Varies each year.

[365]

VIRGINIA SOCIETY OF CERTIFIED PUBLIC ACCOUNTANTS MINORITY UNDERGRADUATE SCHOLARSHIP

Virginia Society of Certified Public Accountants
   Education Foundation
Attn: Educational Foundation
4309 Cox Road
P.O. Box 4620
Glen Allen, VA 23058-4620
(804) 270-5344   Toll-free: (800) 733-8272
Fax: (804) 273-1741   E-mail: vscpa@vscpa.com
Web: www.vscpa.com

Purpose To provide financial assistance to minority students enrolled in an undergraduate accounting program in Virginia.

Eligibility Applicants must be minority students (African Americans, Hispanic Americans, Native American Indians, or Asian Pacific Americans) currently enrolled in a Virginia college or university undergraduate accounting program.

They must be U.S. citizens, be majoring in accounting, have completed at least 6 hours of accounting, be currently registered for 3 more credit hours of accounting, and have a GPA of 3.0 or higher. Along with their applications, they must submit a 1-page essay on how they are financing their education, how they plan to use their accounting education, and why they should be awarded this scholarship. Selection is based on the essay (50%), an official undergraduate transcript (15%), a current resume, (25%), and a faculty letter of recommendation (10%).

Financial data A stipend is awarded (amount not specified). A total of $10,000 is available for this program each year.

Duration 1 year.

Number awarded Varies each year; recently, 3 of these scholarships were awarded.

Deadline April of each year.

[366]
WARNER NORCROSS & JUDD PARALEGAL ASSISTANT STUDIES SCHOLARSHIP

Grand Rapids Community Foundation
Attn: Scholarship Coordinator
209-C Waters Building
161 Ottawa Avenue N.W., 209-C
Grand Rapids, MI 49503-2757
(616) 454-1751, ext. 103   Fax: (616) 454-6455
E-mail: rbishop@grfoundation.org
Web: www.grfoundation.org

Purpose To provide financial assistance to minority residents of Michigan who are interested in working on a paralegal degree at an institution in the state.

Eligibility This program is open to minority students currently residing in Michigan. Applicants must be accepted at or enrolled in an accredited public or private 2- or 4-year college or university with a declared major in paralegal/legal assistant studies. The institution must also be in Michigan.

Financial data The stipend is $2,000.

Duration 1 year.

Additional information Funding for this program is provided by the law firm Warner Norcross & Judd LLP.

Number awarded 1 each year.

Deadline April of each year.

[367]
WARNER NORCROSS & JUDD SECRETARIAL STUDIES SCHOLARSHIP

Grand Rapids Community Foundation
Attn: Scholarship Coordinator
209-C Waters Building
161 Ottawa Avenue N.W., 209-C
Grand Rapids, MI 49503-2757
(616) 454-1751, ext. 103   Fax: (616) 454-6455
E-mail: rbishop@grfoundation.org
Web: www.grfoundation.org

Purpose To provide financial assistance to minority residents of Michigan who are interested in enrolling in a legal assistant/secretarial program at an institution in the state.

Eligibility This program is open to minority students currently residing in Michigan. Applicants must be accepted at or enrolled in an accredited public or private 2- or 4-year college, university, vocational school, or business school with a declared major in legal assistant/legal secretarial studies. The institution must also be in Michigan.

Financial data The stipend is $1,000.

Duration 1 year.

Additional information Funding for this program is provided by the law firm Warner Norcross & Judd LLP.

Number awarded 1 each year.

Deadline April of each year.

[368]
WARREN G. MAGNUSON EDUCATIONAL SUPPORT PERSONNEL SCHOLARSHIP GRANT

Washington Education Association
32032 Weyerhaeuser Way South
P.O. Box 9100
Federal Way, WA 98063-9100
(253) 765-7029   Toll-free: (800) 622-3393, ext. 7029
E-mail: cmartinez@washingtonea.org
Web: www.washingtonea.org

Purpose To provide funding to Educational Support Personnel (ESP) members of the Washington Education Association (WEA), particularly minority members, who are interested in taking classes to obtain an initial teaching certificate.

Eligibility This program is open to WEA/ESP members who are engaged in course work related to obtaining an initial teaching certificate. Applicants must submit a plan for obtaining an initial certificate, a letter describing their passion to become a teacher, evidence of activities and/or leadership in the association, and 3 to 5 letters of reference. Minority members of the association are especially encouraged to apply; 1 of the scholarships is reserved for them.

Financial data The stipend is $1,000.

Duration These are 1-time grants.

Number awarded 3 each year, including 1 reserved for a minority member.

Deadline February of each year.

[369]
WASA/PEMCO 21ST CENTURY EDUCATOR SCHOLARSHIP

Washington Association of School Administrators
825 Fifth Avenue, S.E.
Olympia, WA 98501
(360) 943-5717   Toll-free: (800) 859-9272
Fax: (360) 352-2043   E-mail: selder@wasa-oly.org
Web: www.wasa-oly.org

Purpose To provide financial assistance to minority and other high school seniors in the state of Washington who are interested in majoring in education in college.

Eligibility This program is open to high school seniors who are enrolled in a Washington public or accredited private school, have a GPA of 3.0 or higher, and intend to major and prepare for a career in K-12 education. Applicants must submit a completed application form, a criteria essay, a goals essay, 3 reference letters, and an official grades transcript. They compete in 3 applicant pools: eastern Washington, western Washington, and minorities. Selection is based on leadership, community service, honors and awards, student activities, and educational goals.

Financial data The stipend is $1,000 per year.

Duration 4 years.

Additional information This program is sponsored jointly by the Washington Association of School Administrators (WASA) and the PEMCO Foundation. Faxed applications will not be accepted.

Number awarded 3 each year: 1 to a minority student, 1 to a student from eastern Washington, and 1 to a student from western Washington.

Deadline March of each year.

[370]
WASHINGTON BUREAU MINORITY SCHOLARSHIPS

Knight Ridder Newspapers-Washington Bureau
Attn: Anthony Pugh
700 12th Street, N.W., Suite 1000
Washington, DC 20005-3994
(202) 383-6013   Fax: (202) 383-3738
E-mail: tpugh@krwashington.com
Web: www.krwashington.com

Purpose To provide financial assistance to minority high school seniors from the Washington, D.C. area who are interested in attending college to prepare for a career in the newspaper industry.

Eligibility This program is open to minority seniors graduating from high schools in the metropolitan area of Washington, D.C. Applicants must be able to demonstrate an interest in journalism, but they are not required to have been school newspaper reporters or editors. They may be photographers, graphic artists, computer experts, delivery workers with an interest in circulation, or business and advertising staff members. Along with their application, they must submit a transcript of grades (with a GPA of 3.0 or higher), SAT/ACT scores, 2 letters of recommendation, a list of journalism or business experience, information on extracurricular activities, up to 5 samples of work with bylines (for journalism applicants), and a 500-word essay on why they want to prepare for a career in journalism or communication business.

Financial data The stipend is $1,000.

Duration 1 year.

Additional information The recipients of these scholarships are entered into competition for the Knight Ridder Minority Scholarship Program of $40,000 over 4 years.

Number awarded 2 each year.

Deadline January of each year.

[371]
WASHINGTON MUTUAL MINORITY TEACHER SCHOLARSHIP

Independent Colleges of Washington
600 Stewart Street, Suite 600
Seattle, WA 98101
(206) 623-4494   Fax: (206) 625-9621
E-mail: info@icwashington.org
Web: www.icwashington.org

Purpose To provide financial assistance to minority students preparing for a career in teaching at colleges and universities that are members of Independent Colleges of Washington (ICW).

Eligibility This program is open to minority students at ICW-member colleges and universities. Applicants must be able to demonstrate financial need and a commitment to preparing for a career as a teacher (through either selection of a major or course load). They must submit a 1-page essay on why they are interested in a career in teaching. Selection criteria include education courses taken, activities, and community service.

Financial data The stipend is $3,000.

Duration 1 year; nonrenewable.

Additional information The ICW-member institutions are Gonzaga University, Heritage College, Pacific Lutheran University, Saint Martin's College, Seattle Pacific University, Seattle University, University of Puget Sound, Walla Walla College, Whitman College, and Whitworth College.

Number awarded Multiple scholarships are awarded each year.

Deadline April of each year.

[372]
WASHINGTON NASA SPACE GRANT CONSORTIUM UNDERGRADUATE SCHOLARSHIPS

Washington NASA Space Grant Consortium
c/o University of Washington
401A Johnson Hall
Box 351310
Seattle, WA 98195-1310
(206) 543-1943   Toll-free: (800) 659-1943
Fax: (206) 543-0179
Web: www.waspacegrant.org/undergr.html

Purpose To provide financial assistance for college to minority and other students in Washington who wish to study science, engineering, or mathematics with an emphasis on space.

Eligibility This program is open to residents of Washington who are attending or planning to attend institutions that are members of the Washington NASA Space Grant Consortium. Applicants must be interested in majoring in space-related aspects of science, engineering, or mathematics. U.S. citizenship is required. The program values diversity and strongly encourages women and minorities to apply.

Financial data Each participating college or university determines its awards.

Duration 1 year; may be renewed.

Additional information This program is funded by the U.S. National Aeronautics and Space Administration (NASA). Members of the consortium include Northwest Indian College, Seattle Central Community College, the University of Washington, and Washington State University.

Number awarded Varies each year.

Deadline Each participating college or university establishes its own deadline.

[373]
WASHINGTON POST YOUNG JOURNALISTS DEVELOPMENT PROGRAM

Washington Post
Attn: Public Relations Department
1150 15th Street, N.W.
Washington, DC 20071
(202) 334-7969
Web: washpost.com

Purpose To provide financial assistance to minority and other high school seniors in the Washington, D.C. area who are interested in preparing for a career in newspaper journalism.

Eligibility This program is open to high school seniors in 19 designated public school systems in the Washington, D.C. area. Applicants must have an interest in a print journalism career and a command of the English language. All students are eligible, but special emphasis is placed on participation by minority students. From the original applicants, a group is selected to participate in a program of 4 Saturday seminars at *The Washington Post*. During those seminars, conducted by the newspaper's reporters and editors, students produce a newspaper or magazine story. Scholarship winners are selected on the basis of those stories, attendance and participation in the seminars, and financial need.

Financial data The stipend is $2,500.

Duration 1 year; nonrenewable.

Additional information The eligible public school systems are those in Washington, D.C.; the counties of Anne Arundel, Calvert, Charles, Frederick, Howard, Montgomery, Prince George's, and St. Mary's in Maryland; the cities of Alexandria, Falls Church, Manassas, and Manassas Park in Virginia; and the counties of Arlington, Fairfax, Fauquier, Loudoun, Prince William, and Stafford in Virginia. This program, which began in 1997, is offered in collaboration with the National Association of Hispanic Journalists and the Asian American Journalists Association

Number awarded Recently, 19 students were selected to participate in the seminar. From among those, 2 were chosen to receive scholarships.

Deadline February of each year.

[374]
WASHINGTON STATE GEAR UP SCHOLARSHIP PROGRAM

Washington Higher Education Coordinating Board
917 Lakeridge Way
P.O. Box 43430
Olympia, WA 98504-3430
(360) 753-7833   Fax: (360) 753-7808
TDD: (360) 753-7809   E-mail: johnmcl@hecb.wa.gov
Web: www.hecb.wa.gov/CollegePrep/gu/guindex.asp

Purpose To provide financial and other assistance for college to low-income, disadvantaged middle and high school students in selected areas throughout Washington.

Eligibility This program is open to students in grades 7-12 in Washington communities who are low income and at risk. Participants receive tutoring and academic and career counseling, visit college campuses, perform community service, meet regularly with mentors, and attend informational seminars on such topics as financial aid, admissions, career planning, and student success strategies. Dur-

ing their junior and senior years, they get help preparing for college entrance examinations and completing admissions and financial aid applications.

Financial data Participants receive stipends and scholarships for college.

Duration Up to 4 years, provided the recipient remains drug-, crime-, and alcohol-free; maintains a GPA of 2.0 or higher; and participates in community service projects.

Additional information The communities currently participating in this program are Aberdeen, Elma, Hoquiam, Inchelium, Quincy, Seattle, Spokane, Tacoma, Taholah, Wapato, White Swan, and Yakima. GEAR UP is a federal program that stands for Gaining Early Awareness and Readiness for Undergraduate Programs. In Washington, it operates as a partnership among the Higher Education Coordinating Board, the Office of the Governor, and the University of Washington. It began operating in 1999 as the successor to the National Early Intervention Scholarship and Partnership Program.

Number awarded Currently, 1,200 students in grades 7-12 are participating.

[375]
WASHINGTON STATE NEED GRANT

Washington Higher Education Coordinating Board
917 Lakeridge Way
P.O. Box 43430
Olympia, WA 98504-3430
(360) 753-7851   Fax: (360) 753-7808
TDD: (360) 753-7809   E-mail: info@hecb.wa.gov
Web: www.hecb.wa.gov

Purpose To provide financial assistance for undergraduate study to Washington residents who come from a low-income or disadvantaged family.

Eligibility This program is open to residents of Washington whose family income is equal to or less than 55% of the state median (currently defined as $18,000 for a family of 1 ranging to $48,000 for a family of 8) or who are disadvantaged (defined to mean a student who by reasons of adverse cultural, educational, environmental, experiential, or familial circumstance is unlikely to aspire to, or enroll in, higher education). Applicants must be enrolled or planning to enroll at least half time in an eligible certificate, bachelor's degree, or first associate degree program. They may not be working on a degree in theology.

Financial data The stipend depends on the type of institution the recipient attends. Recently, it was $1,908 per year at community, technical, and private career colleges; $3,026 at public comprehensive universities (Central Washington University, Eastern Washington University, The Evergreen State College, and Western Washington University); $3,798 at public research universities (University of Washington and Washington State University); or $4,032 at independent universities.

Duration 1 academic year; renewal is possible for up to 3 additional years.

Additional information Consideration is automatic with the institution's receipt of the student's completed financial aid application. This program began in 1969.

Number awarded Varies each year; recently, more than 49,000 students received about $106 million in benefits from this program.

Deadline Varies according to the participating institution; generally in October of each year.

[376]
WEAC SCHOLARSHIPS

Wisconsin Education Association Council
33 Nob Hill Drive
P.O. Box 8003
Madison, WI 53708-8003
(608) 276-7711   Toll-free: (800) 362-8034
Web: www.weac.org/AboutWEA/scholarship.htm

Purpose To provide financial assistance for college to high school seniors whose parent is a member of the Wisconsin Education Association Council (WEAC) and who plan to study education in college.

Eligibility This program is open to high school seniors whose parent is an active WEAC member, an active retired member, or a parent who died while holding a WEAC membership. Applicants must rank in the top 25% of their graduating class or have a GPA of 3.0 or higher, plan to major or minor in education in college, and intend to teach in Wisconsin. Selection is based primarily on GPA, a 300-word essay, letters of recommendation, and school and community activities. Secondary consideration may be given to other factors, including financial need. The Kathy Mann Memorial Scholarship is reserved for a minority student.

Financial data The stipend is $1,450 per year.

Duration 4 years, provided the recipient remains eligible.

Number awarded 4 each year. If no minority student applies, the Kathy Mann Memorial Scholarship is awarded to a fourth non-minority applicant.

Deadline February of each year.

[377]
WEST VIRGINIA SPACE GRANT CONSORTIUM UNDERGRADUATE NASA SPACE GRANT FELLOWSHIPS

West Virginia Space Grant Consortium
c/o West Virginia University
College of Engineering and Mineral Resources
G-68 Engineering Sciences Building
P.O. Box 6070
Morgantown, WV 26506-6070
(304) 293-4099, ext. 3737   Fax: (304) 293-4970
E-mail: nasa@cemr.wvu.edu
Web: www.nasa.wvu.edu/scholarships.htm

Purpose To provide financial assistance to minority and other high school seniors who wish to attend academic institutions affiliated with the West Virginia Space Grant Consortium to prepare for a career in space-related science or engineering.

Eligibility This program is open to high school seniors in West Virginia who are planning to attend a college or university that is a member of the West Virginia Space Grant Consortium. U.S. citizenship is required. Selection is based on academic record and desire to prepare for a career in science or engineering. The consortium is a component of the Space Grant program of the U.S. National Aeronautics and Space Administration (NASA). Women and minorities are strongly encouraged to apply.

Financial data The program provides payment of full tuition, fees, room, and board.

Duration 4 years.

Additional information Funding for this program is provided by NASA. During the summers, some recipients work at a NASA center on a project under the supervision of a NASA advisor; others work with researchers at their respective colleges. The consortium includes Bethany College, Fairmont State College, Marshall University, Salem International University, Shepherd College, West Liberty State College, West Virginia Institute of Technology, West Virginia State College, West Virginia University, West Virginia Wesleyan College, and Wheeling-Jesuit University.

Number awarded Varies each year.

Deadline Each participating college or university establishes its own deadline.

[378]
WEST VIRGINIA SPACE GRANT CONSORTIUM UNDERGRADUATE SCHOLARSHIP PROGRAM

West Virginia Space Grant Consortium
c/o West Virginia University
College of Engineering and Mineral Resources
G-68 Engineering Sciences Building
P.O. Box 6070
Morgantown, WV 26506-6070
(304) 293-4099, ext. 3737   Fax: (304) 293-4970
E-mail: nasa@cemr.wvu.edu
Web: www.nasa.wvu.edu/scholarships.htm

Purpose To provide financial assistance to minority and other undergraduates at academic institutions affiliated with the West Virginia Space Grant Consortium who wish to prepare for a career in space-related science or engineering.

Eligibility This program is open to undergraduates at member institutions of the consortium. Applicants must be U.S. citizens and West Virginia residents. Selection is based on academic record and desire to prepare for a career in science or engineering. The consortium is a component of the Space Grant program of the U.S. National Aeronautics and Space Administration (NASA). Women and minorities are strongly encouraged to apply.

Financial data Stipends are either $2,000 or $1,000.

Duration 1 year.

Additional information Funding for this program is provided by NASA. In addition to their class work, recipients either work with faculty members in their major department on a research project or participate in the Consortium Challenge Program by working with elementary students on their science projects. The consortium members are Bethany College, Fairmont State College, Marshall University, Salem International University, Shepherd College, West Liberty State College, West Virginia Institute of Technology, West Virginia State College, West Virginia University, West Virginia Wesleyan College, and Wheeling-Jesuit University.

Number awarded Varies each year.

Deadline Each participating college or university establishes its own deadline.

[379]
WESTERN REGION KOREAN AMERICAN SCHOLARSHIPS

Korean American Scholarship Foundation
Western Region
Attn: Scholarship Committee
3435 Wilshire Boulevard, Suite 2450B
Los Angeles, CA 90010
(213) 380-KASF   Fax: (213) 380-KASF
E-mail: western@kasf.org
Web: www.kasf.org

Purpose To provide financial assistance to Korean American undergraduate and graduate students attending college in the western states.

Eligibility This program is open to full-time Korean American students who have completed at least 1 year of study at a 4-year college, graduate school, or professional school. Applicants may be residents of any state as long as they attend school in the western region (Alaska, Arizona, California, Colorado, Hawaii, Idaho, Montana, Nevada, New Mexico, Oregon, Utah, Washington, or Wyoming). Selection is based on academic achievement, community service, school activities, and financial need.

Financial data Stipends range from $1,000 to $2,000.

Duration 1 year; renewable.

Number awarded Varies each year. Recently, 60 of these scholarships were awarded.

Deadline February of each year.

[380]
WILLIAM ORR DINGWALL FOUNDATION GRANT

William Orr Dingwall Foundation
43 Topaz Way
San Francisco, CA 04131
(415) 641-7142   Fax: (415) 824-9609
E-mail: woding@aol.com
Web: www.wod.org/e_grant.html

Purpose To provide financial assistance to 1) undergraduates or graduate students of Korean descent or 2) graduate students of any nationality who are interested in studying the neural bases of language.

Eligibility Eligible to apply for this support are 1) undergraduate or graduate students of Korean or other Asian descent (may be majoring in any field) or 2) graduate students of any nationality who are interested in studying the neural bases of language. There are no residency requirements. Selection is based on academic record and evidence of financial need.

Financial data Grants up to $18,000 per year are awarded, although the actual amount paid will depend on the grantee's justified financial need. Stipends are paid directly to the recipient.

Duration 3 years; may be extended for 1 additional year.

Additional information Recipients must maintain at least a 3.0 GPA.

Deadline January of each year.

[381]
WILLIAM RUCKER GREENWOOD SCHOLARSHIP

Association for Women Geoscientists
Attn: AWG Foundation
P.O. Box 30645
Lincoln, NE 68503-0645
E-mail: awgscholarship@yahoo.com
Web: www.awg.org/members/po_scholarships.html

Purpose To provide financial assistance to minority women working on an undergraduate or graduate degree in the geosciences in the Potomac Bay region.

Eligibility This program is open to minority women who are currently enrolled as full-time undergraduate or graduate geoscience majors in an accredited, degree-granting college or university in Delaware, the District of Columbia, Maryland, Virginia, or West Virginia. Selection is based on the applicant's 1) awareness of the importance of community outreach as demonstrated by participation in geoscience or earth science educational activities, and 2) potential for leadership as a future geoscience professional.

Financial data The stipend is $1,000. The recipient also is granted a 1-year membership in the Association for Women Geoscientists (AWG).

Duration 1 year.

Additional information This program is sponsored by the AWG Potomac Area Chapter. Information is also available from Laurel M. Bybell, U.S. Geological Survey, 926 National Center, Reston, VA 20192.

Number awarded 1 each year.

Deadline April of each year.

[382]
WILLIE KEE MEMORIAL FELLOWSHIP

Asian American Journalists Association-San Francisco
   Bay Area Chapter
c/o Nerissa Pacio, Scholarship Co-Chair
San Jose Mercury News
750 Ridder Park Drive
San Jose, CA 95190
(408) 920-5827   Fax: (408) 271-3786
E-mail: aaja@aajasf.org
Web: www.aajasf.org

Purpose To provide financial assistance to residents of the San Francisco Bay area who have a strong interest in Asian American affairs and are working on a degree in a field related to broadcasting.

Eligibility This program is open to students who are residing in the San Francisco Bay area or who are originally from the area and are attending college out of state or out of the country. Applicants must have demonstrated a strong interest in Asian American or Asian affairs and in preparing for a career in photography, editing, or other broadcast arts. Preference is given to members of the Asian American Journalists Association, especially those who are regular volunteers.

Financial data The stipend is $1,000.

Duration 1 year.

Additional information This program was established in 2003 to honor the first Asian American television news cameraman in the Bay area.

Number awarded 1 each year.

Deadline April of each year.

[383]
WISCONSIN INSTITUTE OF CERTIFIED PUBLIC ACCOUNTANTS MINORITY SCHOLARSHIPS

Wisconsin Institute of Certified Public Accountants
Attn: WICPA Educational Foundation
235 North Executive Drive, Suite 200
P.O. Box 1010
Brookfield, WI 53008-1010
(414) 785-0445
Toll-free: (800) 772-6939 (within WI and MN)
Fax: (414) 785-0838   E-mail: Tammy@wicpa.org
Web: www.wicpa.org

Purpose To provide financial assistance to minority high school seniors in Wisconsin who are interested in majoring in accounting.

Eligibility This program is open to high school seniors who are residents of Wisconsin and African American, Hispanic, Native American, Indian, or Asian. Applicants must have earned a GPA of 3.0 or higher, be planning to attend a Wisconsin college or university, and be planning to begin academic work leading to an accounting major and a bachelor's degree.

Financial data The stipend is $375 per academic semester for the first 2 years, $500 per semester during the third year, and $750 per semester during the fourth year. The total award is $4,000 over 4 years. Funds may be used only for tuition and books.

Duration 4 years.

Number awarded Varies each year; recently, 2 of these scholarships were awarded.

Deadline February of each year.

[384]
WISCONSIN MINORITY UNDERGRADUATE RETENTION GRANTS

Wisconsin Higher Educational Aids Board
131 West Wilson Street, Room 902
P.O. Box 7885
Madison, WI 53707-7885
(608) 267-2212   Fax: (608) 267-2808
E-mail: mary.kuzdas@heab.state.wi.us
Web: heab.state.wi.us/programs.html

Purpose To provide financial assistance to minorities in Wisconsin who are currently enrolled in college.

Eligibility African Americans, Hispanic Americans, and American Indians in Wisconsin are eligible to apply if they are enrolled as sophomores, juniors, seniors, or fifth-year undergraduates in a 4-year nonprofit institution or as second-year students in a 2-year program at a public vocational institution in the state. Grants are also available to students who were admitted to the United States after December 31, 1975 and who are a former citizen of Laos, Vietnam, or Cambodia or whose ancestor was a citizen of 1 of those countries. They must be nominated by their institution and be able to demonstrate financial need.

Financial data Stipends range from $250 to $2,500 per year.

Duration Up to 4 years.

Additional information The Wisconsin Higher Educational Aids Board administers this program for students in private nonprofit institutions and public vocational institutions. The University of Wisconsin has a similar program for students attending any of the branches of that system. Eligible students should apply through their school's financial aid office.

Number awarded Varies each year.

Deadline Deadline dates vary by institution; check with your school's financial aid office.

[385]
WISCONSIN TALENT INCENTIVE PROGRAM (TIP) GRANTS

Wisconsin Higher Educational Aids Board
131 West Wilson Street, Room 902
P.O. Box 7885
Madison, WI 53707-7885
(608) 266-1665   Fax: (608) 267-2808
E-mail: john.whitt@heab.state.wi.us
Web: heab.state.wi.us/programs.html

Purpose To provide financial assistance for college to needy and educationally disadvantaged students in Wisconsin.

Eligibility This program is open to residents of Wisconsin entering a college or university in the state who meet requirements of both financial need and educational disadvantage. Financial need qualifications include 1) family contribution (a dependent student whose expected parent contribution is $200 or less, an independent student with dependents whose academic year contribution is $200 or less, or an independent student with no dependents whose maximum contribution is $1,200 or less); 2) AFDC benefits (a dependent student whose family is receiving AFDC benefits or an independent student who is receiving AFDC benefits); or 3) unemployment (a dependent student whose parents are ineligible for unemployment compensation and have no current income from employment, or an independent student and spouse, if married, who are ineligible for unemployment compensation and have no current income from employment). Educational disadvantage qualifications include students who are 1) minorities (African American, Native American, Hispanic, or southeast Asian); 2) enrolled in a special academic support program due to insufficient academic preparation; 3) a first-generation college student (neither parent graduated from a 4-year college or university); 4) disabled according to the Department of Workforce Development, Division of Vocational Rehabilitation; 5) currently or formerly incarcerated in a correctional institution; or 6) from an environmental and academic background that deters the pursuit of educational plans. Students already in college are not eligible.

Financial data Grants range up to $1,800 per year.

Duration 1 year; may be renewed up to 4 additional years provided the recipient continues to be a Wisconsin resident enrolled at least half time in a degree or certificate program, makes satisfactory academic progress, demonstrates financial need, and remains enrolled continuously from semester to semester and from year to year. If recipients withdraw from school or cease to attend classes for any reason (other than medical necessity), they may not reapply.

Number awarded Varies each year.

[386]
WORLDSTUDIO FOUNDATION SCHOLARSHIPS

Worldstudio Foundation
200 Varick Street, Suite 507
New York, NY 10014
(212) 366-1317, ext. 18   Fax: (212) 807-0024
E-mail: scholarshipcoordinator@worldstudio.org
Web: www.worldstudio.org/schol/index.html

Purpose To provide financial assistance to undergraduate and graduate students, especially minorities, who wish to study fine or commercial arts, design, or architecture.

Eligibility This program is open to undergraduate and graduate students who are currently enrolled or planning to enroll at an accredited college or university and major in 1 of the following areas: advertising (art direction only), architecture, crafts, environmental graphics, fashion design, film/video (direction or cinematography only), film/theater design (including set, lighting, and costume design), fine arts, furniture design, graphic design, industrial/product design, interior design, landscape architecture, new media, photography, surface/textile design, or urban planning. Although not required, minority status is a significant factor in the selection process. International students may apply if they are enrolled at a U.S. college or university. Applicants must have a GPA of 2.0 or higher. Along with their application, they must submit a 600-word statement of purpose that includes a brief autobiography, an explanation of how their experiences have influenced their creative work and/or their career plans, and how they see themselves contributing to the community at large in the future. Selection is based on that statement, the quality of submitted work, financial need, minority status, and academic record.

Financial data Basic scholarships range from $1,000 to $2,000, but awards between $3,000 and $5,000 are also presented at the discretion of the jury. Honorable mentions are $100. Funds are paid directly to the recipient's school.

Duration 1 academic year. Recipients may reapply.

Additional information The foundation encourages the scholarship recipients to focus on ways that their work can address issues of social and environmental responsibility. This program includes the following named awards: the Sherry and Gary Baker Award, the Bobolink Foundation Award, the Bombay Sapphire Awards, the Richard and Jean Coyne Family Foundation Awards, the David A. Dechman Foundation Awards, the Philip and Edina Jennison Award, the Kraus Family Foundation Awards, the Dena McKelvey Award. the New York Design Center Award, the Rudin Foundation Awards, the Starr Foundation Awards, and the John F. Wright III Award.

Number awarded Varies each year; recently, 24 scholarships and 7 honorable mentions were awarded.

Deadline March of each year.

[387]
WORLDSTUDIO FOUNDATION SPECIAL ANIMATION AND ILLUSTRATION SCHOLARSHIPS

Worldstudio Foundation
200 Varick Street, Suite 507
New York, NY 10014
(212) 366-1317, ext. 18   Fax: (212) 807-0024
E-mail: scholarshipcoordinator@worldstudio.org
Web: www.worldstudio.org/schol/specawards.html

Purpose To provide financial assistance to members of disadvantaged and ethnic minority groups who wish to study illustration, animation, or cartooning in college.

Eligibility This program is open to members of disadvantaged or minority groups who are currently enrolled or planning to enroll in an accredited college or university in the United States. Applicants must be majoring or planning to major in illustration, animation, or cartooning. They must submit their most recent college or high school transcripts, documentation of financial need, a portfolio of their work, and a 600-word statement of purpose that includes a brief autobiography and how they plan to contribute to the community. International students are also eligible. Selection is based on the quality of submitted work, the strength of the written statement of purpose, financial need, and academic record.

Financial data The stipend is $1,500. Funds are paid directly to the recipient's school.

Duration 1 academic year. Recipients may reapply.

Additional information This program was established in 2002 with funding from the W.K. Kellogg Foundation.

Number awarded 25 each year.

Deadline March of each year.

[388]
WPS RESOURCES FOUNDATION BUSINESS AND TECHNOLOGY SCHOLARSHIPS

Wisconsin Public Service Corporation
Attn: WPS Resources Foundation, Inc.
c/o Scholarship Assessment Service
P.O. Box 5189
Appleton, WI 54912-5189
(920) 832-8322
Web: www.wpsr.com/community/minoritybus.asp

Purpose To provide financial assistance to women and minority upper-division students who are majoring in business or engineering at selected universities.

Eligibility This program is open to women and African American, Native American, Asian American, and Hispanic students who are enrolled full time as a junior or senior at a participating university with a GPA of 2.8 or higher. They must be majoring in business or engineering (chemical, civil, computer, electrical, environmental, industrial, or mechanical). Along with their application, they must submit 1) a 250-word essay on why they chose their current major and what career they hope to enter after graduation, and 2) a 350-word essay on a selection of topics that relate to challenges facing the energy industry.

Financial data The stipend is $1,500.

Duration 1 year; may be renewed if the recipient remains in good academic standing.

Additional information The participating universities are Marquette University, Michigan Technological University,

Milwaukee School of Engineering, University of Wisconsin at Green Bay, University of Wisconsin at Platteville, University of Wisconsin at Madison, University of Minnesota, Iowa State University, St. Norbert College, Notre Dame University, and University of Michigan at Ann Arbor.

Number awarded Varies each year; recently, 15 of these scholarships were awarded.

Deadline January of each year.

[389]
WTS PUGET SOUND CHAPTER SCHOLARSHIP

Women's Transportation Seminar-Puget Sound Chapter
c/o Lorelei Mesic, Scholarship Co-Chair
W&H Pacific
3350 Monte Villa Parkway
Bothell, WA 98021-8972
(425) 951-4872   Fax: (425) 951-4808
E-mail: lmesic@whpacific.com
Web: www.wtspugetsound.org/nscholarships.html

Purpose To provide financial assistance to women undergraduate and graduate students, particularly minority women, from Washington who are working on a degree related to transportation and have financial need.

Eligibility This program is open to women who are residents of Washington, studying at a college in the state, or working as an intern in the state. Applicants must be currently enrolled in an undergraduate or graduate degree program in a transportation-related field, such as engineering, planning, finance, or logistics. They must have a GPA of 3.0 or higher and plans to prepare for a career in a transportation-related field. Minority candidates are encouraged to apply. Along with their application, they must submit a 500-word statement about their career goals after graduation, their financial need, and why they think they should receive this scholarship award. Selection is based on transportation goals, academic record, transportation-related activities or job skills, and financial need.

Financial data The stipend is $1,500.

Duration 1 year.

Additional information The winner is also nominated for scholarships offered by the national organization of the Women's Transportation Seminar.

Number awarded 1 each year.

Deadline October of each year.

[390]
WTS/ITS WASHINGTON INTELLIGENT TRANSPORTATION SYSTEMS SCHOLARSHIP

Women's Transportation Seminar-Puget Sound Chapter
c/o Lorelei Mesic, Scholarship Co-Chair
W&H Pacific
3350 Monte Villa Parkway
Bothell, WA 98021-8972
(425) 951-4872   Fax: (425) 951-4808
E-mail: lmesic@whpacific.com
Web: www.wtspugetsound.org/nscholarships.html

Purpose To provide financial assistance to minority and other undergraduate and graduate students from Washington working on a degree related to intelligent transportation systems (ITS).

Eligibility This program is open to students who are residents of Washington, studying at a college in the state, or working as an intern in the state. Applicants must be currently enrolled in an undergraduate or graduate degree program related to the design, implementation, operation, and maintenance of ITS technologies. They must be majoring in transportation or a related field, including transportation engineering, systems engineering, electrical engineering, planning, finance, or logistics, and be taking courses in such ITS-related fields of study as computer science, electronics, and digital communications. In addition, they must have a GPA of 3.0 or higher and plans to prepare for a career in a transportation-related field. Minority candidates are encouraged to apply. Along with their application, they must submit a 500-word statement about their career goals after graduation, how those relate to ITS, and why they think they should receive this scholarship award. Selection is based on that statement, academic record, and transportation-related activities or job skills. Financial need is not considered.

Financial data The stipend is $1,500.

Duration 1 year.

Additional information This program is co-sponsored by ITS Washington.

Number awarded 1 each year.

Deadline October of each year.

[391]
XEROX TECHNICAL MINORITY SCHOLARSHIP PROGRAM

Xerox Corporation
Attn: Technical Minority Scholarship Program
150 State Street, Fourth Floor
Rochester, NY 14614
(585) 422-7689   E-mail: xtmsp@imcouncil.com
Web: www.xerox.com

Purpose To provide financial assistance to minorities interested in undergraduate or graduate education in the sciences and/or engineering.

Eligibility This program is open to minorities (people of African American, Asian, Pacific Islander, Native American, Native Alaskan, or Hispanic descent) working full time on an undergraduate or graduate degree in chemistry, computing and software systems, engineering (chemical, computer, electrical, imaging, manufacturing, mechanical, optical, or software), information management, laser optics, material science, physics, or printing management science. Applicants must be U.S. citizens or permanent residents with a GPA of 3.0 or higher and attending, or planning to attend, a 4-year college or university.

Financial data The maximum stipend is $1,000 per year.

Duration 1 year.

Number awarded Approximately 150 each year.

Deadline September of each year.

[392]
YALE NEW HAVEN HOSPITAL MINORITY NURSING AND ALLIED HEALTH SCHOLARSHIPS

Yale New Haven Hospital
Attn: Human Resources
20 York Street
New Haven, CT 06510-3202
(203) 688-5226   Fax: (203) 688-6670
E-mail: lacamera@ynhh.org
Web: www.ynhh.org/ynhch/ch_comm.html#career

Purpose To provide financial assistance to minority high school seniors in Connecticut interested in studying nursing or allied health fields in college.

Eligibility This program is open to graduating seniors at high schools in Connecticut who are members of minority groups. Applicants must be interested in attending a 4-year college or university with an accredited program in nursing, respiratory therapy, medical technology, pharmacy, or radiation therapy. Selection is based on academic record, teacher evaluations, an essay, and extracurricular activities.

Financial data The stipend is $1,500 per year.

Duration 1 year.

Number awarded 4 each year.

Deadline February of each year.

[393]
YOSHIKO TANAKA MEMORIAL SCHOLARSHIP

Japanese American Citizens League
Attn: National Scholarship Awards
1765 Sutter Street
San Francisco, CA 94115
(415) 921-5225   Fax: (415) 931-4671
E-mail: jacl@jacl.org
Web: www.jacl.org/scholarships.html

Purpose To provide financial assistance for college to student members of the Japanese American Citizens League (JACL), especially those studying Japanese language or U.S.-Japan relations.

Eligibility This program is open to JACL members who are currently enrolled or planning to reenter a college, university, trade school, business college, or other institution of higher learning. Applicants must submit a statement describing their current level of involvement in the Japanese American community or Asian Pacific community and how they will continue their involvement in future years. Selection is based on academic record, extracurricular activities, financial need, and community involvement. Preference is given to applicants planning to study Japanese language, Japanese culture, and/or U.S.-Japan relations.

Financial data The stipend depends on the availability of funds but usually ranges from $1,000 to $5,000.

Duration 1 year; nonrenewable.

Additional information Applications must be submitted to the JACL National Scholarship Program, c/o San Diego JACL Chapter, 1031 25th Street, San Diego, CA 92102.

Number awarded 1 each year.

Deadline March of each year.

[394]
YOUTHFORCE 2020 SCHOLARSHIP

Turner Construction Company
Attn: Community Affairs Coordinator
375 Hudson Street
New York, NY 10014
(212) 229-6480   Fax: (212) 229-6260
Web: www.turnerconstruction.com

Purpose To provide financial assistance to minority and female high school seniors in New York City who are interested in a career in the construction industry.

Eligibility This program is open to seniors at high schools in New York City who have been accepted into a 4-year college program in architecture, civil engineering, construction management, electrical engineering, or mechanical engineering. Applicants must be minorities or women interested in preparing for a career in the construction industry. They must have a cumulative GPA of "B-" (80%) or higher, an excellent SAT score, and a record of school and community activities. Along with their application, they must submit an essay (350 to 500 words) on "Why I want to prepare for a career in construction."

Financial data The stipend is $2,000 per year.

Duration 4 years.

Additional information This program was established in 1989. The company offers a paid internship during the summer after the completion of the first year of college.

Number awarded 4 each year.

Deadline May of each year.

[395]
YUTAKA NAKAZAWA MEMORIAL SCHOLARSHIP

Japanese American Citizens League
Attn: National Scholarship Awards
1765 Sutter Street
San Francisco, CA 94115
(415) 921-5225   Fax: (415) 931-4671
E-mail: jacl@jacl.org
Web: www.jacl.org/scholarships.html

Purpose To provide financial assistance for college to student members of the Japanese American Citizens League (JACL) who are high school seniors.

Eligibility This program is open to JACL members who are high school seniors interested in attending a college, university, trade school, business college, or other institution of higher learning. Applicants must submit a statement describing their current level of involvement in the Japanese American community or Asian Pacific community and how they will continue their involvement in future years. Selection is based on academic record, extracurricular activities, and community involvement.

Financial data The stipend depends on the availability of funds but usually ranges from $1,000 to $5,000.

Duration 1 year; nonrenewable.

Additional information Applications must be submitted to the local JACL chapter.

Number awarded 1 each year.

Deadline February of each year.

Fellowships

Described here are 260 funding programs open to Asian Americans that are to be used to fund studies on the graduate (for a master's degree, doctorate, professional degree, or specialist's certificate) or postgraduate level in the United States. Usually no return of service or repayment is required. Note: other funding opportunities for Asian Americans on the graduate or postgraduate level are also described in the Loans, Grants, Awards, and Internships sections. So, if you are looking for a particular program and don't find it in this section, be sure to check the Program Title Index to see if it is covered elsewhere in the directory.

[396]
AAJA FELLOWSHIP PROGRAM

Asian American Journalists Association
Attn: Professional Programs Coordinator
1182 Market Street, Suite 320
San Francisco, CA 94102
(415) 346-2051, ext. 107   Fax: (415) 346-6343
E-mail: albertl@aaja.org
Web: www.aaja.org

Purpose To provide financial assistance to members of the Asian American Journalism Association (AAJA) interested in participating in short-term training and skills development programs

Eligibility This program is open to full and associate members of AAJA who have at least 3 years of professional experience. Applicants must be interested in attending a short-term training or skills development program. Their news organization must be willing to grant a leave of absence to attend the program. Along with their application, they must submit brief essays on their financial need and resources, how the fellowship will improve their professional skills, the impact the additional training will have on their ability to serve the Asian Pacific American community, and how they propose to share the knowledge and experiences gained from the fellowship with other AAJA members. Selection is based on the essays, work samples, a resume, and 2 letters of recommendation.

Financial data Grants of up to $1,000 are awarded. Funds must be used to defray tuition, travel, food, lodging, and other related training costs.

Duration 1 year; may be renewed.

Number awarded 4 each year.

Deadline Applications may be submitted at any time.

[397]
AAUW CAREER DEVELOPMENT GRANTS

American Association of University Women
Attn: AAUW Educational Foundation
301 ACT Drive, Department 177
P.O. Box 4030
Iowa City, IA 52243-4030
(319) 337-1716   Fax: (319) 337-1204
E-mail: aauw@act.org
Web: www.aauw.org

Purpose To provide financial assistance to women (particularly women of color) who are seeking career advancement, career change, or reentry into the work force.

Eligibility This program is open to women who are U.S. citizens or permanent residents, have earned a bachelor's degree, received their most recent degree more than 4 years ago, and plan to work toward a master's degree, second bachelor's degree, or specialized training in technical or professional fields. Applicants must be planning to undertake course work at an accredited 2- or 4-year college or university (or a technical school that is licensed, accredited, or approved by the U.S. Department of Education). Special consideration is given to qualified members of the American Association of University Women (AAUW), women of color, women working on their first advanced degree, and women working on degrees in nontraditional fields. Doctoral students and candidates eligible for other fellowship programs of the AAUW may not apply for these grants.

Financial data The awards range from $2,000 to $8,000. The funds are to be used for tuition, fees, books, supplies, local transportation, and dependent care.

Duration 1 year, beginning in July; nonrenewable.

Number awarded Approximately 60 each year.

Deadline December of each year.

[398]
ABE AND ESTHER HAGIWARA STUDENT AID AWARD

Japanese American Citizens League
Attn: National Scholarship Awards
1765 Sutter Street
San Francisco, CA 94115
(415) 921-5225   Fax: (415) 931-4671
E-mail: jacl@jacl.org
Web: www.jacl.org/scholarships.html

Purpose To provide financial assistance for college or graduate school to student members of the Japanese American Citizens League (JACL) who can demonstrate severe financial need.

Eligibility This program is open to JACL members who are enrolled or planning to enroll in a college, university, trade school, or business college. Applicants must be undergraduate or graduate students who are able to demonstrate that, without this aid, they will have to delay or terminate their education. They must submit a statement describing their current level of involvement in the Japanese American community or Asian Pacific community and how they will continue their involvement in future years. Selection is based on financial need, academic record, extracurricular activities, and community involvement.

Financial data The stipend depends on the availability of funds but usually ranges from $1,000 to $5,000.

Duration 1 year; nonrenewable.

Additional information Applications must be submitted to the JACL National Scholarship Program, c/o San Diego JACL Chapter, 1031 25th Street, San Diego, CA 92102.

Number awarded At least 1 each year.

Deadline March of each year.

[399]
ACCOUNTANCY BOARD OF OHIO EDUCATION ASSISTANCE PROGRAM

Accountancy Board of Ohio
77 South High Street, 18th Floor
Columbus, OH 43215-6128
(614) 466-4135   Fax: (614) 466-2628
Web: acc.ohio.gov/edrule.html

Purpose To provide financial assistance to minority and financially disadvantaged students enrolled in an accounting education program at Ohio academic institutions approved by the Accountancy Board of Ohio.

Eligibility This program is open to minority and financially disadvantaged Ohio residents enrolled full time as sophomores, juniors, or seniors in an accounting program at an accredited college or university in the state. Students who remain in good standing at their institutions and who enter a qualified fifth-year program are also eligible, if funds are available. Minority is defined as people with significant ancestry from Africa (excluding the Middle East), Asia (excluding the Middle East), Central America and the Caribbean islands, South America, and the islands of the Pacific Ocean. Financial disadvantage is defined according to information provided on the Free Application for Federal Student Aid (FAFSA). U.S. citizenship or permanent resident status is required.

Financial data The amount of the stipend is determined annually but does not exceed the in-state tuition at Ohio public universities.

Duration 1 year; nonrenewable.

Number awarded Several each year.

Deadline May or November of each year.

[400]
ADRIENNE M. AND CHARLES SHELBY ROOKS FELLOWSHIP FOR RACIAL AND ETHNIC THEOLOGICAL STUDENTS

United Church of Christ
Attn: Local Church Ministries
700 Prospect Avenue East
Cleveland, OH 44115-1100
(216) 736-3865   Fax: (216) 736-3783
E-mail: lcm@ucc.org
Web: www.ucc.org/education/scholarships

Purpose To provide financial assistance to minority students who are either enrolled at an accredited seminary preparing for a career of service in the United Church of Christ or working on a doctoral degree in the field of religion.

Eligibility This program is open to members of a congregation of the United Church of Christ who are from an underrepresented ethnic group (African American, Hispanic American, Asian American, Native American Indian, or Pacific Islander). Applicants must be either 1) enrolled in an accredited school of theology in the United States or Canada with the intent to become a pastor or teacher within the United Church of Christ, or 2) doctoral (Ph.D., Th.D., or Ed.D.) students within a field related to religious studies. Seminary students must have a GPA in all postsecondary work of 3.0 or higher and must have begun the in-care process; preference is given to students who have demonstrated leadership through a history of service to the church and scholarship through exceptional academic performance. For doctoral students, preference is given to applicants who have demonstrated academic excellence, teaching effectiveness, and commitment to the United Church of Christ and who intend to become professors in colleges, seminaries, or graduate schools.

Financial data Grants range from $500 to $5,000 per year.

Duration 1 year; may be renewed.

Number awarded Varies each year; recently, 21 of these scholarships, worth $97,000, were awarded.

Deadline February of each year.

[401]
AETNA/NCEMNA SCHOLARS PROGRAM

National Coalition of Ethnic Minority Nurse
  Associations
c/o Dr. Betty Smith Williams, President
6101 West Centinela Avenue, Suite 378
Culver City, CA 90230
(310) 258-9515   Fax: (310) 258-9513
E-mail: bwilliams@ncemna.org
Web: www.ncemna.org/scholarships.html

Purpose To provide financial assistance to nursing students who are members of constituent organizations of the National Coalition of Ethnic Minority Nurse Associations (NCEMNA) working on a 4-year or master's degree.

Eligibility This program is open to members of the 5 associations that comprise NCEMNA: the Asian American/Pacific Islander Nurses Association, Inc. (AAPINA), the National Alaska Native American Indian Nurses Association, Inc. (NANAINA), the National Association of Hispanic Nurses, Inc. (NAHN), the National Black Nurses Association, Inc. (NBNA), and the Philippine Nurses Association of America, Inc. (PNAA). Applicants must be currently attending or applying to a 4-year or master's degree program in nursing. Along with their application, they must submit a letter of reference, demonstration of leadership and involvement in the ethnic community, and statement of career goals.

Financial data The stipend is $2,000.

Duration 1 year.

Additional information This program was established in 2004 with a grant from the Aetna Foundation.

Number awarded 5 each year: 1 nominee from each of the constituent associations.

[402]
ALBERT W. DENT STUDENT SCHOLARSHIP

American College of Healthcare Executives
One North Franklin Street, Suite 1700
Chicago, IL 60606-3529
(312) 424-2800   Fax: (312) 424-0023
E-mail: ache@ache.org
Web: www.ache.org

Purpose To provide financial assistance to minority graduate student members of the American College of Healthcare Executives.

Eligibility This program is open to student associates of the organization in good standing. Applicants must be minority students enrolled full time in a health care management graduate program, able to demonstrate financial need, and a U.S. or Canadian citizen.

Financial data The stipend is $3,500.

Duration 1 year.

Additional information The program was established and named in honor of Dr. Albert W. Dent, the foundation's first Black fellow and president emeritus of Dillard University.

Number awarded Varies each year.

Deadline March of each year.

[403]
AMELIA KEMP MEMORIAL SCHOLARSHIP

Women of the Evangelical Lutheran Church in America
Attn: Scholarships
8765 West Higgins Road
Chicago, IL 60631-4189
(773) 380-2730   Toll-free: (800) 638-3522, ext. 2730
Fax: (773) 380-2419   E-mail: womenelca@elca.org
Web: www.womenoftheelca.org

Purpose To provide financial assistance to lay women of color who are members of Evangelical Lutheran Church of America (ELCA) congregations and who wish to study on the undergraduate, graduate, professional, or vocational school level.

Eligibility These scholarships are available to ELCA lay women of color who are at least 21 years of age and have experienced an interruption of at least 2 years in their education since high school. Applicants must have been admitted to an educational institution to prepare for a career in other than a church-certified profession. U.S. citizenship is required.

Financial data The amount of the award varies, depending on the availability of funds.

Duration Up to 2 years.

Number awarded Varies each year, depending upon the funds available.

Deadline February of each year.

[404]
AMERICAN ASSOCIATION OF JAPANESE UNIVERSITY WOMEN SCHOLARSHIP PROGRAM

American Association of Japanese University Women
c/o Ms. Reiko Yamashita, Scholarship Committee Co-Chair
15325 South Menlo Avenue
Gardena, CA 90247-4240

Purpose To provide financial assistance to female students currently enrolled in upper-division or graduate classes in California.

Eligibility This program is open to female students enrolled in accredited colleges or universities in California. They must have junior, senior, or graduate standing. Applicants must be a contributor to U.S.-Japan relations, cultural exchanges, and leadership development in the areas of their designated field of study. To apply, they must submit a current resume, an official transcript of the past 2 years of college work, 2 letters of recommendation, and an essay (up to 2 pages in English or 1,200 characters in Japanese) on 1 of the following topics: 1) what I hope to accomplish in my field of study to develop leadership and role model qualities; or 2) thoughts on how my field of study can contribute to U.S.-Japan relations and benefit international relations.

Financial data The stipend is $1,000.

Duration 1 year.

Additional information The association was founded in 1970 to promote the education of women as well as to contribute to U.S.-Japan relations, cultural exchanges, and leadership development. Requests for applications must include a stamped self-addressed envelope.

Number awarded 1 or more each year.

Deadline September of each year.

[405]
AMERICAN ASSOCIATION OF OBSTETRICIANS AND GYNECOLOGISTS FOUNDATION SCHOLARSHIPS

American Association of Obstetricians and Gynecologists Foundation
Attn: Administrative Director
409 12th Street, S.W.
Washington, DC 20024-2188
(202) 863-1647   Fax: (202) 554-0453
E-mail: ejones@acog.org
Web: www.agosonline.org

Purpose To provide funding to physicians (particularly minorities and women) interested in a program of research training in obstetrics and gynecology.

Eligibility Applicants must have an M.D. degree and be eligible for the certification process of the American Board of Obstetrics and Gynecology (ABOG). They must document departmental planning for a significant research training experience to be conducted by 1 or more faculty mentors. There is no formal application form, but departments must supply a description of the candidate's qualifications, including a curriculum vitae, bibliography, prior training, past research experience, and evidence of completion of residency training in obstetrics and gynecology; a comprehensive description of the proposed training program; a description of departmental resources appropriate to the training; a list of other research grants, training grants, or scholarships previously or currently held by the applicant; and a budget. Applicants for the scholarship sponsored by ABOG must verify that 90% of their time and effort will be dedicated to the research training and conduct of research. Applicants for the scholarship sponsored by the Society for Maternal-Fetal Medicine (SMFM) must also have completed MFM subspecialty training or be in the second or third year of an ABOG-approved MFM training program at the time of applying. Candidates for that scholarship must also be members or associate members of the SMFM. Preference for both awards is given to training in areas currently underrepresented in obstetrics and gynecology. A personal interview may be requested. Priority is given to individuals who have not previously received extramural funding for research training. Women and minority candidates are strongly encouraged to apply. Selection is based on the scholarly, clinical, and research qualifications of the candidate; evidence of the candidate's commitment to an investigative career in academic obstetrics and gynecology in the United States or Canada; qualifications of the sponsoring department and mentor; and quality of the research project.

Financial data The grant is $100,000 per year, of which at least $5,000 but not more than $15,000 must be used for employee benefits. In addition, sufficient funds to support travel to the annual fellows' retreat must be set aside. The balance of the funds may be used for salary, technical support, and supplies. The grant co-sponsored by the SMFM must be matched by an institutional commitment of at least $30,000 per year.

Duration 1 year; may be renewed for 2 additional years, based on satisfactory progress of the scholar.

Number awarded 2 each year: 1 co-sponsored by ABOG and 1 co-sponsored by SMFM.

Deadline August of each year.

[406]
AMERICAN BAR ASSOCIATION LEGAL OPPORTUNITY SCHOLARSHIP

American Bar Association
Attn: Fund for Justice and Education
321 North Clark Street
Chicago, IL 60610
(312) 988-5415   Fax: (312) 988-6392
E-mail: fje@staff.abanet.org
Web: www.abanet.org/fje/losfpage.html

Purpose To provide financial assistance to racial and ethnic minority students who are interested in attending law school.

Eligibility This program is open to racial and ethnic minority college graduates who are interested in attending an ABA-accredited law school. Only students beginning law school may apply; students who have completed 1 or more semesters of law school are not eligible. Applicants must have a cumulative GPA of 2.5 or higher and be citizens or permanent residents of the United States. Financial need must be demonstrated.

Financial data The stipend is $5,000 per year.

Duration 1 year; may be renewed for 2 additional years if satisfactory performance in law school has been achieved.

Additional information This program began in the 2000-01 academic year.

Number awarded Approximately 20 each year.

Deadline February of each year.

[407]
AMERICAN COLLEGE OF SPORTS MEDICINE GRADUATE SCHOLARSHIPS FOR MINORITIES AND WOMEN

American College of Sports Medicine
Attn: Research Review Committee
401 West Michigan Street
P.O. Box 1440
Indianapolis, IN 46206-1440
(317) 637-9200   Fax: (317) 637-7817
E-mail: mwayne@acsm.org
Web: www.acsm.org/grants/scholarships.htm

Purpose To provide financial assistance to minority and women graduate students who are interested in preparing for a career in sports medicine or exercise science.

Eligibility This program is open to minorities and women who have been accepted in a full-time master's, Ph.D., M.D., or equivalent degree program in sports medicine, exercise science, or other related field. Minorities are defined as American Indians, Alaskan Natives, Asians, Pacific Islanders, Blacks, and Hispanics. Applicants must submit 3 letters of professional recommendation (including at least 1 from a current member of the American College of Sports Medicine), evidence of participation in sports medicine or exercise science (including documentation of research and scholarly activities), transcripts, GRE or MCAT scores, and a 300-word description of short- and long-term career goals.

Financial data The stipend is $1,500 per year. Funds are to be used to cover tuition and/or fees.

Duration 1 year; may be renewed for up to 3 additional years.

Additional information Recipients are given a 1 year's free membership in the American College of Sports Medicine.

Deadline April of each year.

[408]
AMERICAN SOCIETY OF CRIMINOLOGY GRADUATE FELLOWSHIPS FOR ETHNIC MINORITIES

American Society of Criminology
Attn: Awards Committee
1314 Kinnear Road, Suite 212
Columbus, OH 43212-1156
(614) 292-9207   Fax: (614) 292-6767
E-mail: asc41@infinet.com
Web: www.asc41.com/minorfel.htm

Purpose To provide financial assistance to ethnic minority doctoral students in criminology and criminal justice.

Eligibility This program is open to African American, Asian American, Latino, and Native American doctoral students planning to enter the field of criminology and criminal justice. Applicants must submit an up-to-date curriculum vitae; an indication of race or ethnicity; copies of undergraduate and graduate transcripts; a statement of need and prospects for other financial assistance; a letter describing career plans, salient experiences, and nature of interest in criminology and criminal justice; and 3 letters of reference.

Financial data Stipends up to $6,000 are available.

Duration 1 year.

Additional information This fellowship was first awarded in 1989.

Number awarded 3 each year.

Deadline February of each year.

[409]
AMERICAN SPEECH-LANGUAGE-HEARING FOUNDATION SCHOLARSHIP FOR MINORITY STUDENTS

American Speech-Language-Hearing Foundation
Attn: Graduate Student Scholarship Competition
10801 Rockville Pike
Rockville, MD 20852-3279
(301) 897-5700   Toll-free: (800) 498-2071
Fax: (301) 571-0457   TTY: (800) 498-2071
E-mail: foundation@asha.org
Web: www.ashfoundation.org

Purpose To provide financial assistance to minority graduate students in communication sciences and disorders programs.

Eligibility This program is open to full-time graduate students who are enrolled in communication sciences and disorders programs, with preference given to U.S. citizens who are members of a racial or ethnic minority group. Selection is based on academic promise and outstanding academic achievement. Master's (but not doctoral) candidates must be enrolled in an ASHA Educational Standards Board (ESB) accredited program.

Financial data The stipend ranges from $2,000 to $4,000. Funds must be used for educational support (e.g., tuition, books, school living expenses), not for personal or conference travel.

Duration 1 year.
Number awarded 1 each year.
Deadline June of each year.

[410]
ANGELFIRE SCHOLARSHIP

Datatel Scholars Foundation
4375 Fair Lakes Court
Fairfax, VA 22033
(703) 968-9000, ext. 4549   Toll-free: (800) 486-4332
Fax: (703) 968-4573   E-mail: scholars@datatel.com
Web: www.datatel.com

Purpose To provide financial assistance to graduating high school seniors, continuing college students, and graduate students who will be studying at a Datatel client school and are veterans, veterans' dependents, or refugees from southeast Asia.

Eligibility This program is open to 1) veterans who served in the Asian theater (Vietnam, Cambodia, or Laos) between 1964 and 1975; 2) their spouses and children; 3) refugees from Vietnam, Cambodia, or Laos; and 4) veterans who served in Operation Desert Storm, Operation Enduring Freedom, and/or Operation Iraqi Freedom. Applicants must attend a Datatel client college or university during the upcoming school year. They must first apply to their institution, which selects 2 semifinalists and forwards their applications to the sponsor. Along with they application, they must include a 1,000-word personal statement that discusses how the conflict has affected them personally, summarizes how the conflict has impacted their educational goals, and describes how being awarded this scholarship will help them achieve their goals. Selection is based on the quality of the personal statement (40%), academic merit (30%), achievements and civic involvement (20%), and 2 letters of recommendation (10%).

Financial data Stipends are $2,400, $1,600, or $1,000, depending upon the cost of undergraduate tuition at the participating institution. Funds are paid directly to the institution.

Duration 1 year.

Additional information Datatel, Inc. produces advanced information technology solutions for higher education. It has more than 470 client sites in the United States and Canada. This scholarship was created to commemorate those who lost their lives in Vietnam or Iraq and is named after a memorial administered by the Disabled American Veterans Association in Angelfire, New Mexico.

Number awarded Varies each year. Recently, 10 of these scholarships were awarded: 7 at $2,400, 2 at $1,600, and 1 at $1,000.

Deadline Students must submit online applications to their institution or organization by January of each year.

[411]
ANHEUSER-BUSCH NAPABA LAW FOUNDATION PRESIDENTIAL SCHOLARSHIPS

National Asian Pacific American Bar Association
Attn: NAPABA Law Foundation
910 17th Street, N.W., Suite 315
Washington, DC 20006
(202) 775-9555   Fax: (202) 775-9333
E-mail: foundation@napaba.org
Web: www.napaba.org

Purpose To provide financial assistance to law students interested in serving the Asian Pacific American community.

Eligibility This program is open to students at accredited law schools in the United States. Applicants must demonstrate leadership potential to serve the Asian Pacific American community upon graduation. They must submit 500-word essays on 1) the most significant experiences in their background that have shaped and demonstrated their commitment to serving the needs of Asian Pacific Americans; and 2) how they intend to serve the needs of the Asian Pacific American community in their future legal career. Selection is based on demonstrated commitment to and interest in pro bono and/or public interest legal work, financial need, leadership potential, maturity and responsibility, and commitment to serving the needs of the Asian Pacific American community.

Financial data The stipend is $5,000 per year.

Duration 1 year.

Additional information This program is supported by Anheuser-Busch Companies, Inc.

Number awarded 2 each year.

Deadline September of each year.

[412]
APALA SCHOLARSHIP

Asian Pacific American Librarians Association
Attn: Executive Director
3735 Palomar Centre, Suite 150
PMB 26
Lexington, KY 40513
E-mail: lhjen00@uky.edu
Web: www.apalaweb.org/awards/scholarship.htm

Purpose To provide financial assistance to students of Asian or Pacific descent who are working on a graduate library degree.

Eligibility Eligible to apply are students of Asian or Pacific background who are enrolled or have been accepted into a master's program or doctoral degree program in library or information science at a library school accredited by the American Library Association. Applicants must be citizens or permanent residents of the United States or Canada.

Financial data Stipends are either $1,000 or $500.

Duration 1 year; recipients may reapply, but they may not receive an award for more than 2 consecutive years.

Additional information Recipients may attend school on either a part-time or full-time basis. Recipients must join and be active members of the association, which is an affiliate of the American Library Association.

Number awarded 2 each year: 1 at $1,000 and 1 at $500.

Deadline March of each year.

[413]
ASCA FOUNDATION SCHOLARSHIPS

American School Counselor Association
Attn: ASCA Foundation
1101 King Street, Suite 625
Alexandria, VA 22314
(703) 683-ASCA   Toll-free: (800) 306-4722
Fax: (703) 683-1619
E-mail: asca@schoolcounselor.org
Web: www.schoolcounselor.org

Purpose To provide financial assistance for graduate school to members of the American School Counselor Association (ASCA), especially males and minorities.

Eligibility This program is open to ASCA members working on a master's degree in school counseling. Applicants must submit a 2-page essay on how school counselors should be held accountable for fulfilling their duties and responsibilities. Males and minorities are especially encouraged to apply.

Financial data The stipend is $1,000.

Duration 1 year.

Additional information Support for this program is provided by Anheuser-Busch.

Number awarded Up to 10 each year.

Deadline October of each year.

[414]
ASEI GRADUATE SCHOLARSHIPS

American Society of Engineers of Indian Origin
c/o Ramu Ramamurthy, Scholarship Committee Chair
47790 Pavillon Road
Canton, MI 48188
(248) 226-6895   Fax: (248) 226-7166
E-mail: awards@aseimichigan.org.
Web: www.aseio.org

Purpose To provide financial assistance to graduate students of Indian origin (from India) who are working on a degree in architecture, engineering, or related areas.

Eligibility This program is open to graduate students of Indian origin (by birth, ancestry, or relation). Applicants must be enrolled full time at an accredited college or university in the United States and working on a degree in engineering, architecture, computer science, or allied science with a GPA of 3.5 or higher. Selection is based on demonstrated ability, academic achievement (including GPA, honors, and awards), career objectives, faculty recommendations, involvement in science fair and campus activities, financial hardship, and industrial exposure (including part-time work and internships).

Financial data The stipend is $1,000.

Duration 1 year.

Number awarded Several each year.

Deadline June of each year.

[415]
ASIAN BAR ASSOCIATION OF WASHINGTON SCHOLARSHIPS

Asian Bar Association of Washington
c/o Clinton Foy
Heller Ehrman White & McAuliffe LLP
701 Fifth Avenue
Seattle, WA 98104-7098
(206) 389-6043   E-mail: cfoy@hewm.com
Web: www.abaw.org/scholarships.html

Purpose To provide financial assistance to Asian American law students in Washington.

Eligibility This program is open to students currently attending law school in the state of Washington. Along with their applications, students must submit a 2-page cover letter that describes their interest in the scholarship and contributions made to the Asian community. They must also submit a resume, copy of their most recent law school transcript, and 2 letters of reference.

Financial data The stipend is $2,000.

Duration 1 year.

Number awarded 3 each year.

Deadline September of each year.

[416]
ASIAN CHURCH MULTIPLICATION TEAM SCHOLARSHIPS

Southern Baptist Convention
North American Mission Board
Attn: Church Multiplication Team
4200 North Point Parkway
Alpharetta, GA 30022-4176
(770) 410-6235   Fax: (770) 410-6012
E-mail: jdoyle@namb.net
Web: www.namb.net

Purpose To provide financial assistance to Asian American Baptists interested in religious vocations.

Eligibility This program is open to Asian Americans who are U.S. citizens involved in some type of approved Baptist ministry. Applicants must be able to demonstrate financial need. Only students in accredited institutions working toward a basic college (bachelor's) or seminary (M.Div.) degree are eligible. As part of the selection process, applicants must submit an essay describing their interest in and commitment to a Christian vocation.

Financial data The maximum grants are $500 per year for students attending accredited colleges, $600 per year for students in non-Southern Baptist Convention seminaries, and $850 per year for students at 1 of the 6 Southern Baptist Convention seminaries.

Duration 1 year; renewable.

Additional information The 6 Southern Baptist seminaries are Golden Gate Baptist Theological Seminary (Mill Valley, California), Midwestern Baptist Theological Seminary (Kansas City, Missouri), New Orleans Baptist Theological Seminary (New Orleans, Louisiana), Southeastern Baptist Theological Seminary (Wake Forest, North Carolina), Southern Baptist Theological Seminary (Louisville, Kentucky), and Southwestern Baptist Theological Seminary (Fort Worth, Texas).

Number awarded Varies each year.

Deadline Applications may be submitted at any time, but they must be received at least 1 month (preferably sooner) before the student enrolls in a school.

[417]
ASTRAZENECA FELLOWSHIP/FACULTY TRANSITION AWARDS

Foundation for Digestive Health and Nutrition
Attn: Research Awards Coordinator
4930 Del Ray Avenue
Bethesda, MD 20814-2512
(301) 222-4005   Fax: (301) 222-4010
E-mail: info@fdhn.org
Web: www.fdhn.org

Purpose To provide funding to physicians (especially those who are minority group members or women) for research training in an area of gastrointestinal, liver function, or related diseases.

Eligibility This program is open to trainee members of the American Gastroenterological Association (AGA) who are M.D.s or M.D./Ph.D.s currently holding a gastroenterology-related fellowship at an accredited North American institution. Applicants must be committed to an academic career; have completed 2 years of research training at the start of this award; be sponsored by an AGA member who directs a gastroenterology-related unit that is engaged in research training in a North American medical school, affiliated teaching hospital, or research institute; and be cosponsored by the director of a basic research laboratory (or other comparable laboratory) who is committed to the training and development of the applicant. Minorities and women investigators are strongly encouraged to apply. Selection is based on novelty, feasibility, and significance of the proposal; attributes of the candidate; record and commitment of the sponsors; and the institutional and laboratory environment.

Financial data The stipend is $40,000 per year. Funds are to be used as salary support for the recipient. Indirect costs are not allowed.

Duration 2 years.

Additional information This award is administered by the Foundation for Digestive Health and Nutrition (FDHN) and sponsored by the AGA with support from AstraZeneca Pharmaceuticals, L.P. Finalists for the award are interviewed. Although the host institution may supplement the award, the applicant may not concurrently have a similar training award or grant from another organization. All publications coming from work funded by this program must acknowledge the support of the award.

Number awarded Up to 4 each year.

Deadline September of each year.

[418]
ATLANTA CHAPTER OF AAJA SCHOLARSHIPS

Asian American Journalists Association-Atlanta Chapter
c/o Patti Tom, President
Primedia Business Magazines
6151 Powers Ferry Road, Suite 200
Atlanta, GA 30339
(770) 618-0310   (770) 618-0204
E-mail: ptom@primediabusiness.com
Web: chapters.aaja.org/Atlanta

Purpose To provide financial assistance to Asian American undergraduate and graduate students in the Southeast who are interested in preparing for a career in journalism.

Eligibility This program is open to Asian American graduate or undergraduate students enrolled in an accredited college or university in the Southeast. Applicants must be interested in preparing for a career in print, photo, or broadcast journalism.

Financial data Stipends are $1,000 or $250.

Duration 1 year.

Number awarded Varies each year. Recently, 4 of these scholarships were awarded: 3 at $1,000 and 1 at $250.

Deadline October of each year.

[419]
BALFOUR PHI DELTA PHI MINORITY SCHOLARSHIP PROGRAM

Phi Delta Phi International Legal Fraternity
1426 21st Street, N.W., First Floor
Washington, DC 20036
(202) 223-6801   Toll-free: (800) 368-5606
Fax: (202) 223-6808   E-mail: info@phideltaphi.org
Web: www.phideltaphi.org

Purpose To provide financial assistance to minorities who are members of Phi Delta Phi International Legal Fraternity.

Eligibility All ethnic minority members of the legal fraternity are eligible to apply for this scholarship. Selection is based on participation, ethics, and scholastics.

Financial data The stipend is $3,000 per year.

Duration 1 year.

Additional information This scholarship was established in 1997. Funding for this scholarship comes from the Lloyd G. Balfour Foundation.

Number awarded 1 each year.

Deadline October of each year.

[420]
BAY AREA MINORITY LAW STUDENT SCHOLARSHIPS

Bar Association of San Francisco
c/o Raquel Cabading, Director, Minority Law Student
     Scholarship Program
465 California Street, Suite 1100
San Francisco, CA 94104-1826
(415) 782-8916   E-mail: rcabading@sfbar.org
Web: www.sfbar.org/charitable/scholarships.aspx

Purpose To provide financial assistance to students of color interested in attending law school in northern California.

Eligibility This program is open to students of color (African Americans, Native Americans, Latinos/Chicanos, and southeast Asians) who accept offers of admission from designated law schools in northern California. Applicants must submit a 500-word essay on obstacles they have overcome in pursuing their education and the qualities and talents they would bring to the legal profession. Financial need is considered in the selection process.

Financial data The stipend is $10,000 per year.

Duration 3 years.

Additional information This program was established in 1998. Since then, more than 600 students have applied for these scholarships and nearly 50 have been awarded. The designated law schools are Boalt, Davis, Golden Gate University, Hastings, McGeorge, Santa Clara University, Stanford, and University of San Francisco.

Number awarded Varies each year; recently, 2 of these scholarships were awarded.

Deadline May of each year.

[421]
BEHAVIORAL SCIENCES POSTDOCTORAL FELLOWSHIPS IN EPILEPSY

Epilepsy Foundation
Attn: Research Department
4351 Garden City Drive
Landover, MD 20785-7223
(301) 459-3700   Toll-free: (800) EFA-1000
Fax: (301) 577-2684   TDD: (800) 332-2070
E-mail: grants@efa.org
Web: www.epilepsyfoundation.org

Purpose To provide funding to postdoctorates (especially minorities, women, and persons with disabilities) in the behavioral sciences who wish to pursue research training in an area related to epilepsy.

Eligibility Individuals who have received their doctoral degree in a behavioral science field by the time the fellowship begins and desire additional postdoctoral research experience in epilepsy may apply. Academic faculty holding the rank of instructor or above are not eligible, nor are graduate or medical students, medical residents, permanent government employees, or employees of private industry. Appropriate fields of study in the behavioral sciences include sociology, social work, anthropology, nursing, economics, and others relevant to epilepsy research and practice. Because these fellowships are designed as training opportunities, the quality of the training plans and environment are considered in the selection process. Other selection criteria include the scientific quality of the proposed research, a statement regarding the relevance of the research to epilepsy, the applicant's qualifications, and the preceptor's qualifications. Applications from women, members of minority groups, and people with disabilities are especially encouraged. U.S. citizenship is not required, but the research must be conducted in the United States.

Financial data Grants up to $30,000 per year are available.

Duration 1 year.

Number awarded Varies each year; recently, 2 of these fellowships were awarded.

Deadline February of each year.

[422]
BELVA DAVIS DIVERSITY SCHOLARSHIP

American Women in Radio and Television-Golden Gate Chapter
c/o Jackie Wright
UPN Bay Area, KBHK-TV
855 Battery Street
San Francisco, CA 94111-1597
(415) 765-8725   E-mail: jwright@kbhktv.com
Web: www.awrtgold.org/pages/scholarship.htm

Purpose To provide financial assistance to minority students in the San Francisco Bay area who are interested in a career as a broadcast journalist.

Eligibility This program is open to students who have been enrolled for at least 2 years in a San Francisco Bay area high school, 4-year college or university, or graduate school. Applicants must be members of minority groups who are preparing for a career as a broadcast journalist. Selection is based on educational achievements, journalistic achievements and plans, leadership experience, extracurricular activities, community involvement, academic goals, overall future plans and goals, and financial need.

Financial data A stipend is awarded.

Duration 1 year.

Additional information This program was established in 1999.

Number awarded 1 each year.

Deadline May of each year.

[423]
BEVERLY YIP SCHOLARSHIPS

Union of Pan Asian Communities
Attn: Development Coordinator
1031 25th Street
San Diego, CA 92102
(619) 232-6454   Fax: (619) 235-9002
E-mail: info@upacsd.com
Web: www.upacsd.com/programs.html

Purpose To provide financial assistance to Asian and Pacific Islander residents of San Diego County, California who are interested in studying designated fields in college.

Eligibility This program is open residents of San Diego County, California who are Asian, Pacific Islander, or of refugee status. Applicants may be high school seniors, undergraduates, or graduate student, but they must be studying health and human services, international relations, psychology, social work, criminal justice, health promotion and disease prevention, engineering, business, or science. Along with their application, they must submit an autobiographical statement, documentation of financial need, and 2 letters of recommendation.

Financial data The stipend is $1,000.

Duration 1 year.

Number awarded 3 each year.

Deadline February of each year.

[424]
BILL BERNBACH MINORITY SCHOLARSHIP FUND

American Association of Advertising Agencies
Attn: Manager of Diversity Programs
405 Lexington Avenue, 18th Floor
New York, NY 10174-1801
(212) 682-2500   Toll-free: (800) 676-9333
Fax: (212) 682-8391   E-mail: tiffany@aaaa.org
Web: www.aaaa.org/diversity/foundation/funds.htm

Purpose To provide financial assistance to multicultural students interested in working on a graduate degree in advertising.

Eligibility This program is open to African Americans, Asian Americans, Hispanic Americans, and Native Americans who are interested in studying the advertising creative arts at designated institutions. Applicants must have already received an undergraduate degree and be able to demonstrate financial need. As part of the selection process, they must submit 10 samples of creative work in their respective field of expertise.

Financial data The stipend is $5,000.

Duration Most awards are for 2 years.

Additional information This program began in 1997 and currently provides scholarships to students at the Adcenter at Virginia Commonwealth University, the Creative Circus and the Portfolio Center in Atlanta, and the Miami Ad School.

Number awarded 4 each year.

[425]
BOARD OF GOVERNORS MEDICAL SCHOLARSHIP PROGRAM

North Carolina State Education Assistance Authority
Attn: Scholarship and Grant Services
10 T.W. Alexander Drive
P.O. Box 14103
Research Triangle Park, NC 27709-4103
(919) 549-8614   Toll-free: (800) 700-1775
Fax: (919) 549-8481   E-mail: information@ncseaa.edu
Web: www.ncseaa.edu

Purpose To provide financial assistance to residents (especially minorities) of North Carolina who have been admitted to a medical school in the state.

Eligibility Students must be nominated for this program. Nominees must be residents of North Carolina, be able to demonstrate financial need, express an intent to practice medicine in North Carolina, and have been accepted for admission to 1 of the 4 medical schools in North Carolina: Bowman Gray School of Medicine at Wake Forest University, Duke University School of Medicine, East Carolina University School of Medicine, and the University of North Carolina at Chapel Hill School of Medicine. Minorities are especially encouraged to apply.

Financial data Each scholarship provides a stipend of $5,000 a year, plus tuition and mandatory fees.

Duration 1 year; renewable up to 3 additional years, provided the recipient makes satisfactory academic progress, continues to have financial need, and remains interested in medical practice in North Carolina.

Number awarded 20 new awards are granted each year. Recently, a total of 81 students were receiving $1,637,085 in support through this program

Deadline April of each year.

[426]
BOR-UEI CHEN SCHOLARSHIPS

Photonics Society of Chinese-Americans
c/o Chun-Ching Shih
1517 Via Fernandez
Palos Verdes Estates, CA 90274
E-mail: cc.shih.ngc.com
Web: www.psc-a.org

Purpose To provide financial assistance to Chinese American graduate students in the field of optical communications and photonic devices.

Eligibility This program is open to Chinese American graduate students at universities in the United States. Applicants must be majoring in a field related to optical communications and photonic devices. Selection is based on the merits of the candidate's research work as documented by publications in technical journals, conference presentations, and recommendations from the candidate's sponsor or advisor.

Financial data The stipend is $1,000.

Duration 1 year.

Additional information These scholarships were first awarded in 1995.

Number awarded 1 or 2 each year.

Deadline January of each year.

[427]
BOSTON CHAPTER MINORITY SCHOLARSHIP

Special Libraries Association-Boston Chapter
Attn: Danielle Green Barney, Co-Chair, Affirmative
  Action Committee
6 Warren Road
Framingham, MA 01702
(617) 495-8306   Fax: (617) 496-3811
E-mail: dbarney@hbs.edu
Web: www.sla.org/chapter/cbos/awards.htm

Purpose To provide financial assistance for library education to minority graduate students from New England.

Eligibility This program is open to members of minority groups (African Americans, Hispanics, Asian Americans, Pacific Islanders, Native Hawaiians, American Indians, and Alaskan Natives) who are enrolled or planning to enroll in an accredited graduate library science program. Applicants must be residents of New England or attending school in the region. They must submit an essay (500 to 750 words) on their interest and experience in special libraries. Financial need is not considered in the selection process.

Financial data The stipend is $2,000.

Duration 1 year.

Number awarded 1 each year.

Deadline April of each year.

[428]
BUNCHIRO TAMESA SCHOLARSHIP

Japanese American Citizens League-Seattle Chapter
P.O. Box 18558
Seattle, WA 98118-0558
(206) 622-4098   E-mail: email@jaclseattle.org
Web: www.jaclseattle.org

Purpose To provide financial assistance for college or graduate school to residents of the Seattle, Washington area who are of Japanese ancestry or from a family that is a member of the Japanese American Citizens League (JACL).

Eligibility This program is open to Seattle (Washington) area residents who are of Japanese ancestry or members of JACL families. Applicants must be entering their freshman year of college or graduate school. As part of their application, they must submit a list of extracurricular and community activities, 2 letters of recommendation, a list of awards or recognitions they have earned, and a 500-word essay on the legacy of the Japanese American community in American society.

Financial data The stipend is $1,000.

Duration 1 year.

Additional information Information is also available from May Namba, 2324 N.W. 94th Street, Seattle, WA 98117.

Number awarded 1 each year.

Deadline March of each year.

[429]
C. CLYDE FERGUSON LAW SCHOLARSHIP

New Jersey Commission on Higher Education
Attn: Educational Opportunity Fund
20 West State Street, Seventh Floor
P.O. Box 542
Trenton, NJ 08625-0542
(609) 984-2709   Fax: (609) 292-7225
E-mail: nj_che@che.state.nj.us
Web: www.state.nj.us

Purpose To provide financial assistance to disadvantaged and minority students who want to study law in New Jersey.

Eligibility Applicants must be disadvantaged students or members of an ethnic minority group that has been historically underrepresented in the legal profession. They must have been New Jersey residents for at least 12 months before receiving the award. They must plan to enroll full time in the Minority Student Program at law schools in New Jersey (Rutgers University School of Law at Newark, Rutgers University School of Law at Camden, or Seton Hall Law School). Applicants may be former or current undergraduate recipients of the New Jersey Educational Opportunity Fund (EOF) grant or students who would have met the undergraduate EOF grant eligibility requirements. Financial need must be demonstrated.

Financial data Awards are based on financial need. In no case, however, can awards exceed the maximum amount of tuition, fees, room, and board charged at Rutgers University School of Law at Newark.

Duration 1 year; may be renewed.

[430]
CAAM SCHOLARSHIPS

Chinese American Association of Minnesota
Attn: Scholarship Program
P.O. Box 582584
Minneapolis, MN 55458-2584
Web: www.caam.org/pages/scholarships.htm

Purpose To provide financial assistance for college or graduate school to Minnesota residents of Chinese descent.

Eligibility This program is open to Minnesota residents of Chinese descent who are enrolled or planning to enroll full time at a postsecondary school, college, or graduate school. Applicants must submit an essay on the role their Chinese heritage has played in their work, study, and accomplishments. Selection is based on academic record, leadership qualities, and community service; financial need is also considered for some awards. Membership in the Chinese American Association of Minnesota (CAAM) is not required. Priority is given to applicants who have not previously received a CAAM scholarship.

Financial data The stipend is $1,000.

Duration 1 year.

Additional information Recipients who are not CAAM members are expected to become members for at least 2 years.

Number awarded At least 5 each year.

Deadline September of each year.

[431]
CALA SCHOLARSHIP

Chinese American Librarians Association
c/o Sha Li Zhang, Scholarship Committee Chair
University of North Carolina at Greensboro
Jackson Library
P.O. Box 26170
Greensboro, NC 27402-6170
(336) 334-4705   Fax: (336) 334-5399
E-mail: slzhang@uncg.edu
Web: www.cala-web.org

Purpose To provide financial assistance to Chinese American students interested in working on a graduate degree in library or information science.

Eligibility This program is open to students enrolled full time in an accredited library school and working on a master's or doctoral degree. Applicants must be of Chinese nationality or Chinese descent. They must submit a resume and a personal statement of 300 to 500 words on their past experiences, career interests, and commitment to information science.

Financial data The stipend is $1,000.

Duration 1 year.

Additional information This program was established in 2004.

Number awarded 1 each year.

Deadline April of each year.

[432]

CALIFORNIA STATE PSYCHOLOGICAL ASSOCIATION FOUNDATION MINORITY SCHOLARSHIP PROGRAM

California State Psychological Association Foundation
Attn: Scholarship Coordinator
3835 North Freeway Boulevard, Suite 240
Sacramento, CA 95834-1955
(916) 286-7979   Fax: (916) 325-9790
Web: fdncenter.org

Purpose To provide financial assistance to minority students interested in working on a doctoral degree in psychology in California.

Eligibility Applicants must be full-time graduate students who are enrolled or accepted in a doctoral-level psychology program at an accredited California school. Applicants must belong to 1 of the following ethnic groups: Black/African American, Hispanic/Latino, Asian/Asian American, American Indian/Alaskan Native, or Pacific Islander. Along with their application, they must submit 3 to 5 letters of recommendation, an official transcript, and documentation of financial need. Selection is based on potential for completing doctoral-level work in psychology. No distinction or preference is made for practitioner versus academic programs. Priority is given to applicants with demonstrated community involvement or leadership, whose graduate program focuses on ethnic minority cultural issues, and who plan to work with direct delivery of services to a culturally diverse population in either private or public settings.

Financial data The stipend is $2,000.

Duration 1 year; nonrenewable.

Additional information This program was established in 1991.

Number awarded 3 each year: 1 each to a first-, second-, and third-year doctoral student.

Deadline October of each year.

[433]

CAMS SCHOLARSHIP PROGRAM

Chinese American Medical Society
Attn: Dr. H.H. Wang, Executive Director
281 Edgewood Avenue
Teaneck, NJ 07666
(201) 833-1506   Fax: (201) 833-8252
E-mail: hw5@columbia.edu
Web: www.camsociety.org/programs.htm

Purpose To provide financial assistance to Chinese Americans who are interested in studying, conducting research, or teaching in the medical and dental fields.

Eligibility This program is open to Chinese or Chinese Americans who need financial assistance to complete their study, research, or teaching in the field of medicine and/or dentistry. At the time of application, they must be residing in the United States (either as resident aliens or American citizens). Applicants must be enrolled at an approved medical/dental school in the United States or have a research position in an approved institution. Special consideration is given to applicants with research projects relating to health care of the Chinese.

Financial data The scholarships range from $1,000 to $1,500.

Duration 1 year; recipients may reapply.

Additional information This program includes the Esther Lim Memorial Scholarship, established in 1989, and the Ruth Liu Memorial Scholarship, established in 1996. Information is also available from David Wang, M.D., CAMS Scholarship Committee Chairman, 171 East 84th Street, Suite 33B, New York, NY 10028, (201) 833-7244, E-mail: dwang007@yahoo.com. Recipients who do not complete their planned study, research, or teaching must make a pro-rated refund to the society.

Number awarded Varies; recently, 3 to 5 scholarships have been awarded each year.

Deadline March of each year.

[434]

CANFIT PROGRAM SCHOLARSHIPS

California Adolescent Nutrition, Physical Education, and
   Culinary Arts Scholarships
2140 Shattuck Avenue, Suite 610
Berkeley, CA 94704
(510) 644-1533   Toll-free: (800) 200-3131
Fax: (510) 644-1535   E-mail: info@canfit.org
Web: www.canfit.org/scholarships.html

Purpose To provide financial assistance to minority undergraduate and graduate students who are studying nutrition, physical education, or culinary arts in California.

Eligibility Eligible to apply are American Indians/Alaska Natives, African Americans, Asians/Pacific Islanders, and Latinos/Hispanics who are enrolled in either: 1) an approved master's or doctoral graduate program in nutrition, public health nutrition, or physical education or in a preprofessional practice program approved by the American Dietetic Association at an accredited university in California; or, 2) an approved bachelor's or professional certificate program in culinary arts, nutrition, or physical education at an accredited university or college in California. Graduate student applicants must have completed at least 12 units of graduate course work and have a cumulative GPA of 3.0 or higher; undergraduate applicants must have completed 50 semester units or the equivalent of college credits and have a cumulative GPA of 2.5 or higher. Selection is based on financial need, academic goals, and community nutrition or physical education activities.

Financial data Graduate stipends are $1,000 each and undergraduate stipends are $500 per year.

Additional information A goal of the California Adolescent Nutrition and Fitness (CANFit) program is to improve the nutritional status and physical fitness of California's low-income multi-ethnic youth aged 10 to 14. By offering these scholarships, the program hopes to encourage more students to consider careers in adolescent nutrition and fitness.

Number awarded 5 graduate scholarships and 10 undergraduate scholarships are available each year.

Deadline March of each year.

[435]
CAPS SCHOLARSHIPS

Chinese American Physicians Society
c/o Lawrence Ng, Award Committee Chair
345 Ninth Street, Suite 204
Oakland, CA 94607-4206
Fax: (510) 839-0988 E-mail: scholarship@caps-ca.org
Web: www.caps-ca.org/scholarship.html

Purpose To provide financial assistance to medical students (especially Chinese and other Asian American students) in the United States.

Eligibility This program is open to students attending or planning to attend a U.S. medical school. Preference is given to those willing to serve Asian American communities after graduation. Along with their application, they must submit a 500-word essay on the cause of the mental health crisis facing Asian American communities and possible solutions. Selection is based on the essay, academic achievement, financial need, and Asian American community service.

Financial data Stipends range from $2,000 to $3,000 per year.

Duration 1 year; may be renewed.

Number awarded Up to 8 each year.

Deadline September of each year.

[436]
CARL A. SCOTT BOOK SCHOLARSHIPS

Council on Social Work Education
Attn: Chair, Carl A. Scott Memorial Fund
1725 Duke Street, Suite 500
Alexandria, VA 22314-3457
(703) 683-8080   Fax: (703) 683-8099
E-mail: eafrancis@cswe.org
Web: www.cswe.org

Purpose To provide financial assistance to ethnic minority social work students in their last year of study for a baccalaureate or master's degree.

Eligibility This program is open to students from ethnic groups of color (African American, Asian American, Mexican American, Puerto Rican, and American Indian) who are in the last year of study for a social work degree in an accredited baccalaureate or master's degree program. Applicants must have a cumulative GPA of 3.0 or higher and be enrolled full time. They must demonstrate a commitment to work for equity and social justice in social work.

Financial data The award is $500.

Duration This is a 1-time award.

Number awarded 2 each year.

Deadline May of each year.

[437]
CATHY L. BROCK MEMORIAL SCHOLARSHIP

Institute for Diversity in Health Management
Attn: Education Program Coordinator
One North Franklin Street, 28th Floor
Chicago, IL 60606
Toll-free: (800) 233-0996   Fax: (312) 422-4566
E-mail: clopez@aha.org
Web: www.diversityconnection.com

Purpose To provide financial assistance to minorities who are entering or continuing graduate students in health care management or business management.

Eligibility This program is open to members of ethnic minority groups who are either accepted to graduate school or first- or second-year graduate students. Applicants must be accepted or enrolled in an accredited program in health care management or business management and have a GPA of 3.0 or higher. They must demonstrate commitment to a career in health services administration, financial need, solid extracurricular and community service activities, and a strong interest and experience in finance. U.S. citizenship or permanent resident status is required.

Financial data The stipend is $1,000.

Duration 1 year.

Number awarded 1 or more each year, depending on the availability of funds.

Deadline October of each year.

[438]
CAVE MEMORIAL AWARD

National Optometric Association
c/o Dr. Charles Comer, Association Manager
3723 Main Street
P.O. Box F
East Chicago, IL 46312
Toll-free: (877) 394-2020   Fax: (219) 398-1077
E-mail: ccomer2@aol.com
Web: www.natoptassoc.org

Purpose To provide financial assistance to members (particularly members who are minorities) of the National Optometric Student Association (NOSA).

Eligibility This program is open to NOSA members enrolled in a school or college of optometry. Applicants must have a GPA of 2.5 or higher and be able to demonstrate community involvement. Along with their application, they must submit a 2-page statement on their career goals, community and college involvement, and how they feel they can affect minority communities in a positive way. Financial need is considered in the selection process.

Financial data The stipend is $500.

Duration 1 year.

Additional information The National Optometric Association was founded in 1969 with the goal of recruiting minority students for schools and colleges of optometry. It remains committed to improving the quality and accessibility of eye care in minority and other historically underserved communities.

Number awarded 1 each year.

Deadline April of each year.

[439]
CAY DRACHNIK MINORITIES FUND

American Art Therapy Association, Inc.
Attn: Scholarships and Grants Committee
1202 Allanson Road
Mundelein, IL 60060-3808
(847) 949-6064   Toll-free: (888) 290-0878
Fax: (847) 566-4580   E-mail: info@arttherapy.org
Web: www.arttherapy.org

Purpose To help to pay for the books needed by minority students who are members of the American Art Therapy Association (AATA).

Eligibility This program is open to minority student AATA members accepted or enrolled in a graduate art therapy program approved by the association. They must be able to demonstrate financial need. Applications must include transcripts, 2 letters of reference, a student financial information form, and a 2-page essay that contains a brief biography and a statement of career goals.

Financial data The fund provides from $200 to $500 for the purchase of books.

Duration 1 year.

Deadline June of each year.

[440]
CENTOCOR EXCELLENCE IN IBD CLINICAL RESEARCH AWARDS

Foundation for Digestive Health and Nutrition
Attn: Research Awards Coordinator
4930 Del Ray Avenue
Bethesda, MD 20814-2512
(301) 222-4005   Fax: (301) 222-4010
E-mail: info@fdhn.org
Web: www.fdhn.org

Purpose To provide funding to senior gastroenterology fellows (especially minorities and women) interested in preparing for a research career in inflammatory bowel diseases (IBD).

Eligibility This program is open to trainee members of the American Gastroenterological Association (AGA) who have an M.D. or equivalent degree. Applicants must be currently enrolled in an accredited gastroenterology-related fellowship at a U.S. institution and committed to an academic career. They must be interested in additional full-time research training in IBD clinical science to acquire modern laboratory skills. Their sponsor must be an AGA member engaged in research training at an academic gastroenterology-related unit of a medical school, affiliated teaching hospital, or research institute. A co-sponsor must be the director of a clinical or other comparable laboratory who is committed to the training and development of the applicant. The institution must provide them with at least 75% protected time. Women and minority investigators are strongly encouraged to apply. Selection is based on novelty, feasibility, and significance of the proposal; attributes of the candidate; record and commitment of the sponsors; and the institutional and laboratory environment.

Financial data The grant is $70,000 per year. No institutional indirect costs are allowed.

Duration 1 year; nonrenewable.

Additional information This program is administered by the Foundation for Digestive Health and Nutrition (FDHN) with support from Centocor, Inc. and the AGA.

Number awarded 5 each year.

Deadline January of each year.

[441]
CHIYOKO AND THOMAS SHIMAZAKI SCHOLARSHIP

Japanese American Citizens League
Attn: National Scholarship Awards
1765 Sutter Street
San Francisco, CA 94115
(415) 921-5225   Fax: (415) 931-4671
E-mail: jacl@jacl.org
Web: www.jacl.org/scholarships.html

Purpose To provide financial assistance to student members of the Japanese American Citizens League (JACL) who are interested in preparing for a career in medicine.

Eligibility This program is open to JACL members who are interested in preparing for a career in the medical field. Applicants must submit a statement describing their current level of involvement in the Japanese American community or Asian Pacific community and how they will continue their involvement in future years. Selection is based on academic record, extracurricular activities, financial need, and community involvement.

Financial data The stipend depends on the availability of funds but usually ranges from $1,000 to $5,000.

Duration 1 year; nonrenewable.

Additional information Applications must be submitted to the JACL National Scholarship Program, c/o San Diego JACL Chapter, 1031 25th Street, San Diego, CA 92102.

Number awarded At least 1 each year.

Deadline March of each year.

[442]
CHUNGHI HONG PARK SCHOLARSHIP

Korean-American Scientists and Engineers Association
1952 Gallows Drive, Suite 300
Vienna, VA 22182
(703) 748-1221   Fax: (703) 748-1331
E-mail: sejong@ksea.org
Web: www.ksea.org

Purpose To provide financial assistance to women who are undergraduate or graduate student members of the Korean-American Scientists and Engineers Association (KSEA).

Eligibility This program is open to women who are Korean American undergraduate or graduate students, graduated from a high school in the United States, are KSEA members, and are majoring in science, engineering, or a related field. Along with their application, they must submit a 500-word essay on either of the following topics: 1) their career goals and intended contributions to society, or 2) the meaning of Korean heritage in their life. Selection is based on the essay (20%), work experience and extracurricular activities (20%), recommendation letters (30%), and academic performance (30%).

Financial data The stipend is $1,000.

Duration 1 year.

Number awarded 2 each year.
Deadline February of each year.

[443]
CJAAA SCHOLARSHIP PROGRAM

California Japanese American Alumni Association
Attn: Ron Yamada
P.O. Box 15235
San Francisco, CA 94115-0235
(650) 802-0939   E-mail: scholarships@cjaaa.org
Web: www.cjaaa.org/scholarship.html

Purpose To provide financial assistance to undergraduate or graduate students of Japanese American descent who are currently enrolled at 1 of the University of California campuses.

Eligibility This program is open to continuing or returning undergraduate or graduate students of Japanese American descent who are attending 1 of the University of California campuses. They must be American citizens and may be studying in any field or discipline. A GPA of 3.0 or higher is strongly recommended but not required. Applicants interested in participating in the University of California Education Abroad Program in Japan must have a GPA of 3.5 or higher. Selection is based on academic excellence, commitment to community and social concerns, personal attributes, and financial need (in that order).

Financial data Stipends range from $1,000 to $3,000. The Moriaki "Mo" Noguchi Memorial Scholarship of $3,000 is given to the top overall candidate. The George Kondo Award is at least $1,000 and is awarded to the applicant with the best community service record. The Yori Wada Award is $2,000 and is awarded to the applicant with the most outstanding record of public service. The stipend for a student accepted to the University of California Education Abroad Program ranges from $2,500 to $5,000.

Duration 1 year; nonrenewable.
Number awarded 5 to 15 each year.
Deadline April of each year.

[444]
CLA SCHOLARSHIP FOR MINORITY STUDENTS IN MEMORY OF EDNA YELLAND

California Library Association
717 20th Street, Suite 200
Sacramento, CA 95814
(916) 447-8541   Fax: (916) 447-8394
E-mail: info@cla-net.org
Web: www.cla-net.org/awards/ednayelland.php

Purpose To provide financial assistance to students of ethnic minority origin in California who are interested in preparing for a career in library or information science.

Eligibility This program is open to California residents who are members of ethnic minority groups (American Indian, African American/Black, Mexican American/Chicano, Latino/Hispanic, Asian American, Pacific Islander, or Filipino). Applicants must be enrolled or accepted for enrollment in a master's program at an accredited graduate library school in California. Evidence of financial need and U.S. citizenship or permanent resident status must be submitted. Finalists are interviewed.

Financial data The stipend is $2,500.

Duration 1 academic year.
Additional information This fellowship is named for the executive secretary of the California Library Association from 1947 to 1963 who worked to promote the goals of the California Library Association and the profession. Until 1985, it was named the Edna Yelland Memorial Scholarship.
Number awarded 3 each year.
Deadline May of each year.

[445]
CLINICAL RESEARCH POST-DOCTORAL FELLOWSHIP PROGRAM

American Nurses Association
Attn: Ethnic Minority Fellowship Programs
600 Maryland Avenue, S.W., Suite 100 West
Washington, DC 20024-2571
(202) 651-7244   Fax: (202) 651-7007
E-mail: emfp@ana.org
Web: www.nursingworld.org

Purpose To provide funding to postdoctoral minority nurses interested in a program of research and study on psychiatric, mental health, and substance abuse issues that impact the lives of ethnic minority people.

Eligibility This program is open to doctoral-prepared nurses who are members of an ethnic or racial minority group, including but not limited to Blacks or African Americans, Hispanics or Latinos, American Indians and Alaska Natives, Asians and Asian Americans, and Native Hawaiians and other Pacific Islanders. Applicants must be able to demonstrate a commitment to a research career in nursing and psychiatric/mental health issues affecting ethnic minority populations. They must be interested in a program of full-time postdoctoral study, with a research focus on such issues of concern to minority populations as child abuse, violence in intimate relationships, mental health disorders, substance abuse, mental health service utilization, and stigma as a barrier to mental health care and personal resilience. U.S. citizenship or permanent resident status and membership in the American Nurses Association are required.

Financial data The stipend is $28,260 per year.
Duration Up to 2 years.
Additional information Funds for this program are provided by the Substance Abuse and Mental Health Services Administration.
Number awarded 1 or more each year.

[446]
CLINICAL RESEARCH PRE-DOCTORAL FELLOWSHIP PROGRAM

American Nurses Association
Attn: Ethnic Minority Fellowship Programs
600 Maryland Avenue, S.W., Suite 100 West
Washington, DC 20024-2571
(202) 651-7244   Fax: (202) 651-7007
E-mail: emfp@ana.org
Web: www.nursingworld.org

Purpose To provide financial assistance to minority nurses who are doctoral candidates interested in psychiatric, mental health, and substance abuse issues that impact the lives of ethnic minority people.

Eligibility This program is open to nurses who have a master's degree and are members of an ethnic or racial minority group, including but not limited to Blacks or African Americans, Hispanics or Latinos, American Indians and Alaska Natives, Asians and Asian Americans, and Native Hawaiians and other Pacific Islanders. Applicants must be able to demonstrate a commitment to a research career in nursing and psychiatric/mental health issues affecting ethnic minority populations. They must be interested in a program of full-time doctoral study, with a research focus on such issues of concern to minority populations as child abuse, violence in intimate relationships, mental health disorders, substance abuse, mental health service utilization, and stigma as a barrier to mental health care and personal resilience. U.S. citizenship or permanent resident status and membership in the American Nurses Association are required. Selection is based on research potential, scholarship, writing ability, knowledge of broad issues in mental health nursing, and professional commitment to ethnic minority concerns.

Financial data Fellows receive a stipend of $20,772 per year and $5,000 in tuition assistance.

Duration 3 to 5 years.

Additional information Funds for this program are provided by the Substance Abuse and Mental Health Services Administration.

Number awarded 1 or more each year.

Deadline February of each year.

[447]
CONNECTICUT COMMUNITY COLLEGE MINORITY TEACHING FELLOWSHIPS

Connecticut Community College System
Attn: System Officer for Diversity Awareness
61 Woodland Street
Hartford, CT 06105-9949
(860) 244-7606   Fax: (860) 566-6624
E-mail: karmstrong@commnet.edu
Web: www.commnet.edu/minority_fellowship.asp

Purpose To provide financial assistance and work experience to graduate students, especially minorities, in Connecticut who are interested in preparing for a career in community college teaching or administration.

Eligibility This program is open to graduate students who have completed at least 6 credits of graduate work and have indicated an interest in a career in community colleges. Applicants must be willing to commit to at least 1 year of employment in the Connecticut Community College System. Although all qualified graduate students are eligible, the program encourages applicants to register who strengthen the racial and cultural diversity of the minority fellow registry. That includes, in particular, making all possible efforts to recruit from historically underrepresented people (Asians, Blacks, and Hispanics).

Financial data Fellows receive a stipend of $3,500 per semester.

Duration 1 year; may be renewed.

Additional information Fellows are expected to dedicate 9 hours per week to the program. They spend 6 hours per week in teaching-related activities under the supervision of a mentor. During the second semester, they assist the mentor in teaching a course. The remaining time is spent on program and campus orientation activities, attendance at relevant faculty or staff meetings, and participation in other college meetings or professional development activities.

Number awarded Up to 13 each year: 1 at each of the 12 colleges in the system and 1 in the chancellor's office.

[448]
CONNECTICUT SPECIAL EDUCATION TEACHER INCENTIVE GRANT

Connecticut Department of Higher Education
Attn: Education and Employment Information Center
61 Woodland Street
Hartford, CT 06105-2326
(860) 947-1846   Toll-free: (800) 842-0229 (within CT)
Fax: (860) 947-1311   E-mail: setig@ctdhe.org
Web: www.ctdhe.org/SFA/sfa.htm

Purpose To provide financial assistance to undergraduate and graduate students (particularly underrepresented minorities) in Connecticut who are preparing for a career as a special education teacher.

Eligibility This program is open to full-time juniors and seniors and full- or part-time graduate students who are residents of Connecticut. Applicants must be enrolled in 1) special education teacher preparation programs at selected universities in Connecticut; or 2) out-of-state teacher preparation programs seeking cross-endorsement for teaching "low-incidence student" areas. They must be nominated by the dean of education at their school and have a stated intent to teach in a Connecticut public school, an approved private special education facility, or a Regional Educational Service Center. Priority is given to minority (African American, Hispanic/Latino, Asian American, and Native American) and bilingual students and to Connecticut residents enrolled in an approved out-of-state program.

Financial data The stipend is $5,000 per year for full-time study or $2,000 per year for part-time graduate study.

Duration 1 year.

Additional information The approved in-state programs are at Central Connecticut State University, Fairfield University, Saint Joseph College, Southern Connecticut State University, University of Connecticut, and University of Hartford. The programs for students seeking cross-endorsement certification for teaching students who are blind and partially-sighted or visually impaired are at Hunter College of CUNY (New York, New York), Dominican College (Orangeburg, New York), Teachers College of Columbia University (New York, New York), and University of Northern Colorado (Greeley, Colorado). The programs for students seeking cross-endorsement certification for teaching students who are deaf or hearing-impaired are at Hunter College, Teachers College, Clarke School for the Deaf at Smith College (Northampton, Massachusetts), and Boston University (Boston, Massachusetts).

Number awarded Varies each year.

Deadline August of each year.

[449]
CORA AGUDA MANAYAN FUND

Hawai'i Community Foundation
Attn: Scholarship Department
1164 Bishop Street, Suite 800
Honolulu, HI 96813
(808) 537-6333   Toll-free: (888) 731-3863
Fax: (808) 521-6286
E-mail: scholarships@hcf-hawaii.org
Web: www.hawaiicommunityfoundation.org

Purpose To provide financial assistance to Hawaii residents of Filipino ancestry who are interested in preparing for a career in the health field.

Eligibility This program is open to Hawaii residents of Filipino ancestry who are interested in studying in Hawaii as full-time students and majoring in a health-related field (on the undergraduate or graduate school level). They must be able to demonstrate academic achievement (GPA of 2.7 or higher), good moral character, and financial need. In addition to filling out the standard application form, they must write a short statement indicating their reasons for attending college, their planned course of study, and their career goals.

Financial data The amounts of the awards depend on the availability of funds and the need of the recipient; recently, stipends averaged $1,000.

Duration 1 year.

Number awarded Varies each year; recently, 15 of these scholarships were awarded.

Deadline February of each year.

[450]
COX FOUNDATION SCHOLARSHIPS

Asian American Journalists Association
Attn: Student Programs Coordinator
1182 Market Street, Suite 320
San Francisco, CA 94102
(415) 346-2051, ext. 102   Fax: (415) 346-6343
E-mail: brandons@aaja.org
Web: www.aaja.org

Purpose To provide financial assistance to student members of the Asian American Journalists Association (AAJA) interested in careers in broadcast, photo, or print journalism.

Eligibility This program is open to AAJA members who are high school seniors or college students (graduate or undergraduate) enrolled full time in accredited institutions. Applicants must submit a 500-word essay on their involvement or interest in the Asian American community and how, if they are awarded this scholarship, they would contribute to the field of journalism and/or media issues involving the Asian American and Pacific Islander community. Selection is based on scholastic ability, commitment to journalism, sensitivity to Asian American and Pacific Islander issues as demonstrated by community involvement, journalistic ability, and financial need.

Financial data The stipend is $2,500.

Duration 1 year; may be renewed.

Additional information This program is supported by the Cox Foundation.

Number awarded Varies each year.

Deadline April of each year.

[451]
CROWELL & MORING DIVERSITY IN THE LEGAL PROFESSION SCHOLARSHIPS

Crowell & Moring LLP
Attn: Diversity in the Legal Profession Scholarship
1001 Pennsylvania Avenue, N.W.
Washington, DC 20004-2595
(202) 624-2849   Fax: (202) 628-5116
E-mail: scholarship@crowell.com
Web: www.crowell.com/diversityscholarship

Purpose To provide financial assistance to minority students from any state attending a law school in the District of Columbia.

Eligibility This program is open to students of racial or ethnic minority origin (American Indian/Alaskan Native, Black/African American or African, Hispanic/Latino, or Asian/Pacific Islander). Applicants must be enrolled in the first year (or second year for students in a part-time or joint degree program) at an accredited law school in the District of Columbia. They must submit a personal statement of 1,000 words or less on 1) significant obstacles, disadvantages, and/or challenges that they have overcome in pursuit of a legal education; and 2) how they plan to use their legal education upon completion of law school and how they foresee this scholarship assisting in that regard. Selection is based on academic performance, leadership skills, work experience, community service, special accomplishments and honors, and financial need.

Financial data Stipends are $10,000 or $7,500.

Duration 1 year.

Additional information This program was established in 2005.

Number awarded 3 each year: 1 at $10,000 and 2 at $7,500.

Deadline April of each year.

[452]
CSCPA ETHNIC DIVERSITY SCHOLARSHIPS FOR COLLEGE STUDENTS

Colorado Society of Certified Public Accountants
Attn: CSCPA Educational Foundation
7979 East Tufts Avenue, Suite 500
Denver, CO 80237-2845
(303) 741-8613   Toll-free: (800) 523-9082 (within CO)
Fax: (303) 773-6344   E-mail: gmantz@cocpa.org
Web: www.cocpa.org

Purpose To provide financial assistance to minority undergraduate or graduate students in Colorado who are studying accounting.

Eligibility This program is open to African Americans, Hispanics, Asian Americans, American Indians, and Pacific Islanders studying at a college or university in Colorado at the associate, baccalaureate, or graduate level. Applicants must have completed at least 1 intermediate accounting class, be declared accounting majors, have completed at least 8 semester hours of accounting classes, and have a GPA of at least 3.0. Selection is based first on scholastic achievement and second on financial need.

Financial data The stipend is $1,000. Funds are paid directly to the recipient's school to be used for books, tuition, room, board, fees, and expenses.

Duration 1 year; recipients may reapply.

Number awarded 2 each year.

Deadline June of each year.

[453]
D. AUGUSTUS STRAKER SCHOLARSHIP

D. Augustus Straker Bar Association
Attn: Foundation Board
P.O. Box 1898
Troy, MI 48099-1898
Web: www.michbar.org/localbars/straker/home.html

Purpose To provide financial assistance to minority students at law schools in Michigan.

Eligibility This program is open to minority students enrolled in a certified law school program within the state of Michigan. Applicants must demonstrate scholarly dedication, involvement in school and community activities, and the ability to articulate a vision that indicates prospects for long-term success in the practice of law, especially as it relates to representing minority viewpoints within the system of jurisprudence.

Financial data The stipend is $2,500.

Duration 1 year.

Additional information The D. Augustus Straker Bar Association was founded in 1990 as a proactive organization for African American attorneys. It was named in honor of the first African American attorney to argue a case before the Michigan Supreme Court (in 1890).

Number awarded 2 each year.

Deadline March of each year.

[454]
DAVID TAMOTSU KAGIWADA MEMORIAL SCHOLARSHIP

Christian Church (Disciples of Christ)
Attn: Division of Homeland Ministries
130 East Washington Street
P.O. Box 1986
Indianapolis, IN 46206-1986
(317) 713-2672   Toll-free: (888) DHM-2631
Fax: (317) 635-4426   E-mail: mail@dhm.disciples.org
Web: www.homelandministries.org

Purpose To provide financial assistance to Asian Americans interested in preparing for a career in the ministry of the Christian Church (Disciples of Christ).

Eligibility This program is open to Asian American ministerial students who are members of the Christian Church (Disciples of Christ). Applicants must plan to prepare for the ordained ministry, have at least a "C+" GPA, provide evidence of financial need, be enrolled full time in an accredited school or seminary, provide a transcript of academic work, and be under the care of a regional Commission on the Ministry or in the process of coming under care.

Financial data The stipend is $1,500.

Duration 1 year; may be renewed.

Number awarded Varies each year.

Deadline March of each year.

[455]
DAVIS WRIGHT TREMAINE 1L DIVERSITY SCHOLARSHIP PROGRAM

Davis Wright Tremaine LLP
Attn: Recruiting Administrator
2600 Century Square
1501 Fourth Avenue
Seattle, WA 98101-1688
(206) 622-3150   Fax: (206) 628-7699
E-mail: seattle@dwt.com
Web: www.dwt.com/recruit/diversity.htm

Purpose To provide financial assistance and summer work experience to law students of color.

Eligibility This program is open to first-year law students of color and others of diverse background. Applicants must possess a strong academic record as an undergraduate and in first year of law school, an interest in participating in community and civic opportunities, and a willingness to commit to working in the sponsor's Seattle or Portland office during the summer between their first and second year of law school. They must submit a current resume, a complete undergraduate transcript, grades from the first semester of law school, a short personal essay indicating their interest in the scholarship, a legal writing sample, and 2 or 3 references. Although demonstrated need may be taken into account, applicants need not disclose their financial circumstances.

Financial data The award consists of a $7,500 stipend for second-year tuition and expenses and a paid summer clerkship.

Duration 1 academic year and summer.

Number awarded 3 each year: 2 in the Seattle office and 1 in the Portland office.

Deadline January of each year.

[456]
DELA CRUZ-MILLMAN FILIPINO-AMERICAN NP STUDENT SCHOLARSHIP

American Academy of Nurse Practitioners
Attn: AANP Foundation
P.O. Box 10729
Glendale, AZ 85318-0729
(623) 376-9467   Fax: (623) 376-0369
E-mail: foundation@aanp.org
Web: www.aanp.org

Purpose To provide financial assistance to members of the American Academy of Nurse Practitioners (AANP) from designated states who are of Filipino heritage and working on a master's degree.

Eligibility This program is open to current student and full members of the academy who are enrolled in a M.S.N. degree program as a nurse practitioner (NP). Applicants must be of Filipino or Filipino American heritage and residents of California, Florida, Hawaii, Illinois, Maryland, New Jersey, New York, Texas, Virginia, or Washington. They must have a GPA of 3.2 or higher and have completed at least 25% but no more than 75% of their program requirements.

Financial data The stipend is $1,000. Funds may be used only for educational expenses (tuition, books, equipment, etc.), not for expenses related to master's thesis and/or general research projects.

Duration 1 year.

Additional information This program was established in 1999. There is a $10 application fee.

Number awarded 1 each year.

Deadline April of each year.

[457]
DELL/UNCF CORPORATE SCHOLARS PROGRAM

United Negro College Fund
Attn: Corporate Scholars Program
P.O. Box 1435
Alexandria, VA 22313-9998
Toll-free: (866) 671-7237　E-mail: internship@uncf.org
Web: www.uncf.org/internships/index.asp

Purpose To provide financial assistance and work experience to undergraduate and graduate students, especially minorities, majoring in designated fields and interested in an internship at Dell Computer Corporation's corporate headquarters near Austin, Texas.

Eligibility This program is open to rising juniors and graduate students who are enrolled full time at institutions that are members of the United Negro College Fund (UNCF) or at any other 4-year college or university. Applicants must be majoring in business administration, computer science, engineering (computer, electrical, or mechanical), finance, human resources, management information systems, marketing, or supply chain management with a GPA of 3.0 or higher. Along with their application, they must submit a 1-page essay about themselves and their career goals, including information about their personal background and any particular challenges they have faced. Finalists are interviewed by a team of representatives from Dell, the program's sponsor.

Financial data The program provides a paid summer internship, housing accommodations in Austin, round-trip transportation to and from Austin, and (based on financial need and successful internship performance) a $10,000 scholarship.

Duration 10 to 12 weeks for the internship; 1 year for the scholarship.

Number awarded Varies each year.

Deadline January of each year.

[458]
DELORES A. AUZENNE FELLOWSHIP FOR GRADUATE STUDY

State University System of Florida
Attn: Office of Academic and Student Affairs
325 West Gaines Street, Suite 1501
Tallahassee, FL 32399-1950
(850) 245-0467　　　　　　Fax: (850) 245-9667
E-mail: we're.listening@fldoe.org
Web: www.fldoe.org

Purpose To provide financial assistance to minority students in Florida working on a graduate degree in an underrepresented discipline.

Eligibility Eligible to be nominated are minority students working on a graduate degree at a public university in Florida. Nominees must be enrolled in full-time studies in a discipline in which there is an underrepresentation of the minority group to which they belong. A GPA of 3.0 or higher

and U.S. citizenship or permanent resident status are required.

Financial data The stipend is $5,000 per year.

Duration 1 year; may be renewed if the recipient maintains full-time enrollment and at least a 3.0 GPA.

Additional information This program is administered by the equal opportunity program at each of the 11 State University System of Florida 4-year institutions. Contact that office for further information.

Number awarded 5 each year.

[459]
DR. HILDEGARD E. PEPLAU SCHOLARSHIP

American Psychiatric Nurses Association
Attn: APN Foundation
1555 Wilson Boulevard, Suite 515
Arlington, VA 22209
(703) 243-2443　　　　　　Fax: (703) 243-3390
E-mail: inform@apna.org
Web: www.apna.org/foundation/scholarships.html

Purpose To provide financial assistance to students and registered nurses (especially minorities) working on a degree in nursing.

Eligibility This program is open to students and registered nurses enrolled in an NLN-accredited program in nursing. Applicants must submit 3 essays (each up to 500 words) on the following topics: 1) their career goals, how education will enhance those goals, and their contribution to the profession; 2) their professional activities, involvement, continuing education, and scholarly contributions; and 3) their voluntary community activities. Financial need is not considered in the selection process. Minorities are especially encouraged to apply.

Financial data The stipend is $1,000.

Duration 1 year.

Number awarded 1 or more each year.

Deadline January of each year.

[460]
DR. JOHN HOWLETTE AND C. CLAYTON POWELL STUDENT FOUNDERS AWARD

National Optometric Association
c/o Dr. Charles Comer, Association Manager
3723 Main Street
P.O. Box F
East Chicago, IL 46312
Toll-free: (877) 394-2020　　　　Fax: (219) 398-1077
E-mail: ccomer2@aol.com
Web: www.natoptassoc.org

Purpose To provide financial assistance to members of the National Optometric Student Association (NOSA).

Eligibility This program is open to NOSA members enrolled in the first, second, or third year at a school or college of optometry. Applicants must have a GPA of 3.0 or higher and be able to demonstrate leadership within the profession and community. Along with their application, they must submit a 2-page statement on their career goals, community and college involvement, and how they feel they can affect minority communities in a positive way. Financial need is considered in the selection process.

Financial data The stipend is $500.

Duration 1 year.

Additional information The National Optometric Association was founded in 1969 with the goal of recruiting minority students for schools and colleges of optometry. It remains committed to improving the quality and accessibility of eye care in minority and other historically underserved communities.

Number awarded 1 each year.

Deadline April of each year.

[461]
DR. KIYOSHI SONODA MEMORIAL SCHOLARSHIP

Japanese American Citizens League
Attn: National Scholarship Awards
1765 Sutter Street
San Francisco, CA 94115
(415) 921-5225　　　　Fax: (415) 931-4671
E-mail: jacl@jacl.org
Web: www.jacl.org/scholarships.html

Purpose To provide financial assistance to student members of the Japanese American Citizens League (JACL) who are interested in preparing for a career in dentistry.

Eligibility This program is open to JACL members who are enrolled or planning to enroll in a school of dentistry. Applicants must submit a statement describing their current level of involvement in the Japanese American community or Asian Pacific community and how they will continue their involvement in future years. Selection is based on academic record, extracurricular activities, financial need, and community involvement.

Financial data The stipend depends on the availability of funds but usually ranges from $1,000 to $5,000.

Duration 1 year; nonrenewable.

Additional information Applications must be submitted to the JACL National Scholarship Program, c/o San Diego JACL Chapter, 1031 25th Street, San Diego, CA 92102.

Number awarded At least 1 each year.

Deadline March of each year.

[462]
DR. LESTER CHEN MEMORIAL SCHOLARSHIPS

Chinese American Physicians Society
Attn: Executive Director
345 Ninth Street, Suite 204
Oakland, CA 94607-4206
(510) 895-5539　　　　Fax: (510) 895-5539
E-mail: scholarship@caps-ca.org
Web: www.caps-ca.org

Purpose To provide financial assistance to medical students of Asian descent from the San Francisco Bay area.

Eligibility This program is open to students of Asian ancestry whose hometowns are located in the 9 San Francisco Bay area counties. Applicants must be attending or planning to attend a U.S. medical school. Preference is given to those willing to serve Asian American communities after graduation. Along with their application, they must submit a 500-word essay on the cause of the mental health crisis facing Asian American communities and possible solutions. Selection is based on the essay, academic achievement, financial need, and Asian American community service.

Financial data The stipend ranges from $2,000 to $3,000 per year.

Duration 1 year; may be renewed.

Number awarded 1 or more each year.

Deadline September of each year.

[463]
DR. NANCY FOSTER SCHOLARSHIP PROGRAM

National Oceanic and Atmospheric Administration
Attn: National Ocean Service
Office of the Assistant Administrator
1305 East-West Highway, 13th Floor
Silver Spring, MD 20910-3281
(301) 713-3074　　　　E-mail: fosterscholars@noaa.gov
Web: fosterscholars.noaa.gov

Purpose To provide financial assistance to graduate students, especially minorities and women, who are interested in working on a degree in fields related to marine sciences.

Eligibility This program is open to U.S. citizens, particularly women and members of minority groups, currently working on or intending to work on a master's or doctoral degree in oceanography, marine biology, or maritime archaeology, including the curation, preservation, and display of maritime artifacts. Selection is based on academic record, recommendations, financial need, career goals and objectives, and the applicant's potential for success in a graduate study program.

Financial data The program provides a stipend of $20,000 per year and a tuition allowance of up to $12,000 per year.

Duration Up to 2 years for master's degree students or up to 4 years for doctoral students.

Additional information These scholarships were first awarded in 2001.

Number awarded 4 each year.

Deadline April of each year.

[464]
DRI LAW STUDENT DIVERSITY SCHOLARSHIP

DRI-The Voice of the Defense Bar
Attn: Diversity Scholarship Committee
150 North Michigan Avenue, Suite 300
Chicago, IL 60601
(312) 795-1101　　　　Fax: (312) 795-0747
E-mail: dri@dri.org
Web: www.dir.org/dir/about/diversityawards.cfm

Purpose To provide financial assistance to minority and women law students.

Eligibility This program is open to students entering their second year of law school who are African American, Hispanic, Asian, Pan Asian, Native American, or female. Applicants must submit an essay, up to 1,000 words, on the topic "With the Continuing Decline in the Number of Civil Trials, What Methods Can Defense Lawyers Adopt to Preserve the Civil Jury System?" Selection is based on that essay, demonstrated academic excellence, service to the profession, service to the community, and service to the cause of diversity. Students affiliated with the Association of Trial Lawyers of America as members, student members, or employees are not eligible. Finalists are invited to participate in personal interviews.

Financial data The stipend is $10,000 per year.
Duration 1 year.
Additional information This program was established in 2004.
Number awarded 2 each year.
Deadline September of each year.

[465]
EAST OHIO CONFERENCE BOARD OF ORDAINED MINISTRY ETHNIC MINORITY GRANTS

United Methodist Church-East Ohio Conference
Attn: Board of Ordained Ministry
8800 Cleveland Avenue, N.W.
P.O. Box 2800
North Canton, OH 44720
(330) 499-3972   Toll-free: (800) 831-3972
Fax: (330) 499-3279
Web: www.eocumc.com

Purpose To provide financial assistance to ethnic minority undergraduate and graduate students who are preparing for ordained ministry in the East Ohio Conference.
Eligibility This program is open to ethnic minority college and graduate students who are preparing for ordained ministry in the East Ohio Conference. Students must be recommended to receive this aid either by their District Superintendent or by the District Committee on Ordained Ministry where they hold their relationship. Applicants must attend a college or seminary that is fully accredited by the University Senate. They do not need to be certified candidates. Ethnic minority undergraduate pre-theological students are also eligible.
Financial data The stipend is $500 per year.
Duration 1 year.
Additional information Information is also available from Preston Forbes, Seminary Scholarships and Grants Secretary, 9071 Inverrary Drive, Warren, OH 44484, (330) 856-2631, E-mail: forbes@onecom.com.
Number awarded 1 or more each year.
Deadline September of each year.

[466]
EASTERN REGION KOREAN AMERICAN SCHOLARSHIPS

Korean American Scholarship Foundation
Eastern Region
c/o William S. Lee, Scholarship Committee Chair
10301 Georgia Avenue, Suite 303
Silver Spring, MD 20902
(703) 748-5935   Fax: (703) 748-1874
E-mail: kasfdc@hotmail.com
Web: www.kasf.org

Purpose To provide financial assistance to Korean American undergraduate and graduate students who attend school in the eastern states.
Eligibility This program is open to Korean American students who are currently enrolled in a college or university in an eastern state as a full-time undergraduate or graduate student. Applicants may reside anywhere in the United States as long as they attend school in the eastern region: Delaware, District of Columbia, Kentucky, Maryland, North Carolina, Pennsylvania, Virginia, and West Virginia. Selec-

tion is based on academic achievement, school activities, community service, and financial need.
Financial data Stipends range from $350 to $5,000.
Duration 1 year; renewable.
Number awarded Varies each year. Recently, 65 of these scholarships were awarded: 1 at $5,000, 20 at $2,000, 3 at $1,500, 33 at $1,000, 2 at $500, and 6 at $350.
Deadline May of each year.

[467]
EDUCATIONAL ADVANCEMENT GRADUATE SCHOLARSHIPS

American Association of Critical-Care Nurses
Attn: Educational Advancement Scholarships
101 Columbia
Aliso Viejo, CA 92656-4109
(949) 362-2000, ext. 338
Toll-free: (800) 899-AACN, ext. 338
Fax: (949) 362-2020   E-mail: info@aacn.org
Web: www.aacn.org

Purpose To assist members of the American Association of Critical-Care Nurses (AACN) who are working on a graduate degree in nursing.
Eligibility This program is open to registered nurses who are current members of the association and enrolled in an accredited master's or doctoral degree program in nursing. Applicants must hold an active R.N. license and be currently working in critical care or have 1 year's experience in the last 3 years. They must have a cumulative GPA of 3.0 or higher. Along with their application, they must submit 1) a 1-page essay on how they see their nursing practice changing as a result of their graduate degree; and 2) a 2-page exemplar (an essay describing a situation in which their intervention made a difference in a patient's outcome). Financial need is not considered in the selection process. Qualified ethnic minority candidates receive at least 20% of these awards.
Financial data The stipend is $1,500. The funds are sent directly to the recipient's college or university and may be used only for tuition, fees, books, and supplies.
Duration 1 year; recipients may reapply.
Number awarded Varies each year; recently, 72 of these scholarships were awarded.
Deadline March of each year.

[468]
EDWARD S. ROTH MANUFACTURING ENGINEERING SCHOLARSHIP

Society of Manufacturing Engineers
Attn: SME Education Foundation
One SME Drive
P.O. Box 930
Dearborn, MI 48121-0930
(313) 425-3304   Toll-free: (800) 733-4763, ext. 3304
Fax: (313) 425-3411   E-mail: foundation@sme.org
Web: www.sme.org

Purpose To provide financial assistance to students (especially minorities) enrolled or planning to enroll in a degree program in manufacturing engineering at selected universities.

Eligibility This program is open to U.S. citizens who are graduating high school seniors or currently-enrolled undergraduate or graduate students. Applicants must be enrolled or planning to enroll as a full-time student at 1 of 13 selected 4-year universities to work on a bachelor's or master's degree in manufacturing engineering. They must have a GPA of 3.0 or higher. Preference is given to 1) students demonstrating financial need, 2) minority students, and 3) students participating in a co-op program. Some preference may also be given to graduating high school seniors and graduate students.

Financial data The stipend is $2,500.

Duration 1 year; may be renewed.

Additional information The eligible institutions are California Polytechnic State University at San Luis Obispo, California State Polytechnic State University at Pomona, University of Miami (Florida), Bradley University, Central State University (Ohio), Miami University (Ohio), Boston University, Worcester Polytechnic Institute, University of Massachusetts, St. Cloud State University, University of Texas-Pan American, Brigham Young University, and Utah State University.

Number awarded 1 each year.

Deadline January of each year.

[469]
EIICHI MATSUSHITA MEMORIAL SCHOLARSHIP FUND

Evangelical Lutheran Church in America
Association of Asians/Pacific Islanders
c/o Rev. Peter Wang
Truth Lutheran Church
110 South Washington Street
Naperville, IL 60540
(630) 416-6476   Fax: (630) 527-9294
Web: www.elca.org

Purpose To provide financial assistance to Asian/Pacific Islanders who wish to receive seminary training to become ordained Lutheran pastors or certified lay teachers.

Eligibility This program is open to students who are of Asian or Pacific Islander background and are attending a Lutheran seminary, have been endorsed by the appropriate synodical or district commissions, have demonstrated financial need, and have received partial financial support from their home congregations. Applicants must include a 250-word statement on their commitment to Asian/Pacific Islander ministry.

Financial data The stipend is $750.

Duration 1 year; may be renewed.

Additional information The scholarship was established by Asian Lutherans in North America. It is administered by Tierrasanta Lutheran Church on behalf of all the seminaries of the 3 Lutheran churches that united in 1988 to form the Evangelical Lutheran Church in America: the Association of Evangelical Lutheran Churches, the American Lutheran Church, and the Lutheran Church in America.

Number awarded 2 each year.

Deadline September of each year.

[470]
EIRO YAMADA MEMORIAL SCHOLARSHIP

Hawai'i Community Foundation
Attn: Scholarship Department
1164 Bishop Street, Suite 800
Honolulu, HI 96813
(808) 537-6333   Toll-free: (888) 731-3863
Fax: (808) 521-6286
E-mail: scholarships@hcf-hawaii.org
Web: www.hawaiicommunityfoundation.org

Purpose To provide financial assistance for college or graduate school to Hawaii residents who are descendants of World War II Japanese American veterans.

Eligibility This program is open to Hawaii residents who are interested in attending college on the undergraduate or graduate school level. Applicants must be a direct descendant of a World War II veteran of the 100th, 442nd, MIS, or 1399th units. They must be able to demonstrate academic achievement (GPA of 2.7 or higher), good moral character, and financial need. In addition to filling out the standard application form, applicants must write a short essay on "The Values I Have Learned from My Japanese American Forefathers" and their personal reflections on the Japanese American experience during World War II.

Financial data The amounts of the awards depend on the availability of funds and the need of the recipient; recently, stipends averaged $500.

Duration 1 year.

Additional information Recipients may attend college in Hawaii or on the mainland. Recipients must be full-time students.

Number awarded Varies each year; recently, 30 of these scholarships were awarded.

Deadline February of each year.

[471]
EIZO AND TOYO SAKUMOTO TRUST SCHOLARSHIPS

Hawai'i Community Foundation
Attn: Scholarship Department
1164 Bishop Street, Suite 800
Honolulu, HI 96813
(808) 537-6333   Toll-free: (888) 731-3863
Fax: (808) 521-6286
E-mail: scholarships@hcf-hawaii.org
Web: www.hawaiicommunityfoundation.org

Purpose To provide financial assistance to Hawaii residents of Japanese ancestry who are interested in attending college or graduate school.

Eligibility This program is open to Hawaii residents of Japanese ancestry who are enrolled in or planning to enroll in an accredited college or university in Hawaii. Applicants must be full-time undergraduate or graduate students and able to demonstrate academic achievement (GPA of 2.7 or higher), good moral character, and financial need. They must have been born in Hawaii.

Financial data The amounts of the awards depend on the availability of funds and the need of the recipient; recently, the stipend was $1,000.

Duration 1 year.

Number awarded Varies each year; recently, 57 of these scholarships were awarded.

Deadline February of each year.

[472]
ELLIOTT C. ROBERTS, SR. SCHOLARSHIP
Institute for Diversity in Health Management
Attn: Education Program Coordinator
One North Franklin Street, 28th Floor
Chicago, IL 60606
Toll-free: (800) 233-0996   Fax: (312) 422-4566
E-mail: clopez@aha.org
Web: www.diversityconnection.com

Purpose To provide financial assistance to minority graduate students in health care management or business management.

Eligibility This program is open to members of ethnic minority groups who are second-year graduate students. Applicants must be accepted or enrolled in an accredited program in health care management or business management and have a GPA of 3.0 or higher. They must demonstrate commitment to a career in health services administration, financial need, solid extracurricular activities, and a commitment to community service. U.S. citizenship or permanent resident status is required.

Financial data The stipend is $1,000.

Duration 1 year.

Number awarded 1 or more each year, depending on the availability of funds.

Deadline October of each year.

[473]
EMAF FELLOWSHIP PROGRAM
Society for Human Resource Management
Attn: Employment Management Association Foundation
1800 Duke Street
Alexandria, VA 22314-3499
(703) 548-3440   Toll-free: (800) 283-SHRM
Fax: (703) 535-6490   TDD: (703) 548-6999
E-mail: wflowers@shrm.org
Web: www.shrm.org/emaf/fellow.asp

Purpose To provide financial assistance to students enrolled or planning to enroll in a graduate program in the human resources field.

Eligibility Students are eligible to apply if they are 1) full-time college seniors who intend to prepare for a career in human resources in a generalist or employment/staffing capacity and have been accepted into an accredited graduate program; 2) full-time graduate students currently working on a degree that will lead them to a career in human resources in a generalist or employment/staffing capacity who have a GPA of 3.0 or higher; or 3) experienced degree holders who are returning to school for the purpose of re-careering or career advancement and have been accepted in an accredited graduate program related to the human resources generalist or employment/staffing field. U.S. citizenship is required. Selection is based on demonstrated scholastic achievement, leadership ability, work experience, and commitment to a career in a human resources field. At least 1 of the awards is designated for a qualified applicant from an ethnic or racial group underrepresented in the profession.

Financial data The stipend is $5,000, payable in 2 equal installments. Funds are made payable jointly to the recipient and the recipient's school.

Duration 1 year; recipients may reapply but may receive only 1 additional award.

Additional information This program includes 1 fellowship designated as the Richard Gast Fellowship. Funding for this program is provided by the Employment Management Association Foundation; the program is administered by Scholarship America, One Scholarship Way, P.O. Box 297, St. Peter, MN 56082, (507) 931-1682, (800) 537-4180, Fax: (507) 931-9168, E-mail: smsinfo@csfa.org.

Number awarded Up to 5 each year.

Deadline January of each year.

[474]
ENVIRONMENTAL EDUCATIONAL SCHOLARSHIP PROGRAM
Missouri Department of Natural Resources
Attn: Environmental Educational Scholarship Program
P.O. Box 176
Jefferson City, MO 65102
(573) 526-8411   Toll-free: (800) 334-6946
TDD: (800) 379-2419
E-mail: daspec@dnr.state.mo.us
Web: www.dnr.state.mo.us/eesp

Purpose To provide financial assistance to underrepresented and minority students from Missouri who are or will be working on a bachelor's or master's degree in an environmental field.

Eligibility This program is open to minority and underrepresented residents of Missouri who have graduated from an accredited high school with a GPA of 3.0 or higher. Students who are already enrolled in college must have a GPA of 2.5 or higher and must be full-time undergraduate or graduate students. Applicants may be 1) engineering students in civil, chemical, environmental, mechanical, or agricultural engineering; 2) environmental students in geology, biology, wildlife management, planning, natural resources, or a closely-related course of study; 3) chemistry students in the field of environmental chemistry; or 4) law enforcement students in environmental law enforcement. They must submit a 1-page essay on their environmental education career goals. Selection is based on the essay, GPA and test scores, school and community activities, leadership, and character.

Financial data A stipend is $2,000 per year.

Duration 1 year; may be renewed if the recipient maintains a GPA of 2.5 or higher and full-time enrollment.

Number awarded Varies each year.

Deadline June of each year.

[475]
EPISCOPAL ASIAMERICA MINISTRY COMMISSION CONTINUING EDUCATION SCHOLARSHIPS AND FELLOWSHIPS

Episcopal Church Center
Attn: Office of Asian American Ministries
815 Second Avenue
New York, NY 10017-4594
(212) 716-6087   Toll-free: (800) 334-7626, ext. 6087
Fax: (212) 867-7652
E-mail: wvergara@episcopalchurch.org
Web: www.episcopalchurch.org

Purpose To provide financial assistance to Asian Americans interested in seeking ordination and serving in a ministry involving Asians in the Episcopal Church.

Eligibility This program is open to Asian students pursuing theological education, including diocesan programs as well as seminary education. Applicants must be a member of an Asian constituency in the Episcopal Church and have begun the process of seeking ordination through a local Episcopal diocese. Scholarships are presented only for full-time study.

Financial data The maximum scholarship is $4,000 per semester for seminary study and $2,500 per semester for diocesan theological study programs.

Duration 1 semester; renewable.

Additional information This program was established in 1991 as part of the Episcopal Legacy Fund for Scholarships Honoring the Memory of the Rev. Dr. Martin Luther King, Jr. Applications must include an essay indicating an understanding of the life and ministry of Dr. King.

Number awarded Varies each year.

Deadline April of each year for the fall semester; August of each year for the spring semester.

[476]
EPISCOPAL ASIAMERICA MINISTRY THEOLOGICAL EDUCATION SCHOLARSHIPS FOR ASIAN AND PACIFIC ISLAND AMERICANS

Episcopal Church Center
Attn: Office of Asian American Ministries
815 Second Avenue
New York, NY 10017-4594
(212) 716-6087   Toll-free: (800) 334-7626, ext. 6087
Fax: (212) 867-7652
E-mail: wvergara@episcopalchurch.org
Web: www.episcopalchurch.org

Purpose To provide financial assistance to Asian and Pacific Island Americans interested in seeking ordination and serving in a ministry involving Asians and Pacific Islanders in the Episcopal Church.

Eligibility This program is open to Asian and Pacific Island students pursuing theological education, including diocesan programs as well as seminary education. Applicants must be a member of an Asian or Pacific Island constituency in the Episcopal Church and have begun the process of seeking ordination through a local Episcopal diocese. Scholarships are presented only for full-time study.

Financial data The maximum scholarship is $4,000 per semester for seminary study or $2,500 per semester for diocesan theological study programs.

Duration 1 semester; renewable.

Additional information This program was established in 1983 with a grant from undesignated funds received through the Venture in Mission Project. Additional funding was received from the Diocese of Southern Virginia.

Number awarded Varies each year.

Deadline April of each year for the fall semester; August of each year for the spring semester.

[477]
ETHNIC IN-SERVICE TRAINING FUND

United Methodist Church
General Board of Higher Education and Ministry
Attn: Section of Chaplains and Related Ministries
1001 19th Avenue South
P.O. Box 340007
Nashville, TN 37203-0007
(615) 340-7392   Fax: (615) 340-7395
E-mail: sespino@gbhem.org
Web: www.gbhem.org/chaplains/mistscholarship.html

Purpose To provide funding to Methodists who are members of racial and ethnic minority groups involved in Clinical Pastoral Education (CPE) for pastoral counseling or hospital chaplaincy.

Eligibility This program is open to racial and ethnic minorities who have been active in a local United Methodist Church. Applicants must have been accepted into an accredited CPE program for pastoral counseling or hospital chaplaincy. They must submit a 2-page paper on their call to the ordained ministry and a 1-page paper on how CPE will enhance their ministry.

Financial data The stipend depends on the need of the recipient, the cost of the program, and the availability of funds.

Number awarded Varies each year.

Deadline March or August of each year.

[478]
ETHNIC MINISTERIAL SCHOLARSHIPS

West Los Angeles United Methodist Church
Attn: Scholarship Committee
1913 Purdue Avenue
Los Angeles, CA 90025
(310) 479-1379   Fax: (310) 478-7756
E-mail: wlaumc@aol.com
Web: www.wlaumc.org

Purpose To provide financial assistance to Japanese American and Asian American seminary students who are preparing for ordained ministry in the United Methodist Church.

Eligibility This program is open to Japanese American and Asian American students at Protestant seminaries in the United States. Applicants must be planning to serve a Japanese American or Asian American congregation of the United Methodist Church as an ordained minister. They must have a GPA of 2.5 or higher. Along with their application, they must submit 2 essays (of 500 words each) on 1) their motivations for preparing for a career in the United Methodist Church, and 2) their concerns for the local church and the United Methodist Church with issues related to Asian Americans and/or Pacific Islanders.

Financial data Stipends range from $250 to $1,000.

Duration 1 year; recipients may reapply.

Additional information This program was established in 1972.

Number awarded Varies each year; recently, 4 of these scholarships were awarded.

Deadline February of each year.

[479]
ETHNIC MINORITY MASTER'S SCHOLARSHIPS IN ONCOLOGY NURSING

Oncology Nursing Society
Attn: ONS Foundation
125 Enterprise Drive
Pittsburgh, PA 15275-1214
(412) 859-6100, ext. 8503   Toll-free: (866) 257-4ONS
Fax: (412) 859-6160   E-mail: foundation@ons.org
Web: www.ons.org

Purpose To provide financial assistance to ethnic minorities interested in working on a master's degree in oncology nursing.

Eligibility The candidate must 1) demonstrate an interest in and commitment to oncology nursing; 2) be enrolled in a graduate nursing degree program at an NLN- or CCNE-accredited school of nursing (the program must have application to oncology nursing); 3) not have previously received a master's scholarship from this sponsor; 4) have a current license to practice as a registered nurse; and 5) be a member of an ethnic minority group (Native American, African American, Asian American, Pacific Islander, Hispanic/Latino, or other ethnic minority background). Applicants must submit an essay of 250 words or less on their role in caring for persons with cancer and a statement of their professional goals and their relationship to the advancement of oncology nursing. Financial need is not considered in the selection process.

Financial data The stipend is $3,000.

Duration 1 year.

Additional information Recipients may attend school on a part-time or full-time basis. This program includes a mentoring component with an individual in the applicant's area of clinical interest. When appropriate, efforts are made to match the applicant and mentor by ethnicity. At the end of each year of scholarship participation, recipients must submit a summary describing their educational activities.

Number awarded 2 each year.

Deadline January of each year.

[480]
EURASIA PREDISSERTATION TRAINING FELLOWSHIPS

Social Science Research Council
Attn: Eurasia Program
810 Seventh Avenue
New York, NY 10019
(212) 377-2700   Fax: (212) 377-2727
E-mail: eurasia@ssrc.org
Web: www.ssrc.org

Purpose To provide funding to graduate students (especially minorities and women) interested in being trained to conduct research related to Eurasia area studies.

Eligibility This program is open to graduate students enrolled in a discipline of the social sciences or humanities that deals with the new states of Eurasia, the Soviet Union, and/or the Russian empire. Research related to the non-Russian states, regions, and peoples is particularly encouraged. Regions and countries currently supported by the program include Armenia, Azerbaijan, Belarus, Georgia, Kazakhstan, Kyrgyzstan, Moldova, Russian Federation, Tajikistan, Turkmenistan, Ukraine, and Uzbekistan; funding is not presently available for research on the Baltic states. Applicants must be in the early stages of their graduate career (preference is given to those in their first or second years) and should not yet have submitted a dissertation prospectus or proposal to their department. They must be interested in the following types of training: language learning at a recognized program in the United States or abroad; formal training away from their home institution to acquire analytical or methodological skills normally unavailable to them; or well-defined exploratory research expressly leading to the formulation of a dissertation proposal. U.S. citizenship or permanent resident status is required. Minorities and women are particularly encouraged to apply.

Financial data Grants range from $3,000 to $7,000. Funds may not be used for tuition or support at the student's home institution.

Duration Awards may be disbursed over a 9-month period, but most grants are from 3 months to 1 semester. No more than 4 months may be spent outside the United States.

Additional information Funding for this program is provided by the U.S. Department of State under the Program for Research and Training on Eastern Europe and the Independent States of the Former Soviet Union (Title VIII).

Number awarded Varies each year; recently, 5 of these fellowships were awarded.

Deadline November of each year.

[481]
FARELLA BRAUN + MARTEL DIVERSITY SCHOLARSHIPS

Farella Braun + Martel LLP
Attn: Henry Fong
235 Montgomery Street
San Francisco, CA 94104
(415) 954-4452   Fax: (415) 954-4480
Web: www.fbm.com

Purpose To provide financial assistance to students from any state who are enrolled at selected law schools in northern California and come from socially and ethnically diverse backgrounds.

Eligibility This program is open to full-time, first-year law students at the University of California's Boalt Hall, the University of California Hastings College of the Law, the University of California at Davis King Hall, Santa Clara University, Golden Gate University, the University of San Francisco, and Stanford University. Applicants must come from socially and ethnically diverse backgrounds. Selection is based on academic accomplishments, ability to balance school with other activities, demonstrated commitment to serving both the legal profession and the community, and financial need. Preference is given to applicants who demonstrate a commitment to working and living in the San Francisco Bay area.

Financial data The stipend is $4,000.

Duration 1 year.

Additional information This program began in 2001.

Number awarded 3 each year.

Deadline April of each year.

[482]
FILIPINO NURSES' ORGANIZATION OF HAWAII SCHOLARSHIP

Hawai'i Community Foundation
Attn: Scholarship Department
1164 Bishop Street, Suite 800
Honolulu, HI 96813
(808) 537-6333   Toll-free: (888) 731-3863
Fax: (808) 521-6286
E-mail: scholarships@hcf-hawaii.org
Web: www.hawaiicommunityfoundation.org

Purpose To provide financial assistance to Hawaii residents of Filipino ancestry who are interested in preparing for a career as a nurse.

Eligibility This program is open to Hawaii residents of Filipino ancestry who are interested in studying in Hawaii or the mainland as full-time students and majoring in nursing. They must be able to demonstrate academic achievement (GPA of 2.7 or higher), good moral character, and financial need.

Financial data The amounts of the awards depend on the availability of funds and the need of the recipient.

Duration 1 year.

Number awarded Varies each year.

Deadline February of each year.

[483]
FINNEGAN HENDERSON DIVERSITY SCHOLARSHIP

Finnegan, Henderson, Farabow, Garrett & Dunner, LLP
Attn: Director of Professional Recruitment and
    Development
1300 I Street, N.W.
Washington, D.C. 20005-3315
(202) 408-4034   Fax: (202) 408-4400
E-mail: suzanne.gentes@finnegan.com
Web: www.finnegan.com

Purpose To provide financial assistance and work experience to minority law students interested in a career in intellectual property law.

Eligibility This program is open to law students from underrepresented minority groups who have demonstrated a commitment to a career in intellectual property law and are currently enrolled either as a first-year full-time student or second-year part-time student. The sponsor defines underrepresented minorities to include American Indians/Alaskan Natives, Blacks/African Americans, Asian Americans/Pacific Islanders, and Hispanics/Latinos. Applicants must have earned an undergraduate degree in life sciences, engineering, or computer science, or have substantial prior trademark experience. Selection is based on academic performance at the undergraduate, graduate (if applicable), and law school level; relevant work experience; com-

munity service; leadership skills; and special accomplishments.

Financial data The stipend is $12,000 per year.

Duration 1 year; may be renewed 1 additional year as long as the recipient completes a summer associateship with the sponsor and maintains of GPA of 3.0 or higher.

Additional information The sponsor, the world's largest intellectual property law firm, established this scholarship in 2003. Summer associateships are available at its offices in Washington, D.C.; Atlanta, Georgia; Cambridge, Massachusetts; Palo Alto, California; or Reston, Virginia.

Number awarded 1 each year.

Deadline May of each year.

[484]
FLORIDA LIBRARY ASSOCIATION MINORITY SCHOLARSHIPS

Florida Library Association
Attn: Chair, Scholarship Committee
1133 West Morse Boulevard, Suite 201
Winter Park, FL 32789-3788
(407) 647-8839   Fax: (407) 629-2502
E-mail: mjs@crowsegal.com
Web: www.flalib.org/library/fla/schol.htm

Purpose To provide financial assistance to minority students working on a graduate degree in library and information science in Florida.

Eligibility This program is open to residents of Florida who are working on a graduate degree in library and information science at schools in the state. Applicants must be members of a minority group: Black/African American, American Indian/Alaska Native, Asian/Pacific Islander, or Hispanic/Latino. They must have some experience in a Florida library and must commit to working in a Florida library for at least 1 year after graduation. Along with their application, they must submit 1) a list of activities, honors, awards, and/or offices held during college and outside college; and 2) a statement of their reasons for entering librarianship and their career goals with respect to Florida libraries.

Financial data The stipend is $2,000 per year.

Duration 1 year.

Number awarded 1 each year.

Deadline January of each year.

[485]
FLORIDA SPACE GRANT CONSORTIUM FELLOWSHIP PROGRAM

Florida Space Grant Consortium
c/o Center for Space Education
Building M6-306, Room 7010
Mail Stop: FSGC
Kennedy Space Center, FL 32899
(321) 452-4301   Fax: (321) 449-0739
E-mail: fsgc@mail.ufl.edu
Web: fsgc.engr.ucf.edu

Purpose To provide financial assistance to graduate students (particularly minorities, women, and persons with disabilities) in space studies at universities participating in the Florida Space Grant Consortium (FSGC).

Eligibility Eligible to be nominated for this program are U.S. citizens who are enrolled full time in master's or doctoral programs at universities participating in the consortium. Nominees must be enrolled in a space-related field of study, broadly defined to include aeronautics, astronautics, remote sensing, atmospheric sciences, and other fundamental sciences and technologies relying on and/or directly impacting space technological resources. Included within that definition are space science; earth observing science; space life sciences; space medicine; space policy, law, and engineering; astronomy and astrophysics; space facilities and applications; and space education. Their undergraduate GPA should be at least 3.5. The program particularly solicits nominations of women, minorities, and students with disabilities.

Financial data The maximum stipend is $20,000 per year for doctoral candidates or $12,000 per year for master's degree students.

Duration 1 year; may be renewed up to 2 additional years for doctoral candidates or 1 additional year for master's degree students, provided the recipient maintains a GPA of 3.5 or higher.

Additional information This program is funded by the U.S. National Aeronautics and Space Administration (NASA). The consortium member universities are Bethune-Cookman College, Eckerd College, Embry-Riddle Aeronautical University, Florida A&M University, Florida Atlantic University, Florida Community Colleges, Florida Gulf Coast University, Florida Institute of Technology, Florida International University, Florida Southern College, Florida State University, University of Central Florida, University of Florida, University of Miami, University of North Florida, University of South Florida, and University of West Florida.

Number awarded 3 or 4 each year.

Deadline Notices of intent must be submitted by January of each year. Completed proposals are due in April.

[486]
FLOYD H. SKINNER LAW SCHOLARSHIPS

Floyd H. Skinner Bar Association
c/o President, Angela T. Ross
Smith Haughley Rice and Roegge
200 Calder Plaza Building
250 Monroe Avenue, N.W.
Grand Rapids, MI 49503-2251
(616) 774-8000   Fax: (616) 774-2461
E-mail: atross@shrr.com

Purpose To provide financial assistance for law school to minorities with a tie to Michigan.

Eligibility This program is open to minority law students who 1) are residents of western Michigan; 2) attend a Michigan law school; or 3) have previously participated in the Grand Rapids Minority Clerkship program. Applicants must be admitted to or currently attending law school full time. Selection is based on academic achievement, demonstrated leadership ability, community activism, and financial need.

Financial data The stipend is $1,000.

Duration 1 year.

Additional information Most members of the Floyd H. Skinner Bar Association are African American attorneys. Information is also available from the Scholarship Committee Chair, James L. Hopewell, Meijer, Inc., Fredrick Meijer

Building 985/4, 2929 Walker Avenue, N.W., Grand Rapids, MI 49544, (616) 453-6711.

Number awarded 1 or more each year, depending on the number of qualified applicants and availability of funds.

Deadline October of each year.

[487]
FOLEY & LARDNER MINORITY SCHOLARSHIP

Foley & Lardner, Attorneys at Law
Attn: Diversity Partner
777 East Wisconsin Avenue
Milwaukee, WI 53202-5367
(414) 297-5520   Fax: (414) 297-4900
E-mail: mmcsweeney@foley.com
Web: www.foley.com

Purpose To provide scholarships to first-year minority students attending selected law schools.

Eligibility Minority students in the first year of law school are eligible to apply if they are attending the following schools: Duke, Florida, Georgetown, Michigan, Northwestern, Stanford, UCLA, or Wisconsin. First-year law students include both summer starters and fall starters. Selection is based on interest in or ties to a city in which the sponsor practices, involvement in community activities and minority student organizations, undergraduate record, and work or personal achievements. Financial need is not a consideration.

Financial data The stipend is $5,000; funds are paid at the beginning of the recipient's second semester in law school and must be applied to tuition, books, fees, and other expenses incident to law school attendance.

Duration 1 semester (the second semester of the first year in law school).

Additional information The U.S. cities in which the sponsor has offices are Chicago, Detroit, Los Angeles, Sacramento, San Diego, Palo Alto, San Francisco, Jacksonville, New York, Orlando, Tallahassee, Tampa, West Palm Beach, Madison, Milwaukee, and Washington, D.C.

Number awarded 8 each year (1 at each of the participating schools).

Deadline September of each year.

[488]
FORE DIVERSITY SCHOLARSHIPS

American Health Information Management Association
Attn: Foundation of Research and Education
233 North Michigan Avenue, Suite 2150
Chicago, IL 60601-5806
(312) 233-1168   Fax: (312) 233-1090
E-mail: fore@ahima.org
Web: www.ahima.org/fore/programs.cfm

Purpose To provide financial assistance to minority members of the American Health Information Management Association (AHIMA) who are interested in working on an undergraduate or graduate degree in health information administration or technology.

Eligibility This program is open to AHIMA members who are enrolled in a health information administration or health information technology program accredited by the Commission on Accreditation of Allied Health Education Programs. Applicants must be minorities, be working on an undergraduate or graduate degree on at least a half-time basis, and have a GPA of 3.0 or higher. U.S. citizenship is required. Selection is based (in order of importance) on GPA and academic achievement, volunteer and work experience, commitment to the health information management profession, suitability to the health information management profession, quality and suitability of references provided, and clarity of application.

Financial data   Stipends range from $1,000 to $5,000.

Duration   1 year; nonrenewable.

Number awarded   Varies each year. Recently, 5 of these scholarships were awarded: 4 to undergraduates and 1 to a graduate student.

Deadline   May of each year.

[489]
FORTUNE BRANDS SCHOLARS PROGRAM

United Negro College Fund
Attn: Corporate Scholars Program
P.O. Box 1435
Alexandria, VA 22313-9998
Toll-free: (866) 671-7237   E-mail: internship@uncf.org
Web: www.uncf.org/internships/index.asp

Purpose   To provide financial assistance and work experience to minorities who are either juniors majoring in fields related to business or law students interested in an internship at corporate headquarters of Fortune Brands.

Eligibility   This program is open to juniors and first- and second-year law students who are members of minority groups. Applicants must have a GPA of 3.0 or higher and an undergraduate major in accounting, finance, human resources, information systems, information technology, or marketing. They must be attending a designated college, university, or law school and be interested in an internship at Fortune Brands corporate headquarters in Lincolnshire, Illinois. Along with their application, they must submit a resume, 2 letters of recommendation, and official transcripts.

Financial data   The program provides a paid internship and (based on successful internship performance) a $7,500 scholarship.

Duration   8 to 10 weeks for the internship; 1 year for the scholarship.

Additional information   Eligible undergraduate institutions are Florida A&M University, Florida State University, Hampton University, Howard University, Morehouse College, North Carolina A&T State University, Northwestern University, Spelman College, University of Chicago, and University of Wisconsin. Participating law schools are those at Howard University, Northwestern University, University of Chicago, and University of Wisconsin.

Number awarded   Varies each year.

Deadline   February of each year.

[490]
FREDRIKSON & BYRON FOUNDATION MINORITY SCHOLARSHIPS

Fredrikson & Byron Foundation
4000 Pillsbury Center
200 South Sixth Street
Minneapolis, MN 55402-1425
(612) 492-7117   Fax: (612) 492-7077
Web: www.fredlaw.com/firm/scholarship.htm

Purpose   To provide financial assistance and summer work experience to minority law students from any state who will be practicing in the Twin Cities area of Minnesota.

Eligibility   This program is open to African American, Asian American, Pacific Islander, Hispanic, Native American, and Alaska Native students enrolled in their first year of law school. Applicants must be interested in practicing law in the Minneapolis-St. Paul area. Along with their application, they must submit 2 recommendations, a writing sample from their first-year legal writing course, transcripts from undergraduate and law school, and a resume. Financial need is not considered.

Financial data   The fellowship stipend is $5,000. The internship portion of the program provides a $1,000 weekly stipend.

Duration   1 year.

Additional information   The scholarship is jointly sponsored by Fredrikson & Byron, P.A. and the Fredrikson & Byron Foundation. Fellows are also eligible to participate in an internship at the firm's offices in Minneapolis.

Number awarded   Up to 2 each year.

Deadline   March of each year.

[491]
GATES MILLENNIUM GRADUATE SCHOLARS PROGRAM

Bill and Melinda Gates Foundation
P.O. Box 10500
Fairfax, VA 22031-8044
Toll-free: (877) 690-GMSP
Web: www.gmsp.org

Purpose   To provide financial assistance for graduate studies in selected subject areas to outstanding low-income minority students.

Eligibility   This program is open to low-income African Americans, Native Alaskans, American Indians, Hispanic Americans, and Asian Pacific Islander Americans who are nominated by a professional educator. Nominees must be U.S. citizens who are enrolled or about to enroll in graduate school to work on a graduate degree in engineering, mathematics, science, education, or library science. They must have a GPA of 3.3 or higher, be able to demonstrate significant financial need, and have demonstrated leadership commitment through participation in community service (i.e., mentoring/tutoring, volunteer work in social service organizations, and involvement in church initiatives), extracurricular activities (student government and athletics), or other activities that reflect leadership abilities.

Financial data   The program covers the full cost of graduate study: tuition, fees, books, and living expenses not paid for by grants and scholarships already committed as part of the recipient's financial aid package.

Duration Up to 4 years (up to and including the doctorate), if the recipient maintains at least a 3.0 GPA.

Additional information This program, established in 1999, is funded by the Bill and Melinda Gates Foundation and administered by the United Negro College Fund with support from the American Indian Graduate Center, the Hispanic Scholarship Fund, and the Organization of Chinese Americans.

Number awarded Under the Gates Millennium Scholars Program, a total of 4,000 students receive support each year.

Deadline January of each year.

[492]
GEORGE A. STRAIT MINORITY STIPEND

American Association of Law Libraries
Attn: Membership Coordinator
53 West Jackson Boulevard, Suite 940
Chicago, IL 60604
(312) 939-4764   Fax: (312) 431-1097
E-mail: membership@aall.org
Web: www.aallnet.org/services/sch_strait.asp

Purpose To provide financial assistance to minority college seniors or college graduates who are interested in becoming law librarians.

Eligibility This program is open to college graduates with meaningful law library experience who are members of minority groups and intend to have a career in law librarianship. Applicants must be degree candidates at an ALA-accredited library school or an ABA-accredited law school. Along with their application, they must submit a personal statement that discusses their interest in law librarianship, reason for applying for this scholarship, career goals as a law librarian, and other pertinent information.

Financial data The stipend is $3,500.

Duration 1 year.

Additional information This program, established in 1990, is currently supported by Thomson West.

Number awarded 1 each year.

Deadline March of each year.

[493]
GEORGE M. BROOKER COLLEGIATE
SCHOLARSHIP FOR MINORITIES

Institute of Real Estate Management Foundation
Attn: Foundation Coordinator
430 North Michigan Avenue
Chicago, IL 60611-4090
(312) 329-6008   Toll-free: (800) 837-0706, ext. 6008
Fax: (312) 410-7908   E-mail: kholmes@irem.org
Web: www.irem.org

Purpose To provide financial assistance to minorities interested in preparing (on the undergraduate or graduate school level) for a career in the real estate management industry.

Eligibility This program is open to junior, senior, and graduate minority (non-Caucasian) students majoring in real estate, preferably with an emphasis on management, asset management, or related fields. Applicants must be interested in beginning a career in real estate management upon graduation. They must have earned a GPA of 3.0 or higher

in their major, have completed at least 2 college courses in real estate, and write an essay (up to 500 words) on why they want to follow a career in real estate management. U.S. citizenship is required. Selection is based on academic success and a demonstrated commitment to a career in real estate management.

Financial data Stipends are $1,000 for undergraduates or $2,500 for graduate students. Funds are disbursed to the institution the student attends to be used only for tuition expenses.

Duration 1 year; nonrenewable.

Number awarded 3 each year: 2 undergraduate awards and 1 graduate award.

Deadline March of each year.

[494]
GEORGE V. POWELL DIVERSITY SCHOLARSHIP

Lane Powell Spears Lubersky LLP
Attn: Administrator of Attorney Recruiting
1420 Fifth Avenue, Suite 4100
Seattle, WA 98101-2338
(206) 223-6123   Fax: (206) 223-7107
E-mail: rodenl@lanepowell.com
Web: www.lanepowell.com

Purpose To provide financial assistance and work experience to law students who will contribute to the diversity of the legal community

Eligibility This program is open to second-year students in good standing at an ABA-accredited law school. Applicants must be able to contribute meaningfully to the diversity of the legal community and have a demonstrated desire to work, live, and eventually practice law in Seattle or Portland. They must submit a cover letter including a statement indicating eligibility to participate in the program, resume, current copy of law school transcript, legal writing sample, and list of 2 or 3 professional or academic references. Selection is based on academic achievement and record of leadership abilities, community service, and involvement in community issues.

Financial data The program provides a stipend of $6,000 for the third year of law school and a paid summer associate clerkship.

Duration 1 year, including the summer.

Additional information This program was established in 2005. Clerkships are provided at the offices of the sponsor in Seattle or Portland.

Number awarded 1 each year.

Deadline October of each year.

[495]
GEORGIA SPACE GRANT CONSORTIUM FELLOWSHIPS

Georgia Space Grant Consortium
c/o Georgia Institute of Technology
Aerospace Engineering
Paul Weber Space Science and Technology Building,
   Room 210
Atlanta, GA 30332-0150
(404) 894-0521   Fax: (404) 894-9313
E-mail: wanda.pierson@aerospace.gatech.edu
Web: www.ae.gatech.edu/research/gsgc

Purpose To provide financial assistance for undergraduate and graduate study of space-related fields to students (particularly minorities, women, and students with disabilities) at member institutions of the Georgia Space Grant Consortium (GSGC).

Eligibility This program is open to U.S. citizens who are undergraduate and graduate students at member institutions of the GSGC. Applicants must be working on a degree in mathematics, science, engineering, computer science, or a technical discipline related to space. Selection is based on transcripts, 3 letters of reference, and an essay of 100 to 500 words on the applicant's professional interests and objectives and their relationship to the field of aerospace. Awards are provided as part of the Space Grant program of the U.S. National Aeronautics and Space Administration, which encourages participation by women, minorities, and people with disabilities.

Financial data A stipend is awarded (amount not specified).

Additional information Institutions that are members of the GSGC include Albany State University, Clark Atlanta University, Columbus State University, Fort Valley State University, Georgia Institute of Technology, Kennesaw State University, Mercer University, Morehouse College, Spelman College, State University of West Georgia, and the University of Georgia. This program is funded by NASA.

Number awarded 1 each year.

[496]
GERALDINE R. DODGE FOUNDATION FELLOWSHIP

College Art Association of America
Attn: Fellowship Program
275 Seventh Avenue
New York, NY 10001-6798
(212) 691-1051, ext. 242   Fax: (212) 627-2381
E-mail: fellowship@collegeart.org
Web: www.collegeart.org/caa/career/fellowship.html

Purpose To provide financial assistance and work experience to art historians from culturally diverse backgrounds who are completing graduate degrees and are interested in working in New Jersey.

Eligibility This program is open to art historians who have been underrepresented in the field because of their race, religion, gender, age, national origin, sexual orientation, disability, or history of economic disadvantage. Applicants must be U.S. citizens or permanent residents and able to demonstrate financial need. They must expect to receive the M.F.A. or Ph.D. degree in the year following application

and then be interested in working at a cultural institution in New Jersey.

Financial data The stipend is $5,000.

Duration 1 year: the final year of the degree program.

Additional information In addition to providing a stipend for the terminal year of their degree program, the College Art Association (CAA) helps fellows search for employment at a museum, art center, college, or university in New Jersey. Upon securing a position, CAA provides a $10,000 subsidy to the employer as part of the fellow's salary. Participating organizations must match this 2:1. In addition to administrative and/or teaching responsibilities, all fellows' positions must include a curatorial or public service component. Salary or stipend, position description, and term of employment will vary and are determined in consultation with individual fellows and their potential employers. This program began in 1993. Funding is provided by the Milton & Sally Avery Arts Foundation, Geraldine R. Dodge Foundation, National Endowment for the Arts, National Endowment for the Humanities, and Terra Foundation for the Arts.

Number awarded 1 each year.

Deadline January of each year.

[497]
GRADUATE FELLOWSHIP IN PHILANTHROPY AND HUMAN RIGHTS

Higher Education Consortium for Urban Affairs
Attn: Graduate Fellowship Coordinator
2233 University Avenue West, Suite 210
St. Paul, MN 55114-1698
(651) 646-8831   Toll-free: (800) 554-1089
E-mail: mshiozawa@hecua.org
Web: www.hecua.org

Purpose To provide financial assistance and work experience to graduate students of color in Minnesota who are interested in working in the fields of philanthropy and human rights.

Eligibility This program is open to graduate students at universities in Minnesota who are members of ethnic or cultural groups historically underrepresented in higher education. Applicants may be studying any academic discipline, but they must be interested in working part time at the Otto Bremer Foundation while they are engaged in study for their graduate degree. Their work for the foundation involves philanthropy and human rights, including social and economic justice, shelter and housing, civic engagement, health disparities and resources, civic engagement, or organizational effectiveness within nonprofits. They must be able to collaborate their academic work with research for nonprofit organizations in Minnesota, Wisconsin, North Dakota, or Montana. Along with their application, they must submit a resume or curriculum vitae, 3 letters of reference, official academic transcripts, and a 1,500-word essay about themselves, their interest and involvement in human rights and social change, and their current research interest in their academic program. Selection is based on how the applicants think, analyze, and write; their definition and commitment to human rights; experiences that predict their potential in human rights, nonprofits, and fulfilling the objectives of the fellowship; current research interest and program; academic merit; and evidence of support from their academic institution.

Financial data Fellows receive $12,000, either as a scholarship (paid directly to them) or as a stipend (paid to their university for tuition).

Duration 1 year.

Additional information This program, established in 2003, is funded by the Otto Bremer Foundation.

Number awarded 3 each year.

Deadline February of each year.

[498]
HAE WON PARK MEMORIAL SCHOLARSHIP

W.O.R.K.: Women's Organization Reaching Koreans
c/o KIWA
3465 West Eighth Street
Los Angeles, CA 90005
Toll-free: (866) 251-5152, ext. 8739
E-mail: workla@onebox.com
Web: www.work-la.org/scholarship.html

Purpose To provide financial assistance to undergraduate and graduate women of Korean heritage.

Eligibility This program is open to women of Korean heritage who are enrolled at an undergraduate or graduate institution and have demonstrated a desire and commitment to serve their community. Applicants must submit 1 letter of recommendation, their transcript, a description of their community involvement, a 250-word statement about themselves, and a 500-word essay on the challenges facing Korean American women and how they would address those.

Financial data The stipend is $1,000.

Duration 1 year.

Additional information This scholarship was established in 1992.

Number awarded 1 each year.

Deadline May of each year.

[499]
HANA SCHOLARSHIPS

United Methodist Church
Attn: General Board of Higher Education and Ministry
Office of Loans and Scholarships
1001 19th Avenue South
P.O. Box 340007
Nashville, TN 37203-0007
(615) 340-7344   Fax: (615) 340-7367
E-mail: umscholar@gbhem.org
Web: www.gbhem.org

Purpose To provide financial assistance to upper-division and graduate Methodist students who are of Hispanic, Asian, Native American, Alaska Native, or Pacific Islander ancestry.

Eligibility This program is open to full-time juniors, seniors, and graduate students at accredited colleges and universities in the United States who have been active, full members of a United Methodist Church for at least 1 year prior to applying. Applicants must have at least 1 parent who is Hispanic, Asian, Native American, Alaska Native, or Pacific Islander. They must be able to demonstrate involvement in their Hispanic, Asian, or Native American (HANA) community. Selection is based on that involvement, aca-

demic ability, and financial need. U.S. citizenship or permanent resident status is required.

Financial data The stipend is $1,000 for undergraduates or $3,000 for graduate students.

Duration 1 year; recipients may reapply.

Number awarded 50 each year.

Deadline March of each year.

[500]
HAWAII CHAPTER OF AAJA SCHOLARSHIPS

Asian American Journalists Association-Hawaii Chapter
Attn: President
P.O. Box 22592
Honolulu, HI 96823-2592
(808) 536-9979   E-mail: aajahawaii@yahoo.com
Web: www.slider.net/~aaja/scholarships.html

Purpose To provide financial assistance to Asian/Pacific Islander students in Hawaii who are interested in careers in broadcast or print journalism.

Eligibility These scholarships are open to Asian/Pacific Islander students in Hawaii who are planning a career in broadcast or print journalism. Applicants may be high school seniors, college undergraduates, or graduate students. They must submit 2 essays of 250 to 500 words each on the following topics: 1) why they want to be a journalist, challenges they foresee, how they can contribute to the profession, and personal characteristics that will prepare them for a journalism career; and 2) involvement or interest in the Asian Pacific American community, how they can contribute to that community in the future, how they can improve coverage of the community as a journalist, and how their ethnic heritage may influence their journalistic perspective. Selection is based on academic achievement, financial need, work samples, recommendations, and the essays.

Financial data Stipends are up to $750.

Duration 1 year; may be renewed.

Number awarded 2 each year.

Deadline April of each year.

[501]
HELENE M. OVERLY MEMORIAL GRADUATE SCHOLARSHIP

Women's Transportation Seminar
Attn: National Headquarters
1666 K Street, N.W., Suite 1100
Washington, DC 20006
(202) 496-4340   Fax: (202) 496-4349
E-mail: wts@wtsnational.org
Web: www.wtsnational.org

Purpose To provide financial assistance to women (particularly minority women) graduate students interested in preparing for a career in transportation.

Eligibility This program is open to women who are enrolled in a graduate degree program in a transportation-related field (e.g., transportation engineering, planning, finance, or logistics). Applicants must have at least a 3.0 GPA and be interested in a career in transportation. They must submit a 750-word statement about their career goals after graduation and why they think they should receive the scholarship award. Applications must be submitted first to a local chapter; the chapters forward selected applications for consideration on the national level. Minority women are particularly encouraged to apply. Selection is based on transportation involvement and goals, job skills, and academic record.

Financial data The stipend is $6,000.

Duration 1 year.

Additional information This program was established in 1981. Local chapters may also award additional funding to winners for their area.

Number awarded 1 each year.

Deadline Applications must be submitted by November to a local WTS chapter.

[502]
HELLER EHRMAN DIVERSITY FELLOWSHIPS

Heller Ehrman White & McAuliffe LLP
Attn: Ethnic Diversity Task Force
275 Middlefield Road
Menlo Park, CA 94025-3506
(650) 324-7171   Fax: (650) 324-0638
E-mail: lkite@hewm.com
Web: www.hewm.com

Purpose To provide financial assistance and work experience to law students who can contribute to the diversity of the legal community.

Eligibility This program is open to first-year law students who show promise of contributing to the diversity of the law student and legal community. Applicants must possess a record of academic, employment, community, and/or other achievement indicating potential for success in law school and in the legal profession. Along with their application, they must submit a statement, up to 500 words, on their interest in the fellowship and how they would contribute to the diversity of the legal profession.

Financial data The program provides a stipend of $7,500 for law school and a paid summer associate clerkship.

Duration 1 year, including the summer.

Additional information This program was established in 2004. Clerkships are provided at offices of the sponsor in each of its 4 regions: Bay Area (San Francisco and Silicon Valley), east coast (New York and Washington, D.C.), northwest (Seattle), and southern California (Los Angeles and San Diego).

Number awarded 4 each year: 1 in each of the firm's regions.

Deadline January of each year.

[503]
HENRY AND CHIYO KUWAHARA CREATIVE ARTS AWARD

Japanese American Citizens League
Attn: National Scholarship Awards
1765 Sutter Street
San Francisco, CA 94115
(415) 921-5225   Fax: (415) 931-4671
E-mail: jacl@jacl.org
Web: www.jacl.org/scholarships.html

Purpose To provide financial assistance to student members of the Japanese American Citizens League (JACL) interested in working on an undergraduate or graduate degree in the creative arts.

Eligibility This program is open to JACL members who are interested in working on an undergraduate or graduate degree in the creative arts. Professional artists are not eligible. Applicants must submit a detailed proposal on the nature of their project, including a time-plan, anticipated date of completion, and itemized budget. They must also submit a statement describing their current level of involvement in the Japanese American community or Asian Pacific community and how they will continue their involvement in future years. Selection is based on academic record, extracurricular activities, and community involvement. Preference is given to students who are interested in creative projects that reflect the Japanese American experience and culture.

Financial data The stipend depends on the availability of funds but usually ranges from $1,000 to $5,000.

Duration 1 year; nonrenewable.

Additional information Applications must be submitted to the JACL National Scholarship Program, c/o San Diego JACL Chapter, 1031 25th Street, San Diego, CA 92102.

Number awarded At least 1 each year.

Deadline March of each year.

[504]
HENRY AND CHIYO KUWAHARA MEMORIAL SCHOLARSHIPS

Japanese American Citizens League
Attn: National Scholarship Awards
1765 Sutter Street
San Francisco, CA 94115
(415) 921-5225   Fax: (415) 931-4671
E-mail: jacl@jacl.org
Web: www.jacl.org/scholarships.html

Purpose To provide financial assistance for undergraduate or graduate study to members of the Japanese American Citizens League (JACL).

Eligibility This program is open to JACL members who are high school seniors, undergraduates, or graduate students. Applicants must be attending or planning to attend a college, university, trade school, or business college. They must submit a statement describing their current level of involvement in the Japanese American community or Asian Pacific community and how they will continue their involvement in future years. Selection is based on academic record, extracurricular activities, financial need, and community involvement.

Financial data The stipend depends on the availability of funds but usually ranges from $1,000 to $5,000.

Duration 1 year; nonrenewable.

Additional information Applications from high school seniors must be submitted to the local JACL chapter. All other applications must be submitted to the JACL National Scholarship Program, c/o San Diego JACL Chapter, 1031 25th Street, San Diego, CA 92102.

Number awarded 6 each year: 2 each to entering freshmen, continuing undergraduates, and entering or currently-enrolled graduate students.

Deadline February of each year for graduating high school seniors; March of each year for current undergraduate or graduate students.

[505]
HERBERT W. NICKENS MEDICAL STUDENT SCHOLARSHIPS

Association of American Medical Colleges
Attn: Division of Diversity Policy and Programs
2450 N Street, N.W.
Washington, DC 20037-1127
(202) 828-0570   Fax: (202) 828-1125
E-mail: nickensawards@aamc.org
Web: www.aamc.org

Purpose To provide financial assistance to medical students who have demonstrated efforts to address the health-care needs of minorities.

Eligibility This program is open to U.S. citizens and permanent residents entering their third year of study at a U.S. allopathic medical school. Each medical school may nominate 1 student for these awards. The letter must describe the nominee's 1) academic achievement through the first and second year, including special awards and honors, clerkships or special research projects, and extracurricular activities in which the student has shown leadership abilities; 2) leadership efforts to eliminate inequities in medical education and health care; and 3) demonstrated leadership efforts in addressing the educational, societal, and health-care needs of minorities. Nominees must submit a curriculum vitae and a 250-word essay that discusses their motivation to pursue a medical career and how they anticipate working to improve the health and health care of minorities.

Financial data The stipend is $5,000.

Duration 1 year.

Number awarded 5 each year.

Deadline March of each year.

[506]
HIV/AIDS RESEARCH FELLOWSHIPS

American Psychological Association
Attn: Minority Fellowship Program
750 First Street, N.E.
Washington, DC 20002-4242
(202) 336-6127   Fax: (202) 336-6012
TDD: (202) 336-6123   E-mail: mfp@apa.org
Web: www.apa.org/mfp/hprogram.html

Purpose To provide financial assistance to psychology doctoral students (especially minorities) who are preparing for a career involving research on HIV/AIDS issues and ethnic minority populations.

Eligibility This program is open to full-time doctoral students who can demonstrate a strong commitment to a career in HIV/AIDS research related to ethnic minorities. Students from the complete range of psychology disciplines are encouraged to apply if their training and research interests are related to mental health and HIV/AIDS. Clinical, counseling, and school psychology students must demonstrate that they will receive substantial training in research and the delivery of services to people with HIV/AIDS. Members of minority groups (African Americans, Alaskan Natives, American Indians, Asian Americans, Hispanics/Latinos, Native Hawaiians, and Pacific Islanders) are especially encouraged to apply. U.S. citizenship or permanent resident status is required. Selection is based on commitment to a career in research that focuses on HIV/AIDS in ethnic minority communities, knowledge of ethnic minor-

ity psychology or HIV/AIDS issues, the fit between career goals and training environment selected, potential for a research career demonstrated through accomplishments and goals, scholarship and grades, and letters of recommendation.

Financial data The stipend is that established by the National Institutes of Health for predoctoral students, currently $20,772 per year.

Duration 1 year; may be renewed for up to 2 additional years.

Additional information Funding is provided by the U.S. National Institute of Mental Health. Students who receive a federally-funded grant from another source may not also accept funds from this program.

Number awarded Varies each year.

Deadline January of each year.

[507]
HMONG NATIONAL DEVELOPMENT EDUCATIONAL SCHOLARSHIPS

Hmong National Development, Inc.
Attn: Educational Scholarships
1112 16th Street, N.W., Suite 110
Washington, DC 20036
(202) 463-2118   Fax: (202) 463-2119
E-mail: info@hndlink.org
Web: www.hndlink.org/scholarships.htm

Purpose To provide financial assistance for college or graduate school to Hmong students in the United States.

Eligibility This program is open to Hmong students who are entering or enrolled in an accredited college or university as a full-time undergraduate or graduate student. Applicants must submit 1) an official transcript; 2) a letter of recommendation; 3) a 1-page resume on their employment history, involvement with community and extracurricular activities, and honors received; and 4) a 3-page essay on a potential goal they plan to achieve within the next 5 years and their plans for overcoming potential obstacles and ultimately achieving their goals.

Financial data The stipend is $500.

Duration 1 year.

Number awarded 10 each year.

Deadline January of each year.

[508]
HOLLY A. CORNELL SCHOLARSHIP

American Water Works Association
Attn: Scholarship Coordinator
6666 West Quincy Avenue
Denver, CO 80235-3098
(303) 347-6206   Fax: (303) 795-7603
E-mail: ncole@awwa.org
Web: www.awwa.org/About/scholars

Purpose To provide financial assistance to outstanding minority and female students interested in pursuing advanced training in the field of water supply and treatment.

Eligibility Minority and female students who anticipate completing the requirements for a master's degree in engineering no sooner than December of the following year are eligible. Students who have been accepted into graduate school but have not yet begun graduate study are encouraged to apply. Recipients of the Larson Aquatic Research Support (LARS) M.S. Scholarship are not eligible for this program. Selection is based on the quality of the applicant's academic record and the potential to provide leadership in the field of water supply and treatment.

Financial data The stipend is $5,000.

Duration 1 year.

Additional information Funding for this program comes from the consulting firm CH2M Hill. The association reserves the right not to make an award for any year in which an outstanding candidate is not identified.

Number awarded 1 each year.

Deadline January of each year.

[509]
HOWARD MAYER BROWN FELLOWSHIP

American Musicological Society
201 South 34th Street
Philadelphia, PA 19104-6313
(215) 898-8698   Toll-free: (888) 611-4AMS
Fax: (215) 573-3673   E-mail: ams@sas.upenn.edu
Web: www.ams-net.org/hmb.html

Purpose To provide financial assistance to minority students who are working on a doctoral degree in the field of musicology.

Eligibility This program is open to members of minority groups historically underrepresented in the field of musicology. In the United States, that includes African Americans, Native Americans, Hispanic Americans, and Asian Americans. In Canada, it refers to visible minorities. Applicants must have completed at least 1 year of academic work at an institution with a graduate program in musicology and be planning to complete a Ph.D. degree in the field. There are no restrictions on research area, age, or sex. Candidates must submit a personal statement summarizing their musical and academic background and stating why they wish to work on an advanced degree in musicology, letters of support from 3 faculty members, a curriculum vitae, and samples of their work (such as term papers or published material). U.S. or Canadian citizenship is required.

Financial data The stipend is $14,000 per year.

Duration 1 year; nonrenewable.

Additional information Information is also available from Ellen T. Harris, Massachusetts Institute of Technology, 4-246, 77 Massachusetts Avenue, Cambridge, MA 02139-4301, E-mail: eharris@mit.edu.

Number awarded 1 each year.

Deadline January of each year.

[510]
HUANG TSO-PING AND WU YAO-YU SCHOLARSHIP

Chinese American Librarians Association
c/o Sha Li Zhang, Scholarship Committee Chair
University of North Carolina at Greensboro
Jackson Library
P.O. Box 26170
Greensboro, NC 27402-6170
(336) 334-4705   Fax: (336) 334-5399
E-mail: slzhang@uncg.edu
Web: www.cala-web.org

Purpose To provide financial assistance to students of Chinese descent or Chinese nationality interested in working on a graduate degree in library or information science.

Eligibility This program is open to students enrolled full time at an accredited school of library and information science in the United States or Canada for a master's or doctoral degree. Applicants must be of Chinese nationality or Chinese descent.

Financial data The stipend is $200 or $500.

Duration 1 year.

Additional information This program was established in 2002.

Number awarded 1 each year.

Deadline April of each year.

[511]
IBM PHD FELLOWSHIP PROGRAM

IBM Corporation
Attn: University Relations
1133 Westchester Avenue
White Plains, NY 10604
Toll-free: (800) IBM-4YOU   TTY: (800) IBM-3383
E-mail: phdfellow@us.ibm.com
Web: www-306.ibm.com

Purpose To provide financial assistance and work experience to students (particularly minorities and women) working on a Ph.D. in a research area of broad interest to IBM.

Eligibility Students nominated for this fellowship should be enrolled full time in an accredited U.S. or Canadian college or university and should have completed at least 1 year of graduate study in the following fields: business, chemistry, computer science, electrical engineering, materials sciences, mathematics, mechanical engineering, physics, or related disciplines. They should be planning a career in research. Nominations must be made by a faculty member and endorsed by the department head. IBM values diversity and encourages nominations of women, minorities, and others who contribute to that diversity. Selection is based on the applicants' potential for research excellence, the degree to which their technical interests align with those of IBM, and academic progress to date.

Financial data Fellows receive tuition, fees, and a stipend of $17,500 per year.

Duration 1 year; may be renewed up to 3 additional years, provided the recipient is renominated, interacts with IBM's technical community, and demonstrates continued progress and achievement.

Additional information Recipients are offered an internship at 1 of the IBM Research Division laboratories and are given an IBM ThinkPad.

Number awarded Varies each year.

Deadline December of each year.

[512]
ILLINOIS MINORITY REAL ESTATE SCHOLARSHIP

Illinois Association of Realtors
Attn: Illinois Real Estate Educational Foundation
3180 Adloff Lane, Suite 400
P.O. Box 19451
Springfield, IL 62794-9451
(217) 529-2600   E-mail: IARaccess@iar.org
Web: www.illinoisrealtor.org/iar/about/minority.htm

Purpose To provide financial assistance to Illinois residents who are members of minority groups and preparing for a career in real estate.

Eligibility This program is open to residents of Illinois who are African American, Hispanic or Latino, Native American, or Asian. Applicants must be interested in preparing for a career in real estate by pursuing: 1) courses to meet Illinois salesperson license requirement; 2) course work to meet Illinois broker license requirement; 3) course work required for Illinois appraisal licensing/certification; 4) professional development unrelated to obtaining license/certification; or 5) an undergraduate or graduate program of study. Along with their application, they must submit information on their employment history, transcripts, evidence of financial need, and an essay that describes their career goals and explains why they believe they should receive scholarship assistance through this program.

Financial data The maximum stipend is $500.

Duration Funds must be used within 24 months of the award date.

Deadline Applications may be submitted at any time, but they must be received at least 12 weeks prior to the beginning of the school term for which financial assistance is requested.

[513]
INTERNATIONAL COMMUNICATIONS INDUSTRIES ASSOCIATION COLLEGE SCHOLARSHIPS

International Communications Industries Association, Inc.
Attn: Director of Strategic Initiatives
11242 Waples Mill Road, Suite 200
Fairfax, VA 22030
(703) 273-7200   Toll-free: (800) 659-7469
Fax: (703) 278-8082   E-mail: dwilbert@infocomm.org
Web: www.infocomm.org

Purpose To provide financial assistance to college students and entering graduate students (especially minorities and women) who are interested in preparing for a career in the audiovisual industry.

Eligibility This program is open to 1) college juniors completing their bachelor's degree in the following year; 2) college seniors who plan to enter graduate school; and 3) students in their final year of study for an associate degree. Applicants must have a GPA of 2.75 or higher in a program of audio, visual, audiovisual, electronics, telecommunications, technical theater, data networking, software development, or information technology. Students in other programs, such as journalism, may be eligible if they can dem-

onstrate a relationship to career goals in the audiovisual industry. Along with their application, they must submit essays on why they are applying for this scholarship, why they are interested in the audiovisual industry, and their professional plans following graduation. Minority and women candidates are especially encouraged to apply. Selection is based on the essays, presentation of the application, GPA, work experience, and letters of recommendation.

Financial data The stipend is $2,500.

Duration 1 year.

Additional information Recipients are required to work during the summer as paid interns with a manufacturer, dealer, designer, or other firm that is a member of the International Communications Industries Association.

Number awarded Varies each year; recently, 7 of these scholarships were awarded.

Deadline April of each year.

[514]
IOWA CONFERENCE ETHNIC MINORITY SCHOLARSHIP

United Methodist Church-Iowa Conference
Attn: Board of Ordained Ministry
500 East Court Avenue, Suite C
Des Moines, IA 50309
(515) 283-1991   Fax: (515) 288-1906
Web: www.iaumc.org

Purpose To provide financial assistance to minority students preparing for ordained ministry under the Iowa Conference of the United Methodist Church.

Eligibility This program is open to certified candidates for ministry who are 1) African Americans, Asian Americans, Hispanic Americans, or Native Americans, and 2) in good standing with their district Committee on Ordained Ministry of the Iowa Conference of the United Methodist Church. Applicants must be enrolled in a graduate school listed by the University Senate and intending to complete a master's degree (either an M.Div. or a master's degree in specialized ministry), be ordained as a deacon or elder, and serve in ministry in the Iowa Conference.

Financial data The stipend is $500 per year. Grants are intended as supplements to the Automatic Grants Program that provides $2,000 per year.

Duration 1 year; may be renewed for up to 2 additional years.

Additional information Information is also available from the Rev. Mike Morgan, 1298 Seventh Avenue, Marion, IA 52302, (319) 377-4856, Fax: (319) 377-5392, E-mail: mike@fumcmarion.org.

Number awarded 1 or more each year.

Deadline May or November of each year.

[515]
JAMES CARLSON MEMORIAL SCHOLARSHIP

Oregon Student Assistance Commission
Attn: Grants and Scholarships Division
1500 Valley River Drive, Suite 100
Eugene, OR 97401-2146
(541) 687-7395   Toll-free: (800) 452-8807, ext. 7395
Fax: (541) 687-7419
E-mail: awardinfo@mercury.osac.state.or.us
Web: www.osac.state.or.us

Purpose To provide financial assistance to Oregon residents (particularly minorities) majoring in education on the undergraduate or graduate school level.

Eligibility This program is open to residents of Oregon who are U.S. citizens or permanent residents. Applicants must be either 1) college seniors or fifth-year students majoring in elementary or secondary education or 2) graduate students working on an elementary or secondary certificate. Full-time enrollment and financial need are required. Priority is given to 1) members of African American, Asian American, Hispanic, or Native American ethnic groups; 2) dependents of members of the Oregon Education Association; and 3) applicants committed to teaching autistic children.

Financial data Stipend amounts vary; recently, they were at least $1,300.

Duration 1 year.

Additional information This program is administered by the Oregon Student Assistance Commission (OSAC) with funds provided by the Oregon Community Foundation, 1221 S.W. Yamhill, Suite 100, Portland, OR 97205, (503) 227-6846, Fax: (503) 274-7771.

Number awarded Varies each year; recently, 3 of these scholarships were awarded.

Deadline February of each year.

[516]
JAMES ECHOLS SCHOLARSHIP

California Association for Health, Physical Education,
 Recreation and Dance
Attn: Chair, Scholarship Committee
1501 El Camino Avenue, Suite 3
Sacramento, CA 95815-2748
(916) 922-3596   Toll-free: (800) 499-3596 (within CA)
Fax: (916) 922-0133   E-mail: cahperd@cahperd.org
Web: www.cahperd.org

Purpose To provide financial assistance to minority student members of the California Association for Health, Physical Education, Recreation and Dance.

Eligibility This program is open to California residents who have been members of the association for at least 60 days and are attending a 2-year or 4-year college or university in California. Applicants must be undergraduate or graduate students majoring in health, physical education, recreation, or dance and have completed at least 60 semester hours of college work. Selection is based on scholastic proficiency (a GPA of 3.0 or higher); leadership ability in school, community, and professional activities; and personal qualities of enthusiasm, cooperativeness, responsibility, initiative, and ability to work with others. This scholarship is awarded to the highest-ranked minority (Asian, African American, Latino, or Native American) applicant.

Financial data The stipend is $750.

Duration 1 year.

Additional information Information is also available from Nicolas Fraire, CAHPERD Scholarship Chair, 3792 Willowpark Drive, San Jose, CA 95118.

Number awarded 1 each year.

Deadline December of each year.

[517]
JAPANESE AMERICAN BAR SCHOLARSHIP

Japanese American Bar Association
Attn: JABA Educational Foundation
c/o Barry S. Morinaka
707 Wilshire Boulevard, Suite 3260
Los Angeles, CA 90017
(213) 624-8697   Fax: (213) 624-8695
E-mail: Bmorinaka@aol.com
Web: www.jabaonline.org

Purpose To provide financial assistance to law students who have participated in the Asian Pacific American community.

Eligibility This program is open to students currently enrolled in law school. Applicants must demonstrate an intention to practice law in southern California. Selection is based on participation in the Asian Pacific American community, academic achievement, and financial need.

Financial data The stipend is $1,000.

Duration 1 year.

Additional information This program, which began in 1984, includes the Justice John F. Aiso Scholarship and the Justice Stephen K. Tamura Scholarship.

Number awarded 1 or more each year.

Deadline December of each year.

[518]
JAPANESE MEDICAL SOCIETY OF AMERICA MEDICAL STUDENT SCHOLARSHIP

Japanese Medical Society of America, Inc.
c/o Yuzuru Anzai, M.D., Scholarship Committee Chair
285 Central Park West, Apartment 3W
New York, NY 10024
(212) 263-8682   Fax: (212) 883-5852
E-mail: yuzuru.anzai@med.nyu.edu
Web: www.jmsa.org

Purpose To provide financial assistance to Japanese American medical school students.

Eligibility This program is open to Japanese Americans who are accepted at or currently enrolled in a medical school in the United States. Applicants must submit a 1-page essay about themselves and how they will be involved in the sponsoring organization's activities. Selection is based on academic excellence, honors and awards, community activities, financial need, and interest in the organization.

Financial data A stipend is awarded (amount not specified).

Duration 1 year.

Deadline February of each year.

[519]
JOHN MCLENDON MEMORIAL MINORITY POSTGRADUATE SCHOLARSHIP AWARD

National Association of Collegiate Directors of Athletics
Attn: NACDA Foundation
24651 Detroit Road
P.O. Box 16428
Cleveland, OH 44116
(440) 892-4000   Fax: (440) 892-4007
E-mail: bhorning@nacda.com
Web: nacda.collegesports.com

Purpose To provide financial assistance and work experience to minority college seniors who are interested in working on a graduate degree in athletics administration.

Eligibility This program is open to minority college students who are seniors, are attending school on a full-time basis, have a GPA of 3.0 or higher, intend to attend graduate school to earn a degree in athletics administration, and are involved on the college or community level. Candidates are not required to be student athletes. Current graduate students are not eligible.

Financial data The stipend is $10,000. In addition, 1 recipient each year is offered the opportunity to serve a 9-month internship in the office of the National Association of Collegiate Directors of Athletics (NACDA).

Duration 1 year.

Additional information Recipients must maintain full-time status during the senior year to retain their eligibility. They must attend NACDA-member institutions.

Number awarded 5 each year.

Deadline January of each year.

[520]
JOHN STANFORD MEMORIAL WLMA SCHOLARSHIP

Washington Library Media Association
P.O. Box 50194
Bellevue, WA 98015-0194
E-mail: wlma@earthlink.net
Web: www.wlma.org/Association/scholar.htm

Purpose To provide financial assistance to ethnic minorities in Washington who are interested in preparing for a library media career.

Eligibility This program is open to residents of Washington who are working toward a library media endorsement or graduate degree in the field. Applicants must be members of an ethnic minority group. They must be working or planning to work in a school library. Along with their application, they must submit documentation of financial need and a description of themselves that includes their plans for the future, interest in librarianship, and plans for further education.

Financial data The stipend is $1,000.

Duration 1 year.

Additional information Information is also available from Camille Hefty, Scholarship Chair, 2728 Webber Court, Steilacoom, WA 98388-2849, (253) 589-3223, E-mail: camille_hefty@fp.k12.wa.us.

Number awarded 1 each year.

Deadline April of each year.

[521]
JUSTICE ALLEN E. BROUSSARD SCHOLARSHIPS

Justice Allen E. Broussard Scholarship Foundation
c/o Jill Dessalines
McKesson Corporation Law Department
One Post Street, 34th Floor
San Francisco, CA 94104-5296
(415) 983-7680
E-mail: scholarship@broussard-scholarship.org
Web: www.broussard-scholarship.org

Purpose To provide financial assistance to minority students from any state enrolled in law schools in the San Francisco Bay area.

Eligibility This program is open to minority students, preferably those entering their first year, at law schools in the Bay area. Applicants must submit a 250-word essay on why they should be awarded this scholarship. Selection is based on the essay, academic record, extracurricular activities (with emphasis on service-oriented extracurricular activities directed toward the enhancement of opportunities for minorities), letters of recommendation, and financial need.

Financial data The stipend is $5,000.

Duration 1 year.

Additional information This program was originally established in 1996.

Number awarded 3 each year.

Deadline March of each year.

[522]
JUSTIN HARUYAMA MINISTERIAL SCHOLARSHIP

Japanese American United Church
Attn: Haruyama Scholarship Committee
255 Seventh Avenue
New York, NY 10001
(212) 242-9444   Fax: (212) 242-5274
E-mail: pastor@jauc.org
Web: www.jauc.org

Purpose To provide financial assistance to Protestant seminary students who are interested in serving Japanese American congregations.

Eligibility This program is open to students enrolled full time at an accredited Protestant seminary in the United States. Applicants must be working on a ministerial degree in order to serve Japanese American congregations. Along with their application, they must submit 2 letters of recommendation, a transcript of grades, information on their financial situation, and a brief statement of their spiritual journey.

Financial data A stipend is awarded (amount not specified).

Duration 1 year; may be renewed.

Number awarded 1 or more each year.

Deadline May of each year.

[523]
KALA SINGH MEMORIAL SCHOLARSHIP

American Speech-Language-Hearing Foundation
Attn: Graduate Student Scholarship Competition
10801 Rockville Pike
Rockville, MD 20852-3279
(301) 897-5700   Toll-free: (800) 498-2071
Fax: (301) 571-0457   TTY: (800) 498-2071
E-mail: foundation@asha.org
Web: www.ashfoundation.org

Purpose To provide financial assistance to international or minority students who are interested in working on a graduate degree in communication sciences and disorders.

Eligibility Applicants must be college graduates who are accepted for graduate study in the United States in a communication sciences and disorders program or enrolled as a full-time graduate student. The fund gives priority to foreign or minority (American Indian, Alaskan Native, Asian, Pacific Islander, Black, Hispanic) students. Students who previously received a scholarship from the American Speech-Language-Hearing Foundation are not eligible.

Financial data The stipend ranges from $2,000 to $4,000. Funds must be used for educational support (e.g., tuition, books, school living expenses), not for personal or conference travel.

Duration The award is granted annually.

Number awarded 1 each year.

Deadline June of each year.

[524]
KALPANA CHAWLA SCHOLARSHIP AWARD

American Society of Engineers of Indian Origin
c/o Ramu Ramamurthy, Scholarship Committee Chair
47790 Pavillon Road
Canton, MI 48188
(248) 226-6895   Fax: (248) 226-7166
E-mail: awards@aseimichigan.org.
Web: www.aseio.org

Purpose To provide financial assistance to graduate students of Indian origin (from India) who are working on a degree in aerospace.

Eligibility This program is open to graduate students of Indian origin (by birth, ancestry, or relation). They must be enrolled full time at an accredited college or university in the United States and working on a degree in an aerospace discipline with a GPA of 3.5 or higher. Selection is based on academic excellence, technical excellence, and leadership excellence.

Financial data The stipend is $3,000.

Duration 1 year.

Additional information This program was established in 2003 with support from Ford Motor Company.

Number awarded 1 each year.

Deadline June of each year.

[525]
KEN INOUYE SCHOLARSHIP

Society of Professional Journalists-Greater Los Angeles
     Professional Chapter
c/o Christopher Burnett, Scholarship Chair
California State University at Long Beach
Department of Journalism
1250 Bellflower Boulevard
Long Beach, CA 90840-4601
(562) 985-5779   E-mail: cburnett@csulb.edu
Web: www.spj.org/losangeles

Purpose To provide financial assistance to minority undergraduate and graduate students in southern California who are interested in preparing for careers in journalism.

Eligibility Minority college juniors, seniors, or graduate students who are interested in careers in journalism (but not public relations, advertising, publicity, law, or a related field) are eligible to apply if they are residents of or attending school in Los Angeles, Ventura, or Orange counties, California. Applicants should be enrolled as journalism majors, but if their university does not offer such a major they may present other evidence of intent to prepare for a career in the field. Selection is based on evidence of unusual accomplishment and potential to advance in a news career; financial need is considered only if 2 or more applicants are equally qualified.

Financial data Stipends range from $500 to $1,000.

Duration 1 year; may be renewed.

Additional information The sponsor reserves the right to split the scholarship equally if 2 or more applicants appear equally qualified or to make no award if there are no promising applicants.

Number awarded 1 each year.

Deadline April of each year.

[526]
KENNETH B. CHANG MEMORIAL SCHOLARSHIPS

Korean American Bar Association of Southern
     California
c/o WonKoo Chang
Los Angeles City Attorney's Office
201 North Main Street, Suite 1600
Los Angeles, CA 90012
(213) 978-7907   E-mail: wonkoochang@attbi.com
Web: www.kabasocal.org

Purpose To provide financial assistance to students at law schools in southern California who have been active in the Asian Pacific Islander community.

Eligibility This program is open to students currently enrolled at law schools in southern California. Applicants must be able to demonstrate a commitment to the Korean American community and/or Asian Pacific Islander community through past, current, or future contributions.

Financial data The stipend is $1,000.

Duration 1 year.

Number awarded 2 each year.

Deadline March of each year.

[527]
KSEA SCHOLARSHIPS

Korean-American Scientists and Engineers Association
1952 Gallows Drive, Suite 300
Vienna, VA 22182
(703) 748-1221   Fax: (703) 748-1331
E-mail: sejong@ksea.org
Web: www.ksea.org

Purpose To provide financial assistance to undergraduate and graduate student members of the Korean-American Scientists and Engineers Association (KSEA).

Eligibility This program is open to Korean American undergraduate and graduate students who graduated from a high school in the United States, are KSEA members, and are majoring in science, engineering, or a related field. Along with their application, they must submit a 500-word essay on either of the following topics: 1) their career goals and intended contributions to society, or 2) the meaning of Korean heritage in their life. Selection is based on the essay (20%), work experience and extracurricular activities (20%), recommendation letters (30%), and academic performance (30%).

Financial data The stipend is $1,000.

Duration 1 year.

Additional information This program includes the following named scholarships: the Inyong Ham Scholarship, the Yohan and Rumie Cho Scholarship, the Shoon Kyung Kim Scholarship, the Nam Sook and Je Hyun Kim Scholarship, and the Hyundai Scholarships.

Number awarded Varies each year.

Deadline February of each year.

[528]
KUSCO SCHOLARSHIPS FOR GRADUATE STUDENTS

Korean-American Scientists and Engineers Association
1952 Gallows Drive, Suite 300
Vienna, VA 22182
(703) 748-1221   Fax: (703) 748-1331
E-mail: sejong@ksea.org
Web: www.ksea.org

Purpose To provide financial assistance to graduate student members of the Korean-American Scientists and Engineers Association (KSEA).

Eligibility This program is open to Korean American graduate students who graduated from a high school in the United States, are KSEA members, and are majoring in science or engineering. Students preparing for a career in medical practice are not eligible. Along with their application, they must submit a 500-word essay on either of the following topics: 1) their career goals and intended contributions to society, or 2) the meaning of Korean heritage in their life. Selection is based on the essay (20%), work experience and extracurricular activities (20%), recommendation letters (30%), and academic performance (30%).

Financial data The stipend is $1,000.

Duration 1 year.

Additional information This program, established in 2005, is supported by the Korea-US Science Cooperation Center (KUSCO).

Number awarded 14 each year.

Deadline February of each year.

[529]
LAWRENCE R. FOSTER MEMORIAL SCHOLARSHIP

Oregon Student Assistance Commission
Attn: Grants and Scholarships Division
1500 Valley River Drive, Suite 100
Eugene, OR 97401-2146
(541) 687-7395   Toll-free: (800) 452-8807, ext. 7395
Fax: (541) 687-7419
E-mail: awardinfo@mercury.osac.state.or.us
Web: www.osac.state.or.us

Purpose To provide financial assistance for college or graduate school to residents of Oregon (particularly minorities) who are interested in preparing for a public health career.

Eligibility This program is open to residents of Oregon who are attending a 4-year college or university in any state to prepare for a career in public health (not private practice). First preference is given to applicants who are either working in public health or enrolled as graduate students in that field. Second preference is given to undergraduates entering the junior or senior year of a health program, including nursing, medical technology, and physician assistant. A general preference is given to applicants from diverse cultures. Along with their application, they must submit a 1- to 2-page essay on their interest, experience, and future plans for a public health career

Financial data Stipend amounts vary; recently, they were at least $4,167.

Duration 1 year.

Additional information This program is administered by the Oregon Student Assistance Commission (OSAC) with funds provided by the Oregon Community Foundation, 1221 S.W. Yamhill, Suite 100, Portland, OR 97205, (503) 227-6846, Fax: (503) 274-7771.

Number awarded Varies each year; recently, 6 of these scholarships were awarded.

Deadline February of each year.

[530]
LIBRARY AND INFORMATION TECHNOLOGY ASSOCIATION/OCLC MINORITY SCHOLARSHIP

American Library Association
Attn: Library and Information Technology Association
50 East Huron Street
Chicago, IL 60611-2795
(312) 280-4270   Toll-free: (800) 545-2433, ext. 4270
Fax: (312) 280-3257   TDD: (312) 944-7298
TDD: (888) 814-7692   E-mail: lita@ala.org
Web: www.lita.org

Purpose To provide financial assistance to minority graduate students interested in preparing for a career in library automation.

Eligibility Applicants must be American or Canadian citizens, interested in working on a master's degree in library/information science (with a focus on library automation), and a member of 1 of the following ethnic groups: American Indian, Alaskan Native, Asian, Pacific Islander, African American, or Hispanic. The award is based on academic excellence, leadership potential, evidence of a commitment to a career in library automation and information technology, and prior activity and experience in those fields. Economic need is considered when all other criteria are equal.

Financial data The stipend is $3,000.

Duration 1 year.

Additional information This scholarship, first awarded in 1991, is funded by Online Computer Library Center (OCLC) and administered by the Library and Information Technology Association (LITA) of the American Library Association.

Number awarded 1 each year.

Deadline February of each year.

[531]
LIM, RUGER & KIM SCHOLARSHIP

National Asian Pacific American Bar Association
Attn: NAPABA Law Foundation
910 17th Street, N.W., Suite 315
Washington, DC 20006
(202) 775-9555   Fax: (202) 775-9333
E-mail: foundation@napaba.org
Web: www.napaba.org

Purpose To provide financial assistance to law students interested in serving the Asian Pacific American community.

Eligibility This program is open to students at accredited law schools in the United States. Applicants must demonstrate leadership potential to serve the Asian Pacific American community upon graduation. They must submit 500-word essays on 1) the most significant experiences in their background that have shaped and demonstrated their commitment to serving the needs of Asian Pacific Americans; and 2) how they intend to serve the needs of the Asian Pacific American community in their future legal career. Selection is based on demonstrated commitment to and interest in pro bono and/or public interest legal work, financial need, leadership potential, maturity and responsibility, and commitment to serving the needs of the Asian Pacific American community.

Financial data The stipend is $2,500 per year.

Duration 1 year.

Additional information This program was established in 2004 by the Los Angeles law firm of Lim, Ruger & Kim.

Number awarded 1 each year.

Deadline September of each year.

[532]
LIONEL C. BARROWS MINORITY DOCTORAL STUDENT SCHOLARSHIP

Association for Education in Journalism and Mass
    Communication
Attn: Communication Theory and Methodology Division
234 Outlet Pointe Boulevard, Suite A
Columbia, SC 29210-5667
(803) 798-0271   Fax: (803) 772-3509
E-mail: aejmc@aejmc.org
Web: www.aejmc.org

Purpose To provide financial assistance to minorities who are interested in working on a doctorate in mass communication.

Eligibility This program is open to minority students enrolled in a Ph.D. program in journalism and mass communication. Applicants must submit 2 letters of recommendation, a resume, and a brief letter outlining their research interests and career plans. Membership in the association is not required, but applicants must be U.S. citizens or permanent residents. Selection is based on the likelihood that the applicant's work will contribute to communication theory and/or methodology.

Financial data The stipend is $1,400.

Duration 1 year.

Additional information This program began in 1972. Information is also available from Michael S. Shapiro, Cornell University, Department of Communication, 319 Kennedy Hall, Ithaca, NY 14853, (607) 255-6356, E-mail: mas29@cornell.edu.

Number awarded 1 each year.

Deadline June of each year.

[533]
LITA/LSSI MINORITY SCHOLARSHIP

American Library Association
Attn: Library and Information Technology Association
50 East Huron Street
Chicago, IL 60611-2795
(312) 280-4270   Toll-free: (800) 545-2433, ext. 4270
Fax: (312) 280-3257   TDD: (312) 944-7298
TDD: (888) 814-7692   E-mail: lita@ala.org
Web: www.lita.org

Purpose To provide financial assistance to minority graduate students interested in preparing for a career in library automation.

Eligibility Applicants must be American or Canadian citizens, interested in working on a master's degree in library/information science (with a focus on library automation), and a member of 1 of the following ethnic groups: American Indian, Alaskan Native, Asian, Pacific Islander, African American, or Hispanic. The award is based on academic excellence, leadership potential, evidence of a commitment to a career in library automation and information technology, and prior activity and experience in those fields. Economic need is considered only when all other criteria are equal.

Financial data The stipend is $2,500.

Duration 1 year.

Additional information This scholarship, first awarded in 1995, is funded by Library Systems & Services, Inc. (LSSI) and administered by the Library and Information Technology Association (LITA) of the American Library Association.

Number awarded 1 each year.

Deadline February of each year.

[534]
LOS ANGELES CHAPTER OF AAJA GENERAL SCHOLARSHIPS

Asian American Journalists Association-Los Angeles
Chapter
231 East Third Street
Los Angeles, CA 90013-1494
Web: www.aaja-la.org/scholarshipandfellowship

Purpose To provide financial assistance to Asian/Pacific Islander students in southern California who are interested in careers in journalism.

Eligibility These scholarships are open to Asian/Pacific Islander students who are planning a career in broadcast, photo, or print journalism. Applicants may be high school seniors, college undergraduates, or graduate students who are either permanently residing in or attending a school in the southern California region. They do not need to be a journalism, photojournalism, or communications major, but applicants must intend to pursue a journalism career. Selection is based on commitment to the field of journalism, scholastic achievement, journalistic ability and potential, a sensitivity to Asian American issues, community involvement, and financial need.

Financial data Stipends range from $500 to $1,000.

Duration 1 year; may be renewed.

Additional information Information is also available from Henry Fuhrmann, Los Angeles Times, 202 West First Street, Los Angeles, CA 90012, E-mail: henry.fuhrmann@latimes.com.

Number awarded Varies each year. Recently, 9 of these scholarships were awarded: 1 at $1,000, 4 at $750, and 4 at $500.

Deadline May of each year.

[535]
MAGOICHI AND SHIZUKO KATO MEMORIAL SCHOLARSHIP

Japanese American Citizens League
Attn: National Scholarship Awards
1765 Sutter Street
San Francisco, CA 94115
(415) 921-5225   Fax: (415) 931-4671
E-mail: jacl@jacl.org
Web: www.jacl.org/scholarships.html

Purpose To provide financial assistance for graduate study to members of the Japanese American Citizens League (JACL).

Eligibility This program is open to JACL members who are attending or planning to attend an accredited college or university as a graduate student. Applicants must submit a statement describing their current level of involvement in the Japanese American community or Asian Pacific community and how they will continue their involvement in future years. Selection is based on academic record, extracurricular activities, financial need, and community involvement. Preference is given to applicants planning a career in medicine or the ministry.

Financial data The stipend depends on the availability of funds but usually ranges from $1,000 to $5,000.

Duration 1 year; nonrenewable.

Additional information Applications must be submitted to the JACL National Scholarship Program, c/o San Diego JACL Chapter, 1031 25th Street, San Diego, CA 92102.

Number awarded 1 each year.

Deadline March of each year.

[536]
MARRIAGE AND FAMILY THERAPY MINORITY FELLOWSHIP PROGRAM

American Association for Marriage and Family Therapy
Attn: Awards Committee
112 South Alfred Street
Alexandria, VA 22314
(703) 838-9808   Fax: (703) 838-9805
Web: www.aamft.org

Purpose To provide financial assistance to minority students enrolled in graduate and post-degree training programs in marriage and family therapy.

Eligibility Eligible to apply are minority students (including African Americans, Hispanics, Native Americans, Asian Americans, and Pacific Islanders) enrolled in university graduate education programs or post-degree institutes that provide training in marriage and family therapy. They must be citizens of the United States or Canada and show promise in and commitment to a career in marital and family therapy education, research, or practice. Along with their application, they must submit a personal statement explaining how their racial or ethnic background has had an impact on them and their career decision; the statement should include their professional interests, goals, and commitment to the field of marriage and family therapy.

Financial data The stipend is $1,000. Awardees also receive a plaque and funding to attend the association's annual conference.

Duration 1 year.

Additional information This program began in 1986.

Number awarded Up to 3 each year.

Deadline January of each year.

[537]
MARTIN LUTHER KING, JR. MEMORIAL SCHOLARSHIP FUND

California Teachers Association
Attn: Human Rights Department
P.O. Box 921
Burlingame, CA 94011-0921
(650) 552-5370   E-mail: scholarships@cta.org
Web: www.cta.org

Purpose To provide financial assistance for college or graduate school to racial and ethnic minorities in California who are members of the California Teachers Association (CTA), children of members, or members of the Student CTA.

Eligibility This program is open to members of a racial or ethnic minority group who are 1) active CTA members; 2) dependent children of active, retired-life, or deceased CTA members; or 3) members of Student CTA. Applicants must be interested in preparing for a teaching career in public education or already engaged in such a career.

Financial data Stipends vary each year, depending upon the amount of contributions received and the financial need of individual recipients.

Duration 1 year.

Number awarded Varies each year. Recently, 23 of these scholarships were awarded: 10 to CTA members, 8 to children of CTA members, and 5 to Student CTA members.

Deadline March of each year.

[538]
MENTAL HEALTH AND SUBSTANCE ABUSE SERVICES FELLOWSHIP

American Psychological Association
Attn: Minority Fellowship Program
750 First Street, N.E.
Washington, DC 20002-4242
(202) 336-6127   Fax: (202) 336-6012
TDD: (202) 336-6123   E-mail: mfp@apa.org
Web: www.apa.org/mfp/cprogram.html

Purpose To provide financial assistance to doctoral students committed to providing mental health and substance abuse services to ethnic minority populations.

Eligibility Applicants must be U.S. citizens or permanent residents, enrolled full time in an accredited doctoral program, and committed to a career in psychology related to ethnic minority mental health and substance abuse services. Members of ethnic minority groups (African Americans, Hispanics/Latinos, American Indians, Alaskan Natives, Asian Americans, Native Hawaiians, and other Pacific Islanders) are especially encouraged to apply. Preference is given to students specializing in clinical, school, and counseling psychology. Students of any other specialty will be considered if they plan careers in which their training will lead to delivery of mental health or substance abuse services to ethnic minority populations. Selection is based on commitment to ethnic minority health and substance abuse services, knowledge of ethnic minority psychology or mental health issues, the fit between career goals and training environment selected, potential to become a culturally competent mental health service provider demonstrated through accomplishments and goals, scholarship and grades, and letters of recommendation.

Financial data The stipend is the amount established by the National Institutes of Health for predoctoral students, currently $20,772 per year.

Duration 1 academic or calendar year; may be renewed for up to 2 additional years.

Additional information Funding is provided by the U.S. Substance Abuse and Mental Health Services Administration.

Number awarded Varies each year.

Deadline January of each year.

[539]
MENTAL HEALTH RESEARCH FELLOWSHIP

American Psychological Association
Attn: Minority Fellowship Program
750 First Street, N.E.
Washington, DC 20002-4242
(202) 336-6127   Fax: (202) 336-6012
TDD: (202) 336-6123   E-mail: mfp@apa.org
Web: www.apa.org/mfp/rprogram.html

Purpose To provide financial assistance to doctoral students interested in preparing for a career in mental health or psychological research as it relates to ethnic minority populations.

Eligibility Applicants must be U.S. citizens or permanent residents, enrolled full time in an accredited doctoral program, and committed to a career as a researcher specializing in mental health issues of concern to ethnic minority populations. African American Hispanic/Latino, American Indian, Asian American, Alaskan Native, Native Hawaiian, and other Pacific Islander students are especially encouraged to apply. Students specializing in all disciplines of psychology are eligible as long as their training and research interests are related to mental health. Selection is based on commitment to a career in research that focuses on ethnic minority mental health, knowledge of ethnic minority psychology or mental health issues, fit between career goals and training environment selected, potential for a research career as demonstrated through accomplishments and productivity, scholarship and grades, and letters of recommendation.

Financial data The stipend is the amount established by the National Institutes of Health for predoctoral students, currently $20,772 per year.

Duration 1 academic or calendar year; may be renewed for up to 2 additional years.

Additional information Funding is provided by the U.S. National Institute of Mental Health, a component of the National Institutes of Health.

Number awarded Varies each year; recently, 22 of these fellowships were awarded.

Deadline January of each year.

[540]
MFT MINORITY SUPERVISION STIPEND PROGRAM

American Association for Marriage and Family Therapy
Attn: Awards Committee
112 South Alfred Street
Alexandria, VA 22314
(703) 838-9808   Fax: (703) 838-9805
Web: www.aamft.org

Purpose To support the recruitment, training, and retention of minorities as supervisors in the field of marriage and family therapy.

Eligibility Eligible to apply are minority individuals (including African Americans, Hispanics, Native Americans, Asian Americans, and Pacific Islanders) enrolled in a program to become marriage and family therapy supervisors approved by the American Association for Marriage and Family Therapy (AAMFT). Applicants must be U.S. or Canadian citizens or permanent visa residents and hold a graduate degree in marriage and family therapy or a related discipline. Information on financial need is not required but is a significant factor considered in the review process.

Financial data Awardees receive up to $750 to offset the cost of supervision, waiver of the supervision application processing fee, and waiver of the registration fee to attend the AAMFT conference.

Duration 1 year.

Additional information This program began in 1990.

Number awarded Up to 2 each year.

Deadline January of each year.

[541]
MICHELE CLARK FELLOWSHIP

Radio and Television News Directors Foundation
1600 K Street, N.W., Suite 700
Washington, DC 20006-2838
(202) 467-5218   Fax: (202) 223-4007
E-mail: karenb@rtndf.org
Web: www.rtndf.org/asfi/fellowships/minority.html

Purpose To provide financial assistance for professional development to minority journalists employed in electronic news.

Eligibility This program is open to minority journalists employed in television or radio news who have 10 years or less of full-time experience. Applications must include samples of the journalist's work done as the member of a news staff, with a script and tape (audio or video) up to 15 minutes.

Financial data The grant is $1,000 plus an all-expense paid trip to the international convention of the Radio-Television News Directors Association held that year.

Duration The grant is presented annually.

Additional information The grant, named for CBS journalist Michele Clark, may be used in any way to improve the craft and enhance the excellence of the recipient's news operation.

Number awarded 1 each year.

Deadline April of each year.

[542]
MIDEASTERN REGION KOREAN AMERICAN SCHOLARSHIPS

Korean American Scholarship Foundation
Mideastern Region
c/o Chang S. Choi, Scholarship Committee Chair
6410 Lahser Road
Bloomfield Hills, MI 48301
(248) 752-3180   Fax: (248) 644-0507
E-mail: cschoi@comcast.net
Web: www.kasf.org

Purpose To provide financial assistance to Korean American undergraduate and graduate students who attend school in Indiana, Michigan, or Ohio.

Eligibility This program is open to Korean American students who are currently enrolled in a college or university as full-time undergraduate or graduate students. Applicants may reside anywhere in the United States as long as they attend school in Indiana, Michigan, or Ohio. Selection is based on academic achievement, school activities, community service, and financial need.

Financial data Stipends range from $1,000 to $2,000.

Duration 1 year; renewable.

Number awarded Varies each year. Recently, the midwestern regional chapter (which then included the current mideastern regional chapter) awarded 69 of these scholarships.

Deadline March of each year.

[543]
MIDWESTERN REGION KOREAN AMERICAN SCHOLARSHIPS

Korean American Scholarship Foundation
Midwestern Region
c/o Tony S. Hahm, Scholarship Committee Chair
P.O. Box 0416
Northbrook, IL 60065-0416
(847) 797-1291   Fax: (847) 797-1304
E-mail: tonyhahm@yahoo.com
Web: www.kasf.org

Purpose To provide financial assistance to Korean American undergraduate and graduate students who attend school in the Midwest.

Eligibility This program is open to Korean American students who are currently enrolled in a college or university in the midwestern states as full-time undergraduate or graduate students. Applicants may reside anywhere in the United States as long as they attend school in the midwest region: Illinois, Iowa, Kansas, Minnesota, Missouri, Nebraska, North Dakota, South Dakota, and Wisconsin. Selection is based on academic achievement, school activities, community service, and financial need.

Financial data Stipends range from $1,000 to $2,000.

Duration 1 year; renewable.

Number awarded Varies each year. Recently, the midwestern regional chapter (which then included the current mideastern regional chapter) awarded 69 of these scholarships.

Deadline June of each year.

[544]
MILDRED COLODNY SCHOLARSHIP FOR GRADUATE STUDY IN HISTORIC PRESERVATION

National Trust for Historic Preservation
Attn: Scholarship Coordinator
1785 Massachusetts Avenue, N.W.
Washington, DC 20036-2117
(202) 588-6124   Toll-free: (800) 944-NTHP, ext. 6124
Fax: (202) 588-6059   E-mail: david_field@nthp.org
Web: www.nthp.org/help/colodny.html

Purpose To provide financial assistance and summer work experience to graduate students (particularly minority students) interested in working on a degree in a field related to historic preservation.

Eligibility Eligible to apply are students in their final year of undergraduate study intending to enroll in a graduate program in historic preservation and graduate students enrolled in or intending to enroll in historic preservation programs; these programs may be in a department of history, architecture, American studies, urban planning, museum studies, or a related field with a primary emphasis on historic preservation. Applicants must submit an essay in which they discuss their career goals and how their pursuit of a graduate preservation degree relates to those goals, including evidence of their interest in, commitment to, and/or potential for leadership in the field of preservation. Selection is based on the essay, a resume, 2 letters of recommendation, academic transcripts, and financial need. Applications are especially encouraged from people of diverse racial, ethnic, cultural, and economic backgrounds.

Financial data The program provides a stipend of up to $15,000 towards graduate school tuition, a stipend of $5,000 for a summer internship with the sponsor following the student's first year of study, and up to $1,500 towards the student's attendance at a National Preservation Conference.

Duration 1 year; nonrenewable.

Additional information Internships may be completed at 1) the sponsor's Washington, D.C. office; 2) a regional office or historic museum site; or 3) the offices of 1 of the sponsor's partner organizations.

Number awarded 1 each year.

Deadline February of each year.

[545]
MINORITIES IN GOVERNMENT FINANCE SCHOLARSHIP

Government Finance Officers Association
Attn: Scholarship Committee
203 North LaSalle Street, Suite 2700
Chicago, IL 60601-1210
(312) 977-9700   Fax: (312) 977-4806
Web: www.gfoa.org/services/scholarships.shtml

Purpose To provide financial assistance to minority upper-division and graduate students who are preparing for a career in state and local government finance.

Eligibility This program is open to upper-division and graduate students who are preparing for a career in public finance with a major in public administration, accounting, finance, political science, economics, or business administration (with a specific focus on government or nonprofit management). Applicants must be members of a minority group, citizens or permanent residents of the United States or Canada, and able to provide a letter of recommendation from a representative of their school. Selection is based on career plans, academic record, plan of study, letters of recommendation, and GPA. Financial need is not considered.

Financial data The stipend is $5,000.

Duration 1 year.

Additional information Funding for this program is provided by Fidelity Investments Tax-Exempt Services Company.

Number awarded 1 or more each year.

Deadline February of each year.

[546]
MINORITY FACULTY DEVELOPMENT SCHOLARSHIP AWARD IN PHYSICAL THERAPY

American Physical Therapy Association
Attn: Department of Minority/International Affairs
1111 North Fairfax Street
Alexandria, VA 22314-1488
(703) 706-3144   Toll-free: (800) 999-APTA, ext. 3144
Fax: (703) 706-8519   TDD: (703) 683-6748
E-mail: min-intl@apta.org
Web: www.apta.org

Purpose To provide financial assistance to minority faculty members in physical therapy who are interested in working on a doctoral degree.

Eligibility This program is open to U.S. citizens and permanent residents who are members of the following minority groups: African American or Black, Asian, Native Hawaiian or other Pacific Islander, American Indian or Alaska Native, or Hispanic/Latino. Applicants must be full-time faculty members, teaching in an accredited or developing professional physical therapist education program, who will have completed the equivalent of 2 full semesters of post-professional doctoral course work. They must possess a license to practice physical therapy in a U.S. jurisdiction and be enrolled as a student in an accredited post-professional doctoral program whose content has a demonstrated relationship to physical therapy. Along with their application, they must submit transcripts of all post-professional doctoral course work, a curriculum vitae, and a plan of study for attaining the doctoral degree. Selection is based on 1) demonstrated evidence of contributions in the area of minority affairs and services; 2) contributions to the professional of physical therapy; and 3) scholastic achievement.

Financial data A stipend is awarded (amount not specified).

Duration 1 year.

Additional information This program was established in 1999.

Number awarded 1 or more each year.

Deadline November of each year.

[547]
MINORITY FELLOWSHIP PROGRAM IN MENTAL HEALTH

American Sociological Association
Attn: Minority Affairs Program
1307 New York Avenue, N.W., Suite 700
Washington, DC 20005-4701
(202) 383-9005, ext. 322   Fax: (202) 638-0882
TDD: (202) 872-0486
E-mail: minority.affairs@asanet.org
Web: www.asanet.org

Purpose To provide financial assistance to minority doctoral candidates in sociology who are interested in preparing to conduct research on mental health issues relating to minority groups.

Eligibility These fellowships are available to U.S. citizens or permanent residents who are Blacks/African Americans, Latinos (e.g., Chicanos, Puerto Ricans, Cubans), American Indians or Alaskan Natives, Asian Americans (e.g., southeast Asian, Japanese, Chinese, Korean), or Pacific Islanders (e.g., Filipino, Samoan, Hawaiian, Guamanian). The competition is open to students beginning or continuing study in sociology at the doctoral level. Selection is based on commitment to research in mental health and mental illness, scholarship, writing ability, research potential, and financial need.

Financial data The stipend is $20,772 per year.

Duration 1 year; renewable for 3 additional years.

Additional information This program is funded by a grant from the U.S. National Institute of Mental Health, a component of the National Institutes of Health. Upon completion of their studies, recipients are expected to engage in mental health and mental illness research and/or teaching for a period equal to the period of support beyond 12 months.

Number awarded 10 to 12 each year.

Deadline January of each year.

[548]
MINORITY NEUROSCIENCE POSTDOCTORAL FELLOWSHIP PROGRAM

Society for Neuroscience
Attn: Education Department
11 Dupont Circle, N.W., Suite 500
Washington, DC 20036
(202) 462-6688　　　　　　　　　Fax: (202) 462-9740
E-mail: info@sfn.org
Web: apu.sfn.org

Purpose To provide funding to minority postdoctoral fellows participating in mental health related neuroscience research and training programs.

Eligibility This program is open to postdoctoral fellows in neuroscience who are members of traditionally underrepresented racial and ethnic minority groups (African Americans, Hispanics, Native Americans, Alaskan Natives, Asians, and Pacific Islanders). Applicants must be U.S. citizens or permanent residents enrolled in a program of research and training to prepare for a career in neuroscience research laboratories. Along with their application, they must submit 2 academic letters of recommendation, a 1- to 2-page essay describing their area of interest and research goals in neuroscience, a 1- to 2-page essay describing how their career goals are consistent with the goals of the program to increase diversity in neuroscience, undergraduate and graduate transcripts, a current resume or curriculum vitae, copies of papers and abstracts they have authored or co-authored, a 1-page summary of their dissertation, and a biosketch of the home institution advisor (if available).

Financial data Fellows receive a stipend that is based on number of years of postdoctoral experience, in accordance with standard National Research Service Award guidelines (currently, ranging from $35,568 per year for no experience to $51,036 for 7 or more years). Other benefits include travel assistance and registration to attend the annual meeting of the Society for Neuroscience (SfN), enrichment programs that include funds to participate in activities outside the fellow's home laboratory, and mentoring opportunities with a mentor chosen from the SfN membership.

Duration 2 years, contingent upon adequate research progress and academic standing.

Additional information This program, established in 1991, is sponsored largely by the National Institute of Mental Health with additional support from the National Institute of Neurological Disorders and Stroke. Information is also available from Joanne Berger-Sweeney, Wellesley College, Department of Biological Sciences, 106 Central Street, Wellesley, MA 02481-8203, (781) 283-3503, Fax: (781) 283-3704, E-mail: mnfp@wellesley.edu.

Number awarded 5 each year.

Deadline March, August, or December of each year.

[549]
MINORITY NEUROSCIENCE PREDOCTORAL FELLOWSHIP PROGRAM

Society for Neuroscience
Attn: Education Department
11 Dupont Circle, N.W., Suite 500
Washington, DC 20036
(202) 462-6688　　　　　　　　　Fax: (202) 462-9740
E-mail: info@sfn.org
Web: apu.sfn.org

Purpose To provide funding to minority graduate students participating in mental health related neuroscience research and training programs.

Eligibility This program is open to doctoral students in neuroscience who are members of traditionally underrepresented racial and ethnic minority groups (African Americans, Hispanics, Native Americans, Alaskan Natives, Asians, and Pacific Islanders). Applicants must be U.S. citizens or permanent residents enrolled in a program of research and training to prepare for a career in neuroscience research laboratories. Along with their application, they must submit 2 academic letters of recommendation, a 1- to 2-page essay describing their area of interest and research goals in neuroscience, a 1- to 2-page essay describing how their career goals are consistent with the goals of the program to increase diversity in neuroscience, undergraduate and graduate transcripts, a current resume or curriculum vitae, copies of papers and abstracts they have authored or co-authored, and a biosketch of the home institution advisor (if available).

Financial data Fellows receive a stipend in accordance with standard National Research Service Award guidelines (currently, $20,772 per year). Other benefits include travel assistance and registration to attend the annual meeting of the Society for Neuroscience (SfN), enrichment programs that include funds to participate in activities outside the fellow's home laboratory, and mentoring opportunities with a mentor chosen from the SfN membership.

Duration 3 years, contingent upon adequate research progress and academic standing.

Additional information This program, established in 1991, is sponsored largely by the National Institute of Mental Health with additional support from the National Institute of Neurological Disorders and Stroke. Information is also available from Joanne Berger-Sweeney, Wellesley College, Department of Biological Sciences, 106 Central Street, Wellesley, MA 02481-8203, (781) 283-3503, Fax: (781) 283-3704, E-mail: mnfp@wellesley.edu.

Number awarded 12 each year.

Deadline August of each year.

[550]
MINORU TAZUMA SCHOLARSHIP

Japanese American Citizens League-Seattle Chapter
P.O. Box 18558
Seattle, WA 98118-0558
(206) 622-4098   E-mail: email@jaclseattle.org
Web: www.jaclseattle.org

Purpose To provide financial assistance for college or graduate school to residents of the Seattle, Washington area who are of Japanese ancestry or from a family that is a member of the Japanese American Citizens League (JACL).

Eligibility This program is open to Seattle (Washington) area residents who are of Japanese ancestry or members of JACL families. Applicants must be entering their freshman year of college or graduate school. As part of their application, they must submit a list of extracurricular and community activities, 2 letters of recommendation, a list of awards or recognitions they have earned, and a 500-word essay on the legacy of the Japanese American community in American society.

Financial data The stipend is $1,000.

Duration 1 year.

Additional information Information is also available from May Namba, 2324 N.W. 94th Street, Seattle, WA 98117.

Number awarded 1 each year.

Deadline March of each year.

[551]
MINORU YASUI MEMORIAL SCHOLARSHIP

Japanese American Citizens League
Attn: National Scholarship Awards
1765 Sutter Street
San Francisco, CA 94115
(415) 921-5225   Fax: (415) 931-4671
E-mail: jacl@jacl.org
Web: www.jacl.org/scholarships.html

Purpose To provide financial assistance for graduate study to members of the Japanese American Citizens League (JACL).

Eligibility This program is open to JACL members who are attending or planning to attend an accredited college or university as a graduate student. Applicants must submit a statement describing their current level of involvement in the Japanese American community or Asian Pacific community and how they will continue their involvement in future years. Selection is based on academic record, extracurricular activities, financial need, and community involvement. Preference is given to applicants with a strong interest in human and civil rights; fields of study may also include sociology, law, or education.

Financial data The stipend depends on the availability of funds but usually ranges from $1,000 to $5,000.

Duration 1 year; nonrenewable.

Additional information Applications must be submitted to the JACL National Scholarship Program, c/o San Diego JACL Chapter, 1031 25th Street, San Diego, CA 92102.

Number awarded At least 1 each year.

Deadline March of each year.

[552]
MINORU YASUI MEMORIAL SCHOLARSHIP AWARD

Asian American Journalists Association
Attn: Student Programs Coordinator
1182 Market Street, Suite 320
San Francisco, CA 94102
(415) 346-2051, ext. 102   Fax: (415) 346-6343
E-mail: brandons@aaja.org
Web: www.aaja.org

Purpose To provide financial assistance to male Asian American students who are members of the Asian American Journalists Association (AAJA) and interested in a career in broadcast journalism.

Eligibility This program is open to Asian American male high school seniors, undergraduates, or graduate students enrolled full time at an accredited college or university in a broadcast journalism program. Applicants must be AAJA members. Along with their application, they must submit a 500-word essay on their involvement or interest in the Asian American community and how, if they are awarded this scholarship, they would contribute to the field of journalism and/or media issues involving the Asian American and Pacific Islander community. Selection is based on scholastic ability, commitment to journalism, sensitivity to Asian American and Pacific Islander issues as demonstrated by community involvement, journalistic ability, and financial need.

Financial data The stipend is $2,000.

Duration 1 year.

Additional information This scholarship honors Minoru Yasui, a civil rights advocate and attorney who was 1 of 3 Nisei to challenge the internment of Japanese Americans during World War II.

Number awarded 1 each year.

Deadline April of each year.

[553]
MINORU YASUI SCHOLARSHIPS

Asian Pacific American Bar Association of Colorado
P.O. Box 3011
Denver, CO 80201
E-mail: bseo@gorsuch.com
Web: www.apaba.8k.com

Purpose To provide financial assistance to Asian American law students in Colorado.

Eligibility This program is open to students at law schools in Colorado. Applicants must demonstrate a record of public service to the Asian community in the state.

Financial data The stipend is $1,000. The recipients' law schools match the award so the total is $2,000.

Duration 1 year.

Additional information This program, which began in 1996, is supported by Anheuser-Busch Companies, Inc.

Number awarded 2 each year: 1 at the University of Colorado Law School and 1 at the University of Denver Law School.

[554]
MLA SCHOLARSHIP FOR MINORITY STUDENTS

Medical Library Association
Attn: Professional Development Department
65 East Wacker Place, Suite 1900
Chicago, IL 60601-7298
(312) 419-9094, ext. 28   Fax: (312) 419-8950
E-mail: mlapd2@mlahq.org
Web: www.mlanet.org/awards/grants/minstud.html

Purpose   To assist minority students interested in preparing for a career in medical librarianship.

Eligibility   This program is open to racial minority students (Asians, African Americans, Hispanics, Native Americans, or Pacific Islander Americans) who are entering a graduate program in librarianship or who have completed less than half of their academic requirements for the master's degree in library science. They must be interested in preparing for a career in medical librarianship. Selection is based on academic record, letters of reference, professional potential, and the applicant's statement of career objectives. U.S. or Canadian citizenship or permanent resident status is required.

Financial data   The stipend is $5,000.

Duration   1 year.

Additional information   This scholarship was first awarded in 1973.

Number awarded   1 each year.

Deadline   November of each year.

[555]
MLA/ARL LEADERSHIP AND CAREER DEVELOPMENT PROGRAM

Medical Library Association
Attn: Professional Development Department
65 East Wacker Place, Suite 1900
Chicago, IL 60601-7298
(312) 419-9094, ext. 28   Fax: (312) 419-8950
E-mail: mlapd2@mlahq.org
Web: www.mlanet.org

Purpose   To provide an opportunity for minority mid-career librarians to engage in leadership and career development activities.

Eligibility   This program is open to mid-career professionals at academic and research libraries. Applicants must be members of minority ethnic groups (African Americans, Hispanics, Asians, Native Americans, or Pacific Islanders). They must be interested in taking advantage of advancement and leadership opportunities.

Financial data   The stipend is $6,000.

Duration   1 year.

Additional information   This program is jointly managed by the Medical Library Association (MLA) and the Association of Research Libraries (ARL) with funding from the National Library of Medicine.

Number awarded   2 each year.

[556]
MORRIS SCHOLARSHIP

Morris Scholarship Fund
Attn: Scholarship Selection Committee
525 S.W. Fifth Street, Suite A
Des Moines, IA 50309-4501
(515) 282-8192   Fax: (515) 282-9117
E-mail: morris@assoc-mgmt.com
Web: www.morrisscholarship.org

Purpose   To provide financial assistance to minority undergraduate, graduate, and law students in Iowa.

Eligibility   This program is open to minority students (African Americans, Asian/Pacific Islanders, Hispanics, or Native Americans) who are interested in studying at a college, graduate school, or law school. Applicants must be either Iowa residents and high school graduates who are attending a college or university anywhere in the United States or non-Iowa residents who are attending a college or university in Iowa; preference is given to native Iowans who are attending an Iowa college or university. Along with their application, they must submit an essay of 250 to 500 words on why they are applying for this scholarship, activities or organizations in which they are involved, and their future plans. Selection is based on the essay, academic achievement (GPA of 2.5 or higher), community service, and financial need.

Financial data   The stipend is $1,500 per year.

Duration   1 year; may be renewed.

Additional information   This fund was established in 1978 in honor of the J.B. Morris family, who founded the Iowa branch of the National Association for the Advancement of Colored People and published the *Iowa Bystander* newspaper.

Number awarded   Varies each year; recently, 11 of these scholarships were awarded.

Deadline   January of each year.

[557]
NAPABA LAW FOUNDATION SCHOLARSHIPS

National Asian Pacific American Bar Association
Attn: NAPABA Law Foundation
910 17th Street, N.W., Suite 315
Washington, DC 20006
(202) 775-9555   Fax: (202) 775-9333
E-mail: foundation@napaba.org
Web: www.napaba.org

Purpose   To provide financial assistance to law students interested in serving the Asian Pacific American community.

Eligibility   This program is open to students at accredited law schools in the United States. Applicants must demonstrate leadership potential to serve the Asian Pacific American community upon graduation. They must submit 500-word essays on 1) the most significant experiences in their background that have shaped and demonstrated their commitment to serving the needs of Asian Pacific Americans; and 2) how they intend to serve the needs of the Asian Pacific American community in their future legal career. Selection is based on demonstrated commitment to and interest in pro bono and/or public interest legal work, financial need, leadership potential, maturity and responsibility, and commitment to serving the needs of the Asian Pacific American community.

Financial data The stipend is $2,500 per year.

Duration 1 year.

Additional information These scholarships were first awarded in 1995. In 2003, 1 of the scholarships was named the Chris Nakamura Scholarship in honor of a leader of the Asian Pacific American legal community of Arizona. Information is also available from Parkin Lee, New York Life Investment Management, LLC, 51 Madison Avenue, Room 1104, New York, NY 10010.

Number awarded 8 to 10 each year.

Deadline September of each year.

[558]
NASA-DESGC GRADUATE STUDENT FELLOWSHIPS

Delaware Space Grant Consortium
c/o University of Delaware
Bartol Research Institute
104 Center Mall, #217
Newark, DE 19716-4793
(302) 831-1094   Fax: (302) 831-1843
E-mail: desgc@bartol.udel.edu
Web: www.delspace.org

Purpose To provide financial support to graduate students (particularly minority, women, and disabled students) in Delaware and Pennsylvania involved in space-related studies.

Eligibility This program is open to graduate students at member institutions of the Delaware Space Grant Consortium (DESGC) embarking on or involved in aerospace-related research, technology, or design. Fields of interest have included astronomy, chemical engineering, geography, marine studies, materials science, mechanical engineering, and physics. U.S. citizenship is required. The DESGC is a component of the U.S. National Aeronautics and Space Administration (NASA) Space Grant program, which encourages applications from women, minorities, and persons with disabilities.

Financial data This program covers tuition and provides stipends.

Duration 1 year; may be renewed.

Additional information This program, established in 1991, is funded by NASA. Members of the consortium include Delaware State University (Dover, Delaware), Delaware Technical and Community College (Dover, Georgetown, Newark, and Wilmington, Delaware), Franklin and Marshall College (Lancaster, Pennsylvania), Gettysburg College (Gettysburg, Pennsylvania), Lehigh University (Bethlehem, Pennsylvania), Swarthmore College (Swarthmore, Pennsylvania), University of Delaware (Newark, Delaware), Villanova University (Villanova, Pennsylvania), and Wilmington College (New Castle, Delaware).

Number awarded Varies each year; since this program was established, it has awarded 45 fellowships to 27 graduate students.

Deadline February of each year.

[559]
NASP MINORITY SCHOLARSHIP

National Association of School Psychologists
Attn: Education and Research Trust
4340 East-West Highway, Suite 402
Bethesda, MD 20814
(301) 657-0270, ext. 234   Fax: (301) 657-0275
TTY: (301) 657-4155   E-mail: kbritton@naspweb.org
Web: www.nasponline.org/about_nasp/minority.html

Purpose To provide financial assistance to minority graduate students enrolled in a school psychology program.

Eligibility This program is open to minority students who are U.S. citizens enrolled in a regionally-accredited school psychology program in the United States. Applicants must have a GPA of 3.0 or higher. Doctoral candidates are not eligible. Applications must be accompanied by 1) a resume that includes undergraduate and/or graduate schools attended, awards and honors, student and professional activities, work and volunteer experiences, research and publications, workshops or other presentations, and any special skills, training, or experience, such as bilingualism, teaching experience, or mental health experience; 2) a statement, up to 1,000 words, of professional goals; 3) at least 2 letters of recommendation, including at least 1 from a faculty member from their undergraduate or graduate studies (if a first-year student) or at least 1 from a faculty member of their school psychology program (if a second- or third-year student); 4) a completed financial statement; 5) an official transcript of all graduate course work (first-year students may submit an official undergraduate transcript); 6) other personal accomplishments that the applicant wishes to be considered; and 7) a letter of acceptance from a school psychology program for first-year applicants.

Financial data The stipend is $5,000.

Duration 1 year; may be renewed up to 2 additional years.

Number awarded 1 each year.

Deadline January of each year.

[560]
NATIONAL CRUSADE SCHOLARSHIP PROGRAM

United Methodist Church
Attn: General Board of Global Ministries
475 Riverside Drive, Room 1351
New York, NY 10115
(212) 870-3787   Toll-free: (800) 654-5929
E-mail: Scholars@gbgm-umc.org
Web: www.gbgm-umc.org

Purpose To provide financial assistance to minority students who are interested in attending graduate school to prepare for leadership within the United Methodist Church.

Eligibility This program is open to U.S. citizens and permanent residents who are ethnic and racial minority graduate students (African Americans, Hispanic Americans, Pacific/Asian Americans, and Native Americans). They must be working on their first graduate degree (M.Div., M.A., Ph.D., D.D.S., M.D., M.Ed., M.B.A., or other graduate degree). Preference is given to members of the United Methodist Church and to persons entering Christian vocations. Applicants should be committed to preparing themselves for leadership in mission to church and society and serving for at least 10 years. Financial need must be demonstrated.

Financial data The amount awarded varies, depending upon the availability of funds and the need of the recipient. Recently, stipends ranged from $1,000 to $2,500.

Duration Up to 3 years, but only to complete 1 degree.

Additional information These awards are funded by the World Communion Offering received in United Methodist churches on the first Sunday in October.

Number awarded Varies each year; recently, 23 of these scholarships were awarded.

Deadline January of each year.

[561]
NATIONAL DEFENSE SCIENCE AND ENGINEERING GRADUATE FELLOWSHIP PROGRAM

American Society for Engineering Education
Attn: NDSEG Fellowship Program
1818 N Street, N.W., Suite 600
Washington, DC 20036-2479
(202) 331-3516   Fax: (202) 265-8504
E-mail: ndseg@asee.org
Web: www.asee.org/ndseg

Purpose To provide financial assistance to doctoral students (particularly minorities, women, and students with disabilities) in the areas of science and engineering that are of military importance.

Eligibility Graduate students in the following specialties are eligible: aeronautical and astronautical engineering; biosciences, including toxicology; chemical engineering; chemistry; civil engineering; cognitive, neural, and behavioral sciences; computer and computational sciences; electrical engineering; geosciences, including terrain, water, and air; materials science and engineering; mathematics; mechanical engineering; naval architecture and ocean engineering; oceanography; and physics, including optics. Applicants must be U.S. citizens or nationals in the final year of undergraduate study or the first year of graduate study and planning to work on a doctoral degree in 1 of the indicated specialties. Applications are particularly encouraged from women, members of ethnic minority groups (American Indians, African Americans, Hispanics or Latinos, Native Hawaiians, Alaska Natives, Asians, and Pacific Islanders), and persons with disabilities. Selection is based on all available evidence of ability, including academic records, letters of recommendation, and GRE scores.

Financial data The annual stipend is $30,500 for the first year, $31,000 for the second year; and $31,500 for the third year; the program also pays the recipient's institution full tuition and required fees (not to include room and board). An additional allowance may be considered for a student with a disability.

Duration 3 years, as long as satisfactory academic progress is maintained.

Additional information This program is sponsored by the Army Research Office, the Air Force Office of Scientific Research, and the Office of Naval Research. Recipients do not incur any military or other service obligation. They must attend school on a full-time basis.

Number awarded Approximately 180 each year.

Deadline January of each year.

[562]
NATIONAL HEART, LUNG, AND BLOOD INSTITUTE MENTORED CAREER AWARD FOR FACULTY AT MINORITY INSTITUTIONS

National Heart, Lung, and Blood Institute
Attn: Division of Extramural Affairs
6701 Rockledge Drive, Room 10135
Bethesda, MD 20892-7950
(301) 435-0222   Fax: (301) 480-1060
E-mail: tm280y@nih.gov
Web: www.nhlbi.nih.gov

Purpose To provide funding to faculty investigators at minority schools interested in receiving further research training in areas relevant to cardiovascular, pulmonary, and hematologic diseases.

Eligibility Candidates for this award must be faculty members who are U.S. citizens, nationals, or permanent residents at the time of application; have a doctoral degree or equivalent in a biomedical or behavioral science; wish to receive specialized training in cardiovascular, pulmonary, hematologic, or sleep disorders research; have the background and potential to benefit from the training; and are committed to providing research opportunities and cultivating an interest in research for students from disadvantaged backgrounds at their institution. They must be teaching at a college or university with student enrollment drawn substantially from minority ethnic groups (including African Americans/Blacks, Hispanics, American Indians, Alaska Native, and non-Asian Pacific Islanders). Candidates must identify and complete arrangements with a mentor (at the same institution or at a collaborating research center) who is recognized as an accomplished investigator in the research area proposed and who will provide guidance for their development and research plans. They are also encouraged to recruit at least 1 and up to 2 students from disadvantaged backgrounds, including racial and ethnic minorities at their institution, to serve as research assistants.

Financial data The awardee receives salary support of up to $75,000 per year plus fringe benefits. Student research assistants receive up to $10 per hour. Support for up to 5% of the mentor's salary during the summer experience may also be awarded. In addition, up to $36,000 per year may be provided for research project requirements and related support (e.g., technical personnel costs, supplies, equipment, candidate travel, telephone charges, publication costs, and tuition for necessary courses). Facilities and administrative costs may be reimbursed at the rate of 8% of total direct costs.

Duration Academic years and summers for 3 to 5 years.

Additional information Awardees must commit 100% of their effort during summer and/or off-quarter periods and at least 25% of their effort during the academic year.

Number awarded Varies each year.

Deadline Letters of intent must be submitted by May of each year; final applications are due in June.

[563]

NATIONAL KOREAN PRESBYTERIAN WOMEN GRANTS

National Korean Presbyterian Women
c/o Shin Ok Chang (Lee), Moderator
82 Dartmouth Street
Forest Hill, NY 11375
(718) 575-0373   E-mail: sochanglee@hotmail.com
Web: www.pcusa.org/korean/org-nkpw.htm

Purpose To provide financial assistance to Korean American women preparing for ministry in the Presbyterian Church.

Eligibility This program is open to second-generation Korean American women who are entering their third semester of full-time study at a Presbyterian seminary. Selection is based on academic ability and leadership skills.

Financial data The stipend is $1,000.

Duration 1 year.

Deadline May of each year.

[564]

NATIONAL TONGAN AMERICAN SOCIETY SCHOLARSHIPS

National Tongan American Society
Attn: Director
2480 South Main Street, Suite 108
Salt Lake City, UT 84115
(801) 467-8712
Web: www.planet-tonga.com/NTAS/education.htm

Purpose To provide financial assistance to undergraduate and graduate students of Tongan background.

Eligibility Applicants must be of Tongan background and enrolled full time as an undergraduate or graduate student. They must submit a completed application, a college and/or high school transcript, a Student Aid Report (SAR), and 2 letters of recommendation. Selection is based on GPA (10 points), extracurricular activities (25 points), statement of goals (10 points), letters of recommendation (5 points), financial need (25 points), and special considerations (e.g., single parent home, disability, etc., 25 points).

Financial data Stipends are awarded (amounts not specified).

Duration 1 year.

Number awarded Several each year.

Deadline May of each year.

[565]

NATIONAL URBAN FELLOWS PROGRAM

National Urban Fellows, Inc.
Attn: Program Director
59 John Street, Suite 310
New York, NY 10038
(212) 349-6200   Fax: (212) 349-7478
E-mail: lbenitez@nuf.org
Web: www.nuf.org

Purpose To provide mid-career minority and women public sector professionals with an opportunity to strengthen leadership skills through an academic program coupled with a mentorship.

Eligibility This program is open to minorities and women who are U.S. citizens, have a bachelor's degree, have at least 3 years of administrative or managerial experience, have demonstrated exceptional ability and leadership potential, meet academic admission requirements, have a high standard of integrity and work ethic, and are committed to the solution of urban problems. Applicants must a 1,000-word autobiographical statement and a 1,000-word statement on their career goals. Semifinalists are interviewed.

Financial data The stipend is $25,000. The program also provides full payment of tuition, a relocation allowance of $500, a book allowance of $500, and reimbursement for program-related travel.

Duration 14 months.

Additional information The program begins with a summer semester of study at Bernard M. Baruch College of the City University of New York. Following this, fellows spend 9 months in mentorship assignments with a senior administrator in a government agency, a major nonprofit, or a foundation. The final summer is spent in another semester of study at Baruch College. Fellows who successfully complete all requirements are granted a master's of public administration from that college. A $35 processing fee must accompany each application.

Number awarded Varies; approximately 20 each year.

Deadline February of each year.

[566]

NCAA ETHNIC MINORITY POSTGRADUATE SCHOLARSHIP PROGRAM

National Collegiate Athletic Association
Attn: Leadership Advisory Board
700 West Washington Avenue
P.O. Box 6222
Indianapolis, IN 46206-6222
(317) 917-6477   Fax: (317) 917-6888
Web: www.ncaa.org

Purpose To provide funding to ethnic minority graduate students who are interested in preparing for a career in intercollegiate athletics.

Eligibility This program is open to members of minority groups who have been accepted into a program at a National Collegiate Athletic Association (NCAA) member institution that will prepare them for a career in intercollegiate athletics (athletics administrator, coach, athletic trainer, or other career that provides a direct service to intercollegiate athletics). Applicants must be U.S. citizens, have performed with distinction as a student body member at their respective undergraduate institution, and be entering the first semester or term of their postgraduate studies. Selection is based on the applicant's involvement in extracurricular activities, course work, commitment to preparing for a career in intercollegiate athletics, and promise for success in that career. Financial need is not considered.

Financial data The stipend is $6,000; funds are paid to the college or university of the recipient's choice.

Duration 1 year; nonrenewable.

Number awarded 16 each year; 3 of the scholarships are reserved for applicants who completed undergraduate study at an NCAA Division III institution.

Deadline February of each year.

[567]

NELLIE STONE JOHNSON SCHOLARSHIP

Minnesota State University Student Association
Attn: Scholarship
108 Como Avenue
St. Paul, MN 55103-1820
(651) 224-1518   Fax: (651) 224-9753
E-mail: nsj@msusa.net
Web: www.msusa.net/nellie_stjo.html

Purpose To provide financial assistance to racial minority union members and their families who are interested in working on an undergraduate or graduate degree at a Minnesota state college or university.

Eligibility This program is open to students in 2-year, undergraduate, and graduate programs at a Minnesota state university, community college, or consolidated campus. Applicants must be a minority (Asian, American Indian, Alaska Native, Black/African American, Hispanic/Latino, Native Hawaiian, or Pacific Islander) union member or the child, grandchild, or spouse of a minority union member. They must submit a 2-page statement about their background, educational goals, career goals, and other activities that may impact the cause of human or civil rights. Awards may be reserved for women. Preference is given to Minnesota residents. A personal or telephone interview may be required.

Financial data Stipends range from $500 to $2,000.

Duration 1 year; may be renewed up to 3 additional years for student working on a bachelor's degree, 1 additional year for students working on a master's degree, or 1 additional year for students in a community or technical college program.

Number awarded 1 or more each year. If multiple awards are made, at least 1 recipient must be female.

Deadline March of each year.

[568]

NISABURO AIBARA MEMORIAL SCHOLARSHIP

Japanese American Citizens League
Attn: National Scholarship Awards
1765 Sutter Street
San Francisco, CA 94115
(415) 921-5225   Fax: (415) 931-4671
E-mail: jacl@jacl.org
Web: www.jacl.org/scholarships.html

Purpose To provide financial assistance for graduate study to members of the Japanese American Citizens League (JACL).

Eligibility This program is open to JACL members who are attending or planning to attend an accredited college or university as a graduate student. Applicants must submit a statement describing their current level of involvement in the Japanese American community or Asian Pacific community and how they will continue their involvement in future years. Selection is based on academic record, extracurricular activities, financial need, and community involvement.

Financial data The stipend depends on the availability of funds but usually ranges from $1,000 to $5,000.

Duration 1 year; nonrenewable.

Additional information The funds for this program are provided by the Turlock Social Club of California, in honor of the late Issei pioneer. Applications must be submitted to the JACL National Scholarship Program, c/o San Diego JACL Chapter, 1031 25th Street, San Diego, CA 92102.

Number awarded At least 1 each year.

Deadline March of each year.

[569]

NISEI VETERANS' COMMITTEE SCHOLARSHIP PROGRAM

Nisei Veterans' Committee, Inc.
Attn: Debbie McQuilken
6336 N.E. 138th Place
Seattle, WA 98144
(206) 721-5359   E-mail: debbiemcqu@aol.com

Purpose To provide financial assistance for college or graduate school to Japanese Americans and others in Seattle who are related to members of the Nisei Veterans' Committee (NVC).

Eligibility This program is open to Japanese Americans and others who are direct descendants or relatives of a member of the Nisei Veterans' Committee or its Women's Auxiliary. The Nisei Veterans' Committee Scholarship and the Women's Auxiliary Scholarship are limited to high school seniors. The Shiro Kashino Memorial Scholarships are also open to college and graduate students. Applicants must be residents of the Seattle area. Selection is based on leadership ability, activity in the Japanese American community, volunteer service to the NVC, pride in their Japanese American heritage, personality, athletic excellence, academic standards, and humanitarian qualities.

Financial data The stipend is normally $1,500 per year.

Duration 1 year.

Number awarded 6 each year, including 4 designated as Shiro Kashino Memorial Scholarships.

Deadline January of each year.

[570]

NORTHEASTERN REGION KOREAN AMERICAN SCHOLARSHIPS

Korean American Scholarship Foundation
NorthEastern Region
c/o William Kim, Scholarship Committee Chair
51 West Overlook
Port Washington, NY 11050
(516) 883-1142   Fax: (516) 883-1964
E-mail: wkim@alson.com
Web: www.kasf.org

Purpose To provide financial assistance to Korean American undergraduate and graduate students who attend school in the northeastern states.

Eligibility This program is open to Korean American students who are currently enrolled in a college or university in a northeastern state as a full-time undergraduate or graduate student. Applicants may reside anywhere in the United States as long as they attend school in the northeastern region: Connecticut, Maine, Massachusetts, New Hampshire, New Jersey, New York, Rhode Island, and Vermont. Selection is based on academic achievement, school activities, community service, and financial need.

Financial data Stipends range from $1,000 to $2,000.

Duration 1 year; renewable.

Number awarded Varies each year; recently, 60 of these scholarships were awarded
Deadline June of each year.

[571]
NSCA MINORITY SCHOLARSHIPS

National Strength and Conditioning Association
Attn: Foundation
1955 North Union Boulevard
P.O. Box 9908
Colorado Springs, CO 80932-0908
(719) 632-6722   Toll-free: (800) 815-6826
Fax: (719) 632-6367   E-mail: foundation@nsca-lift.org
Web: www.nsca-lift.org/foundation

Purpose To provide financial assistance to members of the National Strength and Conditioning Association (NSCA) who are minorities interested in preparing for a career in strength training and conditioning.

Eligibility This program is open to members who are minorities and have been accepted into an accredited postsecondary institution to work on a graduate degree in the strength and conditioning field. They must submit a 500-word essay describing their course of study, career goals, and financial need.

Financial data The stipend is $1,000.

Duration 1 year.

Additional information The NSCA is a nonprofit organization of strength and conditioning professionals, including coaches, athletic trainers, physical therapists, educators, researchers, and physicians. This program was first offered in 2003.

Number awarded 2 each year.

Deadline March of each year.

[572]
OAHU COUNCIL OF FILIPINO CATHOLIC CLUBS SCHOLARSHIP PROGRAM

Oahu Council of Filipino Catholic Clubs
Attn: Josie Rayray, Information and Education
   Committee
47-464 Poomau Street
Kaneohe, HI 96744
(808) 266-9893

Purpose To provide financial assistance for high school, college, or seminary to descendants of members of the Oahu Council of Filipino Catholic Clubs.

Eligibility This program is open to high school, college, and seminary students from Hawaii whose parents or grandparents have been members of the organization for at least 1 year. Applicants must be 1) Filipino Catholics attending Catholic colleges or high schools or non-Catholic colleges, or 2) Filipino students attending a seminary or convent. They must have a GPA of 3.0 or higher and be able to demonstrate financial need. Along with their application, they must submit an essay about their significant experiences, accomplishments, future goals, and service to school, church, and community. An interview is required.

Financial data A stipend is awarded (amount not specified).

Duration 1 year.

Number awarded Several each year.

Deadline July of each year.

[573]
ONE-YEAR-ON-CAMPUS PROGRAM

Sandia National Laboratories
Attn: Staffing Department 3535
MS-1023
P.O. Box 5800
Albuquerque, NM 87185-1023
(505) 844-3441   Fax: (505) 844-6636
E-mail: pacover@sandia.gov
Web: www.sandia.gov/employment/index.html

Purpose To enable minority students to obtain a master's degree in engineering or computer science and also work at Sandia National Laboratories.

Eligibility This program is open to minority students with a bachelor's degree in engineering or computer science and a GPA of 3.2 or higher. Participants must apply to 3 schools jointly selected by the program and themselves. They must be prepared to obtain a master's degree within 1 year. The fields of study (not all fields are available at all participating universities) include computer science, electrical engineering, mechanical engineering, civil engineering, chemical engineering, nuclear engineering, materials sciences, and petroleum engineering. Applicants must be interested in working at the sponsor's laboratories during the summer between graduation from college and the beginning of their graduate program, and then following completion of their master's degree.

Financial data Participants receive a competitive salary while working at the laboratories on a full-time basis and a stipend while attending school.

Duration 1 year.

Additional information During their summer assignment, participants work at the laboratories, either in Albuquerque, New Mexico or in Livermore, California. Upon successful completion of the program, they return to Sandia's hiring organization as a full-time member of the technical staff. This program began in 1968. Application to schools where students received their undergraduate degree is not recommended. After the schools accept an applicant, the choice of a school is made jointly by the laboratories and the participant.

Number awarded Varies each year; since the program began, more than 350 engineers and computer scientists have gone to work at Sandia with master's degrees.

[574]
OPERATION JUMP START II SCHOLARSHIPS

American Association of Advertising Agencies
Attn: Manager of Diversity Programs
405 Lexington Avenue, 18th Floor
New York, NY 10174-1801
(212) 682-2500   Toll-free: (800) 676-9333
Fax: (212) 682-8391   E-mail: tiffany@aaaa.org
Web: www.aaaa.org/diversity/foundation/funds.htm

Purpose To provide financial assistance to multicultural art directors and copywriters interested in working on a graduate degree in advertising.

Eligibility This program is open to African Americans, Asian Americans, Hispanic Americans, and Native Americans who are interested in studying the advertising creative arts at designated institutions. Applicants must have already received an undergraduate degree and be able to demonstrate financial need. As part of the selection process, they must submit 10 samples of creative work in their respective field of expertise.

Financial data The stipend is $10,000.

Duration Most awards are for 2 years.

Additional information This program began in 2002 and currently provides scholarships to students at the Adcenter at Virginia Commonwealth University, the Creative Circus and the Portfolio Center in Atlanta, the Miami Ad School, the University of Texas at Austin, Pratt Institute, the Minneapolis College of Art and Design, and the Art Center College of Design at Pasadena.

Number awarded 20 each year.

[575]
ORANGE COUNTY ASIAN AMERICAN BAR FOUNDATION SCHOLARSHIPS

Orange County Asian American Bar Foundation
7700 Irvine Center Drive
Irvine, CA 92618
(949) 585-0088   Fax: (949) 585-0008

Purpose To provide financial assistance to students at law schools in southern California who have been active in the Asian American community.

Eligibility This program is open to students from any state who are in their first or second year of law school in southern California. Evening students in their third year of study are also eligible. Selection is based on the applicant's service to, and/or leadership in, the Asian American community and commitment to continue providing such service and/or leadership.

Financial data The stipend is $1,000.

Duration 1 year.

Number awarded 2 each year.

Deadline March of each year.

[576]
ORGANIC CHEMISTRY GRADUATE STUDENT FELLOWSHIPS

American Chemical Society
Division of Organic Chemistry
1155 16th Street, N.W.
Washington, DC 20036
(202) 872-4408   Toll-free: (800) 227-5558
E-mail: divisions@acs.org
Web: www.organicdivision.org/fellowships.html

Purpose To provide financial assistance to advanced doctoral students (particularly minorities and women) in organic chemistry.

Eligibility This program is open to students working toward a Ph.D. degree in organic chemistry who have completed the second year of graduate study by the time the fellowship period begins. Applicants must submit 3 letters of recommendation, a resume, and a short essay on a research area of their choice. U.S. citizenship or permanent resident status is required. Selection is based primarily on evidence of research accomplishment. Applications from women and minorities are especially encouraged.

Financial data The stipend is $20,000. Fellows also receive travel support to present a poster of their work at the National Organic Symposium.

Duration 1 year.

Additional information This program was established in 1982. It includes the Emmanuil Troyansky Fellowship. Information is also available from Scott Rychnovsky, University of California at Irvine, School of Physical Sciences, 3038A FRH, Mail Code 2025, Irvine, CA 92697, (949) 824-8292, Fax: (949) 824-6369, E-mail: srychnov@uci.edu.

Number awarded Varies each year; recently, 14 of these fellowships were awarded.

Deadline May of each year.

[577]
OSB SCHOLARSHIPS

Oregon State Bar
Attn: Affirmative Action Program
5200 S.W. Meadows Road
P.O. Box 1689
Lake Oswego, OR 97035-0889
(503) 431-6338
Toll-free: (800) 452-8260, ext. 338 (within OR)
Fax: (503) 598-6938   E-mail: dgigoux@osbar.org
Web: www.osbar.org

Purpose To provide financial assistance to minority students in Oregon who are currently attending law school.

Eligibility This program is open to minority (African American, Asian, Hispanic, Native American) students who are entering or attending an Oregon law school and planning to practice law in Oregon upon graduation. Along with their application, they must submit 1) a personal statement on their history of disadvantage or barriers to educational advancement, personal experiences of discrimination, extraordinary financial obligations, composition of immediate family, extraordinary health or medical needs, and languages in which they are fluent; and 2) a state bar statement in which they describe their intention to practice law in Oregon and how they will improve the quality of legal service or increase access to justice in Oregon. Selection is based on financial need (30%), the personal statement (25%), the state bar statement (25%), community activities (10%), and employment history (10%).

Financial data The stipend is $1,000 per semester. Funds are credited to the recipient's law school tuition account.

Duration 1 year; recipients may reapply.

Additional information Recipients are encouraged to contribute monetarily to the Oregon State Bar's affirmative action program once they become employed.

Number awarded 8 each year.

Deadline February of each year.

[578]
PABA FELLOWSHIP

Philippine American Bar Association of Los Angeles
c/o Avelino J. Halagao, Jr.
400 Continental Boulevard, Sixth Floor
El Segundo, CA 90245
(310) 426-2323   E-mail: ajhalagao@netsperanto.com
Web: www.philconnect.com/paba/students.html

Purpose To provide financial assistance and work experience to Asian American/Pacific Islanders attending law school in the Los Angeles area.

Eligibility This program is open to Asian American/Pacific Islander students at law schools in the Los Angeles area. Applicants must be interested in a clerkship at the Asian Pacific American Legal Center of Southern California (APALC). Selection is based on academic accomplishment, past and potential community contributions, and financial need.

Financial data The stipend is $2,500.

Duration 1 year.

Additional information The awardee must work 8 to 10 hours per week during the spring or summer at APALC.

Number awarded 1 each year.

Deadline January of each year.

[579]
PABA SCHOLARSHIPS

Philippine American Bar Association of Los Angeles
c/o Avelino J. Halagao, Jr.
400 Continental Boulevard, Sixth Floor
El Segundo, CA 90245
(310) 426-2323   E-mail: ajhalagao@netsperanto.com
Web: www.philconnect.com/paba/students.html

Purpose To provide financial assistance to Asian American/Pacific Islanders attending law school in the Los Angeles area.

Eligibility This program is open to Asian American/Pacific Islander students at law schools in the Los Angeles area. Selection is based on academic accomplishment, past and potential community contributions, and financial need.

Financial data The stipend is $750.

Duration 1 year.

Number awarded 2 each year.

Deadline January of each year.

[580]
PATRICK D. MCJULIEN MINORITY GRADUATE SCHOLARSHIP

Association for Educational Communications and
  Technology
Attn: ECT Foundation
1800 North Stonelake Drive, Suite 2
Bloomington, IN 47408
(812) 335-7675   Toll-free: (877) 677-AECT
Web: www.aect.org

Purpose To provide financial assistance to minority members of the Association for Educational Communications and Technology (AECT) working on a doctorate in the field of educational communications and technology.

Eligibility This program is open to AECT members who are members of minority groups. Applicants must be full-time graduate students enrolled in a degree-granting program in educational technology at the masters (M.S.), specialist (Ed.S.), or doctoral (Ph.D., Ed.D.) levels with a GPA of 3.0 or higher. Along with their application, they must submit an essay on what they believe to be an important issue confronting minorities in the field of media and 3 letters of recommendation.

Financial data The stipend is $250 or $500.

Duration 1 year.

Additional information Information is also available from K.J. Saville, AECT Awards Chair, (906) 227-2413, E-mail: ksaville@nmu.edu.

Number awarded 1 each year.

Deadline October of each year.

[581]
PAUL D. WHITE SCHOLARSHIP

Baker & Hostetler LLP
Attn: Kathleen Ferdico
3200 National City Center
1900 East Ninth Street
Cleveland, OH 44114-3485
(216) 861-7092   Fax: (216) 696-0740
Web: www.bakerlaw.com

Purpose To provide financial assistance and summer work experience to minority students at selected law schools.

Eligibility This program is open to first- and second-year law students of African American, Hispanic, Asian American, or American Indian descent. Applicants must be attending 1 of the following schools that currently participate in the program: Case Western Reserve School of Law, Cleveland-Marshall School of Law, Howard University School of Law, Ohio State University Moritz School of Law, University of Michigan School of Law, the University of Texas School of Law, University of California at Los Angeles School of Law, University of Cincinnati College of Law, University of Denver College of Law, University of Florida Levin College of Law, and University of Colorado School of Law.

Financial data The program provides a stipend of $5,000 and a paid summer clerkship with the sponsoring firm.

Duration 1 year, including the following summer.

Number awarded 1 each year.

[582]
PEDIATRIC/VISION THERAPY AWARD

National Optometric Association
c/o Dr. Charles Comer, Association Manager
3723 Main Street
P.O. Box F
East Chicago, IL 46312
Toll-free: (877) 394-2020   Fax: (219) 398-1077
E-mail: ccomer2@aol.com
Web: www.natoptassoc.org

Purpose To provide financial assistance to members of the National Optometric Student Association (NOSA).

Eligibility This program is open to NOSA members enrolled in the third or fourth year at a school or college of optometry. Applicants must have a GPA of 2.5 or higher and be able to demonstrate community involvement. Along with their application, they must submit a 300-word essay demonstrating their aspirations as an optometrist and commitment to serve their community related to pediatric optometry or vision therapy. Financial need is considered in the selection process.

Financial data   The stipend is $500.

Duration   1 year.

Additional information   The National Optometric Association was founded in 1969 with the goal of recruiting minority students for schools and colleges of optometry. It remains committed to improving the quality and accessibility of eye care in minority and other historically underserved communities.

Number awarded   1 each year.

Deadline   April of each year.

[583]
PFIZER/UNCF CORPORATE SCHOLARS PROGRAM

United Negro College Fund
Attn: Corporate Scholars Program
P.O. Box 1435
Alexandria, VA 22313-9998
Toll-free: (866) 671-7237   E-mail: internship@uncf.org
Web: www.uncf.org/internships/index.asp

Purpose   To provide financial assistance and work experience to minority undergraduate and graduate students majoring in designated fields and interested in an internship at a Pfizer facility.

Eligibility   This program is open to sophomores, juniors, graduate students, and first-year law students who are African American, Hispanic American, Asian/Pacific Islander American, or American Indian/Alaskan Native. Applicants must have a GPA of 3.0 or higher and be enrolled at an institution that is a member of the United Negro College Fund (UNCF) or at another targeted college or university. They must be working on 1) a bachelor's degree in animal science, business, chemistry (organic or analytical), human resources, logistics, microbiology, organizational development, operations management, pre-veterinary medicine, or supply chain management; 2) a master's degree in chemistry (organic or analytical), finance, human resources, or organizational development; or 3) a law degree. Eligibility is limited to U.S. citizens, permanent residents, asylees, refugees, and lawful temporary residents. Along with their application, they must submit a 1-page essay about themselves and their career goals, including information about their interest in Pfizer (the program's sponsor), their personal background, and any particular challenges they have faced.

Financial data   The program provides an internship stipend of up to $5,000, housing accommodations near Pfizer Corporate facilities, and (based on successful internship performance) a $15,000 scholarship.

Duration   8 to 10 weeks for the internship; 1 year for the scholarship.

Additional information   Opportunities for first-year law students include the summer internship only.

Number awarded   Varies each year.

Deadline   January of each year.

[584]
PHILIPPINE NURSES ASSOCIATION OF AMERICA SCHOLARSHIP

Philippine Nurses Association of America
c/o Mila Velasquez, President
20127 Avenida Pamplona
Cerritos, CA 90703
(562) 860-4428   E-mail: pnaa@pnaa03.org
Web: www.pnaamerica.net

Purpose   To provide financial assistance for graduate school to members of the Philippine Nurses Association of America (PNAA).

Eligibility   This program is open to PNAA members who are enrolled or admitted at an accredited program for a master's degree in nursing, post-master's study, or doctoral degree. Applicants must have a GPA of 3.0 or higher. They must submit a 150-word essay on their professional career goals, an academic transcript, and 2 letters of recommendation.

Financial data   The stipend is $1,000.

Duration   1 year.

Additional information   Information is also available from Josie Villanueva, Scholarship Chair, 24556 Mando Drive, Laguna Niguel, CA 92677-4079, (949) 831-4247, E-mail: jphine5150@aol.com.

Number awarded   1 or more each year.

[585]
PORTLAND CHAPTER AAJA SCHOLARSHIPS

Asian American Journalists Association-Portland
    Chapter
c/o Tracy Jan
The Oregonian
Metro East News Bureau
295 N.E. Second Street
Gresham, OR 97030
(503) 294-5970
E-mail: tracyjan@news.oregonian.com
Web: chapters.aaja.org/Portland/scholar.html

Purpose   To provide financial assistance to undergraduate and graduate journalism students in Oregon and southwestern Washington area who have been involved in the Asian American community.

Eligibility   This program is open to high school seniors, undergraduates, and graduate students who live or attend school in Oregon or the Vancouver, Washington area. Applicants must be enrolled or planning to enroll full time in a journalism program and be able to demonstrate involvement in the Asian American community. Along with their application, they must submit an essay (up to 750 words) on how they became interested in journalism or how they see themselves contributing to the Asian American community. They must also submit work samples (print: up to 3 articles; radio: up to 3 different stories on standard audio tapes; television: up to 3 different stories on a VHS tape; photojournalism: a portfolio of up to 15 entries). Selection is based on scholastic ability, commitment to journalism, sensitivity to Asian American issues as demonstrated by community involvement, journalistic ability, and financial need.

Financial data   Stipends up to $2,000 are available.

Duration   1 year.

Number awarded   1 each year.

Deadline March of each year.

[586]
POSTDOCTORAL FELLOWSHIP IN MENTAL HEALTH AND SUBSTANCE ABUSE SERVICES

American Psychological Association
Attn: Minority Fellowship Program
750 First Street, N.E.
Washington, DC 20002-4242
(202) 336-6127   Fax: (202) 336-6012
TDD: (202) 336-6123   E-mail: mfp@apa.org
Web: www.apa.org/mfp/postdocpsych.html

Purpose To provide financial assistance to minority and other postdoctoral scholars interested in a program of research training related to providing mental health and substance abuse services to ethnic minority populations.

Eligibility This program is open to U.S. citizens and permanent residents who received a doctoral degree in psychology in the last 5 years. Applicants must be interested in participating in a program of training under a qualified sponsor for research, delivery of services, or policy related to substance abuse and its relationship to the mental health or psychological well-being of ethnic minorities. Members of ethnic minority groups (African Americans, Hispanics/Latinos, American Indians, Alaskan Natives, Asian Americans, Native Hawaiians, and other Pacific Islanders) are especially encouraged to apply. Selection is based on commitment to a career in ethnic minority mental health service delivery, research, or policy; qualifications of the sponsor; the fit between career goals and training environment selected; merit of the training proposal; potential demonstrated through accomplishments and goals; and appropriateness to goals of the program.

Financial data The stipend depends on the number of years of research experience and is equivalent to the standard postdoctoral stipend level of the National Institutes of Health (currently ranging from $35,568 for no years of experience to $51,036 for 7 or more years of experience).

Duration 1 academic or calendar year; may be renewed for up to 2 additional years.

Additional information Funding is provided by the U.S. Substance Abuse and Mental Health Services Administration.

Number awarded Varies each year.

Deadline January of each year.

[587]
POSTDOCTORAL FELLOWSHIPS IN THE NEUROSCIENCES

American Psychological Association
Attn: Minority Fellowship Program
750 First Street, N.E.
Washington, DC 20002-4242
(202) 336-6127   Fax: (202) 336-6012
TDD: (202) 336-6123   E-mail: mfp@apa.org
Web: www.apa.org/mfp/pdprogram.html

Purpose To provide funding to minority postdoctorates who are interested in pursuing research training in neuroscience.

Eligibility This program is open to all U.S. citizens and permanent residents who have a Ph.D. or M.D. degree with appropriate research experience in neuroscience or an applied discipline, such as cell or molecular biology or immunology. Applicants must have career goals that are consistent with those of the program: 1) to increase ethnic and racial diversity among neuroscience researchers with a special emphasis on increasing the numbers of underrepresented ethnic minorities; and 2) to increase numbers of neuroscientists whose work is related to the federal initiative to eliminate health disparities. They must be interested in engaging in postdoctoral research training in behavioral neuroscience, cellular neurobiology, cognitive neuroscience, computational neuroscience, developmental neurobiology, membrane biophysics, molecular neurobiology, neuroanatomy, neurobiology of aging, neurobiology of disease, neurochemistry, neurogenetics, neuroimmunology, neuropathology, neuropharmacology, neurophysiology, neurotoxicology, or systems neuroscience. Students identified as underrepresented ethnic minorities in the neurosciences (African Americans, Native Americans, Hispanic Americans, and Pacific Islanders) are especially encouraged to apply. Selection is based on scholarship, research experience and potential, a research proposal, the suitability of the proposed laboratory and mentor, commitment to a research career in neuroscience, writing ability, and appropriateness to program goal.

Financial data The stipend depends on the number of years of research experience and is equivalent to the standard postdoctoral stipend level of the National Institutes of Health (currently ranging from $35,568 for no years of experience to $51,036 for 7 or more years of experience). The fellowship also provides travel funds to attend the annual meeting of the Society for Neuroscience.

Duration 1 year; may be renewed for up to 1 additional year.

Additional information The program was established in 1987. It is funded by the U.S. National Institute of Mental Health of the National Institutes of Health and administered by the American Psychological Association.

Number awarded Varies each year.

Deadline January of each year.

[588]
POSTDOCTORAL RESEARCH FELLOWSHIPS IN EPILEPSY

Epilepsy Foundation
Attn: Research Department
4351 Garden City Drive
Landover, MD 20785-7223
(301) 459-3700   Toll-free: (800) EFA-1000
Fax: (301) 577-2684   TDD: (800) 332-2070
E-mail: grants@efa.org
Web: www.epilepsyfoundation.org

Purpose To provide funding for a program of postdoctoral training to minority and other physicians and scientists committed to epilepsy research.

Eligibility Applicants must have a doctoral degree (M.D., Ph.D., or equivalent) and be a resident or postdoctoral fellow at a university, medical school, research institution, or medical center. They must be interested in participating in a training experience and research project that has potential significance for understanding the causes, treatment, or consequences of epilepsy. The program is geared toward applicants who will be trained in research in epilepsy rather than those who use epilepsy as a tool for research in other fields. Equal consideration is given to applicants interested in acquiring experience either in basic laboratory research or in the conduct of human clinical studies. Academic faculty holding the rank of instructor or higher are not eligible, nor are graduate or medical students, medical residents, permanent government employees, or employees of private industry. Applications from women, members of minority groups, and people with disabilities are especially encouraged. Selection is based on scientific quality of the proposed research, a statement regarding its relevance to epilepsy, the applicant's qualifications, the preceptor's qualifications, and the adequacy of facility and related epilepsy programs at the institution.

Financial data The grant is $40,000. No indirect costs are covered.

Duration 1 year.

Additional information Support for this program is provided by many individuals, families, and corporations, especially the American Epilepsy Society, Abbott Laboratories, Ortho-McNeil Pharmaceutical, and Pfizer Inc. The fellowship must be carried out at a facility in the United States where there is an ongoing epilepsy research program.

Number awarded Varies each year; recently, 13 of these fellowships were awarded.

Deadline August of each year.

[589]
PRESBYTERIAN CHURCH CONTINUING EDUCATION GRANT AND LOAN PROGRAM

Presbyterian Church (USA)
Attn: Office of Financial Aid for Studies
100 Witherspoon Street, Room M-052
Louisville, KY 40202-1396
(502) 569-5735   Toll-free: (888) 728-7228, ext. 5735
Fax: (502) 569-8766   E-mail: LBryan@ctr.pcusa.org
Web: www.pcusa.org

Purpose To provide financial assistance for continuing education, in the form of educational grants and loans, to minority and other professional church workers of the Presbyterian Church (USA) and doctoral candidates who are church members.

Eligibility This program is open to 1) PC(USA) ministers and lay professionals who have served a congregation of 150 or fewer members for at least 3 years; and 2) PC(USA) church members enrolled in a D.Min, Ph.D., or equivalent program in religious studies. Ministers and lay professionals must be planning to attend a program of study that will lead to certification, course work at an accredited institution, or a national event sponsored by PC(USA). The study, course work, or event must be approved by a church session, presbytery, or synod. Events must be at least 3 days in duration. For church members working on a Ph.D. degree, preference is given to women and racial ethnic applicants attending PC(USA) theological institutions, colleges, or universities. U.S. citizenship or permanent resident status is required.

Financial data For ministers and lay professionals, grants for events range from $100 to $500 and grants for study or course work range from $100 to $1,000. For doctoral candidates, grants range from $500 to $1,000. The maximum loan is $2,000 per year.

Duration 1 year. Ministers and lay professionals at small churches are eligible for unlimited renewal of grants. Candidates for a D.Min. degree may renew their grants for a total of 3 years. Candidates for a Ph.D. or equivalent degree may renew their grants for a total of 4 years. Loans may be renewed to a maximum of $6,000.

Number awarded Varies each year.

Deadline November of each year.

[590]
PROCTER & GAMBLE SCHOLARSHIP

Franklin Pierce Law Center
Attn: Assistant Dean for Admissions
Two White Street
Concord, NH 03301
(603) 228-9217   E-mail: kmcdonald@piercelaw.edu
Web: www.piercelaw.edu/finan/GambleSchol.htm

Purpose To provide an opportunity for law students, especially women and minorities, to study patent and intellectual property law as a visiting scholar at Franklin Pierce Law Center in Concord, New Hampshire.

Eligibility This program is open to full-time second- and third-year students at law schools in the United States and Canada. Applicants must be interested in a program of study in patent and intellectual property law at the center. They must have sufficient undergraduate scientific and/or technical education to be admitted to the patent bar, including work in biology, biochemistry, botany, electronics technology, engineering (all types, especially civil, computer, and industrial), food technology, general chemistry, marine technology, microbiology, molecular biology, organic chemistry, pharmacology, physics, and textile technology. Their home school must agree to apply a year's credits earned at another school toward the J.D. degree. Preference is given to members of groups underrepresented among lawyers practicing patent law, including women and minorities.

Financial data The stipend is $5,000. Scholars must pay the tuition charged either by the Franklin Pierce Law Center or their home school, whichever is less.

Duration 1 academic year.

Additional information This program is sponsored by the Procter & Gamble Company.

Number awarded 1 each year.

Deadline April of each year.

[591]
PROFESSIONAL DEVELOPMENT FELLOWSHIPS FOR DOCTORAL CANDIDATES IN ART HISTORY

College Art Association of America
Attn: Fellowship Program
275 Seventh Avenue
New York, NY 10001-6798
(212) 691-1051, ext. 248   Fax: (212) 627-2381
E-mail: fellowship@collegeart.org
Web: www.collegeart.org/caa/career/fellowship.html

Purpose To provide financial assistance to doctoral candidates from socially and economically diverse backgrounds who are completing a Ph.D. degree in art history.

Eligibility This program is open to Ph.D. candidates in art history who have been underrepresented in the field because of their race, religion, gender, age, national origin, sexual orientation, disability, or financial status. Applicants must be U.S. citizens or permanent residents and able to demonstrate financial need. They must expect to receive the Ph.D. degree in the year following application.

Financial data The stipend is $5,000.

Duration 1 year: the final year of the degree program.

Additional information In addition to providing a stipend for the terminal year of their degree program, the College Art Association (CAA) helps fellows search for employment at a museum, art center, college, or university. Upon securing a position, CAA provides a $10,000 subsidy to the employer as part of the fellow's salary. Participating organizations must match this 2:1. In addition to administrative and/or teaching responsibilities, all fellows' positions must include a curatorial or public service component. Salary or stipend, position description, and term of employment will vary and are determined in consultation with individual fellows and their potential employers. This program began in 1993. Funding is provided by the Milton & Sally Avery Arts Foundation, Geraldine R. Dodge Foundation, National Endowment for the Arts, National Endowment for the Humanities, and Terra Foundation for the Arts.

Number awarded 1 each year.

Deadline January of each year.

[592]
PROFESSIONAL DEVELOPMENT FELLOWSHIPS FOR MASTER OF FINE ARTS CANDIDATES

College Art Association of America
Attn: Fellowship Program
275 Seventh Avenue
New York, NY 10001-6798
(212) 691-1051, ext. 248   Fax: (212) 627-2381
E-mail: fellowship@collegeart.org
Web: www.collegeart.org/caa/career/fellowship.html

Purpose To provide financial assistance to graduate students from socially and economically diverse backgrounds who are completing an M.F.A. degree in art history.

Eligibility This program is open to M.F.A. candidates in art history who have been underrepresented in the field because of their race, religion, gender, age, national origin, sexual orientation, disability, or financial status. Applicants must be U.S. citizens or permanent residents and able to demonstrate financial need. They must expect to receive the M.F.A. degree in the year following application.

Financial data The stipend is $5,000.

Duration 1 year: the final year of the degree program.

Additional information In addition to providing a stipend for the terminal year of their degree program, the College Art Association (CAA) helps fellows search for employment at a museum, art center, college, or university. Upon securing a position, CAA provides a $10,000 subsidy to the employer as part of the fellow's salary. Participating organizations must match this 2:1. In addition to administrative and/or teaching responsibilities, all fellows' positions must include a curatorial or public service component. Salary or stipend, position description, and term of employment will vary and are determined in consultation with individual fellows and their potential employers. This program began in 1993. Funding is provided by the Milton & Sally Avery Arts Foundation, Geraldine R. Dodge Foundation, National Endowment for the Arts, National Endowment for the Humanities, and Terra Foundation for the Arts.

Number awarded 1 each year.

Deadline January of each year.

[593]
PUBLIC POLICY AND INTERNATIONAL AFFAIRS FELLOWSHIPS

Public Policy and International Affairs Fellowship
   Program
c/o Association for Public Policy Analysis and
   Management
2100 M Street, N.W., Suite 610
P.O. Box 18766
Washington, DC 20037
(202) 496-0130   Fax: (202) 496-0134
E-mail: ppia@ppiaprogram.org
Web: www.ppiaprogram.org/programs/eligibility.php

Purpose To provide financial assistance to minority undergraduate students who are interested in preparing for graduate study in the fields of public policy and/or international affairs.

Eligibility This program is open to people of color historically underrepresented in public policy and international affairs, including African Americans, Asian Americans, Pacific Islanders, Hispanic Americans, Alaska Natives, and Native Americans. In most cases, most persons enter the program when they apply to participate in a summer institute following the junior year of college. Applicants must be U.S. citizens or permanent residents interested in a summer institute in public policy and international affairs. They must first apply directly to the summer institute. Following participation in that institute, they apply for graduate study in fields of their choice at more than 30 designated universities. For a list of participating institutions, contact the sponsor.

Financial data During the summer institute portion of the program, participants receive transportation to and from the institute site, room and board, and a $1,000 stipend. More than 30 graduate programs in public policy and/or international affairs have agreed to waive application fees and grant fellowships of at least $5,000 to students who have participated in the summer institutes.

Duration 1 summer and 1 academic year.

Additional information This program was established in 1981 when the Alfred P. Sloan Foundation provided a grant to the Association for Public Policy Analysis and Management (APPAM). From 1981 through 1988, participants were known as Sloan Fellows. From 1989 through 1995, the program was supported by the Ford Foundation and administered by the Woodrow Wilson National Fellowship Administration, so participants were known as Woodrow Wilson Fellows in Public Policy and International Affairs. Beginning in 1995, the program's name was shortened to the Public Policy and International Affairs Fellowship Program (PPIA) and its administration was moved to the Academy for Educational Development. To complement APPAM's role, the Association of Professional Schools of International Affairs (APSIA) also became an institutional sponsor. In 1999, the Ford Foundation ended its support for PPIA effective with the student cohort that participated in summer institutes in 1999. The APPAM and APSIA incorporated PPIA as an independent organization and operated the summer institutes in 2000. In 2001, the National Association of Schools of Public Affairs and Administration (NASPAA) also became a sponsor of PPIA. Beginning in summer of that year, summer institutes have been held at 4 universities: the Summer Program in Public Policy and International Affairs at the Gerald R. Ford School of Public Policy at the University of Michigan, the Maryland Leadership Institute at the School of Public Affairs at the University of Maryland, the UCPPIA Summer Institute at the Richard & Rhoda Goldman School of Public Policy at the University of California at Berkeley, and the Junior Summer Institute at the Woodrow Wilson School of Public and International Affairs at Princeton University. For information on those institutes, contact the respective school.

Number awarded   Varies each year.

[594]
PUGET SOUND CHAPTER HELENE M. OVERLY MEMORIAL SCHOLARSHIP

Women's Transportation Seminar-Puget Sound Chapter
c/o Lorelei Mesic, Scholarship Co-Chair
W&H Pacific
3350 Monte Villa Parkway
Bothell, WA 98021-8972
(425) 951-4872   Fax: (425) 951-4808
E-mail: lmesic@whpacific.com
Web: www.wtspugetsound.org/nscholarships.html

Purpose   To provide financial assistance to women graduate students, particularly minority women, from Washington who are working on a degree related to transportation.

Eligibility   This program is open to women who are residents of Washington, studying at a college in the state, or working as an intern in the state. Applicants must be currently enrolled in a graduate degree program in a transportation-related field, such as engineering, planning, finance, or logistics. They must have a GPA of 3.0 or higher and plans to prepare for a career in a transportation-related field. Minority candidates are encouraged to apply. Along with their application, they must submit a 750-word statement about their career goals after graduation and why they think they should receive this scholarship award. Selection is based on that statement, academic record, and transportation-related activities or job skills. Financial need is not considered.

Financial data   The stipend is $1,700.

Duration   1 year.

Additional information   The winner is also nominated for scholarships offered by the national organization of the Women's Transportation Seminar.

Number awarded   1 each year.

Deadline   October of each year.

[595]
RACIAL ETHNIC SUPPLEMENTAL GRANTS

Presbyterian Church (USA)
Attn: Office of Financial Aid for Studies
100 Witherspoon Street, Room M-052
Louisville, KY 40202-1396
(502) 569-5735   Toll-free: (888) 728-7228, ext. 5735
Fax: (502) 569-8766   E-mail: LBryan@ctr.pcusa.org
Web: www.pcusa.org

Purpose   To provide financial assistance to minority graduate students who are Presbyterian Church (USA) members interested in preparing for church occupations.

Eligibility   This program is open to racial/ethnic graduate students (Asian American, African American, Hispanic American, Native American, or Alaska Native) who are enrolled full time at a PC(USA) seminary or accredited theological institution approved by their Committee on Preparation for Ministry. Applicants must be working on 1) an M.Div. degree and enrolled as an inquirer or candidate by a PC(USA) presbytery, or 2) an M.A.C.E. degree and preparing for a church occupation. They must be PC(USA) members, U.S. citizens or permanent residents, able to demonstrate financial need, and recommended by the financial aid officer at their theological institution.

Financial data   Stipends range from $500 to $1,000 per year. Funds are intended as supplements to students who have been awarded a Presbyterian Study Grant but still demonstrate remaining financial need.

Duration   1 year; may be renewed up to 2 additional years.

Number awarded   Varies each year.

Deadline   September of each year.

[596]
RACIAL ETHNIC THEOLOGICAL EDUCATION SCHOLARSHIP FUND

Synod of Southern California and Hawaii
Attn: Racial Ethnic Pastoral Leadership Work Group
1501 Wilshire Boulevard
Los Angeles, CA 90017-2205
(213) 483-3840, ext. 255   Fax: (213) 483-4275
E-mail: LeonFanniel@synod.org
Web: www.synod.org/REPL/schol.html

Purpose   To provide financial assistance to members of racial minority groups in the Presbyterian Church (USA) Synod of Southern California and Hawaii who are preparing for a career as a pastor or other church vocation.

Eligibility   Applicants must be under care of a presbytery within the Synod of Southern California and Hawaii. They must be members of racial ethnic groups interested in becoming a Presbyterian pastor or other church worker (e.g., commissioned lay pastor, certified Christian educator) and serving in a racial ethnic ministry within the PC(USA). Racial ethnic persons who already have an M.Div. degree and are from another denomination in correspondence with the PC(USA) and are seeking to meet PC(USA) requirements for ordination or transfer may also be eligible if they plan to serve in a racial ethnic congregation or an approved specialized ministry. Applicants must submit documentation of financial need, recommendations from the appropriate presbytery committee or session, a current transcript, and essays on their goals and objectives.

Financial data The stipend is $2,000 per year.

Duration 1 year; may be renewed.

Additional information These scholarships were first awarded in 1984.

Number awarded Varies each year.

Deadline April of each year.

[597]
RAILROAD AND MINE WORKERS MEMORIAL SCHOLARSHIP

Japanese American Citizens League
Attn: National Scholarship Awards
1765 Sutter Street
San Francisco, CA 94115
(415) 921-5225   Fax: (415) 931-4671
E-mail: jacl@jacl.org
Web: www.jacl.org/scholarships.html

Purpose To provide financial assistance for graduate study to members of the Japanese American Citizens League (JACL).

Eligibility This program is open to JACL members who are attending or planning to attend an accredited college or university as a graduate student. Applicants must submit a statement describing their current level of involvement in the Japanese American community or Asian Pacific community and how they will continue their involvement in future years. Selection is based on academic record, extracurricular activities, financial need, and community involvement.

Financial data The stipend depends on the availability of funds but usually ranges from $1,000 to $5,000.

Duration 1 year; nonrenewable.

Additional information Applications must be submitted to the JACL National Scholarship Program, c/o San Diego JACL Chapter, 1031 25th Street, San Diego, CA 92102.

Number awarded At least 1 each year.

Deadline March of each year.

[598]
RALPH W. SHRADER DIVERSITY SCHOLARSHIPS

Armed Forces Communications and Electronics
   Association
Attn: AFCEA Educational Foundation
4400 Fair Lakes Court
Fairfax, VA 22033-3899
(703) 631-6149   Toll-free: (800) 336-4583, ext. 6149
Fax: (703) 631-4693   E-mail: scholarship@afcea.org
Web: www.afcea.org

Purpose To provide financial assistance to master's degree students in fields related to communications and electronics.

Eligibility This program is open to students working on a master's degree who are U.S. citizens attending an accredited college or university in the United States. Applicants must be enrolled full time and studying electronics, engineering (aerospace, chemical, electrical, computer, communications, or systems), physics, communications technology, mathematics, computer science or technology, or information management systems. At least 1 of these scholarships is set aside for a woman or a minority.

Financial data The stipend is $3,000. Funds are paid directly to the recipient.

Duration 1 year.

Number awarded 5 each year, at least 1 of which is for a woman or minority candidate.

Deadline January of each year.

[599]
RDW GROUP, INC. MINORITY SCHOLARSHIP FOR COMMUNICATIONS

Rhode Island Foundation
Attn: Scholarship Coordinator
One Union Station
Providence, RI 02903
(401) 274-4564   Fax: (401) 751-7983
E-mail: libbym@rifoundation.org
Web: www.rifoundation.org

Purpose To provide financial assistance to Rhode Island students of color interested in preparing for a career in communications.

Eligibility This program is open to minority undergraduate and graduate students who are Rhode Island residents. Applicants must intend to major in communications (including computer graphics, art, cinematography, or other fields that would prepare them for a career in advertising). They must be able to demonstrate financial need and a commitment to a career in communications. Along with their application, they must submit an essay (up to 300 words) on the impact they would like to have on the communications field.

Financial data The stipend is $2,000.

Duration 1 year; nonrenewable.

Additional information This program is sponsored by the RDW Group, Inc.

Number awarded 1 each year.

Deadline April of each year.

[600]
RESEARCH AND TRAINING FELLOWSHIPS IN EPILEPSY FOR CLINICIANS

Epilepsy Foundation
Attn: Research Department
4351 Garden City Drive
Landover, MD 20785-7223
(301) 459-3700   Toll-free: (800) EFA-1000
Fax: (301) 577-2684   TDD: (800) 332-2070
E-mail: clinical_postdocs@efa.org
Web: www.epilepsyfoundation.org

Purpose To provide funding to minority and other clinically trained professionals interested in gaining additional training in order to develop an epilepsy research program.

Eligibility Applicants must have an M.D., D.O., Ph.D., D.S., or equivalent degree and be a clinical or postdoctoral fellow at a university, medical school, or other appropriate research institution. Holders of other doctoral-level degrees (e.g., Pharm.D., D.S.N.) may also be eligible. Candidates must be interested in a program of research training that may include mechanisms of epilepsy, novel therapeutic approaches, clinical trials, development of new technologies, or behavioral and psychosocial impact of epilepsy. The training program may consist of both didactic training and a supervised research experience that is designed to develop the necessary knowledge and skills in the chosen area of research and foster the career goals of the candidate. Academic faculty holding the rank of instructor or higher are not eligible, nor are graduate or medical students, medical residents, permanent government employees, or employees of private industry. Applications from women, members of minority groups, and people with disabilities are especially encouraged. Selection is based on the quality of the proposed research training program, the applicant's qualifications, the preceptor's qualifications, and the adequacy of clinical training, research facilities, and other epilepsy-related programs at the institution.

Financial data The grant is $40,000. No indirect costs are provided.

Duration 1 year.

Additional information Support for this program is provided by many individuals, families, and corporations, especially the American Epilepsy Society, Abbott Laboratories, Ortho-McNeil Pharmaceutical, and Pfizer Inc. Grantees are expected to spend at least 50% of their time dedicated to research training and conducting research.

Number awarded Varies each year; recently, 5 of these fellowships were awarded.

Deadline October of each year.

[601]
REVEREND H. JOHN YAMASHITA MEMORIAL SCHOLARSHIP

Japanese American Citizens League
Attn: National Scholarship Awards
1765 Sutter Street
San Francisco, CA 94115
(415) 921-5225   Fax: (415) 931-4671
E-mail: jacl@jacl.org
Web: www.jacl.org/scholarships.html

Purpose To provide financial assistance for graduate study to members of the Japanese American Citizens League (JACL).

Eligibility This program is open to JACL members who are attending or planning to attend an accredited college or university as a graduate student. Applicants must submit a statement describing their current level of involvement in the Japanese American community or Asian Pacific community and how they will continue their involvement in future years. Selection is based on academic record, extracurricular activities, financial need, and community involvement.

Financial data The stipend depends on the availability of funds but usually ranges from $1,000 to $5,000.

Duration 1 year; nonrenewable.

Additional information Applications must be submitted to the JACL National Scholarship Program, c/o San Diego JACL Chapter, 1031 25th Street, San Diego, CA 92102.

Number awarded At least 1 each year.

Deadline March of each year.

[602]
RICHARD AND HELEN BROWN COREM SCHOLARSHIPS

United Church of Christ
Parish Life and Leadership Ministry Team
Attn: Minister for Grants, Scholarships, and Resources
700 Prospect Avenue East
Cleveland, OH 44115-1100
(216) 736-3839   Fax: (216) 736-3783
E-mail: jeffersv@ucc.org
Web: www.ucc.org/education/scholarships

Purpose To provide financial assistance to minority seminary students who are interested in becoming a pastor in the United Church of Christ (UCC).

Eligibility This program is open to students at accredited seminaries who have been members of a UCC congregation for at least 1 year. Applicants must work through 1 of the member bodies of the Council for Racial and Ethnic Ministries (COREM): United Black Christians (UBC), Council of Hispanic Ministries (CHM), Pacific Islander and Asian American Ministries (PAAM), or Council for American Indian Ministries (CAIM). They must 1) have a GPA of 3.0 or higher, 2) be enrolled in a course of study leading to ordained ministry, 3) be in care of an association or conference at the time of application, and 4) demonstrate leadership ability through participation in their local church, association, conference, or academic environment.

Financial data Stipends are approximately $10,000 per year.

Duration 1 year.

Additional information Information on the UBC is available from the Minister for African American Relations, (216) 736-2189. Information on the CHM is available from the Minister for Hispanic Relations, (216) 736-2193. Information on the PAAM is available from the Minister for Pacific Islander and Asian American Relations, (216) 736-2195. Information on the CAIM is available from the Minister for Native American Relations, (216) 736-2194.

Number awarded Varies each year; recently, 5 scholarships were awarded by UBC, 5 by CHM, 3 by PAAM, and 1 by CAIM.

[603]
RICHARD D. HAILEY LAW STUDENT SCHOLARSHIPS

Association of Trial Lawyers of America
Attn: Minority Caucus
1050 31st Street, N.W.
Washington, DC 20007
(202) 944-2827   Toll-free: (800) 424-2725
Fax: (202) 298-6849   E-mail: info@astlahq.org
Web: www.atla.org/members/lawstud/Hailey.aspx

Purpose To provide financial assistance for law school to minority student members of the Association of Trial Lawyers of America (ATLA).

Eligibility This program is open to African American, Hispanic, Asian American, Native American, and biracial members of the association who are enrolled in the first or second year of law school. Selection is based on commitment to the association, involvement in student chapter activities, desire to represent victims, interest and proficiency of skills in trial advocacy, and financial need. Applicants must submit a 500-word essay on how they meet those criteria and 3 letters of recommendation.

Financial data The stipend is $1,000.

Duration 1 year.

Number awarded Up to 6 each year.

Deadline May of each year.

[604]
RISK AND DEVELOPMENT FIELD RESEARCH GRANTS

Social Science Research Council
Attn: Program in Applied Economics
810 Seventh Avenue
New York, NY 10019
(212) 377-2700   Fax: (212) 377-2727
E-mail: pae@ssrc.org
Web: www.ssrc.org/pae

Purpose To provide funding to minority and other doctoral students and postdoctoral scholars interested in conducting research on risk and uncertainty in economics.

Eligibility This program is open to 1) full-time graduate students enrolled in economics and related Ph.D. programs (e.g., development studies or agricultural economics) at U.S. universities; and 2) scholars who have completed a Ph.D. in economics and related fields within the past 5 years and have a current position at a U.S. academic or nonprofit research institution. There are no citizenship, nationality, or (for graduate students) residency requirements. Applicants must be interested in conducting field research into questions of risk and uncertainty in the context of developing economies. Preference is given to proposals that include interdisciplinary and novel approaches, with an aim to create a better understanding of the way that individuals, institutions, and policymakers perceive and respond to situations of risk and uncertainty. Minorities and women are particularly encouraged to apply.

Financial data The stipend is $5,000 for graduate students or $15,000 for postdoctoral scholars. Funds must be used for field research, not general support or dissertation write-up.

Duration 1 year.

Additional information This program, established in 1997 as the Program in Applied Economics, is administered by the Social Science Research Council with funds provided by the John D. and Catherine T. MacArthur Foundation.

Number awarded Varies each year; recently, 17 graduate student and 4 postdoctoral fellowships were awarded.

Deadline January of each year.

[605]
ROBERT TOIGO FOUNDATION FELLOWSHIPS

Robert Toigo Foundation
Attn: Fellowship Program Administrator
1230 Preservation Park Way
Oakland, CA 94612
(510) 763-5771   Fax: (510) 763-5778
E-mail: info@toigofoundation.org
Web: www.toigofoundation.org

Purpose To provide financial assistance to minority students working on a master's degree in business administration or related field.

Eligibility This program is open to members of minority groups (of African American, Hispanic, Native American/Alaskan Native, or Asian/Pacific Islander descent) who have been accepted to an M.B.A. program as a full-time student. Applicants must be preparing for a career in finance, including (but not limited to) investment management, investment banking, corporate finance, real estate, private equity, venture capital, sales and trading, research, or financial services consulting.

Financial data The stipend is $5,000 per year.

Duration 2 years.

Number awarded Approximately 50 each year.

Deadline February of each year.

[606]
RYU FAMILY FOUNDATION SCHOLARSHIP GRANTS

Ryu Family Foundation, Inc.
901 Murray Road
East Hanover, NJ 07936
(973) 560-9696   Fax: (973) 560-0661

Purpose To provide financial assistance to Korean and Korean American undergraduate and graduate students in the Northeast.

Eligibility To qualify for this assistance, applicants must be Korean American (U.S. citizen) or Korean (permanent resident status); be enrolled full time and working on an undergraduate or graduate degree; have a GPA of 3.5 or higher; be able to document financial need; and be either residing or attending college in 1 of the following 10 northeastern states: Connecticut, Delaware, Maine, Massachusetts, New Hampshire, New Jersey, New York, Pennsylvania, Rhode Island, or Vermont. All applicants must submit a 500-word essay on a subject that changes annually.

Financial data A stipend is awarded (amount not specified). Checks are made out jointly to the recipient and the recipient's school.

Duration 1 year; may be renewed for 1 additional year.

Additional information Recipients who reside in the designated northeastern states may attend school in any state.

Deadline November of each year.

[607]
SABBATICALS FOR LONG-TIME ACTIVISTS OF COLOR

Alston/Bannerman Fellowship Program
1627 Lancaster Street
Baltimore, MD 21231
(410) 327-6220   Fax: (501) 421-5862
E-mail: info@AlstonBannerman.org
Web: www.AlstonBannerman.org

Purpose To finance a sabbatical for people of color who have been community activists for at least 10 years.

Eligibility This program is open to persons of color (people of African, Latino, Asian, Pacific Islander, Native American, or Arab descent) who are U.S. residents and have at least 10 years of experience as community activists. Applicants must be committed to continuing to work for social change. Preference is given to applicants whose work attacks root causes of injustice by organizing those affected to take collective action; challenges the systems that perpetrate injustice and effects institutional change; builds their community's capacity for self-determination and develops grassroots leadership; acknowledges the cultural values of the community; creates accountable participatory structures in which community members have decision-making power; and contributes to building a movement for social change by making connections between issues, developing alliances with other constituencies, and collaborating with other organizations. Individuals are ineligible if they only provide services (such as substance abuse counseling, after-school programs, HIV-AIDS outreach, or shelter for the homeless) or if they advocate on behalf of a community without directly involving the members of that community in asserting their own interests and choosing their own leadership. An equal number of men and women are selected.

Financial data The stipend is $15,000.

Duration The sabbaticals are to be 3 months or longer.

Additional information Fellows are encouraged to use their sabbaticals to engage in activities that are substantially different from their normal routine. Activities during the sabbatical must strengthen the recipient's ability to contribute to social change in the future. This program was established in 1987 as the Bannerman Fellowship Program. Its name was changed in 2002. Sabbaticals must be taken within 1 year of receipt of the award. Fellows must submit a report on their sabbatical.

Number awarded At least 10 each year. Since 1988, more than 140 fellowships have been awarded.

Deadline November of each year.

[608]
SAJA SCHOLARSHIPS

South Asian Journalists Association
c/o Sreenath Sreenivasan
Columbia Graduate School of Journalism
2950 Broadway
New York, NY 10027
(212) 854-5979   Fax: (212) 854-7837
E-mail: ss221@Columbia.edu
Web: www.saja.org/scholarships.html

Purpose To provide financial assistance for undergraduate and graduate study to journalism students of south Asian descent.

Eligibility This program is open to students of south Asian descent (including Bangladesh, Bhutan, India, Maldives, Nepal, Pakistan, and Sri Lanka; Indo-Caribbeans are also eligible). Applicants must be serious about preparing for a journalism career and must provide evidence they plan to do so through courses, internships, or freelancing. They may be 1) high school seniors about to enroll in an accredited college or university; 2) current students in an accredited college or university in the United States or Canada; or 3) students enrolled or about to enter a graduate program in the United States or Canada. Applicants with financial hardship are given special consideration. Selection is based on interest in journalism, writing skills, participation and enthusiasm in the sponsoring organization, reasons for entering journalism, and financial need.

Financial data The stipends are $1,000 for high school seniors and current college students or $1,500 for graduate students.

Duration 1 year.

Additional information Recipients are expected to give back to the South Asian Journalists Association (SAJA) by volunteering at the annual convention or at other events during the year.

Number awarded 3 each year: 1 to a high school senior entering college, 1 to a current college student, and 2 to graduate students.

Deadline February of each year.

[609]
SAN FRANCISCO BAY AREA CHAPTER OF AAJA SCHOLARSHIPS

Asian American Journalists Association-San Francisco Bay Area Chapter
c/o Nerissa Pacio, Scholarship Co-Chair
San Jose Mercury News
750 Ridder Park Drive
San Jose, CA 95190
(408) 920-5827   Fax: (408) 271-3786
E-mail: aaja@aajasf.org
Web: www.aajasf.org

Purpose To provide financial assistance to Asian American students in the San Francisco Bay area who are interested in careers in broadcast or print journalism.

Eligibility These scholarships are open to Asian American students who either attend school in the San Francisco Bay area or reside in northern California and attend school elsewhere. Applicants may be high school seniors entering college in the following fall, undergraduates, or graduate students. Students do not need to be majoring in journalism, radio/television, photojournalism, or mass communications, but they must demonstrate serious intent to prepare for a career in journalism. Selection is based on scholastic achievement, commitment to journalism, sensitivity to Asian American issues as demonstrated by community involvement, journalistic ability, and financial need.

Financial data Stipends range from $500 to $2,500.

Duration 1 year; may be renewed.

Number awarded Varies each year. Recently, 9 of these scholarships were awarded: 1 at $2,500 (the Ken Wong Memorial Award), 3 at $2,000 (AAJA ChevronTexaco Awards), 2 at $1,500 (AAJA Shamrock Awards), and 3 at $500.

Deadline April of each year.

[610]
SCCLA SCHOLARSHIPS AND FELLOWSHIPS

Southern California Chinese Lawyers Association
Attn: Scholarship Fund
P.O. Box 861959
Los Angeles, CA 90086-1959
Web: www.sccla.org/aboutsccla.htm

Purpose To provide financial assistance and work experience to Asian Pacific American law students in southern California.

Eligibility This program is open to Asian Pacific American students at law schools in southern California. Applicants for scholarships may be in any year of law school, including entering first-year students and fourth-year evening students. Applicants for fellowships may be in any year, but they must also be interested in serving a clerkship at the Asian Pacific American Legal Center in Los Angeles for 10 to 15 hours per semester. Selection is based on academic accomplishment, financial need, and potential contribution to the Chinese American community.

Financial data The stipend is $1,500 for fellowships or $1,000 for scholarships.

Duration 1 year.

Additional information This program includes the following named scholarships: the Ming Y. Moy Memorial Scholarship, the Justice Elwood Lui Scholarship, the Lee Gum Low Presidential Scholarship, and the Margaret and Ned Good Scholarships. Information is also available from Philip H. Lam, Deputy City Attorney, Intellectual Property Counsel, 111 North Hope Street, Suite 340, Los Angeles, CA 90012, (213) 367-4520, Fax: (213) 367-4588, E-mail: Philip.lam@ladwp.com, and from Will Niu, Warmuth & Niu, LLP, 400 South Atlantic Boulevard, Suite 203, Monterey Park, CA 91754, (626) 282-6868.

Number awarded Varies each year; recently, 15 of these scholarships and fellowships were awarded.

Deadline February of each year.

[611]
SELECTED PROFESSIONS FELLOWSHIPS FOR WOMEN OF COLOR

American Association of University Women
Attn: AAUW Educational Foundation
301 ACT Drive, Department 177
P.O. Box 4030
Iowa City, IA 52243-4030
(319) 337-1716   Fax: (319) 337-1204
E-mail: aauw@act.org
Web: www.aauw.org

Purpose To aid women of color who are in their final year of graduate training in the fields of business administration, law, or medicine.

Eligibility This program is open to women of color who are entering their final year of graduate study in these historically underrepresented fields: business administration (M.B.A., E.M.B.A.), law (J.D.), and medicine (M.D., D.O.). Women in medical programs may apply for either their third or final year of study. U.S. citizenship or permanent resident status is required. Special consideration is given to applicants who demonstrate professional promise in innovative or neglected areas of research and/or practice in public interest concerns.

Financial data Stipends range from $5,000 to $12,000 for the academic year.

Duration 1 academic year, beginning in September.

Deadline January of each year.

[612]
SHEILA SUEN LAI SCHOLARSHIP OF LIBRARY AND INFORMATION SCIENCE

Chinese American Librarians Association
c/o Sha Li Zhang, Scholarship Committee Chair
University of North Carolina at Greensboro
Jackson Library
P.O. Box 26170
Greensboro, NC 27402-6170
(336) 334-4705   Fax: (336) 334-5399
E-mail: slzhang@uncg.edu
Web: www.cala-web.org

Purpose To provide financial assistance to Chinese American students interested in working on a graduate degree in library or information science.

Eligibility This program is open to students enrolled full time in an accredited library school and working on a master's or doctoral degree. Applicants must be of Chinese nationality or Chinese descent. They must submit verification of admission to an accredited graduate program as a full-time student and/or proof of current full-time enrollment status, curriculum vitae, personal statement, official transcript, and 3 letters of recommendation.

Financial data The stipend is $500.

Duration 1 year.

Additional information The program was established in 1989. The donor of the scholarship, Ms. Sheila Lai, is the Executive Director of the Chinese American Librarians Association and a reference librarian at California State University at Sacramento.

Number awarded 1 each year.

Deadline April of each year.

[613]
SHO SATO MEMORIAL SCHOLARSHIP

Japanese American Citizens League
Attn: National Scholarship Awards
1765 Sutter Street
San Francisco, CA 94115
(415) 921-5225   Fax: (415) 931-4671
E-mail: jacl@jacl.org
Web: www.jacl.org/scholarships.html

Purpose To provide financial assistance to student members of the Japanese American Citizens League (JACL) who are interested in preparing for a career in law.

Eligibility This program is open to JACL members who are currently enrolled or planning to enroll in an accredited law school. Applicants must submit a statement describing their present level of involvement in the Japanese American Community or Asian Pacific community and how they will continue their involvement in future years. Selection is based on academic record, extracurricular activities, financial need, and community involvement.

Financial data The stipend depends on the availability of funds but usually ranges from $1,000 to $5,000.

Duration 1 year; nonrenewable.

Additional information Applications must be submitted to the JACL National Scholarship Program, c/o San Diego JACL Chapter, 1031 25th Street, San Diego, CA 92102.

Number awarded 1 each year.

Deadline March of each year.

[614]
S.I. NEWHOUSE FOUNDATION SCHOLARSHIPS

Asian American Journalists Association
Attn: Student Programs Coordinator
1182 Market Street, Suite 320
San Francisco, CA 94102
(415) 346-2051, ext. 102   Fax: (415) 346-6343
E-mail: brandons@aaja.org
Web: www.aaja.org

Purpose To provide financial assistance and summer work experience in print journalism to members of the Asian American Journalists Association (AAJA) who are undergraduate or graduate students.

Eligibility This program is open to all students but especially welcomes applications from historically underrepresented Asian Pacific American groups, including southeast Asians (Vietnamese, Cambodians, and Hmong), south Asians, and Pacific Islanders. Applicants may be graduating high school seniors who declare journalism as a major or undergraduate or graduate students working on a degree in journalism and a career in print journalism. AAJA membership is required. Along with their application, they must submit a 500-word essay on their involvement or interest in the Asian American community and how, if they are awarded this scholarship, they would contribute to the field of journalism and/or media issues involving the Asian American and Pacific Islander community. Selection is based on scholastic ability, commitment to journalism, sensitivity to Asian American and Pacific Islander issues as demonstrated by community involvement, journalistic ability, and financial need.

Financial data Stipends range from $1,000 to $5,000.

Duration 4 years for a graduating high school senior; 1 year for current undergraduate or graduate students.

Additional information This program began in 1994; it is funded by Newhouse News Service and administered by AAJA. Recipients are also eligible for summer internships with a Newhouse publication.

Number awarded Varies each year; recently, 7 of these scholarships (2 at $5,000, 3 at $4,000, 1 at $2,000, and 1 at $1,000) were awarded.

Deadline April of each year.

[615]
SIDNEY B. WILLIAMS, JR. INTELLECTUAL PROPERTY LAW SCHOOL SCHOLARSHIPS

American Intellectual Property Law Association
Attn: American Intellectual Property Law Education
  Foundation
485 Kinderkamack Road
Oradell, NY 07649
(201) 634-1870   Fax: (201) 634-1871
E-mail: admin@aiplef.org
Web: www.aiplef.org/scholarships/sidney_b_williams

Purpose To provide financial assistance to minority law school students who are interested in preparing for a career in intellectual property law.

Eligibility This program is open to members of minority groups currently enrolled in or accepted to an ABA-accredited law school. Applicants must be U.S. citizens with a demonstrated intent to engage in the full-time practice of intellectual property law. Along with their application, they

must submit a 250-word essay on how this scholarship will make a difference to them in meeting their goal of engaging in the full-time practice of intellectual property law and why they intend to do so. Selection is based on 1) demonstrated commitment to developing a career in intellectual property law; 2) academic performance at the undergraduate, graduate, and law school levels (as applicable); 3) general factors, such as leadership skills, community activities, or special accomplishments; and 4) financial need.

Financial data The stipend is $10,000 per year. Funds may be used for tuition, fees, books, supplies, room, board, and a patent bar review course.

Duration 1 year; may be renewed if the recipient maintains a GPA of 2.0 or higher.

Additional information This program, which began in 2002, is administered by the Thurgood Marshall Scholarship Fund, 90 William Street, Suite 1203, New York, NY 10038, (212) 573-8888, Fax: (212) 573-8497, E-mail: pallen@tmsf.org Additional funding is provided by the American Intellectual Property Law Association, the American Bar Association's Section of Intellectual Property Law, and the Minority Corporate Counsel Association. The first class of recipients included a Chinese American, an Asian Pacific American, Mexican Americans, and African Americans. Recipients are required to join and maintain membership in the American Intellectual Property Law Association.

Number awarded Varies each year; recently, 9 of these scholarships were awarded.

Deadline February of each year.

[616]
SLA AFFIRMATIVE ACTION SCHOLARSHIP

Special Libraries Association
Attn: Scholarships
331 South Patrick Street
Alexandria, VA 22314-3501
(703) 647-4900   Fax: (703) 647-4901
E-mail: sla@sla.org
Web: www.sla.org

Purpose To provide financial assistance to minority group members who are interested in preparing for a career in the fields of library or information science in the United States or Canada.

Eligibility To be eligible, applicants must be U.S. citizens or permanent residents; members of a racial minority group (Black, Hispanic, Asian, Pacific Islander, American Indian, or Alaskan Native); enrolled or accepted for enrollment in a recognized school of library or information science; and in financial need. Preference is given to members of the Special Libraries Association and to persons who have worked in and for special libraries.

Financial data The stipend is $6,000.

Duration 3 quarters or 2 semesters.

Number awarded 1 each year.

Deadline October of each year.

[617]
SOUTH ASIAN BAR ASSOCIATION OF SOUTHERN CALIFORNIA SCHOLARSHIPS

South Asian Bar Association of Southern California
c/o Nimish P. Patel, Executive Director
Richardson & Patel LLP
10900 Wilshire Boulevard, Suite 500
Los Angeles, CA 90024
(310) 208-1182   Fax: (310) 208-1154
E-mail: npatel@richardsonpatel.com
Web: www.sabasc.org

Purpose To provide financial assistance for law school to southern Californian members of the South Asian Bar Association (SABA).

Eligibility This program is open to law students who are current members of the SABA, of south Asian ancestry, and legal residents of southern California. Applicants must be enrolled or planning to enroll in law school. Selection is based on commitment and devotion to public interest and activism and service within the south Asian community and/or the larger southern California community.

Financial data The stipend is $500.

Duration 1 year.

Number awarded 2 each year.

Deadline March of each year.

[618]
SOUTHEAST EUROPEAN LANGUAGE TRAINING GRANTS FOR INDIVIDUALS

American Council of Learned Societies
Attn: Office of Fellowships and Grants
633 Third Avenue, 8C
New York, NY 10017-6795
(212) 697-1505   Fax: (212) 949-8058
E-mail: grants@acls.org
Web: www.acls.org/eeguide.htm

Purpose To provide financial support to graduate students and others (particularly minorities and women) interested in studying southeastern European languages during the summer.

Eligibility Applicants must have completed at least a 4-year college degree. They must be interested in a program of training, primarily in intensive courses offered by institutions of higher education in the United States, in the languages of southeastern Europe, including Albanian, Bosnian-Croatian-Serbian, Bulgarian, Macedonian, or Romanian. The language course may be at the beginning, intermediate, or advanced level. The awards are intended for people who will use those languages in academic research or teaching. Preference is given to applicants who 1) cannot study their chosen language at their home institution, 2) will be continuing the study of that language in the following year, and 3) have been or are beginning language study early in their academic career. Applications are particularly encouraged from women and members of minority groups.

Financial data Grants up to $2,000 are available.

Duration Summer months.

Additional information This program, reinstituted in 2002, is supported by the U.S. Department of State under the Research and Training for Eastern Europe and the Independent States of the Former Soviet Union Act of 1983 (Title VIII).

Number awarded Approximately 10 each year.

Deadline January of each year.

[619]
SOUTHERN REGION KOREAN AMERICAN SCHOLARSHIPS

Korean American Scholarship Foundation
Southern Region
c/o Dr. Sam Sook Chung, Scholarship Committee Chair
2989 Preston Drive
Rex, GA 30273
(770) 968-6768   E-mail: southern@kasf.org
Web: www.kasf.org

Purpose To provide financial assistance to Korean American undergraduate and graduate students who attend school in the southern states.

Eligibility This program is open to Korean American students who are currently enrolled in a college or university in the southern states as full-time undergraduate or graduate students. Applicants may reside anywhere in the United States as long as they attend school in the southern region: Alabama, Arkansas, Florida, Georgia, Louisiana, Mississippi, Oklahoma, South Carolina, Tennessee, and Texas. Selection is based on academic achievement, school activities, community service, and financial need.

Financial data Stipends range from $1,000 to $2,000.

Duration 1 year; renewable.

Number awarded Varies each year. Recently, 39 of these scholarships, worth $42,700, were awarded.

Deadline June of each year.

[620]
SPECTRUM INITIATIVE SCHOLARSHIPS

American Library Association
Attn: Office for Diversity
50 East Huron Street
Chicago, IL 60611-2795
(312) 280-4276   Toll-free: (800) 545-2433, ext. 4276
Fax: (312) 280-3256   TDD: (312) 944-7298
TDD: (888) 814-7692   E-mail: diversity@ala.org
Web: www.ala.org

Purpose To provide financial assistance to minority students interested in working on a degree in librarianship.

Eligibility This program is open to ethnic minority students (African American or Black, Asian, Native Hawaiian or Pacific Islander, Latino or Hispanic, and American Indian or Alaska Native). Applicants must be U.S. or Canadian citizens or permanent residents who are planning to attend an accredited school of library science. Selection is based on academic leadership, outstanding service, commitment to a career in librarianship, statements indicating the nature of the applicant's library and other work experience, letters of reference, and personal presentation.

Financial data The stipend is $5,000 per year.

Duration 1 year; nonrenewable.

Additional information This program began in 1998. It is administered by a joint committee of the American Library Association (ALA). Funding is provided by outside contributions and returns from the ALA Future Fund and the Giles and Leo Albert Funds.

Number awarded 50 each year.

Deadline   February of each year.

[621]
SREB DOCTORAL SCHOLARS PROGRAM

Southern Regional Education Board
592 10th Street N.W.
Atlanta, GA 30318-5790
(404) 875-9211, ext. 273   Fax: (404) 872-1477
E-mail: doctoral.scholars@sreb.org
Web: www.sreb.org/programs/dsp/dspindex.asp

Purpose   To provide financial assistance to minority students who wish to work on a doctoral degree in the sciences at designated universities in the southern states.

Eligibility   This program is open to U.S. citizens who are members of racial/ethnic minority groups (Native Americans, Hispanic Americans, Asian Americans, and African Americans) and hold or will receive a bachelor's degree from an accredited college or university. Applicants must intend to work on a Ph.D. in science, mathematics, engineering, or science or mathematics education at a participating institution. They must indicate an interest in becoming a college professor at an institution in the South. Students who are already enrolled in a doctoral program are not eligible. Study for professional degrees, such as the M.D., D.D.S., J.D., or D.V.M., as well as graduate study in education leading to an Ed.D., does not qualify.

Financial data   Scholars receive waiver of tuition and fees (in or out of state) for up to 5 years, an annual stipend of $15,000 for 3 years, an annual allowance for professional development activities, and reimbursement of travel expenses to attend the Doctoral Scholars annual meeting.

Duration   Up to 5 years.

Number awarded   Varies each year; recently, the program was supporting 208 scholars at 54 institutions in 22 states.

Deadline   March of each year.

[622]
STAN BECK FELLOWSHIP

Entomological Society of America
Attn: Entomological Foundation
9332 Annapolis Road, Suite 210
Lanham, MD 20706-3150
(301) 459-9082   Fax: (301) 459-9084
E-mail: melodie@entfdn.org
Web: www.entfdn.org/beck.html

Purpose   To assist "needy" students working on an undergraduate or graduate degree in science who are nominated by members of the Entomological Society of America (ESA).

Eligibility   This program is open to students working on an undergraduate or graduate degree in entomology at a college or university in Canada, Mexico, or the United States. Candidates must be nominated by members of the society. They must be "needy" students; for the purposes of this program, need may be based on physical limitations, or economic, minority, or environmental conditions.

Financial data   The stipend is $2,000 per year.

Duration   1 year; may be renewed up to 3 additional years.

Additional information   Recipients are expected to be present at the society's annual meeting, where the award will be presented.

Number awarded   1 or more each year.

Deadline   June of each year.

[623]
SUBSTANCE ABUSE RESEARCH FELLOWSHIPS

American Psychological Association
Attn: Minority Fellowship Program
750 First Street, N.E.
Washington, DC 20002-4242
(202) 336-6127   Fax: (202) 336-6012
TDD: (202) 336-6123   E-mail: mfp@apa.org
Web: www.apa.org/mfp/sarprogram.html

Purpose   To provide financial assistance to psychology doctoral students (especially minorities) who are preparing for a career involving research on substance abuse issues and ethnic minority populations.

Eligibility   This program is open to full-time doctoral students who can demonstrate a strong commitment to a career in substance abuse research and the mental health or psychological well-being of ethnic minorities. Students from all psychology disciplines are encouraged to apply if their training and research interests are related to mental health and substance abuse. Clinical, counseling, and school psychology students may be eligible if they intend to specialize in substance abuse treatment and research. Members of minority groups (African Americans, Alaskan Natives, American Indians, Asian Americans, Hispanics/Latinos, Native Hawaiians, and Pacific Islanders) are especially encouraged to apply. U.S. citizenship or permanent resident status is required. Selection is based on commitment to a career in research that focuses on substance abuse in ethnic minority communities, knowledge of ethnic minority psychology or mental health issues, the fit between career goals and training environment selected, potential for a research career demonstrated through accomplishments and goals, scholarship and grades, and letters of recommendation.

Financial data   The stipend is the amount established by the National Institutes of Health for predoctoral students, currently $20,772 per year.

Duration   1 year; may be renewed for up to 2 additional years.

Additional information   Funding is provided by the U.S. National Institute of Mental Health. Students who receive a federally-funded grant from another source may not also accept funds from this program.

Number awarded   Varies each year.

Deadline   January of each year.

[624]
SYNOD OF LAKES AND PRAIRIES RACIAL ETHNIC SCHOLARSHIPS

Synod of Lakes and Prairies
Attn: Committee on Racial Ethnic Ministry
8012 Cedar Avenue, South
Bloomington, MN 55425-1210
(952) 854-0144   Fax: (952) 854-6690
E-mail: office@lakesandprairies.org
Web: www.lakesandprairies.org

Purpose To provide financial assistance to minority residents of the Presbyterian Church (USA) Synod of Lakes and Prairies who are studying for the ministry.

Eligibility This program is open to members of Presbyterian churches within the Synod of Lakes and Prairies (Iowa, Minnesota, Nebraska, North Dakota, South Dakota, and Wisconsin). Applicants must be members of ethnic minority groups studying for the ministry.

Financial data Stipends range from $850 to $3,500.

Duration 1 year.

Number awarded Varies each year; recently, 9 of these scholarships were awarded.

Deadline September of each year.

[625]
SYNOD OF THE COVENANT ETHNIC THEOLOGICAL SCHOLARSHIPS

Synod of the Covenant
Attn: CECA Ethnic Scholarship Committee
1911 Indianwood Circle, Suite B
Maumee, OH 43537-4063
(419) 754-4050
Toll-free: (800) 848-1030 (within MI and OH)
Web: www.synodofthecovenant.org

Purpose To provide financial assistance to ethnic students working on a degree at an approved Presbyterian theological institution (with priority given to Presbyterian applicants from Ohio and Michigan).

Eligibility This program is open to ethnic individuals enrolled in church vocations at approved Presbyterian theological institutions. Priority is given to Presbyterian applicants from the states of Michigan and Ohio. Financial need is considered in the selection process.

Financial data Students may be awarded a maximum of $1,500 on initial application. They may receive up to $2,000 on subsequent applications with evidence of continuing progress. Funds are made payable to the session for distribution.

Duration Students are eligible to receive scholarships 1 time per year, up to a maximum of 5 years.

Number awarded Varies each year.

Deadline September of each year for fall semester; February of each year for spring semester.

[626]
TED SCRIPPS FELLOWSHIPS IN ENVIRONMENTAL JOURNALISM

University of Colorado at Boulder
Attn: Center for Environmental Journalism
1511 University Avenue
Campus Box 478
Boulder, CO 80309-0478
(303) 492-4114   E-mail: cej@colorado.edu
Web: www.colorado.edu/journalism/cej

Purpose To provide minority and other journalists with an opportunity to gain more knowledge about environmental issues at the University of Colorado at Boulder.

Eligibility This program is open to full-time U.S. print and broadcast journalists who have at least 5 years' professional experience and have completed an undergraduate degree. Applicants may be general assignment reporters, editors, producers, environmental reporters, or full-time freelancers. Prior experience in covering the environment is not required. Professionals in such related fields as teaching, public relations, or advertising are not eligible. Applicants must be interested in a program at the university that includes classes, weekly seminars, and field trips. They also must engage in independent study expected to lead to a significant piece of journalistic work. Applications are especially encouraged from women, ethnic minorities, disabled persons, and veterans (particularly veterans of the Vietnam era).

Financial data The program covers tuition and fees and pays a $44,000 stipend. Employers are strongly encouraged to continue benefits, including health insurance.

Duration 9 months.

Additional information This program, established in 1992 at the University of Michigan and transferred to the University of Colorado in 1997, is supported by the Scripps Howard Foundation. This is a non-degree program. Fellows must obtain a leave of absence from their regular employment and must return to their job following the fellowship.

Number awarded 5 each year.

Deadline February of each year.

[627]
TEXAS CHAPTER SCHOLARSHIPS

Asian American Journalists Association-Texas Chapter
c/o Julie Tam, Scholarship Chair
KLTV-TV ABC 7
105 West Ferguson
P.O. Box 957
Tyler, TX 75710
(903) 597-5588   Fax: (903) 510-7847
E-mail: julie@julietam.com
Web: chapters.aaja.org/Texas/schol.html

Purpose To provide financial assistance to members of the Asian American Journalists Association (AAJA) in Texas who are working on an undergraduate or graduate degree in journalism.

Eligibility This program is open to graduating high school seniors, undergraduates, and graduate students who are either Texas residents or planning to attend an accredited college or university in Texas. Applicants must be AAJA members. Along with their application, they must submit a 250-word autobiography that explains why they are interested in a career in journalism, a 500-word essay on the role of ethnic diversity in news coverage (both for the subjects of the news events and also the journalists involved), their most recent official transcript, a statement of financial need, 2 letters of recommendation, and a resume. Work samples to be submitted are 2 legible clips from print journalism students; 3 to 5 prints or slides with captions or descriptions from print photojournalism students; 2 VHS taped excerpts with corresponding scripts from television broadcast students; 2 edited VHS excepts from television photojournalism students; 3 taped cassette excerpts with corresponding scripts from radio broadcast students; or 3 legible online articles from web journalism students. Selection is based on commitment to the field of journalism, awareness of Asian American issues, journalistic ability, scholastic ability, and financial need.

Financial data The stipend is $1,000 per year.

Duration 1 year.

Number awarded 2 each year.

Deadline April of each year.

[628]
TEXAS LIBRARY ASSOCIATION SPECTRUM SCHOLARSHIP

Texas Library Association
Attn: Director of Administration
3355 Bee Cave Road, Suite 401
Austin, TX 78746-6763
(512) 328-1518   Toll-free: (800) 580-2TLA
Fax: (512) 328-8852   E-mail: tla@txla.org
Web: www.txla.org

Purpose To provide additional funding to students at schools of library and information studies in Texas who have received a Spectrum Scholarship for minorities from the American Library Association (ALA).

Eligibility This program is open to recipients of ALA Spectrum Scholarships who are enrolled in a master's degree program in library and information studies at a Texas university. Applicants must be African American, Latino or Hispanic, Asian or Pacific Islander, or Native American. They must be members of the Texas Library Association (TLA) and agree to work for 2 years in a Texas library following completion of their master's degree requirements.

Financial data The stipend is $2,000.

Duration 1 year.

Number awarded 1 or more each year.

[629]
TEXAS YOUNG LAWYERS ASSOCIATION MINORITY SCHOLARSHIP PROGRAM

Texas Young Lawyers Association
Attn: Minority Involvement Committee
1414 Colorado, Suite 400-B
P.O. Box 12487
Austin, TX 78711-2487
(512) 463-1463, ext. 6429
Toll-free: (800) 204-2222, ext. 6429
Fax: (512) 463-1503
Web: www.tyla.org

Purpose To provide financial assistance to minorities and women attending law school in Texas.

Eligibility This program is open to members of recognized minority groups, including but not limited to women, African Americans, Hispanics, Asian Americans, and Native Americans. Applicants must be attending an ABA-accredited law school in Texas. Selection is based on participation in extracurricular activities inside and outside law school and financial need.

Financial data The stipend is $1,000.

Duration 1 year.

Number awarded 1 at each accredited law school in Texas.

Deadline October of each year.

[630]
THIRD WAVE FOUNDATION WOODLAKE SCHOLARSHIPS

Third Wave Foundation
511 West 25th Street, Suite 301
New York, NY 10002
(212) 675-0700   Fax: (212) 255-6653
E-mail: info@thirdwavefoundation.org
Web: www.thirdwavefoundation.org

Purpose To provide educational assistance to undergraduate and graduate women of color who have been involved as social change activists.

Eligibility This program is open to full-time and part-time students under 30 years of age who are enrolled in, or have been accepted to, an accredited university, college, vocational/technical school, community college, or graduate school. Applicants must be women of color who place greater emphasis on social justice and the struggle for justice and equality over academic performance and who integrate social justice into all areas of their lives. They must submit 500-word essays on 1) their current social change involvement and how it relates to their educational and life goals; and 2) if they would describe themselves as a feminist and why. Graduate students and students planning to study abroad through a U.S. university program are also eligible. Selection is based on financial need and commitment to social justice work.

Financial data Stipends are $3,000 or $1,000 per year.

Duration 1 year.

Number awarded Varies each year. Recently, 8 of these scholarships were awarded: 6 at $3,000 and 2 at $1,000.

Deadline March or September of each year.

[631]
THOMAS T. HAYASHI MEMORIAL SCHOLARSHIPS

Japanese American Citizens League
Attn: National Scholarship Awards
1765 Sutter Street
San Francisco, CA 94115
(415) 921-5225   Fax: (415) 931-4671
E-mail: jacl@jacl.org
Web: www.jacl.org/scholarships.html

Purpose To provide financial assistance to student members of the Japanese American Citizens League (JACL) who are interested in preparing for a career in law.

Eligibility This program is open to JACL members who are currently enrolled or planning to enroll in an accredited law school. Applicants must submit a statement describing their current level of involvement in the Japanese American community or Asian Pacific community and how they will continue their involvement in future years. Selection is based on academic record, extracurricular activities, financial need, and community involvement. Special consideration is given to applicants who demonstrate an interest in entering the legal profession as a means of securing justice for the disadvantaged.

Financial data The stipend depends on the availability of funds but usually ranges from $1,000 to $5,000.

Duration 1 year; nonrenewable.

Additional information Applications must be submitted to the JACL National Scholarship Program, c/o San Diego JACL Chapter, 1031 25th Street, San Diego, CA 92102.

Number awarded 1 each year.

Deadline March of each year.

[632]
THZ FO FARM FUND

Hawai'i Community Foundation
Attn: Scholarship Department
1164 Bishop Street, Suite 800
Honolulu, HI 96813
(808) 537-6333   Toll-free: (888) 731-3863
Fax: (808) 521-6286
E-mail: scholarships@hcf-hawaii.org
Web: www.hawaiicommunityfoundation.org

Purpose To provide financial assistance to Hawaii residents of Chinese descent who are interested in studying gerontology on the undergraduate or graduate school level.

Eligibility This program is open to high school seniors, high school graduates, and college students in Hawaii who are of Chinese ancestry and are interested in studying gerontology as full-time undergraduate or graduate students. They must be able to demonstrate academic achievement (GPA of 2.7 or higher), good moral character, and financial need. In addition to filling out the standard application form, applicants must write a short statement indicating their reasons for attending college, their planned course of study, and their career goals.

Financial data The amounts of the awards depend on the availability of funds and the need of the recipient; recently, stipends averaged $1,500.

Duration 1 year.

Additional information Recipients may attend college in Hawaii or on the mainland.

Number awarded Varies each year; recently, 2 of these scholarships were awarded.

Deadline February of each year.

[633]
T.P. WANG SCHOLARSHIP

Chinese Professional Club of Houston
Attn: John Loh, Scholarship Committee Chair
P.O. Box 941682
Houston, TX 77094-8682
(832) 428-8832
Web: www.cpchouston.com/scholarship.htm

Purpose To provide financial assistance for college, graduate school, or other study activities to members of the Chinese Professional Club (CPC) of Houston and their families.

Eligibility This program is open to CPC members and their offspring who are interested in undergraduate, graduate, leadership, or community service development studies. Applicants for undergraduate or graduate study must submit 2 essays (1 on themselves and their aspirations, 1 on either being a Chinese American living in the United States or a person or event that has had the greatest influence on their lives); transcripts; a list of academic honors, awards, and scholarships; a list of extracurricular activities and personal initiatives; and 2 letters of recommendation. Applicants for non-academic study must submit a personal resume, 2 letters of recommendation, and an essay, of 300 to 500 words, on their aspirations and how the scholarship can help to achieve their goals.

Financial data A stipend is awarded (amount not specified). Funds must be used for payment of tuition.

Duration 1 year.

Additional information This scholarship was established in 2002.

Number awarded 1 each year.

Deadline November of each year.

[634]
TRANSPORTATION FELLOWSHIP PROGRAM

North Central Texas Council of Governments
Attn: Transportation Department
616 Six Flags Drive, Centerpoint Two
P.O. Box 5888
Arlington, TX 76005-5888
(817) 608-2325   Fax: (817) 640-7806
E-mail: lucile@dwfinfo.com
Web: www.dfwinfo.com/trans/fellowship

Purpose To provide financial assistance and work experience to ethnic minorities, women, and economically disadvantaged persons who are interested in obtaining a master's degree in Texas in preparation for a career in the field of transportation.

Eligibility This program is open to ethnic minorities (African Americans, Hispanics, American Indians, Alaskan Natives, Asians, and Pacific Islanders), women, and those who are economically disadvantaged. Only U.S. citizens or permanent residents may apply. Applicants must be interested in obtaining a master's degree at a participating university in Texas as preparation for a career in transportation. They must be pursuing a degree in an approved program of study (transportation planning, urban and regional planning, urban or spatial geography, transportation/environmental sciences, logistics, transportation or civil engineering, transportation law, transportation management, or geographic information systems). Full-time enrollment is required. Selection is based on 1) financial need; 2) interest in, and commitment to, a professional career in transportation; and 3) the applicant's ability to complete the academic and work placement responsibilities of the program.

Financial data Fellowships in the amount of $2,000 each will be awarded on a yearly basis. One-half of each award will be distributed in each of the fall and spring semesters. Funds are to be used for tuition, fees, books, and/or educational supplies.

Duration 1 year; may be renewed if the recipient maintains a GPA of 3.0 or higher.

Additional information The Federal Highway Administration, Federal Transit Administration, and the Texas Department of Transportation fund this program through the sponsor's Unified Planning Work Program for Regional Transportation Planning. Fellows are assigned to an internship in a local government in that area. Universities currently participating in the program are the University of North Texas, the University of Texas at Arlington, and the University of Texas at Dallas. Fellows are required to agree to make a good-faith effort to obtain employment in community-building fields for at least 2 consecutive years after graduation.

Deadline July of each year.

[635]
UNDERREPRESENTED MENTAL HEALTH MINORITY RESEARCH FELLOWSHIP PROGRAM

Council on Social Work Education
Attn: Minority Fellowship Program
1725 Duke Street, Suite 500
Alexandria, VA 22314-3457
(703) 683-8080, ext. 217   Fax: (703) 683-8099
E-mail: mfp@cswe.org
Web: www.cswe.org

Purpose To provide funding to racial minority members interested in preparing for a career in mental health research.

Eligibility This program is open to U.S. citizens and permanent residents who have been underrepresented in the field of social work. These include but are not limited to the following groups: American Indians/Alaskan Natives, Asian/Pacific Islanders (e.g., Chinese, East Indians, South Asians, Filipinos, Hawaiians, Japanese, Koreans, and Samoans), Blacks, and Hispanics (e.g., Mexicans/Chicanos, Puerto Ricans, Cubans, Central or South Americans). Applicants must be interested in enrolling in a doctoral-level social work program that provides strong research courses and research training in mental health. They must be interested in working on a doctoral degree as a full-time student.

Financial data Awards provide a stipend of $16,500 per year and tuition support at the rate of 100% of the first $3,000 and 60% of the remaining tuition.

Duration 1 academic year; renewable for 2 additional years if funds are available and the recipient makes satisfactory progress toward the degree objectives.

Additional information This program has been funded since 1974 by the National Institute of Mental Health of the National Institutes of Health.

Deadline February of each year.

[636]
UNITARIAN UNIVERSALIST ASSOCIATION INCENTIVE GRANTS

Unitarian Universalist Association
Attn: Office of Ministerial Credentialing
25 Beacon Street
Boston, MA 02108-2800
(617) 948-6403   Fax: (617) 742-2875
E-mail: cmay@uua.org
Web: www.uua.org

Purpose To provide financial aid to persons of color who the Unitarian Universalist Association is interested in attracting to the ministry.

Eligibility These grants are offered to persons of color who the association is particularly interested in attracting to Unitarian Universalist ministry to promote racial, cultural, or class diversity. Applicants must be in their first year of study. Decisions regarding potential recipients are made in consultation with the schools. Selection is based on merit.

Financial data A stipend is awarded (amount not specified).

Duration 1 year; nonrenewable.

Additional information In subsequent years, recipients may apply for the association's General Financial Aid Grants.

Number awarded Varies each year.

Deadline April of each year.

[637]
UNITED METHODIST SCHOLARSHIP PROGRAM

United Methodist Church
Attn: General Board of Higher Education and Ministry
Office of Loans and Scholarships
1001 19th Avenue South
P.O. Box 340007
Nashville, TN 37203-0007
(615) 340-7344   Fax: (615) 340-7367
E-mail: umscholar@gbhem.org
Web: www.gbhem.org

Purpose To provide financial assistance to undergraduate and graduate students attending schools affiliated with the United Methodist Church.

Eligibility This program is open to U.S. citizens and permanent residents who have been active, full members of a United Methodist Church for at least 1 year prior to applying; members of the A.M.E., A.M.E. Zion, and other "Methodist" denominations are not eligible. Undergraduates must have been admitted to a full-time degree program at a United Methodist-related college or university and have a GPA of 2.5 or above. Most graduate scholarships are designated for persons working on a degree in theological studies (M.Div., D.Min., Ph.D.) or higher education administration, or for older adults changing their careers. Some scholarships are designated for racial ethnic undergraduate or graduate students. Applications are available from the financial aid office of the United Methodist school the applicant attends or from the chair of their annual conference Board of Higher Education and Campus Ministry.

Financial data The funding is intended to supplement the students' own resources.

Duration 1 year; renewal policies are set by participating universities.

Number awarded Varies each year.

[638]
UNITED METHODIST WOMEN OF COLOR SCHOLARS PROGRAM

United Methodist Church
Attn: General Board of Higher Education and Ministry
Office of Loans and Scholarships
1001 19th Avenue South
P.O. Box 340007
Nashville, TN 37203-0007
(615) 340-7344 Fax: (615) 340-7367
E-mail: umscholar@gbhem.org
Web: www.gbhem.org

Purpose To provide financial assistance to Methodist women of color who are working on a doctoral degree.

Eligibility This program is open to women of color (have at least 1 parent who is African American, Hispanic, Asian, Native American, Alaska Native, or Pacific Islander) who have a M.Div. degree. Applicants must have been active, full members of a United Methodist Church for at least 3 years prior to applying. They must be enrolled full time in a degree program at the Ph.D. or Th.D. level to prepare for a career teaching at a United Methodist seminary.

Financial data The maximum stipend is $10,000.

Duration 1 year.

Number awarded Varies each year; recently, 10 of these scholarships were awarded.

Deadline January of each year.

[639]
USA FUNDS ACCESS TO EDUCATION SCHOLARSHIPS

Scholarship America
Attn: Scholarship Management Services
One Scholarship Way
P.O. Box 297
St. Peter, MN 56082
(507) 931-1682 Toll-free: (800) 537-4180
Fax: (507) 931-9168
E-mail: scholarship@usafunds.org
Web: www.usafunds.org

Purpose To provide financial assistance to undergraduate and graduate students, especially those who are members of ethnic minority groups or have physical disabilities.

Eligibility This program is open to high school seniors and graduates who plan to enroll or are already enrolled in full-time undergraduate or graduate course work at an accredited 2- or 4-year college, university, or vocational/technical school. Half-time undergraduate students are also eligible. Up to 50% of the awards are targeted at students who have a documented physical disability or are a member of an ethnic minority group, including but not limited to Native Hawaiian, Alaskan Native, Black/African American, Asian, Pacific Islander, American Indian, or Hispanic/Latino. Residents of 49 states (residents of Hawaii are eligible for a separate program), the District of Columbia, Puerto Rico, Guam, the U.S. Virgin Islands, and all U.S. territories and commonwealths are eligible. Preference is given to applicants from the following states: Arizona, Indiana, Kansas, Maryland, Mississippi, Nevada, and Wyoming.

Applicants must also be U.S. citizens or eligible noncitizens and come from a family with an annual adjusted gross income of $35,000 or less. In addition to financial need, selection is based on past academic performance and future potential, leadership and participation in school and community activities, work experience, career and educational aspirations, and goals.

Financial data The stipend is $1,500 per year for full-time undergraduate or graduate students or $750 per year for half-time undergraduate students. Funds are paid jointly to the student and the school.

Duration 1 year; may be renewed until the student receives a final degree or certificate or until the total award to a student reaches $6,000, whichever comes first. Renewal requires the recipient to maintain a GPA of 2.5 or higher.

Additional information This program, established in 2000, is sponsored by USA Funds, which serves as the education loan guarantor and administrator in the 7 states where the program gives preference.

Number awarded Varies each year; recently, a total of $2.85 million was available for this program.

Deadline March of each year.

[640]
USA FUNDS HAWAII SILVER ANNIVERSARY SCHOLARSHIPS

Scholarship America
Attn: Scholarship Management Services
One Scholarship Way
P.O. Box 297
St. Peter, MN 56082
(507) 931-1682 Toll-free: (800) 537-4180
Fax: (507) 931-9168
E-mail: scholarship@usafunds.org
Web: www.usafunds.org

Purpose To provide financial assistance to undergraduate and graduate students from Hawaii, especially those who are members of ethnic minority groups or have physical disabilities.

Eligibility This program is open to high school seniors and graduates who are residents of Hawaii planning to enroll or already enrolled in full-time undergraduate or graduate course work at an accredited 2- or 4-year college, university, or vocational/technical school. Half-time undergraduate students are also eligible. Up to 50% of the awards are targeted at students who have a documented physical disability or are a member of an ethnic minority group, including but not limited to Native Hawaiian, Alaskan Native, Black/African American, Asian, Pacific Islander, American Indian, or Hispanic/Latino. Applicants must also be U.S. citizens or eligible noncitizens and come from a family with an annual adjusted gross income of $50,000 or less. In addition to financial need, selection is based on past academic performance and future potential, leadership and participation in school and community activities, work experience, career and educational aspirations, and goals.

Financial data The stipend is $1,500 per year for full-time undergraduate or graduate students or $750 per year for half-time undergraduate students. Funds are paid jointly to the student and the school.

Duration 1 year; may be renewed until the student receives a final degree or certificate or until the total award to a student reaches $6,000, whichever comes first. Renewal requires the recipient to maintain a GPA of 2.5 or higher.

Additional information This program, first offered in 2004, is sponsored by SMS Hawaii, the USA Funds affiliate that serves as the education loan guarantor and administrator in Hawaii and 7 other states. Information is also available from SMS Hawaii, 1314 South King Street, Suite 861, Honolulu, HI 96814, (808) 593-2262, (866) 497-USAF, ext. 7573, Fax: (808) 593-8268, E-mail: lteniya@usafunds.org.

Number awarded Varies each year; recently, a total of $300,000 was available for this program.

Deadline March of each year.

[641]
VAMA SCHOLARSHIP PROGRAM

Vietnamese American Medical Association
6255 University Avenue, Suite A-2
San Diego, CA 92115
(619) 583-0553   Fax: (619) 583-5702
Web: vmausa.org

Purpose To provide financial assistance to medical students with an interest in serving the Vietnamese American community.

Eligibility This program is open to students enrolled in their third year at an accredited medical school in the United States. Applicants must be able to demonstrate a strong interest in serving the Vietnamese communities in the United States when they complete their training. Along with their application, they must submit a letter from the financial aid office of their medical school verifying the amount of other assistance they are receiving, a letter of recommendation, their medical school transcript, and a 600-word essay describing the reason why they wish to serve Vietnamese communities in the United States, including the specific location where they plan to practice. Preference is given to applicants who demonstrate the greatest financial need.

Financial data Stipends range from $1,000 to $2,000.

Duration 1 year.

Number awarded Varies each year.

Deadline April of each year.

[642]
VIETNAMESE AMERICAN BAR ASSOCIATION OF NORTHERN CALIFORNIA STUDENT RECOGNITION AWARDS.

Vietnamese American Bar Association of Northern
   California
c/o Jacqui Duong
Office of the County Counsel
373 West Julian Street, Suite 300
San Jose, CA 95110
(408) 491-4217

Purpose To provide financial assistance to students at law schools in northern California who have been active in the Asian American community.

Eligibility This program is open to students at law schools in northern California. Applicants must submit the following: law school GPA or class rank, a resume or curric-

ulum vitae, and a 2-page essay on how they have demonstrated a commitment to the Asian American community and/or the rights of Asian Americans (e.g., community service), why they think they should be recognized for past and present contributions, and how they view their future involvement in the community.

Financial data Stipends are $1,000 or $500.

Duration 1 year.

Additional information This scholarship is not offered every year. Check with the sponsor to determine its availability.

Number awarded Varies each year.

Deadline March of each year.

[643]
VIRGIL HAWKINS FELLOWSHIP PROGRAM

State University System of Florida
Attn: Office of Academic and Student Affairs
325 West Gaines Street, Suite 1501
Tallahassee, FL 32399-1950
(850) 245-0467   Fax: (850) 245-9667
E-mail: we're.listening@fldoe.org
Web: www.fldoe.org

Purpose To provide financial assistance to minorities in Florida who are interested in legal careers.

Eligibility First-year minority students who are attending law schools at accredited state universities in Florida are eligible to apply.

Financial data The stipend is $14,000 per year.

Duration 1 year; renewable up to 2 additional years.

Additional information This program is administered by the equal opportunity program at each of the public institutions in Florida that have a law school. Contact that office for further information.

Number awarded Varies each year; recently, more than $200,000 was available for this program.

[644]
WARNER NORCROSS & JUDD LAW SCHOOL STUDIES SCHOLARSHIP

Grand Rapids Community Foundation
Attn: Scholarship Coordinator
209-C Waters Building
161 Ottawa Avenue N.W., 209-C
Grand Rapids, MI 49503-2757
(616) 454-1751, ext. 103   Fax: (616) 454-6455
E-mail: rbishop@grfoundation.org
Web: www.grfoundation.org

Purpose To provide financial assistance for law school to minorities with a residential connection to Michigan.

Eligibility This program is open to minority students entering, accepted at, or currently attending an accredited law school within the United States. Applicants must be residents of Michigan or have a connection to the state (e.g., family members reside in the state, student previously resided in the state, student attended a school in the state).

Financial data The stipend is $5,000.

Duration 1 year.

Additional information Funding for this program is provided by the law firm Warner Norcross & Judd LLP.

Number awarded 1 each year.
Deadline April of each year.

[645]
WESTERN REGION KOREAN AMERICAN SCHOLARSHIPS

Korean American Scholarship Foundation
Western Region
Attn: Scholarship Committee
3435 Wilshire Boulevard, Suite 2450B
Los Angeles, CA 90010
(213) 380-KASF   Fax: (213) 380-KASF
E-mail: western@kasf.org
Web: www.kasf.org

Purpose To provide financial assistance to Korean American undergraduate and graduate students attending college in the western states.
Eligibility This program is open to full-time Korean American students who have completed at least 1 year of study at a 4-year college, graduate school, or professional school. Applicants may be residents of any state as long as they attend school in the western region (Alaska, Arizona, California, Colorado, Hawaii, Idaho, Montana, Nevada, New Mexico, Oregon, Utah, Washington, or Wyoming). Selection is based on academic achievement, community service, school activities, and financial need.
Financial data Stipends range from $1,000 to $2,000.
Duration 1 year; renewable.
Number awarded Varies each year. Recently, 60 of these scholarships were awarded.
Deadline February of each year.

[646]
WILEY MANUEL LAW FOUNDATION SCHOLARSHIPS

Wiley Manuel Law Foundation
c/o Law Offices of George Holland
1970 Broadway, Suite 900
Oakland, CA 94612
(510) 465-4100

Purpose To provide financial assistance to minority students from any state enrolled in law schools in northern California.
Eligibility This program is open to minority students entering their third year at law schools in northern California. Applicants should exemplify the qualities of the late Justice Wiley Manuel. Selection is based on financial need, scholarship, commitment, and community service.
Financial data The stipend is approximately $1,500.
Duration 1 year.
Number awarded Varies each year; recently, 7 of these scholarships were awarded.
Deadline March of each year.

[647]
WILLIAM G. ANDERSON, D.O. SCHOLARSHIP FOR MINORITY STUDENTS

American Osteopathic Foundation
Attn: Program Manager
142 East Ontario Street
Chicago, IL 60611-2864
(312) 202-8232   Toll-free: (800) 621-1773
Fax: (312) 202-8216
E-mail: vheck@aof-foundation.org
Web: www.aof-foundation.org

Purpose To provide financial assistance to minority students enrolled in colleges of osteopathic medicine.
Eligibility This program is open to minority (African American, Native American, Asian American, Pacific Islander, or Hispanic) students entering their second, third, or fourth year at an accredited college of osteopathic medicine. Applicants must demonstrate academic achievement and outstanding leadership qualities.
Financial data The stipend is $5,000.
Duration 1 year.
Additional information This program was established in 1998.
Number awarded 1 each year.

[648]
WILLIAM ORR DINGWALL FOUNDATION GRANT

William Orr Dingwall Foundation
43 Topaz Way
San Francisco, CA 04131
(415) 641-7142   Fax: (415) 824-9609
E-mail: woding@aol.com
Web: www.wod.org/e_grant.html

Purpose To provide financial assistance to 1) undergraduates or graduate students of Korean descent or 2) graduate students of any nationality who are interested in studying the neural bases of language.
Eligibility Eligible to apply for this support are 1) undergraduate or graduate students of Korean or other Asian descent (may be majoring in any field) or 2) graduate students of any nationality who are interested in studying the neural bases of language. There are no residency requirements. Selection is based on academic record and evidence of financial need.
Financial data Grants up to $18,000 per year are awarded, although the actual amount paid will depend on the grantee's justified financial need. Stipends are paid directly to the recipient.
Duration 3 years; may be extended for 1 additional year.
Additional information Recipients must maintain at least a 3.0 GPA.
Deadline January of each year.

[649]

WILLIAM RUCKER GREENWOOD SCHOLARSHIP

Association for Women Geoscientists
Attn: AWG Foundation
P.O. Box 30645
Lincoln, NE 68503-0645
E-mail: awgscholarship@yahoo.com
Web: www.awg.org/members/po_scholarships.html

Purpose To provide financial assistance to minority women working on an undergraduate or graduate degree in the geosciences in the Potomac Bay region.

Eligibility This program is open to minority women who are currently enrolled as full-time undergraduate or graduate geoscience majors in an accredited, degree-granting college or university in Delaware, the District of Columbia, Maryland, Virginia, or West Virginia. Selection is based on the applicant's 1) awareness of the importance of community outreach as demonstrated by participation in geoscience or earth science educational activities, and 2) potential for leadership as a future geoscience professional.

Financial data The stipend is $1,000. The recipient also is granted a 1-year membership in the Association for Women Geoscientists (AWG).

Duration 1 year.

Additional information This program is sponsored by the AWG Potomac Area Chapter. Information is also available from Laurel M. Bybell, U.S. Geological Survey, 926 National Center, Reston, VA 20192.

Number awarded 1 each year.

Deadline April of each year.

[650]

W.K. KELLOGG FOUNDATION FELLOWSHIP PROGRAM IN HEALTH RESEARCH

National Medical Fellowships, Inc.
Attn: Scholarship Program
5 Hanover Square, 15th Floor
New York, NY 10004
(212) 483-8880   Fax: (212) 483-8897
E-mail: info@nmfonline.org
Web: www.nmf-online.org

Purpose To provide financial assistance to minorities enrolled in a doctoral program in health policy research who are committed to working with underserved populations.

Eligibility This program is open to members of minority groups (African Americans, Native Americans, Asians, and Hispanics) enrolled in doctoral programs in public health, social policy, or health policy (Ph.D., Dr.P.H., or Sc.D.). Applicants must demonstrate a willingness to complete relevant dissertation research and a commitment to work with underserved populations upon completion of the doctorate. They must include an essay of 500 to 1,000 words discussing their reasons for applying for a fellowship, their qualifications, how it will support their career plans, and which of 4 areas of focus (health policy, men's health, mental health, substance abuse) most interests them and why.

Financial data Fellowships cover tuition, fees, and a partial living stipend.

Duration Up to 5 years: 2 years to do the necessary course work and 3 years to complete the dissertation.

Additional information The program was created in 1998 with grant support from the W.K. Kellogg Foundation.

Recently, it operated at 8 institutions: the RAND Graduate School, the Heller Graduate School at Brandeis University, the Joseph L. Mailman School of Public Health at Columbia University, the Harvard School of Public Health, the Johns Hopkins School of Hygiene and Public Health, the UCLA School of Public Health, the University of Michigan School of Public Health, and the University of Pennsylvania. Information is also available from the sponsor's Washington office at 1627 K Street, N.W., Suite 1200, Washington, DC 20006-1702, (202) 296-4431, Fax: (202) 293-1990.

Number awarded 5 each year.

Deadline June of each year.

[651]

WOLVERINE BAR FOUNDATION SCHOLARSHIP

Wolverine Bar Association
Attn: Wolverine Bar Foundation
645 Griswold, Suite 961
Detroit, MI 48226
(313) 962-0250   Fax: (313) 962-5906
Web: www.michbar.org/localbars/wolverine/web.html

Purpose To provide financial assistance for law school to Michigan minority students.

Eligibility This program is open to minority law students who are either currently enrolled in a Michigan law school or are Michigan residents enrolled in an out-of-state law school. Applicants must be in at least their second year of law school. Selection is based on financial need, merit, and an interview.

Financial data The stipend is at least $1,000.

Duration 1 year; nonrenewable.

Additional information The Wolverine Bar Association was established by a number of African American attorneys during the 1930s. It was the successor to the Harlan Law Club, founded in 1919 by attorneys in the Detroit area who were excluded from other local bar associations in Michigan. Information is also available from the Scholarship Committee co-chairs, Kimberly D. Stevens, (313) 235-7711, E-mail: kds0183@hotmail.com, or Vanessa Peterson Williams, (313) 877-7000, E-mail: vpwilliams@mbpia.com.

Number awarded 1 or more each year.

Deadline January of each year.

[652]

WORLDSTUDIO FOUNDATION SCHOLARSHIPS

Worldstudio Foundation
200 Varick Street, Suite 507
New York, NY 10014
(212) 366-1317, ext. 18   Fax: (212) 807-0024
E-mail: scholarshipcoordinator@worldstudio.org
Web: www.worldstudio.org/schol/index.html

Purpose To provide financial assistance to undergraduate and graduate students, especially minorities, who wish to study fine or commercial arts, design, or architecture.

Eligibility This program is open to undergraduate and graduate students who are currently enrolled or planning to enroll at an accredited college or university and major in 1 of the following areas: advertising (art direction only), architecture, crafts, environmental graphics, fashion design, film/video (direction or cinematography only), film/theater design (including set, lighting, and costume design), fine arts, furniture design, graphic design, industrial/product design, interior design, landscape architecture, new media, photography, surface/textile design, or urban planning. Although not required, minority status is a significant factor in the selection process. International students may apply if they are enrolled at a U.S. college or university. Applicants must have a GPA of 2.0 or higher. Along with their application, they must submit a 600-word statement of purpose that includes a brief autobiography, an explanation of how their experiences have influenced their creative work and/or their career plans, and how they see themselves contributing to the community at large in the future. Selection is based on that statement, the quality of submitted work, financial need, minority status, and academic record.

Financial data Basic scholarships range from $1,000 to $2,000, but awards between $3,000 and $5,000 are also presented at the discretion of the jury. Honorable mentions are $100. Funds are paid directly to the recipient's school.

Duration 1 academic year. Recipients may reapply.

Additional information The foundation encourages the scholarship recipients to focus on ways that their work can address issues of social and environmental responsibility. This program includes the following named awards: the Sherry and Gary Baker Award, the Bobolink Foundation Award, the Bombay Sapphire Awards, the Richard and Jean Coyne Family Foundation Awards, the David A. Dechman Foundation Awards, the Philip and Edina Jennison Award, the Kraus Family Foundation Awards, the Dena McKelvey Award. the New York Design Center Award, the Rudin Foundation Awards, the Starr Foundation Awards, and the John F. Wright III Award.

Number awarded Varies each year; recently, 24 scholarships and 7 honorable mentions were awarded.

Deadline March of each year.

[653]
WTS PUGET SOUND CHAPTER SCHOLARSHIP

Women's Transportation Seminar-Puget Sound Chapter
c/o Lorelei Mesic, Scholarship Co-Chair
W&H Pacific
3350 Monte Villa Parkway
Bothell, WA 98021-8972
(425) 951-4872   Fax: (425) 951-4808
E-mail: lmesic@whpacific.com
Web: www.wtspugetsound.org/nscholarships.html

Purpose To provide financial assistance to women undergraduate and graduate students, particularly minority women, from Washington who are working on a degree related to transportation and have financial need.

Eligibility This program is open to women who are residents of Washington, studying at a college in the state, or working as an intern in the state. Applicants must be currently enrolled in an undergraduate or graduate degree program in a transportation-related field, such as engineering, planning, finance, or logistics. They must have a GPA of 3.0 or higher and plans to prepare for a career in a transportation-related field. Minority candidates are encouraged to apply. Along with their application, they must submit a 500-word statement about their career goals after graduation, their financial need, and why they think they should receive this scholarship award. Selection is based on transportation

goals, academic record, transportation-related activities or job skills, and financial need.

Financial data The stipend is $1,500.

Duration 1 year.

Additional information The winner is also nominated for scholarships offered by the national organization of the Women's Transportation Seminar.

Number awarded 1 each year.

Deadline October of each year.

[654]
WTS/ITS WASHINGTON INTELLIGENT TRANSPORTATION SYSTEMS SCHOLARSHIP

Women's Transportation Seminar-Puget Sound Chapter
c/o Lorelei Mesic, Scholarship Co-Chair
W&H Pacific
3350 Monte Villa Parkway
Bothell, WA 98021-8972
(425) 951-4872   Fax: (425) 951-4808
E-mail: lmesic@whpacific.com
Web: www.wtspugetsound.org/nscholarships.html

Purpose To provide financial assistance to minority and other undergraduate and graduate students from Washington working on a degree related to intelligent transportation systems (ITS).

Eligibility This program is open to students who are residents of Washington, studying at a college in the state, or working as an intern in the state. Applicants must be currently enrolled in an undergraduate or graduate degree program related to the design, implementation, operation, and maintenance of ITS technologies. They must be majoring in transportation or a related field, including transportation engineering, systems engineering, electrical engineering, planning, finance, or logistics, and be taking courses in such ITS-related fields of study as computer science, electronics, and digital communications. In addition, they must have a GPA of 3.0 or higher and plans to prepare for a career in a transportation-related field. Minority candidates are encouraged to apply. Along with their application, they must submit a 500-word statement about their career goals after graduation, how those relate to ITS, and why they think they should receive this scholarship award. Selection is based on that statement, academic record, and transportation-related activities or job skills. Financial need is not considered.

Financial data The stipend is $1,500.

Duration 1 year.

Additional information This program is co-sponsored by ITS Washington.

Number awarded 1 each year.

Deadline October of each year.

[655]
XEROX TECHNICAL MINORITY SCHOLARSHIP PROGRAM

Xerox Corporation
Attn: Technical Minority Scholarship Program
150 State Street, Fourth Floor
Rochester, NY 14614
(585) 422-7689   E-mail: xtmsp@imcouncil.com
Web: www.xerox.com

Purpose To provide financial assistance to minorities interested in undergraduate or graduate education in the sciences and/or engineering.

Eligibility This program is open to minorities (people of African American, Asian, Pacific Islander, Native American, Native Alaskan, or Hispanic descent) working full time on an undergraduate or graduate degree in chemistry, computing and software systems, engineering (chemical, computer, electrical, imaging, manufacturing, mechanical, optical, or software), information management, laser optics, material science, physics, or printing management science. Applicants must be U.S. citizens or permanent residents with a GPA of 3.0 or higher and attending, or planning to attend, a 4-year college or university.

Financial data The maximum stipend is $1,000 per year.

Duration 1 year.

Number awarded Approximately 150 each year.

Deadline September of each year.

Loans

Described here are 36 programs open to Asian Americans that provide money which must eventually be repaid—in cash or in service and with or without interest. Included here are traditional loans, loans-for-service, and forgivable loans. If you are looking for a particular program and don't find it in this section, be sure to check the Program Title Index to see if it is covered elsewhere in the directory.

[656]
ARKANSAS MINORITY MASTERS FELLOWS PROGRAM

Arkansas Department of Higher Education
Attn: Financial Aid Division
114 East Capitol Avenue
Little Rock, AR 72201-3818
(501) 371-2050   Toll-free: (800) 54-STUDY
Fax: (501) 371-2001   E-mail: finaid@adhe.arknet.edu
Web: www.arkansashighered.com/mmasters.html

Purpose To provide fellowship/loans to minority graduate students in Arkansas who want to become teachers in selected subject areas.

Eligibility Applicants must be minority (African American, Hispanic, Native American, or Asian American) residents of Arkansas who are U.S. citizens and enrolled as full-time master's degree students at an Arkansas public or independent institution with a cumulative GPA of 2.75 or higher. Also eligible are minority students in the fifth year of a 5-year teacher certification program. Recipients must be willing to teach in an Arkansas public school or public institution of higher education for at least 2 years after completion of their education. Preference is given to applicants who completed their baccalaureate degrees within the previous 2 years.

Financial data The stipend is up to $7,500 per year for full-time students (or up to $2,500 per summer for part-time summer students). This is a fellowship/loan program. The loan will be forgiven at the rate of 50% for each year the recipient teaches full time in an Arkansas public school or public institution of higher education. If the recipient does not attend college on a full-time basis, withdraws from an approved teacher education program, or does not fulfill the required teaching obligation, the loan must be repaid in full with interest at a rate up to 5 percentage points above the Federal Reserve discount rate.

Duration 1 year; may be renewed if the recipient remains a full-time student with a GPA of 3.0 or higher.

Number awarded Varies each year; recently, 25 of these fellowship/loans were approved.

Deadline May of each year.

[657]
ARKANSAS MINORITY TEACHER SCHOLARS PROGRAM

Arkansas Department of Higher Education
Attn: Financial Aid Division
114 East Capitol Avenue
Little Rock, AR 72201-3818
(501) 371-2050   Toll-free: (800) 54-STUDY
Fax: (501) 371-2001   E-mail: finaid@adhe.arknet.edu
Web: www.arkansashighered.com/mteachers.html

Purpose To provide scholarship/loans to minority undergraduates in Arkansas who want to become teachers.

Eligibility Applicants must be minority (African American, Native American, Hispanic, or Asian American) residents of Arkansas who are U.S. citizens and enrolled as full-time juniors or seniors in an approved teacher certification program at an Arkansas public or independent 4-year institution. They must have a cumulative GPA of 2.5 or higher and be willing to teach in an Arkansas public school for at least 5 years after completion of their teaching certificate (3 years

if the teaching is in 1 of the 42 counties of Arkansas designated as the Delta Region; or if the teaching is in mathematics, science, or foreign language; or if the recipient is an African American male and teaches at the elementary level; or if the service is as a guidance counselor).

Financial data Awards up to $5,000 per year are available. This is a scholarship/loan program. The loan will be forgiven at the rate of 20% for each year the recipient teaches full time in an Arkansas public school (or 33% per year if the obligation is fulfilled in 3 years as described above). If the loan is not forgiven by service, it must be repaid with interest at a rate up to 5% points above the Federal Reserve discount rate.

Duration 1 year; may be renewed for 1 additional year if the recipient remains a full-time student with a GPA of 2.5 or higher.

Number awarded Varies each year; recently, 97 of these scholarship/loans were approved.

Deadline May of each year.

[658]
CALIFORNIA STATE UNIVERSITY FORGIVABLE LOAN/DOCTORAL INCENTIVE PROGRAM

California State University
Office of the Chancellor
Attn: Human Resources
401 Golden Shore, Fourth Floor
Long Beach, CA 90802-4210
(562) 951-4426   Fax: (562) 951-4954
E-mail: forgivableloan@calstate.edu
Web: www.calstate.edu/HR/FLP/index.shtml

Purpose To provide forgivable loans to graduate students who can help increase the diversity of persons qualified to compete for instructional faculty positions at campuses of the California State University (CSU) system.

Eligibility This program is open to new and continuing full-time students enrolled in a doctoral program anywhere in the United States, whether affiliated with a CSU campus or not. Applicants must present a plan of support from a full-time CSU faculty sponsor who will agree to advise and support the candidate throughout doctoral study. Selection is based on the applicant's academic record; professional qualifications; and relevant background, experience, and motivation to educate a diverse student body in the CSU system. The elements considered include unconditional acceptance into a specific doctoral program, quality of the proposed doctoral program, and other experiences or skills that enhance the potential of the candidate to educate a diverse student body; those experiences and characteristics may include experience working with persons who have a wide range of backgrounds and perspectives, research interests related to educating an increasingly diverse student body, a history of successfully overcoming economic disadvantage and adversity, experience in a variety of cultural environments, and being a first-generation college student. Special consideration is given to candidates whose proposed area of study falls where CSU campuses anticipate the greatest difficulty in filling instructional faculty positions.

Financial data Participants receive up to $10,000 per year or a maximum of $30,000 over 5 years. The loans are converted to fellowships at the rate of 20% of the total loan amount for each postdoctoral year that the program participant teaches, for up to 5 years. Thus, the entire loan will be forgiven after the recipient has taught full time for 5 years on a CSU campus. Recipients who do not teach on a CSU campus or who discontinue full-time studies will be required to repay the total loan amount within a 15-year period at the rate established for other student loans. The minimum repayment required for a $30,000 loan is approximately $287 per month to amortize the 8% per annum loan over a 15-year period. Waiver of loan obligations can be made in those exceptional cases where graduate work was discontinued for valid reasons and where repayment of the loan would cause an unnecessary or undue hardship.

Duration Up to 5 years.

Additional information This program began in 1987. It has loaned $32.4 million to 1,385 doctoral students enrolled in universities throughout the nation and abroad.

Number awarded Varies each year.

Deadline The deadline varies at different CSU campuses but typically falls in February of each year.

[659]
CENTRAL INTELLIGENCE AGENCY UNDERGRADUATE SCHOLARSHIP PROGRAM

Central Intelligence Agency
Attn: Recruitment Center
P.O. Box 4090
Reston, VA 20195
Toll-free: (800) 368-3886
Web: www.cia.gov/employment/student.html

Purpose To provide scholarship/loans and work experience to high school seniors and college sophomores, especially minorities and people with disabilities, who are interested in working for the Central Intelligence Agency (CIA) after graduation from college.

Eligibility This program is open to U.S. citizens who are either high school seniors or college sophomores. Seniors must be at least 18 years of age by April of the year they apply and have minimum scores of 21 on the ACT (or the equivalent on the SAT). College sophomores must have a GPA of 3.0 or higher. All applicants must be able to demonstrate financial need (household income of $70,000 or less for a family of 4 or $80,000 or less for a family of 5 or more) and be able to meet the same employment standards as permanent employees of the CIA. An explicit goal of the program is to attract minorities and students with disabilities to a career with the CIA.

Financial data Scholars are provided a salary and up to $18,000 per year for tuition, fees, books, and supplies. They must agree to continue employment with the CIA after college graduation for a period 1.5 times the length of their college support.

Duration 1 year; may be renewed if the student maintains a GPA of 3.0 or higher and full-time enrollment in a 4- or 5-year college program.

Additional information Scholars work each summer at a CIA facility. In addition to a salary, they receive the cost of transportation between school and the Washington, D.C. area and a housing allowance.

Number awarded Varies each year.

Deadline October of each year.

[660]
CENTRAL VALLEY NURSING SCHOLARSHIP PROGRAM

Health Professions Education Foundation
Attn: Program Administrator
818 K Street, Suite 210
Sacramento, CA 95814
(916) 324-6500   Toll-free: (800) 773-1669
Fax: (916) 324-6585
Web: www.healthprofessions.ca.gov

Purpose To provide scholarship/loans to underrepresented residents of California who plan to work on an associate, baccalaureate, or master's degree in nursing at an institution in the state's Central Valley and then provide direct patient care in a medically underserved area in the region.

Eligibility This program is open to California residents who are enrolled or accepted for enrollment in an associate, baccalaureate, or master's degree nursing program in 6 counties of the Central Valley (Fresno, Kern, Kings, Madera, Merced, or Tulare). Applicants must quality as underrepresented and/or economically disadvantaged. They must agree to begin a 2-year service obligation immediately following graduation by practicing full-time nursing in direct patient care in a medically underserved area within the 6-county region. U.S. citizenship or permanent resident status is required.

Financial data Stipends range from $8,000 to $12,000 per year. Recipients who fail to meet the service obligation must repay all funds received.

Duration 1 year; may be renewed provided the recipient maintains at least half-time enrollment and a GPA of 2.0 or higher.

Additional information This program, established in 2002, is funded by a grant from the California Endowment.

Number awarded Varies each year; recently, 44 of these scholarships (worth $402,000) were awarded, including 27 for associate degree students, 14 for baccalaureate degree students, and 3 for master's degree students.

Deadline Applications are accepted biennially, in May or October of even-numbered years.

[661]
DEFENSE INTELLIGENCE AGENCY UNDERGRADUATE TRAINING ASSISTANCE PROGRAM

Defense Intelligence Agency
Attn: DAH-2
Bolling Air Force Base
Building 6000
Washington, DC 20340-5100
(202) 231-4713   Fax: (202) 231-4889
TTY: (202) 231-5002
Web: www.dia.mil/Careers/Programs/utap.html

Purpose To provide loans-for-service and work experience to women, minority, and disabled high school seniors interested in majoring in specified fields and working for the U.S. Defense Intelligence Agency (DIA).

Eligibility This program is open to women, minorities, and individuals with disabilities who are graduating high school seniors and interested in majoring in 1 of the following fields in college: geography, foreign area studies, international relations, or political science. Applicants must have a high school GPA of 3.0 or higher, have an ACT score of 21 or higher (or the equivalent SAT score), be able to demonstrate financial need (household income ceiling of $65,000 for a family of 4 or $80,000 for a family of 5 or more), be U.S. citizens and from a family of U.S. citizens, and demonstrate leadership abilities through extracurricular activities, civic involvement, volunteer work, or part-time employment.

Financial data Students accepted into this program receive tuition (up to $18,000 per year) at an accredited college or university selected by the student and endorsed by the sponsor; reimbursement for books and needed supplies; an annual salary to cover college room and board expenses and for summer employment; and a position at the sponsoring agency after graduation. Recipients must work for DIA after college graduation for at least 1 and a half times the length of study. For participants who leave DIA earlier than scheduled, the agency arranges for payments to reimburse DIA for the total cost of education (including the employee's pay and allowances).

Duration 4 years.

Additional information Recipients are provided a challenging summer internship and guaranteed a job at the agency in their field of study upon graduation. Recipients must attend school on a full-time basis.

Number awarded Only a few are awarded each year.

Deadline November of each year.

[662]
DIANE YU LOAN REPAYMENT ASSISTANCE PROGRAM

National Asian Pacific American Bar Association
Attn: NAPABA Law Foundation
910 17th Street, N.W., Suite 315
Washington, DC 20006
(202) 775-9555   Fax: (202) 775-9333
E-mail: foundation@napaba.org
Web: www.napaba.org

Purpose To provide funding for educational loan repayment to recent law graduates interested in serving the Asian Pacific American community.

Eligibility This program is open to recent graduates of accredited law schools in the United States. Applicants must demonstrate leadership potential to serve the Asian Pacific American community. They must submit 500-word essays on 1) the most significant experiences in their background that have shaped and demonstrated their commitment to serving the needs of Asian Pacific Americans; and 2) how they intend to serve the needs of the Asian Pacific American community in their future legal career.

Financial data The program awards recipients $5,000 per year to be applied to their educational debt.

Duration 2 years.

Additional information This program was established in 2004.

Number awarded 1 each year.

Deadline September of each year.

[663]
DIRECT FARM LOANS FOR SOCIALLY DISADVANTAGED PERSONS

Department of Agriculture
Farm Service Agency
Attn: Office of Minority and Socially Disadvantaged
    Farmers Assistance
1400 Independence Avenue, S.W.
Washington, DC 20250-0568
(202) 720-1584   Toll-free: (866) 538-2610
Fax: (202) 720-5398   Fax: (866) 480-2824
E-mail: msda@wdc.usda.gov
Web: www.fsa.usda.gov

Purpose To lend money to eligible members of socially disadvantaged groups for the purchase or operation of family-size farms or ranches.

Eligibility For the purposes of this program, a "socially disadvantaged group" is 1 whose members "have been subjected to racial, ethnic, or gender prejudice because of their identity as members of a group without regard to their individual qualities." Those groups are women, African Americans, American Indians, Alaskan Natives, Hispanics, Asian Americans, and Pacific Islanders. Applicants may be seeking either farm ownership loans (to purchase or enlarge a farm or ranch, purchase easements or rights of way needed in the farm's operation, erect or improve buildings such as a dwelling or barn, promote soil and water conservation, or pay closing costs) or farm operating loans (to purchase livestock, poultry, farm and home equipment, feed, seed, fertilizer, chemicals, hail and other crop insurance, food, clothing, medical care, and hired labor). Loans are made to individuals, partnerships, joint operations, corporations, and cooperatives primarily and directly engaged in farming and ranching on family-size operations; a family-size farm is defined as a farm that a family can operate and manage itself. In addition to belonging to a "socially disadvantaged group," borrowers must have a satisfactory history of meeting credit obligations, have 3 years of experience in operating a farm or ranch for an ownership loan or 1 year's experience within the last 5 years for an operating loan, be a U.S. citizen or legal resident, possess the legal capacity to incur the obligations of a loan or credit sale, and be unable to obtain sufficient credit elsewhere at reasonable rates.

Financial data The maximum loan is $200,000. Interest rates are set periodically according to the federal government's cost of borrowing.

Duration Repayment terms are generally up to 40 years for ownership loans or 1 to 7 years for operating loans.

Deadline Applications may be submitted at any time.

[664]
DIVERSIFYING HIGHER EDUCATION FACULTY IN ILLINOIS

Southern Illinois University at Carbondale
Attn: DFI Administrative Office
900 South Normal
Woody Hall C-224
Carbondale, IL 62901-4723
(618) 453-4558   E-mail: fellows@siu.edu
Web: www.dfi.siu.edu

Purpose To provide fellowship/loans to minority students interested in enrolling in graduate school programs in Illinois to prepare for a career in higher education.

Eligibility This program is open to 1) residents of Illinois who have received a high school diploma or postsecondary degree from an educational institution in the state; and 2) registered voters in Illinois with 3 or more years of residency in the state. Applicants must be members of a minority group traditionally underrepresented in graduate school enrollment in Illinois (African Americans, Hispanic Americans, Native Americans, or Asian Americans) and have been admitted to a graduate program in the state to work on a doctoral or master's degree and prepare for a career in teaching or administration at an Illinois postsecondary institution or Illinois higher education governing board. They must have a GPA of 2.75 or higher in the last 60 hours of undergraduate work or 3.2 or higher in at least 9 hours of graduate study and be able to demonstrate financial need. Along with their application, they must submit statements on their educational and career goals (including their rationale for selecting their major field of study, the relationship between the selected major and future plans, and their research interest and academic preparation) and on their underrepresented status (including how their underrepresented status influenced their personal and academic development and why they should be awarded a fellowship designated specifically for underrepresented groups in higher education).

Financial data Stipends range between $12,500 and $16,000 per year for full-time enrollment. Some participating institutions also provide a tuition waiver or scholarship. This is a fellowship/loan program. Recipients must agree to accept a position, in teaching or administration, at an Illinois postsecondary educational institution, on an Illinois higher education governing or coordinating board, or at a state agency in an education-related position. Recipients failing to fulfill the conditions of the award are required to repay 20% of the total award.

Duration Up to 2 years for master's degree students; up to 4 years for doctoral students.

Additional information The Illinois General Assembly established this program in 2004 as a successor to 2 earlier programs (both established in 1985); the Illinois Consortium for Educational Opportunity Program (ICEOP) and the Illinois Minority Graduate Incentive Program (IMGIP).

Deadline February of each year.

[665]
EXTENDED OPPORTUNITY PROGRAMS AND SERVICES LOANS

California Community Colleges
Attn: Student Services and Special Programs Division
1102 Q Street
Sacramento, CA 95814-6511
(916) 323-0453   Fax: (916) 327-8232
Web: www.cccco.edu/ss/ss.htm

Purpose To provide California community college students (especially minorities) with emergency loans to meet unexpected or untimely costs for books, college supplies, transportation, or housing.

Eligibility To receive support under this program, students must be residents of California, be enrolled full time in a California community college, not have completed more than 70 units of course work in any combination of postsecondary institutions, be educationally disadvantaged, and be able to demonstrate financial need. Up to 10% of the EOPS students at each college may enroll for only 9 units; students with disabilities may enroll for fewer units, based on their disability. Educationally disadvantaged students include those who are not qualified to enroll in the minimum level English or mathematics course at their college, did not graduate from high school or obtain the GED, graduated from high school with a GPA below 2.5, previously enrolled in remedial education, or met other factors described in their college's plan, such as first-generation college student, member of underrepresented group at the college, or English not the primary language.

Financial data Loans may not exceed $500 in a single academic year and must be repaid within the academic year in which the loan was made.

Duration 1 year.

Additional information EOPS students are also eligible for other support in the form of counseling, tutoring, registration assistance, orientation, child care, transportation, and cultural activities. Students apply to their community college, not to the sponsoring organization.

Number awarded Varies each year; recently, 223 students statewide received EOPS loans.

Deadline Varies by participating institution.

[666]
GOLDEN APPLE SCHOLARS OF ILLINOIS

Golden Apple Foundation
Attn: Director of Scholars, Recruitment and Placement
8 South Michigan Avenue, Suite 700
Chicago, IL 60603-3463
(312) 407-0433, ext. 105   Fax: (312) 407-0344
E-mail: kilduff@goldenapple.org
Web: www.goldenapple.org/scholars.htm

Purpose To provide scholarship/loans to high school seniors (particularly minorities) in Illinois who wish to study education at an Illinois college and teach in the state.

Eligibility This program is open to high school seniors at schools in Illinois. Students must be nominated by a teacher, principal, guidance counselor, or other non-family adult; self-nominations are also accepted. Nominees must be committed to teaching as a profession and must be interested in attending 1 of 53 designated colleges and universities in Illinois. A limited number of openings are also available to sophomores at those designated Illinois institutions. The program strongly encourages nomination of prospective teachers for which there is currently a shortage, especially minority and bilingual teachers.

Financial data Scholars receive a scholarship/loan of $2,500 per year to apply toward their educational expenses and a stipend of $2,000 per year for participating in a summer teaching internship. If they complete a bachelor's degree and teach for 5 years in an Illinois school of need, the loan is forgiven. Schools of need are defined as those either having Chapter I status by the U.S. Department of Education or having mediocre to poor PSAE or ISAT scores.

Duration 4 years, provided the recipient maintains a GPA of 2.0 or higher during the freshman year and 2.5 or higher in subsequent years. Students who enter the program as sophomores receive 2 years of support.

Additional information During the annual summer institutes, scholars participate in teaching internships and seminars on the art and craft of teaching. This program was established in 1988.

Number awarded Up to 100 each year.

Deadline Nominations must be submitted by November of each year.

[667]
GUARANTEED FARM LOANS FOR SOCIALLY DISADVANTAGED PERSONS

Department of Agriculture
Farm Service Agency
Attn: Office of Minority and Socially Disadvantaged
   Farmers Assistance
1400 Independence Avenue, S.W.
Washington, DC 20250-0568
(202) 720-1584   Toll-free: (866) 538-2610
Fax: (202) 720-5398   Fax: (866) 480-2824
E-mail: msda@wdc.usda.gov
Web: www.fsa.usda.gov

Purpose To guarantee loans to eligible members of socially disadvantaged groups for the purchase or operation of family-size farms or ranches.

Eligibility For the purposes of this program, a "socially disadvantaged group" is 1 whose members "have been subjected to racial, ethnic, or gender prejudice because of their identity as members of a group without regard to their individual qualities." Those groups are women, African Americans, American Indians, Alaskan Natives, Hispanic Americans, Asian Americans, and Pacific Islanders. Applicants may be seeking guarantees of loans either for farm ownership (to purchase or enlarge a farm or ranch, purchase easements or rights of way needed in the farm's operation, erect or improve buildings such as a dwelling or barn, promote soil and water conservation, or pay closing costs) or farm operation (to purchase livestock, poultry, farm and home equipment, feed, seed, fertilizer, chemicals, hail and other crop insurance, food, clothing, medical care, and hired labor). Guarantees are provided on loans by lending institutions subject to federal or state supervision. Loans are made to individuals, partnerships, joint operations, corporations, and cooperatives primarily and directly engaged in farming and ranching on family-size operations; a family-size farm is defined as a farm that a family can operate and manage itself. In addition to belonging to a "socially disad-

vantaged group," borrowers must have a satisfactory history of meeting credit obligations, have 3 years of experience in operating a farm or ranch for an ownership loan or 1 year's experience within the last 5 years for an operating loan, be a U.S. citizen or legal resident, possess the legal capacity to incur the obligations of a loan or credit sale, and be unable to obtain sufficient credit elsewhere at reasonable rates.

Financial data The size of the loan is agreed upon by the borrower and the lender, but the maximum indebtedness of loans guaranteed by the Farm Service Agency (FSA) may not exceed $762,000. Interest rates can be fixed or variable, as agreed upon by the borrower and the lender, but may not exceed the rate the lender charges its average farm customer. FSA guarantees up to 95% of the loan principal and interest against loss.

Duration Repayment terms are generally up to 40 years for ownership loans or 1 to 7 years for operating loans.

Deadline Applications may be submitted at any time.

[668]
ILLINOIS FUTURE TEACHER CORPS PROGRAM

Illinois Student Assistance Commission
Attn: Scholarship and Grant Services
1755 Lake Cook Road
Deerfield, IL 60015-5209
(847) 948-8550   Toll-free: (800) 899-ISAC
Fax: (847) 831-8549   TDD: (847) 831-8326, ext. 2822
E-mail: collegezone@isac.org
Web: www.collegezone.com

Purpose To provide scholarship/loans to minority and other college students in Illinois who are interested in training or retraining for a teaching career in academic shortage areas.

Eligibility This program is open to Illinois residents who are enrolled at the junior level or higher at an institution of higher education in the state. Applicants must be planning to prepare for a career as a preschool, elementary, or secondary school teacher. Priority is given to students working on a degree in designated teacher shortage disciplines, making a commitment to teach at a hard-to-staff school, and/or planning to teach minority students. Recently, the teacher shortage disciplines included behavior disordered, bilingual teacher (K-12), cross categorical (seeking certification in 2 or more areas of special education), general special education (including blind and deaf specialties and early childhood special education), learning disabled, mathematics (K-12), music (K-12), physical education (K-12), reading and English language arts (K-12), and speech and language impaired. Priority is given to renewal applicants. Selection is based on cumulative GPA, expected family contribution, and minority student status.

Financial data This program pays tuition and fees, room and board, or a commuter allowance at academic institutions in Illinois. The maximum award is $5,000 or $10,000 (and may even be increased by an additional $5,000), depending on the teaching commitment the recipient makes. Funds are paid directly to the school. This is a scholarship/loan program. Recipients must agree to teach in an Illinois public, private, or parochial preschool, elementary school, or secondary school for 1 year for each full year of assistance received. The teaching obligation must be completed within 5 years of completion of the degree or certificate program for which the scholarship was awarded. That time period may be extended if the recipient serves in the U.S. armed forces, enrolls full time in a graduate program related to teaching, becomes temporarily disabled, is unable to find employment as a teacher, or takes additional courses on at least a half-time basis to teach in a specialized teacher shortage discipline. Recipients who fail to honor this work obligation must repay the award with interest.

Duration 1 year; may be renewed.

Additional information This program was formerly known as the David A. DeBolt Teacher Shortage Scholarship Program.

Number awarded Varies each year, depending on the availability of funds.

Deadline Priority consideration is given to applications submitted by February of each year.

[669]
ILLINOIS PODIATRIC MEDICAL STUDENT SCHOLARSHIPS

Illinois Department of Public Health
Attn: Center for Rural Health
535 West Jefferson Street
Springfield, IL 62761
(217) 782-4977   Fax: (217) 782-3987
TTY: (800) 547-0466   E-mail: mailus@idph.state.il.us
Web: www.idph.state.il.us

Purpose To provide scholarship/loans to Illinois residents (particularly minorities) who are interested in working on a degree in podiatry at an institution in the state.

Eligibility This program is open to Illinois residents who are studying podiatric medicine, or have been accepted for enrollment, in a podiatry school in the state. Selection is based, in order, on the following factors: interest in pursuing podiatric medicine, previous experience with medically underserved populations, previous experience in the health care delivery system (with preference given to those whose experience has involved a primary care specialty area), academic capability as reported by the applicant's podiatric medical school, financial need, years of podiatric medical school remaining, interest in providing podiatric care to Illinois residents in designated shortage areas, and length of residence in Illinois. U.S. citizenship is required. Preference is given to minority students.

Financial data Funding is provided to cover the cost of tuition and matriculation fees. This is a scholarship/loan program. Within 30 days after Illinois licensure to practice podiatric medicine, the recipient must provide primary health care in a designated shortage area of Illinois for 1 year per academic year of scholarship support. The service must be a full-time, office-based practice providing direct patient care. Scholarship recipients who fail to fulfill their obligation to practice in designated shortage areas must pay a sum equal to 3 times the amount of the annual scholarship grant for each year the recipient fails to fulfill the obligation.

Duration Up to 2 years.

Number awarded Varies each year.

Deadline May of each year.

[670]
KANSAS TEACHER SERVICE SCHOLARSHIPS

Kansas Board of Regents
Attn: Student Financial Aid
1000 S.W. Jackson Street, Suite 520
Topeka, KS 66612-1368
(785) 296-3518   Fax: (785) 296-0983
E-mail: dlindeman@ksbor.org
Web: www.kansasregents.com

Purpose To provide scholarship/loans to high school seniors, high school graduates, and selected undergraduates (particularly minorities) who are interested in preparing for a career as a teacher in Kansas.

Eligibility This program is open to Kansas residents who plan to enter the teaching profession in specific curriculum areas; recently, those included special education, mathematics, and science. Applicants must submit evidence of completion of the Kansas Scholars Curriculum (4 years of English, 4 years of mathematics, 3 years of science, 3 years of social studies, 2 years of foreign language, and 1 year of computer technology), ACT or SAT scores, high school GPA, high school class rank, and (if relevant) college transcripts and letters of recommendation from a college or university official. First priority goes to applicants who are in the final 2 years of study in teacher education and have submitted a college transcript and 1 letter of recommendation from a college official. Special consideration is given to minority applicants (academic performance being similar), because minorities continue to be underrepresented in the teaching profession in Kansas schools. Second priority goes to students who have completed the Kansas Scholars Curriculum and have competitive GPAs, ACT scores, and class rank.

Financial data Participants receive $5,000 per year. This is a scholarship/loan program. Recipients must teach in Kansas 1 year for every year of funding received, or they must repay the amount received with interest at 5% over the federal PLUS rate. The teaching must be in the specific curriculum area or in an underserved geographic area (recently including Wichita, Leavenworth, Garden City, and Kansas City).

Duration 1 year; may be renewed for up to 3 additional years or up to 4 additional years for designated 5-year courses of study requiring graduate work.

Additional information There is a $10 application fee.

Number awarded Approximately 100 each year.

Deadline March of each year.

[671]
KENTUCKY MINORITY EDUCATOR RECRUITMENT AND RETENTION SCHOLARSHIPS

Kentucky Department of Education
Attn: Division of Minority Educator Recruitment and
   Retention
500 Mero Street, 17th Floor
Frankfort, KY 40601
(502) 564-1479   Fax: (502) 564-6952
E-mail: bpelphre@kde.state.ky.us
Web: www.education.ky.gov

Purpose To provide forgivable loans to minority undergraduate and graduate students enrolled in Kentucky public institutions who want to become teachers.

Eligibility This program is open to residents of Kentucky who are undergraduate or graduate students pursuing initial teacher certification at a public university or community college in the state. Applicants must have a GPA of 2.5 or higher and either maintain full-time enrollment or be a part-time student within 18 semester hours of receiving a teacher education degree. U.S. citizenship is required.

Financial data Awards up to $5,000 per year are available. This is a scholarship/loan program. Recipients are required to teach 1 semester in Kentucky for each semester or summer term the scholarship is received. If they fail to fulfill that requirement, the scholarship converts to a loan at 12% interest.

Duration 1 year; may be renewed.

Additional information The Kentucky General Assembly established this program in 1992.

Number awarded Varies each year.

Deadline Each state college of teacher education sets its own deadline.

[672]
MENTAL HEALTH SUBSTANCE ABUSE CLINICAL FELLOWSHIP PROGRAM

Council on Social Work Education
Attn: Minority Fellowship Program
1725 Duke Street, Suite 500
Alexandria, VA 22314-3457
(703) 683-8080, ext. 217   Fax: (703) 683-8099
E-mail: mfp@cswe.org
Web: www.cswe.org

Purpose To provide forgivable loans to racial minority members interested in preparing for a clinical career in the mental health fields.

Eligibility This program is open to U.S. citizens and permanent residents who have been underrepresented in the field of social work. These include but are not limited to the following groups: American Indians/Alaskan Natives, Asian/Pacific Islanders (e.g., Chinese, East Indians, South Asians, Filipinos, Hawaiians, Japanese, Koreans, and Samoans), Blacks, and Hispanics (e.g., Mexicans/Chicanos, Puerto Ricans, Cubans, Central or South Americans). Applicants must be interested in and committed to a career in mental health and/or substance abuse with specialization in the delivery of services of ethnic and racial minority groups. They must have a master's degree in social work and be accepted to or enrolled in a full-time doctoral degree program.

Financial data Awards provide a stipend of $16,500 per year and tuition support to a maximum of $3,000.

Duration 1 academic year; renewable for 2 additional years if funds are available and the recipient makes satisfactory progress toward the degree objectives.

Additional information This program has been funded since 1978 by the Center for Mental Health Services of the Substance Abuse and Mental Health Services Administration.

Deadline February of each year.

[673]
MINORITY TEACHERS OF ILLINOIS SCHOLARSHIP PROGRAM

Illinois Student Assistance Commission
Attn: Scholarship and Grant Services
1755 Lake Cook Road
Deerfield, IL 60015-5209
(847) 948-8550   Toll-free: (800) 899-ISAC
Fax: (847) 831-8549   TDD: (847) 831-8326, ext. 2822
E-mail: collegezone@isac.org
Web: www.collegezone.com

Purpose To provide scholarship/loans to minority students in Illinois who plan to become teachers at the preschool, elementary, or secondary level.

Eligibility Applicants must be Illinois residents, U.S. citizens or eligible noncitizens, members of a minority group (African American/Black, Hispanic American, Asian American, or Native American), and high school graduates or holders of a General Educational Development (GED) certificate. They must be enrolled in college full time at the sophomore level or above, have a GPA of 2.5 or higher, not be in default on any student loan, and be enrolled or accepted for enrollment in a teacher education program.

Financial data Grants up to $5,000 per year are awarded. This is a scholarship/loan program. Recipients must agree to teach full time 1 year for each year of support received. The teaching agreement may be fulfilled at a public, private, or parochial preschool, elementary school, or secondary school in Illinois; at least 30% of the student body at those schools must be minority. It must be fulfilled within the 5-year period following the completion of the undergraduate program for which the scholarship was awarded. The time period may be extended if the recipient serves in the U.S. armed forces, enrolls full time in a graduate program related to teaching, becomes temporarily disabled, is unable to find employment as a teacher at a qualifying school, or takes additional courses on at least a half-time basis to obtain certification as a teacher in Illinois. Recipients who fail to honor this work obligation must repay the award with 5% interest.

Duration 1 year.

Number awarded Varies each year.

Deadline Priority consideration is given to applications received by February of each year.

[674]
MISSOURI MINORITY TEACHER EDUCATION SCHOLARSHIP PROGRAM

Missouri Department of Elementary and Secondary
  Education
Attn: Teacher Quality and Urban Education
205 Jefferson Street
P.O. Box 480
Jefferson City, MO 65102-0480
(573) 751-1668   Fax: (573) 526-3580
E-mail: lharriso@mail.dese.state.mo.us
Web: www.dese.state.mo.us

Purpose To provide scholarship/loans to minority high school seniors, high school graduates, and college students in Missouri who are interested in preparing for a teaching career in mathematics or science.

Eligibility This program is open to Missouri residents who are African American, Asian American, Hispanic American, or Native American. Applicants must be 1) high school seniors, college students, or returning adults (without a degree) who ranked in the top 25% of their high school class and scored at or above the 75th percentile on the ACT or SAT examination; 2) individuals who have completed 30 college hours with a cumulative GPA of 3.0 or better; or 3) baccalaureate degree-holders who are returning to an approved mathematics or science program. All applicants must attend an approved teacher education program at a community college, 4-year college, or university in Missouri. Selection is based on academic performance, the quantity and quality of school and community activities, range of interests and activities, leadership abilities, interpersonal skills, and desire to enter the field of education.

Financial data The stipend is $3,000 per year. This is a scholarship/loan program. Recipients must commit to teaching in a Missouri public elementary or secondary school for 5 years following graduation. If they fail to fulfill that obligation, they must repay the state portion of the scholarship.

Duration Up to 4 years.

Number awarded 100 each year.

Deadline February of each year.

[675]
MISSOURI PROFESSIONAL AND PRACTICAL NURSING STUDENT LOAN PROGRAM

Missouri Department of Health and Senior Services
Attn: Primary Care and Rural Health
P.O. Box 570
Jefferson City, MO 65102-0570
(573) 751-6400   Toll-free: (800) 891-7415
Fax: (573) 751-6041
Web: www.dhss.state.mo.us

Purpose To provide scholarship/loans to nursing students (particularly minorities) in Missouri who agree to work in an "area of need" in the state.

Eligibility This program is open to residents of Missouri who have lived for 1 or more years in the state for purposes other than attending an educational institution. Applicants must have applied for acceptance into a full-time course of study leading to an associate degree, a diploma, a bachelor of science, or a master of science degree in nursing, or leading to the completion of educational requirements for a licensed practical nurse. The educational institution must have a Missouri program approved by the State Board of Nursing for participation in this program. Priority is given to residents of underserved areas, minority persons, and previous recipients of these loans.

Financial data The maximum loan is $5,000 per year for professional nursing education or $2,500 per year for practical nursing education. This is a scholarship/loan program. Loans are forgiven at the rate of 25% per year for qualifying employment in an area of defined need (a geographic area or a nursing specialty that is experiencing a shortage of nurses in Missouri). If the loan is not forgiven by service, it must be repaid at 9.5% interest.

Duration 1 year; may be renewed as long as the recipient is enrolled in an approved program.

Number awarded Varies each year.

Deadline June or December of each year.

[676]
NORTH CAROLINA PRINCIPAL FELLOWS PROGRAM

North Carolina Principal Fellows Commission
Attn: Director
P.O. Box 4440
Chapel Hill, NC 27515-4440
(919) 962-4575   Fax: (919) 962-0488
E-mail: mupdike@northcarolina.edu
Web: www.ga.unc.edu/Principal_Fellows

Purpose To provide scholarship/loans to minority and other students in North Carolina who are interested in working on a master's degree in educational administration.

Eligibility This program is open to residents of North Carolina who have at least 4 years of successful teaching or other relevant experience. Applicants must have been admitted as a full-time first-year student in a master's degree program in educational administration at 1 of the following institutions: Appalachian State University, East Carolina University, Fayetteville State University, North Carolina A&T State University, North Carolina Central University, North Carolina State University, University of North Carolina at Chapel Hill, University of North Carolina at Charlotte, University of North Carolina at Greensboro, University of North Carolina at Wilmington, or Western Carolina University. They must be willing to complete the school administrator program supported by the scholarship, pass the school administration certification examination within 24 months following graduation, and provide 4 years of full-time service as a school administrator in North Carolina within 6 months. U.S. citizenship is required. The sponsor specifically encourages women and minorities to apply. Selection is based on undergraduate academic record (GPA of 3.2 or higher), leadership and management potential, communication skills, and moral and ethical standards.

Financial data These scholarship/loans are $20,000 per year for full-time study. Funds are to be used to pay for tuition, fees, and living expenses while in the program. Should the recipient not complete the educational program or not serve in an eligible school administration position in North Carolina for 4 years within 6 years of completing the program, the funds must be repaid at an interest rate of 10%.

Duration 2 years: the first year is devoted to full-time academic study at 1 of the participating schools in North Carolina and the second year is spent as an intern at a public school in the state.

Additional information This program was established by the North Carolina General Assembly in 1993 and became effective for the 1994-95 academic year. It is now cosponsored by the North Carolina Principal Fellows Commission and the North Carolina State Education Assistance Authority. Recipients may not be employed full time during the 2-year period. To satisfy the requirements of this scholarship/loan program, recipients must seek, obtain, and maintain employment as an assistant principal or principal in a public school or a U.S. government school in North Carolina for 4 years after graduation.

Number awarded Up to 200 each year.

Deadline January of each year.

[677]
NORTH CAROLINA TEACHING FELLOWS SCHOLARSHIP PROGRAM

North Carolina Teaching Fellows Commission
Koger Center, Cumberland Building
3739 National Drive, Suite 210
Raleigh, NC 27612
(919) 781-6833   Fax: (919) 781-6527
E-mail: tfellows@ncforum.org
Web: www.teachingfellows.org

Purpose To provide scholarship/loans to minority and other high school seniors in North Carolina who wish to prepare for a career in teaching.

Eligibility This program is open to seniors at high schools in North Carolina who are interested in preparing for a career as a teacher and have been accepted for enrollment at a participating school in the state. Applicants must demonstrate superior achievement on the basis of high school grades, class standing, SAT scores, a writing sample, community service, extracurricular activities, and references from teachers and members of the community. U.S. citizenship is required. A particular goal of the program is to recruit and retain greater numbers of male and minority teacher education candidates in North Carolina.

Financial data The maximum stipend is $6,500 per year. This is a scholarship/loan program; recipients must teach in a North Carolina public school 1 year for each year of support received. If they cannot fulfill the service requirement, they must repay the loan with 10% interest.

Duration 1 year; renewable for up to 3 additional years if the recipient maintains full-time enrollment and a GPA of 2.25 or higher for the freshman year and 2.50 or higher in the sophomore year.

Additional information The participating schools are Appalachian State University, East Carolina University, Elon College, Meredith College, North Carolina A&T State University, University of North Carolina at Asheville, North Carolina Central University, North Carolina State University, University of North Carolina at Pembroke, University of North Carolina at Chapel Hill, University of North Carolina at Charlotte, University of North Carolina at Greensboro, University of North Carolina at Wilmington, and Western Carolina University. This program was established in 1986 and the first fellows were named in 1987.

Number awarded Up to 400 each year. Approximately 20% of the program's recipients are minority and 30% are male.

Deadline October of each year.

[678]
NORTH CAROLINA UNDERGRADUATE NURSE SCHOLARS PROGRAM

North Carolina State Education Assistance Authority
Attn: Scholarship and Grant Services
10 T.W. Alexander Drive
P.O. Box 14103
Research Triangle Park, NC 27709-4103
(919) 549-8614   Toll-free: (800) 700-1775
Fax: (919) 549-8481   E-mail: information@ncseaa.edu
Web: www.ncseaa.edu

Purpose To provide scholarship/loans to minority and other students in North Carolina who wish to prepare for a career in nursing.

Eligibility Applicants must be high school seniors, high school graduates, or currently-enrolled college students who are U.S. citizens, North Carolina residents, and interested in becoming a nurse. Students must plan to enter a North Carolina college, university, or hospital that prepares students for licensure as a registered nurse. Applications are encouraged from nontraditional students, including older individuals, ethnic minorities, males, and individuals with previous careers and/or degrees who are pursuing nursing studies. U.S. citizenship and full-time enrollment are required. Selection is based on academic achievement, leadership potential, and the promise of service as a registered nurse in North Carolina; financial need is not considered.

Financial data Annual stipends are $3,000 for candidates for an associate degree, $3,000 for candidates for a diploma in nursing, or $5,000 or $3,000 for students in a B.S.N. program. This is a scholarship/loan program; 1 year of full-time work as a nurse in North Carolina cancels 1 year of support under this program. Recipients who fail to honor the work obligation must repay the balance plus 10% interest.

Duration 1 year; may be renewed 1 additional year by candidates for an associate degree, registered nurses completing a B.S.N. degree, and community college transfer students and juniors in a B.S.N. program, or for 3 additional years by freshmen and nontraditional students in a B.S.N. program.

Additional information The North Carolina General Assembly created this program in 1989; the first recipients were funded for the 1990-91 academic year.

Number awarded Varies; generally, up to 450 new undergraduate degree awards are made each year. Recently, a total of 834 students were receiving $3,414,500 through this program.

Deadline February of each year for B.S.N. programs; May of each year for A.D.N. and diploma students.

[679]
PAT AND DICK HAZEL MINORITY SCHOLARSHIP AWARD

Community Foundation of the Eastern Shore, Inc.
200 West Main Street
P.O. Box 156
Salisbury, MD 21803-0156
(410) 742-9911   Fax: (410) 742-6638
E-mail: cfes@cfes.org
Web: www.cfes.org/grants/scholarships.cfm

Purpose To provide scholarship/loans to minority high school seniors who are preparing for a teaching career in selected counties of Maryland.

Eligibility This program is open to minority residents of Wicomico, Somerset, and Worcester counties, in Maryland. Applicants must be high school seniors who have been admitted as a full-time student by a college or university in Maryland or Delaware. They must be planning for a career as a teacher and must indicate a willingness to teach for 2 years in the 3 counties following graduation. The application package must include a completed application form, a 1-page essay on why they want to teach, official high school transcripts, the letter of acceptance from their college or university, a summary of financial assistance from their college or university's financial aid office, a copy of their parents' or guardian's most recent income tax return, and 2 letters of recommendation. Selection is based on financial need, community involvement, academic achievement, and extracurricular activities.

Financial data Generally, annual stipends not do exceed $2,000. Funds are paid to the recipient's school and must be used for tuition, fees, and books.

Duration 1 year; may be renewed if the recipient continues to meet eligibility requirements and maintains a GPA of 2.5 or higher.

Deadline April of each year.

[680]
PRESBYTERIAN CHURCH CONTINUING EDUCATION GRANT AND LOAN PROGRAM

Presbyterian Church (USA)
Attn: Office of Financial Aid for Studies
100 Witherspoon Street, Room M-052
Louisville, KY 40202-1396
(502) 569-5735   Toll-free: (888) 728-7228, ext. 5735
Fax: (502) 569-8766   E-mail: LBryan@ctr.pcusa.org
Web: www.pcusa.org

Purpose To provide financial assistance for continuing education, in the form of educational grants and loans, to minority and other professional church workers of the Presbyterian Church (USA) and doctoral candidates who are church members.

Eligibility This program is open to 1) PC(USA) ministers and lay professionals who have served a congregation of 150 or fewer members for at least 3 years; and 2) PC(USA) church members enrolled in a D.Min, Ph.D., or equivalent program in religious studies. Ministers and lay professionals must be planning to attend a program of study that will lead to certification, course work at an accredited institution, or a national event sponsored by PC(USA). The study, course work, or event must be approved by a church session, presbytery, or synod. Events must be at least 3 days in duration. For church members working on a Ph.D. degree, preference is given to women and racial ethnic applicants attending PC(USA) theological institutions, colleges, or universities. U.S. citizenship or permanent resident status is required.

Financial data For ministers and lay professionals, grants for events range from $100 to $500 and grants for study or course work range from $100 to $1,000. For doctoral candidates, grants range from $500 to $1,000. The maximum loan is $2,000 per year.

Duration 1 year. Ministers and lay professionals at small churches are eligible for unlimited renewal of grants. Candidates for a D.Min. degree may renew their grants for a total of 3 years. Candidates for a Ph.D. or equivalent degree may renew their grants for a total of 4 years. Loans may be renewed to a maximum of $6,000.

Number awarded Varies each year.

Deadline November of each year.

[681]
PRIMARY CARE RESOURCE INITIATIVE FOR MISSOURI

Missouri Department of Health and Senior Services
Attn: Primary Care and Rural Health
P.O. Box 570
Jefferson City, MO 65102-0570
(573) 751-6400   Toll-free: (800) 891-7415
Fax: (573) 751-6041
Web: www.dhss.state.mo.us

Purpose To provide scholarship/loans to minority and other residents of Missouri who are interested in working as a health care professional in an underserved area of the state following graduation.

Eligibility This program is open to residents of Missouri who have lived for 1 or more years in the state for purposes other than attending an educational institution. Applicants must have been accepted by or currently be attending a Missouri school offering a course of study leading to a degree as 1) a doctor of allopathic (M.D.) or osteopathic (D.O.) medicine; 2) a doctor of dentistry (D.D.S.); 3) a bachelor of science (B.S.) in a field leading to acceptance into a school of medicine or into a master of science (M.S.N.) degree program leading to certification as a primary care advanced practice nurse; or 4) a bachelor of science (B.S.) in dental hygiene. Physicians and dentists in primary care residency programs are also eligible. Priority is given to residents of medically underserved areas in Missouri, minority group members, and previous recipients.

Financial data For undergraduate students enrolled in an accredited bachelor of science degree in dental hygiene, nursing, or a pre-medicine or pre-dental program, the maximum loan is $5,000 per year for full-time enrollment. Medical (M.D. or D.O.) students are eligible for loans in the amount of tuition, to a maximum of $25,000 per year. Students in 6-year medical programs may receive $10,000 per year for the first 2 years and up to $25,000 per year for the last 4 years. Physicians and dentists in primary care residency programs are eligible for loans of $10,000 per year. This is a scholarship/loan program. Loans of 5 years or more are forgiven at the rate of 20% per year for qualifying employment in an area of defined need (a geographic area or a population that is experiencing a shortage of primary health care providers in Missouri). Loans for less than 5 years are forgiven on a year-for-year basis. If the loan is not forgiven by service, it must be repaid within 48 months at 9.5% interest.

Duration Full-time undergraduate students may receive up to 4 loans. part-time Medical students may receive loans for up to 4 or 6 years, depending on the length of their program. Physicians and dentists in primary care residency programs may receive up to 3 years of loans.

Additional information This program is also known as the PRIMO Loan Program.

Number awarded Varies each year.

Deadline June or December of each year.

[682]
STOKES EDUCATIONAL SCHOLARSHIP PROGRAM

National Security Agency
Office of Recruitment and Staffing (Stokes)
9800 Savage Road, Suite 6779
P.O. Box 1661, Suite 6779
Fort Meade, MD 20755-6779
Toll-free: (866) 672-4473
Web: www.nsa.gov/programs/employ/utp.cfm

Purpose To provide minority and other high school seniors with scholarship/loans and work experience at the National Security Agency (NSA).

Eligibility This program is open to graduating high school seniors, particularly minorities, who 1) are planning a college major in electrical or computer engineering, computer science, mathematics, or foreign languages (recent language interests included Amharic, Arabic, Chinese, Dari, modern Greek, Hindi, Japanese, Korean, Pashto, Persian/Farsi, Somali, Swahili, Turkish, and Urdu/Punjabi); 2) have minimum scores of 25 on the ACT (or the equivalent on the SAT); 3) have a GPA of 3.0 or higher; 4) are U.S. citizens; and 5) demonstrate leadership abilities. Also eligible are college sophomores who are U.S. citizens, have a GPA of 3.0 or higher, and have completed 6 credits in 1 of the core languages. Applicants must include a 1-page essay on why they want to have a career with the NSA.

Financial data Participants receive college tuition for 4 years, reimbursement for books and certain fees, a year-round salary, and a housing allowance and travel reimbursement during summer employment if the distance between the agency and school exceeds 75 miles. Following graduation, participants must work for the agency for 1 and a half times their length of study, usually 5 years. Students who leave agency employment earlier must repay the tuition cost.

Duration 4 years, followed by employment at the agency for 5 years.

Additional information Participants must attend classes full time and work at the agency during the summer in jobs tailored to their course of study. They must maintain at least a 3.0 GPA. This program, established in 1986, was formerly known as the National Security Agency Undergraduate Training Program.

Number awarded Varies each year.

Deadline November of each year.

[683]
TENNESSEE MINORITY TEACHING FELLOWS PROGRAM

Tennessee Student Assistance Corporation
Parkway Towers
404 James Robertson Parkway, Suite 1950
Nashville, TN 37243-0820
(615) 741-1346   Toll-free: (800) 342-1663
Fax: (615) 741-6101   E-mail: tsac@mail.state.tn.us
Web: www.tnscholardollars.com

Purpose To provide scholarship/loans to minority Tennesseans who wish to enter the teaching field.

Eligibility This program is open to minority residents of Tennessee who are either high school seniors planning to attend a college or university in the state or continuing college students at a Tennessee college or university. High

school seniors must have a GPA of 2.75 or higher and either have an ACT score of at least 18 (or its SAT equivalent) or rank in the top 25% of their high school class. Continuing college students must have a college GPA of 2.5 or higher. All applicants must agree to teach at the K-12 level in a Tennessee public school following graduation from college.

Financial data The scholarship/loan is $5,000 per year. Recipients incur an obligation to teach at the K-12 level in a Tennessee public school 1 year for each year the award is received.

Duration 1 year; may be renewed for up to 3 additional years.

Additional information This program was established in 1989.

Number awarded 20 new awards are granted each year.

Deadline April of each year.

[684]
TEXAS DEPARTMENT OF TRANSPORTATION CONDITIONAL GRANT PROGRAM

Texas Department of Transportation
Attn: Employment Opportunities Section
125 East 11th Street
Austin, TX 78701-2483
(512) 416-4976
Web: www.dot.state.tx.us/employment/recruiting.htm

Purpose To provide scholarship/loans to minorities and women in Texas who are interested in majoring in designated areas and then working for the Texas Department of Transportation.

Eligibility This program is open to minorities (Black, Hispanic, American Indian, Asian, Pacific Islander) and women who are residents of Texas. High school applicants must have a GPA of 3.0 or higher or at least 21 on the ACT (or the equivalent on the SAT); plan to attend an accredited 4-year public college or university in Texas as a full-time student; plan to major in civil engineering; be willing to work for the Texas Department of Transportation for at least 2 years after graduation; and not be more than 30 days delinquent on any child support obligation. College or university applicants must have a GPA of 2.5 or higher; be attending a 4-year public college or university in Texas; be taking at least 12 hours per semester; have declared a major in civil engineering; be willing to work for the Texas Department of Transportation for at least 2 years after graduation; not be in repayment status for a previously-awarded Conditional Grant; and be no more than 30 days delinquent on any child support obligation.

Financial data The grant covers tuition, fees and a stipend, up to a maximum of $3,000 per semester or $6,000 per year. The exact amount awarded is based on the recipient's documented financial need. This is a scholarship/loan program. Recipients must repay the full amount of the grant if they fail to graduate, or maintain a cumulative GPA of 2.5 or higher, or stay in school, or stay in an approved major, or work for the Texas Department of Transportation for the required period of time.

Duration 1 year; may be renewed.

Additional information Recipients must attend school on a full-time basis (at least 12 hours per semester), maintain a GPA of 2.5 or higher, graduate in an approved major, and work for the Texas Department of Transportation for at least 2 years.

Number awarded   Varies each year.

Deadline   February of each year.

[685]
VERMONT LOAN FORGIVENESS FOR CULTURALLY DIVERSE EDUCATION STUDENTS

Vermont Teacher Diversity Scholarship Program
Attn: Director
P.O. Box 359
Waterbury, VT 05676-0359
(802) 241-3379   Fax: (802) 241-3369
E-mail: phyl.newbeck@vsc.edu
Web: templeton.vsc.edu/teacherdiversity

Purpose   To forgive the educational loans of students from diverse racial and ethnic backgrounds at colleges in Vermont who wish to become public school teachers in the state.

Eligibility   This program is open to students enrolled or planning to enroll at designated colleges and universities in Vermont to prepare for licensure as a public school teacher. Applicants must come from diverse racial and ethnic backgrounds and be willing to become teachers in the Vermont public school system. As part of their application, they must submit brief essays on why they believe it is important for children in grades K-12 to be exposed to teachers from diverse backgrounds, why they believe their particular background is appropriate for them to be considered for this program, why they want to be a teacher, the experiences they have had that have prepared them for the challenge of teaching, and the challenges they expect to experience as a person whose background may differ from the majority culture. Selection is based on racial and ethnic diversity, leadership qualities, experience working with children, employment history (if applicable), educational history, commitment to teaching in Vermont, understanding of diversity and issues related to power and privilege in the United States, and academic potential. Preference is given to residents of Vermont, but students from all states are encouraged to apply.

Financial data   If participants in this program are hired as public school teachers in Vermont, $4,000 of their college loans are forgiven for each year they teach.

Duration   Participants may receive up to 3 years of loan forgiveness (for a total of $12,000).

Additional information   This program, formerly known as Coming Home, operates in partnership with several organizations in the state (including the Vermont Student Assistance Corporation, the Vermont Department of Education, and Vermont-NEA) and with 16 designated colleges and universities in the states. Participants in this program are not required to attend those schools, but they are encouraged to investigate them.

Number awarded   Varies each year; recently, 10 of the program's scholars were working on a degree in education at a participating Vermont college or university.

Deadline   March or October of each year.

[686]
VIRGINIA MEDICAL SCHOLARSHIP PROGRAM

Virginia Department of Health
Attn: Center for Primary Care and Rural Health
1500 East Main Street, Suite 227
Richmond, VA 23219
(804) 786-4891   Fax: (804) 371-0116
Web: www.vdh.state.va.us

Purpose   To provide loans-for-service to minority and other medical students who are willing to practice as primary care physicians in Virginia.

Eligibility   This program is open to medical students pursuing primary care medical education at designated schools in Virginia and Tennessee. Graduate medical students in the first year of a primary care residency are also eligible. Primary care specialties include family practice, general internal medicine, pediatrics, and obstetrics/gynecology. Applicants must intend to practice in underserved areas within Virginia. Preference is given to residents of Virginia, residents from rural and medically underserved areas, and minority students.

Financial data   The maximum assistance is $10,000 per year. Repayment begins after completion of a 3-year residency (or 4 years for obstetrics/gynecology). Repayment is made through practice as a primary care physician in Virginia Medically Underserved Areas (VMUAs) designated by the Board of Health.

Duration   1 year; may be renewed for up to 4 additional years, for a total loan of $50,000.

Additional information   The designated schools are Eastern Virginia Medical School of the Medical College of Hampton Roads (Norfolk, Virginia), the University of Virginia School of Medicine (Charlottesville, Virginia), the Medical College of Virginia of the Virginia Commonwealth University (Richmond, Virginia), James H. Quillen College of Medicine of East Tennessee State University (Johnson City, Tennessee), and Pikeville College School of Osteopathic Medicine (Pikeville, Kentucky).

Number awarded   Varies each year; 4 scholarships are set aside for East Tennessee State University and the number assigned to the 3 Virginia schools is determined by the funding provided by the Virginia General Assembly.

Deadline   Deadlines are established by the directors of financial aid at the participating medical schools.

[687]
VIRGINIA NURSE PRACTITIONER/NURSE MIDWIFE SCHOLARSHIP PROGRAM

Virginia Department of Health
Attn: Office of Health Policy and Planning
109 Governor Street, 1016 East Office
P.O. Box 2448
Richmond, VA 23218
(804) 864-7433   Fax: (804) 864-7440
E-mail: Margie.Thomas@vdh.virginia.gov
Web: www.vdh.state.va.us

Purpose   To provide forgivable loans to minority and other nursing students in Virginia who are willing to work as nurse practitioners and/or midwives in the state following graduation.

Eligibility   This program is open to residents of Virginia who are enrolled or accepted for enrollment full time at a nurse practitioner program in the state or a nurse midwifery program in a nearby state. Applicants must have a cumulative GPA of at least 3.0 in undergraduate and/or graduate courses. Preference is given to 1) residents of designated medically underserved areas of Virginia; 2) students enrolled in family practice, obstetrics and gynecology, pediatric, adult health, and geriatric nurse practitioner programs; and 3) minority students. Selection is based on scholastic achievement, character, and stated commitment to postgraduate employment in a medically underserved area of Virginia.

Financial data The amount of the award depends on the availability of funds. Recipients must agree to serve in a designated medically underserved area of Virginia for a period of years equal to the number of years of scholarship support received. The required service must begin within 2 years of the recipient's graduation and must be in a facility that provides services to persons who are unable to pay for the service and that participates in all government-sponsored insurance programs designed to assure full access to medical care service for covered persons. If the recipient fails to complete the course of study, or pass the licensing examination, or provide the required service, all scholarship funds received must be repaid with interest.

Duration 1 year; may be renewed for 1 additional year.

Number awarded Varies each year.

Deadline June of each year.

[688]
VIRGINIA TEACHING SCHOLARSHIP LOAN PROGRAM

Virginia Department of Education
Attn: Division of Teacher Education and Licensure
P.O. Box 2120
Richmond, VA 23218-2120
(804) 371-2475   Toll-free: (800) 292-3820
Fax: (804) 786-6759
Web: www.pen.k12.va.us

Purpose To provide scholarship/loans to upper-division and graduate students in Virginia who are interested in a career in teaching.

Eligibility This program is open to Virginia residents who are enrolled full or part time as a junior, senior, or graduate student in a state-approved teacher preparation program in Virginia with a GPA of 2.7 or higher. Applicants must agree to engage in full-time teaching in designated teacher shortage areas within Virginia following graduation. Males interested in teaching at the elementary and middle school levels and people of color in all teaching areas also qualify.

Financial data The scholarship/loan is $3,720 per year. Loans are forgiven at the rate of $2,000 for each year the recipient teaches in designated teacher shortage areas. If the recipient fails to fulfill the teaching service requirement, the loan must be repaid with interest.

Duration 1 year; may be renewed 1 additional year.

Additional information Critical shortage teaching areas in Virginia are currently identified as foreign languages, science (including, in order of priority preference, physics, earth science, chemistry, and biology), all areas of special education (severe emotional disturbances, hearing disabilities, learning disabilities, mental retardation, severe disabilities, visual disabilities, early childhood special education,

and speech-language pathology), career and technical education (including technology education, trade and industrial education, business education, and family and consumer sciences), mathematics, English as a second language, middle grades 6-8, library media K-12, art preK-12, and reading specialist.

Number awarded Varies each year. Recently, 163 of these scholarship/loans were granted, including 47 in special education, 20 in science, 4 in foreign language, 2 in technology education, 24 in mathematics, 4 in English as a second language, 1 in library media, 3 for reading specialists, 1 in agricultural education, 22 for males in elementary or middle grades, and 35 for people of color.

[689]
WELLS FARGO ASIAN AMERICAN SMALL BUSINESS LOAN PROGRAM

Wells Fargo Bank
Attn: National Business Banking Center
P.O. Box 340214
Sacramento, CA 95834-0214
Toll-free: (800) 35-WELLS, ext. 450
Web: www.wellsfargo.com

Purpose To loan money to Asian American-owned businesses.

Eligibility To qualify for a loan, Asian American business owners must have a satisfactory personal and business credit history, have been in business for at least 3 years, have a profitable business with sufficient cash flow to meet their new and current financial obligations, and have not declared bankruptcy in the past 10 years. Applicants may be interested in 1) an unsecured, revolving line of credit; 2) financing for new and used machinery, equipment, and vehicles; or 3) equity loans or lines of credit secured by commercial real estate.

Financial data This program offers unsecured, revolving lines of credit up to $100,000, equipment loans up to $50,000, and equity loans from $25,000 to $250,000. Interest rates are variable.

Number awarded Varies each year. This program, established in 2002, has a goal of lending $2 billion over 10 years to Asian American small business owners.

Deadline Applications may be requested at any time.

[690]
WISCONSIN MINORITY BUSINESS DEVELOPMENT LOAN PROGRAM

Wisconsin Department of Commerce
Attn: Bureau of Minority Business Development
201 West Washington Avenue
P.O. Box 7970
Madison, WI 53707-7970
(608) 267-9550   Fax: (608) 267-2829
E-mail: MBD@commerce.state.wi.us
Web: www.commerce.state.wi.us

Purpose To provide low-interest loans to businesses owned by minorities in Wisconsin.

Eligibility This program is open to businesses in Wisconsin that have completed a comprehensive business plan and that are at least 51% owned by a Black, Hispanic, American Indian, Eskimo, Asian Pacific, Asian Indian, Aleut, or Native Hawaiian. Applicants must be interested in a loan for land, construction, acquisition of an existing business, purchase of equipment, or working capital. Factors considered in loan approval include whether the applicant has at least 2 years of relevant work experience, if the applicant's education and/or training is relevant to the proposed business venture, if the applicant has cash reserves (equity) necessary to invest in the proposed business, if a local bank and/or other local organization has made a funding commitment to the project, if the business will have a positive economic impact upon the local community, the number of jobs that will be created or retained, if the proposed business will have a negative impact upon other local businesses, and if the proposed business will be located in a target area.

Financial data Loan amounts vary. Ideally, this loan should provide 25% of total investment; other financing should include 5% from personal equity, 45% from a bank loan, and 25% from a development corporation. Interest rates are fixed at levels below market rates, typically 4%.

Duration Real estate loans are for 10 to 15 years, equipment loans for 5 to 10 years, and working capital loans for 5 to 7 years.

Number awarded Varies each year.

Deadline Applications may be submitted at any time.

[691]
WISCONSIN MINORITY TEACHER LOANS

Wisconsin Higher Educational Aids Board
131 West Wilson Street, Room 902
P.O. Box 7885
Madison, WI 53707-7885
(608) 267-2212   Fax: (608) 267-2808
E-mail: mary.kuzdas@heab.state.wi.us
Web: heab.state.wi.us/programs.html

Purpose To provide scholarship/loans to minorities in Wisconsin who are interested in teaching in Wisconsin school districts with large minority enrollments.

Eligibility African Americans, Hispanic Americans, and American Indians in Wisconsin are eligible to apply if they are enrolled full time as juniors or seniors in an independent or public institution in the state. The program also includes students who were admitted to the United States after December 31, 1975 and who are a former citizen of Laos, Vietnam, or Cambodia or whose ancestor was a citizen of 1 of those countries. Applicants must be enrolled in a program leading to teaching licensure and must agree to teach in a Wisconsin school district in which minority students constitute at least 29% of total enrollment or in a school district participating in the inter-district pupil transfer program.

Financial data Scholarship/loans are provided up to $2,500 per year. For each year the student teaches in an eligible school district, 25% of the loan is forgiven; if the student does not teach in an eligible district, the loan must be repaid at an interest rate of 5%.

Duration 1 year; may be renewed 1 additional year.

Additional information Eligible students should apply through their school's financial aid office.

Number awarded Varies each year.

Deadline Deadline dates vary by institution; check with your school's financial aid office.

Grants

Described here are 135 programs that provide funds to Asian Americans for innovative efforts, travel, projects, creative activities, or research on any level (from undergraduate to postdoctorate and professional). In some cases, proposals may be submitted by institutions or organizations only; in others, individual Asian Americans may submit proposals directly. If you are looking for a particular program and don't find it in this section, be sure to check the Program Title Index to see if it is covered elsewhere in the directory.

[692]
ABC TALENT DEVELOPMENT SCHOLARSHIP-GRANT PROGRAM

ABC Entertainment
Attn: Talent Development Programs
500 South Buena Vista Street
Burbank, CA 91521-4390
(818) 460-7770   E-mail: abc.fellowships@abc.com
Web: www.abctalendevelopment.com

Purpose To provide funding to emerging artists (including high school, college, and graduate students) from diverse backgrounds in selected cities throughout the United States who are interested in completing a creative project.

Eligibility This program is open to high school, college, and graduate students from Chicago, Houston, Los Angeles, Minneapolis, New York, Raleigh-Durham, and Washington, D.C. Applications must be submitted through participating sponsors (high schools, colleges, universities, or civic, social service, or professional organizations) in those communities. Emerging artists who are members of sponsoring organizations are also eligible to apply. Many of the designated sponsors focus on service to minorities and students with disabilities, because a goal of the program is to discover, develop, and encourage creative talent from diverse backgrounds. Applicants must be proposing to complete an existing creative project. They must submit a work resume, personal bio, essay of 500 to 800 words on their career goals and interest in the field, and samples of the proposed project. If the project involves a screenplay or television script, submissions must include a treatment, 10 pages of proposed story idea, and a detailed budget. If the project involves a video, submissions must include a sample reel of a previously completed film or video project, a proposal, and a detailed budget. Material that may not be submitted in support of an application includes published material (e.g., short stories), scripts adapted from other material not indicative of writing for television or film, sequels to motion pictures, plays, magazine articles, drawings, projects that have been fully executed creatively (i.e., polished scripts or videos needing post production only), or projects that have been previously entered into a competition or festival.

Financial data Individuals receive grants of $20,000 to help finance the development of their project. Sponsoring organizations with winning submissions receive $10,000 grants to further develop their creative programs.

Duration 1 year.

Additional information Selected participants are paired with a mentor at Walt Disney Studios or ABC Entertainment. The program concludes with a 3-day workshop in Los Angeles. Recently, the sponsoring organizations included the International Latino Cultural Center of Chicago, the Mille Lacs Band of Ojibwe, American Indian Artists, Inc, the International Agency for Minority Artist Affairs, National Hispanic Foundation for the Arts, National Asian American Telecommunications Association, National Association for the Advancement of Colored People, and the Media Access Office of the California Governor's Committee on Employment of People with Disabilities. This program began in 2001.

Number awarded Varies each year; recently, 16 of these grants were awarded.

Deadline December of each year.

[693]
ABE FELLOWSHIP PROGRAM

Social Science Research Council
Attn: Japan Program
810 Seventh Avenue
New York, NY 10019
(212) 377-2700   Fax: (212) 377-2727
E-mail: abe@ssrc.org
Web: www.ssrc.org/fellowships/abe

Purpose To provide funding to postdoctoral scholars (particularly minorities and women) interested in conducting research on contemporary policy-relevant affairs in Japan.

Eligibility This program is open to American and Japanese research professionals who have doctorate-equivalent or professional experience (other nationals affiliated with an American or Japanese institution are also eligible to apply). Applicants should be interested in conducting multidisciplinary research on topics of pressing global concern. Currently, research must focus on the 3 themes of global issues, problems common to industrial and industrializing societies, and issues that pertain to U.S.-Japan relations. Within those 3 themes, research may address issues related to technology and society; consumption, labor, and markets; human security; civil society; bioethics; aging societies and other life-span issues; transnational economic relations; sustainable development and global environmental issues; and foreign assistance. Previous language training is not a prerequisite for this fellowship. Minorities and women are particularly encouraged to apply.

Financial data The terms of the fellowship include a base award and funds to pay supplementary research and travel expenses as necessary for completion of the research project.

Duration The program provides support for 3 to 12 months over a 24-month period.

Additional information Fellows are expected to affiliate with an American or Japanese institution appropriate to their research aims. In addition to receiving fellowship awards, fellows attend annual Abe Fellows Conferences, which promote the development of an international network of scholars concerned with research on contemporary policy issues. Funds are provided by the Japan Foundation's Center for Global Partnership. Fellows should plan to spend at least one third of their tenure abroad in Japan or the United States.

Deadline August of each year.

[694]
ABF POSTDOCTORAL FELLOWSHIPS IN LAW AND SOCIAL SCIENCE

American Bar Foundation
Attn: Assistant Director
750 North Lake Shore Drive
Chicago, IL 60611
(312) 988-6500   Fax: (312) 988-6579
E-mail: fellowships@abfn.org
Web: www.abf-sociolegal.org/Fellowship/index.html

Purpose To provide funding to postdoctoral scholars (particularly minorities) who wish to conduct research on law, the legal profession, and legal institutions.

Eligibility Applications are invited from junior scholars who completed all requirements for their Ph.D. within the past 2 years; in exceptional circumstances, candidates with a J.D. who have substantial social science training may also be considered. Proposed research must be in the general area of sociolegal studies or in social scientific approaches to law, the legal profession, or legal institutions and legal processes. Applications must include 1) a sample of written work; 2) 2 letters of recommendation; 3) a curriculum vitae; and 4) a statement describing research interests and achievements to date and plans for the fellowship period. Minority candidates are especially encouraged to apply.

Financial data The stipend is $30,000 per year; fringe benefits are also provided. Fellows may request up to $3,500 each fellowship year for research support. Relocation expenses of up to $1,000 may be reimbursed on application.

Duration 1 year; may be renewed for 1 additional year.

Additional information Fellows are offered access to the computing and word processing facilities of the American Bar Foundation and the libraries of Northwestern University and the University of Chicago. This program was established in 1996. Fellowships must be held in residence at the American Bar Foundation. Appointments to the fellowship are full time; fellows are not permitted to undertake other work.

Number awarded 2 each year.

Deadline January of each year.

[695]
ACLS FELLOWSHIPS

American Council of Learned Societies
Attn: Office of Fellowships and Grants
633 Third Avenue, 8C
New York, NY 10017-6795
(212) 697-1505   Fax: (212) 949-8058
E-mail: grants@acls.org
Web: www.acls.org/felguide.htm

Purpose To provide research funding to scholars (particularly minorities and women) in all disciplines of the humanities and the humanities-related social sciences.

Eligibility This program is open to scholars at all stages of their careers who received a Ph.D. degree at least 2 years previously. Established scholars who can demonstrate the equivalent of the Ph.D. in publications and professional experience may also qualify. Applicants must be U.S. citizens or permanent residents who have not held supported leave time for at least 3 years prior to the start of the proposed research. Appropriate fields of specialization include, but are not limited to, anthropology, archaeology, art history, economics, film, geography, history, languages and literatures, law, linguistics, musicology, philosophy, political science, psychology, religion, rhetoric and communication, and sociology. Proposals in those fields of the social sciences are eligible only if they employ predominantly humanistic approaches (e.g., economic history, law and literature, political philosophy). Proposals in interdisciplinary and cross-disciplinary studies are welcome, as are proposals focused on any geographic region or on any cultural or linguistic group. Awards are available at 3 academic levels: full professor, associate professor, and assistant professor. Applications are particularly invited from women and members of minority groups.

Financial data The maximum grant is $50,000 for full professors and equivalent, $40,000 for associate professors and equivalent, or $30,000 for assistant professors and equivalent. Normally, fellowships are intended as salary replacement and may be held concurrently with other fellowships, grants, and sabbatical pay, up to an amount equal to the candidate's current academic year salary.

Duration 6 to 12 months.

Additional information This program is supported in part by funding from the Ford Foundation, the Andrew W. Mellon Foundation, the National Endowment for the Humanities, the William and Flora Hewlett Foundation, and the Rockefeller Foundation.

Number awarded Varies each year. Recently, 68 of these fellowships were awarded: 17 to full professors, 16 to associate professors, 34 to assistant professors (including 27 designated as ACLS/Andrew W. Mellon Foundation Junior Faculty Fellowships and 1 designated as an ACLS/Oscar Handlin Fellowship), and 1 independent scholar.

Deadline September of each year.

[696]
ACLS/SSRC/NEH INTERNATIONAL AND AREA STUDIES FELLOWSHIPS

American Council of Learned Societies
Attn: Office of Fellowships and Grants
633 Third Avenue, 8C
New York, NY 10017-6795
(212) 697-1505   Fax: (212) 949-8058
E-mail: grants@acls.org
Web: www.acls.org/felguide.htm

Purpose To provide funding to postdoctoral scholars (particularly minorities and women) interested in conducting humanities-related research on the societies and cultures of Asia, Africa, the Near and Middle East, Latin America and the Caribbean, eastern Europe, and the former Soviet Union.

Eligibility This program is open to U.S. citizens and residents who have lived in the United States for at least 3 years. Applicants must have a Ph.D. degree and not have received supported research leave time for at least 3 years prior to the start of the proposed research. They must be interested in conducting humanities and humanities-related social science research on the societies and cultures of Asia, Africa, the Middle East, Latin America and the Caribbean, east Europe, or the former Soviet Union. Selection is based on the intellectual merit of the proposed research and the likelihood that it will produce significant and innovative scholarship. Applications are particularly invited from women and members of minority groups.

Financial data The maximum grant is $50,000 for full professors and equivalent, $40,000 for associate professors and equivalent, or $30,000 for assistant professors and equivalent. These fellowships may not be held concurrently with another major fellowship.

Duration 6 to 12 months.

Additional information This program is jointly supported by the American Council of Learned Societies (ACLS) and the Social Science Research Council (SSRC), with funding provided by the National Endowment for the Humanities (NEH).

Number awarded Approximately 10 each year.

Deadline September of each year.

[697]
AMERICAN ANTHROPOLOGICAL ASSOCIATION MINORITY DISSERTATION FELLOWSHIP PROGRAM

American Anthropological Association
Attn: Department of Academic Relations
2200 Wilson Boulevard, Suite 600
Arlington, VA 22201-3357
(703) 528-1902   Fax: (703) 528-3546
E-mail: academic@aaanet.org
Web: www.aaanet.org

Purpose To provide funding to minorities who are working on a Ph.D. dissertation in anthropology.

Eligibility Native American, African American, Latino(a), and Asian American doctoral students who have been admitted to degree candidacy in anthropology are invited to apply. Applicants must be U.S. citizens, enrolled in a full-time academic program leading to a doctoral degree in anthropology, and members of the American Anthropological Association. They must have a record of outstanding academic success, have had their dissertation proposal approved by their dissertation committee prior to application, be writing a dissertation in an area of anthropological research, and need funding to complete the dissertation. To apply, students must submit an application form, a cover letter, a research plan summary, a curriculum vitae, a statement regarding employment, a disclosure statement providing information about other sources of available and pending financial support, 3 letters of recommendation, and an official transcript from their doctoral program. Selection is based on the quality of the submitted information and the judged likelihood that the applicant will have a good chance at completing the dissertation. Consideration is also given to the implications of the applicant's research to issues and concerns of the U.S. historically disadvantaged populations, relevant service to the community, and future plans.

Financial data The stipend is $10,000. Funds are sent in 2 installments (in September and in January) to the recipient's institution.

Duration 1 year; nonrenewable.

Number awarded 1 each year.

Deadline February of each year.

[698]
AMERICAN ASSOCIATION OF OBSTETRICIANS AND GYNECOLOGISTS FOUNDATION SCHOLARSHIPS

American Association of Obstetricians and
  Gynecologists Foundation
Attn: Administrative Director
409 12th Street, S.W.
Washington, DC 20024-2188
(202) 863-1647   Fax: (202) 554-0453
E-mail: ejones@acog.org
Web: www.agosonline.org

Purpose To provide funding to physicians (particularly minorities and women) interested in a program of research training in obstetrics and gynecology.

Eligibility Applicants must have an M.D. degree and be eligible for the certification process of the American Board of Obstetrics and Gynecology (ABOG). They must document departmental planning for a significant research training experience to be conducted by 1 or more faculty mentors. There is no formal application form, but departments must supply a description of the candidate's qualifications, including a curriculum vitae, bibliography, prior training, past research experience, and evidence of completion of residency training in obstetrics and gynecology; a comprehensive description of the proposed training program; a description of departmental resources appropriate to the training; a list of other research grants, training grants, or scholarships previously or currently held by the applicant; and a budget. Applicants for the scholarship sponsored by ABOG must verify that 90% of their time and effort will be dedicated to the research training and conduct of research. Applicants for the scholarship sponsored by the Society for Maternal-Fetal Medicine (SMFM) must also have completed MFM subspecialty training or be in the second or third year of an ABOG-approved MFM training program at the time of applying. Candidates for that scholarship must also be members or associate members of the SMFM. Preference for both awards is given to training in areas currently underrepresented in obstetrics and gynecology. A personal interview may be requested. Priority is given to individuals who have not previously received extramural funding for research training. Women and minority candidates are strongly encouraged to apply. Selection is based on the scholarly, clinical, and research qualifications of the candidate; evidence of the candidate's commitment to an investigative career in academic obstetrics and gynecology in the United States or Canada; qualifications of the sponsoring department and mentor; and quality of the research project.

Financial data The grant is $100,000 per year, of which at least $5,000 but not more than $15,000 must be used for employee benefits. In addition, sufficient funds to support travel to the annual fellows' retreat must be set aside. The balance of the funds may be used for salary, technical support, and supplies. The grant co-sponsored by the SMFM must be matched by an institutional commitment of at least $30,000 per year.

Duration 1 year; may be renewed for 2 additional years, based on satisfactory progress of the scholar.

Number awarded 2 each year: 1 co-sponsored by ABOG and 1 co-sponsored by SMFM.

Deadline August of each year.

[699]
AMERICAN EDUCATIONAL RESEARCH ASSOCIATION MINORITY FELLOWSHIP PROGRAM

American Educational Research Association
1230 17th Street, N.W.
Washington, DC 20036-3078
(202) 223-9485   Fax: (202) 775-1824
Web: www.aera.net/programs/minority

Purpose To provide funding to minority doctoral students writing their dissertation on educational research.

Eligibility This program is open to U.S. citizens and native residents of a U.S. possession who have advanced to candidacy and successfully defended their Ph.D./Ed.D. dissertation research proposal. Applicants must plan to work full time on their dissertation in educational research. This program is targeted for members of groups historically underrepresented in higher education (African Americans, American Indians, Alaskan Natives, Filipino Americans, Native Pacific Islanders, Mexican Americans, and Puerto Ricans). Selection is based on scholarly achievements and publications, letters of recommendation, quality and significance of the proposed research, and commitment of the applicant's faculty mentor to the goals of the program.

Financial data The grant is $12,000 per year; nonrenewable. Also, up to $1,000 is provided to pay for travel to the sponsor's annual conference.

Duration 1 year; may be renewed for 1 additional year upon demonstration of satisfactory progress.

Additional information The association also sponsors a number of other funding programs that give special attention to applications submitted by minorities, including the AERA/IES Dissertation Grants Program, AERA/IES Postdoctoral Fellowship Program, AERA/IES Research Grants Program, American Educational Research Association Dissertation Grants Program, American Educational Research Association Fellows Program, American Educational Research Association Postdoctoral Fellows Program, American Educational Research Association Research Fellows Program, American Educational Research Association Research Grants Program.

Number awarded 2 each year.

Deadline February of each year.

[700]
ANDREW W. MELLON FOUNDATION EARLY CAREER FELLOWSHIP IN ECONOMIC STUDIES

Brookings Institution
Attn: Mellon Fellows Program
1775 Massachusetts Avenue, N.W.
Washington, DC 20036-2188
(202) 797-6104   Fax: (202) 797-6181
E-mail: erobinson@brookings.edu
Web: www.brookings.edu/admin/eswebmellon.htm

Purpose To provide funding to economists (particularly minorities and women) who are interested in conducting an independent research project in residence at the Brookings Institution.

Eligibility This program is open to economists, especially junior faculty members who have between 2 and 6 years of teaching experience. Applicants should have a Ph.D. or equivalent and an expressed interest in analyzing applied and policy issues and empirical research. They must submit a curriculum vitae, a 500-word research proposal, 2 letters of recommendation, and copies of up to 5 significant publications and working papers. The institution particularly encourages applications from women and members of minority groups.

Financial data Fellows receive a salary and partial support for staff and research assistance.

Duration 1 year.

Additional information Fellows participate in workshops and conferences at the institution. Funding for this program is provided by the Andrew W. Mellon Foundation. Fellows are expected to pursue their research at the Brookings Institution.

Number awarded 1 or more each year.

Deadline November of each year.

[701]
APA MINORITY MEDICAL STUDENT SUMMER MENTORING PROGRAM

American Psychiatric Association
Attn: Department of Minority and National Affairs
1000 Wilson Boulevard, Suite 1825
Arlington, VA 22209-3901
(703) 907-8653   Toll-free: (888) 35-PSYCH
Fax: (703) 907-7852   E-mail: mking@psych.org
Web: www.psych.org

Purpose To provide funding to minority medical students who are interested in working on a summer project with a psychiatrist mentor.

Eligibility This program is open to minority medical students who are interested in psychiatric issues. Minorities include American Indians, Alaska Natives, Native Hawaiians, Asian Americans, Hispanic/Latinos, and African Americans. Applicants must be interested in working with a psychiatrist mentor, primarily on clinical work with underserved minority populations and mental health care disparities. Work settings may be in a research, academic, or clinical environment. Most of them are inner-city or rural, preferably those dealing with psychiatric subspecialties, particularly substance abuse and geriatrics. Selection is based on interest of the medical student and the specialty of the mentor, practice setting, and geographic proximity of the mentor to the student.

Financial data Fellowships provide $1,500 for living expenses and up to another $1,500 for out-of-pocket expenses directly related to the conduct of the fellowship.

Duration Summer months.

Number awarded Varies each year.

Deadline February of each year.

[702]
ARCTIC RESEARCH OPPORTUNITIES

National Science Foundation
Attn: Office of Polar Programs
4201 Wilson Boulevard, Room 755S
Arlington, VA 22230
(703) 292-8029   Fax: (703) 292-9082
TDD: (703) 292-5090
Web: www.nsf.gov/od/opp

Purpose To provide funding (particularly to minorities, women, and persons with disabilities) for research related to the Arctic.

Eligibility This program is open to investigators affiliated with U.S. universities, research institutions, or other organizations, including local or state governments. Applicants must be proposing to conduct research in the 3 program areas of Arctic Natural Sciences (including atmospheric sciences, biological sciences, earth sciences, glaciology, and ocean sciences); Arctic Social Sciences (including anthropology, archaeology, economics, geography, linguistics, political science, psychology, science and technology studies, sociology, traditional knowledge, and related subjects); and Arctic System Science (encompassing 3 components: 1) how do human activities interact with changes in the Arctic to affect the sustainability of ecosystems and societies? 2) what are the limits of Arctic system predictability? and 3) how will changes in Arctic cycles and feedbacks affect Arctic and global systems?). Proposals should involve field studies in the Arctic, although projects outside the Arctic but directly related to Arctic science and engineering are also considered, as are related laboratory and theoretical studies. The program particularly encourages proposals from women, minorities, and persons with disabilities.

Financial data The amounts of the awards depend on the nature of the proposal and the availability of funds.

Number awarded Varies each year. Recently, this program awarded 130 to 160 grants worth approximately $66 million.

Deadline August or February of each year.

[703]
ASA/NSF/BLS SENIOR RESEARCH FELLOW PROGRAM

American Statistical Association
Attn: Fellowship Program
1429 Duke Street, Suite 200
Alexandria, VA 22314-3415
(703) 684-1221   Toll-free: (888) 231-3473
Fax: (703) 684-2037   E-mail: asainfo@amstat.org
Web: www.amstat.org/research_grants

Purpose To provide funding to senior researchers (particularly minorities and women) interested in conducting research in residence at the Bureau of Labor Statistics (BLS).

Eligibility This program is open to scholars interested in conducting research in the broad field of labor economics and statistics that is of interest to the BLS. Applicants must be planning to work in residence, using BLS data and facilities, and interacting with BLS staff. They should have a recognized research record and considerable expertise in their area of proposed research. Selection is based on the applicability of the proposed research to BLS programs, the value of the proposed research to science, and the quality of the applicant's research record. Qualified women and members of minority groups are especially encouraged to apply.

Financial data The stipends paid to senior research fellows are commensurate with their qualifications and experience. Fellows also receive fringe benefits and a travel allowance.

Duration The usual term is 6 to 12 months, although the duration is flexible.

Additional information Fellows are given an opportunity to conduct their research in residence and interact with staff. Funding for this program is provided by the National Science Foundation (NSF). Information is also available from the Office of Survey Methods Research, Attn: Stephen Cohen, 2 Massachusetts Avenue, N.E., Room 4915, Washington, DC 20212, (202) 691-7400, E-mail: Cohen.Steve@bls.gov, and the Office of Employment Research and Program Development, Attn: James Spletzer, 2 Massachusetts Avenue, N.E., Room 4945, Washington, DC 20212, (202) 691-7393, E-mail: Spletzer.Jim@bls.gov.

Number awarded Varies each year.

Deadline December of each year.

[704]
ASIAN AMERICAN STUDIES POSTDOCTORAL AND VISITING SCHOLARS FELLOWSHIP PROGRAM

University of California at Los Angeles
Asian American Studies Center
Attn: IAC Coordinator
3230 Campbell Hall
P.O. Box 951546
Los Angeles, CA 90095-1546
(310) 825-2974   Fax: (310) 206-9844
Web: www.gdnet.ucla.edu/iacweb/pstweber.htm

Purpose To provide financial support to scholars interested in conducting research in Asian American studies at UCLA's Asian American Studies Center.

Eligibility Applicants must have completed a doctoral degree in Asian American or related studies. They must be interested in teaching or conducting research at UCLA's Asian American Studies Center. UCLA faculty, students, and staff are not eligible. U.S. citizenship or permanent resident status is required.

Financial data Fellows receive a stipend of $30,000 to $35,000 (depending on rank, experience, and date of completion of the Ph.D.), health benefits, and up to $4,000 in research support.

Duration 1 academic year; may be renewed.

Additional information Fellows must teach or do research in the programs of the center. The award is offered in conjunction with UCLA's Institute of American Cultures (IAC).

Number awarded 1 each year.

Deadline January of each year.

[705]
ASTRAZENECA FELLOWSHIP/FACULTY TRANSITION AWARDS

Foundation for Digestive Health and Nutrition
Attn: Research Awards Coordinator
4930 Del Ray Avenue
Bethesda, MD 20814-2512
(301) 222-4005   Fax: (301) 222-4010
E-mail: info@fdhn.org
Web: www.fdhn.org

Purpose To provide funding to physicians (especially those who are minority group members or women) for research training in an area of gastrointestinal, liver function, or related diseases.

Eligibility This program is open to trainee members of the American Gastroenterological Association (AGA) who are M.D.s or M.D./Ph.D.s currently holding a gastroenterology-related fellowship at an accredited North American institution. Applicants must be committed to an academic career; have completed 2 years of research training at the start of this award; be sponsored by an AGA member who directs a gastroenterology-related unit that is engaged in research training in a North American medical school, affiliated teaching hospital, or research institute; and be cosponsored by the director of a basic research laboratory (or other comparable laboratory) who is committed to the training and development of the applicant. Minorities and women investigators are strongly encouraged to apply. Selection is based on novelty, feasibility, and significance of the proposal; attributes of the candidate; record and commitment of the sponsors; and the institutional and laboratory environment.

Financial data The stipend is $40,000 per year. Funds are to be used as salary support for the recipient. Indirect costs are not allowed.

Duration 2 years.

Additional information This award is administered by the Foundation for Digestive Health and Nutrition (FDHN) and sponsored by the AGA with support from AstraZeneca Pharmaceuticals, L.P. Finalists for the award are interviewed. Although the host institution may supplement the award, the applicant may not concurrently have a similar training award or grant from another organization. All publications coming from work funded by this program must acknowledge the support of the award.

Number awarded Up to 4 each year.

Deadline September of each year.

[706]
BEHAVIORAL SCIENCES POSTDOCTORAL FELLOWSHIPS IN EPILEPSY

Epilepsy Foundation
Attn: Research Department
4351 Garden City Drive
Landover, MD 20785-7223
(301) 459-3700   Toll-free: (800) EFA-1000
Fax: (301) 577-2684   TDD: (800) 332-2070
E-mail: grants@efa.org
Web: www.epilepsyfoundation.org

Purpose To provide funding to postdoctorates (especially minorities, women, and persons with disabilities) in the behavioral sciences who wish to pursue research training in an area related to epilepsy.

Eligibility Individuals who have received their doctoral degree in a behavioral science field by the time the fellowship begins and desire additional postdoctoral research experience in epilepsy may apply. Academic faculty holding the rank of instructor or above are not eligible, nor are graduate or medical students, medical residents, permanent government employees, or employees of private industry. Appropriate fields of study in the behavioral sciences include sociology, social work, anthropology, nursing, economics, and others relevant to epilepsy research and practice. Because these fellowships are designed as training opportunities, the quality of the training plans and environment are considered in the selection process. Other selection criteria include the scientific quality of the proposed research, a statement regarding the relevance of the research to epilepsy, the applicant's qualifications, and the preceptor's qualifications. Applications from women, members of minority groups, and people with disabilities are especially encouraged. U.S. citizenship is not required, but the research must be conducted in the United States.

Financial data Grants up to $30,000 per year are available.

Duration 1 year.

Number awarded Varies each year; recently, 2 of these fellowships were awarded.

Deadline February of each year.

[707]
BEHAVIORAL SCIENCES STUDENT FELLOWSHIPS IN EPILEPSY

Epilepsy Foundation
Attn: Research Department
4351 Garden City Drive
Landover, MD 20785-7223
(301) 459-3700   Toll-free: (800) EFA-1000
Fax: (301) 577-2684   TDD: (800) 332-2070
E-mail: grants@efa.org
Web: www.epilepsyfoundation.org

Purpose To provide funding to undergraduate and graduate students (minorities, women, and persons with disabilities) interested in working on a summer research training project in a field relevant to epilepsy.

Eligibility This program is open to undergraduate and graduate students in a behavioral science program relevant to epilepsy research or clinical care, including, but not limited to, sociology, social work, psychology, anthropology, nursing, economics, vocational rehabilitation, counseling, and political science. Applicants must be interested in working on an epilepsy research project under the supervision of a qualified mentor. Because the program is designed as a training opportunity, the quality of the training plans and environment are considered in the selection process. Other selection criteria include the quality of the proposed project, the relevance of the proposed work to epilepsy, the applicant's interest in the field of epilepsy, the applicant's qualifications, and the mentor's qualifications, including his or her commitment to the student and the project. U.S. citizenship is not required, but the project must be conducted in the United States. Applications from women, members of minority groups, and people with disabilities are especially encouraged. The program is not intended for students working on a dissertation research project.

Financial data The grant is $3,000.

Duration 3 months during the summer.

Additional information This program is supported by the American Epilepsy Society, Abbott Laboratories, Ortho-McNeil Pharmaceutical Corporation, and Pfizer Inc.

Number awarded Varies each year; recently, 4 of these fellowships were awarded.

Deadline March of each year.

[708]
BERNARD L. MAJEWSKI FELLOWSHIP

University of Wyoming
Attn: American Heritage Center
P.O. Box 3924
Laramie, WY 82071-3924
(307) 766-4114   Fax: (307) 766-5511
E-mail: ahc@uwyo.edu
Web: ahc.uwyo.edu

Purpose To provide funding to scholars (especially minorities) who are interested in using the resources at the University of Wyoming's American Heritage Center to conduct research in economic geology.

Eligibility This program is open to scholars who are interested in conducting research at the center in the history of economic geology. For purposes of the fellowship, economic geology is defined as the activities of exploration and development of petroleum and base, precious, and industrial minerals, including basic geological research. Acceptable related fields include history; oral history; historical archaeology pertaining to economic geology, environmental, and natural resources history; and business or economic history related to economic geology. Applicants must be recognized scholars in 1 of those fields of research. They should have a record of publication in the field or show significant potential for publication. Young scholars, minorities, and multi-disciplinary researchers are encouraged to apply.

Financial data The grant is $2,500, paid in 2 installments: $500 upon the applicant's acceptance of the fellowship and $2,000 upon completion of the first research session at the American Heritage Center.

Duration 1 calendar year.

Additional information This program began in 1998.

Number awarded 1 each year.

Deadline February of each year.

[709]
BYRD FELLOWSHIP PROGRAM

Ohio State University
Byrd Polar Research Center
Attn: Fellowship Committee
Scott Hall Room 108
1090 Carmack Road
Columbus, OH 43210-1002
(614) 292-6531   Fax: (614) 292-4697
Web: www-bprc.mps.ohio-state.edu

Purpose To provide funding to postdoctorates (particularly minorities and other special groups) interested in conducting research on the Arctic or Antarctic areas at Ohio State University.

Eligibility This program is open to postdoctorates of superior academic background who are interested in conducting advanced research on either Arctic or Antarctic problems at the Byrd Polar Research Center at Ohio State University. Applicants must have received their doctorates within the past 5 years. Each application should include a statement of general research interest, a description of the specific research to be conducted during the fellowship, and a curriculum vitae. Women, minorities, Vietnam-era veterans, disabled veterans, and individuals with disabilities are particularly encouraged to apply.

Financial data The stipend is $35,000 per year; an allowance of $3,000 for research and travel is also provided.

Duration 18 months.

Additional information This program was established by a major gift from the Byrd Foundation in memory of Rear Admiral Richard Evelyn Byrd and Marie Ames Byrd, his wife. Except for field work or other research activities requiring absence from campus, fellows are expected to be in residence at the university for the duration of the program.

Deadline April of each year.

[710]
BYRON HANKE FELLOWSHIP FOR GRADUATE RESEARCH ON COMMUNITY ASSOCIATIONS

Community Associations Institute
Attn: Foundation for Community Association Research
225 Reinekers Lane, Suite 300
Alexandria, VA 22314-2875
(703) 548-8600, ext. 340   Fax: (703) 684-1581
E-mail: smclaughlin@caionline.org
Web: www.cairf.org/schol/hanke.html

Purpose To provide funding to graduate students (particularly minorities) interested in working on research related to community associations.

Eligibility Applicants must be enrolled in an accredited master's, doctoral, or law program. They may be working in any subject area, but their proposed research must relate to community associations (organizations that govern common-interest communities of any kind—condominiums, cooperatives, townhouse developments, planned unit developments, and other developments where homeowners support an association with mandatory financial assessments and are subject to use and aesthetic restrictions). The proposed research may deal with management, institutions, organization and administration, public policy, architecture, as well as political, economic, social, and intellectual trends in community association housing. Academic disciplines include law, economics, sociology, and urban planning. The foundation is especially interested in substantive papers from the social sciences which place community association housing within political or economic organizational models. Minority applicants are particularly encouraged to apply. Selection is based on academic achievement, faculty recommendations, demonstrated research and writing ability, and nature of the proposed topic and its benefit to the study and understanding of community associations.

Financial data Grants range from $2,000 to $4,000. Funds are paid in 2 equal installments and may be used for tuition, books, or other educational expenses.

Duration 1 year.

Additional information The foundation may publish the final project. Recipients must provide the foundation with a copy of their final project.

Deadline Applications may be submitted at any time.

[711]
CAMS SCHOLARSHIP PROGRAM

Chinese American Medical Society
Attn: Dr. H.H. Wang, Executive Director
281 Edgewood Avenue
Teaneck, NJ 07666
(201) 833-1506   Fax: (201) 833-8252
E-mail: hw5@columbia.edu
Web: www.camsociety.org/programs.htm

Purpose To provide financial assistance to Chinese Americans who are interested in studying, conducting research, or teaching in the medical and dental fields.

Eligibility This program is open to Chinese or Chinese Americans who need financial assistance to complete their study, research, or teaching in the field of medicine and/or dentistry. At the time of application, they must be residing in the United States (either as resident aliens or American citizens). Applicants must be enrolled at an approved medical/dental school in the United States or have a research position in an approved institution. Special consideration is given to applicants with research projects relating to health care of the Chinese.

Financial data The scholarships range from $1,000 to $1,500.

Duration 1 year; recipients may reapply.

Additional information This program includes the Esther Lim Memorial Scholarship, established in 1989, and the Ruth Liu Memorial Scholarship, established in 1996. Information is also available from David Wang, M.D., CAMS Scholarship Committee Chairman, 171 East 84th Street, Suite 33B, New York, NY 10028, (201) 833-7244, E-mail: dwang007@yahoo.com. Recipients who do not complete their planned study, research, or teaching must make a pro-rated refund to the society.

Number awarded Varies; recently, 3 to 5 scholarships have been awarded each year.

Deadline March of each year.

[712]
CAMS SUMMER RESEARCH OUTREACH PROGRAM

Chinese American Medical Society
Attn: Dr. H.H. Wang, Executive Director
281 Edgewood Avenue
Teaneck, NJ 07666
(201) 833-1506   Fax: (201) 833-8252
E-mail: hw5@columbia.edu
Web: www.camsociety.org/programs.htm

Purpose To provide funding to Chinese American medical students who are interested in working on a summer research project.

Eligibility This program is open to Chinese or Chinese Americans who are enrolled in a medical school in the United States and are interested in working on a research project. The research can be basic science or clinical. Preference is given to proposals related to health problems of the Chinese.

Financial data The stipend is $300 per week, up to 8 weeks.

Duration Up to 8 weeks during the summer.

Additional information A written report is expected at the conclusion of the project.

Number awarded Varies each year.

Deadline February of each year.

[713]
CARNEGIE INSTITUTION OF WASHINGTON POSTDOCTORAL FELLOWSHIPS

Carnegie Institution of Washington
1530 P Street, N.W.
Washington, DC 20005-1910
(202) 387-6400   Fax: (202) 387-8092
Web: www.carnegieinstitution.org

Purpose To encourage the development of researchers (particularly minorities and women) in the fields of astronomy, geophysics, physics and related subjects, plant biology, and embryology.

Eligibility Qualified scientists who have obtained the doctoral degree are eligible. Candidates are evaluated on the basis of academic record, recommendations of professors and associates, and growth potential. Special efforts are made to recruit qualified minorities and women.

Financial data Stipends average approximately $15,000 each year; in addition to financial support, fellows receive the use of the institution's laboratory and observational facilities, including special equipment when needed. Some travel funds are provided.

Duration 1 to 2 years.

Additional information Facilities of the Carnegie Institution include the Department of Embryology in Baltimore, Maryland, the Department of Plant Biology and the Department of Global Ecology in Stanford, California, the Geophysical Laboratory and the Department of Terrestrial Magnetism in Washington, D.C., and the Observatories in Pasadena, California and Las Campanas, Chile. Fellowships are tenable at the institution's facilities only.

Number awarded More than 200 postdoctoral fellows are in residence each year.

Deadline Applications should be submitted at least 1 year in advance.

[714]
CARNEGIE INSTITUTION OF WASHINGTON PREDOCTORAL FELLOWSHIPS

Carnegie Institution of Washington
1530 P Street, N.W.
Washington, DC 20005-1910
(202) 387-6400   Fax: (202) 387-8092
Web: www.carnegieinstitution.org

Purpose To provide funding to doctoral candidates (particularly minorities and women) conducting thesis research in the sciences.

Eligibility Doctoral students from universities situated near Carnegie departments or other major universities may apply for funding to carry out their thesis research using Carnegie Institution facilities if they are working in the following areas: embryology, global ecology, plant biology, or astronomy. Special consideration is given to applications submitted by women and minorities.

Financial data The amount awarded varies, depending upon the scope of the funded research.

Duration 1 academic year, generally starting in July.

Additional information The relevant Carnegie facilities are the Department of Embryology on the grounds of The Johns Hopkins University (Baltimore, Maryland), the Departments of Plant Biology and Global Ecology on the Stanford University campus (Stanford, California), and the Observatories situated near the California Institute of Technology (Pasadena, California).

Number awarded Varies each year.

Deadline December of each year.

[715]
CDC/PRC MINORITY FELLOWSHIPS

Association of Schools of Public Health
Attn: Atlanta Office
2872 Woodcock Boulevard, Suite 211
Atlanta, GA 30341
(770) 455-6898   E-mail: hward@asph.org
Web: www.asph.org

Purpose To provide an opportunity for minority doctoral students to conduct research at Prevention Research Centers (PRCs) funded by the U.S. Centers for Disease Control and Prevention (CDC).

Eligibility This program is open to minority (African American/Black American, Hispanic/Latino, American Indian/Alaska Native, and Asian/Pacific Islander) students working on a doctoral degree at a school of public health with a CDC-funded PRC. Applicants must be proposing to conduct a research project that is related to the PRC activities and is endorsed by the PRC director. Along with their application, they must submit an essay (2 pages or less) on why they are interested in this fellowship, including specific ideas regarding their interest in the opportunity, benefits they expect to receive from the fellowship experience, how the experience will shape their future career plans, and how the proposed project will advance the field of public health prevention research. Selection is based on the essay (30 points), strength of credentials (20 points), and the project proposal (50 points). U.S. citizenship or permanent resident status is required.

Financial data The stipend is $22,500 per year. Fellows are also reimbursed up to $2,500 per year for health-related expenses, project-related travel, tuition, journal subscriptions, and association dues.

Duration 2 years.

Additional information Currently, PRCs are funded at 28 universities: University of Alabama at Birmingham, University of Albany, University of Arizona, Boston University, University of California at Berkeley, University of California at Los Angeles, University of Colorado, Columbia University, Harvard University, University of Illinois at Chicago, University of Iowa, Johns Hopkins University, University of Kentucky, University of Michigan, University of Minnesota, Morehouse School of Medicine, University of New Mexico, University of North Carolina at Chapel Hill, University of Oklahoma, University of Pittsburgh, St. Louis University, University of South Carolina, University of South Florida, University of Texas at Houston, Tulane University, University of Washington, West Virginia University, and Yale University.

Number awarded Varies each year; recently, 4 of these fellowships were awarded.

Deadline January of each year.

[716]
CENTOCOR EXCELLENCE IN IBD CLINICAL RESEARCH AWARDS

Foundation for Digestive Health and Nutrition
Attn: Research Awards Coordinator
4930 Del Ray Avenue
Bethesda, MD 20814-2512
(301) 222-4005   Fax: (301) 222-4010
E-mail: info@fdhn.org
Web: www.fdhn.org

Purpose To provide funding to senior gastroenterology fellows (especially minorities and women) interested in preparing for a research career in inflammatory bowel diseases (IBD).

Eligibility This program is open to trainee members of the American Gastroenterological Association (AGA) who have an M.D. or equivalent degree. Applicants must be currently enrolled in an accredited gastroenterology-related fellowship at a U.S. institution and committed to an academic career. They must be interested in additional full-time research training in IBD clinical science to acquire modern laboratory skills. Their sponsor must be an AGA member engaged in research training at an academic gastroenterology-related unit of a medical school, affiliated teaching hospital, or research institute. A co-sponsor must be the director of a clinical or other comparable laboratory who is committed to the training and development of the applicant. The institution must provide them with at least 75% protected time. Women and minority investigators are strongly encouraged to apply. Selection is based on novelty, feasibility, and significance of the proposal; attributes of the candidate; record and commitment of the sponsors; and the institutional and laboratory environment.

Financial data The grant is $70,000 per year. No institutional indirect costs are allowed.

Duration 1 year; nonrenewable.

Additional information This program is administered by the Foundation for Digestive Health and Nutrition (FDHN) with support from Centocor, Inc. and the AGA.

Number awarded 5 each year.

Deadline January of each year.

[717]
CHARLES A. RYSKAMP RESEARCH FELLOWSHIPS

American Council of Learned Societies
Attn: Office of Fellowships and Grants
633 Third Avenue, 8C
New York, NY 10017-6795
(212) 697-1505   Fax: (212) 949-8058
E-mail: grants@acls.org
Web: www.acls.org/rysguide.htm

Purpose To provide financial assistance to advanced assistant professors (particularly minorities and women) in all disciplines of the humanities and the humanities-related social sciences.

Eligibility This program is open to tenure-track faculty members at the advanced assistant professor level and untenured associate professors in the humanities and related social sciences. Applicants must have successfully completed their institution's last reappointment review before tenure review. They must have a Ph.D. or equivalent degree and be employed at an academic institution in the

United States. Appropriate fields of specialization include, but are not limited to, anthropology, archaeology, art history, economics, film, geography, history, languages and literatures, law, linguistics, musicology, philosophy, political science, psychology, religion, rhetoric and communication, and sociology. Proposals in the social sciences are eligible only if they employ predominantly humanistic approaches (e.g., law and literature, political philosophy). Proposals in interdisciplinary and cross-disciplinary studies are welcome, as are proposals focused on any geographic region or on any cultural or linguistic group. Applicants are encouraged to spend substantial periods of their leaves in residential interdisciplinary centers, research libraries, or other scholarly archives in the United States or abroad. Applications are particularly invited from women and members of minority groups.

Financial data Fellows receive a stipend of $60,000, a fund of $2,500 for research and travel, and the possibility of an additional summer's support, if justified by a persuasive case.

Duration 1 academic year (9 months) plus an additional summer's research (2 months) if justified.

Additional information This program, first available for the 2002-03 academic year, is supported by funding from the Andrew W. Mellon Foundation.

Number awarded Up to 12 each year.

Deadline September of each year.

[718]
CIRES VISITING FACULTY, POSTDOCTORAL, AND SABBATICAL FELLOWSHIPS

University of Colorado at Boulder
Attn: Cooperative Institute for Research in
    Environmental Sciences
Campus Box 216
Boulder, CO 80309-0216
(303) 492-8773   Fax: (303) 492-1149
E-mail: cires@cires.colorado.edu
Web: cires.colorado.edu/cires.vf.html

Purpose To provide an opportunity for scholars (particularly minorities) to conduct research in the sciences at the Cooperative Institute for Research in Environmental Sciences (CIRES) at the University of Colorado.

Eligibility This program is open to Ph.D. scientists at all levels and to faculty planning sabbatical leave. Recent Ph.D. recipients and those affiliated with minority institutions are especially encouraged to apply. Scientists from all countries are eligible. Applicants must be interested in conducting research at CIRES in the following areas: advanced observing and modeling systems, climate system variability, geodynamics, planetary metabolism, and regional processes. Selection is based on the likelihood of interactions between the visiting fellows and the scientists at CIRES and the degree to which both parties will benefit from the exchange of new ideas.

Financial data The salary is commensurate with qualifications, current salary, and cost of living considerations.

Duration 1 year; the program may begin at anytime during the year.

Additional information This program is sponsored jointly by the University of Colorado and the National Oce-

anic and Atmospheric Administration (with support from other public and private sources).

Number awarded Up to 6 each year.

Deadline December of each year.

[719]
CLINICAL RESEARCH POST-DOCTORAL FELLOWSHIP PROGRAM

American Nurses Association
Attn: Ethnic Minority Fellowship Programs
600 Maryland Avenue, S.W., Suite 100 West
Washington, DC 20024-2571
(202) 651-7244   Fax: (202) 651-7007
E-mail: emfp@ana.org
Web: www.nursingworld.org

Purpose To provide funding to postdoctoral minority nurses interested in a program of research and study on psychiatric, mental health, and substance abuse issues that impact the lives of ethnic minority people.

Eligibility This program is open to doctoral-prepared nurses who are members of an ethnic or racial minority group, including but not limited to Blacks or African Americans, Hispanics or Latinos, American Indians and Alaska Natives, Asians and Asian Americans, and Native Hawaiians and other Pacific Islanders. Applicants must be able to demonstrate a commitment to a research career in nursing and psychiatric/mental health issues affecting ethnic minority populations. They must be interested in a program of full-time postdoctoral study, with a research focus on such issues of concern to minority populations as child abuse, violence in intimate relationships, mental health disorders, substance abuse, mental health service utilization, and stigma as a barrier to mental health care and personal resilience. U.S. citizenship or permanent resident status and membership in the American Nurses Association are required.

Financial data The stipend is $28,260 per year.

Duration Up to 2 years.

Additional information Funds for this program are provided by the Substance Abuse and Mental Health Services Administration.

Number awarded 1 or more each year.

[720]
CLINICAL RESEARCH PRE-DOCTORAL FELLOWSHIP PROGRAM

American Nurses Association
Attn: Ethnic Minority Fellowship Programs
600 Maryland Avenue, S.W., Suite 100 West
Washington, DC 20024-2571
(202) 651-7244   Fax: (202) 651-7007
E-mail: emfp@ana.org
Web: www.nursingworld.org

Purpose To provide financial assistance to minority nurses who are doctoral candidates interested in psychiatric, mental health, and substance abuse issues that impact the lives of ethnic minority people.

Eligibility This program is open to nurses who have a master's degree and are members of an ethnic or racial minority group, including but not limited to Blacks or African Americans, Hispanics or Latinos, American Indians and

Alaska Natives, Asians and Asian Americans, and Native Hawaiians and other Pacific Islanders. Applicants must be able to demonstrate a commitment to a research career in nursing and psychiatric/mental health issues affecting ethnic minority populations. They must be interested in a program of full-time doctoral study, with a research focus on such issues of concern to minority populations as child abuse, violence in intimate relationships, mental health disorders, substance abuse, mental health service utilization, and stigma as a barrier to mental health care and personal resilience. U.S. citizenship or permanent resident status and membership in the American Nurses Association are required. Selection is based on research potential, scholarship, writing ability, knowledge of broad issues in mental health nursing, and professional commitment to ethnic minority concerns.

Financial data Fellows receive a stipend of $20,772 per year and $5,000 in tuition assistance.

Duration 3 to 5 years.

Additional information Funds for this program are provided by the Substance Abuse and Mental Health Services Administration.

Number awarded 1 or more each year.

Deadline February of each year.

[721]
CMS DISSERTATION FELLOWSHIPS

Centers for Medicare & Medicaid Services
Attn: Acquisition and Grants Group
C2-21-15
7500 Security Boulevard
Baltimore, MD 21244-1850
(410) 786-5701   Toll-free: (877) 267-2323
TTY: (410) 786-0727   TTY: (866) 226-1819
Web: cms.hhs.gov/researchers/priorities/grants.asp

Purpose To provide financial assistance to doctoral candidates (particularly minorities and women) writing dissertations in various social science disciplines that focus on health care financing and delivery issues.

Eligibility Students enrolled in an accredited doctoral degree program in social, management, or health sciences may apply for these research grants if they are sponsored by their universities and conducting or intending to conduct research on issues related to the delivery or financing of health care services. Topics of special interest to the Centers for Medicare & Medicaid Services (CMS) include monitoring and evaluating CMS programs; improving managed care payment and delivery; improving fee-for-service payment and delivery; future trends influencing our programs; strengthening Medicaid, State Children's Health Insurance Program (SCHIP), and state programs; meeting the needs of vulnerable populations; outcomes, quality, and performance; and building research capacity. Applicants must have completed all course work and academic requirements for the doctoral degree, other than the research and dissertation. Applications from minority and women researchers are specifically encouraged. Selection is based on topic significance (25 points), research design (50 points), support structure (15 points), and budgetary appropriateness (10 points).

Financial data The budget for direct costs (investigator's salary, travel, data processing, and supplies) may be up to $30,000; the sponsoring university may receive indirect costs of up to 8% of direct costs.

Additional information Until 2001, the Centers for Medicare & Medicaid Services was known as the Health Care Financing Administration. Applications must be submitted jointly by the student and the university, but funds are dispensed only to the university.

Number awarded Varies each year; recently, 9 of these grants were awarded.

Deadline October of each year.

[722]
COMMUNITY ACTION GRANTS

American Association of University Women
Attn: AAUW Educational Foundation
301 ACT Drive, Department 177
P.O. Box 4030
Iowa City, IA 52243-4030
(319) 337-1716   Fax: (319) 337-1204
E-mail: aauw@act.org
Web: www.aauw.org

Purpose To provide seed money to branches or divisions of the American Association of University Women (AAUW) or to individual women (particularly women of color) for projects or nondegree research that promotes education and equity for women and girls.

Eligibility This program is open to individual women who are U.S. citizens or permanent residents, AAUW branches, AAUW state organizations, and local community-based nonprofit organizations. Applicants must be proposing projects that have direct public impact, are nonpartisan, and take place within the United States or its territories. They must focus on K-12 and community college girls' and women's achievements in mathematics, science, or technology; the proposal must involve planning activities and coalition building during the first year and implementation and evaluation the following year. Special consideration is given to AAUW branch and state applicants who seek partners for collaborative projects; collaborators can include local schools or school districts, businesses, and other community-based organizations. Applications from women of color and underrepresented groups as well as applications for projects that meet the needs of underserved populations are especially encouraged.

Financial data Grants range from $5,000 to $10,000. Funds are to be used for such project-related expenses as office space and mailing, promotional materials, honoraria, and transportation. Funds cannot cover salaries for project directors or regular, ongoing overhead costs for any organization.

Duration 2 years.

Number awarded Varies each year.

Deadline January of each year.

[723]
CONTEMPLATIVE PRACTICE FELLOWSHIPS

American Council of Learned Societies
Attn: Office of Fellowships and Grants
633 Third Avenue, 8C
New York, NY 10017-6795
(212) 697-1505   Fax: (212) 949-8058
E-mail: grants@acls.org
Web: www.acls.org/conprac.htm

Purpose To provide funding to college faculty members (particularly minorities and women) interested in conducting research leading to the development of courses and teaching materials that integrate contemplative practices into courses.

Eligibility This program is open to full-time faculty members at accredited academic institutions in the arts, humanities, and humanities-related sciences and social sciences. There are no citizenship requirements. Applicants must be interested in conducting individual or collaborative research to advance scholarship in the field of contemplative practices and to encourage innovative pedagogy and course design. Methodologies that include practical and experiential approaches to the subject matter are especially welcome. Proposals of particular interest are those in which classroom contemplative practices are related clearly to the content of the course itself. Applications are particularly invited from women and members of minority groups.

Financial data The maximum grant is $10,000.

Duration 1 semester or 1 summer.

Additional information This program is sponsored by the Center for Contemplative Mind in Society and funded by the Fetzer Institute.

Number awarded Approximately 6 each year.

Deadline November of each year.

[724]
COVAD BROADBAND ENTREPRENEUR AWARD

Association for Enterprise Opportunity
1601 North Kent Street, Suite 1101
Arlington, VA 22209
(703) 841-7760   Fax: (703) 841-7748
E-mail: aeo@assoceo.org
Web: www.microenterpriseworks.org/projects/covad

Purpose To provide funding to entrepreneurs (especially women, minorities, and people with disabilities) who are interested in obtaining broadband access to the Internet.

Eligibility This program is open to low- and moderate-income entrepreneurs who have 5 or fewer employees, $35,000 or less cash on hand, and no access to traditional bank loans. Preference is given to entrepreneurs who are women, minorities, or people with disabilities. Applicants must be based in and/or serve clients within the service area of Covad Communications Group, Inc. in the following states: Arizona, California, Illinois, Massachusetts, Michigan, New Mexico, Pennsylvania, or Tennessee. They must own or have regular access to a computer and be able to implement installation of broadband within 30 days of the grant award. It is not necessary that entrepreneurs have existing access to the Internet or an e-mail address as long as they intend to use the grant funds to set up Internet and e-mail service. They must submit a cover letter and busi-

ness plan that demonstrate how broadband access will improve and strengthen their business.

Financial data Grants provide a $500 cash award (which may be used for purchase of a new computer) and free Covad broadband installation and service for 1 year. The total value of the grant is more than $2,500.

Duration These are 1-time grants.

Additional information Covad Communications Group, Inc. established this program in 2003 and selected the Association for Enterprise Opportunity (AEO) to administer it. Information is available from 10 local partners selected by AEO to process and forward applications. Those 10 local organizations are CHARO Community Development Corporation of Los Angeles, Community Business Network of Boston, Detroit Entrepreneurship Institute, Inc. of Detroit, New Mexico Community Development Loan Fund of Albuquerque, Renaissance Entrepreneurship Center of San Francisco, Self-Employment Loan Fund of Phoenix, Start Up of East Palo Alto, California, The Abilities Fund of Centerville, Iowa, Women's Opportunities Resource Center of Philadelphia, and Women's Self-Employment Project of Chicago.

Number awarded Up to 144 each year.

Deadline Each of the 10 local partners sets its own deadline date.

[725]
CULTURAL ANTHROPOLOGY GRANTS FOR HIGH RISK EXPLORATORY RESEARCH

National Science Foundation
Directorate for Social, Behavioral, and Economic
    Sciences
Attn: Division of Behavioral and Cognitive Sciences
4201 Wilson Boulevard, Room 995
Arlington, VA 22230
(703) 292-8758   TDD: (703) 292-9068
E-mail: splattne@nsf.gov
Web: www.nsf.gov/sbe/bcs/anthro/highrisk.htm

Purpose To provide funding to scholars (particularly minorities, women, and persons with disabilities) interested in conducting high-risk research in cultural anthropology.

Eligibility This program is open to scholars interested in conducting research projects in anthropology that might be considered too risky for normal review procedures. A project is considered risky if the data may not be obtainable in spite of all reasonable preparation on the researcher's part. Proposals for extremely urgent research where access to the data may not be available in the normal review schedule, even with all reasonable preparation by the researcher, are also appropriate for this program. Graduate students are not eligible to apply. Women, minorities, and persons with disabilities are strongly encouraged to participate in this program.

Financial data Grants up to $25,000, including indirect costs, are available.

Number awarded Varies each year, depending on the availability of funds.

Deadline Applications may be submitted at any time.

[726]
CULTURAL ANTHROPOLOGY RESEARCH EXPERIENCE FOR GRADUATES SUPPLEMENTS

National Science Foundation
Directorate for Social, Behavioral, and Economic
  Sciences
Attn: Division of Behavioral and Cognitive Sciences
4201 Wilson Boulevard, Room 995
Arlington, VA 22230
(703) 292-8758   TDD: (703) 292-9068
E-mail: splattne@nsf.gov
Web: www.nsf.gov/sbe/sber/anthro

Purpose To provide funding to graduate students (particularly minorities, women, and persons with disabilities) interested in conducting dissertation research in cultural anthropology.

Eligibility Applications may be submitted through regular university channels by dissertation advisors on behalf of graduate students in cultural anthropology. The faculty member must be a principal investigator on a research grant from the National Science Foundation. The application must be for supplemental funds for a doctoral student's closely mentored but independent research experience. The student's research should be a creative project, not a clerk or assistant's task. Selection is based on the appropriateness and value of the educational experience for the student participant, particularly the independence and theoretical significance of the student's activities and the quality of the supervision. Each principal investigator normally may seek funding for only 1 graduate student; exceptions are considered for training additional qualified students who are members of underrepresented groups. Women, minorities, and persons with disabilities are strongly encouraged to participate in this program.

Financial data Supplemental grants up to $5,000 are available. Institutions are encouraged to treat these supplements like dissertation research grants (which incur no indirect costs).

Duration 1 year.

Number awarded Varies each year, depending on the availability of funds.

Deadline January of each year.

[727]
DESGC SUMMER SCHOLARSHIPS

Delaware Space Grant Consortium
c/o University of Delaware
Bartol Research Institute
104 Center Mall, #217
Newark, DE 19716-4793
(302) 831-1094   Fax: (302) 831-1843
E-mail: desgc@bartol.udel.edu
Web: www.delspace.org

Purpose To provide funding to undergraduate students (particularly minorities, women, and persons with disabilities) in Delaware and Pennsylvania for summer research on space-related subjects.

Eligibility This program is open to undergraduate students at member or affiliate colleges and universities of the Delaware Space Grant Consortium (DESGC). Applicants must have a proven interest and aptitude for space-related studies and be proposing a summer research project. U.S.

citizenship is required. The DESGC is a component of the U.S. National Aeronautics and Space Administration (NASA) Space Grant program, which encourages applications from women, minorities, and persons with disabilities.

Financial data A stipend is provided (amount not specified).

Duration Summer months.

Additional information This program, established in 1994, is funded by NASA. Members of the consortium include Delaware State University (Dover, Delaware), Delaware Technical and Community College (Dover, Georgetown, Newark, and Wilmington, Delaware), Franklin and Marshall College (Lancaster, Pennsylvania), Gettysburg College (Gettysburg, Pennsylvania), Lehigh University (Bethlehem, Pennsylvania), Swarthmore College (Swarthmore, Pennsylvania), University of Delaware (Newark, Delaware), Villanova University (Villanova, Pennsylvania), and Wilmington College (New Castle, Delaware).

Number awarded Varies each year; recently, 10 of these scholarships were awarded.

Deadline February of each year.

[728]
DISSERTATION FELLOWSHIPS IN EAST EUROPEAN STUDIES

American Council of Learned Societies
Attn: Office of Fellowships and Grants
633 Third Avenue, 8C
New York, NY 10017-6795
(212) 697-1505   Fax: (212) 949-8058
E-mail: grants@acls.org
Web: www.acls.org/eeguide.htm

Purpose To provide funding to doctoral candidates (particularly minorities and women) interested in conducting dissertation research in the social sciences and humanities relating to eastern Europe.

Eligibility This program is open to U.S. citizens or permanent residents who have completed all requirements for a doctorate in east European studies except the dissertation. Applicants may be working in any discipline of the humanities and the social sciences, including comparative work considering more than 1 country of eastern Europe or relating east European societies to those of other parts of the world. Most awards are for work on southeast Europe, including Albania, Bosnia and Herzegovina, Bulgaria, Croatia, Macedonia, Romania, and Serbia and Montenegro (including Kosovo). A few awards may be available for work on the Czech Republic, Estonia, Hungary, Latvia, Lithuania, Poland, Slovakia, and Slovenia. The fellowships are intended to support dissertation writing in the United States after research is complete, although short visits to the countries of eastern Europe may be proposed. Selection is based on the scholarly potential of the applicant, the quality and scholarly importance of the proposed work, and its importance to the development of east European studies. Applications are particularly invited from women and members of minority groups.

Financial data The maximum stipend is $17,000. Recipients' home universities are required (consistent with their policies and regulations) to provide or to waive normal academic year tuition payments or to provide alternative cost-sharing support.

Duration 1 year.

Additional information This program is sponsored jointly by the American Council of Learned Societies, (ACLS) and the Social Science Research Council, funded by the U.S. Department of State under the Research and Training for Eastern Europe and the Independent States of the Former Soviet Union Act of 1983 (Title VIII) but administered by ACLS.

Number awarded Approximately 10 each year.

Deadline November of each year.

[729]
DISSERTATION FELLOWSHIPS OF THE MINORITY SCHOLAR-IN-RESIDENCE PROGRAM

Consortium for a Strong Minority Presence at Liberal
    Arts Colleges
c/o Administrative Assistant, President's Office
Grinnell College
1121 Park Street
Grinnell, IA 50112-1690
(641) 269-3000   E-mail: cousins@grinnell.edu
Web: www.grinnell.edu/dean/csmp

Purpose To provide an opportunity for minority scholars to work on their dissertation while in residence at selected liberal arts colleges.

Eligibility This program is open to African American, Asian American, Hispanic American, and Native American doctoral candidates who have completed all the requirements for the Ph.D. or M.F.A. except the dissertation. Applicants must be interested in a residency at a member institution of the Consortium for a Strong Minority Presence at Liberal Arts Colleges during which they will complete their dissertation.

Financial data Dissertation fellows receive a stipend based on the average salary paid to instructors at the participating college. Modest funds are made available to finance the fellow's proposed research, subject to the usual institutional procedures.

Duration 1 year.

Additional information The following schools are participating in the program: Bowdoin College, Bryn Mawr College, Carleton College, Claremont McKenna College, Coe College, College of Wooster, Colorado College, Denison University, DePauw University, Dickinson College, Gettysburg College, Grinnell College, Hamilton College, Haverford College, Hope College, Juniata College, Lewis and Clark College, Luther College, Macalester College, Mount Holyoke College, Oberlin College, Occidental College, Pitzer College, Pomona College, Rhodes College, St. Olaf College, Skidmore College, Southwestern University, Swarthmore College, Trinity University, University of the South, Vassar College, Wellesley College, Wheaton College, Whitman College, and Willamette University. Fellows are expected to teach at least 1 course, participate in departmental seminars, and interact with students.

Number awarded Varies each year.

Deadline November of each year.

[730]
DOCTORAL DISSERTATION FELLOWSHIPS IN LAW AND SOCIAL SCIENCE

American Bar Foundation
Attn: Assistant Director
750 North Lake Shore Drive
Chicago, IL 60611
(312) 988-6500   Fax: (312) 988-6579
E-mail: fellowships@abfn.org
Web: www.abf-sociolegal.org/Fellowship/pre.html

Purpose To provide funding to doctoral candidates (particularly minorities) who wish to conduct research on law, the legal profession, and legal institutions.

Eligibility Applications are invited from outstanding students who are candidates for a Ph.D. degree in the social sciences. They must have completed all doctoral requirements except the dissertation. Proposed research must be in the general area of sociolegal studies or in social scientific approaches to law, the legal profession, or legal institutions. The dissertation must address critical issues in the field and show promise of making a major contribution to social scientific understanding of law and legal processes. Applications must include 1) transcripts of graduate work; 2) 2 letters of recommendation; 3) a curriculum vitae; and 4) a dissertation prospectus or proposal with an outline of the substance and methodology of the intended research. Minority students are especially encouraged to apply.

Financial data The stipend is $15,000 per year. Fellows also may request up to $1,000 each fellowship year to reimburse expenses associated with dissertation research, travel to meet with dissertation advisors, and travel to conferences at which papers are presented. Moving expenses of up to $1,000 may be reimbursed on application.

Duration 1 year; may be renewed for 1 additional year.

Additional information Fellows are offered access to the computing and word processing facilities of the American Bar Foundation and the libraries of Northwestern University and the University of Chicago. This program was established in 1987. Fellowships must be held in residence at the American Bar Foundation. Appointments to the fellowship are full time; fellows are not permitted to undertake other work.

Number awarded 2 each year.

Deadline January of each year.

[731]
DR. SUZANNE LEGO RESEARCH GRANT

American Psychiatric Nurses Association
Attn: APN Foundation
1555 Wilson Boulevard, Suite 515
Arlington, VA 22209
(703) 243-2443   Fax: (703) 243-3390
E-mail: inform@apna.org
Web: www.apna.org/foundation/scholarships.html

Purpose To provide funding to graduate students and registered nurses (especially minorities) interested in conducting a research project in the field of psychiatric nursing.

Eligibility This program is open to registered nurses with at least a master's degree in psychiatric mental health nursing or a related field. Students completing a master's thesis or doctoral dissertation may also apply if their thesis or dissertation committee approves. Applicants must be proposing to conduct a research project on psychotherapeutic interventions in nursing. Selection is based on the scientific merit of the proposal and its potential for knowledge development of psychotherapeutic interventions relevant to the practice of psychiatric nursing. Minorities are especially encouraged to apply.

Financial data The grant is $1,000. Funds are not provided for principal or co-investigator's salary, educational assistance such as tuition or textbooks, travel, presenting a paper or attending a conference, or purchase of personal computers or other equipment.

Duration 1 year.

Number awarded 1 or more each year.

Deadline January of each year.

[732]
EDUCATIONAL TESTING SERVICE POSTDOCTORAL FELLOWSHIP AWARD PROGRAM

Educational Testing Service
Attn: Fellowships
Rosedale Road
MS 09-R
Princeton, NJ 08541-0001
(609) 734-1806   E-mail: fellowships@ets.org
Web: www.ets.org/research/fellowships.html

Purpose To provide financial assistance to postdoctorates (especially minorities and women) who wish to conduct independent research at the Educational Testing Service (ETS).

Eligibility Applicants must have a doctorate in a relevant discipline and be able to provide evidence of prior research. They must be interested in conducting research at ETS in 1 of the following areas: computer science, education, learning, literacy, minority issues, policy research, psychology, statistics, teaching, educational technology, or testing issues (including alternate forms of assessment for special populations and new forms of assessment). Selection is based on the scholarship and importance of the proposed research. An explicit goal of the program is to increase the number of women and minority professionals in educational measurement and related fields.

Financial data The stipend is $50,000 per year; fellows and their families also receive limited reimbursement for relocation expenses.

Duration 1 year, normally beginning in September.

Additional information Fellows work with senior staff at the Educational Testing Service in Princeton, New Jersey.

Number awarded Up to 3 each year.

Deadline January of each year.

[733]
EDUCATIONAL TESTING SERVICE VISITING SCHOLAR PROGRAM

Educational Testing Service
Attn: Visiting Scholar Program
Rosedale Road
MS 18-N
Princeton, NJ 08541-0001
(609) 683-2473   Fax: (609) 683-2800
E-mail: egilmore@ets.org
Web: www.ets.org/research/fellowships.html

Purpose To provide funding to postdoctoral scholars or color who wish to learn more about issues related to minorities at the Educational Testing Service (ETS).

Eligibility This program is open to members of underrepresented groups who are experienced liberal arts community college or university teachers or administrators. Applicants must be interested in spending time at the ETS campus studying issues related to test design and development and learning to write and review test questions and related materials for a variety of testing programs, including elementary and secondary education tests, college admission and placement tests, graduate admission tests, professional assessments for teachers and administrators, and international assessments.

Financial data The stipend is set in relation to compensation at the home institution. Scholars and their families also receive reimbursement for relocation expenses.

Duration 4 weeks during the summer.

Additional information Fellows work with senior staff at ETS in Princeton, New Jersey and have access to senior research staff. This program was established in 2000.

Number awarded Several each year.

Deadline January of each year.

[734]
EDWARD AND SALLY VAN LIER FELLOWSHIP COMPETITION

Asian American Writers' Workshop
Attn: Van Lier Fellowship
16 West 32nd Street, Suite 10A
New York, NY 10001-3808
(212) 494-0061   Fax: (212) 494-0062
E-mail: desk@aaww.org
Web: www.aaww.org/publications/submission.html

Purpose To provide financial assistance and other literary guidance to Asian American writers from New York City.

Eligibility This program is open to U.S. citizens of Asian descent who reside in New York City (all 5 boroughs). Applicants must be 30 years of age or younger, be a current member of the Asian American Writers' Workshop, and not be currently enrolled in an M.F.A. creative writing program. They must submit a work-in-progress in poetry, fiction, or creative nonfiction.

Financial data Fellows receive a cash stipend of $2,500 for living expenses, free enrollment in writing workshops, access to computers, use of the reading room collection, and connections to publishing professionals and established writers who offer feedback on manuscripts and advice on getting published.

Additional information This program was established in 1993.

Number awarded 3 each year.
Deadline December of each year.

[735]
ELSEVIER RESEARCH INITIATIVE AWARD

Foundation for Digestive Health and Nutrition
Attn: Research Awards Coordinator
4930 Del Ray Avenue
Bethesda, MD 20814-2512
(301) 222-4005   Fax: (301) 222-4010
E-mail: info@fdhn.org
Web: www.fdhn.org

Purpose To provide funding to new or established investigators (especially minorities and women) for pilot research projects in areas related to gastroenterology or hepatology.
Eligibility Applicants must have an M.D. or Ph.D. degree (or the equivalent) and a faculty position at an accredited North American institution. They may not hold grants for projects on a similar topic from other agencies. Individual membership in the American Gastroenterology Association (AGA) is required. Women and minority investigators are strongly encouraged to apply. Selection is based on novelty, importance, feasibility, environment, commitment of the institution, and overall likelihood that the project will lead to more substantial grant applications.
Financial data The grant is $25,000 per year. Funds may be used for salary, supplies, or equipment. Indirect costs are not allowed.
Duration 1 year.
Additional information This award is administered by the Foundation for Digestive Health and Nutrition and sponsored by the AGA and Elsevier Science Publishing Company.
Number awarded 1 each year.
Deadline January of each year.

[736]
EPILEPSY FOUNDATION RESEARCH GRANTS PROGRAM

Epilepsy Foundation
Attn: Research Department
4351 Garden City Drive
Landover, MD 20785-7223
(301) 459-3700   Toll-free: (800) EFA-1000
Fax: (301) 577-2684   TDD: (800) 332-2070
E-mail: grants@efa.org
Web: www.epilepsyfoundation.org

Purpose To provide funding to junior investigators (particularly minorities, women, and persons with disabilities) interested in conducting research that will advance the understanding, treatment, and prevention of epilepsy.
Eligibility Applicants must have a doctoral degree and an academic appointment at the level of assistant professor in a university or medical school (or equivalent standing at a research institution or medical center). They must be interested in conducting basic or clinical research in the biological, behavioral, or social sciences related to the causes of epilepsy. Faculty with appointments at the level of associate professor or higher are not eligible. Applications from women, members of minority groups, and people with disabilities are especially encouraged. U.S. citizenship is not

required, but the research must be conducted in the United States. Selection is based on the scientific quality of the research plan, the relevance of the proposed research to epilepsy, the applicant's qualifications, and the adequacy of the institution and facility where research will be conducted.
Financial data The maximum grant is $40,000.
Duration 1 year. An additional year of support may be requested through re-application.
Additional information Support for this program is provided by many individuals, families, and corporations, especially the American Epilepsy Society, Abbott Laboratories, Ortho-McNeil Pharmaceutical, and Pfizer Inc.
Number awarded Varies each year; recently, 7 of these grants were awarded.
Deadline August of each year.

[737]
EPILEPSY RESEARCH AWARDS PROGRAM

American Epilepsy Society
342 North Main Street
West Hartford, CT 06117-2507
(860) 586-7505   Fax: (860) 586-7550
Web: www.aesnet.org

Purpose To provide funding to investigators (particularly minorities and women) anywhere in the world interested in conducting research related to epilepsy.
Eligibility This program is open to active scientists and clinicians working in all aspects of epilepsy. Candidates must be nominated by their home institution. There are no geographic restrictions; nominations from outside the United States and North America are welcome. Nominations of women and members of minority groups are especially encouraged. Selection is based on pioneering research, originality of research, quality of publications, research productivity, relationship of the candidate's work to problems in epilepsy, training activities, other contributions in epilepsy, and productivity over the next decade; all criteria are weighted equally.
Financial data The grant is $50,000. No institutional overhead is allowed.
Additional information This program, established in 1991, is funded by the Milken Family Foundation.
Number awarded 2 each year.
Deadline August of each year.

[738]
ETHNIC MINORITY RESEARCHER AND MENTORSHIP GRANT

Oncology Nursing Society
Attn: Research Team
125 Enterprise Drive
Pittsburgh, PA 15275-1214
(412) 859-6298   Toll-free: (866) 257-4ONS
Fax: (412) 859-6160   E-mail: research@ons.org
Web: www.ons.org

Purpose To provide funding to members of ethnic minority groups interested in conducting oncology nursing research.
Eligibility Principal investigators must be ethnic minority researchers (Native American, African American, Asian

American, Pacific Islander, Hispanic/Latino, or other ethnic minority background). Beginning or novice researchers must utilize a research mentor for consultive services in research design and statistical analyses. Preference is given to projects that involve nurses in the design and conduct of the research activity and that promote theoretically based oncology practice. Graduate students are encouraged to apply for funding that supports work that is considered preliminary in nature or related to their thesis or dissertation.

Financial data The grant is $8,500 ($7,500 for the conduct of the research project and $1,000 for the research mentor or consultant). Funding is not provided for projects that are already completed or nearing completion, payment of tuition, or institutional indirect costs.

Duration Up to 2 years.

Additional information Every effort is made to find an ethnic minority mentor; however, the primary criteria for matching the investigator and mentor is the substantive area of the research and the expertise of the mentor. This program is supported by Ortho Biotech Products, L.P.

Number awarded 1 each year.

Deadline October of each year.

[739]
EURASIA DISSERTATION WRITE-UP FELLOWSHIPS

Social Science Research Council
Attn: Eurasia Program
810 Seventh Avenue
New York, NY 10019
(212) 377-2700   Fax: (212) 377-2727
E-mail: eurasia@ssrc.org
Web: www.ssrc.org

Purpose To provide funding to graduate students (particularly minorities and women) completing a dissertation dealing with Eurasia.

Eligibility This program is open to students who have completed field research for their doctoral dissertation and who plan to work on writing it during the next academic year. Applicants must have been conducting research in a discipline of the social sciences or humanities that deals with the Russian Empire, the Soviet Union, or the New States of Eurasia. Research related to the non-Russian states, regions, and peoples is particularly encouraged. Regions and countries currently supported by the program include Armenia, Azerbaijan, Belarus, Georgia, Kazakhstan, Kyrgyzstan, Moldova, Russian Federation, Tajikistan, Turkmenistan, Ukraine, and Uzbekistan; funding is not presently available for research on the Baltic states. U.S. citizenship or permanent resident status is required. Minorities and women are particularly encouraged to apply.

Financial data Grants up to $15,000 are available.

Duration Up to 1 year.

Additional information Funding for this program is provided by the U.S. Department of State under the Program for Research and Training on Eastern Europe and the Independent States of the Former Soviet Union (Title VIII).

Number awarded Varies each year; recently, 7 of these fellowships were awarded.

Deadline November of each year.

[740]
EURASIA POSTDOCTORAL RESEARCH FELLOWSHIPS

Social Science Research Council
Attn: Eurasia Program
810 Seventh Avenue
New York, NY 10019
(212) 377-2700   Fax: (212) 377-2727
E-mail: eurasia@ssrc.org
Web: www.ssrc.org

Purpose To provide funding to scholars (especially minorities and women) who recently received a Ph.D. in fields related to the study of Eurasia and who wish to engage in further scholarly activity.

Eligibility This program is open to junior faculty and independent scholars who are within the first 5 years of having received their Ph.D., have no more than 3 years' experience in a tenure-track position, and require release time from teaching and administrative duties for the completion of ongoing projects, substantive retooling, and/or preliminary research on new projects. Applicants must be working in a discipline of the social sciences or humanities that deals with the new states of Eurasia, the Soviet Union, and/or the Russian empire. Research related to the non-Russian states, regions, and peoples is particularly encouraged. Regions and countries currently supported by the program include Armenia, Azerbaijan, Belarus, Georgia, Kazakhstan, Kyrgyzstan, Moldova, Russian Federation, Tajikistan, Turkmenistan, Ukraine, and Uzbekistan; funding is not presently available for research on the Baltic states. U.S. citizenship or permanent resident status is required. Minorities and women are particularly encouraged to apply.

Financial data The maximum grant is $20,000. In most cases, scholars should use approximately $15,000 to release themselves from teaching and administrative obligations in their departments and $5,000 for research expenses.

Duration All funds must be expended within no more than 18 to 24 months of receiving the award.

Additional information Funding for this program is provided by the U.S. Department of State under the Program for Research and Training on Eastern Europe and the Independent States of the Former Soviet Union (Title VIII).

Number awarded Varies each year; recently, 3 of these fellowships were awarded.

Deadline November of each year.

[741]
EURASIA TEACHING FELLOWSHIPS

Social Science Research Council
Attn: Eurasia Program
810 Seventh Avenue
New York, NY 10019
(212) 377-2700   Fax: (212) 377-2727
E-mail: eurasia@ssrc.org
Web: www.ssrc.org

Purpose To provide funding to scholars (particularly minorities and women) in fields related to the study of Eurasia who wish to create course curricula.

Eligibility This program is open to faculty at all career levels in a discipline of the social sciences or humanities that deals with the New States of Eurasia, the Soviet Union, and/or the Russian empire. Applicants must be interested in creating original and creative curricula for courses that are completely new or for substantial revisions of a course previously taught. They should have a proven track record of research and teaching in their field of Eurasian studies. Proposals should have an interdisciplinary or comparative outlook, encompass a diverse range of literatures and/or source media (including audio, video, and web content), and make appropriate use of various pedagogical approaches. Proposals that target unique and important student audiences, provide a substantial addition or significantly diversify existing departmental and/or university curricula, or that otherwise fill an important niche or fulfill an instructional gap are especially encouraged. U.S. citizenship or permanent resident status is required. Minorities and women are particularly encouraged to apply.

Financial data The grant is $10,000.

Duration Awardees are expected to demonstrate departmental and institutional support for adding the proposed course to the university's list of offered courses within a 2-year period of time.

Additional information Funding for this program is provided by the U.S. Department of State under the Program for Research and Training on Eastern Europe and the Independent States of the Former Soviet Union (Title VIII).

Number awarded Varies each year.

Deadline January of each year.

[742]
FELLOWSHIPS FOR POSTDOCTORAL RESEARCH IN SOUTHEAST EUROPEAN STUDIES

American Council of Learned Societies
Attn: Office of Fellowships and Grants
633 Third Avenue, 8C
New York, NY 10017-6795
(212) 697-1505   Fax: (212) 949-8058
E-mail: grants@acls.org
Web: www.acls.org/eeguide.htm

Purpose To provide funding to postdoctorates (particularly minorities and women) interested in conducting original research in the social sciences and humanities relating to southeastern Europe.

Eligibility Applicants must be U.S. citizens or permanent residents who hold a Ph.D. degree or equivalent as demonstrated by professional experience and publications. Their field of study must be in the social sciences or humanities relating to Albania, Bosnia and Herzegovina, Bulgaria, Croatia, Macedonia, Romania, or Serbia and Montenegro. Comparative work considering more than 1 country of southeastern Europe or relating southeastern European societies to those of other parts of the world are also supported. All proposals should be for scholarly work, the product of which is to be disseminated in English. Fellowships may not be used for work in western Europe. Selection is based on the scholarly merit of the proposal, its importance to the development of eastern European studies, and the scholarly potential, accomplishments, and financial need of the applicant. Applications are particularly invited from women and members of minority groups.

Financial data Up to $25,000 is provided as a stipend. Funds are intended primarily as salary replacement, but they may be used to supplement sabbatical salaries or awards from other sources.

Duration 6 to 12 consecutive months.

Additional information This program is sponsored jointly by the American Council of Learned Societies, (ACLS) and the Social Science Research Council, funded by the U.S. Department of State under the Research and Training for Eastern Europe and the Independent States of the Former Soviet Union Act of 1983 (Title VIII) but administered by ACLS.

Number awarded 4 or 5 each year.

Deadline November of each year.

[743]
FELLOWSHIPS IN ENVIRONMENTAL REGULATORY IMPLEMENTATION

Resources for the Future
Attn: Coordinator for Academic Programs
1616 P Street, N.W.
Washington, DC 20036-1400
(202) 328-5060   Fax: (202) 939-3460
E-mail: mankin@rff.org
Web: www.rff.org

Purpose To provide funding to postdoctoral researchers (especially minorities and women) who are interested in conducting research that documents the implementation and outcomes of environmental regulation.

Eligibility This program is open to scholars from universities and research organizations who have a doctoral or equivalent degree or equivalent professional research experience. Applicants must be interested in conducting research that examines environmental regulations in practice and can be used to inform regulators, industry, and others of assumptions of environmental laws and policies. The proposed research must be documentary in nature, without arguing in favor of any particular policy or result. Funding is not available for studies balancing costs and benefits or conducting other policy analyses of regulations. Interested scholars must first submit a pre-proposal that describes the project and its expected result, schedule, and budget. Women and minority candidates are strongly encouraged to apply. Preference is given to applicants who have sabbatical or other sources of support from their home institution.

Financial data Fellows receive an annual stipend commensurate with experience, research support, office facilities and limited support for relocation (if they choose to conduct the project at RFF), and funding for travel and conferences. Fellowships do not provide medical insurance or other RFF fringe benefits.

Duration 1 or 2 years.

Additional information Fellows may be in residence at RFF or remain at their current institution. They are requested to visit RFF to discuss progress on their research. This program is supported by the Andrew W. Mellon Foundation.

Number awarded 1 each year.

Deadline Pre-proposals must be submitted by January of each year. Final proposals are due in February.

[744]
FELLOWSHIPS IN SCIENCE AND INTERNATIONAL AFFAIRS

Harvard University
John F. Kennedy School of Government
Belfer Center for Science and International Affairs
Attn: Fellowship Coordinator
79 John F. Kennedy Street
Cambridge, MA 02138
(617) 495-3745   Fax: (617) 495-8963
E-mail: kathleen_siddell@harvard.edu
Web: bcsia.ksg.harvard.edu

Purpose To provide funding for research (by minority and other professionals, postdoctorates, or graduate students) in areas of interest to the Belfer Center for Science and International Affairs at Harvard University in Cambridge, Massachusetts.

Eligibility The postdoctoral fellowship is open to recent recipients of the Ph.D. or equivalent degree, university faculty members, and employees of government, military, international, humanitarian, and private research institutions who have appropriate professional experience. Applicants for predoctoral fellowships must have passed general examinations. Lawyers, economists, physical scientists, and others of diverse disciplinary backgrounds are also welcome to apply. The program especially encourages applications from women, minorities, and citizens of all countries. All applicants must be interested in conducting research in 1 of the 5 major program areas of the center: the international security program; the environment and natural resources program; the science, technology, and public policy program; the World Peace Foundation program on intrastate conflict, conflict prevention, and conflict resolution; and the Caspian Studies program. Fellowships may also be available in other specialized programs, such as science, technology, and globalization; managing the atom; domestic preparedness for terrorism; science and technology for sustainability; and energy technology innovation.

Financial data The stipend is $34,000 for postdoctoral research fellows or $20,000 for predoctoral research fellows. Health insurance is also provided.

Duration 10 months.

Number awarded A limited number each year.

Deadline January of each year.

[745]
FIRST BOOK GRANT PROGRAM FOR MINORITY SCHOLARS

Louisville Institute
Attn: Executive Director
1044 Alta Vista Road
Louisville, KY 40205-1798
(502) 992-5432   Fax: (502) 894-2286
E-mail: info@louisville-institute.org
Web: www.louisville-institute.org

Purpose To provide funding to scholars of color interested in completing a major research and book project that focuses on an aspect of Christianity in North America.

Eligibility This program is open to members of a racial/ethnic minority group (African Americans, Hispanics, Native Americans, Asian Americans, Arab Americans, and Pacific Islanders) who have an earned doctoral degree (nor-

mally the Ph.D. or Th.D.). Applicants must be a pre-tenured faculty member in a full-time, tenure-track position at an accredited institution of higher education (college, university, or seminary) in North America. They must be able to negotiate a full academic year free from teaching and committee responsibilities in order to engage in a scholarly research project leading to the publication of their first (or second) book focusing on an aspect of Christianity in North America. Selection is based on the intellectual quality of the research and writing project, its potential to contribute to scholarship in religion, and the potential contribution of the research to the vitality of North American Christianity.

Financial data The grant is $45,000. Awards are intended to make possible a full academic year of sabbatical research and writing by providing up to half of the grantee's salary and benefits for that year. Funds are paid directly to the grantee's institution, but no indirect costs are allowed.

Duration 1 academic year; nonrenewable.

Additional information The Louisville Institute is located at Louisville Presbyterian Theological Seminary and is supported by the Lilly Endowment. Grantees may not accept other awards that provide a stipend during the tenure of this award and must be released from all teaching and committee responsibilities during the award year.

Number awarded Up to 3 each year.

Deadline February of each year.

[746]
FIVE COLLEGE FELLOWSHIP PROGRAM FOR MINORITY SCHOLARS

Five Colleges, Incorporated
Attn: Five Colleges Fellowship Program Committee
97 Spring Street
Amherst, MA 01002-2324
(413) 256-8316   Fax: (413) 256-0249
E-mail: neckert@fivecolleges.edu
Web: www.fivecolleges.edu

Purpose To provide funding to minority graduate students who have completed all the requirements for the Ph.D. except the dissertation and are interested in teaching at selected colleges in Massachusetts.

Eligibility Fellows are chosen by the host department in each of the 5 participating campuses (Amherst, Hampshire, Mount Holyoke, Smith, and the University of Massachusetts). Applicants must be minority graduate students at an accredited school who have completed all doctoral requirements except the dissertation and are interested in devoting full time to the completion of the dissertation.

Financial data The stipend is $30,000 plus a research grant, fringe benefits, office space, library privileges, and housing assistance.

Duration 9 months, beginning in September.

Additional information Although the primary goal is completion of the dissertation, each fellow also has many opportunities to experience working with students and faculty colleagues on the host campus as well as with those at the other colleges. The fellows are also given an opportunity to teach (generally as a team teacher, in a section of a core course, or in a component within a course). Fellows meet monthly with each other to share their experiences. At Smith College, this program is named Mendenhall Fellowships for Minority Scholars.

Number awarded 5 each year: 1 at each of the participating colleges.

Deadline November of each year.

[747]
FLORIDA SPACE GRANT CONSORTIUM UNDERGRADUATE SPACE RESEARCH PARTICIPATION PROGRAM

Florida Space Grant Consortium
c/o Center for Space Education
Building M6-306, Room 7010
Mail Stop: FSGC
Kennedy Space Center, FL 32899
(321) 452-4301   Fax: (321) 449-0739
E-mail: fsgc@mail.ufl.edu
Web: fsgc.engr.ucf.edu

Purpose To provide funding to undergraduate students (particularly minorities, women, and persons with disabilities) at universities participating in the Florida Space Grant Consortium (FSGC) who wish to work on a summer research project.

Eligibility This program is open to juniors and seniors at colleges and universities that are members of the consortium. Students must be nominated by a faculty member at a consortium institution or by a researcher in a Florida industrial facility who proposes to mentor the student on a summer research project. Students are particularly encouraged to participate at an institution other than their own. Nominees must be enrolled in a space-related field of study, broadly defined to include aeronautics, astronautics, remote sensing, atmospheric sciences, and other fundamental sciences and technologies relying on and/or directly impacting space technological resources. Included within that definition are space science; earth observing science; space life sciences; space medicine; space policy, law, and engineering; space facilities and applications; and space education. The program particularly solicits nominations of women, minorities, and students with disabilities.

Financial data The grant is $3,000, to be used as a student stipend. The sponsoring university or industry may provide additional funds for the student stipend but may not charge for overhead or indirect costs.

Duration 10 weeks during the summer.

Additional information This program is funded by the U.S. National Aeronautics and Space Administration (NASA). The consortium member universities are Bethune-Cookman College, Eckerd College, Embry-Riddle Aeronautical University, Florida A&M University, Florida Atlantic University, Florida Community Colleges, Florida Gulf Coast University, Florida Institute of Technology, Florida International University, Florida Southern College, Florida State University, University of Central Florida, University of Florida, University of Miami, University of North Florida, University of South Florida, and University of West Florida.

Number awarded 15 each year.

Deadline Notices of intent must be submitted by January of each year. Completed proposals are due in March.

[748]
FOREIGN POLICY STUDIES PREDOCTORAL FELLOWSHIPS

Brookings Institution
Attn: Foreign Policy Studies
1775 Massachusetts Avenue, N.W.
Washington, DC 20036-2103
(202) 797-6043   Fax: (202) 797-2481
E-mail: syerkes@brookings.edu
Web: www.brookings.edu/admin/fellowships.htm

Purpose To support predoctoral research on U.S. foreign policy and international relations (particularly by minorities and women) at the Brookings Institution.

Eligibility This program is open to doctoral students who have completed their preliminary examinations and have selected a dissertation topic that directly relates to public policy issues and the major research issues of the Brookings Institution. Candidates cannot apply to conduct research at the institution; they must be nominated by their graduate department. They may be at any stage of their dissertation research. Selection is based on 1) relevance of the topic to contemporary U.S. foreign policy and/or post-Cold War international relations, and 2) evidence that the research will be facilitated by access to the institution's resources or to Washington-based organizations. The institution particularly encourages the nomination of women and minority candidates.

Financial data Fellows receive a stipend of $20,500 for the academic year, supplementary assistance for copying and other essential research requirements up to $750, reimbursement for transportation, health insurance, reimbursement for research-related travel up to $750, and access to computer/library facilities.

Duration 1 year, beginning in September.

Additional information Fellows participate in seminars, conferences, and meetings at the institution. Outstanding dissertations may be published by the institution. Fellows are expected to conduct their research at the Brookings Institution.

Number awarded A limited number are awarded each year.

Deadline Nominations must be submitted by mid-December and applications by mid-February.

[749]
FREDERICK BURKHARDT RESIDENTIAL FELLOWSHIPS FOR RECENTLY TENURED SCHOLARS

American Council of Learned Societies
Attn: Office of Fellowships and Grants
633 Third Avenue, 8C
New York, NY 10017-6795
(212) 697-1505   Fax: (212) 949-8058
E-mail: grants@acls.org
Web: www.acls.org/burkguid.htm

Purpose To provide funding to scholars (particularly minorities and women) in all disciplines of the humanities and the humanities-related social sciences who are interested in conducting research at designated residential centers.

Eligibility This program is open to citizens and permanent residents of the United States who achieved tenure in a humanities or humanities-related social science discipline at a U.S. institution within the past 4 years. Applicants must be interested in conducting research at 1 of 11 participating residential centers in the United States or abroad. Appropriate fields of specialization include, but are not limited to, anthropology, archaeology, art history, economics, film, geography, history, languages and literatures, law, linguistics, musicology, philosophy, political science, psychology, religion, rhetoric and communication, and sociology. Proposals in those fields of the social sciences are eligible only if they employ predominantly humanistic approaches (e.g., economic history, law and literature, political philosophy). Proposals in interdisciplinary and cross-disciplinary studies are welcome, as are proposals focused on any geographic region or on any cultural or linguistic group. Applications are particularly invited from women and members of minority groups.

Financial data The stipend is $75,000. If that stipend exceeds the fellow's normal academic year salary, the excess is available for research and travel expenses.

Duration 1 academic year.

Additional information This program, which began in 1999, is supported by funding from the Andrew W. Mellon Foundation with additional support from the Rockefeller Foundation. The participating residential research centers are the National Humanities Center (Research Triangle Park, North Carolina), the Center for Advanced Study in the Behavioral Sciences (Stanford, California), the Institute for Advanced Study, Schools of Historical Studies and Social Science (Princeton, New Jersey), the Radcliffe Institute for Advanced Study at Harvard University (Cambridge, Massachusetts), the American Antiquarian Society (Worcester, Massachusetts), the Folger Shakespeare Library (Washington, D.C.), the Newberry Library (Chicago, Illinois), the Huntington Library, Art Collections, and Botanical Gardens (San Marino, California), the American Academy in Rome, Collegium Budapest, and Villa I Tatti (Florence, Italy).

Number awarded Up to 11 each year.

Deadline September of each year.

[750]
FRONTIERS IN PHYSIOLOGY PROFESSIONAL DEVELOPMENT FELLOWSHIPS

American Physiological Society
Attn: Education Office
9650 Rockville Pike, Room 3111
Bethesda, MD 20814-3991
(301) 634-7132   Fax: (301) 634-7098
E-mail: education@the-aps.org
Web: www.the-aps.org/education/frontiers/index.htm

Purpose To provide an opportunity for middle/high school life science teachers (particularly minorities) to participate in a summer research project in physiology.

Eligibility This program is open to science teachers at middle schools (grades 6-9) and high schools (grades 9-12) who do not have recent (within 10 years) laboratory experience in physiology or the life sciences, do not have an advanced degree in laboratory science, and are not a candidate for an advanced degree in a laboratory science. Applicants do not need to have extensive mathematics skills, but they must be able to demonstrate a commitment to excellence in teaching, strong observation skills, and a desire to

learn about research first-hand. Teachers who are members of minority groups underrepresented in science (African Americans, Hispanics, and Native Americans) or who teach in schools with a predominance of underrepresented minority students are especially encouraged to apply. Teachers must apply jointly with a member of the American Physiological Society (APS) at a research institution in the same geographic area as their home and school.

Financial data For the summer research experience, teachers receive a stipend of $500 per week (to a maximum of $4,000), a grant of $250 for participation in the summer forum, a grant of $250 for development and field testing of new inquiry-based laboratory or lesson, $400 for completion of online reflections and reading assignments, and $100 for completion of project evaluation activities. For the remainder of the year, they receive $2,500 for reimbursement of travel costs to attend the Science Teaching Forum, $1,000 for reimbursement of travel costs to attend the International Congress of Physiological Sciences, and $300 for materials to field-test a new inquiry-based laboratory or lesson. The maximum total value of the fellowship is $8,800.

Duration 1 year, including 7 to 8 weeks during the summer for participation in the research experience.

Additional information This program enables teachers to work on a summer research project in the laboratory of their APS sponsor, use the Internet to expand their repertory of teaching methods and their network of colleagues, and develop an inquiry-based classroom activity or laboratory, along with a corresponding web page. They also take a break from their summer research to attend a 1-week Science Teaching Forum in Washington D.C. where they work with APS staff, physiologists, and mentors to explore and practice effective teaching methods focused on how to integrate inquiry, equity, and the Internet into their classrooms. This program is supported by the National Center for Research Resources (NCRR) and the National Institute of Diabetes and Digestive and Kidney Diseases (NIDDK). both components of the National Institutes of Health (NIH).

Number awarded Varies each year; recently 16 of these fellowships were awarded.

Deadline January of each year.

[751]
GAIUS CHARLES BOLIN FELLOWSHIPS FOR MINORITY GRADUATE STUDENTS

Williams College
Attn: Dean of the Faculty
Hopkins Hall, Third Floor
800 Main Street
Williamstown, MA 01267
(413) 597-4351   E-mail: gburda@williams.edu
Web: www.williams.edu/admin-depts/deanfac

Purpose To provide financial assistance to minority doctoral students at any school who are interested in teaching courses at Williams College while working on their dissertation.

Eligibility Applicants must be minority graduate students, have completed all doctoral work except for the dissertation, be U.S. citizens, be working on degrees in the humanities or the natural, social, or behavioral sciences, and be willing to teach a course at Williams College. They must submit a full curriculum vitae, a graduate school transcript,

3 letters of recommendation, a copy of their dissertation prospectus, and a description of their teaching interests.

Financial data Fellows receive $31,000 for the academic year, plus housing assistance, office space, computer and library privileges, and a research allowance of up to $4,000.

Duration 1 academic year, beginning in September.

Additional information Bolin fellows are assigned a faculty advisor in the appropriate department. This program was established in 1985. Fellows are expected to teach a 1-semester course. They must be in residence at Williams College for the duration of the fellowship.

Number awarded 2 each year.

Deadline November of each year.

[752]
GEOLOGICAL SOCIETY OF AMERICA GENERAL RESEARCH GRANTS PROGRAM

Geological Society of America
Attn: Program Officer-Grants, Awards and Recognition
3300 Penrose Place
P.O. Box 9140
Boulder, CO 80301-9140
(303) 357-1028   Toll-free: (800) 472-1988, ext. 1028
Fax: (303) 357-1070   E-mail: awards@geosociety.org
Web: www.geosociety.org

Purpose To provide support to graduate student members (particularly minorities, women, and the disabled) of the Geological Society of America (GSA) interested in conducting research at universities in the United States, Canada, Mexico, or Central America.

Eligibility This program is open to GSA members working on a master's or doctoral degree at a university in the United States, Canada, Mexico, or Central America. Applicants must be interested in conducting research on geology. Minorities, women, and persons with disabilities are strongly encouraged to apply. Selection is based on the scientific merits of the problems, the capability of the investigator, and the reasonableness of the budget.

Financial data Grants can be used for the cost of travel, room and board in the field, materials and supplies, and other expenses directly related to the fulfillment of the research contract. Expenses requested for equipment or rental of equipment, film, some supplies, computer time, software, thin sections, and in-house charges for analytical instruments usually provided by a university must be fully justified. Funds cannot be used for the purchase of ordinary field equipment, for maintenance of the families of the grantees and their assistants, as reimbursement for work already accomplished, to attend professional meetings, for thesis preparation, to defray the costs of tuition, or for the employment of persons to conduct research. Recently, grants averaged $1,750.

Duration 1 year.

Additional information In addition to general grants, GSA awards a number of specialized grants: the Gretchen L. Blechschmidt Award for women (especially in the fields of biostratigraphy and/or paleoceanography); the John T. Dillon Alaska Research Award for earth science problems particular to Alaska; the Robert K. Fahnestock Memorial Award for the field of sediment transport or related aspects of fluvial geomorphology; the Lipman Research Award for volcanology and petrology; the Bruce L. "Biff" Reed Award for studies in the tectonic and magmatic evolution of Alaska; the Alexander Sisson Award for studies in Alaska and the Caribbean; the Harold T. Stearns Fellowship Award for work on the geology of the Pacific Islands and the circum-Pacific region; the Parke D. Snavely, Jr. Cascadia Research Fund Award for studies of the Pacific Northwest convergent margin; the Alexander and Geraldine Wanek Fund Award for studies of coal and petroleum; the Charles A. and June R.P. Ross Research Fund Award for stratigraphy; and the John Montagne Fund Award for research in the field of quaternary geology or geomorphology. Furthermore, 9 of the 14 GSA divisions (geophysics, hydrogeology, sedimentary geology, structural geology and tectonics, archaeological geology, coal geology, planetary geology, quaternary geology and geomorphology, and engineering geology) also offer divisional grants. Some of those awards are named: the Allan V. Cox Award of the Geophysics Division, the Claude C. Albritton, Jr. Scholarship of the Archaeological Geology Division, the Antoinette Lierman Medlin Scholarships of the Coal Geology Division, the J. Hoover Mackin Research Grants and the Arthur D. Howard Research Grants of the Quaternary Geology and Geomorphology Division, and the Roy J. Shlemon Scholarship Awards of the Engineering Geology Division. In addition, 4 of the 6 geographic sections (south-central, north-central, southeastern, and northeastern) offer grants to graduate students at universities within their section.

Number awarded Varies each year; recently, the society awarded 224 grants worth more than $400,000 through this and all of its specialized programs.

Deadline January of each year.

[753]
GEOLOGICAL SOCIETY OF AMERICA UNDERGRADUATE STUDENT RESEARCH GRANTS

Geological Society of America
Attn: Program Officer-Grants, Awards and Recognition
3300 Penrose Place
P.O. Box 9140
Boulder, CO 80301-9140
(303) 357-1028   Toll-free: (800) 472-1988, ext. 1028
Fax: (303) 357-1070   E-mail: awards@geosociety.org
Web: www.geosociety.org

Purpose To provide support to undergraduate student members (particularly minorities, women, and the disabled) of the Geological Society of America (GSA) interested in conducting research at universities in designated sections of the United States.

Eligibility This program is open to undergraduate students who are majoring in geology at universities in 4 GSA sections: north-central, northeastern, south-central, and southeastern. Applicants must be student associates of the GSA. Applications from women, minorities, and persons with disabilities are strongly encouraged.

Financial data Grant amounts vary.

Duration 1 year.

Additional information Within the 4 participating sections, information is available from the secretary. For the name and address of the 4 section secretaries, contact the sponsor.

Number awarded 1 or more each year in each of the 4 sections.

Deadline January of each year.

[754]
GEORGE WASHINGTON WILLIAMS FELLOWSHIPS

Independent Press Association
Attn: Executive Editor
2729 Mission Street, Suite 201
San Francisco, CA 94110
(415) 643-4401, ext. 116   Fax: (415) 643-4402
E-mail: gww@indypress.org
Web: www.indypress.org/programs/gwwfellow.html

Purpose To provide journalists of color with an opportunity to engage in public interest and socially responsible journalism.

Eligibility This program is open to journalists of color who have at least 3 years of professional reporting and writing experience. College journalism or internship experience does not qualify as professional experience. Preference is given to applicants with backgrounds in investigative or enterprise reporting. Previous reporting or other experience in the chosen subject area is desirable. The program is open only to U.S. citizens or to foreign journalists who have established relationships with U.S. publications. Applicants must be seeking support for either an individual story or investigative depth reporting. The preferred topics change periodically, but recently included the environment, health care and health care policy, new Americans, the war on terrorism, and gay and lesbian people of color.

Financial data Investigative depth reporting fellows receive $1,500 per month plus expenses to produce 1 or more stories. Individual story fellows are paid a rate equivalent to the going national commercial rate for comparable stories and assisted in placing the story.

Duration 3 to 12 months.

Additional information This program is named in honor of the African American journalist who first exposed conditions in the former Belgian Congo when he published an open letter to King Leopold II in 1890. Fellows are required to complete either a story or series of stories for publication. They may also be expected to attend special events and conferences sponsored by the program to present reports on their work to date and to discuss their own journalistic experiences with interns in the sponsor's student journalism program.

Number awarded 1 or more each year.

Deadline May or November of each year.

[755]
GERALD OSHITA MEMORIAL FELLOWSHIP

Djerassi Resident Artists Program
Attn: Admissions
2325 Bear Gulch Road
Woodside, CA 94062-4405
(650) 747-1250   Fax: (650) 747-0105
E-mail: drap@djerassi.org
Web: www.djerassi.org/oshita.html

Purpose To provide an opportunity for composers of color to participate in the Djerassi Resident Artists Program.

Eligibility This program is open to composers of color interested in utilizing a residency to compose, study,

rehearse, and otherwise advance their own creative projects.

Financial data The fellow is offered housing, meals, studio space, and a stipend of $2,500.

Duration 4 to 5 weeks, from late March through mid-November.

Additional information This fellowship was established in 1994. The program is located in northern California, 45 miles south of San Francisco, on 600 acres of rangeland, redwood forests, and hiking trails.

Number awarded 1 each year.

Deadline February of each year.

[756]
GERTRUDE AND MAURICE GOLDHABER DISTINGUISHED FELLOWSHIPS

Brookhaven National Laboratory
Attn: Dr. Leonard Newman
Building 815E
P.O. Box 5000
Upton, NY 11973-5000
(631) 344-4467   E-mail: newman@bnl.gov
Web: www.bnl.gov/hr/goldhaber.asp

Purpose To provide funding to postdoctoral scientists (particularly minorities and women) interested in conducting research at Brookhaven National Laboratory (BNL).

Eligibility This program is open to scholars who are no more than 3 years past receipt of the Ph.D. and are interested in working at BNL. Candidates must be interested in working in close collaboration with a member of the BNL scientific staff and qualifying for a scientific staff position at BNL upon completion of the appointment. The sponsoring scientist must have an opening and be able to support the candidate at the standard starting salary for postdoctoral research associates. The program especially encourages applications from minorities and women.

Financial data The program provides additional funds to bring the salary to $70,000 per year.

Duration 3 years.

Additional information This program is funded by Battelle Memorial Institute and the State University of New York at Stony Brook.

Number awarded 1 or 2 each year.

[757]
GILBERT F. WHITE POSTDOCTORAL FELLOWSHIP PROGRAM

Resources for the Future
Attn: Coordinator for Academic Programs
1616 P Street, N.W.
Washington, DC 20036-1400
(202) 328-5060   Fax: (202) 939-3460
E-mail: mankin@rff.org
Web: www.rff.org

Purpose To provide funding to postdoctoral researchers (particularly minorities and women) who wish to devote a year to scholarly work at Resources for the Future (RFF) in Washington, D.C.

Eligibility This program is open to individuals in any discipline who have completed their doctoral requirements and are interested in conducting scholarly research at RFF in social or policy science areas that relate to natural resources, energy, or the environment. Teaching and/or research experience at the postdoctoral level is preferred though not essential. Individuals holding positions in government as well as at academic institutions are eligible. Women and minority candidates are strongly encouraged to apply.

Financial data Fellows receive an annual stipend (based on their academic salary) plus research support, office facilities at RFF, and an allowance of up to $1,000 for moving or living expenses. Fellowships do not provide medical insurance or other RFF fringe benefits.

Duration 11 months.

Additional information Fellows are assigned to an RFF research division—the Energy and Natural Resources division, the Quality of the Environment division or the Center for Risk, Resource, and Environmental Management. Fellows are expected to be in residence at Resources for the Future for the duration of the program.

Number awarded 1 each year.

Deadline February of each year.

[758]
GOVERNANCE STUDIES PREDOCTORAL FELLOWSHIPS

Brookings Institution
Attn: Governmental Studies
1775 Massachusetts Avenue, N.W.
Washington, DC 20036-2188
(202) 797-6090   Fax: (202) 797-6144
E-mail: sbinder@brookings.edu
Web: www.brookings.edu/admin/fellowships.htm

Purpose To support predoctoral policy-oriented research in governmental studies (particularly by minorities and women) at the Brookings Institution.

Eligibility This program is open to doctoral students who have completed their preliminary examinations and have selected a dissertation topic that directly relates to the study of public policy and political institutions and thus to the major interests of the Brookings Institution. Candidates cannot apply to conduct research at the institution; they must be nominated by their graduate department. The proposed research should benefit from access to the data, opportunities for interviewing, and consultation with senior staff members afforded by the institution and by residence in Washington, D.C. The institution particularly encourages the nomination of women and minority candidates.

Financial data Fellows receive a stipend of $20,500 for the academic year, supplementary assistance for copying and other essential research requirements up to $750, reimbursement for research-related travel up to $750, health insurance, reimbursement for transportation, and access to computer/library facilities.

Duration 1 year.

Additional information Fellows participate in seminars, conferences, and meetings at the institution. Outstanding dissertations may be published by the institution. Fellows are expected to conduct their research at the Brookings Institution.

Number awarded A limited number are awarded each year.

Deadline Nominations must be submitted by mid-December and applications by mid-February.

[759]
HAMBURG FELLOWSHIP PROGRAM

Stanford University
Center for International Security and Cooperation
Attn: Fellowship Program Coordinator
Encina Hall, Room E210
616 Serra Street
Stanford, CA 94305-6165
(650) 723-9626   Fax: (650) 723-0089
E-mail: barbara.platt@stanford.edu
Web: www.cisac.stanford.edu

Purpose To provide funding to doctoral students (particularly minorities and women) who are interested in working on their dissertation at Stanford University's Center for International Security and Cooperation (which must focus on issues related to preventing deadly conflict).

Eligibility This program is open to advanced doctoral students who have completed all of the curricular and residency requirements at their own institutions and who are engaged in the research and write-up stage of their dissertations in a field related to the prevention of deadly conflict. Applicants must be interested in writing their dissertation at Stanford University's Center for International Security and Cooperation. Fields of study may include anthropology, economics, history, law, political science, sociology, medicine, or the natural and physical sciences. Specific topics might include issues of policing, judiciaries, and civil-military relations; the use of sanctions and other economic tools for the prevention of conflict; early warning mechanisms, mediation processes, and other forms of third-party intervention; environmental degradation and its effects on deadly conflict; the role of non-lethal weapons and other military technologies in preventing conflict; the role of leadership in prevention of conflict. Applications from women and minorities are encouraged.

Financial data The stipend is $20,000. Reimbursement for some travel and health insurance expenses may be available for fellows and their immediate dependents.

Duration 9 months.

Additional information This program began in 1997. It honors Dr. David Hamburg, the retiring president of the Carnegie Corporation of New York, whose gift to the center made the program possible. Fellows join faculty, research staff, and other fellows at the center, where they have an office to ensure their integration into the full spectrum of research activities.

Number awarded Varies each year.

Deadline January of each year.

[760]
HEALTH SCIENCES STUDENT FELLOWSHIPS IN EPILEPSY

Epilepsy Foundation
Attn: Research Department
4351 Garden City Drive
Landover, MD 20785-7223
(301) 459-3700   Toll-free: (800) EFA-1000
Fax: (301) 577-2684   TDD: (800) 332-2070
E-mail: grants@efa.org
Web: www.epilepsyfoundation.org

Purpose To provide financial assistance to medical and health science graduate students (particularly minorities, women, and students with disabilities) interested in working on an epilepsy project during the summer.

Eligibility This program is open to students enrolled, or accepted for enrollment, in a medical school, a doctoral program, or other graduate program. Applicants must have a defined epilepsy-related study or research plan to be carried out under the supervision of a qualified mentor. Because the program is designed as a training opportunity, the quality of the training plans and environment are considered in the selection process. Other selection criteria include the quality of the proposed project, the relevance of the proposed work to epilepsy, the applicant's interest in the field of epilepsy, the applicant's qualifications, and the mentor's qualifications, including his or her commitment to the student and the project. U.S. citizenship is not required, but the project must be conducted in the United States. Applications from women, members of minority groups, and people with disabilities are especially encouraged. The program is not intended for students working on a dissertation research project.

Financial data Stipends are $3,000.

Duration 3 months during the summer.

Additional information Support for this program is provided by many individuals, families, and corporations, especially the American Epilepsy Society, Abbott Laboratories, Ortho-McNeil Pharmaceutical, and Pfizer Inc.

Number awarded Varies each year; recently, 1 of these fellowships was awarded.

Deadline March of each year.

[761]
HENRY LUCE FOUNDATION/ACLS DISSERTATION FELLOWSHIPS IN AMERICAN ART

American Council of Learned Societies
Attn: Office of Fellowships and Grants
633 Third Avenue, 8C
New York, NY 10017-6795
(212) 697-1505   Fax: (212) 949-8058
E-mail: grants@acls.org
Web: www.acls.org/luceguid.htm

Purpose To provide financial assistance to doctoral students (especially minorities and women) interested in conducting dissertation research anywhere in the world on the history of American art.

Eligibility This program is open to Ph.D. candidates in departments of art history whose dissertations are focused on the history of the visual arts in the United States and are object-oriented. Applicants must be proposing to conduct research at their home institution, abroad, or at another

appropriate site. U.S. citizenship or permanent resident status is required. Students preparing theses for a Master of Fine Arts degree are not eligible. Applications are particularly invited from women and members of minority groups.

Financial data The grant is $20,000. Fellowship funds may not be used to pay tuition costs.

Duration 1 year; nonrenewable.

Additional information This program is funded by the Henry Luce Foundation and administered by the American Council of Learned Societies (ACLS).

Number awarded 10 each year.

Deadline November of each year.

[762]
HORIZONS/FRAMELINE FILM AND VIDEO COMPLETION FUND

Frameline
Attn: Film and Video Completion Fund
145 Ninth Street, Suite 300
San Francisco, CA 94103
(415) 703-8650   Fax: (415) 861-1404
E-mail: info@frameline.org
Web: www.frameline.org/fund

Purpose To provide funding to lesbian and gay film/video artists.

Eligibility This program is open to lesbian and gay artists (particularly people of color and women) who are in the last stages of the production of documentary, educational, animated, or experimental projects about or of interest to lesbians, gay men, bisexuals, and transgender people and their communities. Applicants may be independent artists, students, producers, or nonprofit corporations. They must be interested in completion or post-production work, including subtitling or conversion from video to film (or vice versa). In particular, women and people of color are encouraged to apply. Selection is based on financial need, the contribution the grant will make to completing the project, assurances that the project will be completed, and the statement the project makes about lesbian, gay, bisexual, and transgender people and/or issues of concern to them and their communities. Grants are not awarded for script development, research, pre-production, or production work.

Financial data Grants range from $3,000 to $5,000.

Number awarded Varies each year; recently, 4 of these grants were awarded.

Deadline October of each year.

[763]
HUD DOCTORAL DISSERTATION RESEARCH GRANT PROGRAM

Department of Housing and Urban Development
Attn: Office of University Partnerships
451 Seventh Street, S.W., Room 8106
Washington, DC 20410
(800) 245-2691, est. 3181   Fax: (301) 519-5767
E-mail: oup@oup.org
Web: www.oup.org/about/ddrg.html

Purpose To provide funding to doctoral candidates (especially minorities and women) interested in conducting dissertation research related to housing and urban development issues.

Eligibility This program is open to currently-enrolled doctoral candidates in an academic discipline that provides policy-relevant insight on issues in housing and urban development. Applicants must have fully-developed and approved dissertation proposals that can be completed within 2 years and must have completed all written and oral Ph.D. requirements. Funded fields of study have included anthropology, architecture, economics, history, planning, political science, public policy, social work, and sociology. Research must relate to the empowerment principles of the Department of Housing and Urban Development (HUD): a commitment to 1) socially and economically viable communities, 2) stable and supportive families, 3) economic growth, 4) reciprocity and balancing individual rights and responsibilities, and 5) reducing the separation of communities by race and income in American life. Women and minority candidates are encouraged to apply.

Financial data The stipend is $25,000 per year. The program expects that the recipients' universities will support their research by contributing a substantial waiver of tuition and fees, office space, equipment, computer time, or similar items needed to complete the dissertation.

Duration These are 1-time grants.

Additional information This program was established in 1994.

Number awarded Up to 16 each year.

Deadline June of each year.

[764]
ILLINOIS ARTS COUNCIL ETHNIC AND FOLK ARTS MASTER/APPRENTICE PROGRAM

Illinois Arts Council
100 West Randolph, Suite 10-500
Chicago, IL 60601
(312) 814-6750　　Toll-free: (800) 237-6994 (within IL)
Fax: (312) 814-1471　　TTY: (312) 814-4831
E-mail: info@arts.state.il.us
Web: www.state.il.us/agency/iac

Purpose To provide funding to master ethnic and folk artists in Illinois and their apprentices for a program of training in traditional art forms.

Eligibility This program is open to teams of 2 Illinois residents, 1 of whom qualifies as a master artist (an individual who is recognized within his or her community as a person who has achieved the highest possible level of a traditional or classical ethnic art form) and 1 of whom qualifies as an apprentice (an individual with some experience in a traditional or classical ethnic art form who wishes to attain mastery of that art). Ethnic and folk arts are defined as those artistic practices that have a community or family base, express that community's aesthetic heritage and tradition, and have endured through several generations; they should reflect the particular culture of the ethnic, language, regional, tribal, or nationality group from which they spring. The art form may involve traditional crafts, music, dance, or storytelling. Both the master artist and the apprentice must be U.S. citizens or permanent residents who have resided in Illinois for at least 12 months. Selection is based on the artistic quality of both master artist and apprentice as determined by community standards, traditionality of art form and master artist, evidence of apprentice's commitment to the traditional art form, content and feasibility of work

planned for the period of the apprenticeship, and quality and appropriateness of the documentation submitted. Priority is given to apprenticeships that take place outside of institutional settings.

Financial data The honoraria are $2,000 for the master and $1,000 for the apprentice.

Duration Most apprenticeships should include between 80 and 120 hours of instruction.

Number awarded Varies each year.

Deadline August of each year.

[765]
INSTITUTE FOR CIVIL SOCIETY FELLOWSHIPS

Vermont Studio Center
80 Pearl Street
P.O. Box 613
Johnson, VT 05656
(802) 635-2727　　　　Fax: (802) 635-2730
E-mail: info@vermontstudiocenter.org
Web: www.vermontstudiocenter.org

Purpose To provide funding to minority artists from designated cities in several eastern states who are interested in a residency at the Vermont Studio Center in Johnson, Vermont.

Eligibility Eligible to apply for this support are painters, sculptors, printmakers, and photographers who are members of a minority group and residents of New Haven (Connecticut), Jersey City (New Jersey), or Baltimore (Maryland). Applicants must be interested in a residency at the center in Johnson, Vermont. Visual artists must submit up to 20 slides of their work, poets must submit up to 10 pages, and other writers must submit 10 to 15 pages. Selection is based on artistic merit and financial need.

Financial data The residency covers studio space, room, board, lectures, studio visits, and travel expenses.

Duration 4 weeks.

Additional information This program is sponsored by the Institute for Civil Society.

Number awarded 3 each year.

Deadline June of each year.

[766]
INSTITUTE FOR RESEARCH ON POVERTY VISITING SCHOLARS PROGRAM

University of Wisconsin at Madison
Attn: Institute for Research on Poverty
3412 Social Science Building
1180 Observatory Drive
Madison, WI 53706-1393
(608) 262-6358　　　　Fax: (608) 265-3119
E-mail: evanson@ssc.wisc.edu
Web: www.irp.wisc.edu

Purpose To provide minority scholars with an opportunity to visit the Institute for Research on Poverty (IRP) at the University of Wisconsin (UW) at Madison.

Eligibility This program is open to minority scholars, especially those in the beginning years of their academic careers. They are invited to visit UW, interact with its faculty in residence, become acquainted with the staff and resources of IRP, and present lectures. Applicants should submit a letter describing their poverty research interests and experience, the proposed dates for a visit, a current curriculum vitae, and 2 examples of written material.

Financial data Monetary support is provided. Transportation, lodging, and food are covered.

Duration 1 to 2 weeks.

Additional information During their visit, scholars are invited to give a seminar, to work on their own projects, and to confer with an IRP adviser who will arrange for an interchange with other IRP affiliates.

Number awarded Up to 3 each year.

Deadline June of each year.

[767]
INTERNATIONAL SECURITY AND COOPERATION POSTDOCTORAL FELLOWSHIPS

Stanford University
Center for International Security and Cooperation
Attn: Fellowship Program Coordinator
Encina Hall, Room E210
616 Serra Street
Stanford, CA 94305-6165
(650) 723-9626   Fax: (650) 723-0089
E-mail: barbara.platt@stanford.edu
Web: www.cisac.stanford.edu

Purpose To provide funding to postdoctorates (particularly minorities and women) who are interested in conducting research on arms control and international security at Stanford University's Center for International Security and Cooperation.

Eligibility This program is open to scholars who have a Ph.D. or equivalent degree from the United States or abroad. Applicants must be interested in researching international security and arms control issues at the center. Fields of study might include anthropology, economics, history, law, political science, sociology, medicine, or the natural and physical sciences. Topics suitable for support might include the causes and prevention of terrorism; security relationships around the world; U.S.-Russian strategic relations; peacekeeping; prevention of deadly conflicts; U.S. defense and arms control policies; proliferation of nuclear, chemical, and biological weapons; security in south and east Asia; the commercialization of national defense technologies; and ethnic and civil conflict. The center is especially interested in applications from minorities and women.

Financial data The stipend is at least $33,000, depending on experience. Additional funds may be available for dependents and travel.

Duration 9 months.

Number awarded Varies; generally, 2 each year.

Deadline January of each year.

[768]
INTERNATIONAL SECURITY AND COOPERATION PREDOCTORAL FELLOWSHIPS

Stanford University
Center for International Security and Cooperation
Attn: Fellowship Program Coordinator
Encina Hall, Room E210
616 Serra Street
Stanford, CA 94305-6165
(650) 723-9626   Fax: (650) 723-0089
E-mail: barbara.platt@stanford.edu
Web: www.cisac.stanford.edu

Purpose To provide funding to doctoral students, particularly minorities and women, who are interested in writing a dissertation on the problems of arms control and international security at Stanford University's Center for International Security and Cooperation.

Eligibility Students currently enrolled in doctoral programs at academic institutions in the United States who would benefit from access to the facilities offered by the center are eligible to apply. Fields of study might include anthropology, economics, history, law, political science, sociology, medicine, or the natural and physical sciences. Topics suitable for support might include the causes and prevention of terrorism; security relationships around the world; U.S.-Russian strategic relations; peacekeeping; prevention of deadly conflicts; U.S. defense and arms control policies; proliferation of nuclear, chemical, and biological weapons; security in south and east Asia; the commercialization of national defense technologies; and ethnic and civil conflict. The center is especially interested in receiving applications from minorities and women.

Financial data The stipend is $20,000. Additional funds may be available for dependents and travel.

Duration 9 months.

Number awarded Varies; generally, 4 each year.

Deadline January of each year.

[769]
INTERNATIONAL SECURITY AND COOPERATION PROFESSIONAL FELLOWSHIPS

Stanford University
Center for International Security and Cooperation
Attn: Fellowship Program Coordinator
Encina Hall, Room E210
616 Serra Street
Stanford, CA 94305-6165
(650) 723-9626   Fax: (650) 723-0089
E-mail: barbara.platt@stanford.edu
Web: www.cisac.stanford.edu

Purpose To provide funding to professionals (particularly minorities and women) who are interested in conducting research on arms control and international security at Stanford University's Center for International Security and Cooperation.

Eligibility This program is open to military officers or civilian members of the U.S. government, members of military or diplomatic services from other countries, and journalists interested in arms control and international security issues. Applicants must be interested in conducting research on international security and arms control issues at the center. Topics suitable for support might include the causes and prevention of terrorism; security relationships around the world; U.S.-Russian strategic relations; peacekeeping; prevention of deadly conflicts; U.S. defense and arms control policies; proliferation of nuclear, chemical, and biological weapons; security in south and east Asia; the commercialization of national defense technologies; and ethnic and civil conflict. The center is especially interested in applications from minorities and women.

Financial data The stipend depends on experience and is determined on a case-by-case basis. Additional funds may be available for dependents and travel.

Duration 9 months.

Number awarded Varies each year.

Deadline January of each year.

[770]
JEFFREY CAMPBELL GRADUATE FELLOWS PROGRAM

St. Lawrence University
Attn: Human Resources/Office of Equity Programs
Jeffrey Campbell Graduate Fellowship Program
Canton, NY 13617
(315) 229-5509
Web: www.stlawu.edu

Purpose To provide funding to minority graduate students who have completed their course work and are interested in conducting research at St. Lawrence University in New York.

Eligibility This program is open to graduate students who are members of racial or ethnic groups historically underrepresented at the university and in American higher education. Applicants must have completed their course work and preliminary examinations for the Ph.D. or M.F.A. They must be interested in working on their dissertations or terminal degree projects while in residence at the University.

Financial data The stipend is $25,000 per academic year. Additional funds may be available to support travel to conferences and professional meetings. Office space and a personal computer are provided.

Duration 1 academic year.

Additional information This program is named for 1 of the university's early African American graduates. Recipients must teach 1 course a semester in a department or program at St. Lawrence University related to their research interests. In addition, they must present a research-based paper in the fellows' lecture series each semester.

Deadline February of each year.

[771]
JOHN AND ELIZABETH PHILLIPS FELLOWSHIP

Phillips Exeter Academy
Attn: Dean of Faculty
20 Main Street
Exeter, NH 03833-2460
(603) 772-3405   Fax: (603) 772-4393
E-mail: faculty@exeter.edu
Web: www.exeter.edu

Purpose To provide funding to underrepresented teachers interested in a residency at Phillips Exeter Academy in Exeter, New Hampshire.

Eligibility This program is open to scholars and teachers from groups traditionally underrepresented in the secondary school environment who might not otherwise consider teaching in a residential secondary school. Candidates may come from other educational institutions, direct from college or graduate school, or from non-academic settings.

Financial data Fellows receive a competitive salary.

Duration 1 to 3 academic years.

Additional information Fellows live in residence at Phillips Exeter Academy, where they affiliate with a specific academic department and coordinate their teaching responsibilities with a faculty mentor. They serve on important faculty committees and engage in oversight of dormitories, athletics, and extracurricular activities. This fellowship was first offered for the 1998-99 academic year.

Number awarded Up to 4 each year.

[772]
JOSEPH L. FISHER DOCTORAL DISSERTATION FELLOWSHIPS

Resources for the Future
Attn: Coordinator for Academic Programs
1616 P Street, N.W.
Washington, DC 20036-1400
(202) 328-5060   Fax: (202) 939-3460
E-mail: mankin@rff.org
Web: www.rff.org

Purpose To support doctoral dissertation research in economics (particularly by minorities and women) on issues related to the environment, natural resources, or energy.

Eligibility This program is open to graduate students in the final year of research on a dissertation related to the environment, natural resources, or energy. Applicants must submit a brief letter of application and a curriculum vitae, a graduate transcript, a 1-page abstract of the dissertation, a technical summary of the dissertation (up to 2,500 words), a letter from the student's department chair, and 2 letters of recommendation from faculty members on the student's dissertation committee. The technical summary should describe clearly the aim of the dissertation, its significance in relation to the existing literature, and the research methods to be used. Women and minority candidates are strongly encouraged to apply.

Financial data The stipend is $12,000 per year.

Duration 1 academic year.

Additional information It is expected that recipients will not hold other employment during the fellowship period. Recipients must notify Resources for the Future of any financial assistance they receive from any other source for support of doctoral work.

Number awarded 2 or 3 each year.

Deadline February of each year.

[773]
LIBRARY OF CONGRESS FELLOWSHIPS IN INTERNATIONAL STUDIES

American Council of Learned Societies
Attn: Office of Fellowships and Grants
633 Third Avenue, 8C
New York, NY 10017-6795
(212) 697-1505   Fax: (212) 949-8058
E-mail: grants@acls.org
Web: www.acls.org/locguide.htm

Purpose To provide financial assistance to scholars (particularly minorities and women) in all disciplines of the humanities and the social sciences who are interested in using the foreign language collections of the Library of Congress.

Eligibility This program is open to U.S. citizens and permanent residents who hold a Ph.D. in a discipline of the humanities or social sciences. Proposals in multidisciplinary and cross-disciplinary studies are also welcome, as are proposals focused on single or multiple geographical areas. Research must require use of the foreign language collections of the Library of Congress. Preference is given to scholars at an early stage of their career (within 7 years of completing their doctorate). Applicants may be affiliated with any academic institution, although independent scholars are also eligible. Applications are particularly invited from women and members of minority groups.

Financial data The stipend is $3,500 per month.

Duration 4 to 9 months; fellowships may be combined with sabbatical and other fellowship funds to extend the research period up to a total of 12 months.

Additional information This program, established in 2001, is supported by funding from the Andrew W. Mellon Foundation, the Association of American Universities, and the Library of Congress. Additional support for research concerning east or southeast Asia is provided by the Henry Luce Foundation. During the fellowship period, scholars are expected to be engaged in full-time research at the Library of Congress.

Number awarded Up to 10 each year.

Deadline November of each year.

[774]
LILLA JEWEL AWARD FOR WOMEN ARTISTS

McKenzie River Gathering Foundation
Attn: Office Manager
2705 East Burnside, Suite 210
Portland, OR 97214
(503) 289-1517   Toll-free: (800) 489-6743
Fax: (503) 232-1731   E-mail: info@mrgfoundation.org
Web: www.mrgfoundation.org

Purpose To provide funding to women (particularly women of color) who are artists in Oregon.

Eligibility Eligible to apply for this funding are women artists in Oregon. The artistic category rotates on a quadriennial cycle among performing arts (2006), media arts (2007), visual arts (2008), and literary arts and music (2009). Although the award is not based on financial need, the intent is to support a woman artist who lacks traditional access to funding. Selection is based on the artistic impact of the work presented for consideration; whether the artist is a member of another traditionally underfunded group,

such as women of color or lesbians; the ideas embodied in the work as represented in the written application; how the work challenges the status quo and supports the sponsor's mission of progressive social change; and the potential impact of the award on the artist at this point in her career.

Financial data The maximum grant is $4,000.

Duration 1 year.

Additional information This is the only funding available to individuals through the McKenzie River Gathering Foundation.

Number awarded 1 each year.

[775]
LYMAN T. JOHNSON POSTDOCTORAL FELLOWSHIP

University of Kentucky
Attn: Executive Vice President for Research
201 Gillis Building
Lexington, KY 40506-0033
(859) 257-5294   Fax: (859) 323-2800
E-mail: vpr@email.uky.edu
Web: www.rgs.uky.edu/students/postdocs.htm

Purpose To provide an opportunity for recent minority postdoctorates to conduct research at the University of Kentucky (UK).

Eligibility This program is open to minorities who have completed a doctoral degree within the past 2 years in a graduate or professional area in which minorities are under-represented. Applicants must demonstrate evidence of scholarship with competitive potential for a tenure-track faculty appointment at a research university and compatibility of specific research interests with those in doctorate-granting units at the UK. They should submit a letter of application, a curriculum vitae, sample publications or dissertation chapters, a research proposal, 3 letters of recommendation, and a letter from a potential mentor at the university outlining the general research program. U.S. citizenship or permanent resident status is required.

Financial data The fellowship provides a stipend of $35,000 plus $5,000 for support of research activities.

Duration Up to 2 years.

Additional information In addition to conducting an individualized research program under the mentorship of 1 or more UK professors, fellows actively participate in research and teaching as well as service to the university, their profession, and the community. This program began in 1992.

Number awarded 1 each year.

Deadline January or July of each year.

[776]
MANY VOICES RESIDENCIES

Playwrights' Center
2301 Franklin Avenue East
Minneapolis, MN 55406-1099
(612) 332-7481   Fax: (612) 332-6037
E-mail: info@pwcenter.org
Web: www.pwcenter.org/fellowships_MV.htm

Purpose To provide funding for Minnesota playwrights of color so they can spend a year in residence at the Playwrights' Center in Minneapolis.

Eligibility This program is open to playwrights of color who have been citizens or permanent residents of the United States and residents of Minnesota for at least 1 year. Applicants must be interested in playwriting and creating theater in a supportive artists' community at the Playwrights' Center. Selection is based on the applicant's commitment, proven talent, and artistic potential.

Financial data The program provides a stipend of $1,250; a mentorship with an established playwright or theater artist of their choosing; a full scholarship to a center class; a private script workshop with professional actors, directors, and dramaturgs; a public reading with professional actors and an audience discussion; and a 1-year membership in the Playwrights' Center.

Duration 9 months, beginning in October.

Additional information Fellows must be in residence at the Playwrights' Center for the duration of the program. This program is funded by a grant from the Jerome Foundation.

Number awarded 8 each year.

Deadline July of each year.

[777]
MARTIN LUTHER KING, JR., CESAR CHAVEZ, ROSA PARKS VISITING PROFESSORS PROGRAM

University of Michigan
Attn: Office of the Associate Provost—Academic Affairs
503 Thompson Street
3084 Fleming Administration Building 1340
Ann Arbor, MI 48109-1340
(734) 764-3982   Fax: (734) 764-4546
E-mail: provost@umich.edu
Web: www.provost.umich.edu

Purpose To provide funds for minority scholars to visit and lecture/teach at the University of Michigan.

Eligibility Outstanding minority (African American, Asian American, Latino/a (Hispanic) American, and Native American) postdoctorates or scholars/practitioners are eligible to be nominated by University of Michigan department chairs or deans to visit and lecture there. Nominations that include collaborations with other universities are of high priority.

Financial data Visiting Professors receive round-trip transportation and an appropriate honorarium.

Duration Visits range from 1 to 5 days.

Additional information This program was established in 1986. Visiting Professors are expected to lecture or teach at the university, offer at least 1 event open to the general public, and meet with minority campus/community groups, including local K-12 schools.

Number awarded Varies each year.

Deadline January for the summer term; March for the fall term; August for the winter term; and November for the spring term.

[778]
MATHEMATICA SUMMER FELLOWSHIPS

Mathematica Policy Research, Inc.
Attn: Human Resources
600 Alexander Park
P.O. Box 2393
Princeton, NU 08543-2393
(609) 799-3535   Fax: (609) 799-0005
E-mail: HRNJ@mathematica-mpr.com
Web: www.mathinc.com

Purpose To provide an opportunity for graduate students (particularly minority students) in social policy fields to work on an independent summer research project at an office of Mathematica Policy Research, Inc.

Eligibility This program is open to students enrolled in a master's or Ph.D. program in public policy or a social science. Applicants must be interested in conducting independent research on a policy issue of relevance to the economic and social problems of minority groups. Traditionally, that includes those of African American, Hispanic, Asian, and Native American ancestry, although proposals focusing on another group, such as people with disabilities, may be considered. The proposed research must relate to the work of Mathematica, but fellows do not work on Mathematica projects. Qualified minority students are encouraged to apply.

Financial data The stipend is $6,000 (or $2,000 per month). Fellows also receive $500 for project-related expenses.

Duration 3 months during the summer.

Additional information Mathematica offices are located in Princeton (New Jersey), Cambridge (Massachusetts), and Washington, D.C. Fellows may indicate their choice of location, but they are assigned to the office where the work of the research staff meshes best with their topic and interests.

Number awarded Up to 5 each year.

Deadline March of each year.

[779]
MENTAL HEALTH DISSERTATION RESEARCH GRANTS TO INCREASE DIVERSITY IN THE MENTAL HEALTH RESEARCH ARENA

National Institute of Mental Health
Attn: Office for Special Populations
6001 Executive Boulevard, Room 8125
Bethesda, MD 20892-9659
(301) 443-2847   Fax: (301) 443-8022
E-mail: ms265g@nih.gov
Web: www.nimh.nih.gov

Purpose To provide financial support to underrepresented minority doctoral candidates planning to prepare for a research career in any area relevant to mental health and/or mental disorders.

Eligibility This program is open to doctoral candidates conducting dissertation research in a field related to mental health and/or mental disorders at a university, college, or professional school with an accredited doctoral degree granting program. Applicants must be members of an ethnic or racial group that has been determined by their institution to be underrepresented in biomedical or behavioral research. They must be U.S. citizens, nationals, or permanent residents.

Financial data Grants provide up to $30,000 per year in direct costs.

Duration 1 year; may be renewed 1 additional year.

Number awarded Varies each year.

Deadline April, August, or December of each year.

[780]
MFP DISSERTATION SUPPORT

American Nurses Association
Attn: Ethnic Minority Fellowship Programs
600 Maryland Avenue, S.W., Suite 100 West
Washington, DC 20024-2571
(202) 651-7244   Fax: (202) 651-7007
E-mail: emfp@ana.org
Web: www.nursingworld.org

Purpose To provide funding to minority nurses who are working on a dissertation on a topic of interest to the Minority Fellowship Program (MFP) of the American Nurses Association.

Eligibility This program is open to nurses who are completing a doctoral dissertation and are members of an ethnic or racial minority group, including but not limited to Blacks or African Americans, Hispanics or Latinos, American Indians and Alaska Natives, Asians and Asian Americans, and Native Hawaiians and other Pacific Islanders. Applicants must be able to demonstrate a commitment to a research career in nursing and psychiatric/mental health issues affecting ethnic minority populations. They must be working on a doctoral dissertation with a focus on such issues of concern to minority populations as child abuse, violence in intimate relationships, mental health disorders, substance abuse, mental health service utilization, and stigma as a barrier to mental health care and personal resilience. U.S. citizenship or permanent resident status and membership in the American Nurses Association are required.

Financial data Grants range from $1,000 to $5,000.

Duration These are 1-time grants.

Additional information Funds for this program are provided by the Substance Abuse and Mental Health Services Administration.

Number awarded 1 or more each year.

[781]
MILLENDER FELLOWSHIP

Wayne State University
Attn: Associate Provost for Academic Programs
656 West Kirby
4116 Faculty/Administration Building
Detroit, MI 48202
(313) 577-2023   Fax: (313) 577-5666
Web: www.millenderfund.org/fellowship.htm

Purpose To provide professional experience in Detroit to minorities who recently earned a master's degree and are interested in preparing for a public service-oriented career.

Eligibility Prior affiliation with Wayne State University is not required. Eligibility is open to minorities who have a commitment to public service and can demonstrate a record of successful accomplishment in some graduate educational program and/or through equivalent experience.

Applicants must have completed a master's degree (or have equivalent professional experience) by the start of the fellowship. Writing, research, computer, and Internet skills are important.

Financial data The stipend is $30,000 plus fringe benefits. Some funds may be available to assist with moving.

Duration 9 months; nonrenewable.

Additional information Funds for this program come from the Robert L. Millender Sr. Memorial Fund. Fellows work directly with top executives of major public or private nonprofit organizations in Detroit. Previous fellows have served in the office of the mayor of Detroit, Detroit Economic Growth Corporation, New Detroit Inc., Southeastern Michigan Council of Governments, and similar agencies. This program is modeled after the White House and Congressional Fellowship programs. Fellows must devote full time to their assignments. They must live in the Detroit metropolitan area for the duration of the program. A mid-year and a final report are required.

Number awarded 1 each year.

Deadline March of each year.

[782]
MINORITY MEDICAL STUDENT SUMMER EXTERNSHIP IN ADDICTION PSYCHIATRY

American Psychiatric Association
Attn: Department of Minority and National Affairs
1000 Wilson Boulevard, Suite 1825
Arlington, VA 22209-3901
(703) 907-8653   Toll-free: (888) 35-PSYCH
Fax: (703) 907-7852   E-mail: mking@psych.org
Web: www.psych.org

Purpose To provide funding to minority medical students who are interested in working on a research project during the summer with a mentor who specializes in addiction psychiatry.

Eligibility This program is open to minority medical students who have a specific interest in services related to substance abuse treatment and prevention. Minorities include American Indians, Alaska Natives, Native Hawaiians, Asian Americans, Hispanic/Latinos, and African Americans. Applicants must be interested in working with a mentor who specializes in addiction psychiatry. Work settings provide an emphasis on working clinically with or studying underserved minority populations and issues of co-occurring disorders, substance abuse treatment, and mental health disparity. Most of them are in inner-city or rural settings.

Financial data Externships provide $1,500 for travel expenses to go to the work setting of the mentor and up to another $1,500 for out-of-pocket expenses directly related to the conduct of the externship.

Duration 1 month during the summer.

Additional information Funding for this program is provided by the Substance Abuse and Mental Health Services Administration (SAMHSA).

Number awarded 10 each year.

Deadline April of each year.

[783]
MINORITY NEUROSCIENCE POSTDOCTORAL FELLOWSHIP PROGRAM

Society for Neuroscience
Attn: Education Department
11 Dupont Circle, N.W., Suite 500
Washington, DC 20036
(202) 462-6688   Fax: (202) 462-9740
E-mail: info@sfn.org
Web: apu.sfn.org

Purpose To provide funding to minority postdoctoral fellows participating in mental health related neuroscience research and training programs.

Eligibility This program is open to postdoctoral fellows in neuroscience who are members of traditionally underrepresented racial and ethnic minority groups (African Americans, Hispanics, Native Americans, Alaskan Natives, Asians, and Pacific Islanders). Applicants must be U.S. citizens or permanent residents enrolled in a program of research and training to prepare for a career in neuroscience research laboratories. Along with their application, they must submit 2 academic letters of recommendation, a 1- to 2-page essay describing their area of interest and research goals in neuroscience, a 1- to 2-page essay describing how their career goals are consistent with the goals of the program to increase diversity in neuroscience, undergraduate and graduate transcripts, a current resume or curriculum vitae, copies of papers and abstracts they have authored or co-authored, a 1-page summary of their dissertation, and a biosketch of the home institution advisor (if available).

Financial data Fellows receive a stipend that is based on number of years of postdoctoral experience, in accordance with standard National Research Service Award guidelines (currently, ranging from $35,568 per year for no experience to $51,036 for 7 or more years). Other benefits include travel assistance and registration to attend the annual meeting of the Society for Neuroscience (SfN), enrichment programs that include funds to participate in activities outside the fellow's home laboratory, and mentoring opportunities with a mentor chosen from the SfN membership.

Duration 2 years, contingent upon adequate research progress and academic standing.

Additional information This program, established in 1991, is sponsored largely by the National Institute of Mental Health with additional support from the National Institute of Neurological Disorders and Stroke. Information is also available from Joanne Berger-Sweeney, Wellesley College, Department of Biological Sciences, 106 Central Street, Wellesley, MA 02481-8203, (781) 283-3503, Fax: (781) 283-3704, E-mail: mnfp@wellesley.edu.

Number awarded 5 each year.

Deadline March, August, or December of each year.

[784]
MINORITY NEUROSCIENCE PREDOCTORAL FELLOWSHIP PROGRAM

Society for Neuroscience
Attn: Education Department
11 Dupont Circle, N.W., Suite 500
Washington, DC 20036
(202) 462-6688   Fax: (202) 462-9740
E-mail: info@sfn.org
Web: apu.sfn.org

Purpose To provide funding to minority graduate students participating in mental health related neuroscience research and training programs.

Eligibility This program is open to doctoral students in neuroscience who are members of traditionally underrepresented racial and ethnic minority groups (African Americans, Hispanics, Native Americans, Alaskan Natives, Asians, and Pacific Islanders). Applicants must be U.S. citizens or permanent residents enrolled in a program of research and training to prepare for a career in neuroscience research laboratories. Along with their application, they must submit 2 academic letters of recommendation, a 1- to 2-page essay describing their area of interest and research goals in neuroscience, a 1- to 2-page essay describing how their career goals are consistent with the goals of the program to increase diversity in neuroscience, undergraduate and graduate transcripts, a current resume or curriculum vitae, copies of papers and abstracts they have authored or co-authored, and a biosketch of the home institution advisor (if available).

Financial data Fellows receive a stipend in accordance with standard National Research Service Award guidelines (currently, $20,772 per year). Other benefits include travel assistance and registration to attend the annual meeting of the Society for Neuroscience (SfN), enrichment programs that include funds to participate in activities outside the fellow's home laboratory, and mentoring opportunities with a mentor chosen from the SfN membership.

Duration 3 years, contingent upon adequate research progress and academic standing.

Additional information This program, established in 1991, is sponsored largely by the National Institute of Mental Health with additional support from the National Institute of Neurological Disorders and Stroke. Information is also available from Joanne Berger-Sweeney, Wellesley College, Department of Biological Sciences, 106 Central Street, Wellesley, MA 02481-8203, (781) 283-3503, Fax: (781) 283-3704, E-mail: mnfp@wellesley.edu.

Number awarded 12 each year.

Deadline August of each year.

[785]
NAATA MEDIA FUND GRANTS

National Asian American Telecommunications
   Association
Attn: Media Fund
145 Ninth Street, Suite 350
San Francisco, CA 94103
(415) 863-0814   Fax: (415) 863-7428
E-mail: mediafund@naatanet.org
Web: www.naatanet.org

Purpose   To provide funding to producers of public television programs that relate to the Asian American experience.

Eligibility   This program is open to producers who are interested in developing and finishing public television programs on Asian American issues. Preference is given to projects that 1) bring to light underrepresented or unheard voices; 2) place Asian Americans in the context of an increasingly diverse multicultural society; 3) look at issues of universal interest but from a unique Asian American perspective; and 4) expand our definition of the Asian American identity. All programs must be standard broadcast length and in accordance with PBS broadcast specifications. Ineligible projects include those for which the exclusive domestic television broadcast rights are not available; in the script development or research and development stage; intended solely for theatrical release or that are commercial in nature; in which applicant is commissioned, employed, or hired by a commercial or public television station; use funds raised from investors and have a commercial financing structure in place; that are thesis projects or student films co- or solely owned or copywritten, or editorially or fiscally controlled by the school; that are foreign-based, owned, or controlled; that are industrial or promotional projects. Applicants must be U.S. citizens or permanent residents. Selection is based on the potential of the project to provoke thoughtful dialogue about the subject, knowledge and understanding of the subject, thoughtfulness and sensitivity of the approach, ability of the finished program to shed light on the Asian American experience, ability of the production team to carry out the proposed project at the highest standards of quality, soundness of the production and fundraising plans, reasonableness of the budget estimates and considerations, applicant's ability to complete the program on schedule and within budget, and potential of the finished program to get onto national public television.

Financial data   Grants range from $20,000 to $50,000.

Additional information   Funding for this program is provided by the Corporation for Public Broadcasting. The program began in 1990. To date, more than $3 million has been granted to 150 projects. Grants are not unrestricted. Producers must agree to grant the National Asian American Telecommunications Association (NAATA), for no additional fee, exclusive domestic public television distribution rights.

Number awarded   5 to 10 grants are awarded each year.

Deadline   February or August of each year.

[786]
NATIONAL CENTER FOR ATMOSPHERIC RESEARCH POSTDOCTORAL APPOINTMENTS

National Center for Atmospheric Research
Attn: Advanced Study Program
1850 Table Mesa Drive
P.O. Box 3000
Boulder, CO 80307-3000
(303) 497-1598   Fax: (303) 497-1328
E-mail: paulad@ucar.edu
Web: www.asp.ucar.edu/asp/pdann.html

Purpose   To provide funding to recent Ph.D.s (particularly minorities and women) who wish to conduct research at the National Center for Atmospheric Research (NCAR) in Boulder, Colorado.

Eligibility   This program is open to recent Ph.D.s and Sc.D.s in applied mathematics, chemistry, engineering, and physics as well as specialists in atmospheric sciences from such disciplines as biology, economics, geography, geology, and science education. Applicants must be interested in conducting research at the center in atmospheric sciences and global change. Selection is based on the applicant's scientific capability and potential, originality and independence, and ability to take advantage of the research opportunities at center. Applications from women and minorities are encouraged.

Financial data   The stipend is $46,000 in the first year and $47,000 in the second year. Fellows also receive life and health insurance, a relocation allowance (up to $1,000 for travel within the United States or up to $2,500 for travel from abroad), and scientific travel reimbursement up to $1,500 per year.

Duration   2 years.

Additional information   NCAR is operated by the University Corporation for Atmospheric Research (a consortium of 61 universities) and sponsored by the National Science Foundation.

Number awarded   Varies; currently, 7 to 10 each year.

Deadline   January of each year.

[787]
NATIONAL ESTUARINE RESEARCH RESERVE SYSTEM GRADUATE FELLOWSHIPS

National Oceanic and Atmospheric Administration
Office of Ocean and Coastal Resource Management
Attn: Estuarine Reserves Division
Silver Spring Metro Center Building 4, 11th Floor
1305 East-West Highway
Silver Spring, MD 20910
(301) 713-3155, ext. 172   Fax: (301) 713-4363
E-mail: susan.white@noaa.gov
Web: nerrs.noaa.gov/Fellowship

Purpose   To provide funding to minority and other graduate students interested in conducting research within National Estuarine Research Reserves.

Eligibility   This program is open to students admitted to or enrolled in a full-time master's or doctoral program at U.S. accredited universities. Applicants should have completed a majority of their course work at the beginning of their fellowship and have an approved thesis research program focused on improving coastal zone management while providing hands-on training in conducting ecological monitoring. Proposed research topics must address 1 of the following topics: 1) eutrophiation, effects of non-point source pollution and/or nutrient dynamics; 2) habitat conservation and/or restoration; 3) biodiversity and/or the effects of invasive species on estuarine ecosystems; 4) mechanisms for sustaining resources within estuarine ecosystems; or 5) economic, sociological, and/or anthropological research applicable to estuarine ecosystem management. They must be willing to conduct their research within the National Estuarine Research Reserves. Minority students are encouraged to apply.

Financial data The amount of the fellowship is $20,000; at least 30% of total project cost match is required by the applicant (i.e., $7,500 match for a total project cost of $27,000). Requested overhead costs are limited to 10% of the federal amount. Waived overhead costs may be used as match. Funds may be used for any combination of research support, salary, tuition, supplies, or other costs as needed, including overhead.

Duration 1 to 3 years.

Additional information For a list of the National Estuarine Research Reserves, with the name and address of a contact person at each, write to the sponsor. Fellows are required to work with the research coordinator or manager at the host reserve to develop a plan to participate in the reserve's research and/or monitoring program for up to 15 hours per week.

Number awarded Approximately 27 each year.

Deadline October of each year.

[788]
NEW YORK PUBLIC LIBRARY FELLOWSHIPS

American Council of Learned Societies
Attn: Office of Fellowships and Grants
633 Third Avenue, 8C
New York, NY 10017-6795
(212) 697-1505   Fax: (212) 949-8058
E-mail: grants@acls.org
Web: www.acls.org/felguide.htm

Purpose To provide funding to postdoctorates (particularly minorities and women) interested in conducting research at the Dorothy and Lewis B. Cullman Center for Scholars and Writers of the New York Public Library.

Eligibility Applicants must be U.S. citizens or permanent residents who hold a Ph.D. degree and have not held supported research leave time for at least 3 years prior to the start of the proposed research. Applicants must be interested in conducting research in the humanities and humanities-related social sciences at the New York Public Library's Dorothy and Lewis B. Cullman Center for Scholars and Writers. Applications are particularly invited from women and members of minority groups.

Financial data Fellowships provide a maximum stipend of $50,000 and, if necessary, a housing allowance to enable the fellow to live in New York during the fellowship term.

Duration 9 months, beginning in September

Additional information This program was first offered for 1999-2000, the inaugural year of the center. Candidates must also submit a separate application that is available from the New York Public Library, Humanities and Social Sciences Library, Dorothy and Lewis B. Cullman Center for Scholars and Writers, Fifth Avenue and 42nd Street, New

York, NY 10018-2788, E-mail: csw@nypl.org. Fellows are required to be in continuous residence at the center and participate actively in its activities and programs.

Number awarded Up to 5 each year.

Deadline September of each year.

[789]
NEW YORK SEA GRANT AND HUDSON RIVER NATIONAL ESTUARINE RESEARCH RESERVE COOPERATIVE RESEARCH FELLOWSHIP

New York Sea Grant
Attn: Nordica Holochuck, Extension Specialist
10 Westbrook Lane
Kingston, NY 12401-3824
(845) 340-3983   E-mail: nch8@cornell.edu
Web: www.seagrant/sunysb.edu

Purpose To provide funding for master's and doctoral candidates (particularly minorities) who are working on a thesis related to the Hudson River.

Eligibility This program is open to master's and doctoral candidates who are seeking funding for thesis research related to the Hudson River. Although they are preferred, the fellowship is not limited to students in New York state. Minority students are especially encouraged to submit applications. Although research in other areas relevant to the missions of the sponsors may be submitted, proposals that emphasize 1 or more of the following 4 areas are given priority: 1) develop evaluation techniques to measure restoration success and/or remediation techniques to restore disturbed coastal environments and habitat; 2) determine functional impacts/importance of introduced and native species on estuarine wetland ecosystem functioning and develop effective detection and control mechanisms; 3) identify and/or evaluate anthropogenic effects on estuarine wetland ecosystem functions; and 4) identify and/or evaluate relationships between wetland ecosystems and the drainage basin.

Financial data The stipend is $14,000 per year. Another $2,000 per year is provided to cover operational costs (e.g., travel costs and supplies).

Duration 2 years, beginning between June 1 and September 1 of each year.

Additional information This program is jointly sponsored by the New York Sea Grant and the Hudson River National Estuarine Research Reserve. Information is also available from Charles Nieder, Research Coordinator, Hudson River National Estuarine Research Reserve, New York State Department of Environmental Conservation, c/o Bard College Field Station, Annandale, NY 12504, (845) 758-7013, E-mail: wcnieder@gw.dec.state.ny.us. Recipients must submit a 6-month progress report and a final report. They must also make a final oral presentation and/or a poster of research results.

Number awarded 1 each year.

Deadline February of each year.

[790]
N.S. BIENSTOCK FELLOWSHIP

Radio and Television News Directors Foundation
1600 K Street, N.W., Suite 700
Washington, DC 20006-2838
(202) 467-5218   Fax: (202) 223-4007
E-mail: karenb@rtndf.org
Web: www.rtndf.org/asfi/fellowships/minority.html

Purpose To provide financial assistance for professional development to minority journalists employed in electronic news.

Eligibility This program is open to minority journalists employed in electronic news who have 10 years of less of full-time experience. Applications must include samples of the journalist's work done as the member of a news staff, with a script and tape (audio or video) up to 15 minutes.

Financial data The grant is $2,500 plus an all-expense paid trip to the international convention of the Radio-Television News Directors Association held that year.

Duration The grant is presented annually.

Additional information The grant, established in 1999, may be used in any way to improve the craft and enhance the excellence of the recipient's news operation.

Number awarded 1 each year.

Deadline April of each year.

[791]
NUTRITION ACTION FELLOWSHIP

Center for Science in the Public Interest
Attn: Executive Director
1875 Connecticut Avenue, N.W., Suite 300
Washington, DC 20009-5728
(202) 332-9110   Fax: (202) 265-4954
E-mail: cspi@cspinet.org
Web: www.cspinet.org/job/nutrition_fellow.html

Purpose To provide funding to minority and other postdoctorates interested in serving as a nutrition advocate at the Center for Science in the Public Interest.

Eligibility This program is open to recent graduates with a Ph.D. or M.D. who are interested in serving as a nutrition advocate at the center. Applicants should have demonstrated interest in public interest advocacy and nutrition science, food safety, or health policy. They should also be able to demonstrate academic achievement and writing ability. Minorities, women, and persons with disabilities are particularly encouraged to apply.

Financial data The stipend is $35,000. A generous and comprehensive benefits package is also provided.

Duration 1 year, preferably starting in summer.

Additional information Fellows work in the center's Washington office on nutrition science policy and/or food safety issues.

Number awarded 1 each year.

Deadline Applications may be submitted at any time.

[792]
ORGANIZATIONAL LEARNING FOR HOMELAND SECURITY FELLOWSHIP PROGRAM

Stanford University
Center for International Security and Cooperation
Attn: Fellowship Program Coordinator
Encina Hall, Room E210
616 Serra Street
Stanford, CA 94305-6165
(650) 723-9626   Fax: (650) 723-0089
E-mail: barbara.platt@stanford.edu
Web: www.cisac.stanford.edu

Purpose To provide funding to scholars and professionals (particularly minorities and women) who are interested in conducting research on organizational learning and homeland security.

Eligibility This program is open to predoctoral candidates, postdoctoral scholars, scientists, engineers, and professionals (e.g., military officers or civilian members of the U.S. government, members of military or diplomatic services from other countries, and journalists interested in international security issues). Applicants must be interested in conducting research on a broad range of topics related to organizational learning and homeland security. Topics may be historical, with potential lessons for current homeland security issues. Disciplines may include anthropology, computer science, history, law, medicine, operations research, political science, or sociology. Examples of topics suitable for support include (but are not limited to) learning from military and other exercises and simulations; learning from success and failure in intelligence and forecasting; historical interactions and competitive learning between state and non-state organizations; earlier U.S. civil defense efforts, with implications for homeland security; learning from engineering failures, with lessons for homeland security; or causes and prevention of terrorism. Applications from women and minorities are encouraged.

Financial data Stipends are determined on a case-by-case basis commensurate with experience and availability of other funds. Health insurance is provided, and funds are available for travel and other research-related expenses.

Duration 9 months.

Additional information This program, established in 2004, is offered by Stanford University's Center for International Security and Cooperation (CISAC) in cooperation with the Naval Postgraduate School (NPS) in Monterey, California. Fellows must be in residence at CISAC (or split their time between CISAC and NPS) and participate in a monthly seminar held jointly between CISAC and NPS. They are expected to produce a research product (e.g., dissertation chapters, draft article or articles, book manuscript).

Number awarded Varies each year.

Deadline February of each year.

[793]
OSGC RESEARCH PROGRAM

Oklahoma NASA Space Grant Consortium
c/o University of Oklahoma
College of Geosciences
Ditmars House, Suite 5
1623 Cross Center Drive
Norman, Oklahoma 73069
(405) 325-6559   Fax: (405) 325-5537
E-mail: vduca@ou.edu
Web: 129.15.32.115/research/index.html

Purpose To provide funding to minority and other faculty and staff at member institutions of the Oklahoma Space Grant Consortium (OSGC) who are interested in conducting research related to the mission of the U.S. National Aeronautics and Space Administration (NASA).

Eligibility This program provides support for space-related research activities at member and affiliate institutions of the OSGC. Proposals may be submitted by faculty and staff of those institutions 1) to foster multi-disciplinary and multi-university research through special conferences, programs, and correspondence; and 2) to enhance the support infrastructure for faculty to facilitate the pursuit of NASA-related research, including both administrative support and marginal funds for travel and critical equipment or supplies. The OSGC is a component of the NASA Space Grant program, which encourages participation by women, minorities, and persons with disabilities.

Financial data Financing depends on the availability of funds.

Additional information Members of OSGC are Oklahoma State University, the University of Oklahoma, Cameron University, and Langston University. This program is funded by NASA.

[794]
PAUL P. VOURAS DISSERTATION RESEARCH GRANT

Association of American Geographers
Attn: Executive Assistant
1710 16th Street, N.W.
Washington, DC 20009-3198
(202) 234-1450   Fax: (202) 234-2744
E-mail: ekhater@aag.org
Web: www.aag.org

Purpose To provide financial assistance to minority and other members of the Association of American Geographers who are preparing dissertations in geography.

Eligibility Graduate students currently working on a Ph.D. in geography are eligible to apply if they have completed all of the requirements except the dissertation and have been members of the association for at least 1 year prior to submitting an application. Preference is given to minority applicants.

Financial data The amount awarded varies, up to a maximum of $500.

Duration 1 year.

Additional information Funds must be used for direct research expenses only and may not be used to cover overhead costs.

Number awarded 1 each year.

Deadline December of each year.

[795]
PEACE SCHOLAR DISSERTATION FELLOWSHIPS

United States Institute of Peace
Attn: Jennings Randolph Program for International
    Peace
1200 17th Street, N.W., Suite 200
Washington, DC 20036-3011
(202) 429-3886   Fax: (202) 429-6063
TDD: (202) 457-1719   E-mail: fellows@usip.org
Web: www.usip.org/fellows/scholars.html

Purpose To provide financial support to minority and other doctoral candidates working on dissertations that address the nature of international conflict and ways to prevent or end conflict and to sustain peace.

Eligibility This program is open to doctoral candidates, from anywhere in the world, who are enrolled in U.S. universities and conducting dissertation research on international peace and conflict management. Projects from a broad range of disciplines (political science, history, sociology, economics, anthropology, psychology, conflict resolution, and other fields within the humanities and social sciences, including interdisciplinary programs) are welcome. Priority is given to projects that contribute knowledge relevant to the formulation of policy on international peace and conflict issues. Women and members of minority groups are especially encouraged to apply. Selection is based on the candidate's record of achievement and/or leadership potential; the significance and potential of the project for making an important contribution to knowledge, practice, or public understanding; and the quality of the project design and its feasibility within the timetable proposed.

Financial data The stipend is $17,000 per year.

Duration 12 months, beginning in September.

Additional information These fellowships, first awarded in 1988, are tenable at the recipient's university or any other appropriate research site. This program is offered as part of the Jennings Randolph Program for International Peace at the United States Institute of Peace. These awards are not made for projects that constitute policymaking for a government agency or private organization; focus to any substantial degree on conflicts within U.S. domestic society; or adopt a partisan, advocacy, or activist stance.

Number awarded Varies each year; recently, 10 of these fellowships were awarded.

Deadline January of each year.

[796]
PEMBROKE CENTER POSTDOCTORAL FELLOWSHIPS

Brown University
Attn: Pembroke Center for Teaching and Research on
    Women
Box 1958
Providence, RI 02912
(401) 863-2643   Fax: (401) 863-1298
E-mail: Elizabeth_Barboza@Brown.edu
Web: www.pembrokecenter.org/RP-Postdoctoral.asp

Purpose To provide research support for minority and other scholars interested in conducting research at Brown University's Pembroke Center for Teaching and Research on Women on the cross-cultural study of gender.

Eligibility Fellowships are open to scholars in the humanities, social sciences, or life sciences who do not have a tenured position at an American college or university. Applicants must be willing to spend a year in residence at the Pembroke Center for Teaching and Research on Women and participate in a research project related to gender. The project focuses on a theme that changes annually (recently: "The Orders of Time"). The center encourages minority and Third World scholars to apply.

Financial data The stipend is $30,000.

Duration 1 academic year.

Additional information Postdoctoral fellows in residence participate in weekly seminars and present at least 2 public papers during the year, as well as conduct an individual research project. Supplementary funds are available for assistance with travel expenses from abroad. This program includes the following named fellowships: the Nancy L. Buc Postdoctoral Fellowship, the Artemis A.W. and Martha Joukowsky Postdoctoral Fellowship, and the Carol G. Lederer Postdoctoral Fellowship.

Number awarded 3 or 4 each year.

Deadline December of each year.

[797]
PHILIPPINE NURSES ASSOCIATION OF AMERICA FELLOWSHIP PROJECTS

Philippine Nurses Association of America
Attn: PNAA Foundation
11 Heritage Drive
Shrewsbury, NJ 07702
(908) 753-7343   E-mail: Phoebe459@comcast.net
Web: www.pnaamerica.net

Purpose To provide funding for professional development activities to members of the Philippine Nurses Association of America (PNAA).

Eligibility This program is open to PNAA members who are interested in further education, research or other investigation, special project, mentorship, or other professional development activity. Applicants must submit brief statements on their contributions to the PNAA and the nursing profession in general; how they have contributed to the visibility, viability, and vitality of the PNAA and/or their chapter; and their potential for promoting the goals of the PNAA.

Financial data Grants depend on the nature of the proposal and the availability of funds.

Duration Projects must be completed within 1 year.

Additional information The application fee is $50.

Number awarded 1 or more each year.

Deadline May of each year.

[798]
PICKWICK POSTDOCTORAL FELLOWSHIP IN SLEEP

National Sleep Foundation
Attn: Pickwick Club
1522 K Street, N.W., Suite 500
Washington, DC 20005
(202) 347-3471, ext. 203   Fax: (202) 347-3472
E-mail: nsf@sleepfoundation.org
Web: www.sleepfoundation.org

Purpose To enable young researchers, especially minorities, to devote the major portion of their professional effort to the study of sleep and sleep disorders.

Eligibility Applicants for this fellowship must be in recognized North American programs of study or laboratories with strong mentorship in the appropriate area. They must have an M.D., D.V.M., or D.O. degree; the degree or subsequent training must have been completed within the past 5 years. Fellowships are available for basic, applied, or clinical research. Applicants may not have a faculty position or have received an NIH grant. Minorities are specifically encouraged to apply.

Financial data The grant is $40,000 per year.

Duration 1 or 2 years.

Additional information This program was established in 1995. The Pickwick Club is named after the society described in Charles Dickens' *The Pickwick Papers;* the Pickwick Club honors those who, like Mr. Pickwick, are concerned with "a sensation of bodily weariness that in vain contends against an inability to sleep."

Deadline November of each year.

[799]
POETRY MANUSCRIPT COMPETITION FOR PUBLISHED POETS

Asian American Writers' Workshop
Attn: Poetry Competition
16 West 32nd Street, Suite 10A
New York, NY 10001-3808
(212) 494-0061   Fax: (212) 494-0062
E-mail: desk@aaww.org
Web: www.aaww.org/publications/submission.html

Purpose To provide funding for publication of their new work to Asian American poets.

Eligibility This program is open to U.S. citizens of Asian descent, writing in English, who have already published a book of poetry (chapbooks and self-published works are not eligible). Applicants must submit a previously unpublished manuscript of 48 to 100 pages.

Financial data The awardee receives publication of a poetry book (including a standard book contract) and a cash prize of $1,000.

Additional information Funding for the book publication is provided by the Ford Foundation. The book is nationally distributed by Temple University Press.

Number awarded 3 each year.

Deadline December of each year.

[800]

POSTDOCTORAL FELLOWSHIP IN MENTAL HEALTH AND SUBSTANCE ABUSE SERVICES

American Psychological Association
Attn: Minority Fellowship Program
750 First Street, N.E.
Washington, DC 20002-4242
(202) 336-6127   Fax: (202) 336-6012
TDD: (202) 336-6123   E-mail: mfp@apa.org
Web: www.apa.org/mfp/postdocpsych.html

Purpose To provide financial assistance to minority and other postdoctoral scholars interested in a program of research training related to providing mental health and substance abuse services to ethnic minority populations.

Eligibility This program is open to U.S. citizens and permanent residents who received a doctoral degree in psychology in the last 5 years. Applicants must be interested in participating in a program of training under a qualified sponsor for research, delivery of services, or policy related to substance abuse and its relationship to the mental health or psychological well-being of ethnic minorities. Members of ethnic minority groups (African Americans, Hispanics/Latinos, American Indians, Alaskan Natives, Asian Americans, Native Hawaiians, and other Pacific Islanders) are especially encouraged to apply. Selection is based on commitment to a career in ethnic minority mental health service delivery, research, or policy; qualifications of the sponsor; the fit between career goals and training environment selected; merit of the training proposal; potential demonstrated through accomplishments and goals; and appropriateness to goals of the program.

Financial data The stipend depends on the number of years of research experience and is equivalent to the standard postdoctoral stipend level of the National Institutes of Health (currently ranging from $35,568 for no years of experience to $51,036 for 7 or more years of experience).

Duration 1 academic or calendar year; may be renewed for up to 2 additional years.

Additional information Funding is provided by the U.S. Substance Abuse and Mental Health Services Administration.

Number awarded Varies each year.

Deadline January of each year.

[801]

POSTDOCTORAL FELLOWSHIPS IN THE NEUROSCIENCES

American Psychological Association
Attn: Minority Fellowship Program
750 First Street, N.E.
Washington, DC 20002-4242
(202) 336-6127   Fax: (202) 336-6012
TDD: (202) 336-6123   E-mail: mfp@apa.org
Web: www.apa.org/mfp/pdprogram.html

Purpose To provide funding to minority postdoctorates who are interested in pursuing research training in neuroscience.

Eligibility This program is open to all U.S. citizens and permanent residents who have a Ph.D. or M.D. degree with appropriate research experience in neuroscience or an applied discipline, such as cell or molecular biology or immunology. Applicants must have career goals that are consistent with those of the program: 1) to increase ethnic and racial diversity among neuroscience researchers with a special emphasis on increasing the numbers of underrepresented ethnic minorities; and 2) to increase numbers of neuroscientists whose work is related to the federal initiative to eliminate health disparities. They must be interested in engaging in postdoctoral research training in behavioral neuroscience, cellular neurobiology, cognitive neuroscience, computational neuroscience, developmental neurobiology, membrane biophysics, molecular neurobiology, neuroanatomy, neurobiology of aging, neurobiology of disease, neurochemistry, neurogenetics, neuroimmunology, neuropathology, neuropharmacology, neurophysiology, neurotoxicology, or systems neuroscience. Students identified as underrepresented ethnic minorities in the neurosciences (African Americans, Native Americans, Hispanic Americans, and Pacific Islanders) are especially encouraged to apply. Selection is based on scholarship, research experience and potential, a research proposal, the suitability of the proposed laboratory and mentor, commitment to a research career in neuroscience, writing ability, and appropriateness to program goal.

Financial data The stipend depends on the number of years of research experience and is equivalent to the standard postdoctoral stipend level of the National Institutes of Health (currently ranging from $35,568 for no years of experience to $51,036 for 7 or more years of experience). The fellowship also provides travel funds to attend the annual meeting of the Society for Neuroscience.

Duration 1 year; may be renewed for up to 1 additional year.

Additional information The program was established in 1987. It is funded by the U.S. National Institute of Mental Health of the National Institutes of Health and administered by the American Psychological Association.

Number awarded Varies each year.

Deadline January of each year.

[802]

POSTDOCTORAL FELLOWSHIPS OF THE MINORITY SCHOLAR-IN-RESIDENCE PROGRAM

Consortium for a Strong Minority Presence at Liberal
    Arts Colleges
c/o Administrative Assistant, President's Office
Grinnell College
1121 Park Street
Grinnell, IA 50112-1690
(641) 269-3000   E-mail: cousins@grinnell.edu
Web: www.grinnell.edu/dean/csmp

Purpose To make available the facilities of liberal arts colleges to minority scholars who recently received their doctoral/advanced degree.

Eligibility This program is open to African American, Asian American, Hispanic American, and Native American scholars in the liberal arts and engineering who received the Ph.D. or M.F.A. degree within the past 5 years. Applicants must be interested in a residency at a participating institution that is part of the Consortium for a Strong Minority Presence at Liberal Arts Colleges.

Financial data Fellows receive a stipend equivalent to the average salary paid by the host college to beginning assistant professors. Modest funds are made available to finance the fellow's proposed research, subject to the usual institutional procedures.

Duration 1 year.

Additional information The following schools are participating in the program: Bowdoin College, Bryn Mawr College, Carleton College, Claremont McKenna College, Coe College, College of Wooster, Colorado College, Denison University, DePauw University, Dickinson College, Gettysburg College, Grinnell College, Hamilton College, Haverford College, Hope College, Juniata College, Lewis and Clark College, Luther College, Macalester College, Mount Holyoke College, Oberlin College, Occidental College, Pitzer College, Pomona College, Rhodes College, St. Olaf College, Skidmore College, Southwestern University, Swarthmore College, Trinity University, University of the South, Vassar College, Wellesley College, Wheaton College, Whitman College, and Willamette University. Fellows are expected to teach at least 1 course in each academic term of residency, participate in departmental seminars, and interact with students.

Number awarded Varies each year.

Deadline November of each year.

[803]
POSTDOCTORAL FELLOWSHIPS ON SEXUALITY AND POLICY

Social Science Research Council
Attn: Sexuality Research Fellowship Program
810 Seventh Avenue
New York, NY 10019
(212) 377-2700   Fax: (212) 377-2727
E-mail: srfp@ssrc.org
Web: www.ssrc.org/fellowships/sexuality

Purpose To provide financial support for postdoctoral research on sexuality and public policy.

Eligibility This program is open to scholars who received a Ph.D. within the past 10 years and are not already tenured (although they can occupy a tenure-track position). There are no citizenship requirements. Applicants must be interested in conducting research in sexuality that focuses on policy analysis, policy development, and/or implementation and is relevant to local, state, or national concerns. Topics may include (but are not limited to) criminal justice and incarceration; culture, race, and ethnicity; immigration and migration; institutional influences, such as religion, education, or media, on sexuality and social policy; labor, employment, and economics; marriage and family formation; militarization, war, and peacekeeping; pornography; public health, wellness, and health care issues; reproductive health and population issues; sex work and prostitution; sexual development and aging; sexuality and disability; sexual movements, sexual rights, and/or sexual politics; sexual orientation and identity; sexual violence, coercion, abuse, exploitation, and harassment; sexual education and curriculum design, implementation, and evaluation; sexuality and the law; sexuality and the media; sexually-transmitted diseases and infections; and social movements, sexual rights, and/or sexual politics. Applications are invited from a wide range of disciplines and fields, including but not limited to anthropology, demography, economics, education, history, law, linguistics, philosophy, political science, psychology, public health, public policy, and sociology, as well as such

interdisciplinary programs as sociomedical sciences, jurisprudence and social policy, or American, ethnic, family, labor, media, and urban studies; applications from biomedical or other fields outside the social sciences are welcome as long as they are grounded in social science theory and methodology. Policymakers, advocates, service providers, and program administrators who conduct research in various settings (such as business, federal or state government, and community settings) are also eligible. Applicants should work in partnership with another scholar or professional who will function in the advisory capacity of research consultant. The research consultant must have a doctoral degree from a U.S. or accredited foreign university, be able to demonstrate commitment to human sexuality research through previous publication record and experience, and be able to provide substantive expertise to the applicant in specific areas of research methodology, design, and/or policy. Women and members of minority groups are especially encouraged to apply.

Financial data Grants range from $50,000 to $60,000, to cover research costs and living expenses. An additional $5,000 is awarded to the fellow's research consultant.

Duration 1 year.

Additional information Funding for this program is provided by the Ford Foundation.

Number awarded Approximately 6 each year.

Deadline December of each year.

[804]
POSTDOCTORAL RESEARCH FELLOWSHIPS IN EPILEPSY

Epilepsy Foundation
Attn: Research Department
4351 Garden City Drive
Landover, MD 20785-7223
(301) 459-3700   Toll-free: (800) EFA-1000
Fax: (301) 577-2684   TDD: (800) 332-2070
E-mail: grants@efa.org
Web: www.epilepsyfoundation.org

Purpose To provide funding for a program of postdoctoral training to minority and other physicians and scientists committed to epilepsy research.

Eligibility Applicants must have a doctoral degree (M.D., Ph.D., or equivalent) and be a resident or postdoctoral fellow at a university, medical school, research institution, or medical center. They must be interested in participating in a training experience and research project that has potential significance for understanding the causes, treatment, or consequences of epilepsy. The program is geared toward applicants who will be trained in research in epilepsy rather than those who use epilepsy as a tool for research in other fields. Equal consideration is given to applicants interested in acquiring experience either in basic laboratory research or in the conduct of human clinical studies. Academic faculty holding the rank of instructor or higher are not eligible, nor are graduate or medical students, medical residents, permanent government employees, or employees of private industry. Applications from women, members of minority groups, and people with disabilities are especially encouraged. Selection is based on scientific quality of the proposed research, a statement regarding its relevance to epilepsy, the applicant's qualifications, the preceptor's qualifications, and the adequacy of facility and related epilepsy programs at the institution.

Financial data The grant is $40,000. No indirect costs are covered.

Duration 1 year.

Additional information Support for this program is provided by many individuals, families, and corporations, especially the American Epilepsy Society, Abbott Laboratories, Ortho-McNeil Pharmaceutical, and Pfizer Inc. The fellowship must be carried out at a facility in the United States where there is an ongoing epilepsy research program.

Number awarded Varies each year; recently, 13 of these fellowships were awarded.

Deadline August of each year.

[805]
PREDOCTORAL RESEARCH TRAINING FELLOWSHIPS IN EPILEPSY

Epilepsy Foundation
Attn: Research Department
4351 Garden City Drive
Landover, MD 20785-7223
(301) 459-3700	Toll-free: (800) EFA-1000
Fax: (301) 577-2684	TDD: (800) 332-2070
E-mail: grants@efa.org
Web: www.epilepsyfoundation.org

Purpose To provide funding to minority and other doctoral candidates in designated fields for dissertation research on a topic related to epilepsy.

Eligibility This program is open to full-time graduate students working on a Ph.D. in biochemistry, genetics, neuroscience, nursing, pharmacology, pharmacy, physiology, or psychology. Applicants must be conducting dissertation research on a topic relevant to epilepsy under the guidance of a mentor with expertise in the area of epilepsy investigation. Applications from women, members of minority groups, and people with disabilities are especially encouraged. Selection is based on the relevance of the proposed work to epilepsy, the applicant's qualifications, the mentor's qualifications, the scientific quality of the proposed dissertation research, the quality of the training environment for research related to epilepsy, and the adequacy of the facility.

Financial data The grant is $20,000, consisting of $19,000 for a stipend and $1,000 to support travel to attend the annual meeting of the American Epilepsy Society.

Duration 1 year.

Additional information Support for this program, which began in 1998, is provided by many individuals, families, and corporations, especially the American Epilepsy Society, Abbott Laboratories, Ortho-McNeil Pharmaceutical, and Pfizer Inc.

Number awarded Varies each year; recently, 3 of these fellowships were awarded.

Deadline August of each year.

[806]
R. ROBERT & SALLY D. FUNDERBURG RESEARCH SCHOLAR AWARD IN GASTRIC BIOLOGY RELATED TO CANCER

Foundation for Digestive Health and Nutrition
Attn: Research Awards Coordinator
4930 Del Ray Avenue
Bethesda, MD 20814-2512
(301) 222-4005	Fax: (301) 222-4010
E-mail: info@fdhn.org
Web: www.fdhn.org

Purpose To provide funding to minority and other established investigators who are working on research that enhances fundamental understanding of gastric cancer pathobiology.

Eligibility This program is open to faculty at accredited North American institutions who have established themselves as independent investigators in the field of gastric biology, pursuing novel approaches to gastric mucosal cell biology, regeneration and regulation of cell growth, inflammation as precancerous lesions, genetics of gastric carcinoma, oncogenes in gastric epithelial malignancies, epidemiology of gastric cancer, etiology of gastric epithelial malignancies, or clinical research in diagnosis or treatment of gastric carcinoma. Applicants must be individual members of the American Gastroenterological Association (AGA). Women and minority investigators are strongly encouraged to apply. Selection is based on the novelty, feasibility, and significance of the proposal; attributes of the candidate; and the likelihood that support will lead to a research career in the field of gastric biology. Preference is given to novel approaches, especially for initiation of projects by young investigators or established investigators new to the field.

Financial data The award is $25,000 per year. Funds are to be used for the salary of the investigator. Indirect costs are not allowed.

Duration 2 years.

Additional information This program is administered by the Foundation for Digestive Health and Nutrition (FDHN) and sponsored by the AGA.

Number awarded 1 each year.

Deadline September of each year.

[807]
REGINALD F. LEWIS AND CHARLES HAMILTON HOUSTON FELLOWSHIPS FOR LAW TEACHING

Harvard Law School
Attn: Lewis/Houston Committee
Griswold 220
Cambridge, MA 02138
(617) 495-3100
Web: www.law.harvard.edu

Purpose To provide an opportunity for lawyers, especially minorities, to prepare for a career in law teaching by conducting a research project at Harvard Law School.

Eligibility This program is open to law school graduates who will enhance the diversity of the profession; applications from minority candidates are especially encouraged. Applicants must be interested in preparing for a career as a law professor by conducting a research project in the field in which they expect to teach. They must submit a detailed description (3 to 4 pages) of the project, a statement of their interests in teaching, a statement of the fields in which they expect to teach and pursue research, a resume, a copy of their undergraduate and law school transcripts, and 2 letters of reference.

Financial data The stipend is $25,000 per year.

Duration 1 year.

Additional information The Lewis Fellowship is named for a prominent African American graduate of the Harvard Law School; the Houston Fellowship is named for a distinguished lawyer and teacher who was the first African American to serve on the *Harvard Law Review.* Fellows must prepare a major article for publication during the fellowship period; a schedule of research and work must be established with a faculty supervisor. Although fellows may audit courses, they may not be degree candidates.

Number awarded 2 each year.

Deadline February of each year.

[808]
RESEARCH AND TRAINING FELLOWSHIPS IN EPILEPSY FOR CLINICIANS

Epilepsy Foundation
Attn: Research Department
4351 Garden City Drive
Landover, MD 20785-7223
(301) 459-3700   Toll-free: (800) EFA-1000
Fax: (301) 577-2684   TDD: (800) 332-2070
E-mail: clinical_postdocs@efa.org
Web: www.epilepsyfoundation.org

Purpose To provide funding to minority and other clinically trained professionals interested in gaining additional training in order to develop an epilepsy research program.

Eligibility Applicants must have an M.D., D.O., Ph.D., D.S., or equivalent degree and be a clinical or postdoctoral fellow at a university, medical school, or other appropriate research institution. Holders of other doctoral-level degrees (e.g., Pharm.D., D.S.N.) may also be eligible. Candidates must be interested in a program of research training that may include mechanisms of epilepsy, novel therapeutic approaches, clinical trials, development of new technologies, or behavioral and psychosocial impact of epilepsy. The training program may consist of both didactic training and a supervised research experience that is designed to develop the necessary knowledge and skills in the chosen area of research and foster the career goals of the candidate. Academic faculty holding the rank of instructor or higher are not eligible, nor are graduate or medical students, medical residents, permanent government employees, or employees of private industry. Applications from women, members of minority groups, and people with disabilities are especially encouraged. Selection is based on the quality of the proposed research training program, the applicant's qualifications, the preceptor's qualifications, and the adequacy of clinical training, research facilities, and other epilepsy-related programs at the institution.

Financial data The grant is $40,000. No indirect costs are provided.

Duration 1 year.

Additional information Support for this program is provided by many individuals, families, and corporations, especially the American Epilepsy Society, Abbott Laboratories,

Ortho-McNeil Pharmaceutical, and Pfizer Inc. Grantees are expected to spend at least 50% of their time dedicated to research training and conducting research.

Number awarded Varies each year; recently, 5 of these fellowships were awarded.

Deadline October of each year.

[809]
RISK AND DEVELOPMENT FIELD RESEARCH GRANTS

Social Science Research Council
Attn: Program in Applied Economics
810 Seventh Avenue
New York, NY 10019
(212) 377-2700   Fax: (212) 377-2727
E-mail: pae@ssrc.org
Web: www.ssrc.org/pae

Purpose To provide funding to minority and other doctoral students and postdoctoral scholars interested in conducting research on risk and uncertainty in economics.

Eligibility This program is open to 1) full-time graduate students enrolled in economics and related Ph.D. programs (e.g., development studies or agricultural economics) at U.S. universities; and 2) scholars who have completed a Ph.D. in economics and related fields within the past 5 years and have a current position at a U.S. academic or nonprofit research institution. There are no citizenship, nationality, or (for graduate students) residency requirements. Applicants must be interested in conducting field research into questions of risk and uncertainty in the context of developing economies. Preference is given to proposals that include interdisciplinary and novel approaches, with an aim to create a better understanding of the way that individuals, institutions, and policymakers perceive and respond to situations of risk and uncertainty. Minorities and women are particularly encouraged to apply.

Financial data The stipend is $5,000 for graduate students or $15,000 for postdoctoral scholars. Funds must be used for field research, not general support or dissertation write-up.

Duration 1 year.

Additional information This program, established in 1997 as the Program in Applied Economics, is administered by the Social Science Research Council with funds provided by the John D. and Catherine T. MacArthur Foundation.

Number awarded Varies each year; recently, 17 graduate student and 4 postdoctoral fellowships were awarded.

Deadline January of each year.

[810]
SALLY C. TSENG PROFESSIONAL DEVELOPMENT GRANT

Chinese American Librarians Association
c/o Ying Xu, Tseng Grant Ad Hoc Committee Co-Chair
California State University at Los Angeles
John F. Kennedy Memorial Library, 2014 North
5151 State University Drive
Los Angeles, CA 90032-8300
(323) 343-3959   E-mail: yxu2@calstatela.edu
Web: www.cala-web.org

Purpose To provide funding to members of the Chinese American Librarians Association (CALA) who are interested in conducting a research project.

Eligibility This program is open to full-time librarians of Chinese descent who have been CALA members for at least 2 years. Applicants must be interested in conducting a research project in library and information science for which they are qualified and which will result in the advancement of their professional status.

Financial data The grant is $1,000.

Duration 1 year.

Number awarded 1 each year.

Deadline April of each year.

[811]
SCIENCE POLICY AND INTERNATIONAL SECURITY FELLOWSHIP PROGRAM

Stanford University
Center for International Security and Cooperation
Attn: Fellowship Program Coordinator
Encina Hall, Room E210
616 Serra Street
Stanford, CA 94305-6165
(650) 723-9626   Fax: (650) 723-0089
E-mail: barbara.platt@stanford.edu
Web: www.cisac.stanford.edu

Purpose To provide funding to minority and other mid-career scholars who are interested in conducting research on international security or arms control issues at Stanford University's Center for International Security and Cooperation.

Eligibility This program is open to scientists and engineers who have demonstrated excellence in their specialties. Applicants should be interested in conducting interdisciplinary research at the center on such topics as policy issues regarding nuclear, biological, and chemical weapons and delivery systems; prospects for international control of weapons of mass destruction; nuclear weapons safety and security; global diffusion of information technology; assessing antiballistic missile defenses; export controls on high technology; defense conversion; environmental security; and security issues associated with energy development. Fellowships are available for both postdoctoral fellows and mid-career professionals. Scientists in academic and research institutions, government, and industry from both the United States and abroad may apply. The center is particularly interested in receiving applications from minorities or women.

Financial data Stipends are determined on a case-by-case basis commensurate with experience and availability of other funds. Health insurance is provided, and funds are available for travel and other research-related expenses.

Duration 11 months.

Additional information Science fellows pursue research, audit courses, and work with the center's faculty and research staff. They have the opportunity to interact with specialists in arms control, politics, and military affairs.

Number awarded 3 each year.

Deadline February of each year.

[812]
SHEILA SUEN LAI RESEARCH GRANT

Asian Pacific American Librarians Association
Attn: Executive Director
3735 Palomar Centre, Suite 150
PMB 26
Lexington, KY 40513
E-mail: lhjen00@uky.edu
Web: www.apalaweb.org/awards/scholarship.htm

Purpose To provide research funding to members of the Asian Pacific American Librarians Association (APALA).

Eligibility Eligible to apply are APALA members in good standing who have been members for at least 1 year prior to applying. Applicants must have an M.L.S. or M.L.I.S. degree and currently be employed in a professional position in library science or a related field. They must be U.S. citizens or permanent residents. Current recipients of other APALA grants or scholarships are not eligible for this award. A complete grant application must contain a cover letter, a resume or curriculum vitae, a detailed statement of intended research activities, including a budget (up to 5 pages), and, optionally, letters of recommendation or institutional commitment of resources. Incomplete applications will not be considered.

Financial data Grants range up to $1,000.

Duration Grants are awarded annually.

Additional information APALA is an affiliate of the American Library Association. No grant can be used to attend professional association conferences.

Number awarded 1 or more each year.

Deadline February of each year.

[813]
SOUTH CAROLINA SPACE GRANT CONSORTIUM UNDERGRADUATE RESEARCH PROGRAM

South Carolina Space Grant Consortium
c/o College of Charleston
Department of Geology
58 Coming Street, Room 341B
Charleston, SC 29424
(843) 953-7171   Fax: (843) 953-5446
E-mail: colganm@cofc.edu
Web: www.cofc.edu/~scsgrant

Purpose To provide financial assistance for space-related research to minority and other undergraduate students in South Carolina.

Eligibility This program is open to undergraduate students at member institutions of the South Carolina Space Grant Consortium. Applicants should be rising juniors or seniors interested in aerospace and space-related studies, including the basic sciences, astronomy, science education, planetary science, environmental studies, engineering, fine arts, and journalism. U.S. citizenship is required. Selection is based on academic qualifications of the applicant; 2 letters of recommendation; a description of past activities, current interests, and future plans concerning a space science or aerospace-related field; and faculty sponsorship. Women and minorities are encouraged to apply.

Financial data The stipend is $3,000. Up to $500 of the $3,000 will be available for research related expenses, not including any application fees.

Duration 1 academic year or 10 weeks during the summer.

Additional information Members of the consortium are Benedict College, The Citadel, College of Charleston, Clemson University, Coastal Carolina University, Furman University, University of South Carolina, Wofford College, South Carolina State University, The Medical University of South Carolina, and University of the Virgin Islands. This program is funded by the U.S. National Aeronautics and Space Administration

Number awarded Varies each year.

Deadline January of each year.

[814]
SOUTHERN REGIONAL EDUCATION BOARD DISSERTATION-YEAR FELLOWSHIP

Southern Regional Education Board
592 10th Street N.W.
Atlanta, GA 30318-5790
(404) 875-9211, ext. 269   Fax: (404) 872-1477
E-mail: doctoral.scholars@sreb.org
Web: www.sreb.org/programs/dsp/dspindex.asp

Purpose To provide financial assistance to minority students who wish to complete a doctoral dissertation while in residence at a university in the southern states.

Eligibility This program is open to U.S. citizens who are members of racial/ethnic minority groups (Native Americans, Hispanic Americans, Asian Americans, and African Americans) and have completed all requirements for a Ph.D. except the dissertation. Applicants must be in a position to write full time and must expect to complete the dissertation within the year of the fellowship. Eligibility is limited to individuals who plan to become full-time faculty members at a southern institution upon completion of their doctoral degree. It does not include students working on a professional degree (M.D., D.B.A., D.D.S., J.D., and D.V.M.) or doing graduate work leading to the Ed.D.

Financial data Fellows receive waiver of tuition and fees (in or out of state), a stipend of $15,000, and a small grant for research expenses.

Duration 1 year; nonrenewable.

Number awarded Varies each year.

Deadline March of each year.

[815]
SYLVIA TAYLOR JOHNSON MINORITY FELLOWSHIP IN EDUCATIONAL MEASUREMENT

Educational Testing Service
Attn: Fellowships
Rosedale Road
MS 09-R
Princeton, NJ 08541-0001
(609) 734-1806   E-mail: fellowships@ets.org
Web: www.ets.org/research/fellowships/stjmfel.html

Purpose To provide funding to minority scholars who are interested in conducting independent research under the mentorship of senior researchers at the Educational Testing Service (ETS).

Eligibility This program is open to minority scholars who have earned a doctorate within the past 10 years and are U.S. citizens or permanent residents. Applicants must be prepared to conduct independent research at ETS under the mentorship of a senior researcher. They should have a commitment to education and an independent body of scholarship that signals the promise of continuing contributions to educational measurement. Studies focused on issues concerning the education of minority students are especially encouraged. Selection is based on the scholar's record of accomplishment and proposed topic of research.

Financial data The stipend is set in relation to compensation at the home institution. Scholars and their families also receive reimbursement for relocation expenses.

Duration Up to 2 years.

Number awarded 1 each year.

Deadline January of each year.

[816]
UNITED STATES INSTITUTE OF PEACE SENIOR FELLOWSHIPS

United States Institute of Peace
Attn: Jennings Randolph Program for International
    Peace
1200 17th Street, N.W., Suite 200
Washington, DC 20036-3011
(202) 429-3886   Fax: (202) 429-6063
TDD: (202) 457-1719   E-mail: fellows@usip.org
Web: www.usip.org/fellows/srfellows.html

Purpose To provide funding to minority and other professionals who wish to conduct research at the United States Institute of Peace (USIP) in Washington, D.C.

Eligibility This program is open to candidates from a wide variety of professional backgrounds, including governmental and nongovernmental practitioners in international security, peacemaking, and public affairs; scholars and researchers; and media and communications specialists. Fellows may be at any stage of their careers and have any educational background. They should be proposing a research project related to preventive diplomacy, ethnic and regional conflicts, peacekeeping and peace operations, peace settlements, post-conflict reconstruction and reconciliation, democratization and the rule of law, cross-cultural negotiations, U.S. foreign policy in the 21st century, and related topics. Preference is given to projects that demonstrate relevance to the sources and nature of interstate or civil conflict, with ways to prevent, limit, or end violent conflict, and with post-conflict reconstruction and reconciliation. Candidates must be proposing to produce 1 or more products, such as books or monographs published by USIP Press, reports published by the institute, articles for professional or academic journals, op-eds and articles for newspapers or magazines, radio or TV media projects, demonstrations or simulations, teaching curricula, lectures or other public speaking, or workshops, seminars, or symposia, while at the institute. Applicants may be citizens of any country. Women and members of minority groups are especially encouraged to apply. Selection is based on the candidate's record of achievement and/or leadership potential; the significance and potential of the project for making an important contribution to knowledge, practice, or public understanding; and the quality of the project design and its feasibility within the timetable proposed.

Financial data The stipend is based on the fellow's earned income for the preceding year, up to a maximum of $80,000. In the case of candidates from countries with salaries greatly different from the United States, seniority is the basis for calculation. Also provided are transportation to and from Washington, D.C. for the fellow and eligible family members.

Duration Up to 10 months.

Additional information These fellowships, first awarded in 1988, are tenable at the United States Institute of Peace in Washington, D.C., where fellows interact with other fellows and Institute staff by presenting their work and participating in workshops, conferences, and other events. These awards are not made for projects that constitute policymaking for a government agency or private organization; focus to any substantial degree on conflicts within U.S. domestic society, or adopt a partisan, advocacy, or activist stance.

Number awarded Varies each year; recently, 14 of these fellowships were awarded.

Deadline September of each year.

---

[817]
UNIVERSITY OF WISCONSIN VISITING MINORITY SCHOLAR LECTURE PROGRAM

University of Wisconsin at Madison
Attn: Wisconsin Center for Education Research
1025 West Johnson Street, Suite 785
Madison, WI 53706
(608) 263-4200   Fax: (608) 263-6448
E-mail: uw-wcer@education.wisc.edu
Web: www.wcer.wisc.edu

Purpose To make minority scholars and their work in education more visible on the University of Wisconsin (UW) campus.

Eligibility Minority scholars on the faculty of other universities are invited to present lectures on topics related to minorities and education at the University of Wisconsin. Candidates are nominated through a solicitation process within the university's school of education.

Financial data Lecturers receive travel expenses and an honorarium.

Duration Each visit lasts 2 days.

Additional information The visiting scholar makes a general presentation open to the University of Wisconsin's community and meets with a group of minority students at the university to discuss the scholar's work. This program is cosponsored by the University of Wisconsin's School of

Education and the Wisconsin Center for Education Research.

Number awarded 6 each year.

---

[818]
UNIVERSITY POSTDOCTORAL FELLOWSHIP PROGRAM

Ohio State University
Attn: Dean of the Graduate School
250E University Hall
230 North Oval Mall
Columbus, OH 43210-1366
(614) 292-6031   Fax: (614) 292-3656
E-mail: clark.31@osu.edu
Web: www.gradsch.ohio-state.edu

Purpose To provide an opportunity for minority and other recent postdoctorates to conduct research at Ohio State University (OSU).

Eligibility Nominations may be submitted by OSU graduate faculty members who would like to coordinate a fellow's research. Faculty sponsors can host only 1 University Postdoctoral Fellow at a time. Eligible to be nominated are individuals who have held a doctorate or M.F.A. for 5 years or less. Nomination of minority and women candidates is particularly encouraged. Certain categories of persons are ineligible to be nominated: persons with doctoral or M.F.A. degrees from OSU, persons currently on appointment at OSU (or who have held a postdoctoral appointment there), senior faculty (associate or full professors) from other institutions, individuals who received a Ph.D. or M.F.A. more than 5 years ago, and international scholars who would not qualify for a J1 visa. Selection is based on the credentials of the postdoctoral candidates, the reputation of the faculty sponsors and the quality of their research program, the project proposed by the postdoctoral candidates with the guidance of their faculty sponsors, and the extent to which the candidates will enhance the research environment at the university through interactions with faculty, researchers, and graduate students.

Financial data The monthly stipend is $2,000 plus a $500 moving allowance and a $500 travel allowance (to attend professional meetings).

Duration From 9 to 12 months; nonrenewable.

Additional information Fellows are not OSU employees so they may not conduct research required by a grant and may not be asked to teach a course.

Number awarded Approximately 6 each year.

Deadline January of each year.

---

[819]
WALT DISNEY STUDIOS AND ABC ENTERTAINMENT WRITING FELLOWSHIP PROGRAM

Walt Disney Studios and ABC Entertainment
Attn: Writing Fellowship Program
500 South Buena Vista Street
Burbank, CA 91521-4389
(818) 560-6894   E-mail: abc.fellowships@abc.com
Web: www.abctalentdevelopment.com

Purpose To provide support to minority and other writers interested in developing their craft at Walt Disney Studios and ABC Entertainment.

Eligibility This program is open to all writers, although a goal of the program is to seek out and employ culturally and ethnically diverse new writers. Applicants must submit a writing sample; for the feature films division, that should be a completed live-action motion picture screenplay (up to 120 pages) or a full-length 2-to-3 act play; for the television division, the sample should be a full-length script appropriate for a half-hour or 1-hour television series, based on a current prime time television or cable broadcast series.

Financial data The salary is $50,000.

Duration 1 year, beginning in January.

Additional information Fellows train with creative teams either at Walt Disney Studios or ABC Entertainment. This program began in 1990.

Number awarded Up to 11 each year.

Deadline June of each year.

[820]
WASHINGTON NASA SPACE GRANT CONSORTIUM SEED GRANTS FOR FACULTY

Washington NASA Space Grant Consortium
c/o University of Washington
401A Johnson Hall
Box 351310
Seattle, WA 98195-1310
(206) 543-1943   Toll-free: (800) 659-1943
Fax: (206) 543-0179
Web: www.waspacegrant.org/faculty.html

Purpose To provide funding to minority and other faculty at member institutions of the Washington NASA Space Grant Consortium who are interested in conducting space-related research.

Eligibility This program is open to faculty members at institutions that are members of the consortium. Applicants must be interested in initiating research efforts in disciplines relevant to the missions of the U.S. National Aeronautics and Space Administration (NASA) on earth and in space. The program values diversity and strongly encourages women and minorities to apply.

Financial data Grants range from $10,000 to $20,000. Matching funds must be provided.

Duration 1 year.

Additional information This program is funded by NASA. Members of the consortium include Northwest Indian College, Seattle Central Community College, the University of Washington, and Washington State University.

Number awarded 1 each year.

[821]
W.E.B. DUBOIS FELLOWSHIP PROGRAM

Department of Justice
National Institute of Justice
Attn: W.E.B. DuBois Fellowship Program
810 Seventh Street, N.W.
Washington, DC 20531
(202) 616-3233
Web: www.ojp.usdoj.gov/nij/funding.htm

Purpose To provide funding to minority and other junior investigators interested in conducting research on the "con-

fluence of crime, justice, and culture in various societal contexts."

Eligibility This program is open to investigators who have a Ph.D. or other doctoral-level degree or a legal degree of J.D. or higher. Applicants should be early in their careers. They must be interested in conducting research that relates to the following high-priority topics: law enforcement/policing; justice systems (sentencing, courts, prosecution, defense); corrections; investigative and forensic sciences, including DNA; counterterrorism and critical incidents; crime prevention and causes of crime; violence and victimization, including violent crimes; drugs, alcohol, and crime; interoperability, spatial information, and automated systems; and program evaluation. The research should emphasize crime, violence, and the administration of justice in diverse cultural contexts. Because of that focus, the sponsor strongly encourages applications from diverse racial and ethnic backgrounds.

Financial data The grant is approximately $75,000. Funds may be used for salary, fringe benefits, reasonable costs of relocation, travel essential to the project, and office expenses not provided by the sponsor. Indirect costs are limited to 20%.

Duration 6 to 12 months; fellows are required to be in residence at the National Institute of Justice (NIJ) for the first 2 months and may elect to spend all or part of the remainder of the fellowship period either in residence at NIJ or at their home institution.

Number awarded 1 each year.

Deadline January of each year.

[822]
WEST VIRGINIA SPACE GRANT CONSORTIUM GRADUATE FELLOWSHIP PROGRAM

West Virginia Space Grant Consortium
c/o West Virginia University
College of Engineering and Mineral Resources
G-68 Engineering Sciences Building
P.O. Box 6070
Morgantown, WV 26506-6070
(304) 293-4099, ext. 3737   Fax: (304) 293-4970
E-mail: nasa@cemr.wvu.edu
Web: www.nasa.wvu.edu/scholarships.htm

Purpose To provide financial assistance to minority and other graduate students at designated academic institutions affiliated with the West Virginia Space Grant Consortium who wish to conduct research on space-related science or engineering topics.

Eligibility This program is open to graduate students at participating member institutions of the consortium. Applicants must be interested in working on a research project with a faculty member who has received a West Virginia Space Grant Consortium Research Initiation Grant. U.S. citizenship is required. The consortium is a component of the Space Grant program of the U.S. National Aeronautics and Space Administration (NASA). Women and minorities are strongly encouraged to apply.

Financial data The amount of the award for the graduate student depends on the amount of the research grant that the faculty member has received.

Duration 1 year.

Additional information Funding for this program is provided by NASA. The participating consortium members are Marshall University, West Virginia Institute of Technology, West Virginia University, and Wheeling-Jesuit University.
Number awarded Varies each year.

[823]
WEST VIRGINIA SPACE GRANT CONSORTIUM RESEARCH INITIATION GRANTS

West Virginia Space Grant Consortium
c/o West Virginia University
College of Engineering and Mineral Resources
G-68 Engineering Sciences Building
P.O. Box 6070
Morgantown, WV 26506-6070
(304) 293-4099, ext. 3737   Fax: (304) 293-4970
E-mail: nasa@cemr.wvu.edu
Web: www.nasa.wvu.edu/research.htm

Purpose To provide funding for space-related research to minority and other faculty at academic institutions affiliated with the West Virginia Space Grant Consortium.
Eligibility This program is open to faculty members at colleges and universities that are members of the West Virginia Space Grant Consortium. Applicants must be seeking to pursue research in areas of interest to the U.S. National Aeronautics and Space Administration (NASA) and to establish long-term relationships with NASA researchers. U.S. citizenship is required. Selection is based on technical and scientific merit (30 points), potential for future funding and long-term impact (20 points), soundness of approach (20 points), relevance to NASA mission and West Virginia's priorities in science and technology (20 points), and budget (10 points). The consortium is a component of NASA's Space Grant program. Women and minorities are strongly encouraged to apply.
Financial data Grants range from $5,000 to $20,000. The consortium provides two-thirds of the total budget and the researcher's institution must agree to provide the remainder on a cost-sharing basis. At least 35% of the award must be allocated for a graduate student research assistant.
Duration 1 year.
Additional information Funding for this program is provided by NASA. The consortium includes Bethany College, Fairmont State College, Marshall University, Salem International University, Shepherd College, West Liberty State College, West Virginia Institute of Technology, West Virginia State College, West Virginia University, West Virginia Wesleyan College, and Wheeling-Jesuit University.
Number awarded Varies each year; recently, 8 of these grants were awarded.
Deadline March of each year.

[824]
W.K. KELLOGG FOUNDATION FELLOWSHIP PROGRAM IN HEALTH RESEARCH

National Medical Fellowships, Inc.
Attn: Scholarship Program
5 Hanover Square, 15th Floor
New York, NY 10004
(212) 483-8880   Fax: (212) 483-8897
E-mail: info@nmfonline.org
Web: www.nmf-online.org

Purpose To provide financial assistance to minorities enrolled in a doctoral program in health policy research who are committed to working with underserved populations.
Eligibility This program is open to members of minority groups (African Americans, Native Americans, Asians, and Hispanics) enrolled in doctoral programs in public health, social policy, or health policy (Ph.D., Dr.P.H., or Sc.D.). Applicants must demonstrate a willingness to complete relevant dissertation research and a commitment to work with underserved populations upon completion of the doctorate. They must include an essay of 500 to 1,000 words discussing their reasons for applying for a fellowship, their qualifications, how it will support their career plans, and which of 4 areas of focus (health policy, men's health, mental health, substance abuse) most interests them and why.
Financial data Fellowships cover tuition, fees, and a partial living stipend.
Duration Up to 5 years: 2 years to do the necessary course work and 3 years to complete the dissertation.
Additional information The program was created in 1998 with grant support from the W.K. Kellogg Foundation. Recently, it operated at 8 institutions: the RAND Graduate School, the Heller Graduate School at Brandeis University, the Joseph L. Mailman School of Public Health at Columbia University, the Harvard School of Public Health, the Johns Hopkins School of Hygiene and Public Health, the UCLA School of Public Health, the University of Michigan School of Public Health, and the University of Pennsylvania. Information is also available from the sponsor's Washington office at 1627 K Street, N.W., Suite 1200, Washington, DC 20006-1702, (202) 296-4431, Fax: (202) 293-1990.
Number awarded 5 each year.
Deadline June of each year.

[825]
WOMEN'S STUDIES IN RELIGION PROGRAM

Harvard Divinity School
Attn: Director of Women's Studies in Religion Program
45 Francis Avenue
Cambridge, MA 02138
(617) 495-5705   Fax: (617) 495-9489
E-mail: wsrp@hds.harvard.edu
Web: www.hds.harvard.edu/wsrp

Purpose To encourage and support research on the relationship between religion, gender, and culture.
Eligibility This program is open to scholars who have a Ph.D. in the field of religion. Candidates with primary competence in other humanities, social sciences, and public policy fields who have a serious interest in religion and religious professionals with equivalent achievements are also eligible. Applicants should be proposing to conduct research projects at Harvard Divinity School's Women's

Studies in Religion Program (WSRP) on topics related to the history and function of gender in religious traditions, the institutionalization of roles in religious communities, or the interaction between religion and the personal, social, and cultural situations of women. Appropriate topics include feminist theology, Biblical studies, ethics, women's history, and interdisciplinary scholarship on women in world religions. Selection is based on the quality of the applicant's research prospectus, outlining objectives and methods; its fit with the program's research priorities; the significance of the contribution of the proposed research to the study of religion, gender, and culture, and to its field; and agreement to produce a publishable piece of work by the end of the appointment.

Financial data Research associates/visiting lecturers in the WSRP receive a stipend of $40,000 and benefits for a full-time appointment.

Duration 1 academic year, from September to June.

Additional information Fellows at the WSRP devote the majority of their appointments to individual research projects in preparation for publication, meeting together regularly for discussion of research in process. They also teach a semester course related to this research and consult with faculty on current school planning for integration of women's studies into the Harvard Divinity School curriculum. Recipients are required to be in full-time residence at the school while carrying out their research project.

Number awarded 5 each year. The group each year usually includes at least 1 international scholar, 1 scholar working on a non-western tradition, 1 scholar of Judaism, and 1 minority scholar.

Deadline November of each year.

[826]
ZIMMER ORTHOPAEDIC CAREER DEVELOPMENT AWARDS

Orthopaedic Research and Education Foundation
Attn: Vice President, Grants
6300 North River Road, Suite 700
Rosemont, IL 60018-4261
(847) 384-4348　　　　Fax: (847) 698-7806
E-mail: mcquire@oref.org
Web: www.oref.org/grants/grants.html

Purpose To provide funding to new orthopedic surgeons (particularly minorities and women) who are interested in additional training and/or research.

Eligibility This program is open to orthopedic surgeons who have completed formal training within the past 4 years and have a clinical or scientific interest in total joint surgery and/or trauma treatment. Applicants must be interested in a training and/or research program that may involve support for training or investigation, support for travel and furthers training or investigation, or support to provide for special resources required to advance training or investigation. Minority and female surgeons are especially encouraged to apply.

Financial data Grants up to $50,000 per year are awarded.

Duration 1 year.

Additional information Funding for minority surgeons is provided by the J. Robert Gladden Society. Funding for women surgeons is provided by the Ruth Jackson Orthopaedic Society.

Number awarded Varies each year; recently, 8 of these grants were awarded.

Deadline September of each year.

Awards

Described in this section are 25 competitions, prizes, and honoraria open to Asian Americans in recognition or support of creative work, personal accomplishments, professional contributions, or public service. Excluded are prizes received solely as the result of entering contests. If you are looking for a particular program and don't find it in this section, be sure to check the Program Title Index to see if it is covered elsewhere in the directory.

[827]
ANISFIELD-WOLF BOOK AWARDS

Cleveland Foundation
1422 Euclid Avenue, Suite 1300
Cleveland, OH 44115-2001
(216) 861-3810   Fax: (216) 861-1729
E-mail: asktcf@clevefdn.org
Web: www.anisfield-wolf.org

Purpose To recognize and reward recent books that have contributed to an understanding of racism or appreciation of the rich diversity of human cultures.

Eligibility Works published in English during the preceding year that "contribute to our understanding of racism or appreciation of the rich diversity of human cultures" are eligible to be considered. Entries may be either scholarly or imaginative (fiction, poetry, memoir). Plays and screenplays are not eligible, nor are works in progress. Manuscripts and self-published works are not eligible, and no grants are made for completing or publishing manuscripts.

Financial data The prize is $10,000. If more than 1 author is chosen in a given year, the prize is divided equally among the winning books.

Duration The award is presented annually.

Additional information These awards were first presented in 1936. Information is also available from Laura Scharf, 6100 Rockside Woods Boulevard, Suite 350, Cleveland, OH 44131.

Number awarded 3 each year: 1 for fiction, 1 for nonfiction, and 1 for lifetime achievement.

Deadline January of each year.

[828]
ASIAN LAW JOURNAL STUDENT WRITING COMPETITION

Asian Law Journal
Attn: Senior Notes and Comments Editor
University of California, Berkeley
Boalt Hall School of Law
589 Simon Hall
Berkeley, CA 94720
(510) 643-9643   E-mail: asianlj@law.berkeley.edu
Web: www.boalt.org/ALF/main.html

Purpose To recognize and reward outstanding papers written by law students on legal issues affecting Asian Pacific Americans.

Eligibility This competition is open to currently-enrolled law students or recent law school graduates. Submissions must be original, unpublished works (at least 25 pages) exploring legal issues that impact the Asian Pacific American community. Welcomed are focused analyses of individual Asian Pacific American ethnic groups, as well as discussions of domestic or international issues affecting Asian Pacific Americans in general. Possible topics include, but are not limited to: Asian Pacific American political empowerment, the use of "cultural defenses" in criminal law, racial profiling, or Asian Pacific Americans and affirmative action. Entries are judged on relevance, timeliness, thoroughness of research, quality of legal analysis, and clarity of expression.

Financial data The prize is $250 or $500.

Duration The competition is held annually.

Additional information The winning paper is published in the *Asian Law Journal.*

Number awarded 1 each year.

Deadline October of each year.

[829]
BEYOND MARGINS AWARD

PEN American Center
Attn: Beyond Margins Program Assistance
588 Broadway, Suite 303
New York, NY 10012
(212) 334-1660, ext. 110   Fax: (212) 334-2181
E-mail: jmartinez@pen.org
Web: www.pen.org

Purpose To recognize and reward outstanding authors of color from any country.

Eligibility This award is presented to an author of color (African, Arab, Asian, Caribbean, Latino, and Native American) whose book-length writings were published in the United States during the current calendar year. Works of fiction, literary nonfiction, biography/memoir, and other works of literary character are strongly preferred. U.S. citizenship or residency is not required. Nominations must be submitted by publishers or agents.

Financial data The prize is $1,000.

Duration The prizes are awarded annually.

Number awarded 5 each year.

Deadline December of each year.

[830]
CASEY FAMILY SCHOLARSHIPS FOR MALE STUDENTS OF COLOR

Orphan Foundation of America
Attn: Director of Student Services
Tall Oaks Village Center
12020-D North Shore Drive
Reston, VA 20190-4977
(571) 203-0270   Toll-free: (800) 950-4673
Fax: (571) 203-0273 E-mail: scholarships@orphan.org
Web: www.orphan.org/scholarships.html

Purpose To recognize and reward minority male students who have been in foster care and are completing a vocational or undergraduate degree.

Eligibility This program is open to male minority students enrolled in their final year of a vocational program or their senior year of an undergraduate program. Applicants must have aged out of the U.S. foster care system. Along with their application, they must submit 1) verification of their foster care status; 2) documentation of their total outstanding federal loan amount; 3) documentation from their school regarding any outstanding tuition balance they currently owe; and 4) a 5-paragraph essay explaining the single most important thing their postsecondary education has taught them and how they will take that lesson and apply it to their professional and personal life to help ensure their future success. Selection is based on financial need and merit, as commendation for ambition and tenacity in pursuing a higher education.

Financial data Awards range up to $5,000.

Duration These are 1-time awards.

Additional information This program was established in 2004 by Casey Family Programs.

Number awarded Awards are presented until funds are exhausted.

[831]
CHINESE AMERICAN CITIZENS ALLIANCE FOUNDATION ESSAY CONTEST

Chinese American Citizens Alliance
Attn: Scholarship Foundation
763 Yale Street
Los Angeles, CA 90012
(323) 876-4083
Web: www.cacanational.org/foundation-scholar.html

Purpose To recognize and reward high school students of Chinese descent who write outstanding essays on a topic related to Asian Americans.

Eligibility This competition is open to high school students of Chinese descent. Candidates apply through their local lodge of the Chinese American Citizens Alliance and meet at a site arranged by that lodge, usually at 10:00 a.m. on the first Saturday in March. They are given a topic and devote the next 2 hours to writing a 500-word essay, in English, on that topic. Recently, the topic was "One of the most powerful forces in American society today is the mass media, which include newspapers, popular music, movies, and television. Do you believe Asian Americans are depicted fairly in these mainstream media? Provide specific examples to support your views." Selection is based on originality, clarity of thought and expression, and correctness of grammar and spelling.

Financial data Prizes are $1,000 for first place, $800 for second place, $500 for third place, and $100 for merit awards.

Duration The competition is held annually.

Number awarded Varies each year; recently, prizes included 1 first place, 1 second place, 1 third place, and 13 merit awards.

[832]
CHINESE AMERICAN JOURNALIST AWARD

Organization of Chinese Americans, Inc.
1001 Connecticut Avenue, N.W., Suite 601
Washington, DC 20036
(202) 223-5500   Fax: (202) 296-0540
E-mail: oca@ocanatl.org
Web: www.ocanatl.org

Purpose To recognize and reward outstanding Asian Pacific American journalists.

Eligibility This program is open to Asian Pacific American journalists who author the best newspaper, magazine, or other published piece on social, political, economic, or cultural issues facing Chinese Americans and/or Asian Americans. The work must have been printed during the preceding calendar year in a publication with national or international circulation. Submissions may be in English or Chinese, but an English translation for Chinese articles should be included. Selection is based on completeness of the story, accuracy of data used, thoroughness of analysis, importance to the understanding of Chinese American or Asian American issues, and readability of the story.

Financial data Awards are $500 for first prize, $300 for second prize, and $200 for third prize.

Duration The awards are presented annually.

Additional information Asian Pacific Americans are defined to include east Asian Americans, Filipino Americans, Pacific Islander Americans, south Asian Americans, and southeast Asian Americans.

Number awarded 3 each year.

Deadline May of each year.

[833]
DONNA JAMISON LAGO MEMORIAL SCHOLARSHIP

NextGen Network, Inc.
c/o Urbanomics Consulting Group
1010 Wisconsin Avenue, Suite 430
Washington, DC 20007
(202) 298-8226   Fax: (202) 298-8074
E-mail: info@nextgennetwork.com
Web: www.nextgennetwork.com

Purpose To recognize and reward outstanding essays written by minority high school seniors who will be going on to college.

Eligibility This competition is open to ethnic minority high school seniors in good academic standing. Entrants must be U.S. citizens and intending to attend a college or university after graduation. They must submit an essay, from 500 to 1,000 words, on a topic that changes annually; recently, students were invited to write on the following topic: "You have been elected President of the United States. What three initiatives would you want to introduce? Be specific rather than general and give arguments to support your choice." The essay should demonstrate critical thinking, creativity, and strong communication skills.

Financial data Finalists receive $1,500 each; semifinalists receive $1,000 each.

Duration The competition is held annually.

Additional information This program was formerly known as the "Path to Excellence" Scholarship Award.

Number awarded 6 each year: 3 finalists and 3 semifinalists.

Deadline March of each year.

[834]
DR. SUZANNE AHN AWARD FOR CIVIL RIGHTS AND SOCIAL JUSTICE FOR ASIAN AMERICANS

Asian American Journalists Association
1182 Market Street, Suite 320
San Francisco, CA 94102
(415) 346-2051   Fax: (415) 346-6343
E-mail: national@aaja.org
Web: www.aaja.org/programs/awards/ahn

Purpose To recognize and reward journalists who have published or broadcast outstanding coverage of Asian American civil rights and social justice issues.

Eligibility This award is presented to journalists for excellence in coverage of civil rights of Asian Americans and/or issues of social justice for Asian Americans. Nominees do not need to be members of the Asian American Journalists Association (AAJA). Their work must have been published (in newspapers, news services, web sites, magazines, books) or broadcast (on radio or TV). Nominations must be accompanied by supporting materials (up to 5 articles, 10 photographs, 1 book, 1 VHS format tape, or 1 audio cassette) and a 1-page summary of the work. Submissions in other languages must come with an English translation.

Financial data The award consists of $5,000 and a plaque.

Duration The award is presented annually.

Additional information This award, first presented in 2003, is named for a Korean American physician, neurologist, and inventor. Nominations by nonmembers of AAJA must be accompanied by a $25 entry fee.

Number awarded 1 each year.

Deadline June of each year.

[835]
FOUNDERS DISTINGUISHED SENIOR SCHOLAR AWARD

American Association of University Women
Attn: AAUW Educational Foundation
1111 16th Street, N.W.
Washington, DC 20036-4873
(202) 785-7609   Toll-free: (800) 326-AAUW
Fax: (202) 463-7169   TDD: (202) 785-7777
E-mail: foundation@aauw.org
Web: www.aauw.org/fga/awards/fdss.cfm

Purpose To recognize and reward American women (particularly women of color) for a lifetime of scholarly excellence.

Eligibility Eligible for nomination are women scholars who can demonstrate a lifetime of outstanding research, college or university teaching, publications, and positive impact upon women in their profession and community. U.S. citizenship or permanent resident status is required. Selection is based on lifetime commitment to women's issues in the profession or in the community, significance and impact of the nominee's scholarship upon her field, demonstrated excellence in and commitment to teaching and mentoring female college students, and total impact upon her profession and the community. The sponsor strongly encourages nomination of women of color and other underrepresented groups.

Financial data The award is $1,000.

Duration The award is presented annually.

Additional information The award includes a trip to the annual AAUW convention (where the award is presented).

Number awarded 1 each year.

Deadline February of each year.

[836]
GROWING UP ASIAN IN AMERICA CONTEST

Asian Pacific Fund
225 Bush Street, Suite 590
San Francisco, CA 94104
(415) 433-6859   Toll-free: (800) 286-1688
Fax: (415) 433-2425
E-mail: info@asianpacificfund.org
Web: www.asianpacificfund.org/awards/guaa

Purpose To recognize and reward the creative activities of young Asian Americans in the San Francisco Bay area.

Eligibility This contest is open to Asian Americans (including youth of mixed non-Asian and Asian backgrounds) who live or attend school in grades K-12 in the California counties of Alameda, Contra Costa, Marin, Napa, San Francisco, San Mateo, Santa Clara, Solano, and Sonoma. Applicants submit essays, poems, or art. The contest theme changes periodically; recently it was "On Friendship." Students are invited to present their own ideas on the subject, but they should include whether or not growing up Asian in America makes their ideas different. Art and writing entries are judged separately and in separate age categories. Selection is based on creativity and originality, ideas and feelings, and skill in writing or art.

Financial data Winners receive savings bonds of $2,000 for first place, $1,500 for second place, or $1,000 for third place.

Duration The competition is held annually.

Additional information Information about the contest, created in 1995, is available at public schools and libraries in the area.

Number awarded A total of $27,000 in prizes is awarded each year.

Deadline March of each year.

[837]
HARRISON LEE MEMORIAL SCHOLARSHIP AWARD

Chinese American Citizens Alliance-Washington, DC
    Lodge
9302 Christopher Street
Fairfax, VA 22301
(703) 273-7510

Purpose To recognize and reward outstanding essays on "Being an American" written by Chinese American high school seniors in the Washington, D.C. area.

Eligibility Chinese American high school seniors in the metropolitan Washington, D.C. area (including parts of Virginia and Baltimore, Maryland) are invited to write an essay, in English, on "What Does Being an American Mean to Me." Essays must be no more than 500 words. Selection is based on originality, clarity of thought, and expression.

Financial data First prize is $500, second $300, and third $200.

Duration The competition is held annually.

Number awarded 3 each year.

Deadline December of each year.

[838]
HONORABLE THOMAS TANG NATIONAL MOOT COURT COMPETITION SCHOLARSHIPS

National Asian Pacific American Bar Association
Attn: NAPABA Law Foundation
910 17th Street, N.W., Suite 315
Washington, DC 20006
(202) 775-9555   Fax: (202) 775-9333
E-mail: foundation@napaba.org
Web: www.napaba.org

Purpose To recognize and reward law students who participate in a moot court competition sponsored by the National Asian Pacific American Bar Association (NAPABA).

Eligibility This program is open to students at accredited law schools who have completed the first year of study. Applicants must enter the competition as teams of 2 students each. Scholarship awards are presented for the best brief, best oralist, championship team, and runner-up team.

Financial data Awards are a $2,000 scholarship for the championship team, $1,000 scholarship for the runner-up team, $1,000 scholarship for the best brief, and $1,000 scholarship for the best oralist.

Duration The competition is held annually.

Additional information This competition was initiated in 1993 and has been supported since then by Anheuser-Busch. Further information is available from Trudy K. Chow, Hildebrandt International, 150 North Michigan Avenue, Suite 3600, Chicago, IL 60601, (312) 578-0790, Fax: (312) 857-1325, E-mail: TKChow@hildebrandt.com, or the Honorable Alvin T. Wong, State Court of DeKalb County, 608 DeKalb County Courthouse, Decatur, GA 30030, (404) 371-2591. The application fee is $75 per team.

Number awarded 4 each year: 1 first-place team, 1 second-place team, 1 best brief, and 1 best oralist.

Deadline September of each year.

[839]
JAMES A. RAWLEY PRIZE

Organization of American Historians
Attn: Award and Prize Coordinator
112 North Bryan Street
P.O. Box 5457
Bloomington, IN 47408-5457
(812) 855-9852   Fax: (812) 855-0696
E-mail: oahawards@oah.org
Web: www.oah.org

Purpose To recognize and reward outstanding books dealing with race relations in the United States.

Eligibility This award is presented to the author of the outstanding book on the history of race relations in America. Entries must have been published during the current calendar year.

Financial data The award is $1,000 and a certificate.

Duration The award is presented annually.

Additional information The award was established in 1990.

Number awarded 1 each year.

Deadline September of each year.

[840]
MARIE F. PETERS ETHNIC MINORITIES OUTSTANDING ACHIEVEMENT AWARD

National Council on Family Relations
3989 Central Avenue, N.E., Suite 550
Minneapolis, MN 55421
(763) 781-9331   Toll-free: (888) 781-9331
Fax: (763) 781-9348   E-mail: info@ncfr.com
Web: www.ncfr.org/about_us/ncfr_awards.asp

Purpose To recognize and reward minorities who have made significant contributions to the area of ethnic minority families.

Eligibility Members of the National Council on Family Relations (NCFR) who have demonstrated excellence in the area of ethnic minority families are eligible for this award.

Selection is based on leadership and/or mentoring, scholarship and/or service, research, publication, teaching, community service, contribution to the ethnic minorities section, and contribution to the NCFR.

Financial data The award is $1,000 and a plaque.

Duration The award is granted biennially, in odd-numbered years.

Additional information This award, which was established in 1983, is named after a prominent Black researcher and family sociologist who served in many leadership roles in NCFR. It is sponsored by the Ethnic Minorities Section of NCFR.

Number awarded 1 every other year.

Deadline April of odd-numbered years.

[841]
NEW YORK LIBRARY ASSOCIATION MULTICULTURAL AWARD

New York Library Association
Attn: Ethnic Services Round Table
252 Hudson Avenue
Albany, NY 12210-1802
(518) 432-6952   Toll-free: (800) 252-6952
Fax: (518) 427-1697   E-mail: info@nyla.org
Web: www.nyla.org

Purpose To recognize and reward members of the New York Library Association who have contributed to multicultural activities.

Eligibility This program is open to members of the association who have promoted multicultural or multiethnic activities; multilingual activities are not considered. Selection is based on achievement, advocacy and leadership in serving the community in areas of collection development, outreach services, and development of creative multicultural materials and programs.

Financial data The award consists of $500 to be used for the purchase of books published by Routledge Publishers.

Duration The award is presented annually.

Additional information Information is also available from Zahra M. Baird, Multicultural Award Chair, Chappaqua Library, 195 South Greeley Avenue, Chappaqua, NY 10514, E-mail: zbaird@westchesterlibraries.org.

Number awarded 1 each year.

Deadline July of each year.

[842]
OCA-DFW ESSAY CONTEST

Organization of Chinese Americans, Inc.-Dallas/Fort Worth Chapter
Attn: Executive Vice-president
P.O. Box 1281
Rockwall, TX 75087
(972) 577-6538   E-mail: info@ocadfw.org
Web: www.ocadfw.org

Purpose To recognize and reward (with college scholarships) high school students in the Dallas-Fort Worth Metroplex area who submit outstanding essays on a topic of interest to the Dallas/Fort Worth Chapter of the Organization of Chinese Americans (OCA-DFW).

Eligibility This competition is open to juniors and seniors at public and private high schools in the Metroplex area of

Dallas and Fort Worth, Texas. Applicants must submit an essay, up to 500 words in length, on a topic that changes annually but reflects the concerns of OCA-DFW; a recent topic was "What it means to be an American."

Financial data Prizes are $1,500, $750, and $500 scholarships.

Duration The competition is held annually.

Additional information This competition was first held in 2004. The Dallas-Fort Worth Metroplex area is officially defined to include Collin, Dallas, Denton, Ellis, Henderson, Hood, Hunt, Johnson, Kaufman, Parker, Rockwall, and Tarrant counties in Texas.

Number awarded 6 each year: 1 at $1,500, 1 at $750, and 4 at $500.

Deadline March of each year.

[843]
OCA/KFC BRANDS NATIONAL ESSAY CONTEST

Organization of Chinese Americans, Inc.
1001 Connecticut Avenue, N.W., Suite 601
Washington, DC 20036
(202) 223-5500   Fax: (202) 296-0540
E-mail: oca@ocanatl.org
Web: www.ocanatl.org

Purpose To recognize and reward Asian Pacific American high school students who participate in an essay contest.

Eligibility This program is open to Asian Pacific American students in grades 9 through 12. Applicants must submit an essay, from 800 to 1,000 words, on a topic that changes annually; recently, the topic was "As a leader, what is your vision for building unity within the Asian Pacific American community and how will you play a role?" Selection is based on theme and content (50%), organization and development (20%), grammar and mechanics (20%), and style (10%).

Financial data First prize is $1,000, second prize is $500, and third prize is $300.

Duration The contest is held annually.

Additional information This program is sponsored by KFC. Asian Pacific Americans are defined to include east Asian Americans, Filipino Americans, Pacific Islander Americans, south Asian Americans, and southeast Asian Americans.

Number awarded 3 each year.

Deadline May of each year.

[844]
PAVESNP LIFE/WORK CHALLENGE AWARDS

Pennsylvania Association of Vocational Education
    Special Needs Personnel
c/o Vocational Education Services in Pennsylvania
Penn State McKeesport
4000 University Drive
101 Ostermayer
McKeesport, PA 15132
(412) 675-9065
Web: www.pavesnp.org

Purpose To recognize and reward outstanding vocational education students in Pennsylvania who have special needs.

Eligibility Nominations for these awards may be submitted by professionals or paraprofessionals who are members of the Pennsylvania Association of Vocational Education Special Needs Personnel (PAVESNP). Nominees must be enrolled in an approved career and technical program in the current or previous school year and be receiving services from a special needs program (disabled, disadvantaged, or limited-English proficient). They must demonstrate evidence of a personal commitment to maximizing individual potential, social skills that enhance employability, strong personal work ethic, and occupational competence.

Financial data Awards are $500 for first place, $300 for second, and $100 for third.

Duration Awards are presented annually.

Additional information Information is also available from Marjorie Eckman, Overbrook Administrative Center, 2140 Saw Mill Run Boulevard, Pittsburgh, PA 15210.

Number awarded 3 each year.

Deadline January of each year.

[845]
RALPH J. BUNCHE AWARD

American Political Science Association
1527 New Hampshire Avenue, N.W.
Washington, DC 20036-1206
(202) 483-2512   Fax: (202) 483-2657
E-mail: apsa@apsanet.org
Web: www.apsanet.org/section_278.cfm

Purpose To recognize and reward outstanding scholarly books on ethnic/cultural pluralism.

Eligibility Eligible to be nominated (by publishers or individuals) are scholarly political science books issued the previous year that explore issues of ethnic and/or cultural pluralism.

Financial data The award is $500.

Duration The competition is held annually.

Number awarded 1 each year.

Deadline February of each year.

[846]
RECOGNITION AWARD FOR EMERGING SCHOLARS

American Association of University Women
Attn: AAUW Educational Foundation
1111 16th Street, N.W.
Washington, DC 20036-4873
(202) 785-7609   Toll-free: (800) 326-AAUW
Fax: (202) 463-7169   TDD: (202) 785-7777
E-mail: emergingscholar@aauw.org
Web: www.aauw.org/fga/awards/raes.cfm

Purpose To recognize and reward minority and other young women who show promise of future academic distinction.

Eligibility Eligible for nomination are nontenured women faculty members who earned a Ph.D. or equivalent within the past 5 years. They must be U.S. citizens or permanent residents. Selection is based on demonstrated excellence in teaching, a documented and active research record, and evidence of potentially significant contributions to the awardee's field of study. The sponsor strongly encourages the nomination of women of color and other underrepresented groups.

Financial data The award is $5,000.

Duration   The award is presented annually.

Additional information   The award includes a trip to the annual AAUW convention (where the award is presented).

Number awarded   1 each year.

Deadline   Nominations must be submitted by February of each year.

[847]
SAJA STUDENT JOURNALISM AWARDS

South Asian Journalists Association
c/o Sreenath Sreenivasan
Columbia Graduate School of Journalism
2950 Broadway
New York, NY 10027
(212) 854-5979   Fax: (212) 253-4273
E-mail: ss221@Columbia.edu
Web: www.saja.org/awards.html

Purpose   To recognize and reward outstanding reporting on any subject by students of south Asian origin.

Eligibility   Eligible to be considered for these awards are print, broadcast, new media, and photography submitted by south Asian students in the United States or Canada (on any subject). Also eligible are stories for school publications or broadcasts and class work.

Financial data   First prize is $500, second prize is $300, and third prize is $200.

Duration   The competition is held annually.

Number awarded   3 each year.

Deadline   March of each year.

[848]
SPORTS ACHIEVEMENT AWARD

Indian American Heritage Foundation
3818 Gleneagles Drive
Tarzana, CA 91356
(818) 708-3885   E-mail: ashok4u@aol.com
Web: www.la-indiacenter.com

Purpose   To recognize and reward high school seniors in southern California who are of Asian Indian descent who have participated in athletics.

Eligibility   This award is available to seniors graduating from high schools in southern California (south of Fresno) who have at least 1 parent of Asian Indian descent. Applicants must have participated in high school sports activities and have a GPA of 2.0 or higher. They must attend a function of the sponsoring organization at which they take a quiz on India, based on material supplied by the organization. Along with their application, they must submit a 2-page essay on how athletics has affected and influenced their life. Selection is based on their quiz score (15%), the essay (15%), years of athletic training (15%), number of teams on which they have participated (15%), leadership role or captaincy of team (15%), athletics honors and awards (15%), and community involvement (10%).

Financial data   The award is $500 or $250.

Duration   1 year.

Additional information   Material about India for the quiz is sent to the applicant after receipt of a check for $10 and the completed application.

Number awarded   1 each year.

Deadline   April of each year.

[849]
SUMMER WORKSHOPS WRITING COMPETITION FOR MINORITY HIGH SCHOOL STUDENTS

Dow Jones Newspaper Fund
P.O. Box 300
Princeton, NJ 08543-0300
(609) 452-2820   Fax: (609) 520-5804
E-mail: newsfund@wsf.dowjones.com
Web: DJNewspaperFund.dowjones.com

Purpose   To recognize and reward (with college scholarships) outstanding participants in journalism workshops for minority high school students.

Eligibility   Each summer, workshops on college campuses around the country allow minority high school students to experience work on a professional-quality publication. Students are taught to write, report, design, and layout a newspaper on topics relevant to youth. The director of each workshop nominates 1 student who submits an article from the workshop newspaper and an essay on why he/she wants to pursue journalism as a career. The students whose articles and essay are judged most outstanding receive these college scholarships.

Financial data   The award is a college scholarship of $1,000.

Duration   Workshops normally last 2 weeks during the summer. Scholarships are for 1 year and may be renewed for 1 additional year if the recipient maintains a GPA of 2.5 or higher and an interest in journalism.

Additional information   Recently, workshops were held on college campuses in Alabama, Arizona, Arkansas, California, Florida, Illinois, Kentucky, Massachusetts, Minnesota, Mississippi, Missouri, New Jersey, New York, Ohio, Oklahoma, Pennsylvania, South Dakota, Texas, Virginia, Washington, and Wisconsin. For the name and address of the director of each workshop, contact the Newspaper Fund.

Number awarded   8 each year.

[850]
VISUAL AND PERFORMING ARTS AWARD

Indian American Heritage Foundation
3818 Gleneagles Drive
Tarzana, CA 91356
(818) 708-3885   E-mail: ashok4u@aol.com
Web: www.la-indiacenter.com

Purpose   To recognize and reward high school seniors in southern California who are of Asian Indian descent and have participated in visual or performing arts activities.

Eligibility   This award is available to seniors graduating from high schools in southern California (south of Fresno) who have at least 1 parent of Asian Indian descent. Applicants must have participated in visual and performing arts activities and have a GPA of 2.0 or higher. They must attend a function of the sponsoring organization at which they take a quiz on India, based on material supplied by the organization. Along with their application, they must submit a 2-page essay on how learning arts has affected and influenced their life. Selection is based on their quiz score (15%), the essay (15%), years of training (15%), list of events in which they have performed (15%), leadership roles (15%), honors and awards (15%), and community involvement (10%).

Financial data   The award is $250 or $500.

Duration 1 year.

Additional information Material about India for the quiz is sent to the applicant after receipt of a check for $10 and the completed application.

Number awarded 1 each year.

Deadline April of each year.

[851]
WOMEN OF COLOR CAUCUS STUDENT ESSAY AWARD FOR ASIAN AMERICAN WOMEN

National Women's Studies Association
Attn: Women of Color Caucus
7100 Baltimore Avenue, Suite 500
College Park, MD 20740
(301) 403-0525   Fax: (301) 403-4137
E-mail: nwsaoffice@nwsa.org
Web: www.nwsa.org/wocscol.htm

Purpose To recognize and reward outstanding essays by Asian American and Asian women students on feminist issues.

Eligibility This program is open to Asian American and Asian women undergraduates, graduate students, and recent (within 1 year) Ph.D. recipients. Applicants must submit a scholarly essay that provides critical theoretical discussions and/or analyses of issues and experiences of Asian American/Asian women and girls. The focus may be national or international. Manuscripts must be original, unpublished, and between 15 and 25 pages in length.

Financial data The award is approximately $500.

Duration The award is presented annually.

Additional information Information is also available from Pat Washington, 4537 Alamo Drive, San Diego, CA 92115, (619) 582-5383, E-mail: Themorgangirl@aol.com.

Number awarded 1 each year.

Deadline November of each year.

Internships

Described here are 174 work experience programs open to undergraduate, graduate, or postgraduate Asian Americans. Only salaried positions are covered. If you are looking for a particular program and don't find it in this section, be sure to check the Program Title Index to see if it is covered elsewhere in the directory.

[852]
AABA LAW STUDENT SUMMER GRANT

Asian American Bar Association of the Greater Bay
Area
P.O. Box 190517
San Francisco, CA 94119
E-mail: info@aaba-bay.com
Web: www.aaba-bay.com

Purpose To provide funding to law students interested in working on a summer project that will provide legal assistance to the Asian American community in the service area of the Asian American Bar Association of the Greater Bay Area (AABA).

Eligibility This program is open to law students who have obtained a summer position with a nonprofit legal service organization. Applicants must be planning to work on a project or projects that will provide legal assistance to the Asian American community in San Francisco, Alameda, Contra Costa, San Mateo, Marin, or Santa Clara counties in California. The organization must have agreed to supervise the applicant.

Financial data The grant is $3,000.

Duration At least 10 weeks during the summer.

Additional information Information is also available from Allen Kato, Fenwick & West LLP, Embarcadero Center West, 275 Battery Street, San Francisco, CA 94111, (415) 875-2464, Fax: (415) 281-1350, E-mail: akato@fenwick.com, or Garner Weng, Hanson Bridgett, 333 Market Street, Suite 2300, San Francisco, CA 94105, (415) 995-5081, Fax: (415) 541-9366, E-mail: gweng@hansonbridgett.com.

Number awarded 1 or more each year.

Deadline May of each year.

[853]
AAJA INTERNSHIP GRANT FOR BROADCAST

Asian American Journalists Association
Attn: Student Programs Coordinator
1182 Market Street, Suite 320
San Francisco, CA 94102
(415) 346-2051, ext. 102   Fax: (415) 346-6343
E-mail: brandons@aaja.org
Web: www.aaja.org

Purpose To provide a supplemental grant to student members of the Asian American Journalists Association (AAJA) working as a summer intern at a radio or television broadcasting company.

Eligibility This program is open to AAJA members who are full-time college students or recent college graduates. Applicants must have secured a summer internship at a television or radio broadcasting company before they apply. They must submit an essay (150 to 200 words) on why they want to prepare for a career in broadcast journalism and what they want to gain from the experience, a letter of recommendation, a resume, proof of age (at least 18 years), verification of an internship, and statement of financial need.

Financial data The grant is $2,000. Funds must be used to defray the cost-of-living expenses, pay for transportation to the internship site, or supplement low-paying or unpaid internships.

Duration Summer months.

Number awarded 1 each year.

Deadline May of each year.

[854]
AAJA/CHICAGO TRIBUNE PRINT AND NEW MEDIA INTERNSHIP GRANT

Asian American Journalists Association
Attn: Student Programs Coordinator
1182 Market Street, Suite 320
San Francisco, CA 94102
(415) 346-2051, ext. 102   Fax: (415) 346-6343
E-mail: brandons@aaja.org
Web: www.aaja.org

Purpose To provide a supplemental grant to student members of the Asian American Journalists Association (AAJA) participating in print or new media summer internships.

Eligibility This program is open to AAJA members who are full-time college students or recent college graduates. Applicants must have secured a summer internship at a print or online company before they apply. They must submit an essay (150 to 200 words) on why they want to prepare for a career in print or online journalism and what they want to gain from the experience, a letter of recommendation, a resume, proof of age (at least 18 years), verification of an internship, and statement of financial need.

Financial data The grant is $1,500. Funds must be used to defray the cost-of-living expenses, pay for transportation to the internship site, or supplement low-paying or unpaid internships.

Duration Summer months.

Additional information This program is supported by the Chicago Tribune Foundation.

Number awarded 1 or more each year.

Deadline May of each year.

[855]
AAPG SEMESTER INTERNSHIPS IN GEOSCIENCE AND PUBLIC POLICY

American Geological Institute
Attn: Government Affairs Program
4220 King Street
Alexandria, VA 22302-1502
(703) 379-2480   Fax: (703) 379-7563
E-mail: govt@agiweb.org
Web: www.agiweb.org/gap

Purpose To provide work experience to geoscience students (especially minorities and women) who have a strong interest in federal science policy.

Eligibility This program is open to geoscience students who are interested in the public policy aspects of the discipline, especially in energy and resource issues. Applicants must submit official copies of college transcripts, a resume with the names and contact information for 2 references, and a statement of their science and policy interests and what they feel they can contribute to the program. Women and minorities are especially encouraged to apply.

Financial data The stipend is $4,000.

Duration 14 weeks, during the fall or spring semester.

Additional information This program is jointly funded by the American Geological Institute (AGI) and the American Association of Petroleum Geologists (AAPG). Activities for the interns include monitoring and analyzing geoscience-related legislation in Congress, updating legislative and policy information on AGI's web site, attending House and Senate hearings and preparing summaries, responding to information requests from AGI's member societies, and attending meetings with policy-level staff members in Congress, federal agencies, and non-governmental organizations.

Number awarded 2 each semester.

Deadline April of each year for fall internships; October of each year for spring internships.

[856]
ACT SUMMER INTERNSHIP PROGRAM

American College Testing
Attn: Human Resources Department
500 ACT Drive
P.O. Box 168
Iowa City, IA 52243-0168
(319) 337-1763   E-mail: working@act.org
Web: www.act.org/humanresources/jobs/intern.html

Purpose To provide work experience during the summer to graduate students (particularly women and minorities) interested in careers in testing and measurement.

Eligibility This program is open to graduate students enrolled in such fields as educational psychology, measurement, program evaluation, counseling psychology, educational policy, mathematical and applied statistics, industrial or organizational psychology, and counselor education. Selection is based on technical skills, previous practical or work experience, interest in careers in testing, general academic qualifications, and the match of course work and research interests with those of sponsoring mentors. The program is also intended to assist in increasing the number of women and minority professionals in measurement and related fields.

Financial data Interns receive a stipend of $5,000 and round-trip transportation between their graduate institution and Iowa City. A supplemental living allowance of $400 is provided if a spouse and/or children accompany the intern.

Duration 8 weeks during the summer.

Additional information Assignments are available in 4 categories: 1) educational and social research; 2) industrial and organizational psychology; 3) psychometrics and statistics; and 4) vocational and career psychology. Interns work with assigned mentors and participate in weekly seminars led by the professional staff of American College Testing (ACT).

Number awarded Varies each year.

Deadline February of each year.

[857]
AEF FELLOWSHIPS

Asian Pacific American Bar Association Educational
    Fund
P.O. Box 2209
Washington, DC 20013-2209
Fax: (202) 408-4400   E-mail: aef@vvault.com
Web: www.aef-apaba.org/summer/summer.html

Purpose To provide funding to law students interested in interning during the summer with a public interest organization that benefits either the Asian Pacific American commu-

nity or the metropolitan Washington, D.C. community at large.

Eligibility This program is open to law students who have obtained an unpaid internship with a public interest organization (e.g., government organizations and other nonprofits serving the public interest). The organization must be based in the greater Washington, D.C. area and serve either the Asian Pacific American community or the community at large. Applicants must submit an essay, up to 750 words, on the internship, how it will benefit the Asian Pacific American community or the community at large in the metropolitan Washington, D.C. area, and their activities showing past and/or present commitment to public interest and/or Asian Pacific American issues. Preference is given to applicants interning at direct service organizations. Selection is based primarily on the essay, but the applicant's maturity and responsibility are also considered. An effort is made to place fellows in diverse employment settings. The sponsor does not discriminate on the basis of age, sex, disability, race, color, religion, ethnic/national origin, veteran status, or sexual orientation in the award of these fellowships.

Financial data Grants average $3,100.

Duration At least 10 weeks or a total of 400 hours during the summer.

Additional information This program includes the Norman Y. Mineta Anheuser-Busch Fellowship, funded by Anheuser-Busch Companies, Inc., and the GroupMagellan Fellowship funded by GroupMagellan Attorney Placement LLC.

Number awarded Varies each year; recently, 4 of these fellowships were funded.

Deadline April of each year.

[858]
AFSCME/UNCF UNION SCHOLARS PROGRAM

United Negro College Fund
Attn: Corporate Scholars Program
P.O. Box 1435
Alexandria, VA 22313-9998
Toll-free: (866) 671-7237   E-mail: internship@uncf.org
Web: www.uncf.org/internships/index.asp

Purpose To provide financial assistance to students of color who are interested in working during the summer on an organizing campaign for the American Federation of State, County and Municipal Employees (AFSCME).

Eligibility This program is open to students of color, including African Americans, Hispanic Americans, Asian/Pacific Islander Americans, and American Indians/Alaskan Natives. Applicants must be second semester sophomores or juniors and majoring in ethnic studies, women's studies, labor studies, American studies, sociology, anthropology, history, political science, psychology, social work, or economics. They must have a GPA of 2.5 or higher and be interested in working on a union organizing campaign at 1 of several locations in the United States.

Financial data The program provides a stipend of $4,000, on-site housing at their location, a week-long orientation and training, and (based on successful performance during the organizing campaign) a $5,000 scholarship.

Duration 10 weeks for the organizing assignment; 1 year for the scholarship.

Number awarded Varies each year.

Deadline February of each year.

[859]
AIPG SUMMER INTERNSHIPS IN GEOSCIENCE AND PUBLIC POLICY

American Geological Institute
Attn: Government Affairs Program
4220 King Street
Alexandria, VA 22302-1502
(703) 379-2480, ext 212   Fax: (703) 379-7563
E-mail: govt@agiweb.org
Web: www.agiweb.org/gap/interns/internsu.html

Purpose To provide summer work experience to geoscience students (particularly minorities and women) who have a strong interest in federal science policy.

Eligibility This program is open to geoscience students who are interested in the public policy aspects of the discipline, especially legislation pending before Congress. Applicants must submit official copies of college transcripts, a resume with the names and contact information for 2 references, and a statement of their science and policy interests and what they feel they can contribute to the program. Minorities and women are especially encouraged to apply.

Financial data The stipend is $3,500.

Duration 12 weeks during the summer.

Additional information This program is jointly funded by the American Geological Institute (AGI) and the American Institute of Professional Geologists (AIPG). Activities for the interns include monitoring and analyzing geoscience-related legislation in Congress, updating legislative and policy information on AGI's web site, attending House and Senate hearings and preparing summaries, responding to information requests from AGI's member societies, and attending meetings with policy-level staff members in Congress, federal agencies, and non-governmental organizations.

Number awarded 3 each summer.

Deadline March of each year.

[860]
AMERICAN COLLEGE OF HEALTHCARE EXECUTIVES MINORITY INTERNSHIP

American College of Healthcare Executives
Attn: Human Resources Manager
One North Franklin Street, Suite 1700
Chicago, IL 60606-3529
(312) 424-9342   Fax: (312) 424-0023
E-mail: ache@ache.org
Web: www.ache.org/carsvcs/internship.cfm

Purpose To provide minority graduate students who are members of the American College of Healthcare Executives (ACHE) with an opportunity to work at the organization's headquarters.

Eligibility This program is open to ACHE student associates or affiliates who have completed 1 year of graduate study in health care management from an accredited college or university in the United States or Canada. Applicants must be a member of a minority group. They must be interested in working in all major ACHE divisions, including administration, communications, education, executive office, finance, health administration press, management information systems, membership, regional services, and

research and development. Along with their application, they must submit a short statement of interest, a current curriculum vitae, an official undergraduate transcript, and a letter of recommendation.

Financial data The stipend is $16.60 per hour.

Duration 3 months during the summer.

Additional information This program was established in 1991.

Number awarded 1 each year.

Deadline November of each year.

[861]
AMERICAN HEART ASSOCIATION UNDERGRADUATE STUDENT RESEARCH PROGRAM

American Heart Association-Western States Affiliate
Attn: Research Department
1710 Gilbreth Road
Burlingame, CA 94010-1317
(650) 259-6725   Fax: (650) 259-6891
E-mail: research@heart.org
Web: www.americanheart.org

Purpose To provide students (particularly minority and women students) from California, Nevada, and Utah with an opportunity to work on a cardiovascular research project during the summer.

Eligibility This program is open to college students who are enrolled full time at an accredited academic institution at the junior or senior level and interested in a career in heart or stroke research. Applicants must be residents of California, Nevada, or Utah (or attending a college or university in 1 of those states) and interested in a summer internship at a cardiovascular research laboratory in those states. They must have completed the following (or equivalent) courses: 4 semesters (or 6 quarters) of biological sciences, physics, or chemistry; and 1 quarter of calculus, statistics, computational methods, or computer science. Selection is based on an assessment of the student's application, academic record (preference is given to students with superior academic standing), and faculty recommendations. Women and minorities are particularly encouraged to apply.

Financial data Participants receive a $4,000 stipend.

Duration 10 weeks during the summer.

Additional information Participants are assigned to laboratories in California, Nevada, or Utah to work under the direction and supervision of experienced scientists.

Deadline January of each year.

[862]
ANHEUSER-BUSCH/FRANK HORTON FELLOWSHIP PROGRAM

Asian Pacific American Institute for Congressional Studies
Attn: Fellowship Program
1001 Connecticut Avenue, N.W., Suite 835
Washington, DC 20036
(202) 296-9200   Fax: (202) 296-9236
E-mail: apaics@apaics.org
Web: www.apaics.org/apaics_fellow.html

Purpose To provide an opportunity for recent graduates with an interest in issues affecting the Asian American and

Pacific Islander communities to work in the office of a Congressional member, a Congressional committee, or a federal agency.

Eligibility Applicants must have a graduate or bachelor's degree from an accredited educational institution. They must have a demonstrated interest in the political process, public policy issues, and Asian American and Pacific Islander community affairs; relevant work experience; evidence of leadership abilities; oral and written communication skills; a cumulative GPA of 3.3 or higher; U.S. citizenship or permanent resident status; an interest in working in the office of a Congressional member, a Congressional committee, or a federal agency; and an interest in a career in public policy. Along with their application, they must submit an essay on their ideas about an agenda for the Congressional Asian Pacific American Caucus (CAPAC).

Financial data The stipend of $15,000 is intended to cover travel arrangements, housing, and personal expenses. A separate stipend is provided for basic health insurance coverage.

Duration 9 months, starting in September.

Additional information This program is supported by Anheuser-Busch Companies, Inc. Recently, the fellow worked in the office of the vice-chair of the CAPAC.

Number awarded 1 each year.

Deadline January of each year.

[863]
APAICS SUMMER INTERNSHIPS

Asian Pacific American Institute for Congressional
    Studies
Attn: Summer Internship Program
1001 Connecticut Avenue, N.W., Suite 835
Washington, DC 20036
(202) 296-9200   Fax: (202) 296-9236
E-mail: apaics@apaics.org
Web: www.apaics.org/internships.html

Purpose To provide an opportunity for undergraduate students with an interest in issues affecting the Asian American and Pacific Islander communities to work in Washington, D.C. during the summer.

Eligibility This program is open to Asian American and Pacific Islander students currently enrolled in an accredited undergraduate institution; recent (within 90 days) graduates are also eligible. Applicants must be able to demonstrate interest in the political process, public policy issues, and Asian American and Pacific Islander community affairs; leadership abilities; oral and written communication skills; a cumulative GPA of 3.0 or higher; and U.S. citizenship or permanent resident status. They must be interested in working in Congress, federal agencies, or institutions that further the mission of the Asian Pacific American Institute for Congressional Studies (APAICS). Preference is given to students who have not previously had an internship in Washington, D.C.

Financial data The stipend is $2,500.

Duration 9 weeks, starting in June.

Additional information This program is supported by Philip Morris Companies.

Number awarded Varies each year; recently, 13 interns were selected for this program.

Deadline January of each year.

[864]
ARMY JUDGE ADVOCATE GENERAL'S CORPS SUMMER INTERN PROGRAM

U.S. Army
Attn: Judge Advocate Recruiting Office
1777 North Kent Street, Suite 5200
Rosslyn, VA 22209-2194
(703) 696-2822   Toll-free: (866) ARMY-JAG
Fax: (703) 588-0100
Web: www.jagcnet.army.mil

Purpose To provide law students (particularly minorities and women) with an opportunity to gain work experience during the summer in Army legal offices throughout the United States and overseas.

Eligibility This program is open to full-time students enrolled in law schools accredited by the American Bar Association. Applications are accepted both from students who are completing the first year of law school and those completing the second year. Students must be interested in a summer internship with the Army Judge Advocate General's Corps (JAGC). U.S. citizenship is required. The program actively seeks applications from women and minority group members. Selection is based on academic ability and demonstrated leadership potential.

Financial data Interns who have completed the first year of law school are paid at the GS-5 scale, starting at $11.23 per hour. Interns who have completed the second year of law school are paid at the GS-7 scale, starting at $13.91 per hour.

Duration Approximately 60 days, beginning in May or June.

Additional information Interns work under the supervision of an attorney and perform legal research, write briefs and opinions, conduct investigations, interview witnesses, and otherwise assist in preparing civil or criminal cases. Positions are available at Department of the Army legal offices in Washington, D.C. and at Army installations throughout the United States and overseas. These are not military positions. No military obligation is incurred by participating in the summer intern program.

Number awarded 100 per year: 25 first-year students and 75 second-year students.

Deadline February of each year for first-year students; October of each year for second-year students.

[865]
ART PETERS PROGRAM

Philadelphia Inquirer
Attn: Oscar Miller, Director of Recruiting
400 North Broad Street
P.O. Box 8263
Philadelphia, PA 19101
(215) 854-5102   Fax: (215) 854-2578
E-mail: inkyjobs@phillynews.com
Web: www.philly.com/mld/philly

Purpose To provide summer copy editing experience at the *Philadelphia Inquirer* to minority college students interested in careers in journalism.

Eligibility Minority college students entering their sophomore, junior, or senior year in college are eligible to apply if they are interested in the practical work of copy editing. The internship is at the *Philadelphia Inquirer*. Selection is based on experience, potential, academic record, and extracurricular activities.

Financial data The salary is $573 per week.

Duration 10 weeks beginning in June.

Additional information After 1 week of orientation, interns are given their assignments at the *Philadelphia Inquirer:* reporters cover and write stories for the city, business, sports, or features desks; copy editors write headlines and edit articles for those desks or the national/foreign copy desk.

Number awarded 7 each year: 4 in copy-editing and 3 in reporting.

Deadline November of each year.

[866]
ARTTABLE MENTORED INTERNSHIPS

ArtTable Inc.
270 Lafayette Street, Suite 608
New York, NY 10012-3327
(212) 343-1735   Fax: (212) 343-1430
E-mail: women@arttable.org
Web: www.arttable.org

Purpose To provide an opportunity for women art students who are from diverse backgrounds to gain mentored work experience during the summer.

Eligibility This program is open to women from diverse backgrounds who are underrepresented in the visual arts field. Applicants must be 1) in the later years of their undergraduate studies, about to graduate, and contemplating a graduate education; or 2) in the early stages of a terminal degree and seeking career opportunities related to the visual arts professions. They must be interested in working during the summer with a mentor at an art museum or similar facility in New York City, Washington D.C., northern California, or southern California. U.S. citizenship or permanent resident status is required.

Financial data The stipend is $3,000. The hosting institution or mentor receives $500 for administrative and other costs.

Duration 10 weeks during the summer.

Additional information This program began in 2000.

Number awarded 4 each year: 1 in each of the participating locations.

Deadline January of each year.

[867]
ASHA JAINI EMERGING LEADER SCHOLARSHIP

Conference on Asian Pacific American Leadership
Attn: Summer Internships
P.O. Box 65073
Washington, DC 20035-5073
(202) 628-1307   E-mail: info@capal.org
Web: www.capal.org/asha_emerging.html

Purpose To provide funding for summer internships in Washington, D.C. to Asian Pacific American undergraduate students.

Eligibility This program is open to Asian Pacific American continuing undergraduate students (graduating seniors are not eligible) who are interested in a public sector internship within the Washington, D.C. metropolitan area in any of the 3 branches of the federal government, with a state or local

official or government agency, or at a nonprofit organization. Applicants must demonstrate a desire to build skills and develop their commitment to public service and the Asian Pacific American community. Along with their application, they must submit a 750-word essay on their long-term goals, how the summer internship experience will advance those, and their educational, community work, and internship experiences. They must also submit a description of desired internships. Selection is based on demonstrated commitment to public service, including service to the Asian Pacific American community; potential to benefit from the internship; demonstrated leadership and potential for continued growth in leadership skills; and financial need.

Financial data Awardees receive a stipend of $2,000 to help pay expenses during their internship.

Duration At least 6 weeks during the summer.

Additional information The sponsor will find an internship placement for the recipient, based on what it believes to be the best opportunity to develop leadership skills. Recipients must agree to participate in the sponsor's summer Washington Leadership Program.

Number awarded 1 each year.

Deadline April of each year.

[868]
ASHA JAINI MEMORIAL GRADUATE LEADERSHIP FELLOWSHIP

Conference on Asian Pacific American Leadership
Attn: Summer Internships
P.O. Box 65073
Washington, DC 20035-5073
(202) 628-1307   E-mail: info@capal.org
Web: www.capal.org/asha_fellowship.html

Purpose To provide funding for summer internships in Washington, D.C. to Asian Pacific American graduate and law students.

Eligibility This program is open to Asian Pacific American graduate students and recent graduates who have secured a public sector internship within the Washington, D.C. metropolitan area in any of the 3 branches of the federal government, with a state or local official or government agency, or at a nonprofit organization. Applicants may be majoring in any field, including but not limited to nonprofit management, education, public policy, or public interest law. Along with their application, they must submit a 750-word essay on their long-term goals, how the summer internship experience will advance those, and their educational, community work, and internship experiences. They must also submit a 250-word essay on the skills and experience they bring as a mentor, the skills they hope to encourage in younger scholars, and what they might gain from the experience. Selection is based on demonstrated commitment to public service, including service to the Asian Pacific American community; potential to benefit from the internship; demonstrated leadership and potential for continued growth in leadership skills; and financial need.

Financial data Awardees receive a stipend of $2,000 to help pay expenses during their internship.

Duration At least 6 weeks during the summer.

Additional information This program was established in 1991. Recipients are responsible for securing their own internships. They are expected to mentor undergraduate students who participate in the sponsor's internship programs and to help organize, facilitate, and prepare a written evaluation of its summer Washington Leadership Program.

Number awarded   2 each year.

Deadline   April of each year.

[869]
ASIA PACIFIC EXCHANGE SCHOLARSHIPS

Eastman Kodak Company
Attn: Asia Pacific Exchange
343 State Street
Rochester, NY 14650-1193
(585) 724-9388   Fax: (585) 724-9416
E-mail: mimi.lee@kodak.com
Web: www.kodak.com

Purpose   To provide financial assistance and work experience to Asian American high school seniors from the Rochester, New York area who are interested in studying selected business, engineering, or science fields in college.

Eligibility   This program is open to Asian American residents of the Rochester, New York area who are graduating high school seniors. Applicants must be planning to enroll full time in an approved degree program in accounting, chemical engineering, chemistry, computer engineering, computer science, electrical engineering, finance, information systems, logistics, manufacturing engineering, mechanical engineering, optical engineering, optics science, or software engineering. They must have an ACT score of 25 or higher (or the equivalent on the SAT). Selection is based on academic achievement and leadership within the community.

Financial data   The stipend is $10,000 per year.

Duration   4 years, provided the recipient maintains a GPA of 3.0 or higher, full-time enrollment in an approved degree program, and timely progress toward completion of the degree.

Additional information   Recipients are required to complete at least 1 cooperative internship with Kodak.

Number awarded   1 each year.

Deadline   February of each year.

[870]
ASIAN AMERICAN SUMMER INTERN GRANTS

American Baptist Churches USA
Attn: National Ministries
P.O. Box 851
Valley Forge, PA 19482-0851
(610) 768-2067   Toll-free: (800) ABC-3USA, ext. 2067
Fax: (610) 768-2453
E-mail: karen.drummond@abc-usa.org
Web: www.nationalministries.org

Purpose   To provide ministerial experience during the summer to Asian American Baptist seminarians.

Eligibility   This program is open to Asian American seminarians who are interested in gaining local church experience in the summer months. Applicants must be U.S. citizens who have been a member of a church affiliated with American Baptist Churches USA for at least 1 year.

Financial data   The grant is $500; the employing church is expected to match the grant.

Duration   Summer months.

Number awarded   Varies each year.

Deadline   May of each year.

[871]
ATLANTA JOURNAL AND CONSTITUTION MINORITY INTERNSHIPS

Atlanta Journal and Constitution
Attn: Office of Community Affairs
72 Marietta Street, N.W.
Atlanta, GA 30303
(404) 577-5772   E-mail: aeintern@ajc.com
Web: www.ajc.com

Purpose   To provide summer newspaper work experience in Atlanta to Georgia college students of color who are interested in preparing for a career in journalism.

Eligibility   This program is open to Georgia college students of color (Asian Americans, Hispanics, African Americans, and Native Americans) interested in newspaper careers. Applicants must be interested in working at the *Atlanta Journal-Constitution* in the newsroom, online, advertising, accounting, marketing, or information technology department. They must be enrolled as a sophomore or junior at a Georgia college or university (seniors may be considered if they plan to continue on to graduate school), have a cumulative GPA of 3.0 or higher, and have demonstrated an interest in the department where they wish to work (campus publication experience and work with daily deadlines are preferable). Along with their application, they must submit a 500-word essay explaining why they want to be a journalist and how the internship will help them pursue their goals, samples of their work, a resume, and references.

Financial data   Upon successful completion of the internship, participants receive a $1,000 scholarship.

Duration   The internship is 10 weeks during the summer; the scholarship is a 1-year nonrenewable award.

Number awarded   3 each year.

Deadline   January of each year.

[872]
ATTAPONG P. MELLENTHIN MEMORIAL SCHOLARSHIP

Conference on Asian Pacific American Leadership
Attn: Summer Internships
P.O. Box 65073
Washington, DC 20035-5073
(202) 628-1307   E-mail: info@capal.org
Web: www.capal.org

Purpose   To provide funding for summer internships in Washington, D.C. to Asian Pacific American undergraduate students from the Midwest.

Eligibility   This program is open to Asian Pacific American students attending a college or university that is a member of the Midwest Asian American Students Union (MAASU). Applicants must have 1) demonstrated leadership and active involvement in the Asian Pacific American community or with Asian Pacific American student associations; 2) demonstrated interest in public service; 3) oral and written communication skills; and 4) a cumulative GPA of 3.0 or higher. They must be interested in an internship in an institution or agency in Washington, D.C. selected by the Conference on Asian Pacific American Leadership (CAPAL). U.S. citizenship or permanent resident status is required.

Financial data Awardees receive a stipend of $2,000 to help pay expenses during their internship.

Duration At least 10 weeks during the summer.

Additional information This program is co-sponsored and administered by MAASU and CAPAL.

Number awarded 1 each year.

Deadline April of each year.

[873]
BARBARA JORDAN HEALTH POLICY SCHOLARS PROGRAM

Henry J. Kaiser Family Foundation
1330 G Street N.W.
Washington, DC 20005
(202) 347-5270   Fax: (202) 347-5274
E-mail: bischolars@howard.edu
Web: www.kff.org/docs/topics/jordanscholars.html

Purpose To provide minority college seniors and recent graduates with an opportunity to work during the summer in a Congressional office with major health policy responsibilities.

Eligibility This program is open to members of minority groups who are entering or currently enrolled in their senior year of college or who have graduated within the last 12 months from an accredited U.S. college or university. Current law, medical, and graduate students are not eligible. Applicants must demonstrate an active interest in health policy, strong leadership skills, and community commitment. Along with their applications, they must submit 400-word essays on 1) their personal background and how it led them to be interested in health policy, and 2) their views on a current health policy issue. Selection is based on the essays, academic performance, letters of recommendation, and extracurricular activities.

Financial data Scholars receive lodging at Howard University in Washington, D.C., round-trip transportation to Washington, D.C., a daily expense allowance for meals and local transportation, and a stipend of $1,500 upon completion of the program.

Duration 9 weeks during the summer.

Additional information Scholars are first provided with an orientation to the program by its sponsors: Howard University and the Henry J. Kaiser Family Foundation. They are then assigned to work for a Congressional office or committee with significant health policy involvement. This program began in 2000.

Number awarded 16 each year.

Deadline January of each year.

[874]
BAY AREA MINORITY SUMMER CLERKSHIP PROGRAM

Santa Clara County Bar Association
Attn: Minority Access Committee
4 North Second Street, Suite 400
San Jose, CA 95113
(408) 287-2557   Fax: (408) 287-6083
E-mail: info@sccba.com
Web: www.sccba.org

Purpose To provide summer work experience at law firms in the San Francisco Bay area to minority students at law schools in the area.

Eligibility This program is open to first-year students from any state who are enrolled at the following law schools: Golden Gate, Santa Clara, Stanford, University of San Francisco, Boalt, and Hastings. Applicants must be members of minority groups, defined to include Native Americans, Alaska Natives, Asians, Pacific Islanders, sub-continent Indians, African Americans, other Blacks, Puerto Ricans, Mexican Americans, and other Hispanics. They must be interested in summer employment with a large law firm in their choice of 3 Bay area counties: Alameda, San Francisco, and Santa Clara. Selection is based on verbal and written communication skills, leadership, integrity, resourcefulness, and other characteristics that indicate potential for success within the legal community. Grades are not emphasized; life experience, potential, contact with community, and achievement receive strong consideration.

Financial data Students are paid the standard summer clerk salary by their particular employer.

Duration Summer months.

Additional information This program, which began in 1990, is sponsored by the Santa Clara County Bar Association, the Bar Association of San Francisco, and the Alameda County Bar Association.

Number awarded Approximately 20 each year.

Deadline January of each year.

[875]
BUSINESS REPORTING INTERN PROGRAM FOR MINORITY COLLEGE SOPHOMORES AND JUNIORS

Dow Jones Newspaper Fund
P.O. Box 300
Princeton, NJ 08543-0300
(609) 452-2820   Fax: (609) 520-5804
E-mail: newsfund@wsj.dowjones.com
Web: DJNewspaperFund.dowjones.com

Purpose To provide work experience and financial assistance to minority college students who are interested in careers in journalism.

Eligibility This program is open to college sophomores and juniors who are U.S. citizens interested in careers in journalism and participating in a summer internship at a daily newspaper as a business reporter. Applicants must be members of a minority group (African American, Hispanic, Asian American, Pacific Islander, American Indian, or Alaskan Native) enrolled as full-time students. They must submit a resume, 3 to 5 recently-published clips, an list of courses with grades, and a 500-word essay.

Financial data   Interns receive a salary of $350 per week during the summer and a $1,000 scholarship at the successful completion of the program.

Duration   10 weeks for the summer internship; 1 year for the scholarship.

Number awarded   Up to 12 each year.

Deadline   October of each year.

[876]
CAPA INTERNSHIP PROGRAM

Chinese American Political Association
Attn: CAPA Community Education Fund
P.O. Box 4314
Walnut Creek, CA 94596-0314
(925) 945-1901   Fax: (925) 938-2961
E-mail: internapp@capa-news.org
Web: www.capa-news.org/internship.html

Purpose   To provide Chinese American high school seniors and college students from northern California with an opportunity to work in the office of an elected public official in their area during the summer.

Eligibility   This program is open to Chinese American students who will be high school seniors or college students in the following fall. Applicants must be interested in an internship in northern California with elected officials of both political parties at local, county, state, or federal levels. No previous experience is required, but applicants must have a desire to learn more about government, politics, current events, and community service. As part of their application, they must submit a 750-word essay on what they hope to learn from their internship and the skills and perspectives they would bring to the office of an elected official. Membership in the Chinese American Political Association (CAPA) is encouraged but not required.

Financial data   Interns who complete the program receive a stipend (amount not specified).

Duration   Summer months.

Additional information   Recently, assignments were available in the following California communities: Berkeley, Concord, Danville, Martinez, Oakland, Pittsburg, Pleasant Hill, Sacramento, San Francisco, Walnut Creek.

Number awarded   Varies each year; recently, 13 interns participated in this program.

Deadline   February of each year.

[877]
CAPAL SCHOLARSHIP

Conference on Asian Pacific American Leadership
Attn: Summer Internships
P.O. Box 65073
Washington, DC 20035-5073
(202) 628-1307   E-mail: info@capal.org
Web: www.capal.org/capal_state_farm.html

Purpose   To provide funding for summer internships in Washington, D.C. to Asian Pacific American undergraduate students.

Eligibility   This program is open to Asian Pacific American continuing undergraduate students (graduating seniors are not eligible) who are interested in a public sector internship within the Washington, D.C. metropolitan area in any of the 3 branches of the federal government, with a state or local

official or government agency, or at a nonprofit organization. Applicants must have a strong interest in community development, a commitment to public service, and a willingness to better the Asian Pacific American community. Along with their application, they must submit a 750-word essay on their long-term goals, how the summer internship experience will advance those, and their educational, community work, and internship experiences. Selection is based on demonstrated commitment to public service, including service to the Asian Pacific American community; potential to benefit from the internship; demonstrated leadership and potential for continued growth in leadership skills; and financial need.

Financial data   Awardees receive a stipend of $2,000 to help pay expenses during their internship.

Duration   At least 6 weeks during the summer.

Additional information   This program, established in 2001, is sponsored by State Farm Insurance Companies. Recipients are responsible for securing their own internships. They must agree to participate in the sponsor's summer Washington Leadership Program.

Number awarded   1 each year.

Deadline   April of each year.

[878]
CAPITOL HILL NEWS INTERNSHIPS

Radio and Television News Directors Foundation
1600 K Street, N.W., Suite 700
Washington, DC 20006-2838
(202) 467-5218   Fax: (202) 223-4007
E-mail: karenb@rtndf.org
Web: www.rtndf.org/asfi/internships/internships.html

Purpose   To provide work experience to recent graduates (especially minorities) in electronic journalism who are interested in covering Congressional activities in Washington, D.C.

Eligibility   Eligible are recent (within 2 years) college graduates who majored in electronic journalism; preference is given to minority students. Applicants must include an essay explaining why they are interested in this program and how it will help meet their career goals. Excellent writing skills are essential. The sponsor recognizes African Americans, Asian Americans, Hispanic Americans, and Native Americans as minorities.

Financial data   The stipend is $1,000 per month. Interns are responsible for their own housing, travel, and living expenses.

Duration   3 months; the spring program begins in March and the summer program begins in June.

Additional information   Interns cover newsworthy Congressional activities and help coordinate broadcast coverage of those activities; they obtain hands-on experience in the House and Senate radio-TV galleries, working side by side with the Washington press and Congressional staff to cover the political process. The sponsor defines electronic journalism to include radio, television, cable, and online news.

Number awarded   4 each year: 2 in the spring and 2 in the summer.

Deadline   January of each year for the spring program; March of each year for the summer program.

[879]
CARNEGIE INSTITUTION OF WASHINGTON INTERN PROGRAM

Carnegie Institution of Washington
Geophysical Laboratory
Attn: Summer Intern Program Coordinator
5251 Broad Branch Road, N.W.
Washington, DC 20015-1305
(202) 478-8939   Fax: (202) 478-8901
E-mail: s.gramsch@gl.ciw.edu
Web: www.gl.ciw.edu/interns

Purpose To provide an opportunity for undergraduate students (particularly minorities and women) to participate in a research internship at the Carnegie Institution of Washington's Geophysical Laboratory or Department of Terrestrial Magnetism during the summer.

Eligibility This summer program at the Carnegie Institution of Washington is open to undergraduate students working on a degree in astronomy, biology, chemistry, geoscience, materials science, physics, or a related field. Applicants must have completed at least 30 semester hours, but graduating seniors are not eligible. U.S. citizenship or permanent resident status is required. Applicants must be interested in conducting research at the laboratory under the supervision of a staff scientist. Women and minorities are particularly encouraged to apply.

Financial data The stipend is $3,600. Also provided are housing and support for travel expenses to Washington, D.C.

Duration 10 weeks during the summer.

Additional information Funding for this program is provided by a grant from the National Science Foundation's Research Experiences for Undergraduates program.

Number awarded Varies each year; recently, 16 students participated in this program.

Deadline February of each year.

[880]
CASIC STUDENT INTERNSHIP PROGRAM

Chinese American Student Internship Coalition
c/o CAUSE-Vision 21
272 South Los Robles Avenue
Pasadena, CA 91101
(626) 356-9838   Fax: (626)356-9878
E-mail: info@causevision21.org
Web: www.causeusa.org

Purpose To provide Chinese American undergraduate students and high school seniors with an opportunity to work during the summer in the office of an elected official in California or the District of Columbia

Eligibility This program is open to Chinese American undergraduate students and high school seniors who are interested in gaining hands-on experience in the political process and a deeper understanding of issues that impact the Chinese and Asian American communities. Applicants must be available for a summer internship in the office of an elected official in southern California or Washington D.C. Selection is based on letters of recommendation, transcript, community involvement, an essay on public service, and an interview.

Financial data The stipend is $1,000.

Duration Summer months.

Additional information This program, which began in 1991, is supported by several Chinese American associations and administered by Chinese Americans United for Self Empowerment (CAUSE). Interns are expected to work with other interns to complete a joint research project and conduct a final presentation, attend community meetings and meet with various community leaders, conduct voter registration and education drives, attend leadership conferences and seminars, submit journal articles to local newspapers, and visit local radio and television stations.

Number awarded 8 to 12 each year.

[881]
CENTER ON BUDGET AND POLICY PRIORITIES INTERNSHIPS

Center on Budget and Policy Priorities
Attn: Internship Coordinator
820 First Street, N.E., Suite 510
Washington, DC 20002
(202) 408-1095, ext. 386   Fax: (202) 408-1056
E-mail: internship@cbpp.org
Web: www.cbpp.org/internship.html

Purpose To provide work experience at the Center on Budget and Policy Priorities (CBPP) in Washington, D.C. to undergraduates, graduate students, and recent college graduates (particularly those who are minorities or women).

Eligibility This program is open to undergraduates, graduate students, and recent college graduates who are interested in public policy issues affecting low-income families and individuals. Applicants must be interested in working at CBPP in the following areas: media, federal legislation, health policy, housing policy, income security policy, international budget project, national budget and tax policy, outreach campaigns, state budget and tax policy, state low-income initiatives, and food stamps. They should have research, fact-gathering, writing, analytic, and computer skills and a willingness to do administrative as well as substantive tasks. Women and minorities are encouraged to apply.

Financial data Undergraduate students receive $7.50 per hour for a first internship and up to $8.00 per hour subsequently. Graduate students receive $9.00 per hour for a first internship and up to $9.50 per hour subsequently. Students with a master's degree receive $10.00 per hour. Recent college graduates receive $8.00 per hour for a first internship and up to $8.50 per hour subsequently.

Duration 1 semester; may be renewed.

Additional information The center specializes in research and analysis oriented toward practical policy decisions and produces analytic reports that are accessible to public officials at national, state, and local levels, to nonprofit organizations, and to the media.

Number awarded Varies each semester.

Deadline February of each year for summer internships; July of each year for fall internships; November of each year for spring internships.

[882]
CIA UNDERGRADUATE INTERNSHIP PROGRAM

Central Intelligence Agency
Attn: Recruitment Center
P.O. Box 4090
Reston, VA 20195
Toll-free: (800) 368-3886
Web: www.cia.gov/employment/student.html

Purpose To provide work experience at the Central Intelligence Agency (CIA) to undergraduates, especially minorities and people with disabilities.

Eligibility This program is open to undergraduate students, particularly minorities and people with disabilities. Applicants must be U.S. citizens, have a GPA of 3.0 or higher, be available to work in metropolitan Washington, D.C. during the summer or for a semester, and meet the same employment standards as permanent CIA employees. They must be majoring in fields such as accounting, business administration, computer science, economics, engineering, finance, foreign area studies, foreign languages, geography, graphic design, human resources, international relations, logistics, mathematics, military and foreign affairs, national security studies, physical sciences, or political science.

Financial data Student positions offer salaries competitive with the private sector and the same benefits as permanent employees. Student trainees are also eligible to apply for the agency's tuition assistance program.

Duration Interns are required to work either 1) a combination of 1 semester and 1 summer, or 2) 2 90-day summer internships.

Number awarded Varies each year.

Deadline Applications may be submitted at any time, but should be completed 6 to 9 months prior to availability for the first work period and near the end of the applicant's freshman year in college.

[883]
CLEAN THE RAIN ORGANIZING INTERNSHIPS

National Wildlife Federation
Attn: Great Lakes Field Office
213 West Liberty, Suite 200
Ann Arbor, MI 48104-1398
(734) 769-3351   Fax: (734) 769-1449
E-mail: greatlakes@nwf.org
Web: www.nwf.org/greatlakes

Purpose To provide an opportunity for recent graduates (particularly people of color and women) to work on conservation issues at the Great Lakes field office of the National Wildlife Federation.

Eligibility This program is open to college graduates who have a bachelor's degree in biology, chemistry, ecology, environmental science, environmental engineering, natural resources, or other science field. Applicants must be interested in working on organizing aspects of the Clean the Rain project nationally and mercury phaseout work in the Great Lakes states. They must have good organizational skills and excellent communication skills (both oral and written). Familiarity with standard PC word processing, spreadsheet, database, and graphics programs is essential. Some organizing/outreach experience on other campaigns is very helpful. Applications are strongly encouraged from people

of diverse backgrounds, women, people of color, people of all sexual identities, and people with disabilities.

Financial data The stipend is $160 per week. No benefits are provided.

Duration 10 weeks; interns may begin at any time.

Additional information Interns work with partner organizations in deployment and maintenance at field sites; work with other staff in drafting mini-reports on mercury in precipitation in the Great Lakes; assist in planning and coordination of materials for news conferences; assist in preparation and delivery of presentations on the mercury phaseout project; assist in coordination of national advocacy work on mercury reduction legislation and rulemaking; and assist as needed with research and outreach work related to the overall Clean the Rain campaign.

Number awarded Varies each year.

Deadline Applications may be submitted at any time.

[884]
THE CLOISTERS SUMMER INTERNSHIP FOR COLLEGE STUDENTS

Metropolitan Museum of Art
Attn: The Cloisters
Fort Tryon Park
New York, NY 10040
(212) 650-2280
E-mail: cloistersinterns@metmuseum.org
Web: www.metmuseum.org

Purpose To provide art museum work experience during the summer at The Cloisters of the Metropolitan Museum of Art to minority and other college students.

Eligibility This program is open to undergraduate students, especially freshmen and sophomores, who are interested in art and museum careers. They must enjoy working with children and be willing to intern at the Metropolitan Museum of Art. Applicants of diverse backgrounds are particularly encouraged to apply.

Financial data The internship stipend is $2,500.

Duration 9 weeks, beginning in June.

Additional information Interns are assigned to the education department of The Cloisters, the branch museum of the Metropolitan Museum of Art devoted to the art of medieval Europe. They conduct gallery workshops for New York City day campers. This program is funded in part by the Norman and Rosita Winston Foundation, Inc.

Number awarded Varies each year.

Deadline January of each year.

[885]
CONNECTICUT COMMUNITY COLLEGE MINORITY TEACHING FELLOWSHIPS

Connecticut Community College System
Attn: System Officer for Diversity Awareness
61 Woodland Street
Hartford, CT 06105-9949
(860) 244-7606   Fax: (860) 566-6624
E-mail: karmstrong@commnet.edu
Web: www.commnet.edu/minority_fellowship.asp

Purpose To provide financial assistance and work experience to graduate students, especially minorities, in Connecticut who are interested in preparing for a career in community college teaching or administration.

Eligibility This program is open to graduate students who have completed at least 6 credits of graduate work and have indicated an interest in a career in community colleges. Applicants must be willing to commit to at least 1 year of employment in the Connecticut Community College System. Although all qualified graduate students are eligible, the program encourages applicants to register who strengthen the racial and cultural diversity of the minority fellow registry. That includes, in particular, making all possible efforts to recruit from historically underrepresented people (Asians, Blacks, and Hispanics).

Financial data Fellows receive a stipend of $3,500 per semester.

Duration 1 year; may be renewed.

Additional information Fellows are expected to dedicate 9 hours per week to the program. They spend 6 hours per week in teaching-related activities under the supervision of a mentor. During the second semester, they assist the mentor in teaching a course. The remaining time is spent on program and campus orientation activities, attendance at relevant faculty or staff meetings, and participation in other college meetings or professional development activities.

Number awarded Up to 13 each year: 1 at each of the 12 colleges in the system and 1 in the chancellor's office.

[886]
COX NEWSPAPER DIVISION MINORITY JOURNALISM SCHOLARSHIP

Cox Newspapers, Inc.
Attn: Scholarship Administrator
6205 Peachtree Dunwoody Road
P.O. Box 105720
Atlanta, GA 30348
(678) 645-0000
Web: www.coxnews.com

Purpose To provide work experience and financial assistance to minority undergraduate and graduate students from areas served by selected Cox Enterprises newspapers who are preparing for a career in the newspaper industry.

Eligibility This program is open to minority (African American, Hispanic, Asian American, Native American) undergraduate and graduate students interested in newspaper careers. Applicants must be interested in continuing their program of study as well as working as an intern at a participating Cox newspaper. Cox employees and their families are eligible. Each newspaper establishes its own criteria regarding GPA requirements, supporting documentation, and essay requirements. In general, applicants must have demonstrated an interest in the department (newsroom, online, advertising, accounting, marketing, or information technology) in which they would like to intern and be able to demonstrate experience with campus publications and/or daily deadlines.

Financial data All educational expenses are paid for 4 years of college, including room, board, books, and tuition. The approximate total value of the award is $40,000.

Duration The scholarship is awarded for 4 years. The recipient is expected to intern at the newspaper during the summer and holiday breaks throughout the 4 years of college.

Additional information The scholarship is administered by major newspapers owned by the sponsor: the *Atlanta Journal and Constitution, Austin American-Statesman,* and *Palm Beach Post.* Applications are available from the Cox Newspapers headquarters in Atlanta, the offices of the various Cox-owned newspapers, and from guidance offices of high schools in the city selected for the scholarship for that year.

Number awarded 1 each year.

Deadline April of each year.

[887]
COX REPORTING INTERNSHIP

Asian American Journalists Association
Attn: Student Programs Coordinator
1182 Market Street, Suite 320
San Francisco, CA 94102
(415) 346-2051, ext. 102   Fax: (415) 346-6343
E-mail: brandons@aaja.org
Web: www.aaja.org

Purpose To provide members of the Asian American Journalists Association (AAJA) with the opportunity to gain work experience during the summer at the Washington Bureau of Cox Newspapers.

Eligibility This program is open to AAJA members who are college juniors, seniors, graduate students, or recent graduates. Applicants are not required to be journalism majors, but college newspaper experience or a prior internship is preferred. A strong academic record and writing samples are important.

Financial data The stipend is $300 per week. Airfare and a furnished apartment are also provided.

Duration Summer months.

Additional information Interns work as general assignment reporter in the Cox Washington Bureau.

Number awarded 1 each year.

Deadline February of each year.

[888]
C.T. LANG JOURNALISM MINORITY SCHOLARSHIP AND INTERNSHIP

Albuquerque Journal
Attn: Scholarship Committee
7777 Jefferson Street, N.E.
P.O. Drawer J
Albuquerque, NM 87103
(505) 823-7777

Purpose To provide financial assistance and work experience to minority upper-division students in journalism programs at universities in New Mexico.

Eligibility This program is open to minority students majoring or minoring in journalism at a New Mexico university in their junior year with a GPA of 2.5 or higher. Applicants must be enrolled full time. They must be planning a career in newswriting, photography, design, copy editing, or online. Selection is based on clips of published stories, a short autobiography that explains the applicant's interest in the field, a grade transcript, and a letter of recommendation.

Financial data The scholarship is $1,000 per semester; the recipient also receives a paid internship and moving expenses.

Duration The scholarship is for 2 semesters (fall and spring). The internship is for 1 semester.

Additional information This program is funded by the *Albuquerque Journal,* where the internship takes place.

Number awarded 1 each year.

Deadline December of each year.

[889]
CULTURAL RESOURCES DIVERSITY INTERN PROGRAM

Student Conservation Association, Inc.
Attn: Diversity Internships
1800 North Kent Street, Suite 102
Arlington, VA 22209
(703) 524-2441   Fax: (603) 543-1828
E-mail: diversity@thesca.org
Web: www.thesca.org/ci_diversity.cfm

Purpose To provide work experience to ethnically diverse college students and students with disabilities at facilities of the U.S. National Park Service (NPS).

Eligibility This program is open to currently-enrolled students at the sophomore or higher level. Applicants must be U.S. citizens or permanent residents with a GPA of 3.0 or higher. The program is designed to give ethnically diverse students and students with disabilities the opportunity to experience the diversity of careers in the federal sector. Applicants are assigned to a position within the NPS. Possible placements include archaeology and anthropology; historic building preservation; journalism and graphic design; civil and environmental engineering; project management and research; costumed interpretation and living history; landscape architecture; museum studies and library relations; web site design; public relations and outreach; and Native American studies.

Financial data The weekly stipend ranges from $50 to $520, depending on the program and the intern's academic level. Other benefits include a pre-term orientation, transportation to the orientation and the work site, worker's compensation, and accident insurance.

Duration 10 weeks in the summer (beginning in June), 15 weeks in the fall (beginning in September), or 15 weeks in the spring (beginning in January).

Additional information While participating in the internship, students engage in tri-weekly evening career and professional development events, ongoing career counseling, mentoring, and personal and career development services.

Number awarded Approximately 18 each year.

Deadline February of each year for summer; June of each year for fall; November of each year for spring.

[890]
DALMAS A. TAYLOR MEMORIAL SUMMER MINORITY POLICY FELLOWSHIP

Society for the Psychological Study of Social Issues
208 I Street, N.E.
Washington, DC 20002-4340
(202) 675-6956   Fax: (202) 675-6902
E-mail: awards@spssi.org
Web: www.spssi.org/Taylor_flyer.html

Purpose To enable graduate students of color to be involved in the public policy activities of the American Psychological Association (APA) during the summer.

Eligibility This program is open to graduate students who are members of an ethnic minority group (including, but not limited to, African American, Alaskan Native, American Indian, Asian American, Hispanic, and Pacific Islander) and/or have demonstrated a commitment to a career in psychology or a related field with a focus on ethnic minority issues. Applicants must be interested in spending a summer in Washington, D.C. to work on public policy issues in conjunction with the Minority Fellowship Program of the APA. Their application must indicate why they are interested in the fellowship, their previous research experience and current interest, their interest and involvement in ethnic minority psychological issues, and how the fellowship would contribute to their career goals.

Financial data The stipend is $3,000. Housing and travel funds are also provided.

Duration Summer months.

Additional information This program was established in 2000.

Number awarded 1 each year.

Deadline January of each year.

[891]
DAN BRADLEY FELLOWSHIP PROGRAM

Legal Aid Association of California
c/o Public Interest Clearinghouse
47 Kearney Street, Suite 705
San Francisco, CA 94108
(415) 834-0100, ext. 306   Fax: (415) 834-0202
E-mail: laac@pic.org
Web: www.pic.org/laac/laacpage.htm

Purpose To provide funding to law students (particularly students of color) interested in a summer internship with legal services programs that are members of the Legal Aid Association of California (LAAC).

Eligibility This program is open to law students who have a strong interest in working to defend and expand the legal rights of the poor and the disadvantaged. Applicants must be interested in a summer internship with a legal aid services agency that is an LAAC member and that agrees to supervise the student on a major litigation or "impact" advocacy project. Applications must be submitted jointly by the student and a representative of an eligible legal services program. Students must include a personal statement describing their interest in pursuing the fellowship. People of color and students from low-income or working class backgrounds are particularly encouraged to apply.

Financial data The stipend is at least $2,500. The LAAC contributes $2,000 and the program selected to receive the fellow is expected to provide at least an additional $500.

Duration 8 weeks during the summer.
Additional information This program began in 1991.
Number awarded 1 or more each year.
Deadline April of each year.

[892]
DANIEL K. INOUYE FELLOWSHIP PROGRAM

Asian Pacific American Institute for Congressional
  Studies
Attn: Fellowship Program
1001 Connecticut Avenue, N.W., Suite 835
Washington, DC 20036
(202) 296-9200   Fax: (202) 296-9236
E-mail: apaics@apaics.org
Web: www.apaics.org/apaics_fellow.html

Purpose To provide an opportunity for recent graduates with an interest in issues affecting the Asian American and Pacific Islander communities to work in the office of a Congressional member, a Congressional committee, or a federal agency.

Eligibility Applicants must have a graduate or bachelor's degree from an accredited educational institution. They must have a demonstrated interest in the political process, public policy issues, and Asian American and Pacific Islander community affairs; relevant work experience; evidence of leadership abilities; oral and written communication skills; a cumulative GPA of 3.3 or higher; U.S. citizenship or permanent resident status; an interest in working in the office of a Congressional member, a Congressional committee, or a federal agency; and an interest in a career in public policy. Along with their application, they must submit an essay on their ideas about an agenda for the Congressional Asian Pacific American Caucus (CAPAC).

Financial data The stipend of $15,000 is intended to cover travel arrangements, housing, and personal expenses. A separate stipend is provided for basic health insurance coverage.

Duration 9 months, starting in September.

Additional information This program is supported by the Aratani Foundation. Recently, the fellow worked in the office of the chair of the CAPAC.

Number awarded 1 each year.

Deadline January of each year.

[893]
DAVID IBATA PRINT SCHOLARSHIP

Asian American Journalists Association-Chicago
  Chapter
P.O. Box 577639
Chicago, IL 60657-9997
E-mail: chiaaja@aol.com
Web: chapters.aaja.org/Chicago/internships.htm

Purpose To provide funding to members of the Asian American Journalists Association (AAJA) who are interested in a summer internship at a Chicago newspaper.

Eligibility This program is open to AAJA members who are college students or recent graduates. Applicants must be interested in an internship at the *Chicago Tribune.* They must submit a 350-word essay on why they want to be a journalist, a resume, 5 to 7 clips, and a cover letter.

Financial data The stipend is $2,500.

Duration 10 to 12 weeks, during the summer.
Number awarded 1 each year.
Deadline December of each year.

[894]
DAVIS WRIGHT TREMAINE 1L DIVERSITY SCHOLARSHIP PROGRAM

Davis Wright Tremaine LLP
Attn: Recruiting Administrator
2600 Century Square
1501 Fourth Avenue
Seattle, WA 98101-1688
(206) 622-3150   Fax: (206) 628-7699
E-mail: seattle@dwt.com
Web: www.dwt.com/recruit/diversity.htm

Purpose To provide financial assistance and summer work experience to law students of color.

Eligibility This program is open to first-year law students of color and others of diverse background. Applicants must possess a strong academic record as an undergraduate and in first year of law school, an interest in participating in community and civic opportunities, and a willingness to commit to working in the sponsor's Seattle or Portland office during the summer between their first and second year of law school. They must submit a current resume, a complete undergraduate transcript, grades from the first semester of law school, a short personal essay indicating their interest in the scholarship, a legal writing sample, and 2 or 3 references. Although demonstrated need may be taken into account, applicants need not disclose their financial circumstances.

Financial data The award consists of a $7,500 stipend for second-year tuition and expenses and a paid summer clerkship.

Duration 1 academic year and summer.

Number awarded 3 each year: 2 in the Seattle office and 1 in the Portland office.

Deadline January of each year.

[895]
DELL/UNCF CORPORATE SCHOLARS PROGRAM

United Negro College Fund
Attn: Corporate Scholars Program
P.O. Box 1435
Alexandria, VA 22313-9998
Toll-free: (866) 671-7237 E-mail: internship@uncf.org
Web: www.uncf.org/internships/index.asp

Purpose To provide financial assistance and work experience to undergraduate and graduate students, especially minorities, majoring in designated fields and interested in an internship at Dell Computer Corporation's corporate headquarters near Austin, Texas.

Eligibility This program is open to rising juniors and graduate students who are enrolled full time at institutions that are members of the United Negro College Fund (UNCF) or at any other 4-year college or university. Applicants must be majoring in business administration, computer science, engineering (computer, electrical, or mechanical), finance, human resources, management information systems, marketing, or supply chain management with a GPA of 3.0 or higher. Along with their application, they must submit a

1-page essay about themselves and their career goals, including information about their personal background and any particular challenges they have faced. Finalists are interviewed by a team of representatives from Dell, the program's sponsor.

Financial data The program provides a paid summer internship, housing accommodations in Austin, round-trip transportation to and from Austin, and (based on financial need and successful internship performance) a $10,000 scholarship.

Duration 10 to 12 weeks for the internship; 1 year for the scholarship.

Number awarded Varies each year.

Deadline January of each year.

[896]
DENVER BOTANIC GARDENS COLLEGE INTERNSHIPS IN APPLIED HORTICULTURE

Denver Botanic Gardens
Attn: Human Resources
909 York Street
Denver, CO 80206-3799
(720) 865-3531   Fax: (720) 865-3722
E-mail: HR@botanicgardens.org
Web: www.botanicgardens.org

Purpose To provide summer work experience in horticulture to students (especially minorities) at the Denver Botanic Gardens.

Eligibility This internship at the Denver Botanic Gardens is open to graduate students and undergraduates from any state who have completed their sophomore year and have a GPA of 2.5 or higher. Both traditional and nontraditional students, including those making career changes into the field of horticulture, are eligible. Minorities are specifically encouraged to apply.

Financial data A stipend is paid (amount not specified).

Duration 10 weeks during the summer.

Additional information Work assignments include planting, pruning, weeding, and watering on the outside grounds; seeding, transplanting, and propagation in the greenhouses; and tropical display and maintenance in the conservatory and lobby court areas. In addition, educational field trips and special projects help to round-out the program, which highlights gardening in the Front Range of the Colorado Rockies. Participants maintain a plant notebook throughout their internship.

Number awarded Approximately 6 each year.

Deadline February of each year.

[897]
DEPARTMENT OF STATE STUDENT INTERN PROGRAM

Department of State
Attn: Recruitment Division, SA-1
Intern Coordinator
2401 E Street, N.W., Room H518
Washington, DC 20522-0108
(202) 261-8888   Toll-free: (800) JOB-OVERSEAS
Fax: (202) 261-8841
Web: www.careers.state.gov/student/prog_intrn.html

Purpose To provide a work/study opportunity to undergraduate and graduate students (particularly minorities and women) interested in foreign service.

Eligibility This program is open to full- and part-time continuing college and university juniors, seniors, and graduate students. Applications are encouraged from students with a broad range of majors, such as business or public administration, social work, economics, information management, journalism, and the biological and physical sciences, as well as those majors more traditionally identified with international affairs. U.S. citizenship is required. The State Department particularly encourages eligible women and minority students with an interest in foreign affairs to apply.

Financial data Most internships are unpaid. A few paid internships are granted to applicants who can demonstrate financial need. If they qualify for a paid internship, college juniors are placed at the GS-4 level with an annual salary of $20,952; college seniors and first-year graduate students are placed at the GS-5 level with an annual salary of $23,442; second-year graduate students are placed at the GS-7 level with an annual salary of $29,037. Interns placed abroad may also receive housing, medical insurance, a travel allowance, and a dependents' allowance.

Duration Paid internships are available only for 10 weeks during the summer. Unpaid internships are available for 1 semester or quarter during the academic year, or for 10 weeks during the summer.

Additional information About half of all internships are in Washington, D.C., or occasionally in other large cities in the United States. The remaining internships are at embassies and consulates abroad. Depending upon the needs of the department, interns are assigned junior-level professional duties, which may include research, preparing reports, drafting replies to correspondence, working in computer science, analyzing international issues, financial management, intelligence, security, or assisting in cases related to domestic and international law. Interns must agree to return to their schooling immediately upon completion of their internship.

Number awarded Approximately 800 internships are offered each year, but only about 5% of those are paid positions.

Deadline February of each year for fall internships; June of each year for spring internships; October of each year for a summer internships.

[898]
DICK LOUIE MEMORIAL INTERNSHIP FOR AMERICANS OF ASIAN DESCENT

Arthur M. Sackler Gallery
Attn: Intern Coordinator
Freer Building, MRC 707
P.O. Box 37012
Washington, DC 20013-7012
(202) 633-0465   Fax: (202) 357-4911
E-mail: asiaintern@asia.si.edu
Web: www.asia.si.edu/education/dicklouie.htm

Purpose To enable Asian Americans entering or completing their senior year at high schools in the Washington, D.C. area to gain practical experience in a museum setting during the summer.

Eligibility This program is open to graduating seniors and students entering their senior year at high schools in the Washington, D.C. area who are of Asian descent. Applicants must be seeking an internship at the Smithsonian's Arthur M. Sackler Gallery with its renowned collection of Asian art. They need not be planning a career in museum work or Asian studies, but they should be interested in learning about museum work and Asian art.

Financial data The stipend is $1,500.

Duration 6 weeks, beginning in July.

Additional information This internship was established in 1994.

Number awarded 4 each year.

Deadline March of each year.

[899]
DOI DIVERSITY INTERN PROGRAM

Student Conservation Association, Inc.
Attn: Diversity Internships
1800 North Kent Street, Suite 102
Arlington, VA 22209
(703) 524-2441   Fax: (603) 543-1828
E-mail: diversity@thesca.org
Web: www.thesca.org/ci_diversity.cfm

Purpose To provide work experience to ethnically diverse college and graduate students and students with disabilities at federal agencies involved with natural and cultural resources.

Eligibility This program is open to currently-enrolled students at the sophomore or higher level. Applicants must be U.S. citizens or permanent residents with a GPA of 3.0 or higher. The program is designed to give ethnically diverse students and students with disabilities the opportunity to experience the diversity of careers in the federal sector. Applicants are assigned to a position within the U.S. Department of the Interior (DOI). Possible placements include archaeology and anthropology; wildlife and fisheries biology; business administration, accounting, and finance; civil and environmental engineering; computer science, especially GIS applications; human resources; mining and petroleum engineering; communications and public relations; web site and database design; environmental and realty law; geology, hydrology, and geography; Native American studies; interpretation and environmental education; natural resource and range management; public policy and administration; and surveying and mapping.

Financial data The weekly stipend ranges from $50 to $520, depending on the program and the intern's academic level. Other benefits include a pre-term orientation, transportation to the orientation and the work site, worker's compensation, and accident insurance.

Duration 10 weeks in the summer (beginning in June) or 15 weeks in the fall (beginning in September) or spring (beginning in January).

Additional information While participating in the internship, students engage in tri-weekly evening career and professional development events, ongoing career counseling, mentoring, and personal and career development services.

Number awarded Approximately 20 each year.

Deadline February of each year for summer; June of each year for fall; November of each year for spring.

[900]
EATON MULTICULTURAL SCHOLARS PROGRAM

Eaton Corporation
Attn: EMSP
1111 Superior Avenue
Cleveland, OH 44114-2584
(216) 523-4354   E-mail: mildredneumann@eaton.com
Web: www.eatonjobs.com/career/career_choices.asp

Purpose To provide financial assistance and work experience to minority college students interested in a career as an engineer.

Eligibility This program is open to full-time minority students who are U.S. citizens or permanent residents. Applicants must have completed 1 year in an accredited program and have 3 remaining years of course work before completing a bachelor's degree. They must be majoring in computer science/data processing, electrical engineering, or mechanical engineering. Selection is based on academic performance, the student's school recommendation, and an expressed interest in pursuing challenging and rewarding internship assignments.

Financial data Stipends range from $500 to $3,000 per year. Funds are paid directly to the recipient's university to cover the cost of tuition, books, supplies, equipment, and fees.

Duration 3 years.

Additional information In addition to the scholarships, recipients are offered paid summer internships at company headquarters in Cleveland. The target schools participating in this program recently were Cornell, Detroit-Mercy, Florida A&M, Georgia Tech, Illinois at Chicago, Illinois at Urbana-Champaign, Lawrence Technological, Marquette, Massachusetts Institute of Technology, Michigan at Ann Arbor, Michigan at Dearborn, Michigan State, Milwaukee School of Engineering, Minnesota, Morehouse College, North Carolina A&T State, North Carolina State, Northwestern, Notre Dame, Ohio State, Purdue, Southern, Tennessee, Western Michigan, and Wisconsin at Madison. This program was established in 1994. Until 2002, it was known as the Eaton Minority Engineering Scholars Program.

Number awarded Varies each year.

Deadline December of each year.

[901]
EDUCATIONAL TESTING SERVICE SUMMER PROGRAM IN RESEARCH FOR GRADUATE STUDENTS

Educational Testing Service
Attn: Internships
Rosedale Road
MS 07-R
Princeton, NJ 08541-0001
(609) 734-5949   E-mail: internships@ets.org
Web: www.ets.org/research/fellowships.html

Purpose To provide work experience at the Educational Testing Service (ETS) during the summer to minority, women, and other graduate students in educational measurement and related fields.

Eligibility This internship at ETS is open to graduate students who are currently enrolled full time in a doctoral program and have completed at least 1 year of study. Applicants must be working on a doctoral degree in the following areas: computer science, education, learning, linguistics, literacy, minority issues, policy research, psychology, psycholinguistics, psychometrics, statistics, teaching, educational technology, or testing issues (including alternate forms of assessment for special populations and new forms of assessment). Selection is based on academic record and the match of applicant interests with participating ETS researchers. An explicit goal of the program is to attract women and minority graduate students to the field of educational measurement and related disciplines.

Financial data The stipend is $5,000. In addition, participants and their families are reimbursed for travel expenses from their universities to ETS (in Princeton) and back.

Duration 2 months, beginning in June.

Additional information Participants work under the supervision of ETS staff members.

Number awarded Up to 16 each year.

Deadline January of each year.

[902]
EMMA L. BOWEN FOUNDATION INTERNSHIPS

Emma L. Bowen Foundation
Attn: Vice President, Eastern Region
524 West 57th Street
New York, NY 10019
(212) 975-2545   Fax: (212) 975-5884
E-mail: sdrice@cbs.com
Web: www.emmabowenfoundation.com

Purpose To provide minority students with an opportunity to gain work experience during the summer at participating media companies.

Eligibility This program is open to minority students who apply as early as their junior year in high school. Applicants must be interested in working at a media company during the summer and school breaks until they graduate from college. They must have a GPA of 3.0 or higher, plans to attend an accredited 4-year college or university, and an interest in the media industry as a career. Along with their application, they must submit an essay of 500 to 1,000 words on how the media industry helps to create the images that influence our decisions and perceptions on a daily basis.

Financial data Interns receive a stipend of approximately $2,250 and matching compensation of $2,250 to help pay for college tuition and other expenses.

Duration 1 summer; may be renewed until the intern graduates from college if he or she maintains a GPA of 3.0 or higher.

Additional information The sponsoring companies have included ABC, Inc., Adelphia Communications, Broadcast Music Inc., CBS Incorporated, Comcast Foundation, C-SPAN, Fox Television Stations, Inc., Gannett Television, NBC, Paxson Communications, Turner Entertainment Networks, and the Weather Channel. Students in eastern states should use the address of the Vice President, Eastern Region. Students in western states should contact the Vice President, Western Region, CBS Studio Center, Administration Building, Suite 300, 4024 Radford Avenue, Studio City, CA 91604, (818) 655-5708, Fax: (818) 655-8358, E-mail: r.turner@mptp.com.

Number awarded Varies each year; recently, 50 new interns were selected.

[903]
EVERETT PUBLIC SERVICE INTERNSHIPS

Everett Public Internship Program
c/o Co-op America
1612 K Street, N.W., Suite 600
Washington, DC 20006
(202) 872-5335   Fax: (202) 331-8166
E-mail: info@everettinternships.org
Web: www.everettinternships.org

Purpose To provide work experience at public interest organizations during the summer to undergraduate and graduate students (especially minorities) who are interested in preparing for a career in public service.

Eligibility This program is open to undergraduate and graduate students who have completed at least 2 semesters of college and are interested in working in areas of public service at 55 nonprofit organizations throughout the country. Applicants can be majoring in any field as long as they are committed to public interest work. Members of all racial and ethnic groups are eligible, but many of the participating organizations serve predominantly minority communities.

Financial data The salary is $230 per week.

Duration 10 weeks during the summer.

Additional information Most participating organizations are located New York City (including Brooklyn and the Bronx) or Washington, D.C., but others are in Anchorage (Alaska), Boston, Boulder (Colorado), and Brookline (Massachusetts). Applications are submitted directly to the organization where the student wishes to intern. For the addresses and telephone numbers of all the participating organizations, write to the address above.

Number awarded More than 150 each year.

Deadline April of each year.

[904]
FAPAC INTERNSHIPS

Federal Asian Pacific American Council
Attn: Scholarship and Internship Chair
P.O. Box 23184
Washington, DC 20026-3184
E-mail: fapac@fapac.org
Web: www.fapac.org

Purpose To provide an opportunity to undergraduate students to work in the office of the Federal Asian Pacific American Council (FAPAC).

Eligibility This program is open to students currently enrolled in college and available to work 20 hours a week during the spring semester.

Financial data The stipend is $2,000.

Duration 10 to 12 weeks, between March and May.

Additional information FAPAC is an inter-agency organization founded in 1985 to promote equal opportunity and cultural diversity for Asian Pacific Americans within the federal and District of Columbia governments. Interns assist FAPAC executive board members and committee chairs to plan, organize, and coordinate the Congressional Seminar and National Leadership Training Conference. They also have opportunities to network with officials of Asian Pacific American organizations and the federal government. Information is also available from Mai Nguyen, (202) 267-7666, E-mail: Mai.Nguyen@faa.gov.

Number awarded Up to 5 each year.

Deadline March of each year.

[905]
FAYETTEVILLE OBSERVER INTERNSHIPS

Fayetteville Observer
Attn: Managing Editor
458 Whitfield Street
P.O. Box 849
Fayetteville, NC 28302
(910) 486-3558   Toll-free: (800) 722-0457
Web: www.fayettevillenc.com

Purpose To provide work experience during the summer at the *Fayetteville Observer* in North Carolina to college students (particularly minorities) interested in careers in journalism.

Eligibility This program at the *Observer* is open to students from any state, with preference given to sophomores, juniors, and seniors. Applicants must be planning to prepare for a career in news reporting, sports reporting, feature writing, or photography. Minorities are especially encouraged to apply.

Financial data The salary is $300 per week. No other benefits are provided. Interns must provide their own lodging and transportation.

Duration 12 weeks during the summer.

Number awarded 4 each year: 1 each in news reporting, feature writing, sports reporting, and photography.

Deadline February of each year.

[906]
FEDERAL ASIAN PACIFIC AMERICAN COUNCIL SCHOLARSHIP

Conference on Asian Pacific American Leadership
Attn: Summer Internships
P.O. Box 65073
Washington, DC 20035-5073
(202) 628-1307   E-mail: info@capal.org
Web: www.capal.org/fapac_scholarship.html

Purpose To provide funding for summer internships in Washington, D.C. to Asian Pacific American undergraduate students.

Eligibility This program is open to Asian Pacific American continuing undergraduate students (graduating seniors are not eligible) who are interested in a public sector internship in the Washington, D.C. metropolitan area in the executive branch of the federal government or a District of Columbia government agency. Applicants must have a strong commitment to public service and a willingness to better the Asian Pacific American community. Along with their application, they must submit a 750-word essay on their long-term goals, how the summer internship experience will advance those, and their educational, community work, and internship experiences. Selection is based on demonstrated commitment to public service, including service to the Asian Pacific American community; potential to benefit from the internship; demonstrated leadership and potential for continued growth in leadership skills; and financial need.

Financial data Awardees receive a stipend of $2,000 to help pay expenses during their internship.

Duration At least 6 weeks during the summer.

Additional information This program is sponsored by the Federal Asian Pacific American Council, an inter-agency organization founded in 1985 to promote equal opportunity and cultural diversity for Asian Pacific Americans within the federal and District of Columbia governments. Recipients are responsible for securing their own internships. They must agree to participate in the sponsor's summer Washington Leadership Program.

Number awarded 1 each year.

Deadline April of each year.

[907]
FEMINIST MAJORITY FOUNDATION INTERNSHIP PROGRAM

Feminist Majority
Attn: Internship Coordinator
1600 Wilson Boulevard, Suite 801
Arlington, VA 22209
(703) 522-2214   Fax: (703) 522-2219
E-mail: shasannagy@feminist.org
Web: www.feminist.org

Purpose To provide work experience at the Feminist Majority to students (particularly minorities) who aspire to become leaders in the feminist movement.

Eligibility This program is open to feminist undergraduate students of any major. Preference is given to applicants who have prior experience working on women's issues on campus, in their communities, or through a previous internship or job. Applications are especially encouraged from people of color and mathematics and science majors.

Financial data Interns may perform up to 10 hours a week of administrative work at $8 per hour.

Duration 2 months or longer. Full-time internships are available during the summer and full- or part-time internships are offered during the spring and fall.

Additional information Assignments at the Feminist Majority are available in the following project areas: Feminist Majority Leadership Alliance Program, Feminist Majority Foundation Online, Global Feminism, *Ms.* Magazine, National Center for Women and Policing, Women's Health Research, Education Equity Program, and Rock for Choice. Interns work in the Washington, D.C. area (see the contact address) or in the Los Angeles office (433 South Beverly Drive, Beverly Hills, CA 90212, (310) 556-2500, Fax: (310) 556-2509), E-mail: trunning@feminist.org.

Number awarded Varies each year.

Deadline Applications may be submitted at any time; internships begin in September, January, and June of each year.

[908]
FINNEGAN HENDERSON DIVERSITY SCHOLARSHIP

Finnegan, Henderson, Farabow, Garrett & Dunner, LLP
Attn: Director of Professional Recruitment and
   Development
1300 I Street, N.W.
Washington, D.C. 20005-3315
(202) 408-4034   Fax: (202) 408-4400
E-mail: suzanne.gentes@finnegan.com
Web: www.finnegan.com

Purpose To provide financial assistance and work experience to minority law students interested in a career in intellectual property law.

Eligibility This program is open to law students from underrepresented minority groups who have demonstrated a commitment to a career in intellectual property law and are currently enrolled either as a first-year full-time student or second-year part-time student. The sponsor defines underrepresented minorities to include American Indians/Alaskan Natives, Blacks/African Americans, Asian Americans/Pacific Islanders, and Hispanics/Latinos. Applicants must have earned an undergraduate degree in life sciences, engineering, or computer science, or have substantial prior trademark experience. Selection is based on academic performance at the undergraduate, graduate (if applicable), and law school level; relevant work experience; community service; leadership skills; and special accomplishments.

Financial data The stipend is $12,000 per year.

Duration 1 year; may be renewed 1 additional year as long as the recipient completes a summer associateship with the sponsor and maintains of GPA of 3.0 or higher.

Additional information The sponsor, the world's largest intellectual property law firm, established this scholarship in 2003. Summer associateships are available at its offices in Washington, D.C.; Atlanta, Georgia; Cambridge, Massachusetts; Palo Alto, California; or Reston, Virginia.

Number awarded 1 each year.

Deadline May of each year.

[909]
FLORIDA BAR FOUNDATION LEGAL SERVICES SUMMER FELLOWSHIP PROGRAM

Florida Bar Foundation
109 East Church Street, Suite 405
P.O. Box 1553
Orlando, FL 32802-1553
(407) 843-0045   Toll-free: (800) 541-2195
Fax: (407) 839-0287   E-mail: cstawicki@flabarfndn.org
Web: www.flabarfndn.org

Purpose To provide summer work experience at Florida legal assistance providers to students (particularly minority students) from law schools in the state.

Eligibility This program is open to first- and second-year students at accredited Florida law schools. Applicants must be interested in working during the summer at a legal aid and legal services provider funded by Florida's Interest on Trust Accounts (IOTA) program. Minority students are specifically encouraged to apply. Selection is based on experience in working with the low-income community, academic achievement, writing skills, and previous contact with and long-term commitment and interest in public service/pro bono work.

Financial data The stipend is $4,000 for first-year students or $5,000 for second-year students.

Duration 11 weeks during the summer.

Additional information This program was initiated in 1995.

Number awarded 20 each year. Since the program began, 159 students have participated.

Deadline January of each year.

[910]
FLORIDA SOCIETY OF NEWSPAPER EDITORS MINORITY SCHOLARSHIP PROGRAM

Florida Society of Newspaper Editors
c/o Florida Press Association
2636 Mitcham Drive
Tallahassee, FL 32308
(850) 222-5790   Fax: (850) 224-6012
E-mail: info@fsne.org
Web: www.fsne.org/minorityscholar.html

Purpose To provide financial assistance and summer work experience to minority upper-division students majoring in journalism at a college or university in Florida.

Eligibility This program is open to minority students in accredited journalism or mass communication programs at Florida 4-year colleges and universities. Applicants must be full-time students in their junior year, have at least a 3.0 GPA, and be willing to participate in a paid summer internship at a Florida newspaper. Along with their application, they must submit a 300-word autobiographical essay explaining why they want to prepare for a career in print journalism and provide a standard resume, references, and clips or examples of relevant classroom work.

Financial data Winners are given a paid summer internship at a participating newspaper between their junior and senior year. Upon successfully completing the internship, the students are awarded a $3,000 scholarship (paid in 2 equal installments) to be used during their senior year.

Duration 1 summer for the internship; 1 academic year for the scholarship.

Additional information Information is also available from Rosemary Armao, FSNE Scholarship Committee, c/o The Sarasota Herald Tribune, 801 South Tamiami Trail, Sarasota, FL 34230.

Number awarded 1 each year.

Deadline March of each year.

[911]
FORTUNE BRANDS SCHOLARS PROGRAM

United Negro College Fund
Attn: Corporate Scholars Program
P.O. Box 1435
Alexandria, VA 22313-9998
Toll-free: (866) 671-7237   E-mail: internship@uncf.org
Web: www.uncf.org/internships/index.asp

Purpose To provide financial assistance and work experience to minorities who are either juniors majoring in fields related to business or law students interested in an internship at corporate headquarters of Fortune Brands.

Eligibility This program is open to juniors and first- and second-year law students who are members of minority groups. Applicants must have a GPA of 3.0 or higher and an undergraduate major in accounting, finance, human resources, information systems, information technology, or marketing. They must be attending a designated college, university, or law school and be interested in an internship at Fortune Brands corporate headquarters in Lincolnshire, Illinois. Along with their application, they must submit a resume, 2 letters of recommendation, and official transcripts.

Financial data The program provides a paid internship and (based on successful internship performance) a $7,500 scholarship.

Duration 8 to 10 weeks for the internship; 1 year for the scholarship.

Additional information Eligible undergraduate institutions are Florida A&M University, Florida State University, Hampton University, Howard University, Morehouse College, North Carolina A&T State University, Northwestern University, Spelman College, University of Chicago, and University of Wisconsin. Participating law schools are those at Howard University, Northwestern University, University of Chicago, and University of Wisconsin.

Number awarded Varies each year.

Deadline February of each year.

[912]
FRANKLIN WILLIAMS INTERNSHIP

Council on Foreign Relations
Attn: Human Resources Office
58 East 68th Street
New York, NY 10021
(212) 434-9489   Fax: (212) 434-9893
E-mail: humanresources@cfr.org
Web: www.cfr.org

Purpose To provide undergraduate and graduate students (particularly minorities) with an opportunity to gain work experience in international affairs at the Council on Foreign Relations in New York.

Eligibility Applicants should be currently enrolled in either their senior year of an undergraduate program or in a graduate program in the area of international relations or a related field. They should have a record of high academic achievement, proven leadership ability, and previous related internship or work experience. Minority students are strongly encouraged to apply.

Financial data The stipend is $10 per hour.

Duration 1 academic term (fall, spring, or summer). Fall and spring interns are required to make a commitment of at least 12 hours per week. Summer interns may choose to make a full-time commitment.

Additional information Interns work closely with a program director or fellow in either the studies or meetings program and are involved with program coordination, substantive and business writing, research, and budget management. In addition, they are encouraged to attend the council's extensive meetings programs and participate in informal training designed to enhance management and leadership skills.

Number awarded 3 each year: 1 each academic term.

Deadline Applications may be submitted at any time.

[913]
FREDRIKSON & BYRON FOUNDATION MINORITY SCHOLARSHIPS

Fredrikson & Byron Foundation
4000 Pillsbury Center
200 South Sixth Street
Minneapolis, MN 55402-1425
(612) 492-7117   Fax: (612) 492-7077
Web: www.fredlaw.com/firm/scholarship.htm

Purpose To provide financial assistance and summer work experience to minority law students from any state who will be practicing in the Twin Cities area of Minnesota.

Eligibility This program is open to African American, Asian American, Pacific Islander, Hispanic, Native American, and Alaska Native students enrolled in their first year of law school. Applicants must be interested in practicing law in the Minneapolis-St. Paul area. Along with their application, they must submit 2 recommendations, a writing sample from their first-year legal writing course, transcripts from undergraduate and law school, and a resume. Financial need is not considered.

Financial data The fellowship stipend is $5,000. The internship portion of the program provides a $1,000 weekly stipend.

Duration 1 year.

Additional information The scholarship is jointly sponsored by Fredrikson & Byron, P.A. and the Fredrikson & Byron Foundation. Fellows are also eligible to participate in an internship at the firm's offices in Minneapolis.

Number awarded Up to 2 each year.

Deadline March of each year.

[914]
G. RICHARD TUCKER FELLOWSHIP

Center for Applied Linguistics
4646 40th Street, N.W.
Washington, DC 20016-1859
(202) 362-0700   Fax: (202) 362-3740
E-mail: info@cal.org
Web: www.cal.org

Purpose To provide an opportunity for graduate students (particularly minority graduate students) to participate in a research project during the summer at the Center for Applied Linguistics (CAL) in Washington, D.C.

Eligibility This program at CAL is open to candidates for a master's or doctoral degree in any field that is concerned with the study of language. Applicants must be currently enrolled in a degree program in the United States or Canada and must have completed the equivalent of at least 1 year of full-time graduate study. Minorities are especially encouraged to apply. Applicants must be proposing to work with CAL senior staff members on 1 of the center's existing research projects or on a suitable project suggested by themselves; priority is given to proposals that focus on language education, language testing, or language issues related to minorities in the United States or Canada.

Financial data Fellows receive a stipend of $2,400 plus travel expenses up to $1,000.

Duration 4 weeks during the summer.

Number awarded 1 each year.

Deadline April of each year.

[915]
GEORGE V. POWELL DIVERSITY SCHOLARSHIP

Lane Powell Spears Lubersky LLP
Attn: Administrator of Attorney Recruiting
1420 Fifth Avenue, Suite 4100
Seattle, WA 98101-2338
(206) 223-6123   Fax: (206) 223-7107
E-mail: rodenl@lanepowell.com
Web: www.lanepowell.com

Purpose To provide financial assistance and work experience to law students who will contribute to the diversity of the legal community

Eligibility This program is open to second-year students in good standing at an ABA-accredited law school. Applicants must be able to contribute meaningfully to the diversity of the legal community and have a demonstrated desire to work, live, and eventually practice law in Seattle or Portland. They must submit a cover letter including a statement indicating eligibility to participate in the program, resume, current copy of law school transcript, legal writing sample, and list of 2 or 3 professional or academic references. Selection is based on academic achievement and record of leadership abilities, community service, and involvement in community issues.

Financial data The program provides a stipend of $6,000 for the third year of law school and a paid summer associate clerkship.

Duration 1 year, including the summer.

Additional information This program was established in 2005. Clerkships are provided at the offices of the sponsor in Seattle or Portland.

Number awarded 1 each year.

Deadline October of each year.

[916]
GERALDINE R. DODGE FOUNDATION FELLOWSHIP

College Art Association of America
Attn: Fellowship Program
275 Seventh Avenue
New York, NY 10001-6798
(212) 691-1051, ext. 242   Fax: (212) 627-2381
E-mail: fellowship@collegeart.org
Web: www.collegeart.org/caa/career/fellowship.html

Purpose To provide financial assistance and work experience to art historians from culturally diverse backgrounds who are completing graduate degrees and are interested in working in New Jersey.

Eligibility This program is open to art historians who have been underrepresented in the field because of their race, religion, gender, age, national origin, sexual orientation, disability, or history of economic disadvantage. Applicants must be U.S. citizens or permanent residents and able to demonstrate financial need. They must expect to receive the M.F.A. or Ph.D. degree in the year following application and then be interested in working at a cultural institution in New Jersey.

Financial data The stipend is $5,000.

Duration 1 year: the final year of the degree program.

Additional information In addition to providing a stipend for the terminal year of their degree program, the College Art Association (CAA) helps fellows search for employment at a museum, art center, college, or university in New Jersey. Upon securing a position, CAA provides a $10,000 subsidy to the employer as part of the fellow's salary. Participating organizations must match this 2:1. In addition to administrative and/or teaching responsibilities, all fellows' positions must include a curatorial or public service component. Salary or stipend, position description, and term of employment will vary and are determined in consultation with individual fellows and their potential employers. This program began in 1993. Funding is provided by the Milton & Sally Avery Arts Foundation, Geraldine R. Dodge Foundation, National Endowment for the Arts, National Endowment for the Humanities, and Terra Foundation for the Arts.

Number awarded 1 each year.

Deadline January of each year.

[917]
GRADUATE FELLOWSHIP IN PHILANTHROPY AND HUMAN RIGHTS

Higher Education Consortium for Urban Affairs
Attn: Graduate Fellowship Coordinator
2233 University Avenue West, Suite 210
St. Paul, MN 55114-1698
(651) 646-8831   Toll-free: (800) 554-1089
E-mail: mshiozawa@hecua.org
Web: www.hecua.org

Purpose To provide financial assistance and work experience to graduate students of color in Minnesota who are interested in working in the fields of philanthropy and human rights.

Eligibility This program is open to graduate students at universities in Minnesota who are members of ethnic or cultural groups historically underrepresented in higher education. Applicants may be studying any academic discipline, but they must be interested in working part time at the Otto Bremer Foundation while they are engaged in study for their graduate degree. Their work for the foundation involves philanthropy and human rights, including social and economic justice, shelter and housing, civic engagement, health disparities and resources, civic engagement, or organizational effectiveness within nonprofits. They must be able to collaborate their academic work with research for nonprofit organizations in Minnesota, Wisconsin, North Dakota, or Montana. Along with their application, they must submit a resume or curriculum vitae, 3 letters of reference, official academic transcripts, and a 1,500-word essay about themselves, their interest and involvement in human rights and social change, and their current research interest in their academic program. Selection is based on how the applicants think, analyze, and write; their definition and commitment to human rights; experiences that predict their potential in human rights, nonprofits, and fulfilling the objectives of the fellowship; current research interest and program; academic merit; and evidence of support from their academic institution.

Financial data Fellows receive $12,000, either as a scholarship (paid directly to them) or as a stipend (paid to their university for tuition).

Duration 1 year.

Additional information This program, established in 2003, is funded by the Otto Bremer Foundation.

Number awarded 3 each year.

Deadline February of each year.

[918]
HARRY A. BLACKMUN MEMORIAL PUBLIC INTEREST GRANT

California Women's Law Center
3460 Wilshire Boulevard, Suite 1102
Los Angeles, CA 90010
(213) 637-9900　　　　　　Fax: (213) 637-9909
E-mail: amanda@cwlc.org
Web: www.cwlc.org

Purpose To provide summer work experience at the California Women's Law Center (CWLC) to law students (particularly students of color).

Eligibility This program is open to law students interested in advocating for and securing the civil rights of women and girls. Applicants must be interested in working full time at the CWLC under the supervision of a staff attorney. Men, persons with disabilities, and people of color are encouraged to apply.

Financial data The stipend is $4,000.

Duration 10 weeks during the summer.

Number awarded 1 each year.

Deadline January of each year.

[919]
HAYWOOD BURNS MEMORIAL FELLOWSHIPS FOR SOCIAL AND ECONOMIC JUSTICE

National Lawyers Guild
132 Nassau Street, Suite 922
New York, NY 10038
(212) 679-5100　　　　　　Fax: (212) 679-2811
E-mail: nlgno@nlg.org
Web: www.nlg.org

Purpose To provide law students and professionals (especially minorities and women) with summer work experience in progressive legal work.

Eligibility This program is open to law students, legal workers, and lawyers interested in working with civil rights and poverty law groups. Applicants must submit essays on their legal, political, educational, and work experience; their reasons for applying; what they expect to gain from the fellowship; the types of legal and political work they hope to do in the future; how this internship will help them in their goals; the kind of work structure with which they are most comfortable; and how they plan to share their summer experience and skills with others. Women and ethnic minorities are particularly encouraged to apply.

Financial data Interns receive a $2,000 stipend. Recipients are encouraged to seek other funding sources, including law school work-study and fellowship programs.

Duration 10 weeks during the summer; renewable the following year.

Additional information Recently, fellowships were available at the following organizations: the Asian Law Caucus (San Francisco, California), Cleveland Works, Inc. (Cleveland, Ohio), Camden Regional Legal Services, Farmworker Division (Bridgeton, New Jersey), Defender Association of Philadelphia (Philadelphia, Pennsylvania), East Bay Community Law Center (Berkeley, California), Florence Immigrant and Refugee Rights Project, Inc. (Florence, Arizona), Georgia Resource Center (Atlanta, Georgia), Harm Reduction Law Project (New York, New York), Lesbian and Gay Community Services Center (New York, New York), Massachusetts Correctional Legal Services (Boston, Massachusetts), Maurice and Jane Sugar Law Center for Economic and Social Justice (Detroit, Michigan), Meiklejohn Civil Liberties Institute (Berkeley, California), National Housing Law Project (Oakland, California), National Whistleblower Center (Washington, D.C.), Northwest Immigrant Rights Project (Seattle, Washington), Protection and Advocacy, Inc. (Oakland, California), and Southern Arizona People's Law Center (Tucson, Arizona).

Number awarded Approximately 25 each year.

Deadline January of each year.

[920]
HEADQUARTERS PARALEGAL INTERNSHIPS

National Wildlife Federation
Attn: Campus Ecology Coordinator
11100 Wildlife Center Drive
Reston, VA 20190-5362
(703) 438-6000　　　　　　E-mail: internopp@nwf.org
Web: www.nwf.org

Purpose To provide an opportunity for paralegal students (particularly minority students) to gain summer work experience at the headquarters of the National Wildlife Federation.

Eligibility This program is open to paralegal students who have completed enough classes to understand the basics of legal research, client confidentiality, and working with legal documents. Applicants must be able to use Word; proficiency in Excel is a plus. They must also be able to conduct basic legal research online or in a library and to write clear, comprehensive summaries of research in English. Applications are strongly encouraged from people of diverse backgrounds, women, people of color, people of all sexual identities, and people with disabilities.

Financial data The salary is $340 per week for full-time work. A needs-based relocation stipend may be available for those who have experience working within or advocating on behalf of communities traditionally underrepresented, including, but not limited to, Native American, Latino, African American, and Asian American communities.

Duration Summer months, from 20 to 40 hours per week.

Number awarded 1 or more each year.

[921]
HELLER EHRMAN DIVERSITY FELLOWSHIPS

Heller Ehrman White & McAuliffe LLP
Attn: Ethnic Diversity Task Force
275 Middlefield Road
Menlo Park, CA 94025-3506
(650) 324-7171   Fax: (650) 324-0638
E-mail: lkite@hewm.com
Web: www.hewm.com

Purpose To provide financial assistance and work experience to law students who can contribute to the diversity of the legal community.

Eligibility This program is open to first-year law students who show promise of contributing to the diversity of the law student and legal community. Applicants must possess a record of academic, employment, community, and/or other achievement indicating potential for success in law school and in the legal profession. Along with their application, they must submit a statement, up to 500 words, on their interest in the fellowship and how they would contribute to the diversity of the legal profession.

Financial data The program provides a stipend of $7,500 for law school and a paid summer associate clerkship.

Duration 1 year, including the summer.

Additional information This program was established in 2004. Clerkships are provided at offices of the sponsor in each of its 4 regions: Bay Area (San Francisco and Silicon Valley), east coast (New York and Washington, D.C.), northwest (Seattle), and southern California (Los Angeles and San Diego).

Number awarded 4 each year: 1 in each of the firm's regions.

Deadline January of each year.

[922]
HERBERT SCOVILLE JR. PEACE FELLOWSHIP

Herbert Scoville Jr. Peace Fellowship Program
Attn: Program Director
110 Maryland Avenue, N.E., Suite 409
Washington, DC 20002
(202) 543-4100   Fax: (202) 546-5142
E-mail: scoville@clw.org
Web: www.scoville.org

Purpose To provide an opportunity for college graduates (particularly minorities and women) to work with a peace, disarmament, or nuclear arms control organization in Washington, D.C.

Eligibility Applicants must be college graduates who can demonstrate excellent academic accomplishments and a strong interest in issues of peace and security. Prior experience with public-interest activism or advocacy is highly desirable. U.S. citizens receive preference, although foreign nationals residing in the United States are occasionally selected. Complete applications for the fellowship must include 2 letters of reference; a statement describing how the applicant first learned of the program; another essay discussing qualifications, interests, fellowship objectives, and career goals; an essay of up to 1,000 words taking a position on some contemporary, contentious issue; a full curriculum vitae; and transcripts. Preference is given to applicants who have not had substantial prior public interest or government experience in the Washington, D.C. area. Women and people of color are strongly encouraged to apply.

Financial data Fellows receive a stipend of $1,900 per month, health insurance, and travel expenses.

Duration 6 to 9 months, in spring or fall.

Additional information Fellows serve as special project assistants on the staff of 1 of the following 23 participating organizations: Alliance for Nuclear Accountability, Arms Control Association, British American Security Information Council, Center for Defense Information, Center for Nonproliferation Studies, Center for Strategic and Budgetary Assessments, Council for a Livable World Education Fund, Federation of American Scientists, Institute for Energy and Environmental Research, Institute for Science and International Security, Lawyers Alliance for World Security/Committee for National Security, National Security Archive, National Security News Service, Natural Resources Defense Council, Nuclear Control Institute, Peace Action, Physicians for Social Responsibility, Russian American Nuclear Security Advisory Council, Henry L. Stimson Center, 20/20 Vision National Project, Union of Concerned Scientists, Women's Action for New Directions, and World Federalist Association. The program does not provide grant money or scholarships for students.

Number awarded 2 to 4 each semester. To date, more than 100 fellows have been selected.

Deadline January of each year for the fall semester; October for the spring semester.

[923]
IBM PHD FELLOWSHIP PROGRAM

IBM Corporation
Attn: University Relations
1133 Westchester Avenue
White Plains, NY 10604
Toll-free: (800) IBM-4YOU   TTY: (800) IBM-3383
E-mail: phdfellow@us.ibm.com
Web: www-306.ibm.com

Purpose To provide financial assistance and work experience to students (particularly minorities and women) working on a Ph.D. in a research area of broad interest to IBM.

Eligibility Students nominated for this fellowship should be enrolled full time in an accredited U.S. or Canadian college or university and should have completed at least 1 year of graduate study in the following fields: business, chemistry, computer science, electrical engineering, materials sciences, mathematics, mechanical engineering, physics, or related disciplines. They should be planning a career in research. Nominations must be made by a faculty member and endorsed by the department head. IBM values diversity and encourages nominations of women, minorities, and others who contribute to that diversity. Selection is based on the applicants' potential for research excellence, the degree to which their technical interests align with those of IBM, and academic progress to date.

Financial data Fellows receive tuition, fees, and a stipend of $17,500 per year.

Duration 1 year; may be renewed up to 3 additional years, provided the recipient is renominated, interacts with IBM's technical community, and demonstrates continued progress and achievement.

Additional information Recipients are offered an internship at 1 of the IBM Research Division laboratories and are given an IBM ThinkPad.

Number awarded Varies each year.

Deadline December of each year.

[924]
ILLINOIS BROADCASTERS ASSOCIATION MINORITY INTERNSHIPS

Illinois Broadcasters Association
300 North Pershing Street, Suite B
Energy, IL 62933
(618) 942-2139   Fax: (618) 988-9056
E-mail: ilbrdcst@neondsl.com
Web: www.ilba.org

Purpose To provide funding to minority college students in Illinois who are majoring in broadcasting and interested in interning at a radio or television station in the state.

Eligibility This program is open to currently-enrolled minority students majoring in broadcasting at a college or university in Illinois. Applicants must be interested in a fall, spring, or summer internship at a radio or television station that is a member of the Illinois Broadcasters Association. Along with their application, they must submit 1) a 250-word essay on how they expect to benefit from a grant through this program, and 2) at least 2 letters of recommendation from a broadcasting faculty member or professional familiar with their career potential and 1 other letter. The president of the sponsoring organization selects those students nominated by their schools who have the best opportunity to

make it in the world of broadcasting and matches them with internship opportunities that would otherwise be unpaid.

Financial data This program provides a grant to pay the living expenses for the interns in the Illinois communities where they are assigned. The amount of the grant depends on the length of the internship.

Duration 16 weeks in the fall and spring terms or 12 weeks in the summer.

Number awarded 12 each year: 4 in each of the 3 terms.

[925]
INTERNSHIP IN EDUCATIONAL MEDIA

Metropolitan Museum of Art
Attn: Internship Programs
1000 Fifth Avenue
New York, NY 10028-0198
(212) 570-3710   Fax: (212) 570-3782
E-mail: mmainterns@metmuseum.org
Web: www.metmuseum.org

Purpose To provide work experience at the Metropolitan Museum of Art to recent college graduates (particularly minorities) interested in educational media.

Eligibility This internship is available to recent college graduates in museum studies, design, instructional technology, or related fields. Applicants must be interested in planning, creating, and producing publications for families, teachers, students, and the general museum public. Strong computer skills are required. Applicants of diverse backgrounds are encouraged to apply.

Financial data The honorarium is $22,000.

Duration 12 months, beginning in June.

Additional information The intern will acquire skills in preparing materials for print, electronic, and video production.

Number awarded 1 each year.

Deadline January of each year.

[926]
IWPR SUMMER INTERNSHIPS

Institute for Women's Policy Research
Attn: Internship Coordinator
1707 L Street, N.W., Suite 750
Washington, DC 20036
(202) 785-5100   Fax: (202) 833-4362
E-mail: iwpr@iwpr.org
Web: www.iwpr.org/employment_intern.html

Purpose To provide work experience opportunities during the summer at the Institute for Women's Policy Research (IWPR) to minority and other students interested in women's policy issues.

Eligibility This program is open to college students, graduate students, and recent graduates who are interested in economic justice for women. Applicants must have good computer skills, excellent writing and communication skills, and an interest in women's issues. Prior office experience is desirable and a background in the social sciences and/or statistics is preferred. People of all ethnic, cultural, economic, and sexual orientations are encouraged to apply.

Financial data Interns receive a stipend of $100 per week and a local transportation subsidy.

Duration At least 10 weeks; some flexibility can be arranged for starting and ending dates.

Additional information Interns work in Washington D.C. for IWPR, a nonprofit research organization that works primarily on issues related to equal opportunity and economic and social justice for women. They work in 1 of 3 departments: research (reviewing literature, collecting data and resources, gathering information from public officials and organization representatives, and preparing reports and summaries), communications and outreach (handling special requests for public information materials, planning special events, editing and proofreading, and assisting in the maintenance of web activities), or development (grant-writing, nonprofit fundraising, and direct mail programs). The institute gives special emphasis to issues of race, ethnicity, and class in its projects.

Number awarded Varies each year.

Deadline February of each year.

[927]
JACK AND LEWIS RUDIN INTERNSHIPS

Metropolitan Museum of Art
Attn: Internship Programs
1000 Fifth Avenue
New York, NY 10028-0198
(212) 570-3710   Fax: (212) 570-3782
E-mail: mmainterns@metmuseum.org
Web: www.metmuseum.org

Purpose To provide work experience at the Metropolitan Museum of Art during the summer to minority and other students interested in a museum career.

Eligibility This internship is available to college students who show a special interest in preparing for a museum career. Applicants of diverse backgrounds are especially encouraged to apply.

Financial data The honorarium is $3,000.

Duration 10 weeks, beginning in June.

Additional information Interns are assigned to departmental projects (curatorial, administration, or education) at the Metropolitan Museum of Art; other assignments may include giving gallery talks and working at the Visitor Information Center. The assignment is for 35 hours a week. The internships are funded by a grant from Jack and Susan Rudin.

Number awarded 3 each year.

Deadline January of each year.

[928]
JACKIE JOYNER-KERSEE MINORITY INTERNSHIP

Women's Sports Foundation
Attn: Award and Grant Programs Manager
Eisenhower Park
1899 Hempstead Turnpike, Suite 400
East Meadow, NY 11554-1000
(516) 542-4700   Toll-free: (800) 227-3988
Fax: (516) 542-4716   E-mail: wosport@aol.com
Web: www.womenssportsfoundation.org

Purpose To provide work experience at the Women's Sports Foundation to women of color interested in a sports-related career.

Eligibility This program is open to women of color who are undergraduate students, college graduates, graduate students, or women in career change. Applicants must be interested in working at the foundation offices on Long Island, New York. They must submit a personal statement that includes their sports background and current participation, issues and sports topics that interest them, their motivation for interning with the foundation, and what they hope to receive for themselves from the experience. An interview is required.

Financial data The salary is $1,000 per month.

Duration Sessions run from January through May, June through August, and September through December. Interns may complete 1, 2, or 3 sessions consecutively, but they must complete each session in its entirety.

Additional information Assignments are available in the athlete services, development, education, program management, public relations and communications, publications, special events, and web editorial departments. Interns may receive academic credit for their work.

Number awarded 2 or 3 each year.

Deadline Applications should be submitted no later than 120 days prior to the desired internship start date.

[929]
JAMES E. WEBB INTERNSHIPS

Smithsonian Institution
Attn: Office of Fellowships
Victor Building, Suite 9300, MRC 902
P.O. Box 37012
Washington, DC 20013-7012
(202) 275-0655   Fax: (202) 275-0489
E-mail: siofg@si.edu
Web: http:

Purpose To provide summer internship opportunities throughout the Smithsonian Institution to minority students in business or public administration.

Eligibility This program is open to U.S. minority undergraduate seniors and graduate students majoring in areas of business or public administration (finance, human resource management, accounting, or general business administration). Applicants must have a GPA of 3.0 or higher. They must seek placement in offices, museums, and research institutes within the Smithsonian Institution.

Financial data Interns receive a stipend of $450 per week and a travel allowance.

Duration 10 weeks, starting in June.

Number awarded Varies each year.

Deadline January of each year.

[930]
JAMES H. DUNN, JR. MEMORIAL FELLOWSHIP PROGRAM

Office of the Governor
Attn: Department of Central Management Services
503 William G. Stratton Building
Springfield, IL 62706
(217) 524-1381   Fax: (217) 785-7702
TDD: (217) 785-3979
Web: www.illinois.gov/gov/intopportunities.cfm

Purpose To provide recent college graduates (particularly minorities, women, and persons with disabilities) with work experience in the Illinois Governor's office.

Eligibility Applicants may be residents of any state who have completed a bachelor's degree and are interested in working in the Illinois Governor's office or in various agencies under the Governor's jurisdiction. They may have majored in any field, but they must be able to demonstrate a substantial commitment to excellence as evidenced by academic honors, leadership ability, extracurricular activities, and involvement in community or public service. Along with their application, they must submit 1) a 500-word personal statement on the qualities or attributes they will bring to the program, their career goals or plans, how their selection for this program would assist them in achieving those goals, and what they expect to gain from the program; and 2) a 1,000-word essay in which they identify and analyze a public issue that they feel has great impact on state government. A particular goal of the program is to achieve affirmative action through the nomination of qualified minorities, women, and persons with disabilities.

Financial data The stipend is $27,900 per year.

Duration 1 year, beginning in August.

Additional information Assignments are in Springfield and, to a limited extent, in Chicago.

Number awarded Varies each year.

Deadline January of each year.

[931]
JEANNE SPURLOCK MINORITY MEDICAL STUDENT CLINICAL FELLOWSHIP IN CHILD AND ADOLESCENT PSYCHIATRY

American Academy of Child and Adolescent Psychiatry
Attn: Department of Research, Training, and Education
3615 Wisconsin Avenue, N.W.
Washington, DC 20016-3007
(202) 966-7300, ext. 105   Fax: (202) 966-2891
E-mail: emagee@aacap.org
Web: www.aacap.org/research/Spurlck2.htm

Purpose To provide funding to minority medical students who are interested in working with a child and adolescent psychiatrist during the summer.

Eligibility This program is open to African American, Asian American, Native American, Alaska Native, Mexican American, Hispanic, and Pacific Islander students in accredited U.S. medical schools. Applicants must present a plan for a clinical training experience that involves significant contact between the student and a mentor. The plan should include program planning discussions, instruction in treatment planning and implementation, regular meetings with the mentor and other treatment providers, and assigned readings. Clinical assignments may include

responsibility for part of the observation or evaluation, conducting interviews or tests, using rating scales, and psychological or cognitive testing of patients. The training plan should also include discussion of ethical issues in treatment.

Financial data The stipend is $2,500. Fellows also receive reimbursement of travel expenses to attend the annual meeting of the American Academy of Child and Adolescent Psychiatry.

Duration 12 weeks during the summer.

Additional information Upon completion of the training program, the student is required to submit a brief paper summarizing the clinical experience. The fellowship pays expenses for the fellow to attend the academy's annual meeting and present this paper. This program is supported by the Center for Mental Health Services of the Substance Abuse and Mental Health Services Administration.

Number awarded Up to 14 each year.

Deadline March of each year.

[932]
JEANNE SPURLOCK RESEARCH FELLOWSHIP IN DRUG ABUSE AND ADDICTION FOR MINORITY MEDICAL STUDENTS

American Academy of Child and Adolescent Psychiatry
Attn: Department of Research, Training, and Education
3615 Wisconsin Avenue, N.W.
Washington, DC 20016-3007
(202) 966-7300, ext. 105   Fax: (202) 966-2891
E-mail: emagee@aacap.org
Web: www.aacap.org/research/Spurlck1.htm

Purpose To provide funding to minority medical students who are interested in working with a child and adolescent psychiatrist researcher-mentor during the summer on drug abuse and addiction.

Eligibility This program is open to African American, Asian American, Native American, Alaska Native, Mexican American, Hispanic, and Pacific Islander students in accredited U.S. medical schools. Applicants must present a plan for a program of research training in drug abuse and addiction that involves significant contact with a mentor who is an experienced child and adolescent psychiatrist researcher. The plan should include program planning discussions; instruction in research planning and implementation; regular meetings with the mentor, laboratory director, and the research group; and assigned readings. Research assignments may include responsibility for part of the observation or evaluation, developing specific aspects of the research mechanisms, conducting interviews or tests, using rating scales, and psychological or cognitive testing of subjects. The training plan also should include discussion of ethical issues in research, including protocol development, informed consent, collection and storage of raw data, safeguarding data, bias in analyzing data, plagiarism, protection of patients, ethical treatment of animals. etc.

Financial data The stipend is $2,500. Fellows also receive reimbursement of travel expenses to attend the annual meeting of the American Academy of Child and Adolescent Psychiatry.

Duration 12 weeks during the summer.

Additional information Upon completion of the training program, the student is required to submit a brief paper summarizing the research experience. The fellowship pays expenses for the fellow to attend the academy's annual meeting and present this paper. This program is co-sponsored by the National Institute on Drug Abuse.

Number awarded Up to 5 each year.

Deadline March of each year.

[933]
JERE W. THOMPSON, JR. SCHOLARSHIP

Dallas Foundation
Attn: Scholarship Administrator
900 Jackson Street, Suite 150
Dallas, TX 75202
(214) 741-9898   Fax: (214) 741-9848
E-mail: cmcnally@dallasfoundation.org
Web: www.dallasfoundation.org

Purpose To provide financial assistance and work experience to disadvantaged students who are majoring in civil engineering at public universities in Texas.

Eligibility This program is open to disadvantaged students in civil engineering or construction engineering at public colleges and universities in Texas; special consideration is given to residents of counties in the service area of the North Texas Tollway Authority: Collin, Dallas, Denton, or Tarrant. At the time of application, students must be full-time sophomores. Finalists may be interviewed. Financial need is considered in the selection process.

Financial data Stipends range up to $2,000 per semester, beginning in the recipient's junior year; the maximum award is $8,000 over 4 semesters.

Duration 1 semester; may be renewed for up to 3 additional semesters, provided the recipient remains a full-time student, maintains at least a 2.5 GPA, and submits a grade report within 45 days after the end of each semester.

Additional information Recipients of the Thompson Scholarship are given an opportunity for a paid internship in the Dallas area during the summer between their junior and senior year. Assignments are available at the scholarship's sponsors: North Texas Tollway Authority, Brown and Root Services, Carter & Burgess, Inc., and HNTB Companies.

Number awarded 1 each year.

Deadline March of each year.

[934]
JOHN MCLENDON MEMORIAL MINORITY POSTGRADUATE SCHOLARSHIP AWARD

National Association of Collegiate Directors of Athletics
Attn: NACDA Foundation
24651 Detroit Road
P.O. Box 16428
Cleveland, OH 44116
(440) 892-4000   Fax: (440) 892-4007
E-mail: bhorning@nacda.com
Web: nacda.collegesports.com

Purpose To provide financial assistance and work experience to minority college seniors who are interested in working on a graduate degree in athletics administration.

Eligibility This program is open to minority college students who are seniors, are attending school on a full-time basis, have a GPA of 3.0 or higher, intend to attend graduate school to earn a degree in athletics administration, and are involved on the college or community level. Candidates are not required to be student athletes. Current graduate students are not eligible.

Financial data The stipend is $10,000. In addition, 1 recipient each year is offered the opportunity to serve a 9-month internship in the office of the National Association of Collegiate Directors of Athletics (NACDA).

Duration 1 year.

Additional information Recipients must maintain full-time status during the senior year to retain their eligibility. They must attend NACDA-member institutions.

Number awarded 5 each year.

Deadline January of each year.

[935]
JUDGE ROBERT M. TAKASUGI FELLOWSHIPS FOR PUBLIC INTEREST LAW

National Asian Pacific American Bar Association
Attn: NAPABA Law Foundation
910 17th Street, N.W., Suite 315
Washington, DC 20006
(202) 775-9555   Fax: (202) 775-9333
E-mail: foundation@napaba.org
Web: www.napaba.org

Purpose To provide an opportunity for law students in California to gain work experience in public interest law while serving the Asian Pacific American community.

Eligibility This program is open to students at accredited law schools in California. Applicants must demonstrate leadership potential to serve the Asian Pacific American community upon graduation. They must submit a 500-word essay on the most significant experiences in their background that have shaped and demonstrated their commitment to serving the needs of Asian Pacific Americans and how they intend to serve the needs of the Asian Pacific American community in their future legal career. Selection is based on demonstrated commitment to and interest in pro bono and/or public interest legal work, financial need, leadership potential, maturity and responsibility, and commitment to serving the needs of the Asian Pacific American community.

Financial data The stipend is $5,000.

Duration Summer months.

Number awarded 2 each year: 1 for northern California and 1 for southern California.

Deadline September of each year.

[936]
JUDITH L. WEIDMAN RACIAL ETHNIC MINORITY FELLOWSHIP

United Methodist Communications
Attn: Communications Resourcing Team
810 12th Avenue South
P.O. Box 320
Nashville, TN 37202-0320
(615) 742-5481   Toll-free: (888) CRT-4UMC
Fax: (615) 742-5485   E-mail: REM@umcom.org
Web: crt.umc.org/rem

Purpose To provide work experience to Methodists who

are members of minority groups and interested in a communications career.

Eligibility This program is open to United Methodists of racial ethnic minority heritage who are interested in preparing for a career in communications with the United Methodist Church. Applicants must be recent college or seminary graduates who have broad communications training, including work in journalism, mass communications, marketing, public relations, and electronic media. They must be able to understand and speak English proficiently and to relocate for a year. Selection is based on Christian commitment and involvement in the life of the United Methodist Church; achievement as revealed by transcripts, GPA, letters of reference, and work samples; study, experience, and evidence of talent in the field of communications; clarity of purpose and goals for the future; desire to learn how to be a successful United Methodist conference communicator; and potential leadership ability as a professional religion communicators for the United Methodist Church.

Financial data The stipend is $30,000 per year. Benefits and expenses for moving and professional travel are also provided.

Duration 1 year, starting in July.

Additional information Recipients are assigned to 1 of the 65 United Methodist Annual Conferences, the headquarters of local churches within a geographic area. At the Annual Conference, the fellow will be assigned an experienced communicator as a mentor and will work closely with that mentor and with United Methodist Communications in Nashville, Tennessee. Following the successful completion of the fellowship, United Methodist Communications and the participating Annual Conference will assist in a search for permanent employment within the United Methodist Church but cannot guarantee a position.

Number awarded 1 each year.

Deadline March of each year.

[937]
KAISER MEDIA INTERNSHIPS IN URBAN HEALTH REPORTING

Henry J. Kaiser Family Foundation
2400 Sand Hill Road
Menlo Park, CA 94025
(650) 234-9220   Fax: (650) 854-4800
E-mail: pduckham@kff.org
Web: www.kff.org/about/mediafellowships.cfm

Purpose To provide summer work experience to minority college or graduate students who want to specialize in urban public health issues and health reporting.

Eligibility Minority college or graduate students studying journalism or a related field may apply for this internship program if their career goal is to be a reporter on urban health matters. Strong writing skills and previous newsroom reporting experience are essential. Reporting experience and/or academic expertise in health, medical, or science-related issues (or urban affairs) is valuable but not required. Applicants must be U.S. citizens or permanent residents.

Financial data This program provides a stipend of at least $500 per week and all travel expenses.

Duration 12 weeks in the summer.

Additional information This program, sponsored by the Henry J. Kaiser Family Foundation, began in 1994. Each participating news organization selects its own intern; recently, those were the *Atlanta Journal-Constitution, Boston Globe, Los Angeles Times, Detroit Free Press, Mercury News* of San Jose, *The Oregonian* of Portland, *Plain Dealer* of Cleveland, *Sun-Sentinel* of Fort Lauderdale, *Milwaukee Journal Sentinel, Orlando Sentinel, Washington Post,* KXAS/5-TV of Dallas-Fort Worth, WAGA/5-TV of Atlanta, and KTVU/2-TV of San Francisco-Oakland. The program begins with a 1-week orientation program in Washington, D.C. at the National Press Foundation in June and concludes with a 1-week wrap-up in Boston at the end of the summer. In between, interns report and write urban health stories at their host papers or television stations.

Number awarded 14 each year: 1 at each participating news organization.

Deadline Applicants to print organizations should submit their applications prior to the end of November; applicants to broadcast organizations should submit their applications in early January.

[938]
KATU THOMAS R. DARGAN MINORITY SCHOLARSHIP

KATU-TV
Attn: Human Resources
2153 N.E. Sandy Boulevard
P.O. Box 2
Portland, OR 97207-0002
(503) 231-4222
Web: www.katu.com/insidekatu/scholarship.asp

Purpose To provide financial assistance and work experience to minority students from Oregon and Washington who are studying broadcasting or communications in college.

Eligibility This program is open to Native Americans, African Americans, Hispanic Americans, or Asian Americans who are U.S. citizens, currently enrolled in the first, second, or third year at a 4-year college or university or an accredited community college in Oregon or Washington, or, if a resident of Oregon or Washington, at a school in any state. Applicants must be majoring in broadcasting or communications and have a GPA of 3.0 or higher. Community college students must be enrolled in a broadcast curriculum that is transferable to a 4-year accredited university. Finalists will be interviewed. Selection is based on financial need, academic achievement, and an essay on personal and professional goals.

Financial data The stipend is $4,000. Funds are sent directly to the recipient's school.

Duration 1 year; recipients may reapply if they have maintained a GPA of 3.0 or higher.

Additional information Winners are also eligible for a paid internship in selected departments at Fisher Broadcasting/KATU in Portland, Oregon.

Number awarded 1 each year.

Deadline April of each year.

[939]
KNIGHT RIDDER MINORITY SCHOLARS PROGRAM

Knight Ridder, Inc.
Attn: Office of Diversity
50 West San Fernando Street, Suite 1200
San Jose, CA 95113
(408) 938-7734   Fax: (408) 938-7755
Web: www.knightridderscholars.com

Purpose To provide financial assistance and work experience to minority high school seniors who are interested in going to college to prepare for a career in journalism.

Eligibility This program is open to minority seniors graduating from high schools in areas served by Knight Ridder. Applicants must be interested in attending college to prepare for a career in the newspaper industry. They first apply to their local Knight Ridder newspaper and compete for local scholarships; selected winners are then nominated for this award. Both "news" and "business" students are eligible.

Financial data The stipend is $5,000 per year for the freshman and sophomore year and $15,000 per year for the junior and senior year.

Duration 1 year; may be renewed for up to 3 additional years, if the recipient maintains a GPA of 3.0 or higher and satisfactory performance on internships.

Additional information Recipients are offered an internship opportunity at a Knight Ridder newspaper during the summer. News scholars work in the newsroom, writing and editing stories, taking photographs, crafting illustrations, and designing news pages. Business scholars complete internships in advertising, marketing, information technology, circulation, and other areas essential to the industry. At the end of the sophomore year, recipients must agree to work at a Knight Ridder newspaper for 1 year after graduation.

Number awarded Up to 5 each year: 2 for news, 2 for business, and 1 for either.

[940]
KNIGHT RIDDER MINORITY SPECIALTY DEVELOPMENT PROGRAM

Knight Ridder, Inc.
Attn: Office of Diversity
50 West San Fernando Street, Suite 1200
San Jose, CA 95113
(408) 938-7734   Fax: (408) 938-7755
Web: www.kri.com/working/interns.html

Purpose To offer a training program to young minority journalists who are interested in concentrating in a specialty beat or department.

Eligibility Minorities who recently graduated from college with a major in journalism are eligible to apply for internships at selected Knight Ridder newspapers if they are interested in working in an area of the newspaper industry in which minorities are underrepresented, such as high-profile beat assignments, computer-assisted reporting, photojournalism, and graphic arts.

Financial data Salaries are determined by the scale of the participating newspapers.

Duration 1 year.

Additional information Specialty interns are selected by and work at the following Knight Ridder newspapers: the

Detroit Free Press, the *Philadelphia Inquirer,* or the *San Jose Mercury News.* Interns are not guaranteed employment following completion of this program.

Number awarded 1 or more each year.

Deadline December of each year.

[941]
KNIGHT RIDDER ROTATING INTERN PROGRAM

Knight Ridder, Inc.
Attn: Office of Diversity
50 West San Fernando Street, Suite 1200
San Jose, CA 95113
(408) 938-7734   Fax: (408) 938-7755
Web: www.kri.com/working/interns.html

Purpose To offer a training program to young minority journalists who are interested in working at 3 or 4 Knight Ridder newspapers.

Eligibility Minorities who recently graduated from college with a major in journalism are eligible to apply if they are interested in working in a variety of newsrooms, news assignments, and markets.

Financial data Salaries are determined by the scale of the participating newspapers.

Duration 1 year.

Additional information Rotating interns are selected by and work at the following Knight Ridder newspapers: the *News-Democrat* in Belleville, Illinois; the *Contra Costa Times* in Walnut Creek, California; the *Fort Worth Star-Telegram;* or the *Kansas City Star.* Information is available from each of those newspapers and from Reginald Stuart, Coordinator, Knight Ridder Rotating Internship Program, 13102 Tamarack Road, Silver Spring, MD 20904, (301) 879-0085, E-mail: rstuart5@juno.com. Interns are not guaranteed employment following completion of this program.

Number awarded 1 or more each year.

Deadline December of each year.

[942]
LANDMARK SCHOLARS PROGRAM

Landmark Publishing Group
c/o Rich Martin, Managing Editor
The Roanoke Times
201 West Campbell Avenue
Roanoke, VA 24011
(540) 981-3211   Toll-free: (800) 346-1234
E-mail: rich.martin@roanoke.com
Web: www.landmarkcommunications.com

Purpose To provide work experience and financial aid to minority undergraduates who are interested in preparing for a career in journalism.

Eligibility This program is open to minority college sophomores, preferably those with ties to the mid-Atlantic states (Delaware, Maryland, North Carolina, South Carolina, Virginia, and Washington, D.C.). Applicants must be full-time students with a GPA of 2.5 or higher. They must be interested in preparing for a career in print journalism and in an internship as a reporter, photographer, graphic artist, sports writer, copy editor, or page designer.

Financial data The stipend is $5,000 per year. During the summers following their sophomore and junior years, recipients are provided with paid internships. Following graduation, they are offered a 1-year internship with full benefits and the possibility of continued employment.

Duration 2 years (the junior and senior years of college).

Additional information The internships are offered at the *News & Record* in Greensboro, North Carolina, the *Virginian-Pilot* in Norfolk, Virginia, or the *Roanoke Times* in Roanoke, Virginia.

Number awarded 1 or more each year.

Deadline November of each year.

[943]
LEIGH COOK FELLOWSHIP

New Jersey Department of Health and Senior Services
Attn: Office of Minority and Multicultural Health
P.O. Box 360 Suite 501
Trenton, NJ 08625-0360
(609) 292-6962   E-mail: omh@doh.state.nj.us
Web: www.state.nj.us

Purpose To provide financial support for a summer research internship to law, public health, and medical students (particularly minority students) in New Jersey.

Eligibility This program is open to students in medical science, law, or master's of public health programs who are residents of New Jersey attending school in the state or elsewhere. Applicants must be interested in working on a supervised project at the New Jersey Department of Health and Senior Services in Trenton in the areas of minority health, senior services, HIV/AIDS, substance abuse, health insurance, environmental or occupational health, public health, or family health. Minority students are encouraged to apply. Selection is based on commitment to minority and/or public health, as demonstrated by community-based service, volunteer work, public health service advocacy, coalition building, and involvement in student organizations that address minority and public health issues.

Financial data The stipend is $5,000.

Duration 10 to 12 weeks during the summer.

Number awarded 1 each year.

Deadline April of each year.

[944]
LENA CHANG INTERNSHIPS

Nuclear Age Peace Foundation
1187 Coast Village Road, Suite 1
PMB 121
Santa Barbara, CA 93108-2794
(805) 965-3443   Fax: (805) 568-0466
E-mail: youth@napf.org
Web: www.wagingpeace.org

Purpose To provide work experience at the Nuclear Age Peace Foundation in Santa Barbara, California to ethnic minority undergraduate and graduate students.

Eligibility This program is open to ethnic minority students currently enrolled in undergraduate or graduate course work who can demonstrate financial need and academic excellence. Students from the Santa Barbara (California) area may apply for academic year internships. Summer internships are open to students from anywhere in the United States. Applicants must submit their transcript; 2 letters of recommendation; a letter of intent describing their work experience, educational background, field of study,

plans after graduation, and preference for fall, spring, or summer internship; and a copy of their resume or curriculum vitae.

Financial data The stipend is $2,500 for summer; interns are responsible for their own transportation and housing costs. Academic year interns receive $1,250.

Duration The summer internship is 10 weeks of full-time work. Academic year interns are expected to work at least 200 hours.

Number awarded 3 each year: 1 for the summer and 2 for the academic year.

Deadline March of each year for the summer internship; July of each year for fall; December of each year for winter/spring.

[945]
LIBRARY OF CONGRESS JUNIOR FELLOWS PROGRAM

Library of Congress
Library Services
Attn: Junior Fellows Program Coordinator
101 Independence Avenue, S.E., Room LM-642
Washington, DC 20540-4600
(202) 707-5330   Fax: (202) 707-6269
E-mail: jrfell@loc.gov
Web: www.loc.gov/rr/jrfell

Purpose To provide summer work experience at the Library of Congress (LC) to upper-division and graduate students, particularly minorities, women, and students with disabilities.

Eligibility This program at the LC is open to applicants with subject expertise in the following areas: American history and literature; cataloging; history of graphic arts, architecture, design, and engineering; history of photography; film, television and radio; sound recordings; music; rare books and book arts; librarianship; and preservation. Applicants must 1) be juniors or seniors at an accredited college or university, 2) be at the graduate school level, or 3) have completed their degree in the past year. Applications from women, minorities, and persons with disabilities are particularly encouraged. Applications must include the following materials: cover letter, Application for Federal Employment (SF 171) or a resume, letter of recommendation, and official transcript. Telephone interviews are conducted with the most promising applicants.

Financial data Fellows are paid a taxable stipend of $300 per week.

Duration 3 months, beginning in either May or June. Fellows work a 40-hour week.

Additional information Fellows work with primary source materials and assist selected divisions at the Library of Congress in the organization and documentation of archival collections, production of finding aids and bibliographic records, preparation of materials for preservation and service, completion of bibliographical research, and digitization of the Library's historical collections.

Number awarded Varies each year; recently, 6 of these internships were awarded.

Deadline April of each year.

[946]
LIBRARY OF CONGRESS SUMMER INTERNSHIPS

Library of Congress
Library Services
Attn: Affirmative Action and Special Programs Office
101 Independence Avenue, S.E., Room LM-612
Washington, DC 20540-4600
(202) 707-5479   Fax: (202) 707-6269
E-mail: letu@loc.gov
Web: www.loc.gov

Purpose To provide summer work experience at the Library of Congress (LC) to undergraduate and graduate students, particularly minorities, women, and students with disabilities.

Eligibility This program is open to U.S. citizens enrolled at an accredited college, university, or Tribal College at the undergraduate or graduate level. Relevant areas of study include accounting, anthropology, the arts, education, foreign languages, history, information technology, library science, management, photography, and sociology. Applicants must be interested in working during the summer at the Library of Congress. Women, minorities, and persons with disabilities are particularly encouraged to apply.

Financial data The stipend is $1,500.

Duration 10 weeks, beginning in June. Fellows work a 40-hour week.

Additional information Interns work on a number of high-priority projects of the Library of Congress, including digital preservation, audiovisual preservation, and the impact of technology on copyright protection.

Number awarded Varies each year.

Deadline May of each year.

[947]
LIFCHEZ/STRONACH CURATORIAL INTERNSHIPS

Metropolitan Museum of Art
Attn: Internship Programs
1000 Fifth Avenue
New York, NY 10028-0198
(212) 570-3710   Fax: (212) 570-3782
E-mail: mmainterns@metmuseum.org
Web: www.metmuseum.org

Purpose To provide museum work experience at the Metropolitan Museum of Art to disadvantaged graduate students and recent graduates who wish to prepare for a career in art history.

Eligibility This program is open to recent college graduates and students enrolled in master's degree programs in art history. Applicants should come from a background of financial need or other disadvantage that will jeopardize their preparing for a career in art history without the support.

Financial data The honorarium is $15,000.

Duration 9 months, beginning in September.

Additional information Interns are assigned to 1 or more of the Metropolitan Museum of Art's departments, where they work on projects that match their academic background, professional skills, and career goals. This program was reestablished in 1998 with funding from Raymond Lifchez and Judith L. Stronach.

Number awarded 3 each year.

Deadline January of each year.

[948]
LINDA YU BROADCAST SCHOLARSHIP

Asian American Journalists Association-Chicago
    Chapter
P.O. Box 577639
Chicago, IL 60657-9997
E-mail: chiaaja@aol.com
Web: chapters.aaja.org/Chicago/internships.htm

Purpose To provide funding to members of the Asian American Journalists Association (AAJA) who are interested in a summer internship at a Chicago television station.

Eligibility This program is open to AAJA members who are college students or recent graduates. Applicants must be interested in a broadcast news internship at a Chicago television station. They must submit a statement on why they are interested in broadcast journalism and how they expect this internship to help them reach their career goals, a resume, a VHS tape of broadcast work or writing samples, and college transcripts.

Financial data The stipend is $2,500.

Duration 10 to 12 weeks, during the summer.

Additional information Information is also available from Nancy Loo, FOX Chicago, 205 North Michigan Avenue, Chicago, IL 60601.

Number awarded 1 each year.

Deadline January of each year.

[949]
LOS ANGELES CHAPTER OF AAJA INTERNSHIP STIPENDS

Asian American Journalists Association-Los Angeles
    Chapter
231 East Third Street
Los Angeles, CA 90013-1494
Web: www.aaja-la.org

Purpose To provide supplemental funding to members of the Los Angeles chapter of the Asian American Journalists Association (AAJA) who are interested in taking unpaid or low-paying internships.

Eligibility This program is open to students, recent graduates, and beginning professionals who are members of the chapter. Applicants must have already arranged an internship in print, broadcast, or online media journalism. They must submit 1) a cover letter that discusses their involvement with and service to the chapter or AAJA, their interest in and activities involving journalism, and their financial need; 2) a resume; 3) writing samples; and 4) a letter from the media outlet offering the internship that verifies that the internship is unpaid or provides only nominal pay. First-time interns are given priority over applicants who have had previous internships. Selection is based on financial need and the applicant's record of service to and involvement with the chapter or AAJA.

Financial data Grants are $500.

Duration Grants cover 1 trimester (summer, fall, or spring).

Additional information Information is also available from Rachanee Srisavasdi, Orange County Register, 625

Grand Avenue, Santa Ana, CA 92701, E-mail: rsrisavas-di@ocregister.com.

Number awarded 6 each year: 2 each trimester.

Deadline March of each year for summer internships; July of each year for fall internships; November of each year for spring internships.

[950]
MAB FOUNDATION MINORITY INTERNSHIP PROGRAM

Michigan Association of Broadcasters
Attn: MAB Foundation
819 North Washington Avenue
Lansing, MI 48906
(517) 484-7444   Toll-free: (800) YOUR-MAB
Fax: (517) 484-5810   E-mail: mabf@michmab.com
Web: www.michmab.com

Purpose To provide an opportunity for minority students at colleges and universities in Michigan to gain work experience at radio and television stations that are members of the Michigan Association of Broadcasters (MAB).

Eligibility This program is open to minority students enrolled at a Michigan college, university, or vocational school and working on a degree in broadcasting, telecommunications, media studies, engineering, or a related field. Applicants must be interested in an internship at a MAB station for which they will receive academic credit. They must be recommended by their school's faculty.

Financial data The stipend is $1,000.

Number awarded Varies each year.

[951]
MARIAM K. CHAMBERLAIN FELLOWSHIPS

Institute for Women's Policy Research
Attn: Internship Coordinator
1707 L Street, N.W., Suite 750
Washington, DC 20036
(202) 785-5100   Fax: (202) 833-4362
E-mail: iwpr@iwpr.org
Web: www.iwpr.org/employment_fellow.html

Purpose To provide work experience at the Institute for Women's Policy Research (IWPR) to college graduates and graduate students (especially students or color) who are interested in economic justice for women.

Eligibility Applicants for this internship should have at least a bachelor's degree in social science, statistics, or women's studies. Graduate work is desirable but not required. They should have strong quantitative and library research skills and knowledge of women's issues. Familiarity with Microsoft Word and Excel is required; knowledge of STATA, SPSS, SAS, and graphics software is a plus. People of color are especially encouraged to apply.

Financial data The stipend is $1,600 per month and includes health insurance and a public transportation stipend.

Duration 9 months, beginning in September.

Additional information The institute is a nonprofit, scientific research organization that works primarily on issues related to equal opportunity and economic and social justice for women. Recent research topics for the fellow included women's wages, political participation, access to

health care, and other indicators of the status of women on a state-by-state basis; the work and welfare experiences of low-income women on the state and national levels; reforming such income support policies for women as unemployment insurance, family leave, and Social Security; strategies for improving child care access, affordability, and quality; and older women's economic issues.

Number awarded 1 each year.

Deadline February of each year.

[952]
METPRO/EDITING PROGRAM

Newsday
Attn: METPRO/Editing Director
235 Pinelawn Road
Melville, NY 11747-4250
(631) 843-2367   Toll-free: (888) 717-9817, ext. 2367
Fax: (631) 843-4719   E-mail: jobs@newsday.com
Web: www.metpronews.com

Purpose To provide an opportunity for minorities to obtain training for editing positions on daily metropolitan newspapers.

Eligibility Applicants for the Minority Editorial Training Program (METPRO) should be minority (African American, Asian American, Hispanic, American Indian) college graduates with excellent writing skills and an interest in a newspaper career. Selection is based on academic record and potential. Previous professional editing experience is not required.

Financial data Trainees receive a weekly stipend, a monthly housing allowance, and medical benefits for the first year. During the second year, trainees receive compensation and benefits applicable at the newspaper where they are working.

Duration 2 years.

Additional information Participants in this program receive intensive training in editing at *Newsday* during the first year, including a 2-week orientation, 3 weeks of reporting in Queens and on Long Island, 10 weeks of full-time classroom instruction, and 31 weeks of work as editors on *Newsday* copy desks. During the second year, they work for 1 of the 11 Tribune Company newspapers (in Allentown, Pennsylvania; Baltimore, Maryland; Chicago, Illinois; Fort Lauderdale, Florida; Greenwich, Connecticut; Hartford, Connecticut; Los Angeles, California; Melville, New York; Newport News, Virginia; Orlando, Florida; or Stamford, Connecticut).

Number awarded Up to 10 each year.

Deadline January of each year.

[953]
METROPOLITAN MUSEUM OF ART INTERNSHIPS FOR COLLEGE STUDENTS

Metropolitan Museum of Art
Attn: Internship Programs
1000 Fifth Avenue
New York, NY 10028-0198
(212) 570-3710　　　Fax: (212) 570-3782
E-mail: mmainterns@metmuseum.org
Web: www.metmuseum.org

Purpose To provide summer work experience at the Metropolitan Museum of Art to college students, particularly students with diverse backgrounds.

Eligibility These internships are available to college juniors, seniors, and recent graduates who have not yet entered graduate school. Applicants should have a broad background in art history. Freshmen and sophomores are not eligible. Applicants of diverse backgrounds are encouraged to apply.

Financial data The honorarium is $3,000.

Duration 10 weeks, beginning in June.

Additional information Interns are assigned to departmental projects (curatorial, administration, or education) at the Metropolitan Museum of Art; other assignments may include giving gallery talks and working at the Visitor Information Center. The assignment is for 35 hours a week. The internships are funded in part by the Lebensfeld Foundation, the Billy Rose Foundation, the Solow Art and Architecture Foundation, the Ittleson Foundation, and the Tianaderrah Foundation.

Number awarded 14 each year.

Deadline January of each year.

[954]
METROPOLITAN MUSEUM OF ART INTERNSHIPS FOR GRADUATE STUDENTS

Metropolitan Museum of Art
Attn: Internship Programs
1000 Fifth Avenue
New York, NY 10028-0198
(212) 570-3710　　　Fax: (212) 570-3782
E-mail: mmainterns@metmuseum.org
Web: www.metmuseum.org

Purpose To provide summer work experience at the Metropolitan Museum of Art to graduate students, particularly students with diverse backgrounds.

Eligibility These internships are available to individuals who have completed at least 1 year of graduate work in art history or in an allied field. Applicants of diverse backgrounds are encouraged to apply.

Financial data The honorarium is $3,250.

Duration 10 weeks, beginning in June.

Additional information Interns are assigned to research or writing or to a special exhibition at the Metropolitan Museum of Art, depending upon the needs of the department. The assignment is for 35 hours a week. The internships are funded in part by the Lebensfeld Foundation, the Billy Rose Foundation, the Solow Art and Architecture Foundation, the Ittleson Foundation, and the Tianaderrah Foundation.

Number awarded 10 each year.

Deadline January of each year.

[955]
METROPOLITAN MUSEUM OF ART 6-MONTH INTERNSHIPS

Metropolitan Museum of Art
Attn: Internship Programs
1000 Fifth Avenue
New York, NY 10028-0198
(212) 570-3710　　　Fax: (212) 570-3782
E-mail: mmainterns@metmuseum.org
Web: www.metmuseum.org

Purpose To provide work experience at the Metropolitan Museum of Art to candidates who can promote diversity in the profession.

Eligibility This program is open to graduating college seniors, recent graduates, and graduate students in art history or related fields. Selection is based on an essay in which applicants indicate how their selection will promote greater diversity in the national pool of future museum professionals and describe their financial need.

Financial data The stipend is $10,000.

Duration 6 months, beginning in June.

Additional information Interns work at the Metropolitan Museum for 35 hours a week.

Number awarded 2 each year.

Deadline January of each year.

[956]
MIAMI UNIVERSITY MINORITY RESIDENT LIBRARIAN

Miami University
University Libraries
Attn: Dean and University Librarian
King Library, Room 271
Oxford, OH 45056-1878
(513) 529-2800　　　E-mail: hendribn@lib.muohio.edu
Web: www.lib.muohio.edu

Purpose To provide a residency for minority librarians at Miami University.

Eligibility This program is open to minorities who graduated from library school within the past 2 years and are interested in preparing for a career in academic librarianship. Applicants must have a master's degree from a library school accredited by the American Library Association. They should have a familiarity with and knowledge of advancing technologies, an ability to work collegially in a team environment, possess a knowledge of and interest in academic libraries, and demonstrate the ability to establish and maintain good working relationships with faculty, students, and other library users as well as library staff.

Financial data The stipend is $33,500. Benefits include the standard insurance package.

Duration 1 year; may be renewed for 1 additional year.

Additional information Interns are exposed to all areas of the university library's operations, including public, technical, and administrative services. Actual assignments are based on the interests of the intern and the needs of the library.

Number awarded 1 each year.

Deadline June of each year.

[957]
MIKE M. MASAOKA CONGRESSIONAL FELLOW PROGRAM

Japanese American Citizens League
Attn: Washington Office
1001 Connecticut Avenue, N.W., Suite 730
Washington, DC 20036
(202) 223-1240   E-mail: dc@jacl.org
Web: www.jacl.org/masaoka.html

Purpose To provide an opportunity for students involved in the Japanese American community to gain work experience on the staff of a member of Congress.

Eligibility This program is open to U.S. citizens who are college seniors or students in a graduate or professional program. Applicants must be interested in working in Washington on the staff of a member of Congress. Preference is given to those having a demonstrated commitment to Asian American issues, particularly those affecting the Japanese American community. Selection criteria include the applicant's communication skills, both written and verbal, and interest in a career in public service.

Financial data The stipend is $8,500.

Duration 3 and a half months, during either the fall or spring semester.

Number awarded 1 each year.

Deadline March of each year.

[958]
MILDRED COLODNY SCHOLARSHIP FOR GRADUATE STUDY IN HISTORIC PRESERVATION

National Trust for Historic Preservation
Attn: Scholarship Coordinator
1785 Massachusetts Avenue, N.W.
Washington, DC 20036-2117
(202) 588-6124   Toll-free: (800) 944-NTHP, ext. 6124
Fax: (202) 588-6059   E-mail: david_field@nthp.org
Web: www.nthp.org/help/colodny.html

Purpose To provide financial assistance and summer work experience to graduate students (particularly minority students) interested in working on a degree in a field related to historic preservation.

Eligibility Eligible to apply are students in their final year of undergraduate study intending to enroll in a graduate program in historic preservation and graduate students enrolled in or intending to enroll in historic preservation programs; these programs may be in a department of history, architecture, American studies, urban planning, museum studies, or a related field with a primary emphasis on historic preservation. Applicants must submit an essay in which they discuss their career goals and how their pursuit of a graduate preservation degree relates to those goals, including evidence of their interest in, commitment to, and/or potential for leadership in the field of preservation. Selection is based on the essay, a resume, 2 letters of recommendation, academic transcripts, and financial need. Applications are especially encouraged from people of diverse racial, ethnic, cultural, and economic backgrounds.

Financial data The program provides a stipend of up to $15,000 towards graduate school tuition, a stipend of $5,000 for a summer internship with the sponsor following the student's first year of study, and up to $1,500 towards

the student's attendance at a National Preservation Conference.

Duration 1 year; nonrenewable.

Additional information Internships may be completed at 1) the sponsor's Washington, D.C. office; 2) a regional office or historic museum site; or 3) the offices of 1 of the sponsor's partner organizations.

Number awarded 1 each year.

Deadline February of each year.

[959]
MINORITY ACCESS INTERNSHIP

Minority Access, Inc.
Attn: Directory of Internship Program
5214 Baltimore Avenue
Hyattsville, MD 20781
(301) 779-7100   Fax: (301) 779-9812
Web: www.minorityaccess.org

Purpose To provide work experience to minority and other undergraduate and graduate students interested in internships at participating entities in Washington, D.C. and throughout the United States.

Eligibility Applications are accepted from full-time undergraduate and graduate students with at least a 3.0 GPA. Students must be U.S. citizens for most positions. All academic majors are eligible. Interns are selected by participating federal government and other agencies. Most of these are located in Washington, D.C., but placements may be made anywhere in the United States.

Financial data All internships are paid. The weekly salary ranges from $390 for college sophomores to $520 for graduate and professional students. In addition, most internships include paid round-trip travel between home and the internship location.

Duration Spring internships are 5 months, starting in January; summer internships are 3 months, starting in August; fall internships are 4 months, starting in September.

Additional information Minority Access, Inc. is committed to the diversification of institutions, federal agencies and corporations of all kinds and to improving their recruitment, retention, and enhancement of minorities. The majority of interns are placed in the Washington, D.C. metropolitan area. Both full-time and part-time internships are awarded. Students may receive academic credit for full-time internships. Students are expected to pay all housing costs. They are required to attend a pre-employment session in Washington, D.C., all seminars and workshops hosted by Minority Access, and any mandatory activities sponsored by the host agency.

Number awarded Varies each year.

Deadline February of each year for summer internships; July of each year for fall internships; and December of each year for spring internships.

[960]

MINORITY FELLOWSHIP IN ENVIRONMENTAL LAW

New York State Bar Association
Attn: Environmental Law Section
One Elk Street
Albany, NY 12207
(518) 463-3200   Fax: (518) 487-5517
E-mail: kplog@nysba.org
Web: www.nysba.org

Purpose To provide an opportunity for minority law students from New York to work during the summer on legal matters for a government environmental agency or public interest environmental organization in the state.

Eligibility This program is open to members of a minority group (African American, Latino, Native American, Alaskan Native, Asian, or Pacific Islander) who are 1) enrolled in a law school in New York, or 2) New York residents enrolled in a law school in the United States. Applicants must be interested in summer employment working on legal matters for a government environmental agency or public interest environmental organization in New York. They must submit a resume, transcripts, 2 letters of recommendation, and an essay describing their interest in environmental issues and reasons for wanting to participate in the fellowship.

Financial data The stipend is $6,000.

Duration At least 10 weeks during the summer.

Number awarded 1 each year.

Deadline December of each year.

[961]

MINORITY MEDICAL STUDENT SUMMER EXTERNSHIP IN ADDICTION PSYCHIATRY

American Psychiatric Association
Attn: Department of Minority and National Affairs
1000 Wilson Boulevard, Suite 1825
Arlington, VA 22209-3901
(703) 907-8653   Toll-free: (888) 35-PSYCH
Fax: (703) 907-7852   E-mail: mking@psych.org
Web: www.psych.org

Purpose To provide funding to minority medical students who are interested in working on a research project during the summer with a mentor who specializes in addiction psychiatry.

Eligibility This program is open to minority medical students who have a specific interest in services related to substance abuse treatment and prevention. Minorities include American Indians, Alaska Natives, Native Hawaiians, Asian Americans, Hispanic/Latinos, and African Americans. Applicants must be interested in working with a mentor who specializes in addiction psychiatry. Work settings provide an emphasis on working clinically with or studying underserved minority populations and issues of co-occurring disorders, substance abuse treatment, and mental health disparity. Most of them are in inner-city or rural settings.

Financial data Externships provide $1,500 for travel expenses to go to the work setting of the mentor and up to another $1,500 for out-of-pocket expenses directly related to the conduct of the externship.

Duration 1 month during the summer.

Additional information Funding for this program is provided by the Substance Abuse and Mental Health Services Administration (SAMHSA).

Number awarded 10 each year.

Deadline April of each year.

[962]

MULTICULTURAL ADVERTISING INTERN PROGRAM

American Association of Advertising Agencies
Attn: Manager of Diversity Programs
405 Lexington Avenue, 18th Floor
New York, NY 10174-1801
(212) 850-0734   Toll-free: (800) 676-9333
Fax: (212) 573-8968   E-mail: naip@aaaa.org
Web: www.aaaa.org

Purpose To provide racial minority students with summer work experience in advertising agencies and to present them with an overview of the advertising business.

Eligibility This program is open to college juniors, seniors, and graduate students who are Black/African American, Asian/Asian American, Pacific Islander, Hispanic, North American Indian/Native American, or multiracial. Applicants may be majoring in any field, but they must be able to demonstrate a serious commitment to preparing for a career in advertising. They must have a GPA of 3.0 or higher. Students with a cumulative GPA of 2.7 to 2.9 are encouraged to apply, but they must complete an additional essay question. U.S. citizenship or permanent resident status is required.

Financial data Interns are paid a salary of $350 to $400 per week. If they do not live in the area of their host agencies, they may stay in housing arranged by the sponsor. They are responsible for a percentage of the cost of housing and materials.

Duration 10 weeks during the summer.

Additional information Interns may be assigned duties in the following departments: account management, broadcast production, media buying/planning, creative (art direction or copywriting), digital/interactive technologies, print production, strategic/account planning, or traffic.

Number awarded Varies each year; recently, 56 interns were placed in 32 member advertising agency offices located in Boston, Chicago, Detroit, Warren (Michigan), Minneapolis, New York, San Francisco, and Seattle.

Deadline January of each year.

[963]

NASPA MINORITY UNDERGRADUATE FELLOWS PROGRAM

National Association of Student Personnel
  Administrators
Attn: MUFP
1875 Connecticut Avenue, N.W., Suite 418
Washington, DC 20009-5728
(202) 265-7500, ext. 3003   Fax: (202) 797-1157
E-mail: mufp@naspa.org
Web: www.naspa.org/resources/mufp

Purpose To provide summer work experience and leadership training to minorities and students with disabilities who are completing their second year in college.

Eligibility Eligible to be nominated for this program are 1) ethnic minority students (Native, African, Asian, or Hispanic Americans), and 2) students with disabilities. Applicants must be completing their sophomore year in a 4-year institution or their second year in a 2-year transfer program. They must be able to demonstrate academic promise and be interested in a future in higher education.

Financial data Participants are offered a paid summer internship and payment of all expenses to attend the leadership institutes.

Duration The internship lasts 8 weeks during the summer. Leadership institutes last 4 days.

Additional information The program, initiated in the 1989-90 academic year, offers 3 main components: 1) participation in a 1- or 2-year internship or field experience under the guidance of a mentor; 2) participation in a summer leadership institute designed to enhance skill building and career development; and 3) participation in an 8-week paid summer internship designed to encourage the development of future student affairs and higher education administrators. Information is also available from Brian O. Hemphill, MUFP National Coordinator, University of Arkansas, Associate Vice Chancellor and Dean of Students, 325 Administration Building, Fayetteville, AR 72701, (501) 575-5004, E-mail: hemphill@uark.edu.

Number awarded Varies each year; recently, more than 170 undergraduates were participating in the program.

Deadline September of each year.

[964]
NATIONAL MUSEUM FELLOWS PROGRAM FOR MINORITY STUDENTS

Atlanta History Center
Attn: Director, National Museum Fellows Program
130 West Paces Ferry Road, N.W.
Atlanta, GA 30305-1366
(404) 814-4024   Fax: (404) 814-2041
E-mail: bgaines@atlhist.org
Web: www.atlhist.org

Purpose To provide museum training to minority students who are attending designated colleges and universities in selected cities.

Eligibility This program is open to undergraduate students at 9 designated colleges and universities in metropolitan Atlanta and at other academic institutions that operate in conjunction with the Chicago Historical Society, Minnesota Historical Society, Maryland Historical Society, Kentucky Historical Society, and Conner Prairie Museum in Fishers, Indiana. Candidates must be interested in preparing for a museum career and must be nominated by their college or university; each participating institution may nominate 3 students. Nominees must be full-time juniors or seniors in the following academic year with a declared major in a liberal arts discipline. Minority students (African American, Asian American, Latino American, Native American, or any other ethnic group underrepresented in the museum profession) are encouraged to seek nomination from their major professors.

Financial data The stipend is $6,000. Fellows also receive a library of scholarly and professional museum texts and memberships in their home state historical society, the American Association of Museums, and the American Association of State and Local History. Their college or university is asked to provide 2 semesters of course credit at no additional tuition expense.

Duration 12 months.

Additional information This program began in 1994 at the Atlanta History Center, and was expanded in 1998 to include the Chicago Historical Society and the Minnesota Historical Society. In 2002 it expanded again to include the Maryland and Kentucky historical societies and the Conner Prairie Museum. Funding is provided by the Knight Foundation. During the academic year, fellows attend 24 weekly seminars at their home site, where they conduct research and receive hands-on experience in curation, collections care, exhibitions development, interpretive programming, education, development and fundraising, public relations and marketing, and library/archives management. During the summer, fellows perform a 12-week apprenticeship at their home site and travel to the Smithsonian Institution and other museums throughout the United States.

Number awarded Varies each year.

Deadline May of each year.

[965]
NATIONAL MUSEUM OF NATURAL HISTORY RESEARCH TRAINING PROGRAM

National Museum of Natural History
Attn: RTP Program Coordinator
NHB, Room 59A, MRC 166
P.O. Box 37012
Washington, DC 20013-7012
(202) 633-4548   Fax: (202) 786-0153
E-mail: sangrey.mary@nmnh.si.edu
Web: www.nmnh.si.edu/rtp

Purpose To provide undergraduate students (particularly minorities, women, and undergraduates with disabilities) with a summer research training internship at the Smithsonian Institution's National Museum of Natural History in Washington, D.C.

Eligibility This program is open to currently-enrolled undergraduate students interested in preparing for a career in anthropology, botany, entomology, invertebrate zoology, mineral sciences and geology, paleobiology, or vertebrate zoology. Although foreign students may apply, all applicants must be proficient in reading and understanding English. Applications are especially encouraged from women, international and minority students, and persons with disabilities.

Financial data Interns receive a stipend of approximately $3,000, housing, an allowance for transportation to Washington, D.C. (generally $500), and a research allowance (up to $1,000).

Duration 10 weeks during the summer.

Additional information The heart of the program is a research project, designed by the intern in collaboration with a museum staff advisor. In addition, students participate in a laboratory experience and collection workshop; lectures, discussions, tours, and field trips; and other regular museum activities, such as seminars and special lectures. This program receives support from a number of funds within the Smithsonian and from the National Science Foundation through its Research Experiences for Undergraduates (REU) Program and Louis Stokes Alliances for Minority Participation Program.

Number awarded 20 to 24 each year.

Deadline January of each year.

[966]

NATIONAL PUBLIC RADIO INTERNSHIP

Asian American Journalists Association
Attn: Student Programs Coordinator
1182 Market Street, Suite 320
San Francisco, CA 94102
(415) 346-2051, ext. 102   Fax: (415) 346-6343
E-mail: brandons@aaja.org
Web: www.aaja.org

Purpose To provide members of the Asian American Journalists Association (AAJA) with the opportunity to gain work experience during the summer at National Public Radio (NPR) in Washington, D.C.

Eligibility This program is open to AAJA members who are full-time college students or recent college graduates. Applicants must have a serious interest in broadcast journalism. They must submit an essay (150 to 200 words) on why they want to prepare for a career in broadcast journalism and what they want to gain from the experience, a letter of recommendation, a resume, proof of age (at least 18 years), and work samples on CD or cassette tape of their work in radio.

Financial data A stipend is provided (amount not specified).

Duration 10 weeks, starting in late May.

Number awarded 1 each year.

Deadline March of each year.

[967]

NATIONAL SECURITY INTERNSHIP PROGRAM

Pacific Northwest National Laboratory
Attn: Science Education Programs
902 Battelle Boulevard
P.O. Box 999, MS K8-15
Richland, WA 99352
(509) 375-2569   Toll-free: (888) 375-PNNL
E-mail: peg.jarretts@pnl.gov
Web: science-ed.pnl.gov/postings/nsip.stm

Purpose To provide undergraduate and graduate students (particularly minority and female students) with an opportunity to work on a national security-related science research project at Pacific Northwest National Laboratory (PNNL) during the summer.

Eligibility This program is open to undergraduate and graduate students who have a GPA of 3.0 or higher (preferably 3.4 or higher). Applicants should be majoring in chemistry, computer science, electrical engineering, nuclear science, or physics. They must be interested in working at PNNL on a summer science project related to national security. Women and minorities are encouraged to apply. Selection is based on academic achievement, prior experience, and technical interest.

Financial data Interns receive a stipend (amount not specified).

Duration 8 to 12 weeks during the summer; may be extended up to 1 year of part-time work during the academic year.

Additional information Tuition reimbursement is available to interns who agree to work as full-time employees at PNNL for a set period of time following graduation. Interns who accept tuition reimbursement and then fail to complete full-time employment for the specified period of time must repay a prorated portion of the educational expenses.

Number awarded 10 each year.

Deadline January of each year.

[968]

NCAA ETHNIC MINORITY AND WOMEN'S INTERNSHIP PROGRAMS

National Collegiate Athletic Association
Attn: Director of Professional Development
700 West Washington Avenue
P.O. Box 6222
Indianapolis, IN 46206-6222
(317) 917-6222   Fax: (317) 917-6888
E-mail: dmoorman@ncaa.org
Web: www.ncaa.org

Purpose To provide work experience at the National Collegiate Athletic Association (NCAA) office to women or minority college graduates.

Eligibility This program is open to women and ethnic minorities who have completed the requirements for an undergraduate degree. They must have demonstrated a commitment to preparing for a career in intercollegiate athletics and the ability to succeed in such a career.

Financial data Interns receive up to $1,600 per month; this includes a $200 monthly housing allowance.

Duration 1 year, beginning in June.

Additional information Interns work at the NCAA national office in Indianapolis. Positions are available in administrative services, branding and communications, championships, education services, enforcement services, governance, membership services, and men's and women's basketball.

Number awarded Varies each year; recently, 11 of these internships were awarded.

Deadline February of each year.

[969]

NEW YORK CHAPTER INTERNSHIP STIPEND PROGRAM

Asian American Journalists Association-New York
    Chapter
c/o Jennifer Kelleher, Board Member
Newsday
235 Pinelawn Road
Melville, NY 11747
(631) 843-2700   Fax: (631) 843-2953
E-mail: aajanyc@hotmail.com
Web: chapters.aaja.org/NewYork/applications.shtml

Purpose To provide funding to undergraduate and graduate student members of the New York chapter of the Asian American Journalists Association (AAJA) who wish to accept an unpaid or low-paid internship.

Eligibility This program is open to members of the New York chapter of AAJA who are undergraduate or graduate students enrolled in an accredited college or university. Applicants need not be journalism majors, but they must show a serious interest in a career in journalism. They must have accepted an unpaid or low-paid internship. Along with their application, they must submit brief essays on the following: how the internship will contribute to their development as a journalist, their short-term and long-term career goals, their participation in AAJA activities in the past, their participation in other Asian American activities in school or in their community, and their financial need. They must also submit samples of their work: up to 6 writing or editing samples, a 15-minute VHS tape or audiocassette tape, or 3 unmounted photographs. Selection is based on interest in journalism, participation in AAJA, other participation in Asian American issues, value of the internship in leading to a future journalism career, letters of recommendation, and financial need.

Financial data Grants range from $300 to $1,000.

Duration These are 1-time grants.

Additional information Recipients are expected to give back to the organization through future volunteer activity and participation as an active member.

Number awarded Varies each year.

Deadline Applications may be submitted at any time.

[970]
NONPROFIT SECTOR RESEARCH FUND WILLIAM RANDOLPH HEARST ENDOWED SCHOLARSHIP FOR MINORITY STUDENTS

Aspen Institute
Attn: Director, Nonprofit Sector Research Fund
One Dupont Circle, N.W., Suite 700
Washington, DC 20036
(202) 736-5838   Fax: (202) 293-0525
E-mail: nsrf@aspeninstitute.org
Web: www.nonprofitresearch.org

Purpose To provide an opportunity for minority students to learn more about nonprofit activities, including philanthropy and its underlying values, through a summer internship at the Aspen Institute in Washington, D.C.

Eligibility This program at the Aspen Institute is open to minority graduate and undergraduate students. Applicants must be interested in learning about nonprofit organizations by working at the institute, by assisting in preparations for its annual conference, and by engaging in general research and program support for its grantmaking and outreach efforts. They must be able to demonstrate outstanding research skills, background in the social sciences or humanities, writing and communication skills, financial need, and U.S. citizenship.

Financial data Stipends range from $2,500 to $5,000, depending on the recipient's educational level, financial need, and time commitment.

Duration 10 to 12 weeks during the summer.

Additional information This program, established in 1991, is funded by the William Randolph Hearst Foundation.

Number awarded Varies each year.

Deadline March of each year.

[971]
ONEDOT MSI SUMMER INTERNSHIP PROGRAM

ADNET Systems, Inc.
11260 Roger Bacon Drive, Suite 403
Reston, VA 20190
(703) 709-7218   Fax: (703) 709-7219
Web: www.adnet-sys.com

Purpose To provide work experience at offices of the U.S. Department of Transportation (DOT) to minority and disabled students.

Eligibility This program is open to students who are from Historically Black Colleges and Universities (HBCUs), Hispanic Service Institutions (HSIs), Tribal Colleges and Universities (TCUs), Asian American and Pacific Islander communities, and disability communities. Applicants must be U.S. citizens currently enrolled in a college or university as a sophomore or above (including graduate students) with a GPA of 3.0 or higher. They must be interested in an internship with a DOT agency, including the Office of the Secretary, Bureau of Transportation Statistics, Federal Aviation Administration, Federal Highway Administration, Federal Motor Carrier Safety Administration, Federal Railroad Administration, Federal Transit Administration, Maritime Administration, National Highway Traffic Safety Administration, Research and Special Programs Administration, and St. Lawrence Seaway Development Corporation. Jobs have included, but are not limited to, accounting, business, human resources, international affairs, operations, computer science, mathematics, engineering, journalism, and criminal justice. Along with their application, they must submit 200-word statements on 1) their community activities, hobbies, associations, publications, and other relevant experience; and 2) why they want to participate in this program.

Financial data Interns are paid a stipend and receive housing.

Duration 10 weeks in summer or 15 weeks in fall or spring.

Additional information Information on this program is also available from the U.S. Department of Transportation, Office of Civil Rights, Minority Serving Institutions and Educational Partnerships (S-30.10), 400 Seventh Street, S.W., Room 5414A, Washington, DC, (202) 366-8964, Fax: (202) 366-7717, TTY: (202) 366-9696, E-mail: roger.peralta@ost.dot.gov.

Number awarded Varies each year.

Deadline May of each year for summer; July of each year for fall; November of each year for spring.

[972]
OREGON STATE BAR CLERKSHIP STIPENDS

Oregon State Bar
Attn: Affirmative Action Program
5200 S.W. Meadows Road
P.O. Box 1689
Lake Oswego, OR 97035-0889
(503) 431-6338
Toll-free: (800) 452-8260, ext. 338 (within OR)
Fax: (503) 598-6938   E-mail: dgigoux@osbar.org
Web: www.osbar.org

Purpose To provide job opportunities for minority law

students in Oregon and to provide an incentive to prospective employers to hire minority law students in the state.

Eligibility   Applicants must be minority law students (African Americans, Asian Americans, Native Americans, or Hispanic Americans) with financial need. They are not required to be enrolled at a law school in Oregon, but they must demonstrate a commitment to practice in the state. Along with their application, they must submit 1) a personal statement on their history of disadvantage or barriers to educational advancement, personal experiences of discrimination, extraordinary financial obligations, composition of immediate family, extraordinary health or medical needs, and languages in which they are fluent; and 2) a state bar statement in which they describe their intention to practice law in Oregon and how they will improve the quality of legal service or increase access to justice in Oregon. Selection is based on financial need (30%), the personal statement (25%), the state bar statement (25%), community activities (10%), and employment history (10%).

Financial data   This program pays a stipend of $5.00 per hour; the employer must then at least match that stipend.

Duration   1 academic year or summer months.

Additional information   The selected student is responsible for finding work under this program. The job should be in Oregon, although exceptions will be made if the job offers the student special experience not available within the state.

Number awarded   20 each year.

Deadline   January of each year.

[973]
OREGON STATE BAR PUBLIC HONORS FELLOWSHIPS

Oregon State Bar
Attn: Affirmative Action Program
5200 S.W. Meadows Road
P.O. Box 1689
Lake Oswego, OR 97035-0889
(503) 431-6338
Toll-free: (800) 452-8260, ext. 338 (within OR)
Fax: (503) 598-6938   E-mail: dgigoux@osbar.org
Web: www.osbar.org

Purpose   To provide minority law students in Oregon with summer work experience in public interest law.

Eligibility   Qualified minority law students may be nominated by faculty selection committees at Oregon's 3 law schools (Willamette, University of Oregon, and Lewis and Clark) after the completion of their first year of law school. Nominees must have demonstrated a career goal in public interest or public sector law. Each school may nominate up to 5 students. Nominees must submit 1) a personal statement on their history of disadvantage or barriers to educational advancement, personal experiences of discrimination, extraordinary financial obligations, composition of immediate family, extraordinary health or medical needs, and languages in which they are fluent; and 2) a state bar statement in which they describe their intention to practice law in Oregon and how they will improve the quality of legal service or increase access to justice in Oregon. From the nominees of each school, 2 students are selected on the basis of financial need (30%), the personal statement (25%), the state bar statement (25%), and public service (20%).

The information on those students is forwarded to prospective employers in Oregon and they arrange to interview the selectees.

Financial data   Fellows receive a stipend of $4,800.

Duration   3 months during the summer.

Additional information   There is no guarantee that all students selected by the sponsoring organization will receive fellowships at Oregon law firms.

Number awarded   6 each year: 3 from each of the law schools.

Deadline   January of each year.

[974]
THE OREGONIAN MINORITY INTERNSHIP PROGRAM

The Oregonian
Attn: Director of Recruiting and Training
1320 S.W. Broadway
Portland, OR 97201
(503) 221-8039   Fax: (503) 294-5012
E-mail: jobs@news.oregonian.com
Web: www.oregonian.com/newsroom/jobspg1.htm

Purpose   To provide work experience at *The Oregonian* in Portland to minority college graduates who are interested in a career in journalism.

Eligibility   This program is open to recent college graduates who are African American, Asian American, Hispanic, American Indian, or Pacific Islander. Applicants must be committed to a career in newspapers and be interested in an internship at *The Oregonian* that combines practical experience with professional mentoring in 8 specialized areas: arts reporter/critic; business reporter; copy editor/news editor; graphic artist/page designer; local news reporter; medical/science reporter; sports reporter; or photographer/photo editor.

Financial data   A competitive salary is paid.

Duration   2 years.

Additional information   Midway through the second year, interns may apply for any position open on the staff of *The Oregonian;* if no opening is available, assistance is provided in finding another job.

Number awarded   3 each year.

Deadline   February of each year.

[975]
ORGANIZATION OF CHINESE AMERICANS INTERNSHIP PROGRAM

Organization of Chinese Americans, Inc.
1001 Connecticut Avenue, N.W., Suite 601
Washington, DC 20036
(202) 223-5500   Fax: (202) 296-0540
E-mail: oca@ocanatl.org
Web: www.ocanatl.org

Purpose   To provide an opportunity for Asian Pacific American college students to gain summer work experience through the Organization of Chinese Americans (OCA).

Eligibility   This program is open to Asian Pacific American college and graduate students who have a demonstrated interest in public affairs. Applicants must be interested in working at the OCA national office, in a Congressional office, or in a federal agency. Along with their application, they must submit a resume, an academic transcript, an essay on why they want to participate in the internship, and 2 letters of reference. Selection criteria emphasize oral and written communication skills.

Financial data The stipend is $2,000.

Duration 10 weeks in the summer, at the OCA national office, at a Congressional office, or at a federal agency; 10 weeks in the fall, winter, or spring at the OCA national office.

Additional information At the OCA national office, general internships and development internships are available year round. Assignments as public policy, technical, communications and public relations, and scholarship services internships are available only in the summer.

Number awarded Varies each year.

Deadline March of each year for summer; July of each year for fall; November of each year for winter or spring.

[976]
PABA FELLOWSHIP

Philippine American Bar Association of Los Angeles
c/o Avelino J. Halagao, Jr.
400 Continental Boulevard, Sixth Floor
El Segundo, CA 90245
(310) 426-2323   E-mail: ajhalagao@netsperanto.com
Web: www.philconnect.com/paba/students.html

Purpose To provide financial assistance and work experience to Asian American/Pacific Islanders attending law school in the Los Angeles area.

Eligibility This program is open to Asian American/Pacific Islander students at law schools in the Los Angeles area. Applicants must be interested in a clerkship at the Asian Pacific American Legal Center of Southern California (APALC). Selection is based on academic accomplishment, past and potential community contributions, and financial need.

Financial data The stipend is $2,500.

Duration 1 year.

Additional information The awardee must work 8 to 10 hours per week during the spring or summer at APALC.

Number awarded 1 each year.

Deadline January of each year.

[977]
PAUL D. WHITE SCHOLARSHIP

Baker & Hostetler LLP
Attn: Kathleen Ferdico
3200 National City Center
1900 East Ninth Street
Cleveland, OH 44114-3485
(216) 861-7092   Fax: (216) 696-0740
Web: www.bakerlaw.com

Purpose To provide financial assistance and summer work experience to minority students at selected law schools.

Eligibility This program is open to first- and second-year law students of African American, Hispanic, Asian American, or American Indian descent. Applicants must be attending 1 of the following schools that currently participate in the program: Case Western Reserve School of Law, Cleveland-Marshall School of Law, Howard University School of Law, Ohio State University Moritz School of Law,

University of Michigan School of Law, the University of Texas School of Law, University of California at Los Angeles School of Law, University of Cincinnati College of Law, University of Denver College of Law, University of Florida Levin College of Law, and University of Colorado School of Law.

Financial data The program provides a stipend of $5,000 and a paid summer clerkship with the sponsoring firm.

Duration 1 year, including the following summer.

Number awarded 1 each year.

[978]
PAULINE A. YOUNG RESIDENCY

University of Delaware
Library
Attn: Coordinator, Personnel and Staff Development
Newark, DE 19717-5267
(302) 831-1594   Fax: (302) 831-1046
E-mail: jbrewer@udel.edu
Web: www2.lib.udel.edu/personnel/brochure.htm

Purpose To provide full-time professional work experience at the University of Delaware Library to underrepresented minority and other graduates of accredited library schools.

Eligibility This program is open to recent graduates of library schools accredited by the American Library Association Applicants must be able to demonstrate strong written and oral communication skills, an interest in developing a career in academic librarianship, the ability to work independently as well as with colleagues and library users from diverse backgrounds, a willingness to learn, and a desire for professional growth. Members of underrepresented racial and ethnic groups are particularly encouraged to apply.

Financial data Compensation is at the level of assistant librarian; benefits include health coverage, dental insurance, course fee waiver, and relocation assistance.

Duration 2 years; nonrenewable.

Additional information In the first year, residents gain professional experience by rotating through several different areas of the University of Delaware Library. In the second year, they concentrate in 1 area to further specific professional goals. In addition, they are offered opportunities for committee service, specialized training, and professional workshops. Residents are eligible to apply for continuing positions at the library.

Number awarded 1 every other year.

Deadline April of each even-numbered year.

[979]
PEDRO ZAMORA PUBLIC POLICY FELLOWSHIP

AIDS Action
1906 Sunderland Place, N.W.
Washington, DC 20036
(202) 530-8030   Fax: (202) 530-8031
E-mail: zamora@aidsaction.org
Web: www.aidsaction.org/fellowship_new.htm

Purpose To provide work experience at AIDS Action to minority and other undergraduate and graduate students interested in public policy.

Eligibility This program is open to undergraduate and graduate students who can demonstrate strong research, writing, and organizational skills and experience working in a professional office. Familiarity with HIV-related issues and the legislative process is preferred. Applicants must 1) describe their participation in school, work, or extracurricular activities related to HIV and AIDS (e.g., peer prevention programs, volunteer activities); 2) describe their participation in any school or extracurricular activities related to advocacy (e.g., lobbying, political campaigns); 3) explain why they would be the best candidate for this fellowship; and 4) explain how they would use the skills they acquire from the fellowship. People of color, women, gay, lesbian, bisexual, transgender, and HIV-positive individuals are encouraged to apply.

Financial data A stipend is provided (amount not specified).

Duration From 8 to 26 weeks.

Additional information Responsibilities include assisting in researching a variety of public health and civil rights issues related to HIV prevention, treatment, and care; attending Congressional hearings and coalition meetings; monitoring voting records; reviewing the Federal Register and Congressional Record; and preparing correspondence, mailings, and briefing materials. Fellows must commit to a minimum of 30 hours per week at AIDS Action in Washington, D.C.

Number awarded Varies each year.

Deadline March of each year for summer; July of each year for fall; October of each year for spring.

---

[980]
PFIZER/UNCF CORPORATE SCHOLARS PROGRAM

United Negro College Fund
Attn: Corporate Scholars Program
P.O. Box 1435
Alexandria, VA 22313-9998
Toll-free: (866) 671-7237　E-mail: internship@uncf.org
Web: www.uncf.org/internships/index.asp

Purpose To provide financial assistance and work experience to minority undergraduate and graduate students majoring in designated fields and interested in an internship at a Pfizer facility.

Eligibility This program is open to sophomores, juniors, graduate students, and first-year law students who are African American, Hispanic American, Asian/Pacific Islander American, or American Indian/Alaskan Native. Applicants must have a GPA of 3.0 or higher and be enrolled at an institution that is a member of the United Negro College Fund (UNCF) or at another targeted college or university. They must be working on 1) a bachelor's degree in animal science, business, chemistry (organic or analytical), human resources, logistics, microbiology, organizational development, operations management, pre-veterinary medicine, or supply chain management; 2) a master's degree in chemistry (organic or analytical), finance, human resources, or organizational development; or 3) a law degree. Eligibility is limited to U.S. citizens, permanent residents, asylees, refugees, and lawful temporary residents. Along with their application, they must submit a 1-page essay about themselves and their career goals, including information about their interest in Pfizer (the program's sponsor), their personal background, and any particular challenges they have faced.

Financial data The program provides an internship stipend of up to $5,000, housing accommodations near Pfizer

corporate facilities, and (based on successful internship performance) a $15,000 scholarship.

Duration 8 to 10 weeks for the internship; 1 year for the scholarship.

Additional information Opportunities for first-year law students include the summer internship only.

Number awarded Varies each year.

Deadline January of each year.

---

[981]
PGA TOUR DIVERSITY INTERNSHIP PROGRAM

PGA Tour, Inc.
Attn: Diversity Internship Program
100 PGA Tour Boulevard
Ponte Vedra Beach, FL 32082
Toll-free: (800) 556-5400, ext. 3520
E-mail: MIP@mail.pgatour.com
Web: www.pgatour.com

Purpose To provide summer work experience to minority undergraduate and graduate students interested in learning about the business side of golf.

Eligibility This program is open to full-time undergraduates who have completed their sophomore year and graduate students. Applicants must be men or women of African American, Asian American, Native American, or Hispanic descent. International students are eligible if they are legally permitted to work in the United States. Although all interns work in the business side of golf, the ability to play golf or knowledge of the game is not required for most positions.

Financial data Interns receive competitive wages, up to $500 for travel expenses, and (for some) subsidized housing and discounts on company merchandise.

Duration 9 to 13 weeks during the summer.

Additional information This program was established in 1992. Positions are available in communications, corporate marketing, human resources, information systems, international and domestic television, legal department, retail licensing, tournament operations, and professional services. Most assignments are in Ponte Vedra Beach, Florida.

Number awarded Varies each year; recently, 32 of these internships were provided.

Deadline February of each year.

---

[982]
PHILADELPHIA INQUIRER MINORITY GRAPHIC ARTS INTERNSHIP

Philadelphia Inquirer
Attn: Oscar Miller, Director of Recruiting
400 North Broad Street
P.O. Box 8263
Philadelphia, PA 19101
(215) 854-5102　　　　　　　　Fax: (215) 854-2578
E-mail: inkyjobs@phillynews.com
Web: www.philly.com/mld/philly

Purpose To provide graphic design experience during the summer at the *Philadelphia Inquirer* to minority college students interested in careers in journalism.

Eligibility Minority college students entering their sophomore, junior, or senior year in college are eligible to apply if they are interested in working in the art department at the *Philadelphia Inquirer*. Applicants should submit 5 to 7 samples of their work (published or unpublished), a resume, a cover letter, and references.

Financial data The salary is $573 per week.

Duration 10 weeks beginning in June.

Number awarded 1 each year.

Deadline November of each year.

[983]
PHILADELPHIA INQUIRER MINORITY PHOTOJOURNALISM INTERNSHIP

Philadelphia Inquirer
Attn: Director of Photography
P.O. Box 8263
Philadelphia, PA 19101-8263
(215) 854-5045   E-mail: cmurray@phillynews.com
Web: www.philly.com/mld/philly

Purpose To provide summer work experience at the *Philadelphia Inquirer* to minority students who are interested in preparing for a career in photojournalism.

Eligibility Minorities who are fully matriculated undergraduate or graduate students with at least 1 prior internship are eligible to apply if they are interested in gaining work experience in photojournalism at the *Philadelphia Inquirer.* Applicants must submit a portfolio with up to 2 pages of slide duplicates showing creativity in news, general features, sports, and environmental portraiture. At least 1 photo essay should be included.

Financial data The salary is $647 per week.

Duration 10 weeks during the summer.

Additional information A complete set of Nikon equipment is available for use during the internship.

Number awarded 1 each year.

Deadline November of each year.

[984]
PUBLIC INTEREST LAW PROGRAM SUMMER FELLOWSHIP

Public Interest Clearinghouse
Attn: PILP Director
47 Kearney Street, Suite 705
San Francisco, CA 94108
(415) 834-0100, ext. 307   Fax: (415) 834-0202
E-mail: ahamill@pic.org
Web: www.pic.org

Purpose To provide funding to minority and other law students interested in a summer internship in public interest law in California.

Eligibility This program is open to students completing either their first or second year of law school who have a demonstrated commitment to public interest law. Applicants must be interested in a summer internship with a California nonprofit IOLTA-funded organization. Legal services programs in California are given preference. Government programs, including criminal defense or prosecution, are not eligible. The organization must agree to supervise the fellow's work on a substantive legal advocacy project. Students must submit, along with their application, a 2-page personal statement on how their experience (personal, educational, and/or work) demonstrates a commitment to the practice of public interest law, the nature and impact of the work they will perform as well as what they expect to achieve as a fellow, and why this work will help them to realize their post-law school career objectives. People of color, persons from low-income or working class backgrounds, and disabled persons are especially encouraged to apply.

Financial data This program provides a stipend of $2,000, and the sponsoring organization is expected to contribute another $500. Fellows may obtain other funding as long as the total amount earned does not exceed $5,000.

Duration 10 weeks during the summer.

Additional information This program began in 2001.

Number awarded 2 each year: 1 to a law student completing the first year and 1 to a law student completing the second year.

Deadline April of each year.

[985]
RESEARCH AND ENGINEERING APPRENTICESHIP PROGRAM (REAP) FOR HIGH SCHOOL STUDENTS

Academy of Applied Science
1 Maple Street
Concord, NH 03301
(603) 228-0121   Fax: (603) 228-0210
Web: www.aas-world.org/youth_science/reap.html

Purpose To provide an opportunity for disadvantaged high school students to engage in a research apprenticeship in mathematics, science, or technology.

Eligibility Applicants must be economically and socially disadvantaged high school students who have an interest in mathematics, science, or technology. Recipients are selected on the basis of previously demonstrated abilities and interest in science, mathematics, and technology; potential for a successful career in the field as indicated from overall scholastic achievement, aptitude, and interest areas; recommendations of high school teachers and administrators; and an interview.

Financial data Interns receive a salary in accordance with student minimum wage guidelines.

Duration Summer months.

Additional information The program provides intensive summer training for high school students in the laboratories of scientists. The program, established in 1980, is funded by a grant from the U.S. Army Research Office. Students must live at home while they participate in the program and must live in the area where an approved professor lives. The program does not exist in every state.

Number awarded Varies; recently, approximately 120 students were funded at 52 colleges and universities nationwide.

Deadline February of each year.

[986]
RESOURCES FOR THE FUTURE SUMMER INTERNSHIPS

Resources for the Future
Attn: Coordinator for Academic Programs
1616 P Street, N.W.
Washington, DC 20036-1400
(202) 328-5060   Fax: (202) 939-3460
E-mail: mankin@rff.org
Web: www.rff.org

Purpose To provide internships to minority and other undergraduate and graduate students interested in working on research projects in public policy during the summer.

Eligibility Candidates must be in their first or second year of graduate training, with skills in microeconomics, quantitative methods, or occasionally other social and natural sciences. Outstanding undergraduates may also be eligible. Applicants must be interested in an internship in Washington, D.C. in 1 of the divisions of Resources for the Future (RFF): the Center for Risk, Resource, and Environmental Management, the Energy and Natural Resources division, or the Quality of the Environment division. Applicants must be able to work without supervision in a careful and conscientious manner. Women and minority candidates are strongly encouraged to apply. Both U.S. and non-U.S. citizens are eligible, if the latter have proper work and residency documentation.

Financial data The stipend is $375 per week for graduate students or $350 per week for undergraduates.

Duration Summer months; beginning and ending dates can be adjusted to meet particular student needs.

Additional information Interns assist in research projects in complex public policy problems amenable to interdisciplinary analysis, often drawing heavily on economics. Further information on the Center for Risk, Resource, and Environmental Management is available from Marilyn Voigt at (202) 328-5077, Fax: (202) 939-3460, E-mail: voigt@rff.org; on Energy and Natural Resources and on Quality of the Environment from John Mankin at (202) 328-5060, Fax: (202) 939-3460, E-mail: mankin@rff.org.

Deadline March of each year.

[987]
RICHARD B. FISHER SCHOLARSHIP

Morgan Stanley
c/o Joyce Arencibia, IT College Recruiting
750 Seventh Avenue, 30th Floor
New York, NY 10019
(212) 762-4000
E-mail: diversityrecruiting@morganstanley.com
Web: www.morganstanley.com

Purpose To provide financial assistance and work experience to members of minority groups who are preparing for a career in technology within the financial services industry.

Eligibility This program is open to members of minority groups who are enrolled in their sophomore or junior year of college (or the third or fourth year of a 5-year program). Applicants must be enrolled full time and have a GPA of 3.0 or higher. They must be willing to commit to a paid summer internship in the Morgan Stanley Information Technology Division. All majors and disciplines are eligible, but preference is given to students preparing for a career in technol-ogy within the financial services industry. Along with their application, they must submit 1-page essays on 1) why they are applying for this scholarship and why they should be selected as a recipient; 2) a technical project on which they worked, either through a university course or previous work experience, their role in the project, and how they contributed to the end result; and 3) a software, hardware, or new innovative application of existing technology that they would create if they could and the impact it would have. Financial need is not considered in the selection process.

Financial data The stipend is $5,000.

Duration 1 year.

Additional information The program includes a paid summer internship in the Morgan Stanley Information Technology Division in the summer following the time of application.

Number awarded 1 or more each year.

Deadline February of each year.

[988]
ROSWELL L. GILPATRIC INTERNSHIP

Metropolitan Museum of Art
Attn: Internship Programs
1000 Fifth Avenue
New York, NY 10028-0198
(212) 570-3710   Fax: (212) 570-3782
E-mail: mmainterns@metmuseum.org
Web: www.metmuseum.org

Purpose To provide work experience at the Metropolitan Museum of Art during the summer to minority and other students interested in a museum career.

Eligibility This internship is available to college juniors, seniors, recent graduates, and graduate students who show a special interest in preparing for a museum career. Applicants of diverse backgrounds are especially encouraged to apply.

Financial data The honorarium is $3,000 for undergraduate students and recent graduates or $3,250 for graduate students.

Duration 10 weeks, beginning in June.

Additional information Interns are assigned to departmental projects (curatorial, administration, or education) at the Metropolitan Museum of Art; other assignments may include giving gallery talks and working at the Visitor Information Center. The assignment is for 35 hours a week. The internships are funded in part by the Thorne Foundation.

Number awarded 1 each year.

Deadline January of each year.

[989]
RUTH CHANCE LAW FELLOWSHIP

Equal Rights Advocates, Inc.
1663 Mission Street, Suite 250
San Francisco, CA 94103
(415) 621-0672   Fax: (415) 621-6744
E-mail: sgersh@equalrights.org
Web: www.equalrights.org/about/jobs.asp

Purpose To provide work experience at Equal Rights Advocates (ERA) to recent law school graduates who are interested in working for the equal rights of women and minorities.

Eligibility This program is open to recent law school graduates who are licensed to practice law in California. Applicants must be able to demonstrate knowledge of and commitment to women's rights and legal issues affecting women; skill in legal research, analysis, and writing; knowledge of and commitment to civil rights and legal issues affecting people of color and other disadvantaged populations; ability to complete assignments and responsibilities accurately and in a timely manner; proficiency in computer applications; commitment to and involvement with community concerns; verbal and written communication skills; and ability to interact professionally and effectively with co-workers, board members, volunteers, outside counsel, court personnel, organization donors, and guests. Preference is given to applicants who are bilingual in English and Spanish, Cantonese, or Vietnamese.

Financial data The annual salary ranges from $35,000 to $37,500; benefits are also provided.

Duration 1 year, beginning in September.

Additional information Equal Rights Advocates is a nonprofit, public interest law firm that is dedicated to combating the disenfranchisement of women, particularly low-income and minority women. The responsibilities of the fellow include overseeing and coordinating an advice and counseling program, assisting staff attorneys with ongoing litigation, and participating in the firm's public policy and education activities.

Number awarded 1 each year.

Deadline January of each year.

[990]
SCA GENERAL DIVERSITY INTERNSHIPS

Student Conservation Association, Inc.
Attn: Diversity Internships
1800 North Kent Street, Suite 102
Arlington, VA 22209
(703) 524-2441   Fax: (603) 543-1828
E-mail: diversity@thesca.org
Web: www.thesca.org/ci_diversity.cfm

Purpose To provide work experience during the summer to minority and disabled students at private, nonprofit, state, and federal agencies involved in conservation.

Eligibility This program provides summer internships through cooperating federal, state, private, and nonprofit agencies. It is open to currently-enrolled students who have completed at least the freshman year of college with a GPA of 2.5 or higher. U.S. citizenship or permanent resident status is required. Although all students may apply, the program is designed to allow students of color and students with disabilities, traditionally underrepresented in the conservation field, to experience the type of careers available to them. Possible placements include interpretation and environmental education; backcountry patrol; recreation management; archival and museum studies; archaeological surveys; cave studies; historical/cultural resource studies; landscape architecture and planning; biological research and monitoring; and wildlife, forestry, and fisheries management.

Financial data The stipend is $50 per week for internships of 12 weeks or $160 per week for positions of 6 to 12 months. Other benefits include payment of travel expenses, housing, worker's compensation, and accident insurance.

Duration 12-week, 6-month, 9-month, and 1-year positions are available.

Additional information While participating in the fellowship, students engage in ongoing career counseling, mentoring, personal and career development services, and additional training by the professional staff at each host site. Recently, available positions included Golden Gate National Recreation Area (California), Mammoth Cave National Park (Kentucky), Arlingtonians for a Clean Environment (Virginia), Dinosaur National Monument (Colorado), Lassen National Park (California), and Kenai Fjords National Park (Alaska).

Number awarded Approximately 40 each year.

Deadline February of each year.

[991]
SCCLA SCHOLARSHIPS AND FELLOWSHIPS

Southern California Chinese Lawyers Association
Attn: Scholarship Fund
P.O. Box 861959
Los Angeles, CA 90086-1959
Web: www.sccla.org/aboutsccla.htm

Purpose To provide financial assistance and work experience to Asian Pacific American law students in southern California.

Eligibility This program is open to Asian Pacific American students at law schools in southern California. Applicants for scholarships may be in any year of law school, including entering first-year students and fourth-year evening students. Applicants for fellowships may be in any year, but they must also be interested in serving a clerkship at the Asian Pacific American Legal Center in Los Angeles for 10 to 15 hours per semester. Selection is based on academic accomplishment, financial need, and potential contribution to the Chinese American community.

Financial data The stipend is $1,500 for fellowships or $1,000 for scholarships.

Duration 1 year.

Additional information This program includes the following named scholarships: the Ming Y. Moy Memorial Scholarship, the Justice Elwood Lui Scholarship, the Lee Gum Low Presidential Scholarship, and the Margaret and Ned Good Scholarships. Information is also available from Philip H. Lam, Deputy City Attorney, Intellectual Property Counsel, 111 North Hope Street, Suite 340, Los Angeles, CA 90012, (213) 367-4520, Fax: (213) 367-4588, E-mail: Philip.lam@ladwp.com, and from Will Niu, Warmuth & Niu, LLP, 400 South Atlantic Boulevard, Suite 203, Monterey Park, CA 91754, (626) 282-6868.

Number awarded Varies each year; recently, 15 of these scholarships and fellowships were awarded.

Deadline February of each year.

[992]
SCMRE GRADUATE RESEARCH INTERNSHIPS

Smithsonian Center for Materials Research and
Education
Attn: Coordinator of Research and Education
Museum Support Center
4210 Silver Hill Road
Suitland, MD 20746-2863
(301) 238-3700, ext. 121   Fax: (301) 238-3709
E-mail: bishopr@scmre.si.edu
Web: www.si.edu

Purpose To provide funding to minority and other graduate students interested in gaining research experience at the Smithsonian Center for Materials Research and Education (SCMRE).

Eligibility This program is open to graduate students interested in working in an area of SCMRE research programming activity: biogeochemistry; characterizing and preserving natural history collections, photographic materials, and modern materials; preservation science; analysis and characterization of archaeological materials; and conservation treatment and development. Applicants must submit a resume (including transcripts), a statement of experience and intent, and references. Minorities are especially encouraged to apply.

Financial data The stipend is $14,000. Other benefits include a $2,000 travel allowance and health insurance.

Duration 1 year.

Number awarded Varies each year.

Deadline February of each year.

[993]
SCOTTS COMPANY SCHOLARS PROGRAM

Golf Course Superintendents Association of America
Attn: Scholarship and Student Programs Manager
1421 Research Park Drive
Lawrence, KS 66049-3859
(785) 832-3678   Toll-free: (800) 472-7878, ext. 3678
E-mail: psmith@gcsaa.org
Web: www.gcsaa.org

Purpose To provide financial assistance and summer work experience to high school seniors and college students, particularly those from diverse backgrounds, who are preparing for a career in golf management.

Eligibility This program is open to high school seniors and college students (freshmen, sophomores, and juniors) who are interested in preparing for a career in golf management (the "green industry"). Applicants should come from diverse ethnic, cultural, and socioeconomic backgrounds, defined to include women, minorities, and people with disabilities. Selection is based on cultural diversity, academic achievement, extracurricular activities, leadership, employment potential, essay responses, and letters of recommendation. Financial need is not considered. Finalists are selected for summer internships and then compete for scholarships.

Financial data Each intern receives a $500 award. Scholarship stipends are $2,500.

Duration 1 year.

Additional information The program is funded by a permanent endowment established by Scotts Company. Finalists are responsible for securing their own internships.

Number awarded 5 interns and 2 scholarship winners are selected each year.

Deadline February of each year.

[994]
SENATOR PAUL SIMON SCHOLARSHIP

Conference on Asian Pacific American Leadership
Attn: Summer Internships
P.O. Box 65073
Washington, DC 20035-5073
(202) 628-1307   E-mail: info@capal.org
Web: www.capal.org/simon_scholarship.html

Purpose To provide funding for summer internships in Washington, D.C. to Asian Pacific American undergraduate students.

Eligibility This program is open to Asian Pacific American continuing undergraduate students (graduating seniors are not eligible) who are interested in a public sector internship within the Washington, D.C. metropolitan area in any of the 3 branches of the federal government, with a state or local official or government agency, or at a nonprofit organization. Applicants must have a strong interest in community development, a commitment to public service, and a willingness to better the Asian Pacific American community. Along with their application, they must submit a 750-word essay on their long-term goals, how the summer internship experience will advance those, and their educational, community work, and internship experiences. Selection is based on demonstrated commitment to public service, including service to the Asian Pacific American community; potential to benefit from the internship; demonstrated leadership and potential for continued growth in leadership skills; and financial need.

Financial data Awardees receive a stipend of $2,000 to help pay expenses during their internship.

Duration At least 6 weeks during the summer.

Additional information Recipients are responsible for securing their own internships. They must agree to participate in the sponsor's summer Washington Leadership Program.

Number awarded 1 each year.

Deadline April of each year.

[995]
SEO CAREER PROGRAM

Sponsors for Educational Opportunity
Attn: Career Program
30 West 21st Street, Suite 900
New York, NY 10010
(212) 979-2040   Fax: (212) 647-7010
E-mail: careerprogram@seo-usa.org
Web: www.seo-usa.org

Purpose To provide undergraduate students of color with an opportunity to gain summer work experience in selected fields in the United States or Hong Kong.

Eligibility This program is open to undergraduate students of color at colleges and universities in the United States. Applicants must be interested in a summer internship in 1 of the following fields: accounting, asset management, corporate law, global corporate financial leadership, information technology, investment banking, management consulting, or philanthropy. They should be able to demonstrate analytical and quantitative skills, interpersonal and community skills, maturity, and a cumulative GPA of 3.0 or higher. Along with their application, they must submit 1) information on their extracurricular and employment experience; 2) an essay of 75 to 100 words on how the program area to which they are applying related to their professional goals; and 3) an essay of 250 to 400 words on either an example of a time when they had to operate outside their "comfort zone" or their definition of success. Personal interviews are required.

Financial data Stipends range from $600 to $1,000 per week.

Duration 10 weeks during the summer.

Additional information This program was established in 1980. Most internships are available in the New York City metropolitan area (including Connecticut and New Jersey), although some asset management positions are available in San Francisco and investment banking internships are also open in San Francisco and (for students fluent in Mandarin or Korean) in Hong Kong.

Number awarded Varies each year; recently, more than 300 internships were available at more than 40 firms.

Deadline January of each year.

[996]
S.I. NEWHOUSE FOUNDATION SCHOLARSHIPS

Asian American Journalists Association
Attn: Student Programs Coordinator
1182 Market Street, Suite 320
San Francisco, CA 94102
(415) 346-2051, ext. 102   Fax: (415) 346-6343
E-mail: brandons@aaja.org
Web: www.aaja.org

Purpose To provide financial assistance and summer work experience in print journalism to members of the Asian American Journalists Association (AAJA) who are undergraduate or graduate students.

Eligibility This program is open to all students but especially welcomes applications from historically underrepresented Asian Pacific American groups, including southeast Asians (Vietnamese, Cambodians, and Hmong), south Asians, and Pacific Islanders. Applicants may be graduating high school seniors who declare journalism as a major or undergraduate or graduate students working on a degree in journalism and a career in print journalism. AAJA membership is required. Along with their application, they must submit a 500-word essay on their involvement or interest in the Asian American community and how, if they are awarded this scholarship, they would contribute to the field of journalism and/or media issues involving the Asian American and Pacific Islander community. Selection is based on scholastic ability, commitment to journalism, sensitivity to Asian American and Pacific Islander issues as demonstrated by community involvement, journalistic ability, and financial need.

Financial data Stipends range from $1,000 to $5,000.

Duration 4 years for a graduating high school senior; 1 year for current undergraduate or graduate students.

Additional information This program began in 1994; it is funded by Newhouse News Service and administered by

AAJA. Recipients are also eligible for summer internships with a Newhouse publication.

Number awarded Varies each year; recently, 7 of these scholarships (2 at $5,000, 3 at $4,000, 1 at $2,000, and 1 at $1,000) were awarded.

Deadline April of each year.

[997]
SIANI LEE BROADCAST INTERNSHIP

Asian American Journalists Association
Attn: Student Programs Coordinator
1182 Market Street, Suite 320
San Francisco, CA 94102
(415) 346-2051, ext. 102   Fax: (415) 346-6343
E-mail: brandons@aaja.org
Web: www.aaja.org

Purpose To provide summer work experience in broadcast journalism at KYW-TV in Philadelphia to student members of the Asian American Journalists Association (AAJA).

Eligibility This program is open to AAJA members who are enrolled in a college program that gives academic credit for internships. Applicants must have a GPA of 2.7 or higher overall and 3.0 or higher in major courses. They must be able to demonstrate a serious interest in a career in broadcast journalism. Along with their application, they must submit an essay (150 to 200 words) on why they want to undertake this internship and what they want to gain from the experience, work samples on standard VHS tape, transcripts, and a resume.

Financial data The stipend is $2,500. Funds must be used to help defray the cost of travel and lodging.

Duration Summer months.

Additional information Interns work at KYW-TV, the CBS affiliate in Philadelphia, which established this internship in 2002 to honor former employee Siani Lee, the first Asian Pacific American anchor in Philadelphia.

Number awarded 1 each year.

Deadline March of each year.

[998]
SMITHSONIAN MINORITY STUDENT INTERNSHIP

Smithsonian Institution
Attn: Office of Fellowships
Victor Building, Suite 9300, MRC 902
P.O. Box 37012
Washington, DC 20013-7012
(202) 275-0655   Fax: (202) 275-0489
E-mail: siofg@si.edu
Web: www.si.edu/ofg/Applications/MIP/MIPapp.htm

Purpose To provide minority undergraduate or graduate students with the opportunity to work on research or museum procedure projects in specific areas of history, art, or science at the Smithsonian Institution.

Eligibility Internships are offered to minority students who are actively engaged in graduate study at any level or in upper-division undergraduate study. An overall GPA of 3.0 or higher is generally expected. Applicants must be interested in conducting research or working on museum projects in history, art, or science at the institution.

Financial data The program provides a stipend of $400 per week; travel allowances may also be offered.

Duration 10 weeks during the summer or academic year.

Number awarded Varies each year.

Deadline January of each year for summer or fall; October of each year for spring.

[999]
SODEXHO PAN ASIAN NETWORK GROUP SCHOLARSHIP

US Pan Asian American Chamber of Commerce
Attn: Scholarship Coordinator
1329 18th Street, N.W.
Washington, DC 20036
(202) 296-5221   Fax: (202) 296-5225
E-mail: administrator@uspaacc.com
Web: www.uspaacc.com/sodexho

Purpose To provide financial assistance and work experience to Asian American college students

Eligibility This program is open to college sophomores and juniors of Asian heritage who are U.S. citizens or permanent residents. Applicants must be enrolled in full-time study at an accredited 4-year college or university in the United States and working on a degree in business management, preferably food service management, hotel restaurant institution management, facilities management, or similar program leading to a bachelor's degree. They must be willing to commit to a paid internship with Sodexho during the summer. Along with their application, they must submit a 500-word essay on how they plan to use their special talents to achieve their professional goals. Selection is based on academic excellence (GPA of 3.0 or higher), leadership in extracurricular activities, and community service involvement.

Financial data The stipend is $5,000. Funds are paid directly to the recipient's college or university. An additional stipend is paid for the internship.

Duration 1 academic year for the scholarship; 8 weeks for the internship.

Additional information This program, established in 2005, is sponsored by Sodexho and its Pan Asian Network Group (PANG). Funding is not provided for correspondence courses, Internet courses, or study in a country other than the United States.

Number awarded 1 each year.

Deadline February of each year.

[1000]
SPORTS JOURNALISM INSTITUTE

Associated Press Sports Editors
c/o Sandy Bailey
Sports Illustrated
135 West 50th Street
New York, NY 10020
(212) 522-6407   E-mail: Sandy_Bailey@simail.com
Web: apse.dallasnews.com/news/sjiapplication.html

Purpose To provide student journalists (especially those of color) with an opportunity to learn more about sports journalism during the summer.

Eligibility This program is open to college juniors and sophomores, especially members of ethnic and racial minority groups. Applicants must be interested in participating in a summer program that includes a crash course in sports journalism followed by an internship in the sports department of a daily newspaper. They must submit a current college transcript, 2 letters of recommendation, up to 7 writing samples or clips, and an essay of up to 500 words stating why they should be chosen to participate in the program. Selection is based on academic achievement, demonstrated interest in sports journalism as a career, and the essay. Eligibility is not limited to journalism majors.

Financial data All expenses are paid during the crash course segment. A salary is paid during the internship portion. At the conclusion of the program, participants receive a $500 scholarship for the following year of college.

Duration 10 days for the crash course (at the end of June); 7 weeks for the internship (July through mid-August); 1 year for the college scholarship.

Additional information The crash course takes place during the annual convention of the Associated Press Sports Editors (ASPE), which provides funding for this program, along with the Times Mirror Foundation and the New York Daily News. The institute works with the National Association of Black Journalists (NABJ), the Asian American Journalists Association (AAJA), and the National Association of Hispanic Journalists (NAHJ).

Number awarded 10 each year.

Deadline December of each year.

[1001]
ST. PAUL PIONEER PRESS MINORITY INTERNSHIPS

St. Paul Pioneer Press
Attn: Ruben Rosario
345 Cedar Street
St. Paul, MN 55101-1057
(651) 228-5454   Toll-free: (800) 950-9080, ext. 5454
E-mail: rrosario@pioneerpress.com
Web: www.pioneerplanet.com

Purpose To provide summer work experience at the *St. Paul Pioneer Press* to minority college students interested in journalism as a career.

Eligibility This program at the *Pioneer Press* is open to members of minority groups who are college seniors, journalism school graduates, or postgraduate students. Previous journalism intern experience is preferred, but potential, creativity, and a passion for journalism are essential. Applicants must submit a resume, cover letter, 6 to 8 samples of published work (or published slides for photography candidates), names and contact info for 3 references, and a 2-page essay that provides a general idea of their life pursuits.

Financial data Interns receive a salary competitive to that of an entry level reporter.

Duration 10 weeks in the summer.

Additional information Interns work in copy editing, reporting, computer-assisted reporting, photography, and graphic design.

Number awarded 4 each year.

Deadline January of each year.

[1002]
ST. PETERSBURG TIMES 1-YEAR INTERNSHIPS

St. Petersburg Times
Attn: Deputy Managing Editor
490 First Avenue South
P.O. Box 1121
St. Petersburg, FL 33731-1121
(727) 893-8869   Toll-free: (800) 333-7505, ext. 8869
Fax: (727) 892-2257   E-mail: hooker@sptimes.com
Web: www.sptimes.com/internship

Purpose To provide news reporting work experience at the *St. Petersburg Times* to minority and other recent college graduates.

Eligibility This program is open to graduated college seniors from any state who are interested in preparing for a career in the newspaper industry. Applicants should have experience at a college publication and at least 1 professional internship. They must submit a cover letter, resume, 3 references, and 10 or 12 clips that show the range of their work. Preference is given to applicants who will add diversity to the newsroom.

Financial data The salary is $625 per week. Full benefits are provided.

Duration 1 year, beginning in September.

Additional information Interns work in local news reporting at the *St. Petersburg Times.*

Number awarded 2 each year.

Deadline January of each year.

[1003]
STANFORD CHEN INTERNSHIP GRANTS

Asian American Journalists Association
Attn: Student Programs Coordinator
1182 Market Street, Suite 320
San Francisco, CA 94102
(415) 346-2051, ext. 102   Fax: (415) 346-6343
E-mail: brandons@aaja.org
Web: www.aaja.org

Purpose To provide supplemental grants to student members of the Asian American Journalists Association (AAJA) working as interns at small or medium-size news organizations.

Eligibility This program is open to AAJA members who are college juniors or seniors with a serious intent to prepare for a career in print or broadcast journalism. Applicants must be an intern or have been accepted into a journalism internship program with a print or broadcast company. Daily circulation for print companies must be less than 100,000; for broadcast, markets 50 to 100 are eligible. Selection is based on an essay of 150 to 200 words on how an internship at a small to medium-size newspaper or broadcast outlet will benefit the applicant's career, a resume, a letter of recommendation, and financial need.

Financial data The grant is $1,500. Funds must be used to defray the cost-of-living expenses, pay for transportation to the internship site, or supplement low-paying or unpaid internships.

Additional information This program began in 2000.

Number awarded 3 each year, of which 1 is designated for a resident of the Pacific Northwest.

Deadline May of each year.

[1004]
SUMMER RESEARCH PROGRAM IN ECOLOGY

Harvard University
Harvard Forest
324 North Main Street
P.O. Box 68
Petersham, MA 01366-0068
(978) 724-3302   Fax: (978) 724-3595
E-mail: hfapps@fas.harvard.edu
Web: harvardforest.fas.harvard.edu

Purpose To provide an opportunity for minority and other undergraduate students and recent graduates to participate in a summer ecological research project at Harvard Forest in Petersham, Massachusetts.

Eligibility This program is open to undergraduate students and recent graduates interested in participating in a research project at the Forest in collaboration with an investigator from Harvard University, Marine Biological Laboratory Ecosystem Center, University of New Hampshire, or other institutions. The research focuses on the effects of natural and human disturbances on forest ecosystems, including atmospheric pollution, global warming, hurricanes, treefalls, and insect outbreaks. Investigators come from many disciplines, and specific projects center on population and community ecology, paleoecology, land-use history, wildlife biology, biochemistry, soil science, ecophysiology, and atmosphere-biosphere exchanges. Students from diverse backgrounds are strongly encouraged to apply.

Financial data The stipend is $3,600. Free housing and meals are also provided.

Duration 12 weeks during the summer.

Additional information Funding for this program is provided by the National Science Foundation (as part of its Research Experience for Undergraduates Program) and the Andrew W. Mellon Foundation (as part of its United Negro College Fund Summer Internship Program for Ecology Research).

Number awarded Up to 25 each year.

Deadline February of each year.

[1005]
SUMMER TRANSPORTATION INTERNSHIP PROGRAM FOR DIVERSE GROUPS

Department of Transportation
Federal Highway Administration
Attn: Office of Human Resources
HAHR-3, Room 4323
400 Seventh Street, S.W.
Washington, DC 20590
(202) 366-1159
Web: www.fhwa.dot.gov/education/stipdg.htm

Purpose To enable students from diverse groups to gain work experience during the summer at facilities of the U.S. Department of Transportation (DOT).

Eligibility This program is open to undergraduate students who are women, persons with disabilities, and members of diverse social and ethnic groups. Applicants must be U.S. citizens currently enrolled in a degree-granting program of study at an accredited institution of higher learning at the undergraduate (community or junior college, university, college, or Tribal College) or graduate level. They must be entering their junior or senior year (students attending a Tribal College must have completed their "first year" of school). Students who will graduate during the spring or summer are not eligible unless they have been accepted for enrollment in graduate school. Major fields of study include, but are not limited to, aviation, business, criminal justice, economics, engineering, environmental studies, hazardous materials, law, management information systems, marketing, planning, public administration, or transportation management. Applicants must be interested in a summer work experience at various DOT facilities. They must have a GPA of 3.0 or higher. Law students must be entering their second or third year and must be in the upper 30% of their class. Selection is based on an expressed interest in pursuing a transportation-related career, GPA or class standing, a reference from a professor or advisor, the endorsement of the department chair, an essay on transportation interests, areas of interest outside of school, and completeness of application package.

Financial data   A stipend is paid (amount not specified).

Duration   10 weeks during the summer.

Additional information   Assignments are at the DOT headquarters in Washington, D.C., a selected modal administration, or selected field offices around the country.

Number awarded   Varies each year; recently, 17 interns participated in this program.

Deadline   February of each year.

[1006]
TEACH FOR AMERICA FELLOWSHIPS

Teach for America
315 West 36th Street, Sixth Floor
New York, NY 10018
(212) 279-2080   Toll-free: (800) 832-1230
Fax: (212) 279-2081
E-mail: admissions@teachforamerica.org
Web: www.teachforamerica.org/program.html

Purpose   To provide an opportunity for minority and other recent college graduates to serve as teachers in America's rural and urban public school classrooms.

Eligibility   This program recruits students or college graduates for appointments in school districts with severe teacher shortages. A special effort is made to select corps members who are diverse in every respect, particularly with regard to ethnic, racial, and cultural background. All academic majors are eligible, but applicants with a mathematics, science, or engineering major are especially encouraged. No previous education course work is necessary, but a GPA of 2.5 or higher and U.S. citizenship or permanent resident status are required.

Financial data   This program covers major expenses for the summer institute, including room and board and academic materials. It also covers room and board during a regional induction. Corps members are responsible for the cost of transportation to the summer institute, and from the summer institute to their placement site. They are also responsible for their own moving expenses, testing fees, and any necessary credits and district fees. During a transitional period before they begin working, they are eligible for grants and no-interest loans ranging from $1,000 to $5,000, depending on their financial need and cost of living in their assigned region. Teach for America then places recruits in

jobs paying $25,000 to $43,000 per year. This program also has a relationship with AmeriCorps that makes participants eligible for forbearance on student loans during their period of service and to receive an AmeriCorps education award of $4,725 for each year of service.

Duration   2 years.

Additional information   Once selected for this program, participants attend a 5-week summer institute where they receive additional professional development and support. They then travel to their assigned regions for a 1- to 2-week induction, which helps orient them to the schools, school districts, and communities where they will be teaching. Urban assignments are currently available in Atlanta, Baltimore, Chicago, Detroit, Houston, greater New Orleans, Los Angeles, New Jersey, New York City, Phoenix, the San Francisco Bay Area (especially the east bay), St. Louis, and Washington, D.C.; rural assignments are available in south Louisiana, the Mississippi delta (in Arkansas and Mississippi), an Indian reservation in New Mexico, eastern North Carolina, and the Rio Grande Valley of Texas. There is a $25 application fee.

Number awarded   Nearly 2,000 each year.

Deadline   February or October of each year.

[1007]
TRAINEESHIPS IN OCEANOGRAPHY FOR MINORITY UNDERGRADUATES

Woods Hole Oceanographic Institution
Attn: Education Office
Clark Laboratory 223, MS #31
360 Woods Hole Road
Woods Hole, MA 02543-1541
(508) 289-2219   Fax: (508) 457-2188
E-mail: education@whoi.edu
Web: www.whoi.edu

Purpose   To provide work experience to minority group members who are interested in preparing for a career in the marine sciences, oceanographic engineering, or marine policy.

Eligibility   This program is open to ethnic minority undergraduates enrolled in U.S. colleges or universities who have completed at least 2 semesters of study and who are interested in the marine sciences, oceanographic engineering, or marine policy. Applicants must be U.S. citizens or permanent residents and African American or Black; Asian American; Chicano, Mexican American, Puerto Rican or other Hispanic; or Native American.

Financial data   The stipend is $396 per week; trainees may also receive additional support for travel to Woods Hole.

Duration   10 to 12 weeks during the summer or 1 semester during the academic year; renewable.

Additional information   Trainees are assigned advisors who supervise their research programs and supplementary study activities. Some traineeships involve field work or research cruises. This program is sponsored by the Northeast Fisheries Science Center of the National Marine Fisheries Service (U.S. National Oceanic and Atmospheric Administration), the Center for Marine and Coastal Geology (U.S. Geological Survey), and the Office of Naval Research.

Number awarded   4 to 5 each year.

Deadline For a summer appointment, applications must be submitted in February of each year. For the remaining portion of the year, applications may be submitted at any time, but they must be received at least 2 months before the anticipated starting date.

[1008]
TRANSPORTATION SECURITY ADMINISTRATION MINORITY INTERNSHIP PROGRAM

ADNET Systems, Inc.
11260 Roger Bacon Drive, Suite 403
Reston, VA 20190
(703) 709-7218   Fax: (703) 709-7219
Web: www.adnet-sys.com

Purpose To provide work experience at facilities of the U.S. Transportation Security Administration (TSA) to minority and disabled students.

Eligibility This program is open to students who are from Historically Black Colleges and Universities (HBCUs), Hispanic Service Institutions (HSIs), Tribal Colleges and Universities (TCUs), Asian American and Pacific Islander communities, and disability communities. Applicants must be U.S. citizens currently enrolled in a college, university, or law school as a sophomore or above (including graduate students) with a GPA of 3.0 or higher; recent (within 6 months) graduates are also eligible. They must be interested in an internship at a TSA facility. Jobs have included, but are not limited to, accounting, business, human resources, law, computer science, mathematics, journalism, and criminal justice. Along with their application, they must submit 200-word statements on 1) their community activities, hobbies, associations, publications, and other relevant experience; and 2) why they want to participate in this program.

Financial data Interns are paid a stipend and receive housing.

Duration 10 weeks in summer or fall; 15 weeks in spring.

Additional information Recently, assignments were available at TSA facilities in Denver, Detroit, Honolulu, Houston, Miami, Newark, San Francisco, and Washington, D.C.

Number awarded Varies each year.

Deadline April of each year for summer; July of each year for fall; November of each year for spring.

[1009]
UNCF/HOUSEHOLD CORPORATE SCHOLARS PROGRAM

United Negro College Fund
Attn: Corporate Scholars Program
P.O. Box 1435
Alexandria, VA 22313-9998
Toll-free: (866) 671-7237   E-mail: internship@uncf.org
Web: www.uncf.org/internships/index.asp

Purpose To provide financial assistance and work experience to minority and other students majoring in fields related to business.

Eligibility This program is open to rising juniors majoring in accounting, business, computer science, finance, human resources, or marketing with a GPA of 3.0 or higher. Applicants must be interested in an internship with Household International, the program's sponsor, at 1 of the following sites: Bridgewater, New Jersey; Charlotte, North Carolina; Chesapeake, Virginia; Chicago, Illinois; Dallas, Texas; Indianapolis, Indiana; Jacksonville, Florida; Monterey, California; New Castle, Delaware; San Diego, California; or Tampa, Florida. Preference is given to applicants who reside in those areas, but students who live in other areas are also considered. African Americans, Hispanic Americans, American Indians, and Asian Americans are encouraged to apply. Along with their application, students must submit an essay on their personal and career goals and objectives, a letter of recommendation, and an official transcript.

Financial data This program provides a stipend of up to $10,000 per year and a paid internship.

Duration 8 to 10 weeks for the internships; 1 year for the scholarships, which may be renewed.

Number awarded Varies each year.

Deadline February of each year.

[1010]
UNCF/SPRINT SCHOLARS PROGRAM

United Negro College Fund
Attn: Corporate Scholars Program
P.O. Box 1435
Alexandria, VA 22313-9998
Toll-free: (866) 671-7237   E-mail: internship@uncf.org
Web: www.uncf.org/internships/index.asp

Purpose To provide financial assistance and work experience to minority students who are majoring in selected business and science fields.

Eligibility This program is open to members of minority groups who are enrolled full time as juniors or seniors at a 4-year college or university in the United States. Applicants must have a GPA of 3.0 or higher and be majoring in accounting, business, computer engineering, computer information systems, computer science, economics, electrical engineering, finance, industrial engineering, journalism, marketing, management information systems, public relations, or statistics. They must be interested in a summer internship at Sprint. Along with their application, they must submit a 1-page personal statement describing their career interests and goals, a current resume, a letter of recommendation, official transcripts, and a financial need statement.

Financial data This program provides a paid internship and (upon successful completion of the internship) a need-based stipend of up to $7,500.

Duration 10 to 12 weeks for the internships; 1 year for the scholarships.

Additional information This program is sponsored by Sprint. Recipients may attend any of the 39 member institutions of the United Negro College Fund (UNCF), other Historically Black Colleges and Universities (HBCUs), or an accredited majority 4-year college or university.

Number awarded Varies each year.

Deadline October of each year.

[1011]
UNION SUMMER INTERNSHIPS

AFL-CIO
Attn: Union Summer
815 16th Street, N.W.
Washington, DC 20006
(202) 639-6220   Toll-free: (800) 952-2550
Fax: (202) 639-6230   E-mail: unionsummer@aflcio.org
Web: www.aflcio.org/aboutunions/unionsummer

Purpose To provide minority and other college juniors and seniors with a summer opportunity to learn more about social justice through workplace and community organizing.

Eligibility This program is open to college students entering their senior year or planning to graduate. Applicants must be interested in participating in a summer activity to learn more about organizing unions to work for social justice. Desirable qualifications include "strong commitments to social and economic justice, as well as an openness to work with people of a different race, ethnicity, religion or sexual orientation." Applicants should be "people oriented, enthusiastic, energetic, flexible and willing to work long hours on an unpredictable schedule." Previous union experience is not required. Women and people of color are especially encouraged to apply.

Financial data The stipend is $300 per week. Transportation to the site and housing are also provided.

Duration 2 sessions are held each summer, each lasting 5 weeks; the first session begins in June and the second in July. Interns are assigned to 1 of those sessions.

Additional information Internships are conducted at selected sites throughout the country.

Number awarded Varies each year; since this program began in 1996, more than 2,500 students and other activists have participated.

Deadline April of each year.

[1012]
U.S. COAST GUARD MINORITY-SERVING INSTITUTIONS INTERNSHIP PROGRAM

ADNET Systems, Inc.
11260 Roger Bacon Drive, Suite 403
Reston, VA 20190
(703) 709-7218   Fax: (703) 709-7219
Web: www.adnet-sys.com

Purpose To provide summer work experience at facilities of the U.S. Coast Guard to minority and disabled students.

Eligibility This program is open to students who are from Historically Black Colleges and Universities (HBCUs), Hispanic Service Institutions (HSIs), Tribal Colleges and Universities (TCUs), Asian American and Pacific Islander communities, and disability communities. Applicants must be U.S. citizens currently enrolled as a sophomore or higher undergraduate, graduate, or law student with a GPA of 3.0 or higher. They must be interested in an internship at a Coast Guard facility. Jobs have included, but are not limited to, accounting, business, health management, human resources, international affairs, law, computer science, engineering, journalism, and criminal justice. Along with their application, they must submit 200-word statements on 1) their community activities, hobbies, associations, publications, and other relevant experience; and 2) why they want to participate in this program.

Financial data Interns are paid a stipend and receive housing.

Duration 10 weeks in the summer.

Additional information Most openings are at Coast Guard headquarters in Washington, D.C., other recent assignments included Coast Guard facilities in Honolulu (Hawaii), Massena (New York), New London (Connecticut), Norfolk (Virginia), and Topeka (Kansas). Information is also available from Karen Gillaspie, (202) 267-1866.

Number awarded Varies each year.

Deadline April of each year.

[1013]
VAID FELLOWSHIPS

National Gay and Lesbian Task Force
Attn: Policy Institute
214 West 29th Street, Fourth Floor
New York, NY 10001
(212) 604-9830   Fax: (212) 604-9831
E-mail: ngltf@ngltf.org
Web: www.thetaskforce.org/about/vaid.htm

Purpose To provide work experience related to the leadership of people of color in the progressive movement for lesbian, gay, bisexual, and transgendered (LGBT) equality.

Eligibility Applicants must be enrolled in a degree program at least half time as an undergraduate, graduate, or law student or have successfully completed an undergraduate, graduate, or law degree within the preceding 12 months. They should have 1) a desire to work in a multicultural environment where commitment to diversity based on race, ethnic origin, gender, age, sexual orientation, and physical ability is an important institutional value; 2) demonstrated leadership in progressive and/or LGBT communities; 3) extensive research, writing, and critical thinking skills; 4) knowledge of, and commitment to, LGBT issues; and 5) computer proficiency in word processing, database work, e-mail, and Internet research. The program supports and recognizes the leadership of people of color and other emerging leaders in public policy, legal, and social science research.

Financial data The stipend is $400 per week. Fellows are responsible for their own housing and living expenses.

Duration 11 weeks, either in the winter or summer.

Additional information The Policy Institute of the National Gay and Lesbian Task Force (NGLTF), founded in 1995, is the largest think tank in the United States engaged in research, policy analysis, and strategic action to advance equality and understanding of LGBT people. Its activities include the racial and economic justice initiative, family policy issues, aging and youth policy issues, voting behavior and political representation issues, public opinion, workplace benefit and discrimination issues, the impact of anti-LGBT ballot initiatives and the anti-LGBT movement, and documenting basic demographics of the LGBT community.

Number awarded Normally, 1 winter and 3 summer fellows are selected.

Deadline January of each year for winter; March of each year for summer.

[1014]
VILLAGE VOICE/MARY WRIGHT WRITING FELLOWSHIP

Village Voice
Attn: Editorial Department
36 Cooper Square
New York, NY 10003-7118
(212) 475-3300
Web: www.villagevoice.com

Purpose To provide work experience to minority college students interested in interning at the *Village Voice,* a weekly newspaper published in New York City.

Eligibility This program is open to minority college students interested in interning at the *Village Voice.* While journalism experience is not an absolute requirement, candidates should possess research skills, an aptitude for critical thought, and a familiarity with the *Village Voice.* Interested students should submit samples of their written or editorial work, a resume, a letter of recommendation, an application form, and a self-addressed stamped envelope.

Financial data The stipend is $150 per week.

Duration 4 months, usually beginning in January, May/June, or September.

Additional information The *Village Voice* is known for its investigative journalism as well as coverage of cultural events (including reporting on film, art, theater, books, and dance). Interns have the opportunity to work with well-known journalists on the newspaper. College credit may be arranged.

Number awarded Varies each session.

Deadline December for the spring session; March for the summer session; July for the fall semester; November for the winter session.

[1015]
VIRGINIA PRESS ASSOCIATION MINORITY INTERNSHIPS

Virginia Press Association
Attn: Minority Internship Program
11529 Nuckols Road
Glen Allen, VA 23059
(804) 521-7570   Toll-free: (800) 849-8717
Fax: (804) 521-7590   E-mail: arleneh@vpa.net
Web: www.vpa.net

Purpose To provide summer work experience in journalism to minority students in Virginia.

Eligibility This program is open to minority students at the level of sophomore through graduate school who are residents of Virginia or attending a college or university in Virginia. Applicants must have at least a 2.0 GPA, be able to type and/or use a word processor, be willing to move to the location of the host newspaper, and have a driver's license and access to a car. They must be interested in a summer internship at a newspaper in Virginia. Along with their application, they must submit a college transcript, 3 references, a 1-page resume, 3 samples of published work, and a 500-word essay on why they want to work in the newspaper industry and how this internship will help them advance their career plans.

Financial data These are paid internships.

Duration 10 weeks during the summer.

Number awarded 2 each year.

Deadline March of each year.

[1016]
VITO MARZULLO INTERNSHIP PROGRAM

Office of the Governor
Attn: Department of Central Management Services
503 William G. Stratton Building
Springfield, IL 62706
(217) 524-1381   Fax: (217) 785-7702
TDD: (217) 785-3979
Web: www.illinois.gov/gov/intopportunities.cfm

Purpose To provide minority and other recent college graduates with work experience in the Illinois Governor's office.

Eligibility Applicants must be residents of Illinois who have completed a bachelor's degree and are interested in working in the Illinois Governor's office or in various agencies under the Governor's jurisdiction. They may have majored in any field, but they must be able to demonstrate a substantial commitment to excellence as evidenced by academic honors, leadership ability, extracurricular activities, and involvement in community or public service. Along with their application, they must submit 1) a 500-word personal statement on the qualities or attributes they will bring to the program, their career goals or plans, how their selection for this program would assist them in achieving those goals, and what they expect to gain from the program; and 2) a 1,000-word essay in which they identify and analyze a public issue that they feel has great impact on state government. A particular goal of the program is to achieve affirmative action through the nomination of qualified minorities, women, and persons with disabilities.

Financial data The stipend is $27,900 per year.

Duration 1 year, beginning in August.

Additional information Assignments are in Springfield and, to a limited extent, in Chicago.

Number awarded Varies each year.

Deadline January of each year.

[1017]
VSA ARTS INTERNSHIPS

VSA Arts
Attn: Human Resource Manager
1300 Connecticut Avenue, N.W., Suite 700
Washington, DC 20036
(202) 628-2800   Toll-free: (800) 933-8721
Fax: (202) 737-0725   TTY: (202) 737-0645
E-mail: hr@vsarts.org
Web: www.vsarts.org/x214.xml

Purpose To provide work experience in arts education at the Very Special Arts (VSA) program of the John F. Kennedy Center for the Performing Arts.

Eligibility This program is open to upper-division undergraduate and graduate students in arts education, arts administration, museum education, and/or disability fields. Applicants must be interested in working in 1 of the following departments at the VSA office in Washington, D.C.: arts administration, communications, educational research, event planning, exhibition design and fabrication, or information technology. Along with their application, they must submit a cover letter describing their career goals, a resume, 2 letters of recommendation, and writing samples. Minorities and persons with disabilities are encouraged to apply.

Financial data   A stipend of $650 per month may be paid.

Duration   3 months, in the fall (September through December), spring (January through April), or summer (June through August).

Additional information   The sponsor, VSA Arts, was formerly known as Very Special Arts.

Number awarded   1 or more each year.

Deadline   Applications may be submitted at any time.

[1018]
WALT DISNEY STUDIOS AND ABC ENTERTAINMENT WRITING FELLOWSHIP PROGRAM

Walt Disney Studios and ABC Entertainment
Attn: Writing Fellowship Program
500 South Buena Vista Street
Burbank, CA 91521-4389
(818) 560-6894   E-mail: abc.fellowships@abc.com
Web: www.abctalendevelopment.com

Purpose   To provide support to minority and other writers interested in developing their craft at Walt Disney Studios and ABC Entertainment.

Eligibility   This program is open to all writers, although a goal of the program is to seek out and employ culturally and ethnically diverse new writers. Applicants must submit a writing sample; for the feature films division, that should be a completed live-action motion picture screenplay (up to 120 pages) or a full-length 2-to-3 act play; for the television division, the sample should be a full-length script appropriate for a half-hour or 1-hour television series, based on a current prime time television or cable broadcast series.

Financial data   The salary is $50,000.

Duration   1 year, beginning in January.

Additional information   Fellows train with creative teams either at Walt Disney Studios or ABC Entertainment. This program began in 1990.

Number awarded   Up to 11 each year.

Deadline   June of each year.

[1019]
WALTER O. SPOFFORD, JR. MEMORIAL INTERNSHIP

Resources for the Future
Attn: Coordinator for Academic Programs
1616 P Street, N.W.
Washington, DC 20036-1400
(202) 328-5060   Fax: (202) 939-3460
E-mail: mankin@rff.org
Web: www.rff.org

Purpose   To provide summer internships to minority and other graduate students interested in working on Chinese environmental issues at Resources for the Future (RFF).

Eligibility   This program is open to first- or second-year graduate students with a special interest in Chinese environmental issues. Applicants must be interested in an internship in Washington, D.C. at RFF. They should have outstanding policy analysis and writing skills. Women and minority candidates are strongly encouraged to apply. Both

U.S. and non-U.S. citizens (especially Chinese students) are eligible, if the latter have proper work and residency documentation.

Financial data   The stipend depends on individual circumstances. Support for travel expenses and visa assistance are also available.

Duration   The duration of the internship depends on the intern's situation.

Number awarded   1 each year.

Deadline   February of each year.

[1020]
WCVB-TV SUMMER MINORITY INTERNSHIP PROGRAM

WCVB-TV
Attn: Human Resources Department
5 TV Place
Needham, MA 02494-2303
(781) 433-0461   Fax: (781) 449-6682
E-mail: lwalsh@hearstsc.com
Web: www.thebostonchannel.com

Purpose   To provide work experience at WCVB-TV in Boston to minorities who are interested in broadcast journalism as a career.

Eligibility   Applicants must have completed their freshman year, be majoring in some field of broadcasting, be U.S. citizens, and be minorities or others disadvantaged by economic or social conditions. They must be interested in interning at WCVB-TV in Boston.

Financial data   Interns receive the minimum wage for 37.5 hours per week. They also receive funding for meals and transportation.

Duration   12 weeks during the summer.

Additional information   This program at WCVB-TV provides an opportunity for participants to obtain an overview of the television broadcasting field in news, programming, public affairs, or sales. Interns must provide their own transportation.

Number awarded   5 each year.

Deadline   April of each year.

[1021]
WILLIAM KELLY SIMPSON INTERNSHIP FOR EGYPTIAN ART

Metropolitan Museum of Art
Attn: Internship Programs
1000 Fifth Avenue
New York, NY 10028-0198
(212) 570-3710   Fax: (212) 570-3782
E-mail: mmainterns@metmuseum.org
Web: www.metmuseum.org

Purpose   To provide summer work experience at the Metropolitan Museum of Art to minority and other graduate students interested in ancient Egyptian art.

Eligibility   This internship is available to graduate students who have completed the course work for a master's degree in Egyptology or in art history with a main emphasis on ancient Egyptian art. Applicants of diverse backgrounds are encouraged to apply.

Financial data   The honorarium is $3,250.

Duration   10 weeks, beginning in June.

Additional information The intern works with the curatorial staff at the Metropolitan Museum of Art on projects related to the museum's Egyptian collection or a special exhibition. This internship is funded by the Marilyn M. Simpson Charitable Trust

Number awarded 1 each year.

Deadline January of each year.

[1022]
WISE PROGRAM

Washington Internships for Students of Engineering
c/o IEEE-USA
1828 L Street, N.W., Suite 1202
Washington, DC 20036-5104
(202) 785-0017   Fax: (202) 785-0835
E-mail: e.wissolik@ieee.org
Web: www.wise-intern.org/apply.html

Purpose To provide summer work experience in the Washington D.C. area to minority and other engineering students.

Eligibility This program is open to third- and fourth-year undergraduate engineering students and recent graduates beginning study in an engineering policy-related master's program. Interns learn about the operation of government and the interaction between the engineering community and the government in matters of public policy, as well as the way in which engineers can and do contribute to public policy decisions in complex technological matters. Minority students are encouraged to apply. U.S. citizenship is required.

Financial data The stipend is $1,800; lodging and travel expenses are also covered.

Duration 10 weeks, in the summer.

Additional information This internship program is sponsored by a number of engineering and scientific societies, which select and sponsor the student participants. Sponsors include the American Institute of Chemical Engineers (AIChE), the American Nuclear Society (ANS), the American Society of Civil Engineers (ASCE), the American Society of Mechanical Engineers (ASME), the Institute of Electrical and Electronics Engineers (IEEE), the National Science Foundation (NSF), the National Society of Professional Engineers (NSPE), and the Society of Automotive Engineers (SAE). Interns are under the guidance of an engineering professor and receive academic credit. Applicants seeking sponsorship by ANS, ASCE, ASME, or IEEE must be members of those societies.

Number awarded Up to 16 each year.

Deadline December of each year.

[1023]
Y.E.S. TO JOBS COLLEGE PROGRAM

Y.E.S. to Jobs
P.O. Box 3390
Los Angeles, CA 90078-3390
(310) 358-4922   Fax: (310) 358-4330
E-mail: ytjcollegedir@aol.com
Web: www.yestojobs.org

Purpose To provide work experience to minority college students interested in a managerial career in the music industry.

Eligibility This program is open to minority (African American, Asian American, Hispanic American, and Native American) students from 18 to 25 years of age who are actively enrolled in a college or university in Los Angeles or New York. Applicants must have a GPA of 2.5 or higher and an interest in music, media, or business. They must be interested in employment during the fall, winter, or spring in entry level positions at record companies, retail stores, radio and television stations, cable networks, trade publications, film and production companies, public relations and entertainment law firms, or multi-media companies. There is no formal application; interested students must submit a cover letter and resume. The program manager invites selected students to an interview and offers assignments on a first-come, first-served basis.

Financial data Employers establish the salary they pay interns, but most are minimum wage.

Duration The length of the internship varies according to the needs and interests of the employer and the intern.

Additional information This program was established by A&M Records in 1987, and was expanded to include college students in 2003. Y.E.S. stands for Youth Entertainment Summer.

Number awarded Varies each year.

Deadline Applications may be submitted at any time.

[1024]
Y.E.S. TO JOBS HIGH SCHOOL PROGRAM

Y.E.S. to Jobs
P.O. Box 3390
Los Angeles, CA 90078-3390
(310) 358-4922   Fax: (310) 358-4330
E-mail: yestojobs@aol.com
Web: www.yestojobs.org

Purpose To provide summer work experience to minority high school students interested in a managerial career in the music industry.

Eligibility This program is open to minority (African American, Asian American, Hispanic American, and Native American) high school students from 16 to 18 years of age in the following cities: Atlanta, Los Angeles, Miami, Nashville, New York, and Washington, D.C. Applicants must have a GPA of 2.8 or higher, a 90% attendance record in school, and an interest in music, media, or business. They must be interested in full-time summer employment in entry level positions at record companies, retail stores, radio and television stations, cable networks, trade publications, film and production companies, public relations and entertainment law firms, or multi-media companies. Selection is based on self-motivation, dependability, and willingness to take initiative and work hard.

Financial data Employers establish the salary they pay interns, but most are minimum wage.

Duration 8 to 10 weeks during the summer.

Additional information This program was established by A&M Records in 1987, and became a nonprofit organization in 1994. Y.E.S. stands for Youth Entertainment Summer.

Number awarded Varies each year; recently, more than 250 internships were provided.

Deadline February of each year for positions in Los Angeles; March of each year for other cities.

[1025]
ZINA GARRISON MINORITY INTERNSHIP

Women's Sports Foundation
Attn: Award and Grant Programs Manager
Eisenhower Park
1899 Hempstead Turnpike, Suite 400
East Meadow, NY 11554-1000
(516) 542-4700   Toll-free: (800) 227-3988
Fax: (516) 542-4716   E-mail: wosport@aol.com
Web: www.womenssportsfoundation.org

Purpose To provide work experience at the Women's Sports Foundation to women of color interested in a sports-related career.

Eligibility This program is open to women of color who are undergraduate students, college graduates, graduate students, or women in career change. Applicants must be interested in working at the foundation offices on Long Island, New York. They must submit a personal statement that includes their sports background and current participation, issues and sports topics that interest them, their motivation for interning with the foundation, and what they hope to receive for themselves from the experience. An interview is required.

Financial data The salary is $1,000 per month.

Duration Sessions run from January through May, June through August, and September through December. Interns may complete 1, 2, or 3 sessions consecutively, but they must complete each session in its entirety.

Additional information Assignments are available in the athlete services, development, education, program management, public relations and communications, publications, special events, and web editorial departments. Interns may receive academic credit for their work.

Number awarded 2 or 3 each year.

Deadline Applications should be submitted no later than 120 days prior to the desired internship start date.

Indexes

Program Title Index

If you know the name of a particular funding program and want to find out where it is covered in the directory, use the Program Title Index. Here, program titles are arranged alphabetically, word by word. To assist you in your search, every program is listed by all its known names or abbreviations. In addition, we've used an alphabetical code (within parentheses) to help you determine if the program falls within your scope of interest: S = Scholarships; F = Fellowships; L = Loans; G = Grants; A = Awards; and I = Internships. Here's how the code works: if a program is followed (S) 141, the program is described in entry 141 in the Scholarships section. If the same program title is followed by another entry number—for example, (L) 680—the program is also described in entry 680 in the Loans section. Remember: the numbers cited here refer to program entry numbers, not to page numbers in the book.

Illinois Arts Council Ethnic and Folk Arts Master/Apprentice Program, (G) 764

Illinois Broadcasters Association Minority Internships, (I) 924

Illinois Consortium for Educational Opportunity Program. *See* Diversifying Higher Education Faculty in Illinois, entry (L) 664

Illinois Future Teacher Corps Program, (L) 668

Illinois Minority Graduate Incentive Program. *See* Diversifying Higher Education Faculty in Illinois, entry (L) 664

Illinois Minority Real Estate Scholarship, (S) 175, (F) 512

Illinois Podiatric Medical Student Scholarships, (L) 669

India Heritage Award for High School Graduates, (S) 176

Indian American Scholarship Fund Financial Aid Scholarships. *See* IASF Financial Aid Scholarships, entry (S) 173

Indian American Scholarship Fund Merit Scholarships, (S) 177

Ing Memorial Scholarship. *See* Mary Moy Quan Ing Memorial Scholarship, entry (S) 220

Innes Scholarship. *See* SEO Scholars Program, entry (S) 318

Innis Maggiore Scholarship. *See* Cleveland Advertising Association Education Foundation Scholarships, entry (S) 78

Inouye Fellowship Program. *See* Daniel K. Inouye Fellowship Program, entry (I) 892

Inouye Scholarship. *See* Ken Inouye Scholarship, entries (S) 197, (F) 525

Institute for Civil Society Fellowships, (G) 765

Institute for Research on Poverty Visiting Scholars Program, (G) 766

Institute for Women's Policy Research Summer Internships. *See* IWPR Summer Internships, entry (I) 926

International Communications Industries Association College Scholarships, (S) 178, (F) 513

International Communications Industries Association High School Scholarships, (S) 179

International Security and Cooperation Postdoctoral Fellowships, (G) 767

International Security and Cooperation Predoctoral Fellowships, (G) 768

International Security and Cooperation Professional Fellowships, (G) 769

Internship in Educational Media, (I) 925

Inyong Ham Scholarship. *See* KSEA Scholarships, entries (S) 204, (F) 527

Iowa Conference Ethnic Minority Scholarship, (F) 514

Ishimoto Memorial Scholarship. *See* Patricia and Gail Ishimoto Memorial Scholarship, entry (S) 276

Itano Memorial Scholarship. *See* Masao and Sumako Itano Memorial Scholarship, entry (S) 222

ITS Washington Intelligent Transportation Systems Scholarship. *See* WTS/ITS Washington Intelligent Transportation Systems Scholarship, entries (S) 390, (F) 654

IWPR Summer Internships, (I) 926

J. Hoover Mackin Research Grants. *See* Geological Society of America General Research Grants Program, entry (G) 752

Jack and Lewis Rudin Internships, (I) 927

Jackie Chan Scholarships, (S) 180

Jackie Joyner–Kersee Minority Internship, (I) 928

Jackie Robinson Scholarships, (S) 181

Jackson Scholarship Award for Ethnic Minority Gifted/Talented Students with Disabilities. *See* Stanley E. Jackson Scholarship Award for Ethnic Minority Gifted/Talented Students with Disabilities, entry (S) 334

Jackson Scholarship Award for Ethnic Minority Students with Disabilities. *See* Stanley E. Jackson Scholarship Award for Ethnic Minority Students with Disabilities, entry (S) 335

Jaini Emerging Leader Scholarship. *See* Asha Jaini Emerging Leader Scholarship, entry (I) 867

Jaini Memorial Graduate Leadership Fellowship. *See* Asha Jaini Memorial Graduate Leadership Fellowship, entry (I) 868

James A. Rawley Prize, (A) 839

James Carlson Memorial Scholarship, (S) 182, (F) 515

James E. Webb Internships, (I) 929

James Echols Scholarship, (S) 183, (F) 516

James G.K. McClure Educational and Development Fund Scholarships, (S) 184

James H. Dunn, Jr. Memorial Fellowship Program, (I) 930

James J. Wychor Scholarships, (S) 185

James Michener Scholarship. *See* Mari and James Michener Scholarship, entry (S) 217

James S.C. Chao Scholarship. *See* Ruth Mu–Lan Chu and James S.C. Chao Scholarship, entry (S) 304

Japanese American Bar Scholarship, (F) 517

Japanese Medical Society of America Medical Student Scholarship, (F) 518

Japanese Medical Society of America Nursing Student Scholarship, (S) 186

Jasumati B. Patel Memorial Award, (S) 187

Je Hyun Kim Scholarship. *See* KSEA Scholarships, entries (S) 204, (F) 527

Jean Coyne Family Foundation Awards. *See* Worldstudio Foundation Scholarships, entries (S) 386, (F) 652

Jean Marshall Minority Scholarships, (S) 188

Jeanne Spurlock Minority Medical Student Clinical Fellowship in Child and Adolescent Psychiatry, (I) 931

Jeanne Spurlock Research Fellowship in Drug Abuse and Addiction for Minority Medical Students, (I) 932

Jeffrey Campbell Graduate Fellows Program, (G) 770

Jennison Award. *See* Worldstudio Foundation Scholarships, entries (S) 386, (F) 652

Jensen Scholarship. *See* Herbert Jensen Scholarship, entry (S) 167

Jere W. Thompson, Jr. Scholarship, (S) 189, (I) 933

Jewel Award for Women Artists. *See* Lilla Jewel Award for Women Artists, entry (G) 774

Jimmy A. Young Memorial Education Recognition Award, (S) 190

Joe Allman Scholarship, (S) 191

John and Elizabeth Phillips Fellowship, (G) 771

John F. Aiso Scholarship. *See* Japanese American Bar Scholarship, entry (F) 517

John F. Wright III Award. *See* Worldstudio Foundation Scholarships, entries (S) 386, (F) 652

John Hines and Deacon Francis Chao Memorial Scholarship. *See* Father John Hines and Deacon Francis Chao Memorial Scholarship, entry (S) 134

John Howlette and C. Clayton Powell Student Founders Award. *See* Dr. John Howlette and C. Clayton Powell Student Founders Award, entry (F) 460

John McLendon Memorial Minority Postgraduate Scholarship Award, (F) 519, (I) 934

S–Scholarships   F–Fellowships   L–Loans   G–Grants   A–Awards   I–Internships

S–Scholarships   F–Fellowships   L–Loans   G–Grants   A–Awards   I–Internships

Sponsoring Organization Index

The Sponsoring Organization Index makes it easy to identify agencies that offer financial aid primarily or exclusively to minorities. In this index, sponsoring organizations are listed alphabetically, word by word. In addition, we've used an alphabetical code (within parentheses) to help you identify which programs sponsored by these organizations fall within your scope of interest: S = Scholarships; F = Fellowships; L = Loans; G = Grants; A = Awards; and I = Internships. Here's how the code works: if the name of a sponsoring organization is followed by (S) 141, a program sponsored by that organization is described in the Scholarships section in entry 141. If the same sponsoring organization's name is followed by another entry number—for example, (L) 680—the same or a different program sponsored by that organization is described in the Loans chapter in entry 680. Remember: the numbers cited here refer to program entry numbers, not to page numbers in the book.

Abbott Laboratories, (F) 588, 600, (G) 707, 736, 760, 804–805, 808

ABC Entertainment, (G) 692, 819, (I) 1018

ABC, Inc., (I) 902

The Abilities Fund, (G) 724

Academy of Applied Science, (I) 985

Accountancy Board of Ohio, (S) 4, (F) 399

Adelphia Communications, (I) 902

ADNET Systems, Inc., (I) 971, 1008, 1012

Aetna Foundation, (S) 5, (F) 401

AFL–CIO, (I) 1011

AIDS Action, (I) 979

Air Products and Chemicals, Inc., (S) 11

Akron Beacon Journal, (S) 12

Akron General Medical Center, (S) 319

Alameda County Bar Association, (I) 874

Albuquerque Journal, (S) 94, (I) 888

Alston/Bannerman Fellowship Program, (F) 607

American Academy in Rome, (G) 749

American Academy of Child and Adolescent Psychiatry, (I) 931–932

American Academy of Nurse Practitioners, (F) 456

American Anthropological Association, (G) 697

American Antiquarian Society, (G) 749

American Architectural Foundation, (S) 8

American Art Therapy Association, Inc., (F) 439

American Association for Marriage and Family Therapy, (F) 536, 540

American Association for Respiratory Care, (S) 190

American Association of Advertising Agencies, (S) 21, (F) 424, 574, (I) 962

American Association of Critical–Care Nurses, (S) 118, (F) 467

American Association of Japanese University Women, (S) 18, (F) 404

American Association of Law Libraries, (F) 492

American Association of Obstetricians and Gynecologists Foundation, (F) 405, (G) 698

American Association of Petroleum Geologists, (I) 855

American Association of University Women, (F) 397, 611, (G) 722, (A) 835, 846

American Baptist Churches USA, (I) 870

American Bar Association. Fund for Justice and Education, (F) 406

American Bar Association. Section of Intellectual Property Law, (F) 615

American Bar Foundation, (G) 694, 730

American Board of Obstetrics and Gynecology, (F) 405, (G) 698

American Chemical Society. Division of Organic Chemistry, (F) 576

American College of Healthcare Executives, (F) 402, (I) 860

American College of Sports Medicine, (F) 407

American College Testing, (I) 856

American Council of Learned Societies, (F) 618, (G) 695–696, 717, 723, 728, 742, 749, 761, 773, 788

American Dental Hygienists' Association, (S) 19, 80

American Educational Research Association, (G) 699

American Epilepsy Society, (F) 588, 600, (G) 707, 736–737, 760, 804–805, 808

American Federation of State, County and Municipal Employees, (S) 6, (I) 858

American Gastroenterological Association, (F) 417, 440, (G) 705, 716, 735, 806

American Geological Institute, (I) 855, 859

American Health Information Management Association, (S) 144, (F) 488

American Heart Association. Western States Affiliate, (I) 861

American Hotel & Lodging Educational Foundation, (S) 172, 292
American Indian Graduate Center, (S) 151, (F) 491
American Institute of Architects, (S) 8
American Institute of Chemical Engineers, (I) 1022
American Institute of Professional Geologists, (I) 859
American Intellectual Property Law Association, (F) 615
American Library Association. Library and Information Technology Association, (F) 530, 533
American Library Association. Office for Diversity, (F) 620
American Musicological Society, (F) 509
American Nuclear Society, (I) 1022
American Nurses Association, (F) 445–446, (G) 719–720, 780
American Osteopathic Foundation, (F) 647
American Philological Association, (S) 20
American Physical Therapy Association, (S) 237, (F) 546
American Physiological Society, (G) 750
American Political Science Association, (A) 845
American Psychiatric Association, (G) 701, 782, (I) 961
American Psychiatric Nurses Association, (S) 104, (F) 459, (G) 731
American Psychological Association, (F) 506, 538–539, 586–587, 623, (G) 800–801
American School Counselor Association, (F) 413
American Society for Clinical Laboratory Science, (S) 146
American Society for Engineering Education, (F) 561
American Society of Civil Engineers, (I) 1022
American Society of Civil Engineers. Maine Section, (S) 31
American Society of Criminology, (F) 408
American Society of Engineers of Indian Origin, (S) 32, (F) 414, 524
American Society of Mechanical Engineers, (I) 1022
American Society of Radiologic Technologists, (S) 303
American Society of Safety Engineers, (S) 356
American Sociological Association, (F) 547
American Speech–Language–Hearing Foundation, (F) 409, 523
American Statistical Association, (G) 703
American Water Works Association, (F) 508
American Women in Radio and Television. Golden Gate Chapter, (S) 48, (F) 422
Andrew W. Mellon Foundation, (G) 695, 700, 717, 743, 749, 773, (I) 1004
Anheuser–Busch Companies, Inc., (S) 260, (F) 411, 413, 553, (A) 838, (I) 857, 862
Anheuser–Busch Foundation, (S) 23
Appraisal Institute, (S) 27
Aratani Foundation, (I) 892
Arkansas Department of Higher Education, (L) 656–657
Arkansas Game and Fish Commission, (S) 29
Armed Forces Communications and Electronics Association, (F) 598
ArtTable Inc., (I) 866
Asian American Bar Association of the Greater Bay Area, (I) 852
Asian American Journalists Association, (S) 91, 220, 239, 322, 330, 373, (F) 396, 450, 552, 614, (A) 834, (I) 853–854, 887, 966, 996–997, 1000, 1003
Asian American Journalists Association. Arizona Chapter, (S) 1
Asian American Journalists Association. Atlanta Chapter, (S) 43, (F) 418
Asian American Journalists Association. Chicago Chapter, (I) 893, 948

Asian American Journalists Association. Hawaii Chapter, (S) 164, (F) 500
Asian American Journalists Association. Los Angeles Chapter, (S) 213, (F) 534, (I) 949
Asian American Journalists Association. New York Chapter, (S) 256, (I) 969
Asian American Journalists Association. Philadelphia Chapter, (S) 149
Asian American Journalists Association. Portland Chapter, (S) 285, (F) 585
Asian American Journalists Association. San Francisco Bay Area Chapter, (S) 311, 382, (F) 609
Asian American Journalists Association. Seattle Chapter, (S) 264
Asian American Journalists Association. Texas Chapter, (S) 343, (F) 627
Asian American Writers' Workshop, (G) 734, 799
Asian Bar Association of Washington, (F) 415
Asian Business Association of Orange County, (S) 36
Asian Law Journal, (A) 828
Asian McDonald's Owners/Operators Association, (S) 37
Asian Pacific American Bar Association Educational Fund, (I) 857
Asian Pacific American Bar Association of Colorado, (F) 553
Asian Pacific American Institute for Congressional Studies, (I) 862–863, 892
Asian Pacific American Librarians Association, (F) 412, (G) 812
Asian Pacific Fund, (S) 46, 324, (A) 836
Asian & Pacific Islander American Scholarship Fund, (S) 37
Asian Pacific Islander Organization, (S) 26
Asian Pacific State Employees Association, (S) 39
Asian Reporter, (S) 40
Aspen Institute, (I) 970
Associated Colleges of Illinois, (S) 41
Associated Food Dealers of Michigan, (S) 42
Associated Press Sports Editors, (S) 330, (I) 1000
Association for Education in Journalism and Mass Communication, (F) 532
Association for Educational Communications and Technology, (F) 580
Association for Enterprise Opportunity, (G) 724
Association for Public Policy Analysis and Management, (F) 593
Association for Women Geoscientists, (S) 381, (F) 649
Association of American Geographers, (G) 794
Association of American Medical Colleges, (F) 505
Association of American Universities, (G) 773
Association of Chinese American Professionals, (S) 3
Association of Independent Colleges and Universities of Pennsylvania, (S) 11, 229
Association of Indians in America. New Jersey Chapter, (S) 7
Association of Indians in America. South Florida Chapter, (S) 327
Association of National Advertisers, (S) 21
Association of Professional Schools of International Affairs, (F) 593
Association of Research Libraries, (F) 555
Association of Schools of Public Health, (G) 715
Association of Trial Lawyers of America, (F) 603
AstraZeneca Pharmaceuticals, L.P., (F) 417, (G) 705
Atlanta History Center, (I) 964
Atlanta Journal and Constitution, (I) 871

Media Action Network for Asian Americans, (S) 216
Medical Library Association, (F) 554–555
Mercury News, (S) 227–228
Metropolitan Museum of Art, (I) 884, 925, 927, 947, 953–955, 988, 1021
Miami University. Library, (I) 956
Michael Baker Corporation, (S) 229
Michigan Association of Broadcasters, (I) 950
Mid–South Minority Business Council, (S) 300
Midwest Asian American Students Union, (I) 872
Milken Family Foundation, (G) 737
Milton & Sally Avery Arts Foundation, (F) 591–592
Minnesota Association of Counselors of Color, (S) 241
Minnesota Broadcasters Association, (S) 185
Minnesota Historical Society, (I) 964
Minnesota State University Student Association, (S) 254, (F) 567
Minority Access, Inc., (I) 959
Minority Corporate Counsel Association, (F) 615
Minority Educational Foundation of the United States of America, (S) 225
Minority Nurse Magazine, (S) 236
Missouri Department of Elementary and Secondary Education, (L) 674
Missouri Department of Health and Senior Services, (L) 675, 681
Missouri Department of Natural Resources, (S) 126, (F) 474
Missouri Vocational Special Need Association, (S) 247
Monterey County Herald, (S) 244
Morgan Stanley, (S) 296, (I) 987
Morris Scholarship Fund, (S) 245, (F) 556

Nara Bank Scholarship Foundation, (S) 251
National Asian American Telecommunications Association, (G) 785
National Asian Pacific American Bar Association, (F) 411, 531, 557, (L) 662, (A) 838, (I) 935
National Association for Asian and Pacific American Education, (S) 250
National Association of Asian American Professionals. Boston Chapter, (S) 54
National Association of Asian American Professionals. Houston Chapter, (S) 170
National Association of Asian American Professionals. New York Chapter, (S) 248
National Association of Asian American Professionals. Seattle Chapter, (S) 249
National Association of Black Journalists, (S) 330, (I) 1000
National Association of Black Journalists. Seattle Chapter, (S) 264
National Association of Collegiate Directors of Athletics, (F) 519, (I) 934
National Association of Hispanic Journalists, (S) 330, 373, (I) 1000
National Association of School Psychologists, (F) 559
National Association of Schools of Public Affairs and Administration, (F) 593
National Association of Student Personnel Administrators, (I) 963

National Association of Vocational Education Special Needs Personnel, (S) 253
National Center for Atmospheric Research, (G) 786
National Center for Learning Disabilities, (S) 25
National Coalition of Ethnic Minority Nurse Associations, (S) 5, (F) 401
National Collegiate Athletic Association, (F) 566, (I) 968
National Council on Family Relations, (A) 840
National FFA Organization, (S) 14, 47, 53, 135
National Gay and Lesbian Task Force. Policy Institute, (I) 1013
National Humanities Center, (G) 749
National Korean Presbyterian Women, (F) 563
National Lawyers Guild, (I) 919
National Medical Fellowships, Inc., (F) 650, (G) 824
National Minority Junior Golf Scholarship Association, (S) 260
National Naval Officers Association. Washington, D.C. Chapter, (S) 97, 128, 261
National Optometric Association, (F) 438, 460, 582
National Press Club, (S) 124
National Public Radio, (I) 966
National Science Foundation, (G) 703, 786, (I) 879, 965, 1004, 1022
National Science Foundation. Directorate for Social, Behavioral, and Economic Sciences, (G) 725–726
National Science Foundation. Office of Polar Programs, (G) 702
National Sleep Foundation, (G) 798
National Society of Professional Engineers, (I) 1022
National Strength and Conditioning Association, (F) 571
National Student Nurses' Association, (S) 56
National Tongan American Society, (S) 252, 349, (F) 564
National Trust for Historic Preservation, (F) 544, (I) 958
National Urban Fellows, Inc., (F) 565
National Urban League, (S) 157
National Wildlife Federation, (I) 883, 920
National Women's Studies Association, (A) 851
Native American Journalists Association. Seattle Chapter, (S) 264
NBC, (I) 902
Network of Indian Professionals–New York, (S) 255
New Britain Foundation for Public Giving, (S) 15
New Hampshire Charitable Foundation, (S) 243
New Jersey Commission on Higher Education, (F) 429
New Jersey Department of Health and Senior Services, (I) 943
New Jersey Society of Certified Public Accountants, (S) 127
New Jersey State Nurses Association, (S) 188
New Mexico Community Development Loan Fund, (G) 724
New York Library Association, (A) 841
New York Market Radio, (S) 266
New York Public Library. Center for Scholars and Writers, (G) 788
New York Sea Grant, (G) 789
New York State Bar Association. Environmental Law Section, (I) 960
New York University. Department of Journalism and Mass Communication, (S) 257
Newberry Library, (G) 749
Newhouse News Service, (S) 322, (F) 614, (I) 996
Newsday, (I) 952
NextGen Network, Inc., (A) 833
Nisei Student Relocation Commemorative Fund, Inc., (S) 265
Nisei Veterans' Committee, Inc., (S) 259, (F) 569

Norman and Rosita Winston Foundation, Inc., (I) 884
North Carolina Association of Educators, Inc., (S) 219
North Carolina Community College System, (S) 331
North Carolina Principal Fellows Commission, (L) 676
North Carolina State Education Assistance Authority, (F) 425, (L) 676, 678
North Carolina Teaching Fellows Commission, (L) 677
North Central Texas Council of Governments, (F) 634
North Texas Tollway Authority, (S) 189, (I) 933
Northern California Cherry Blossom Scholarship Committee, (S) 73
Northwest Journalists of Color, (S) 264
Nuclear Age Peace Foundation, (I) 944

Oahu Council of Filipino Catholic Clubs, (S) 267, (F) 572
Ohio Newspapers Foundation, (S) 273
Ohio State University. Byrd Polar Research Center, (G) 709
Ohio State University. Graduate School, (G) 818
Oklahoma NASA Space Grant Consortium, (G) 793
Oncology Nursing Society, (S) 130, (F) 479, (G) 738
Online Computer Library Center, (F) 530
Orange County Asian American Bar Foundation, (F) 575
Oregon Community Foundation, (S) 182, 208, (F) 515, 529
Oregon State Bar, (F) 577, (I) 972–973
Oregon Student Assistance Commission, (S) 182, 208, (F) 515, 529
The Oregonian, (I) 974
Organization of American Historians, (A) 839
Organization of Chinese Americans, Inc., (S) 151, 269–272, 357, (F) 491, (A) 832, 843, (I) 975
Organization of Chinese Americans, Inc. Dallas/Fort Worth Chapter, (S) 268, (A) 842
Organization of Chinese Americans of San Mateo County, (S) 242, 274, 281
Orphan Foundation of America, (A) 830
Ortho Biotech Products, L.P., (G) 738
Ortho–McNeil Pharmaceutical Corporation, (F) 588, 600, (G) 707, 736, 760, 804–805, 808
Orthopaedic Research and Education Foundation, (G) 826
Otto Bremer Foundation, (F) 497, (I) 917

Pacific Gas and Electric Company. Filipino Employees Association, (S) 138
Pacific Northwest National Laboratory, (I) 967
Page Education Foundation, (S) 275
Paxson Communications, (I) 902
PEMCO Foundation, (S) 369
PEN American Center, (A) 829
Pennsylvania Association of Vocational Education Special Needs Personnel, (A) 844
Pfizer Inc., (S) 279, (F) 583, 588, 600, (G) 707, 736, 760, 804–805, 808, (I) 980
PGA of America, (S) 260
PGA Tour, Inc., (I) 981
Phi Delta Phi International Legal Fraternity, (F) 419
Phi Tau Phi Scholastic Honor Society. Eastern America Chapter, (S) 280
Philadelphia Foundation, (S) 68

Philadelphia Inquirer, (I) 865, 982–983
Philadelphia Newspapers, Inc., (S) 284
Philip Morris Companies, (I) 863
Philippine American Bar Association of Los Angeles, (F) 578–579, (I) 976
Philippine Nurses Association of America, (F) 584, (G) 797
Phillips Exeter Academy, (G) 771
Photonics Society of Chinese–Americans, (F) 426
Piney Mountain Press, (S) 253
Playwrights' Center, (G) 776
Poughkeepsie Area Chamber of Commerce, (S) 298
Presbyterian Church (USA), (S) 338, (F) 589, 595, (L) 680
Presbyterian Church (USA). Presbytery of Chicago, (S) 24
Presbyterian Church (USA). Synod of Lakes and Prairies, (F) 624
Presbyterian Church (USA). Synod of Southern California and Hawaii, (F) 596
Presbyterian Church (USA). Synod of the Covenant, (S) 340, (F) 625
Presbyterian Church (USA). Synod of the Trinity, (S) 291
Princeton University. Institute for Advanced Study, (G) 749
Private Colleges & Universities, Inc., (S) 287
Procter & Gamble Company, (F) 590
Professor Chen Wen–Chen Memorial Foundation, (S) 105, 288
Public Interest Clearinghouse, (I) 984
Public Policy and International Affairs Fellowship Program, (F) 593
Public Relations Society of America. Puget Sound Chapter, (S) 169
Public Relations Student Society of America, (S) 289

Radcliffe Institute for Advanced Study at Harvard University, (G) 749
Radio and Television News Directors Foundation, (S) 67, 117, 198, (F) 541, (G) 790, (I) 878
RDW Group, Inc., (S) 295, (F) 599
Reformed Church in America, (S) 294
Renaissance Entrepreneurship Center, (G) 724
Resources for the Future, (G) 743, 757, 772, (I) 986, 1019
Rhode Island Foundation, (S) 293, 295, (F) 599
Robert L. Millender Sr. Memorial Fund Inc., (G) 781
Robert Toigo Foundation, (F) 605
Rockefeller Foundation, (G) 695, 749
Routledge, Inc., (A) 841
Ruth Jackson Orthopaedic Society, (G) 826
Ryu Family Foundation, Inc., (S) 305, (F) 606

San Diego Chinese Women's Association, (S) 310
San Diego Foundation, (S) 30
San Luis Obispo Tribune, (S) 348
Sandia National Laboratories, (F) 573
Santa Clara County Bar Association, (I) 874
Scholarship America, (S) 358–359, (F) 473, 639–640
Scholarship Program Administrators, (S) 42
Scotts Company, (S) 316, (I) 993
Scripps Howard Foundation, (F) 626
Seattle Hiroshima Club, (S) 317
Seattle Post–Intelligencer, (S) 264

Residency Index

Some programs listed in this book are restricted to residents of a particular city, county, state, or region. Others are open to applicants wherever they may live. The Residency Index will help you pinpoint programs available only to residents in your area as well as programs that have no residency restrictions at all (these are listed under the term "United States"). To use this index, look up the geographic areas that apply to you (always check the listings under "United States"), jot down the entry numbers listed after the program types that interest you (scholarships, fellowships, etc.), and use those numbers to find the program descriptions in the directory. To help you in your search, we've provided some "see also" references in each index entry. Remember: the numbers cited here refer to program entry numbers, not to page numbers in the book.

Tenability Index

Some programs listed in this book can be used only in specific cities, counties, states, or regions. Others may be used anywhere in the United States (or even abroad). The Tenability Index will help you locate funding that is restricted to a specific area as well as funding that has no tenability restrictions (these are listed under the term "United States"). To use this index, look up the geographic areas where you'd like to go (always check the listings under "United States"), jot down the entry numbers listed after the program types (scholarships, fellowships, etc.) that interest you, and use those numbers to find the program descriptions in the directory. To help you in your search, we've provided some "see also" references in each index entry. Remember: the numbers cited here refer to program entry numbers, not to page numbers in the book.

Subject Index

There are hundreds of different subject areas covered in this directory. You can use the Subject Index to identify both the subject focus and the type (scholarships, fellowships, etc.) of available funding programs. To help you pinpoint your search, we've included hundreds of "see" and "see also" references. In addition to looking for terms that represent your specific subject interest, be sure to check the "General programs" entry; hundreds of funding opportunities are listed there that can be used to support study, research, or other activities in *any* subject area (although the programs may be restricted in other ways). Remember: the numbers cited in this index refer to program entry numbers, not to page numbers in the book.

Labor unions and members: **Scholarships,** 6; **Internships,** 858, 1011. *See also* General programs

Landscape architecture: **Scholarships,** 119, 386; **Fellowships,** 652; **Internships,** 889, 990. *See also* Botany; General programs; Horticulture

Language, Albanian: **Fellowships,** 618. *See also* General programs; Language and linguistics

Language, Amharic: **Loans,** 682. *See also* General programs; Language and linguistics

Language and linguistics: **Scholarships,** 364, 380; **Fellowships,** 648; **Loans,** 657, 688; **Grants,** 695, 702, 717, 749, 803; **Internships,** 882, 901, 914, 946. *See also* General programs; Humanities; names of specific languages

Language, Arabic: **Loans,** 682. *See also* General programs; Language and linguistics

Language, Bulgarian: **Fellowships,** 618. *See also* General programs; Language and linguistics

Language, Chinese: **Loans,** 682. *See also* General programs; Language and linguistics

Language, Dari: **Loans,** 682. *See also* General programs; Language and linguistics

Language, English: **Scholarships,** 52. *See also* English as a second language; General programs; Language and linguistics

Language, Farsi: **Loans,** 682. *See also* General programs; Language and linguistics

Language, Greek: **Loans,** 682. *See also* Classical studies; General programs; Language and linguistics

Language, Hindi: **Loans,** 682. *See also* General programs; Language and linguistics

Language, Japanese: **Scholarships,** 393; **Loans,** 682. *See also* General programs; Language and linguistics

Language, Korean: **Loans,** 682. *See also* General programs; Language and linguistics

Language, Macedonian: **Fellowships,** 618. *See also* General programs; Language and linguistics

Language, Pashto: **Loans,** 682. *See also* General programs; Language and linguistics

Language, Romanian: **Fellowships,** 618. *See also* General programs; Language and linguistics

Language, Serbo–Croatian: **Fellowships,** 618. *See also* General programs; Language and linguistics

Language, Somali: **Loans,** 682. *See also* General programs; Language and linguistics

Language, Swahili: **Loans,** 682. *See also* General programs; Language and linguistics

Language, Turkish: **Loans,** 682. *See also* General programs; Language and linguistics

Language, Urdu: **Loans,** 682. *See also* General programs; Language and linguistics

Language, Yugoslavian. *See* Language, Macedonian; Language, Serbo–Croatian

Latin American studies: **Grants,** 696. *See also* General programs; Humanities

Latino studies. *See* Hispanic American studies

Law enforcement. *See* Criminal justice

Law, general: **Scholarships,** 145, 245, 279; **Fellowships,** 406, 411, 415, 419–420, 429, 451, 453, 455, 464, 481, 483, 485–487, 489–490, 492, 494, 502, 517, 521, 526, 531, 551, 553, 556–557, 575, 577–579, 581, 583, 590, 603, 610–611, 613, 615, 617, 629, 631, 634, 642–644, 646, 651; **Loans,** 662; **Grants,** 694–695, 702, 710, 717, 730, 747, 749, 759, 767–768, 792, 803, 807; **Awards,** 828, 838; **Internships,** 852, 857, 864, 868, 874, 891, 894, 899, 908–909, 911, 913, 915, 918–919, 921, 935, 943, 960, 972, 976–977, 980–981, 984, 989, 991, 995, 1005, 1008, 1012–1013. *See also* Criminal justice; General programs; Paralegal studies; Social sciences; names of legal specialties

Lawyers. *See* Law, general

Leadership: **Internships,** 867. *See also* General programs; Management

Learning disabilities. *See* Disabilities, learning

Legal assistants. *See* Paralegal studies

Legal studies and services. *See* Law, general

Lesbianism. *See* Homosexuality

Librarians. *See* Libraries and librarianship

Libraries and librarianship: **Fellowships,** 412, 427, 431, 444, 484, 491–492, 510, 530, 533, 554–555, 612, 616, 620, 628; **Grants,** 810, 812; **Awards,** 841; **Internships,** 889, 945–946, 956, 978. *See also* Archives; General programs; Information science; Social sciences

Libraries and librarianship, school: **Fellowships,** 520; **Loans,** 688. *See also* General programs; Libraries and librarianship

Life sciences. *See* Biological sciences

Linguistics. *See* Language and linguistics

Literature: **Grants,** 695, 717, 749, 774. *See also* General programs; Humanities; Writers and writing; specific types of literature

Literature, American: **Internships,** 945. *See also* American studies; General programs; Literature

Logistics: **Scholarships,** 33, 160, 215, 279, 321, 389–390; **Fellowships,** 501, 583, 594, 634, 653–654; **Internships,** 869, 882, 980. *See also* General programs; Transportation

Lung disease: **Fellowships,** 562. *See also* Disabilities; General programs; Health and health care; Medical sciences

Macedonian language. *See* Language, Macedonian

Magazines. *See* Journalism; Literature

Management: **Scholarships,** 14, 98, 144, 279, 352, 394; **Fellowships,** 402, 437, 457, 472, 488, 519, 565–566, 583; **Internships,** 860, 895, 934, 946, 968, 980, 995, 1005, 1010, 1023–1024. *See also* General programs; Social sciences

Manufacturing engineering. *See* Engineering, manufacturing

Marine sciences: **Fellowships,** 463, 558; **Grants,** 787; **Internships,** 1007. *See also* General programs; Sciences; names of specific marine sciences

Marketing: **Scholarships,** 12, 78, 92, 98, 141, 145, 157, 202, 206, 227, 244, 336, 348, 351–352; **Fellowships,** 457, 489; **Internships,** 886, 895, 911, 936, 939, 981, 1005, 1009–1010. *See also* Advertising; General programs; Public relations; Sales

Marketing education. *See* Education, business

Marriage. *See* Family relations

Mass communications. *See* Communications

Materials engineering. *See* Engineering, materials

Materials sciences: **Scholarships,** 391; **Fellowships,** 511, 558, 561, 573, 655; **Internships,** 879, 923. *See also* General programs; Physical sciences

Mathematics: **Scholarships,** 151, 155, 364, 372; **Fellowships,** 491, 495, 511, 561, 598, 621; **Loans,** 657, 674, 682, 688; **Grants,** 786; **Internships,** 856, 882, 923, 971, 985, 1006, 1008. *See also* Computer sciences; General programs; Physical sciences; Statistics

Measurement. *See* Testing

Mechanical engineering. *See* Engineering, mechanical

Race relations: **Awards,** 827, 839. *See also* Discrimination, racial; General programs; Minority affairs

Racial discrimination. *See* Discrimination, racial

Racism. *See* Discrimination, racial

Radio: **Scholarships,** 266; **Internships,** 945, 1023–1024. *See also* Communications; General programs

Radiology: **Scholarships,** 303, 392. *See also* General programs; Medical sciences

Reading: **Loans,** 688; **Internships,** 901. *See also* Education; General programs

Real estate: **Scholarships,** 27, 64, 153, 175; **Fellowships,** 493, 512, 605; **Grants,** 710, 763; **Internships,** 881, 899. *See also* General programs

Recreation: **Scholarships,** 111, 183; **Fellowships,** 516; **Internships,** 990. *See also* General programs; names of specific recreational activities

Reentry programs: **Scholarships,** 13, 17, 108, 199, 205, 217, 262, 306, 309, 393; **Fellowships,** 397, 403; **Loans,** 678; **Internships,** 928, 1025. *See also* General programs

Regional planning. *See* City and regional planning

Rehabilitation: **Scholarships,** 125; **Grants,** 707. *See also* General programs; Health and health care; specific types of therapy

Religion and religious activities: **Scholarships,** 35, 112, 131, 267, 297, 354; **Fellowships,** 400, 416, 454, 465, 469, 475–478, 514, 522, 535, 563, 572, 589, 595–596, 602, 624–625, 636–638; **Loans,** 680; **Grants,** 695, 717, 745, 749, 825; **Internships,** 870, 936. *See also* General programs; Humanities; Philosophy

Religious education. *See* Education, religious

Religious reporting: **Scholarships,** 210. *See also* Broadcasting; General programs; Journalism; Religion and religious activities

Resource management: **Scholarships,** 29. *See also* Environmental sciences; General programs; Management

Respiratory therapy: **Scholarships,** 190, 392. *See also* General programs; Health and health care

Retailing. *See* Sales

Risk management: **Grants,** 702. *See also* Business administration; Finance; General programs

Romanian language. *See* Language, Romanian

Safety studies: **Scholarships,** 356. *See also* Engineering; General programs

Sales: **Scholarships,** 174; **Internships,** 981, 1020. *See also* General programs; Marketing

School counselors. *See* Counselors and counseling, school

School libraries and librarians. *See* Libraries and librarianship, school

Schools. *See* Education

Science education. *See* Education, science and mathematics

Science reporting: **Internships,** 974. *See also* Broadcasting; General programs; Journalism; Sciences; Writers and writing

Sciences: **Scholarships,** 49, 76, 151, 204, 333, 372, 377–378; **Fellowships,** 423, 442, 491, 527–528, 621–622; **Loans,** 657, 670, 674; **Grants,** 723, 744, 756, 811, 813; **Internships,** 985, 998, 1006. *See also* General programs; names of specific sciences

Sculpture: **Grants,** 765. *See also* Fine arts; General programs

Secondary education. *See* Education, secondary

Secretarial sciences: **Scholarships,** 367. *See also* General programs

Serbo–Croatian language. *See* Language, Serbo–Croatian

Sex discrimination. *See* Discrimination, sex

Sexuality: **Grants,** 803. *See also* General programs; Medical sciences; Social sciences

Sight impairments. *See* Visual impairments

Sleep and sleep disorders: **Grants,** 798. *See also* General programs; Medical sciences

Social sciences: **Fellowships,** 480; **Grants,** 693–696, 717, 721, 723, 728, 730, 739–742, 749, 751, 757, 773, 778, 788, 795–796; **Internships,** 926, 951, 1013. *See also* General programs; names of specific social sciences

Social services: **Scholarships,** 13, 49, 111; **Fellowships,** 423; **Internships,** 903. *See also* General programs; Social work

Social work: **Scholarships,** 6, 49, 66; **Fellowships,** 421, 423, 436, 635; **Loans,** 672; **Grants,** 706–707, 763; **Internships,** 858, 897. *See also* General programs; Social sciences

Sociology: **Scholarships,** 6, 111; **Fellowships,** 421, 547, 551; **Grants,** 695, 702, 706–707, 710, 717, 749, 759, 763, 767–768, 792, 795, 803; **Awards,** 840; **Internships,** 858, 946. *See also* General programs; Social sciences

Soils science: **Scholarships,** 283; **Internships,** 1004. *See also* Agriculture and agricultural sciences; General programs; Horticulture

Somali language. *See* Language, Somali

Songs. *See* Music

South American studies. *See* Latin American studies

Soviet studies: **Fellowships,** 480; **Grants,** 696, 739–741. *See also* European studies; General programs; Humanities

Space sciences: **Scholarships,** 155, 364, 372, 377–378; **Fellowships,** 485, 495, 524, 558; **Grants,** 727, 747, 793, 813, 820, 822–823. *See also* General programs; Physical sciences

Special education. *See* Education, special

Speech impairments: **Fellowships,** 409, 523. *See also* Disabilities; General programs

Speech pathology: **Loans,** 688. *See also* General programs; Medical sciences; Speech impairments; Speech therapy

Speech therapy: **Fellowships,** 409. *See also* General programs; Health and health care; Speech impairments

Speeches. *See* Oratory

Speleology. *See* Cave studies

Sports. *See* Athletics

Sports medicine: **Fellowships,** 407. *See also* General programs; Medical sciences

Sports reporting: **Scholarships,** 207, 330; **Internships,** 905, 942, 974, 1000. *See also* Broadcasting; General programs; Journalism; Writers and writing

Stage design. *See* Performing arts

Statistics: **Scholarships,** 352; **Grants,** 703, 732; **Internships,** 856, 901, 926, 951, 1010. *See also* General programs; Mathematics

Substance abuse. *See* Alcohol use and abuse; Drug use and abuse

Surveying: **Scholarships,** 136; **Internships,** 899. *See also* General programs

Swahili language. *See* Language, Swahili

Systems engineering. *See* Engineering, systems

Teaching. *See* Education

Technology: **Scholarships,** 144, 296, 364; **Fellowships,** 488, 580; **Loans,** 688; **Grants,** 732, 744; **Internships,** 901, 925,

Calendar Index

Since most funding programs have specific deadline dates, some may have already closed by the time you begin to look for money. You can use the Calendar Index to identify which programs are still open. To do that, go to the type of program (scholarships, fellowships, etc.) that interests you, think about when you'll be able to complete your application forms, go to the appropriate months, jot down the entry numbers listed there, and use those numbers to find the program descriptions in the directory. Keep in mind that the numbers cited here refer to program entry numbers, not to page numbers in the book. Note: not all sponsoring organizations supplied deadline information to us, so not all programs are listed in this index.

Scholarships:

January: 12, 22, 31, 50, 52, 55–56, 69, 89, 98–99, 103–104, 121, 127, 130, 149, 151, 157, 168, 212, 219, 223, 227–228, 244–245, 248, 250, 259, 279, 284, 303, 317, 324, 332, 334–337, 341, 348, 370, 380, 388

February: 6–7, 14, 16–17, 20, 33–34, 37, 39, 46–47, 49, 53–54, 57, 71, 76, 81, 90, 95, 101, 109, 122–124, 135, 137, 139–140, 145, 147, 154, 156, 158, 166–167, 180, 182, 186, 191, 193, 200, 204, 208, 214, 221–222, 233, 240, 246, 276, 278, 282, 296, 304, 307, 309, 313, 316, 319, 323, 325–326, 328, 340, 342, 345, 351, 368, 373, 376, 379, 383, 392, 395

March: 2, 9, 13, 38, 40, 42, 58–59, 61, 65, 70, 73, 82, 97, 100, 108, 110–111, 114, 118, 128, 133, 142, 146, 148, 150, 153, 162, 165–166, 169, 171–172, 174, 181, 189, 194, 199, 205–206, 210, 217–218, 231, 234, 238, 241, 254, 258, 261–262, 265, 268, 273, 285, 299–300, 302, 306, 309–310, 344, 346, 358–359, 361, 369, 386–387, 393

April: 3, 11, 19, 24, 27, 60, 64, 67, 77, 80, 83–85, 91–92, 102, 113, 117, 119, 125, 134, 141, 164, 170, 176–179, 184, 192, 195–198, 201, 203, 220, 225, 229, 239, 242–243, 247, 256–257, 260, 264, 269–272, 274–275, 281, 289, 291, 294–295, 298, 311–312, 314–315, 322, 327, 338, 343, 353, 357, 363, 365–367, 371, 381–382

May: 4, 23, 30, 44, 48, 66, 88, 96, 105–106, 115, 138, 140, 144, 161, 173, 185, 187, 209, 213, 216, 224, 226, 235, 252, 266, 286, 288, 290, 297, 308, 320, 349–350, 394

June: 32, 79, 93, 107, 126, 129, 152, 159, 190, 232, 236, 263, 293, 329, 333

July: 10, 26, 36, 51, 74, 267, 283

August: 87, 360

September: 18, 28, 63, 86, 112, 136, 280, 340, 344, 391

October: 29, 43, 62, 78, 160, 249, 253, 277, 352, 362, 375, 389–390

November: 4, 72, 75, 120, 140, 188, 207, 215, 237, 305, 321, 339, 347, 355–356

December: 1, 8, 25, 94, 116, 163, 183, 230, 251, 287, 330

Any time: 35, 45, 175

Fellowships:

January: 410, 426, 440, 455, 457, 459, 468, 473, 479, 484–485, 491, 496, 502, 506–509, 519, 536, 538–540, 547, 556, 559–561, 569, 578–579, 583, 586–587, 591–592, 598, 604, 611, 618, 623, 638, 648, 651

February: 400, 403, 406, 408, 421, 423, 442, 446, 449, 470–471, 478, 482, 489, 497, 504, 515, 518, 527–530, 533, 544–545, 558, 565–566, 577, 605, 608, 610, 615, 620, 625–626, 632, 635, 645

March: 398, 402, 412, 428, 433–434, 441, 453–454, 461, 467, 477, 490, 492–493, 499, 503–505, 521, 526, 535, 537, 542, 548, 550–551, 567–568, 571, 575, 585, 597, 601, 613, 617, 621, 630–631, 639–640, 642, 646, 652

April: 407, 425, 427, 431, 438, 443, 450–451, 456, 460, 463, 475–476, 481, 500, 510, 513, 520, 525, 541, 552, 582, 590, 596, 599, 609, 612, 614, 627, 636, 641, 644, 649

May: 399, 420, 422, 436, 444, 466, 483, 488, 498, 514, 522, 534, 562–564, 576, 603

June: 409, 414, 439, 452, 474, 523–524, 532, 543, 570, 619, 622, 650

July: 572, 634

August: 405, 448, 475–477, 548–549, 588

September: 404, 411, 415, 417, 430, 435, 462, 464–465, 469, 487, 531, 557, 595, 624–625, 630, 655

October: 413, 418–419, 432, 437, 472, 486, 494, 580, 594, 600, 616, 629, 653–654

November: 399, 480, 501, 514, 546, 554, 589, 606–607, 633

December: 397, 511, 516–517, 548

Any time: 396, 416, 512

Loans:

January: 676

February: 658, 664, 668, 672–674, 684

March: 670, 685

April: 679, 683

May: 656–657, 660, 669

June: 675, 681, 687

September: 662

October: 659–660, 677, 685

November: 661, 666, 680, 682